Children
Behavior and
Development

Children

Behavior and

Development

SECOND EDITION

Boyd R. McCandless

Emory University

HOLT, RINEHART AND WINSTON, INC.
New York   Chicago   San Francisco   Atlanta
Dallas   Montreal   Toronto   London

To Elinore, Beth, Mark, and Christine

During the preparation of this second edition, as in the preparation of the first, they have been very patient with husband and father; and their generally benign influence should be evident, in both subtle and obvious ways, throughout the book.

Preface

M any exciting things have happened in the field of child psychology and development during the six years between the writing of the first and the present edition of this book. The provocative theories of Piaget, a renewed and imaginative approach to cognitive development, more attention to curiosity in the life of the child, investigations of creativity, a proliferating and useful literature concerning infant learning and development, experimental research into effects of methods of child control, and more increasingly sophisticated investigations of sex-typing and identification, refinement of Guilford's theory of the structure of intellect, the beginnings of a substantial literature on "compensatory education," and imaginative research on the relations between body build and social adjustment—these are topics that the author has found particularly fascinating. He hopes the reader finds them equally challenging and involving.

Research has continued apace in older or more traditional areas of child psychology and development. Without sacrificing literature that is of great value simply because it does not carry a recent date line, the author has tried to select from the 1960 to 1966 literature representative samples of the newest and the best in these areas, as well as more extensive samples of the developing topics named in the paragraph above.

In working on this second edition, the author (as one of his children would say) has "had a ball." With respect to the research and theoretical literature of the last six years, the increase in both quantity (staggering) and quality (exceptionally gratifying) is indeed striking. The increase in quantity, of course, demands even more ruthless pruning and selection than was necessary for the first edition. While it would have been fun to include everything—and particularly everything of high quality—such a task is even more impossible than it was six years ago. Thus many worthwhile references, while personally noted and appreciated, must be omitted.

Professionally, the author has had an equally exciting six years: he read page proofs for the first edition under a *punkah* (slowly revolving ceiling fan) in the torrid monsoon weather of West Pakistan. The logistical problems of airmail page proofs (long sheets printed on onion skin), a punkah, and monsoon perspiration were staggering, but interesting and challenging to surmount. The next two years were spent immersed intellectually, emotionally, and physically in the challenging, intensely moving, and almost overwhelming problems of working with a developing nation to achieve a goal of better and more widespread education for its children and youth and its already accredited teachers, as well as its teachers in training. This work carried the author from the remotest villages to the great metropolitan areas of West Pakistan, as well as into East Pakistan and India. The second edition has been strongly influenced by these wonderful two years.

After living in Asia for two years, in the author's judgment, one becomes either a committed activist (there is *so* much to be done that one feels guilty if he is not in the middle of life helping as best he can to *do* what he is best able at a level of direct personal involvement); or he withdraws entirely from directly human welfare-oriented endeavors, because they are too wearing emotionally and physically. The author and his family chose the former path and moved to a setting that combined academia, in the sense of membership in a major psychology department, and clinical work (the Directorship, for the author, of the Indiana University "University Schools Clinic Complex," which was set in the middle of a public school system of about 2500 children ranging in age from the nursery years through high school, but connected, in a training and demonstration capacity, with a large State University). During these years, he worked actively in research on compensatory education for psychosocially disadvantaged preschool-aged children. The influence of these four years, working in a combination of clinical and professorial roles in the midst of the "raw data" of child and adolescent development, is also reflected throughout the second edition. The author hopes and believes that, without lowering scholarly standards, he has also come closer to the real world of the child, his family, and his school.

Finally, there came the chance to develop a program for training research workers for functioning in applied settings (such as the schools) and to combine this with continued involvement in "compensatory education." This opportunity was irresistible and, in the summer of 1966, the author moved to Emory University from which base he also works actively with the Atlanta and DeKalb County, Georgia, public schools. These influences, too, are shown in the second edition.

With the exception of some material on physical growth and the effects of biological (sexual) maturity, the material on adolescence has been removed from the present edition. The physical maturity section has been retained because so many children now achieve pubescence during their elementary-school years (or at least before the age of 14, a traditional cut-off point for child psychology and development books). He has continued to draw, but more sparingly, on relevant research done with young and older adults and on animals. As the literature for children becomes more sophisticated, such sampling from other-than-child populations becomes less necessary. This will become obvious to the reader as he goes through this volume.

The second edition retains the emphasis on learning in a social context that characterized the first edition. Many readers have asked that the section on research design and methods be expanded and the author, agreeing with them, has dealt more in detail with such problems than in the first edition.

Regardless of how a title page reads, no author produces a book alone. It is impossible to say "who helped most." Equally important are colleagues, who keep you on your toes, support you, and if necessary cut you down to size; students, who serve much the same function and who are very good about letting you develop and test your ideas on them; professional readers and editors, who do their best to force an author to organize logically and write coherently; and family, who put up with prolonged preoccupations and irascibility.

A debt of appreciation is still owed to the persons named in the preface of the first edition, whose influence is still clear in the second edition. Ellis D. Evans and Dale B. Harris have been of inestimable help in preparing the second edition, and Larry Barber and Alberta Siegel gave excellent help in planning before the actual writing of the second edition began. Hazel Smith and her assistant, JoEllen Fitzgerald, have given patient and detailed attention to the preparation of the manuscript.

B. R. McC.

Atlanta, Georgia
February 1967

Contents

Children
Behavior and
Development

Culture and the Human Organism

I t's a boy," or "It's a girl." These simple statements of existence and sex-difference are typically the first pieces of information parents acquire about their child. The arrival of the baby starts a chain of evermore complex interactions between parents and the child. This interchange is a two-way street: as the parents learn more about their child, he learns more about them. They use their information to guide and shape *him* and, in a less well-formulated way, he uses the information he gains about them to guide and shape *them*. In other words, the relation between parents and children is reciprocal: parents influence child, child influences parents. This process becomes more complicated both with time and the size of the family. A "tagalong" third child, for example, actually has four parents, to speak psychologically—his true parents and his brothers and/or sisters. Each of them affects him, and he affects each of them.

It is commonly assumed (by the author, as well as almost all other writers about human development), that the parents—the family—exert the most important social-personal influence on the child. It is less commonly granted that the second most important influence on children is the public and private schools they attend.

This book concentrates on these two major influences: families and schools.

The normal new baby—small, complex, primitive—has a head, arms, legs, a torso, the insignia of his sex, and a complicated nervous system that articulates these parts and makes them functional. Of first importance is his set of sense organs. These put him in touch with the world around him. The things this world transmits to him through his eyes, ears, sense of touch, and other senses modify and shape his development. His life pattern will also be affected by such things as whether he is healthy or sickly, has a sturdy or weak physique, or whether (according to the very different standards of the cultural-ethnic group into which he is born) he is good looking or homely. His sex makes a tremendous difference in his development. The efficiency of his "transmitting" nervous system (the nerves and muscles) that helps him put into action the things he receives through his senses is equally important.

Chapter 1 gives a brief sketch of the culture to which United States children and their parents and teachers are exposed. It suggests some of the ways in which the culture affects personality and, finally, it describes the sensory or "culture receptive" equipment and functioning of the normal baby, and his equipment for, in his turn, making an impact on his environment.

Culture and Human Behavior

CLASSES OF BEHAVIOR

Professional workers in child development and educators have used the term the whole child until it has become a cliché—a reference that for many of us almost provokes bored irritation. Yet, like most clichés, there is something about the term to which we should attend. For present purposes, the author wants to talk of the whole child, but not as a "globe" as implied by the term. Rather, he prefers to sketch a method of viewing children that, as a parent and professional worker with children, he has found helpful in the sense that it is less trite than the global concept of whole child and yet it loses little or none of the meaning of the original term. Also, it provides a classification of behavior that seems to make sense to those who work with children. The classification is by no means inclusive. Perhaps more important than the classification itself, is the author's conviction that one cannot, to work productively with children, ignore the interactions or interrelations among the three major classes of behavior as provided in Figure 1.1.

As can be seen from the sketch and its accompanying text, instead of being viewed as a globe, the child is viewed as a rounded triangle. For convenience, the upper corner of this rounded triangle is labeled A for school achievement and academic aptitude. This is not to say that this is the most important corner, but simply that it is the one on which parents and teachers are most likely to concentrate.

The lower-left corner, B, can be thought of as including the personal-social-emotional aspects of the child's behavior. Clinical and school psychologists, counseling and guidance workers, psychiatrists, sociologists, many parents, health and safety officers, as well as others, are likely to focus on these aspects of the child's behavior and characteristics. Yet corner B is neither less nor more crucial than A, nor should either A or B overshadow C.

The lower-right hand corner of the rounded triangle in Figure 1.1, C, represents the child's physical attributes among which may be in-

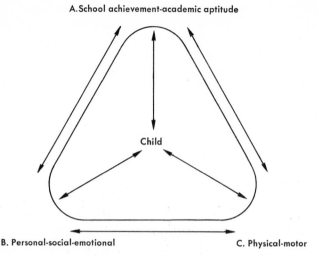

Figure 1.1   A sketch of how the child and his behavior and characteristics may be usefully viewed. The double-headed arrows indicate interactions.

cluded such things as his body type, strength, and motor coordination (both of gross or major and small or fine muscles).

The double-headed arrows in Figure 1.1 indicate interactions. For example, a child can never be separated from his body—its appearance, strength, and so on. He lives with it for twenty-four hours a day from birth until death. It affects his total life and in turn he affects it by such things as overeating, underexercising, getting sufficient sleep, or grooming it well. It also affects his academic-intellectual functions, just as they affect him and interact with his personal-social-emotional behavior and characteristics.

Teachers and the workers in the welfare professions (such as psychologists and social workers) are likely to overlook or under-attend to corner C, while medical doctors and physical education personnel may overstress it while neglecting its interrelating with corners A and B.

The author does not intend for this sketch-classification to be taken as either complete or as a theory. It is simply an illustration-description of what he has found a useful way to guide him and others with whom he has worked in looking at children. Keeping the corners in mind, remembering the various ways different professional and nonprofessional people are likely to pay too much or too little attention to one or another of the different corners, and holding in mind that each corner interacts both with the other two and the child helps one to keep perspective on babies, children or, for that matter, adolescents and adults.

HUMAN CULTURE

The way in which a child *grows,* mentally and physically, is probably affected as much by the way life treats him, by the opportunities he has to learn, and by the richness and emotional atmosphere of his environment as it is by his sensory-neurological and muscular equipment. As has been pointed out, one cannot separate emotional, intellectual, social, and physical development, either logically or for practical reasons. The best possible emotional environment cannot make life simple and easy for deaf, blind, or physically handicapped children. Dorothea McCarthy, 1964, for example, suggests that children born deaf miss the tender-cooing sounds which add so much to the emotional security and intellectual development that hearing babies receive from their mothers. In turn (this illustrates the principles of parent-child interaction mentioned above), such a child is likely to be less responsive to his mother than the hearing baby. The mother may then react negatively to what she regards as his aloofness, and perhaps give him less positive treatment than she has given her fully normal children. Certainly, infants with rugged and efficient muscular and sensory equipment have great advantages in overcoming unfavorable environments.

As we look around us, we see an infinite variety of people, young and old. Some are tall or thin, some short or fat, some medium in build or muscular. They may look (and be) happy or depressed, passive or active. Some are highly intelligent, some dull. Some are rich, some poor. Some love company while others are loners.

Aside from such factors as weight, height, bone structure, eye color, and curliness of hair, these differences which are so apparent even to a casual observer are due largely to the intellectual, social, and emotional learning opportunities these people have had available to them. The broadest term to describe these learning opportunities is *culture.* Each community, each section of each country, and each different country has a culture that is unique, in the sense that it has customs that no other country or region shares. Of course, basic to all cultures are the events of mating, childbirth, and death. Even in dealing with these universals, countries differ among themselves, and different regions in a single country differ from each other.

Sectional differences within the United States are easily discernible. The man from Maine and the man from Louisiana differ. The San Diego girl, in some respects, is a different person from the western Kansas farm girl. Still more widely different, one from another, are the natives

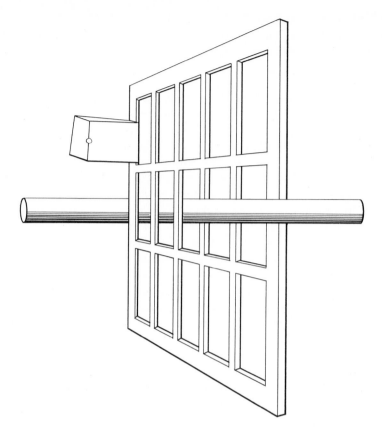

Figure 1.2   The Ames window, with cube and rod attached, in rotation is likely to produce the illusion of sway. (Courtesy of Dr. Hadley Cantril.)

of different countries and widely different cultures. To the Andaman Islander, tears may have a meaning entirely different from the meaning they have to one in Texas (Murphy, Murphy, and Newcomb, 1937).[1] The sexual attitudes and behaviors of the native of New Guinea are very different from those of the boy who was born and brought up in a Presbyterian home in Edinburgh. The youngster from an impoverished family does not react to money in the same way as the child who has never known what it is to be without a dollar for his pleasure or his needs.

The influence of culture on so basic a process as perception is vividly illustrated in an experiment by Allport and Pettigrew (1957). The experiment uses a device called the Ames window (Figure 1.2), which is so

[1] Complete citations of published works will be found in the list of references at the end of this book.

proportioned that, as it rotates, the length of the longer edge is always greater on the retina than the length of the shorter edge. By children and adults in the United States, the rotation of this window is usually perceived as a sway, back and forth in an arc. The experimenters appended to the window a cube and rod, whose rotation was obvious, so that the whole illusion contrasted the sway of the Ames window with the apparent detachment of the cube from the window. According to Allport and Pettigrew, the cube was "usually seen to detach itself and swing without support in a ghostly fashion in front of the window . . . . Similarly, the rod bends, twists or 'cuts through' the mullions in order to accommodate itself to the phenomenal oscillation. The observer finds the bizarre effect both amusing and inexplicable" (p. 105).

This illusion would ordinarily be ascribed to the native or intrinsic structure and function of the human eye. The prediction would be that, regardless of culture, it would occur with equal frequency among normal people who had made ordinary use of their eyes.

Allport and Pettigrew observed that the tribal Zulus of Africa grow up in a circular culture: their houses are round, their kraals are round, and their language does not even include a word for square. They predicted that the more "native" the 10- to 14-year-old boys they used as subjects (that is, the less their experience with cities, windows, and squares), the less frequently they would perceive the illusion. Their findings supported the hypothesis. The youngsters with the least exposure to a culture other than that of the tribe least frequently reported the illusion. There was no difference between *urban* European and *urban* African boys in the frequency with which the illusion was reported.

Allport and Pettigrew provide one of the most convincing illustrations of the point that even so basic or constitutional a human function as perception is culturally affected. More recently, McCandless and Ali (1966) illustrate that culture affects important social attitudes and behaviors. They studied upper-middle class ninth-grade girls. (Definition of the term social class is made later in this chapter; here, the author simply means that most of these girls came from relatively well-educated families with good incomes.) The three groups of girls the authors studied were (1) a group of girls from West Pakistan, reared as Moslems, and attending a prestige girls' school; (2) a group of girls from an equally prestigious and also sex-segregated Roman Catholic day and boarding school; and (3) a group of University School girls. The university school was coeducational. They gave a large number of tests to the girls in each sample and, somewhat surprisingly, found few differences among the three groups. However, skill in sports was much more highly valued by the groups of girls in the sex-segregated schools than by those in the coeducational school. This suggests that when girls spend most of their lives with girls they give much the same importance to sports and

physical skills as boys; but when placed in school with boys, their attention (and possibly values) is diverted to making an impression on the
boys. Thus, the "boyish" value given to being good at sports by the girls
in the girls-only schools becomes of little importance to the coeds.

The sciences concerned with the development of man are in general
agreement that differences between people from different cultures are to
a greater degree due to the learning opportunities provided by these
cultures than they are to basic differences in, for example, sense modalities, brain size, or potential for intellectual, social, and emotional development. Many tentative conclusions, which might almost be called
hunches, have been set forth concerning the influence of culture on
personality; much has been written about this influence; many different
cultures have been studied, some with good and some with poor scientific methods; and a few sound scientific studies have appeared. Where
the methods of science have been applied to the field of culture and personality, the results have been rewarding.

Definition of Culture   As it is usually employed, the term culture is a
loose one. It refers to the general method by which a group of people
organizes its life from the cradle to the grave. The term takes into account
the major group methods of dealing with common life problems. For
most people in the United States the culture includes a two-party
political system and a reasonably formal set of religious behaviors,
usually involving affiliation with a Protestant, Catholic, or Jewish
religious group. Certain methods of handling childbirth are agreed upon
by the majority; most start their children in school at kindergarten age
if the community has a kindergarten, or about 6 years of age in the first
grade. Almost everyone agrees that a high-school education is a desirable
minimum for all children. College is highly regarded by the majority,
and a steadily expanding minority attends.

Most parents begin to turn loose the reins of authority as their children get well into adolescence, although there are social class differences,
and most of them complain about their adolescents' irresponsibility and
inability to handle this independence. The average parent expects his
children to become self-supporting by the time they are between 17 or
18 and 23 or 24 years of age, depending on what the child is attempting
to do with his life vocationally. People are expected to marry somewhere
between approximately 20 and 27 or 28 years, although the age varies
from region to region within the United States and from one group to
another in a given region. The average age of marriage has been steadily
becoming lower for both sexes. Boys are expected to work consistently
and to become good providers for their families. Women may work before marriage but are expected to stay at home and care for the house
and children after marriage, although this expectation is no longer very

strong. It is commonly held that grown children should maintain some ties with their parents, although it is becoming less typical for adults to assume full responsibility for their parents. Old age is treated with reasonable consideration. Death is a sober occasion typically accompanied by elaborate funeral arrangements held, almost always, according to the rituals of the appropriate religious denomination.

It is almost taken for granted that there is corruption in politics but that even the least important person in the community has his rights. It is general to feel prejudice against some race or races, although most deny such feelings: antidemocratic though he may be in practice, the average American has been brought up religiously, within the framework of a democratic ideal, and on the principles of the Constitution and Thomas Jefferson. This upbringing does not make him consistently democratic in his behavior, either toward his fellow men, toward his subordinates or bosses, toward his spouse, or toward his dog, but in the long run he seems to do reasonably well at democracy. The Civil Rights acts of the 1960s have probably speeded democratic behavior and perhaps attitudes.

Young men of average, middle-class families, and probably from less economically secure families, expect to be successful in their careers, to make more money and to have more prestige than their parents had. They in turn pass on similar expectations to their children. Men are nominally the heads of families, but women are actually responsible for more of the total management of the children, the social life of the family, and the spending of money.

It is of such stuff as this that a culture is made. This consists in part of the formal organization of the particular country or community, including the church and the political system, and in part of the commonly accepted standards of behavior in such areas as marriage and sex, work, cooperation versus competition, parenthood, and friendship, by which people informally regulate infinite complexities of daily life. Folklore—and, to a degree, science—attributes a different culture to each country and to each definable group or tribe or community within that country. The Italian has a culture different from that of the German; the northern Italian a culture different from that of the southern Italian; and the Sicilian a different culture still. The Ubangi differs from the Zulu; the Brahmin from the Untouchable. The Zuni differs culturally from the Sioux, and the Sioux from the Nez Perce, and the Pathan from the Panjabi of the Indian-Pakistani plains.

Cultures can be clearly differentiated to the degree that the group in question is isolated geographically and educationally from other groups. The mountaineer culture of eastern Tennessee is easier to specify than the urban culture of New York City or Detroit: residents of New York or Detroit are more likely to be in communication with people from all over the United States and the world than are the inhabitants of eastern

Tennessee. Because of their educational opportunities, they are more likely to be aware of cultural differences, world events, and so on, and to have had a wider variety of socializing experiences. Thus, their culture is likely to be more variable and less easily defined.

Although certain broad practices and expectations apply to all members of a given group, the effective culture is never precisely the same for any two individuals or families in even the simplest, smallest village or tribal community. In so large and complex a community as the United States, one is hard put to find any single factor that applies even to a majority of the population. The loose description of United States culture given a few paragraphs ago probably never applies in all respects to any single person. However, it provides a recognizable pattern and gives the setting within which the American child is born and to which he, his parents, and his teachers react—the pattern that makes them, as an average, different from the average person from any other culture.

Culture, then, consists of the major institutional and social patterns followed by a larger or smaller, but definable, group of persons. The term may be used broadly, in relation to a relatively large social group, or more narrowly, to define the usages of specific subgroups. The culture of the Middle West is often contrasted with that of the East or West Coast; the culture of the Old South is contrasted with that north of the Mason-Dixon line; that of the mandated islands with that of the mainland. Each of these cultures provides a roughly agreed-upon pattern of learning for the children born into it—a pattern different from that of other cultures or subcultures.

Illustrations of Cultural Variation   The vast range of cultural patterns can be clearly exemplified by diverse customs relating to marriage, since mate-taking is a universal custom. The following examples have been randomly selected from observation and anthropological accounts, and range from those common in a Western European culture to practices among the Bushmen of Australia.

> *1.* Boy proposes, girl accepts; they cooperate in getting a marriage license, go with two witnesses to a justice of the peace, and are married without further ado. (United States, informal.)

> *2.* Boy proposes, girl tentatively accepts, girl's father is approached. Diamond is bestowed and engagement announced. Waiting period intervenes while bride buys trousseau, selects bridesmaids and wedding guests; boy chooses ushers. Church is reserved, flowers are ordered, guests are invited; wedding ensues. Reception is held, during which bride changes from white satin and lace to traveling clothes, groom from morning coat to business suit. Newlyweds rush

out front door, pelted by shoes, rice, and confetti, and go on honeymoon. (United States, formal.)

3. Father decides daughter of other father is appropriate for his son. Seeks intermediary, who approaches girl's father. Financial arrangements, as dowry for girl and financial prospects for boy, are discussed; agreement is reached. Time (often years) is allowed for boy and girl, who have never seen each other, to grow up. When the time comes, formal wedding is celebrated with a feast. On wedding night, bride and groom may see each other for first time. (Among others, traditional Chinese.)

On the Indo-Pakistan subcontinent and in many parts of Africa the dowry system (this information comes from news reports and personal experience, 1965–1966) and the pattern of arranged marriages, many of which in Indo-Pakistan are designed to preserve family lands and fortunes, but an equal number of which are a pattern automatically followed by the humblest villager, have become a focus of rebellion by younger people as well as their elders. Some African youths must resort either to crime or live conservatively and thriftily until middle age before they can afford a wife. Indo-Pakistani villagers may assume debts for their children's marriage that require a lifetime to pay.

4. Boy meets and likes girl, courts and wins her. After she has proved she is capable of bearing a sound and healthy child, wedding arrangements are completed between boy's relatives and girl's relatives. Payment is made sometimes by the girl's, sometimes by the boy's family. (Certain African tribes.)

5. Boy meets and is attracted by girl. Their relationship is kept secret, because the adult members of the tribe would pronounce a sentence of death were love interest or matrimonial plans suspected. At an agreed-upon time, boy and girl elope in full flight, pursued by adults of the group. Amnesty is granted the fleeing couple if they reach a particular island. They are reprieved from sentence of death when they return to the tribe, provided they have managed to have a child by that time. (Australian Bush tribe.)

No universal pattern exists for handling any of the major tasks involved in human living. The infinite variety of human custom applies as much to having a baby and caring for him as it does to getting married, worshipping a deity, growing old, and dying.

Social Class   So far in this chapter, variations in culture have mostly been discussed in geographic terms. Another refinement of culture is often postulated: culture as it is affected by social class. According to Davis and Dollard (1940), class is a term that refers to the group with which one "visits, intermarries, and co-belongs . . . to organizations pitched primarily at the social level." Many sociologists separate the United States population into three classes: (1) the *upper* being reasonably free of narrow conventions, but in general law-abiding; conscious to a greater or lesser degree of its own superiority, but secure enough not to need to call it to anyone's attention and secure enough to be reasonably free from acting in any self-conscious manner; (2) the *middle* being ambitious, law-abiding, community-conscious, rather self-conscious; valuing education highly and having a hearty respect, by and large, for the *status quo*; and (3) the *lower,* where most of life's experiences are frustrating; where insecurity is the established pattern; where there is reasonably little hope of social or vocational climbing or of obtaining college degrees or professional status; where violence often occurs; and where sexual behavior is much more forthright and accepted than it is in the other two classes.

The terms upper, middle, and lower, perhaps irritating to the average democratically-minded American, may have been poorly chosen, but they seem to have validity as far as describing culture within a given community is concerned.

There are several different ways of defining social class, and many problems in measuring it. Some define it by parents' educational level (Kinsey, Pomeroy, and Martin, 1948): the higher the educational level, the higher the social-class rating. Others use level of father's occupation as a guide to social class (Sears, Maccoby, and Levin, 1957): professional men, such as doctors or lawyers, for example, are given the highest ranking; unskilled laborers, the lowest classification. A psychological definition of social class has been advanced by Centers (1950, 1951). The concept of social class has been criticized (for example, Loevinger, 1940) as being vague, or false, or useless.

Nonetheless, social class, however defined, has been shown to be associated with important differences in the types of learning experience to which a given child is exposed, the degree of economic security he possesses, the way he is introduced to school, and the way in which fighting and sexuality are introduced to him. It probably plays a part in the way he is fed and trained to go to the toilet, as well as in the way he is disciplined and stimulated intellectually. His social class, finally, is thought to have much to do with the goals he eventually includes in his life pattern: goals of marriage, vocation, and parenthood.

A particularly lasting and effective scale for measuring socio-economic class (Warner, Meeker, and Eells, 1949, as informally updated, for example, in 1966, by such authors as Hodges, McCandless, and Spicker) is widely used today to separate social class into (1) *Upper-upper.* These are the "true United States aristocrats." (2) *Lower-upper.* Such people usually (but not necessarily) have inherited money, are well-educated, and come from "good" but not necessarily "the best" families. (3) *Upper-middle*. Such families have usually "made it on their own, but made it well." In most communities in the United States one finds them among the more successful businessmen, lawyers, bankers, physicians, and ministers from the educated sects. Almost all such men and their families originally came from more humble circumstances. In any university community there is a substantial number of professorial staff which, according to the standards of the community is also upper-middle class. (4) *Lower-middle*. This group is likely to include small businessmen, highly skilled craftsmen, modest farmers, and so on. Clergy of moderate education are usually included here. (5) *Upper-lower*. Speaking subjectively, this seems to be a group on its way up, at least as far as its aspirations for its children are concerned. The wage earners in the families are marginal proprietors, semiskilled but steadily employed fathers and mothers, moonlighting farmers (that is, those who must hold down two jobs to manage financially). (6) *Lower-lower*. Here we find the problem cases each community has: the unskilled worker, irregularly employed; the man or woman who is in-and-out-of-jail, although seldom for serious offenses; families chronically known to welfare or charitable agencies, and so on. Estimates as to the number of this last group vary widely depending on which author one reads, but the proportion of such family heads is probably about 20 percent. These families contribute disproportionately to the public school population. Probably about 30 percent of public school children come from lower-lower class homes. There are indications that percentages for both parents and children from this group are gradually decreasing.

The Family   The relation of family to culture is complex. Although the culture dictates the family form or pattern, the family is the immediate "in group" or small subunit on the basis of which the culture is built and through which it is transmitted to the child. In the United States, the typical or average family is made up of the father (the titular head of the house); the mother (the mainstay of the home); one or more children; and a more or less loosely connected set of uncles, aunts, and grandparents. A large number of families together, subscribing in general to the same customs, makes up a culture; but within a given family, variability is less than between families, so that each family unit in effect constitutes a subculture. No two families interpret the general culture in precisely the same way to their children.

While Australian, British, Canadian, New Zealand, and United States families tend to be nuclear (as made up of the father, mother, and children), the extended family (for example the Indo-Pakistani type family) is probably typical of a larger proportion of the world's population. The extended family (to over-simplify) includes all the male descendants of the oldest man of the family and their wives and children. Orphaned cousins, nephews and nieces, widowed and penniless aunts and sisters, and so on, often form a part of this extended family. In such a family, responsibilities, including child care, are shared, although the families of the patriarch and his sons are the prestige members of the group. Such an organization may be a source of great worry (and satisfaction) to its head(s), and of security from penury and perhaps death to its less fortunate members. It very likely provides great security to young children, since its size and the number of women in it means that they are never long without needed attention, as they may often be in nuclear families.

Motherhood and Infant Care

For about seven out of eight United States couples, marriage is sooner or later followed by the birth of a child. On the basis of interviews with a large number of suburban mothers, Sears, Maccoby, and Levin (1957) rated 62 percent of the mothers of first-born children as delighted when they learned that they were pregnant, while another 19 percent were generally pleased. Fewer than one fifth had mixed feelings or were displeased. Mothers of later children were delighted less frequently than mothers of first children (in 34 percent of the cases) and had mixed feelings or were displeased more often (34 percent). The age of the next-older child markedly affected the sentiments of the mother. For example, when the next-older brother or sister was 21 months of age or less when the child who was the focus of the Sears, Maccoby, and Levin study was born, only 9 percent of the mothers were delighted; but when the next-older child was 55 months or more of age, 52 percent of the mothers expressed delight. Comparable figures for mixed feelings and displeasure were 68 and 32 percent.

PREGNANCY

In the United States, women vary widely in their physical response to pregnancy, just as they do in their psychological response. During the early months of pregnancy, many experience nausea, or morning sickness. For a few, nausea persists throughout the pregnancy. Periods of faintness, food cravings, and moodiness are also frequent. Many modern obstetricians, particularly those with a psychiatric point of view, believe that such symptoms are due in part to the woman's culturally conditioned anxiety; that is, if women fear pregnancy, they expect a difficult time, and, hence, they have a difficult time. Some case-history material suggests that women who genuinely and deeply desire a child, and who have few fears about their ability to bear it and care for it after birth, are less disturbed in health during pregnancy than women who are fearful or ambivalent about having a baby. But this point has not been definitely established.

In other words, culture may affect so apparently physical a condition as the mother's well-being when she is carrying a child. The idea that the early stages of pregnancy are usually accompanied by illness is part of United States folklore, although many women experience well-being from conception to delivery. For most of those who are uneasy early in pregnancy, the frequency and intensity of their symptoms abate after the child quickens, at about four months after conception.

SOME INFLUENCES ON PRENATAL DEVELOPMENT

The baby at birth is essentially the result of the combination of his father's and mother's genes, but environmental influences have also affected him. It is known that mothers who have good diets during pregnancy suffer less from illness and that they threaten to or actually miscarry less frequently than women who have poor diets. Children born to well-nourished mothers have better health records during their first 2 weeks of life, and fewer major diseases afflict them in their first 6 months (Ebbs *et al.*, 1942).

It has also been suggested that precipitately born (short, sharp labor) children and those whose pregnancies were characterized by difficulties such as full or partial *placenta previa* (when the placenta precedes, threatens to precede, or is so located that it may precede the actual birth of the baby) are likely to be hyperactive, hard-to-live with babies and older children (Layman, 1959, author's personal communication). This hyperactivity (at least for boys), has been reported to continue until pubescence when something—perhaps a glandular suppressor variable—intervenes to quiet the child.

Data like these provide a link for the student who wonders why child psychologists use so much writing space (and require so much student reading time) on such topics as prenatal conditions, circumstances of birth, infancy, and the preschool years.

In the days before such tentative research findings were available, these overly active boys would almost certainly have been labeled by their parents, possibly their doctors, and certainly their teachers as chronic troublemakers or even delinquents. Such children usually receive negative, even punitive discipline. The chances are good that this sort of treatment would have moved them into full delinquency.

Since such data have become available, a new way of looking at these children is provided (the group seems to be made up of more boys than girls). The implications are clear: do not regard the child as a *bad* boy who makes mischief simply because he wants to throw the family or classroom into an uproar. Look at him, rather, as a child with a physical condition that is no fault of his own. It may be an obscure type of brain damage or other physical condition that seems not to interfere with normal intellectual development (Dr. Layman reported that the subjects of the study were, on the whole, of well-above average intelligence). The disorder simply makes the boy hyperactive and hard to deal with. Recommendations to parents and teachers might be: be as patient as humanly possible, give time a chance to work, provide constructive outlets for his extra energy whenever possible, and consider his (usually minor) delinquencies with as tolerant an eye as possible. Eventually he may prove not "the type to be hanged but the type to be great." Because of his hyperactivity, he will certainly have had more experiences than the average child and thus more opportunities to learn. If these experiences can be made constructive and wholesome, his condition may actually give him advantages over more passive children.

Also in regard to prenatal development, it has been found that maternal smoking speeds up fetal heart rate; although, nothing is known concerning the significance of this speeding up for either fetal or later life development (Sontag and Wallace, 1935). That it does not damage the unborn child—but possibly helps him—is indicated in a 1966 report by Underwood and co-workers at the 1966 meeting of the American College of Obstetricians and Gynecologists. Nearly 50,000 mothers, half of them smokers, were studied: the babies of the smokers were smaller than average, but had a lower death rate than other premature children. Within a year, they had caught up with the heavier babies of the nonsmoking mothers. The smoking mothers actually had less toxemia of pregnancy than the nonsmoking mothers.

Diseases such as syphilis may affect the fetus devastatingly. The mild disease rubella, or German measles, particularly when it occurs during the first trimester of pregnancy, may result in the birth of a child who is deaf, visually defective, mentally defective (including microcephalic), or afflicted with a pathological heart condition. Combinations of these defects may also occur.

X-ray treatment, especially heavy doses during early pregnancy, may produce disorders of the central nervous system, deformation, blindness, or microcephaly (Murphy, 1929, 1947).

Incompatibility in blood type between mother and infant, where the mother is Rh-negative and the child Rh-positive, may result in brain damage and/or death to the child. This incompatibility affects first-born children less often than it does those born later. With each pregnancy by an Rh-positive father, the Rh-negative mother produces more antibodies, and these antibodies interfere with oxygen distribution in the fetus or newborn. Modern medical techniques, including total replacement of the infant's blood supply immediately or soon after birth, have reduced the danger to the Rh-damaged baby. All couples should be informed about their Rh blood type, since possession of information concerning possible danger helps the specialist avoid the danger.

Examination of the pregnancy histories, birth circumstances, and preschool living circumstances both of normal children and the deviant children described immediately above give the discerning parent, elementary school teacher (and teachers who meet the child later in his development) "extra handles" with which to deal with him, at least in the sense that they understand him better. Improvement in adults' coping techniques may salvage many juvenile lives—or at least improve their destinies.

Until the last few years, there was only one clearly established relation between circumstances of genetics-pregnancy and the relatively rare condition of mongolism or Down's disease (about 1.1 in 1000 births as reported by Gruenberg, 1964, p. 282). Older mothers were known to have Down's disease (or syndrome) babies in greater proportion than younger mothers (Malzberg, 1950). Few if any authorities believed that heredity played any part in producing a Down's syndrome baby. The data are now less clear. Abnormal chromosomal distributions, including the fact that Down's syndrome victims have 47 rather than the usual 46 chromosomes, are characteristic of the disease. The evidence, as summarized in an excellent discussion by Gruenberg (1964, pp. 281–282 and 298–302), continues clear that older mothers are more likely than younger mothers to have babies with Down's disease. Gruenberg presents data that the expectancy for mothers between 15 and 24 of bearing a Down's disease baby is .31 per 1000 births, while for mothers between 45 and 49, the rate is 9.99 (p. 302). First born are more likely than later born children to have the disease.

Causes of the chromosomal abnormality that accompanies and presumably causes Down's disease are still not known, although it is still believed that some factor other than heredity is responsible.

Until the days of antibiotics, these retarded children were not considered as a major "problem" by society, since most of them died young (typically from respiratory disease) and it was generally considered that, even though they had lived beyond the age of 14 or so, they would not become normally pubescent. Hence, society did not consider it likely that the *children* of Down's disease victims might in turn become either problems *to* or the responsibility *of* society (although society has assumed the responsibility of caring for Down's disease victims themselves, since they are almost always mentally retarded, and usually severely so).

Antibiotics and medical research have changed this picture: several cases have occurred of Down's disease girls having babies (some of whom also had the disease, some of whom did not). Thus, the problem of the children of Down's disease victims has already appeared and will probably increase. At present, no clear answers to the present and future problem have appeared.

Until fairly recently, the potential effect of the mother's emotional state on the development of the fetus has been minimized. Old wives' tales about "marking the baby" are not, of course, valid. Yet evidence exists to show that such things as maternal emotional stress, unhappiness in marriage, and extreme rejection of a pregnancy predispose women to uneasy pregnancies, premature births, and possibly miscarriages, and to the production of tense, hyperactive, hard-to-live-with babies (see, Lakin, 1957; Howe, in personal communication, has also provided evidence for this from the Kaui pregnancy study) and other research was discussed immediately above.

Childbirth   Aside from the medical-physiological, little evidence exists concerning the effects of the birth process on the later adjustment of the baby. Prematurity poses psychological as well as physical perils, and is discussed in Chapter 3. Little is known about the effects of severe versus mild delivery, or long as contrasted with moderate or short times of delivery.

The medical aspects of childbirth are of only incidental interest here. Since World War II, the handling of childbirth seems to have become steadily more natural and sensible. There is increasing regard for childbirth as a natural phenomenon, shared by all mammals; the conviction is growing that mothers may not need to be heavily anesthetized during delivery; and there is general agreement that prolonged hospitalization following normal childbirth is unnecessary. Restrictions placed on the activities of the new mother after her return home have also been decreased by physicians and nurses.

Patterns of Child Care   For a majority of American couples, the birth of their first child is what they expect it to be: a time of mature and deep enjoyment. Parenthood is inevitably larded with troubles and cares, illness, financial stresses, and personal annoyances; but over-all it is a deeply satisfying experience. There are, of course, couples too immature to accept children; too sheltered or spoiled themselves to assume full, ungrudging responsibility for their children; or too rigid and dominating to allow their children freedom to grow. But within the limits of their personal make-up and knowledge, almost all do the best they can to promote the welfare of their children. Their practices are influenced by their personalities, singly and together, by the happiness of their marriage, by their intelligence, and by their understanding of child development. But there are relatively few ill-meaning parents, although such certainly exist. This point is one often ignored or forgotten by teachers, child psychologists and psychiatrists, social workers, and the host of persons who write, teach, and counsel about child-rearing methods and parent-child relations. Of course, hard-to-live-with children may also cause hard-to-live-with parents. This vicious interaction intensifies the problems of both the children and their families.

Enough *desperate* conflicts exist between the child and his parent, however (and all the *physical* power is on the side of the parent), so that some states have passed, and many are considering passing, child-abuse laws. Without such laws, doctors or nurses who report serious ill-treatment of a child by his parent(s) run the risk of libel suits. With such laws, the all-too-frequent cases of serious parental mistreatment (this occurs with distressing frequency even with very young infants) can be safely reported to proper authorities. A busy urban general practitioner or pediatrician may find 100 or more such cases per year in his practice, some of which result in the child's death.

Provence (1965) advances several suggestions to account for this. Many mothers, deeply depressed following the birth of a baby, remain able to "put on their faces to go out in public." Alone at home with the baby, they may neglect or abuse him grossly. Other mothers are simply excessively disorganized. The current tendency to release patients from mental hospitals after short periods of treatment (and this practice is probably desirable in the long run and for most people) allows many men and women freedom to become parents before they have recovered fully from their own illness. Regardless of how much the baby is wanted and loved, a new baby adds considerable stress to any home. This increased stress may be more than the partially recovered parent(s) can tolerate. Finally, with the present trend toward ever earlier marriage, many young people become parents before they are emotionally ready for marriage and least of all parenthood. There are undoubtedly other factors contributing to gross child abuse, but such variables as Provence mentions seem plausible in accounting for what seems to be its growing frequency.

An enormous collaborative project involving common methods of gathering data on genetic, pregnancy, and delivery data has been going on for several years; and it will continue (including follow-up data on the children) at least until 1972. Some 40,000 cases will be included in the over-all study, which will undoubtedly have many subparts. The study has been carefully planned and should yield rich results. Its plan is given in a publication by the National Institute of Neurological Diseases and Blindness (1963).

Patterns of parental behavior begin when the infant enters the home. As the authors of one monograph have aptly put it:

> With the arrival of the first baby, the parents are at once plunged into a new situation which is vastly different from pre-parental marital life. The child's coming into the household automatically sets up a more complex social structure and a different

kind of relationship by introducing into the family a completely dependent organism for whose continued existence and happiness the parents are largely responsible. The advent of the baby necessitates many changes in the family schedule; regardless of his virtues, a baby is a far from ideal roomer—he is dirty, noisy, and addicted to highly irregular hours. His presence may restrict the social life of his parents, and his expensive taste for hospitals, doctors, and new clothes may cause them financial embarrassment.[2]

Countless books, pamphlets, and articles have been written advising parents how to handle this "far from ideal roomer." New parents are understandably insecure, faced as they are with an organism whose grip on life seems at best precarious, who cannot tell them either what ails him or what is right with him, who is both unscheduled and unreasonable, yet who possesses a lively flame of ultimate humanity.

Data about family child care (see Frank, 1965) also suggest that studies in the field have been sufficiently inconclusive that almost any definite *simple* recommendation presented by any author can be contradicted by contrary evidence given by another author with a different *simple* recipe. Frank (p. 191) states: "No factors were found in the parent-child interaction of schizophrenics, neurotics, or those with behavior disorders which could be identified as unique to them or which could distinguish one group from the other, or any of the groups from the families of the controls." By *controls* Frank refers to families of normal children. He bases his conclusion on a survey of research of the past forty years.

The next chapter discusses in detail some of the faults of studies of family-child interaction like those on which Frank bases his pessimistic conclusion. However, material presented later in this text suggests that, while simple, specific recommendations for child care may be untenable, research concerning children and their families has resulted in a number of relatively broad or general principles derived from reasonably sound data.

The Infant's Sensory and Response Equipment and Development

INTRODUCTION

In the first part of this chapter, more emphasis was put on the influence of the environment or *setting* for learning than on the infant's *equip-*

2 Reprinted with permission from The American Psychological Association. A. L. Baldwin, from Baldwin, Kalhorn, and Breese, 1945.

ment for learning from and responding to it. As Hebb (1949) and Piaget (from treatments of his work by J. McV. Hunt, 1961, and Flavell, 1963), among others, have pointed out, the infant's transactions with his environment are no more a one-way street than those with his family, as described in the first paragraph of this chapter. From his environment, an infant receives stimuli of all sorts (for example, visual, auditory, and olfactory). He responds to them. His responses result in several possible environmental changes. If they please his parents or caretakers, they are likely to give him more of the same type of stimulation. If they displease the responsible caretaker (and, presumably, displease the baby himself), an attempt is made to remove or reduce the stimuli causing the displeasure. By his own behavior, even at the earliest age, he has considerable success in getting "more of what he wants and less of what he does not want." As a very tiny baby, for example, he can control his food intake by stopping sucking, by dropping off to sleep at the breast or bottle, by sucking vigorously, or by crying to "signify" that he is hungry. As he grows older, his control of his environment so as to suit him becomes greater, partly because he begins, in a primitive way, to "solve problems," such as reaching for or moving toward an object he wants to manipulate. His steadily increasing control of his own body aids this process of selecting stimuli. He can roll from one to another side to seek or avoid a stimulus or pattern of stimuli; he can "shift scenes" by going from his stomach to his back or vice versa. Sitting up, creeping, standing, and walking enable him more and more to obtain stimuli he wants or avoid those he dislikes or is tired of. As a young infant, he begins visual tracking (voluntarily moving his eyes to follow a shifting object). He learns to move his head, localize sounds, and to look at the source of the sound. Of course, "problem solving" and body control go hand in hand and complement each other.

Piaget presents a vivid description of six classes or stages of sensory motor development through which the infant passes in his first 21 to 22 months. This age span is classified by the present author as *infancy:* 21 months is about the age at which normal children change from predominantly nonverbal to verbal organisms. It is at this average age they become "truly human." (Piaget's sensorimotor stages are presented in modified form later in this chapter, after the individual categories of environmental reception-response modalities have been discussed.)

Obviously, an environment has no influence on the individual unless it affects him. This is as true of a baby as of an adult. The impact of environment on babies is made upon their sense organs. At the beginning of life, sense organs receive stimulation from the environment; and the infant responds to this stimulation in rather simple, almost automatic ways. Babies attach no *meaning,* as older children and adults know the term, to stimuli. Light rays strike their eyes, register on the retinas, and are transmitted to the appropriate nervous centers. Reaction is simple: in bright light, the pupils contract and some of the stimulation is shut out; in dim light, the pupils expand and more light reaches the retina. Soon the baby blinks as stimuli approach his eye rapidly; later, more complex responses are made to visual stimuli.

Simple reactions, such as pupil dilation and contraction and the blink reflex, persist through life; but meaning is progressively added to visual stimuli (and all others). Presently, a three-sided figure comes to be distinguished from a circle. Eventually it is labeled as a triangle. A certain face becomes "mother." A given configuration of distance and contrast is recognized as "a place I may fall off," and so on.

By perception, then, is meant awareness of sensory stimuli, attention to them, and attachment of at least some adaptive meaning to them.

When the matter is reduced to its simplest elements, it may be said that an adult functions well or poorly, succeeds or fails, depending on the way he manages his behavior in terms of his perception of himself and the world around him, and on how his perceptions fit with those of the people among whom he lives. His sense organs, the meanings he gives to the sensations he receives and his responses to the stimuli determine this consonance or dissonance.

Such a statement, of course, begs the important question of how he comes to give a certain meaning, or make a certain response, to the stimuli that impinge on him. The elements of these fundamental processes are discussed in Chapter 4.

The bodily equipment by which an infant receives stimulation (his sense modalities) has been classified in different ways, but the following scheme is one commonly used:

1. Vision
2. Hearing, or audition
3. Smell, or olfaction
4. Taste, or gustation
5. Touch, or pressure and contact
6. Touch, or movement (kinesthesis)
7. Pain[3]
8. Temperature, or thermal sensitivity

Until recently, studies of infants have been devoted in large part to determining the nature and function of the sensory equipment with which they came into the world. There are elaborate and highly controlled studies of what and how a baby sees, hears, tastes, and so on. No discussion of infancy can ignore the child's sensory equipment, because it is basic to everything that happens to him for the duration of his life.

---

3 It should be noted that excessive stimulation in any modality may produce pain.

It has been mentioned that the absence of a sensory mode, as in deafness or blindness, leads to problems of living very different from those encountered by normal children.

The sweep of sensory development from infancy to adulthood, or even to the age of 2, is staggering. At birth, the child sees dimly. He has no notion of what he sees, or of what his reaction to it should be. But as an adult, he reacts to the rainy sky, or the slippery pavement; while driving, he attends to the tentative behavior of a pedestrian two blocks away; to the difference in texture between velvet and satin; and to the meaning of the printed pages. On the basis of visual stimuli and the experiences he has had with them, he determines his behavior. The rainy sky suggests a raincoat; the slippery pavement, taking the bus to work. The errant pedestrian causes him to reduce his driving speed; the perception of velvet or satin leads to different sewing responses or a different set of expectations about touching or feeling. The printed page provokes thought, irritation, sympathy, amusement, or some other well-differentiated response.

Although increasing maturity of the sense organs is partly responsible for this increased acuity of perception and response, most of it is due to the learning opportunities afforded the older child or adult—opportunities that the infant has not yet had.

Most authors of books on child psychology and development probably experience considerable conflict in deciding how to treat sensorimotor equipment and development of infants. Their own infancy is long behind them and they have no memory of it. They are also writing for an audience that has no memory of its infancy, and which fails to see the connection between a treatment of infant sensorimotor development and the behavior and characteristics of the older child who is both more "interesting," and with whom they must cope as parents, teachers, or research workers.

Yet the infant's sensorimotor equipment is fundamental to all his later development, and a sensible, functional presentation of it must be given.

Knobloch and Pasamanick (1960) found no differences in sensorimotor status between Negro and white infants; but when the children they studied had reached preschool age, the Negro children were substantially lower on measures of intelligence than the white children. This difference is almost undoubtedly due to the environmental exposures of the two groups of children. As a group, Knobloch's and Pasamanick's Negro children came from homes that were poor in psychological-sociological-economic senses, while the white children's homes offered better opportunities in all three areas. While home data are not given in any detail by Knobloch and Pasamanick, it is not difficult to create a composite picture of the two types of home: for the Negro child (or a white child in similar economic circumstances) there is marginal economic security. This means a number of things: a limited number of toys with which to play, thus a limited chance at the important new learnings which play offers. Homes tend to be overcrowded and usually include a television set that is not used selectively. This means that the child's eyes, ears, and kinesthetic senses are overwhelmed by a mass of stimuli with no chance for him to organize and classify them. So organized and classified, they can thus later be used systematically so as to do well at the sort of problem solving behavior that helps a child earn a high score on an intelligence test or do well with his school work. The white child's home (or that of a Negro child from adequate economic circumstances) is likely to be more organized and less cluttered. There are more drawers in which to put away things. He can count on the family coming together at mealtimes, and he has a set time for going to bed. This helps him with his own "inner clock"—his sense of time and how to organize it. While he will usually have a television set, it will be used selectively rather than constituting one more addition to a generally noisy background. His senses are not overwhelmed; he has time to sort out impressions, give meaning to them, and store them away for later efficient use.

An illustration (anecdotal, not scientific) of how circumstances influence the development of the senses concerns a middle-aged couple whom the author knows well: the husband was born with poor vision. From childhood, he has been extremely nearsighted. The wife's vision was excellent from birth to the present time. To offset his extreme nearsightedness (which was not discovered until he was an adolescent), the husband learned to compensate by using his other senses, to a certain degree as the blind child does: he memorized distances, he learned to reach out to touch the surfaces of walls and sills of doors so that in the dimmest light or complete dark he knew where he was. The wife had no need to make such compensations. From the time of their marriage, they have bickered mildly about their nighttime habits: if the wife gets up for a snack or to tend a child, she immediately switches on all lights along the way, thus arousing her husband from his sleep. If he gets up for similar reasons, the compensations he learned as a small child still serve him: he can move without hesitation or error from one room or floor of the house to the other, occasionally touching something to check his whereabouts, but turning on no lights until he has reached his destination. His wife sleeps peacefully through this; he lies awake until she returns and turns off lights.

VISION

Normal older children and adults react to such characteristics of light as color or hue, brightness, saturation (how much of the hue is present), and length of exposure time. They use these dimensions in discriminative reactions and combine them with stimulation received from the eye muscles in order to judge distance, size, distortion, and so on. Additional information is gained by fusing the separate images received by the two eyes.

The infant has little more than the ability to react by pupillary reaction to different intensities of light, although some believe that the ability to distinguish figure from ground—to perceive primitive contrast —is present from birth (Hebb, 1949). During the developmental process following birth, size and shape constancy are developed. An older child knows that he can blot out the image of a mountain in the distance by holding his hand a few inches from his eyes, or by holding his thumb close to one eye when the other is closed. But he knows that this does not mean that his hand or thumb is larger than the mountain. He has also gained the ability to recognize a circle as a circle, even though it is tilted so that the actual sensory image is one of an oval. The infant has not yet learned clues such as these, which help the older child or adult maintain order in his world.

At birth, normal babies possess organically complete visual equipment. Further visual development and differentiation, particularly around the fovea (the center of direct vision) go on for about 16 weeks after birth (Zubek and Solberg, 1954). Zubek and Solberg describe an investigation of the electrical reaction patterns of the infant eye. Not until about 6 months of age did the thirty-five normal infants studied begin to show reactions to flashes of light rather similar to the responses of adults. At birth, little reaction was present to either moderate or bright light. Three-month-olds showed a slight reaction.

Much evidence exists to show that the infant's use of visual equipment is rudimentary. The following factors probably enter into the inadequate use he makes of vision for the first few days to weeks of his life: birth may be accompanied by mild injury (trauma) to the eye; the shape of the infant eyeball is not well adapted to adult-type vision, in all probability infants are nearsighted; accommodation—the bulging of the lens for close, and thinning or attenuation for distant, stimuli—seems to be present to only a meager degree; and, finally, the infant's eyes do not track well. When the left eye of an adult meets a stimulus, the right eye swings to fix on it. The eyes move in a parallel and coordinated way. Observation of the newborn shows imperfect coordination: the right eye does not necessarily follow the course of the left. The eyes of many infants pursue a relatively uncoordinated course, to the discomfort and surprise of the uninformed adult observer, unaccustomed to seeing a left eye going north, a right eye west or south.

An organism can obviously do nothing about a stimulus until to some degree it can adapt and attend to it. It follows from this that the first useful visual development should be adapting to and fixating on a source of light. Research indicates that this is the case with the human infant. There is some disagreement about when this happens (Sherman and Sherman, 1925; Gesell and Thompson, 1934), but convincing evidence exists (Sherman and Sherman, 1925) to show that the pupillary reflex comes into play two or three hours after birth. The pupillary reflex—the contraction of the pupil in strong light, its dilation in weak light—may be thought of as a protective, adaptive reflex. In response to flashes of light, infants may also show startle responses (a flexion response, not voluntary), Moro reflexes (a tensing of the body, flailing out and retracting of the arms, with roughly coordinated leg movements—a primitive extension response), and the eye-neck response (a throwing back of the head).

Equally good evidence indicates that an infant can fixate at least one eye on a source of light within a few hours after birth, and that by the time he is 2 or 3 days old, he can bring both eyes together to fixate on a light source (Zubek and Solberg, 1954). Efficiency in this fixation, and ability to fixate one thing after another, appear around the fourth week (Gesell and Thompson, 1934).

Ability to follow a moving stimulus—called ocular pursuit or tracking —is the next development in vision. This ability is of obvious biological usefulness, since it is the basis for later crucial avoidance and approach reactions. Although there is lively disagreement about the time at which tracking appears (Pratt, 1954), there is agreement that infants first follow a stimulus that is moving horizontally. When this new skill is fairly well established, the ability to follow a vertically moving stimulus appears. Only later can the infant follow a rotating stimulus. The ages at which these skills appear have been set at $4\frac{1}{2}$, 9, and 10 weeks by one of the more careful investigators in the field (Shirley, 1931). Most studies indicate that some tracking occurs within the first week after birth, but that early tracking movements are jerky and frequently broken up by reversals of direction (McGinnis, 1930).

There is good agreement that infants react to color (Munn, 1938). To arrive at this conclusion, however, different colored and noncolored stimuli must be equated for brightness. This equation must be done by adult standards, since infants are not able to tell us whether something is brighter or darker than something else; hence there is always some question about color vision and color preferences in infancy. One experimenter (Smith, 1936) has found that the responses of boy babies to colored stimuli differ from those of girls very soon after birth. Others have found different reactions to colored and to uncolored light by as early as 15 days of age (Chase, 1937). It seems almost certain that by 6 weeks of age the average baby is making some sort of differential response to color.

Studies of babies' color preferences are numerous (see summaries by

Munn, 1938; Pratt, 1954; and Zubek and Solberg, 1954). The "preference" is ordinarily judged by fixation time: if a baby stares longer at one color than another, it is assumed that he prefers it. According to this criterion, babies prefer yellows and reds at first; yellows lose some of their potency later; older children move toward the adult pattern obtaining for our culture, with blues and greens preferred.

Many of the early studies of color preference were corrected in a 1964 study by Spears. He worked with 4-month-old infants, using very careful controls so as to eliminate as many as possible of the sources of error that might affect his results. His findings are that babies of this age clearly prefer red and blue to gray; that if an object colored according to the baby's preference, but not shaped so as to attract his interest was compared with one of an interesting shape but nonpreferred color, the baby tended to choose by shape rather than color; and that bulls-eye patterns were particularly appealing. His measure of interest was plausible: two stimuli were presented at the same time, and the one at which the youngster looked ·the longest was considered to be his "favorite." "Position preference" can be a serious drawback to this method. Position preference may consist of: (1) a preference for looking to the right (for instance) rather than the left, or (2) inertia, that is, a tendency to keep on looking in the same direction. However, the matter of pattern-preference is not by any means clear, as different studies show different results due to the fact that some authors use one set of patterns and forms, other authors different ones. Preferences probably also change with age, so that the preference established by Spears might have been different if he had used different patterns, or older or younger infants.

This study is particularly interesting, as it has been generally believed that infant's attention-involvement is dominated first by color, second by shape. Color domination is ordinarily considered to be more "primitive" than form domination. Spears, in other words, suggests that "infants may be more sophisticated than we have thought," although he might not approve of having this conclusion attributed to him.

Infants respond differently to different intensities of light. In contrast to behavior of older children and adults, infants are most active in rather dim light, least active in moderate-to-bright light. This tendency to quiet down rather than grow active under conditions of moderate light stimulation may account for the common observation that "babies have their nights and days mixed up." This preference is a matter of considerable inconvenience to the average household. Learning to fit his schedule into that of the adults around him is one of the earliest learning tasks of the child and one for which his original sensory equipment and patterns of behavior equip him poorly.

One possible explanation of the frustrating reversal of nights and days manifested by infants has been provided indirectly by Hebb (1949,

1955). He and his students and co-workers have amassed evidence indicating that the human organism can become "stimulus hungry." College students, placed in soundproof darkness, touching as little as possible, and smelling nothing, soon grow exceedingly disturbed, even experiencing visual and auditory hallucinations (Bexton et al., 1954; Heron et al., 1956). After release from such experiences of extreme sensory deprivation, their work efficiency suffers for some time. However, there has been some difficulty in replicating these studies. Perhaps the infant's exasperating relaxation during the day—full of sights, sounds, and smells—is due to a surfeit of stimulation. But, during the quiet, dark night, he grows stimulus-hungry and comes briskly to, seeking stimulation or providing it for himself. Sullivan also suggests that extreme anxiety may cause sleep.

During the four months following early infancy, visual perception and response become much more acute, and enormous amounts of learning occur. The 6-month-old child can apparently distinguish between his father and mother, between familiar and strange adults, and between expressions of pleasure and disapproval. He forms clear images, reaches for things and grasps them with moderate accuracy. He definitely possesses the ability to distinguish colors; his judgment of distance is fair, although he makes determined efforts to reach things outside his normal grasp when he sees them and registers the seeing. He has probably outgrown his baby tendency to be least active in the light, most active in the dark. He recognizes certain toys as favorites; he often shows a degree of alarm when placed in strange situations. In general, he has become an exceedingly complicated visual receptor and reactor.

All these things come about through the interaction of his different senses and his own behavior. The study summarized below illustrates this.

In 1964, White and Castle reported on a group of infants who would ordinarily have been reared with little contact with adults. In the judgment of most professional workers in the field, including the author, this means they would not have enough stimulation to develop normal visual function. Some infants (the experimental group) were given small amounts of extra handling during their first 5 weeks of life. A control (no extra handling) group showed significantly less visual interest in their environments at the end of the study. Such a study relates to kinesthesis (the sensations from and reaction to being handled) as much as it does to vision. In other words, it illustrates the interaction among the different senses: how one can facilitate another or, presumably, how deficiency in one can retard others.

Interaction of vision with the environment, of course, is influenced by the parts of the environment that have special appeal for the baby. Thomas' 1965 study indicates that as they grow older, more complex stimuli in the environment hold the baby's interest longer than simpler stimuli (his younger group of infants ranged in age from 2 to 14 weeks, his older babies from 15 to 26 weeks). Speculating, we might say this is a good thing: the more complex the phenomena investigated (looked at, in this case), the richer the experience, and the more to be learned.

Visual perception of depth, its time of onset, and its development are particularly important. If he has not yet developed it, the baby cannot manage the reaching, manipulating behavior that is necessary for him to learn about the world around him. This reaching, manipulating behavior coordinates with and further sharpens visual functioning, and plays an important role in the child's learning about the "permanence of objects" (a concept that will be further defined and developed as Piaget is discussed later in this chapter). Manipulative behavior also helps a child develop discrimination and acuity of smell and taste (sometimes in ways that bother parents, such as when he reaches accurately for something a mother does not consider hygienic, and pops it immediately in his mouth). Accurate depth perception can result in a harmless or painful learning experience (he reaches unerringly for the cat, pulls its tail, and gets scratched). But learning about pain (as long as a child is not seriously injured) is just as necessary a lesson as learning about pleasure. In a study by Polak, Emde, and Spitz (1964), to determine when depth perception begins for twenty-three infants, the authors judged that a child could perceive depth when he responded differently to a human face and a colored, same-sized picture of the same face (a rather clever, valid-seeming technique). According to this criterion, their babies were able to perceive depth by or slightly earlier than 3 months of age.

No discussion of depth perception is complete without mentioning the interesting, original work of Eleanor J. Gibson (1963). She has developed an intriguing device which she refers to as the "visual cliff." In her tests of babies (with whom she cannot work until they can crawl: thus the population she reports on in the article referred to immediately above ranges from $6\frac{1}{2}$ to 12 months old), her visual cliff consists of a raised center runway. A strong sheet of glass extends outward on either side of the runway. On one side, the shallow side, a textured pattern is placed immediately under the glass. The same textured pattern is placed much further below the glass on the other side. If human infants of the ages she has studied have depth perception, they should avoid the deep side.

Her prediction was supported, since "The great majority of them avoided the deep side, despite the entreaties of their mothers and tempting toys. We are ready to assert, therefore, that perception of depth has developed as soon as locomotion is possible in this young organism" (p. 12). She believes that development of depth perception, at least of this self-protective sort (keeping oneself from falling off things) does not depend on having had experiences in "stepping down, climbing up, or walking into things" (p. 12). Her implication is that such depth perception is unlearned, or "native," although this does not follow from her data: any baby, by the time he is $6\frac{1}{2}$ months old (the youngest of her subjects) has had an endless set of chances to develop concepts of up and down: he has been picked up, he has been put down, he has been carried, he has been held on laps, typically he has rolled off a couch or chair on which he has been placed, and so on. Finally, as anyone who has ever cared for a crawling baby can testify, his depth perception is by no means accurate enough to keep him from falling off things. One of a parent's most constant preoccupations is to keep him from doing exactly that!

Scientists as well as parents have long puzzled over what the world really looks like to infants. No one can ever answer this question directly, of course, since no baby can tell us. One of the great early psychologist-philosophers, William James, has suggested that the infant's world is a "big, booming, buzzing confusion." Indirect evidence about the infant's visual perception of his world has been gleaned from observations and reports of people who, after a lifetime of blindness, have had their sight suddenly restored; this evidence supports James's position. Von Senden's observations on a number of such cases have been reported by Hebb (1949).

These newly-sighted people cannot discriminate cubes from squares nor squares from triangles without handling them patiently, and checking and rechecking their visual images with the touch modality to which they have become accustomed. While in the hospital following surgery, some learned color names that they retained eleven months later, whereas they forgot the names of geometric forms. They were shown an egg, a potato, and a cube of sugar until they could name them promptly; but when these objects were put into colored light, they were not recognized. A cube of sugar could be named easily when placed on a table or in another person's hand, but not when it was hung by a thread with a change in background.

For normal older children and adults, the perception and differentiation of squares, cubes, circles, and so forth is so prompt that we think of it as automatic or inborn. This does not seem to be the case. Hebb believes that recognition of such common figures is the result of perceptual learning; that they can be recognized and identified only after a gradual process during which contrast, or the figure-ground relation, dominates perception first; then, separate and laborious attention is given to each part of the figure; until finally, with increasing speed and accuracy, the whole is identified as a whole. The baby, according to Hebb, comes into the world with only a "primitive, sensorily determined unity." This unity is simply the figure-ground relation (the infant can see a solid blot of ink on an indefinite white background, but ascribes no formal characteristics either to the figure or to the ground). Later the human organism perceives "nonsensory unities" such as the corner of a room, the middle of a rope, or the foreground of a scene; and finally he arrives at "identity," which involves seeing both the similarities and differences of a given thing in relation to other things.

Observation of the development of a baby in his first year suggests that he is attempting to become acquainted with all of his environment with all of his senses: he pokes, fondles, clutches, tastes, rubs, smells, manipulates with both hands and feet, stares long and quietly, observes things from far away, brings them near. It is as though he were trying to coordinate each sense with every other as well as with all the objects (including people and animals) he can encompass with his senses. Piaget, as discussed later, makes interesting analyses of this behavior.

HEARING

No sense operates in isolation, and responses made to stimuli to one or more sense modalities feed back to the modalities still more and different stimuli in an endless circle. It is best then, keeping this in mind, to proceed with a brief summary of infant hearing. There has recently been renewed scientific interest in this area for a number of reasons: to wit, the infant's sensorium and his reactions to his environment's input are *the* foundation for all his future behavior. He does *not* unfold naturally like a flower, as many earlier authors have said (implicitly and explicitly). He "unfolds" according to the way he *learns* or is *taught* to develop. In other words, the idea that development is an inevitable sequence occurring more or less independently of the environment is untenable. Biology may dictate a sequence but environment can change the direction and speed of the sequence, limit or extend its potential level of competence or efficiency, and even inhibit it entirely.

As might be expected, the young research workers who have become interested in the field have developed interesting and precise new instruments. They are much more sophisticated than their elders about research methods and scientific procedures. But each works with different instruments, babies of different ages and types and in different settings, as well as with different stimuli. Hence, their results are often seemingly contradictory.

It can still be safely said that adults and older children distinguish the pitch of sounds (whether they are high or low) and loudness or intensity, quality or timbre, and duration. There is some disagreement about whether the infant responds at all to sound immediately after birth. The fact that some have been observed to do so and our knowledge that the hearing structures are reasonably complete at birth lead us to believe that the newborn *can* respond to sound. He may be relatively insensitive to auditory stimuli for the first few days after birth, probably because his ear cavities are filled with amniotic fluid. But this drains off after the first few hours or days of life and from then on increasingly frequent and adaptive reactions to sounds can be observed.

There are well-controlled studies (Sontag and Richards, 1938; Bernard and Sontag, 1947) which indicate that babies respond to sound before birth and that their response is independent of physical vibration (response is made to sound itself, not to mechanical vibration). Loud, sharp sounds produce a reaction from the time of birth in most infants; and the range of responses increases rapidly during the first two weeks of life as the ears clear (Pratt *et al.*, 1930). There does not appear to be much reaction to the ordinarily-pitched human voice until about the fourth week (Hetzer and Tudor-Hart, 1927).

Experiments by Stubbs (1934) demonstrated that very young infants react principally to loudness and duration of sound. Tuning forks, pure-tone whistles, and other types of stimuli have been used to study infants' reactions to both pitch and intensity. No differential reactions to high and low tones have been conclusively shown, although some investigators (see Pratt, 1954) claim that high tones excite, low tones soothe very young children. The common-sense lore of the lullaby may be based on such a concept. Rough discrimination of sound pitch exists in babies 1 to 4 days old. They will show different patterns of breathing and leg movement for a 200 rather than for a 1000 cycle per second sound, but not between a 200 and a 500 cycle pair of sounds (Leventhal and Lipsitt, 1964). As far as loudness is concerned, new research fits well enough with old. For example, Bartoshuk (1964) shows that the louder the sound, the greater the acceleration of heart rate (presumably, the higher the heart rate, the more excited or potentially excitable the baby is).

We used to be able to say that short, intense noises disturb children but that they begin to adapt to these sounds after 10 to 15 seconds (Haller, 1932; Stubbs, 1934). But new findings have been made by Eisenberg *et al.* (1964); Kaye and Levin (1963); and Keen (1964). Keen finds that it takes a sound lasting at least 10 seconds to change or stop a baby's sucking behavior. Eisenberg *et al.*, agree, but Kaye and Levin find no change in sucking behavior even for sounds lasting up to 15 seconds (actually a long time for a baby and even for an adult; let the reader try counting off 15 seconds while doing absolutely nothing else).

In other words, we are not nearly so sure what to think about babies and their reactions to sound as we thought we were even six years ago when the first edition of this book was written. Far from being upset about this, the author is pleased: disagreement in the literature stirs up interest; puts the different authors into communication with each other; causes them to repeat each other's studies, define the conditions of their own studies more carefully and, all in all, eventually produces better scientific groundwork.

Although no statistically significant results were secured, the author cannot resist mentioning one impeccably designed and conducted study in the area of audition (Casler, 1965). The study is impeccable in the sense that the subjects, while few in number, were well matched and almost every experimental variable that could produce a source of error in the results was eliminated or controlled for. Another virtue of the study is that Casler describes his procedure in sufficient detail and so precisely that others can repeat it. Casler wanted to find out if giving orphanage infants extra verbal stimulation would speed up their verbal development. This, in turn, would presumably indicate that their intelligence had improved. His experimenters first secured the babies' attention. After having done so, they stared blankly at the babies' midriffs (so as to avoid visual contact with the baby or give the baby possible cues from the experimenters' facial expressions). While staring blankly, they counted aloud to the infants in a monotone according to a prearranged and carefully controlled schedule.

It is likely, however, that the controls used by Casler were too rigid. Probably the monotonous counting was so unlike the verbalization a baby gets from his mother or nurse that it had little effect on him. About all Casler demonstrated is that babies from 19 to 59 weeks of age attend to the human voice, but the study is significant in that it can be used as a model for infant research since it is well designed.

In fairness to Casler, it should be added that he has more positive results from an equally well-controlled study in the area of kinesthesis (Casler, 1965).

Also, findings from June Miller's 1963 study of 3-, 4-, and 5-month-old Negro and Caucasian babies failed to show sex or ethnic (race) differences to several different types of sound.

It was originally believed that fear of loud noises was a basic, inborn emotional response, although practical experience with infants and experimental results demonstrate that no two children react in exactly the same way to any stimulus, including sudden sounds (see Pratt, 1954). Where one child may show what we judge to be real terror, another may sleep unperturbed through almost any degree of intense noise.

The auditory pattern from the end of the first few weeks of the child's life—a period that might well be called one of sensory stabilization—to the sixth month is not essentially different from that described for vision. Ability to localize sound, absent in the newborn but obviously of as much biological importance as the ability to fixate and follow moving visual stimuli, comes into play at about the twentieth week (Gesell, 1925). At first inefficient and halting, this ability improves steadily and is moderately accurate by 6 months. By the end of his first half-year, the baby reacts with pleasure to the parental voice; can apparently distinguish scolding or threatening sounds from comforting or loving and protective sounds; frequently exhibits pleasure in music; demonstrates by moving his head that he can follow a sound stimulus, such as a ticking watch, as it is moved in his immediate vicinity; may react to street noises, such as fire sirens or dogs barking; and, in general, has begun to develop a method of differential sound response similar to an adult's. He may pitch his own voice differently as different pitches of sound are produced for him, although not until much later does the average child attempt to reproduce a melody.

SMELL

Partly because in our twentieth-century culture the sense of smell is of relatively little survival value for man, and partly because he makes less use of smell than of his other senses, there is considerably less research on infants' olfactory development than on visual and auditory development.

Research on the sense of smell as separate from taste is difficult. The mouth and nose are intimately connected. Stimuli applied to the nostrils are likely to enter the mouth and affect taste organs. The same difficulty confounds attempts to investigate taste independently. Intense olfactory stimuli, such as ammonia, are also likely to result in pain and sneeze stimulation, thus making the problem of research still more difficult.

However, newborn babies have at one time or another been subjected experimentally to stimulation with such varied substances as ammonia, acetic acid, oil of cloves, anise, essence of lavender, valerian, turpentine, lemon, and many others (Pratt et al., 1930; Disher, 1934). Conclusions have been conflicting because it is often not known whether the responses observed—catalogued as approaching, withdrawing, sucking, smiling, and so on—were due to direct nerve stimulation or the more indirect neural stimulation involved in smell proper.

Very pungent odors, such as from ammonia, seem to produce vigorous responses of withdrawal or displeasure. According to one investigator (see Pratt, 1954), some substances, such as anise oil, seem to produce pleasure.

The renewed interest in the sensorium of the new baby, discussed under the heading of "Hearing," has not resulted in as much growth in knowledge of olfaction as for vision and hearing. This may be because smell is so hard to study and the sense plays a relatively minor role in survival in an industrialized society.

However, two excellent studies have come from the Brown University laboratories (from which, incidentally, some of the best and most sophisticated research in infancy is emerging). Engen, Lipsitt, and Kaye (1963) observed changes in breathing and activity following different types and patterns of olfactory stimulation. They studied twenty babies from 32 to

68 hours of age. First, infants of this tender age definitely *did* respond to odors (such as those of asafetida and anise oil); second, at least for these two substances, the infant adapted (became more indifferent) to repeated applications of the stimuli; third, infants did not react differentially to what adults ordinarily consider pleasant and unpleasant odors. Fourth, the order in which the stimuli were presented affected the nature and amount of the infants' reactions and fifth, increased refinement of response occurred as the babies had more experience with the stimuli (in other words, the babies *learned*). In the second study (Lipsitt, Engen, and Kaye, 1963), it was demonstrated that the developmental-learning rate of newborns is rapid: 4-day-olds were more sensitive (more often showed reactions) than 1-day-olds to asafetida stimulation.

In short, in the very young infant there seems to be a crude reaction to at least certain pungent or penetrating odors, perhaps due more to pain than to smell. More refined reactions, which have been likened to pleasure or displeasure, accompany other odors. Whether the sense of smell is acting independently is doubtful, although at present we can conclude that the smell in the newborn is functional, at least in a crude way.

The transition from relatively unlearned to learned, acculturated, methods of responding to odors is less easily mapped than for vision and hearing. Presumably the same process of increasingly refined discrimination and reaction occurs, although the less prominent place of odor in our culture appears to prevent a high-level development of responses. We know that, as we move up the phylogenetic or evolutionary scale from primitive vertebrates to higher mammals and man, an increasingly smaller proportion of the brain is devoted to the rhinencephalon, or small brain; and in man this comprises only a small patch on the brain's undersurface (Zubek and Solberg, 1954). There are, of course, species variations in this progression.

Although the proportion of man's brain devoted to smell is relatively small, he possesses a good, although customarily underdeveloped, sense of smell—better than that of many of the lower species—and, if we are to believe the folklore about trackers and hunters from the so-called primitive tribes, he can use it acutely when necessary.

Despite the lack of scientific knowledge about the development and role of the sense of smell, ordinary observation suggests that odors have deep cultural and emotional significance, and that learning has produced this significance. To those who have grown up in a Western European culture, such as the United States, the odor of human feces and urine produces reactions that range from mild distaste to nausea. But human urine is valued as a hairdressing among the Eskimos. Perspiration odors are considered to evoke withdrawal reactions. We react negatively to stuffy smells, positively to fresh ones. The odors of spring incite pleasure, relaxation, thoughts of love. Certain perfumes are commonly advertised, and cartooned, as arousing erotic reactions in the human male.

These responses to smells are learned in early childhood in conjunction with major training, pleasure, and pain situations. They appear to be primitive in that they are more often emotional and physical than intellectual and logical, and they seem to be remarkably resistant to change or retraining.

Research and theory about learning, discussed in Chapter 4, include suggestions about how the sense of smell enters into emotionally tinged responses that affect, for example, much of our social, sexual, and food-choice behavior. Some of these responses are adaptive, or helpful; others are maladaptive. For example, it is *not* helpful to an elementary-school teacher if she becomes nauseated when one of her charges throws up.

Although we know little about the development of the sense of smell from the time of birth, when it is apparently nonfunctional, to adulthood, when its influence is pervasive, its effect on behavior is such that more thinking and research in this area are clearly required.

TASTE

Adult taste sensations have been analyzed into four basic tastes: sweet, sour, bitter, and salt. The complex and subtle tastes we experience—numbering at least into the hundreds—are partially due to the sense of smell. The difficulty of studying taste independently of smell and pain has been discussed in the preceding section. Little research on taste has been done with people beyond the age of early infancy and has concerned itself principally with the acuity of the sense of taste and the frequency of taste buds. The indications are that the acuity of this sense lessens with maturity and old age and that there is an actual decrease in the number of taste buds, possibly starting at birth.

As is true of the sense of smell, taste is considered of relatively minor importance in learning compared with sight or hearing, and it has been studied less adequately. Certain findings are, however, agreed upon by most investigators. The preferred taste sensation for infants is sweetness, as in sugar or saccharine solutions. Preference has been judged by presence or amount of sucking and other approach reactions. Even in the very early days after birth, children have shown increased sucking responses to sugar solutions (see Pratt, 1954), and have manifested what adult observers believed were signs of pleasure. These same taste sensations disturb the pulse and breathing rate less than any of the other taste sensations. Sour stimuli seem to be next favored by infants and are also responded to by sucking, although the sucking is less vigorous than with a sweet stimulus. The infant's breathing and circulation are disturbed more by sour solutions than they are by sweet solutions or salt. Salt solutions cause considerable breathing and circulation disturbance, as do bitter solutions, and interrupt the infant's sucking. Babies definitely avoid bitter solutions, and some observers maintain that infants make grimaces characteristic of dislike and disgust when they are offered solutions of quinine (see Pratt, 1954).

Babies in the first few weeks of life show avoidance of certain foods. Whether this is due to the taste, smell, or texture of the foods is not known, but each of the three factors probably enters into the reaction. Many foods will be rejected at the first feeding, apparently without prior learning.

Of course, in many such instances the child has formed certain associations to given types of food or stimulation and merely transfers similar patterns of response to the new food.

The sense of taste is central in the adjustment of the older child and the adult, but taste is so interwoven with the sense of smell and food texture that it is difficult to say just which sense modality is associated with later food preferences or rejections. Studies of adults suggest a relationship between good personal adjustment and lack of food dislikes: people who have few dislikes for certain reasonably common and basic foods show better personal adjustment than those with many food dislikes. Such a finding, of course, holds for groups but not necessarily for any given individual.

Poorly adjusted adults and older children, as is well known, frequently attach their symptoms of maladjustment to physical life processes —they develop psychosomatic symptoms. Peculiar taste preferences, digestive disorders, breathing difficulties, heart "flutters," and so forth, are often symptoms of emotional problems. Since food is essential to life, and since the senses of taste and smell are inextricably bound up with eating, it is important to build up predominantly pleasant associations with these senses and with the entire process of eating.

TOUCH (PRESSURE OR CONTACT)

Studies of pressure independent of contact are difficult to carry out with infants, because it is hard to separate touch or pressure from pain or taste, for example. Even casual observation indicates that the infant reacts in some fashion or another to various types of pressure on most surfaces of his body. Reactions to touch have been observed by the third month of fetal life. Touch sensitivity follows the cephalocaudal course of development: it seems to begin in the lip-nose area and move downward.

With increase in the length of fetal as well as infant life, reactions to touch become increasingly more specific. Different parts of the body are differentially sensitive, as each of us knows from experience with his own body; but systematic explorations of the sensitivity of the entire body are lacking.

Stimulation of the sole of the foot produces a reflex response called the Babinski or plantar response. Some investigators (Zubek and Solberg, 1954) think of these as separate responses. The Babinski can be demonstrated by drawing the convex nail of the little or ring finger lightly from the infant's heel in the direction of his toes. In very early infancy this reflex is ordinarily a fanning or extension of the toes; toward the sixth month it becomes a curling or flexion of the toes for most infants (the plantar phase), and deviation from the normal course of development is used as an indicator of possible neural damage.

Stimulation of the facial areas leads to head-turning in the direction of the contact, markedly so when the infant is awake and hungry, less so when awake and replete, little or not at all when he is asleep. The closer the touch is to the lip area, the more likely it is that head-turning and sucking will occur. Infants apparently do not respond to tickling as such, although some report that the child will show withdrawing movements; nor to itching powder as such or, if at all, very slowly. As is generally true of all of his responses, the infant responds massively to strong stimuli; that is, he reacts all over but less strongly when replete or asleep, more strongly when hungry and awake, and always with a poor sense of direction. However, with repeated trials, he is usually able to locate a bothersome sensation or make an adaptive response, such as approaching and sucking the nipple.

The infant's reactions to skin conditions, binding clothes, and so on, all seem to be less acute than they will be later. He apparently recovers quickly (until he has learned to respond by fright or crying) from bumps, bruises, or pricks. In general, compared with older children and adults, he appears to require stronger stimuli in all sense modalities before he makes a response. However, he quickly learns the meaning of certain pressures and skin sensations, just as he learns refinements of reaction to stimuli in any other sense modality. His adaptation to the breast or bottle grows steadily more refined. At 6 months a slight push here or pull there will usually produce signs of cooperation in dressing. Certain pressures that were originally struggled against, such as hats and caps, are accepted or looked forward to at 6 months. Responses to tactile or touch sensations are reasonably refined, and the 6-month-old baby often seems to enjoy contact for the sake of contact: stroking, patting, and other caressing stimuli to which no attention was paid in early infancy.

MOVEMENT

Kinesthesis, the muscle sense, pervades all of living. Through kinesthesis we "know where we are and where we are going." From about the fourth fetal month, stimulus receptors located in muscles, tendons, joints, and perhaps around blood vessels (see Zubek and Solberg, 1954) report constantly to the brain or spinal nerves sensations that later lead the human to know whether he is sitting, standing, or lying down; the degree of flexion or extension; and the amount, direction, and force of movement of his body and its parts. Even before anything like conscious awareness can be assumed to exist, these sensory reports lead to attempts to correct position, or to approach or withdraw or make other adaptive movements.

The effect of moving the child's body or some part of it through space has been studied less painstakingly than have his reactions to touch. Watson (1924, 1928), one of the earliest psychologists interested in babies, maintained that sudden "dropping" of an infant invariably produced signs of fear, and that such fear was inborn. Later studies and casual observations of infants indicate that this is not true of all babies. It may be that a child's response to such a situation is a function of his basic reactivity; some have held that it depends on the degree of security he feels. In other words, the meaning of responses to loss of support is not agreed on. Probably a majority of small babies show the Moro or startle response to loss of support, and for many this will be followed by crying and signs of agitation and excitement.

Watson also held that restraint or inhibition of the child's ability to move was the basic cause of rage. Careful observation by others has failed to support his position, and many now believe that the infant's response to having his arms held is related to how he has learned to regard such restraint. If he senses hostility or rejection in the holding, he may show signs of rage; but if the restraint is loving or matter-of-course, no emotional response will appear. In many cultures swaddling is so complete that babies are virtually immobilized; but no satisfactory evidence exists that these babies are full of rage. Indeed, the Hopis, among whom confining cradle boards have been frequently used, are among the most peaceful of people.

Infants' spontaneous movements are varied but relatively uncontrolled. Babies seem almost to have a drive toward activity; and it is through random, massive activity that the muscle coordinations which result in sitting, creeping, and walking slowly evolve. When very young infants are held erect, stepping movements may occur, although these are different in pattern from those that later constitute walking. Such stepping movements usually disappear after the first few weeks of life.

By the time the child is 6 months of age he has learned much about being moved and moving himself. Infants, depending partially on how they have been handled, may take delight in centrifugal-type games— being danced with, whirled, and rotated by adults; in height—being lifted above the adult's head; in sensations of loss of support—imitations of dropping. Other babies show concern and purposeful although panicky grasping responses to such activities, often followed by crying. These differential responses are primarily a function of learning, although individual differences appear that, to ordinary observation, scarcely seem to be so attributable. Certainly infants at birth show pronounced differences in reactivity: for example, before learning can possibly have influenced behavior greatly, some children startle when support is lost while others show little or no reaction; some startle and cry in response to loud sounds while others are passive. Because of these differences in reactivity, similar learning experiences have very different effects on different babies.

The author has already mentioned the White and Castle (1964) study. They gave extra handling to one group of infants from a barren environment, withheld it from another. The children who received the extra handling later showed more visual interest in their environments (see the section on "Vision," this volume).

Along somewhat the same lines, Casler (1965) has conducted an extremely well-controlled study. In his own words, his experimenters practiced "stroking any accessible part of the baby's skin, except for the hands and the mouth region" (p. 151). His study seems to involve *Touch: Pressure or Contact* at least as much as *Touch: Movement or Kinesthesis,* so might perhaps have been included in the immediately preceding section. He included only sixteen orphanage infants in the study, who were 4 to 59 weeks old when the experiment began; but his experimental and control groups were well-matched and the study has a pattern similar to and all the virtues ascribed to his study of verbal stimulation, previously discussed. It should be added that his "orphanage" was actually a relatively temporary "way stop" for infants and kindergartners at least temporarily without permanent homes.

The infants received a total of 1000 minutes of preplanned tactile stimulation over a total of ten weeks, just as was true in his verbal stimulation study. The commonly used Gesell Developmental Schedule was given both before and after the treatment (this was also true for the verbal stimulation study.) The Gesell yields an over-all score for developmental level, 100 being considered average; and subscores for language, adaptive, personal-social, and motor areas of development. For all five general or subscores, both groups decreased in quotients over the ten-week period (this is typical of children living in institutions, but the decline found in this study may also be due partly to the construction of the Gesell instrument). Casler concludes that "with the exception of the motor subtest, the mean decline of the experimental group is approximately one-half that of the control group" (p. 157). These changes are striking although none of them is statistically significant (this term is explained more fully in Chapter 2), probably because Casler worked with such a small number of subjects and the babies varied so much among themselves. It may also be true for this study as for the verbal stimulation experiment, that Casler limited his treatment variable (stroking) so rigidly that he did not make a massive enough impact on his experimental group to produce a significant difference between them and the controls. While tight controls are desirable and are all too infrequently found in child and other areas of psychology, they can be so rigorous that the experiment loses its connection with the real-life conditions it is designed to test.

This is suggested by the fact that Dennis and Sayegh (1965) working with institutionalized infants in Beirut, Lebanon, selected thirteen infants, ranging in age from 7.2 to 18.7 months, none of whom could sit alone, even when placed in a sitting position. They matched five of the babies who were to serve as experimental subjects fairly well for age (both chronological and developmental—how mature they were in behavior) with eight controls. The experimental group was given an hour of supplementary experience per day for fifteen days: this involved their being taken out of their cribs, carried to an experimental room, given a number of interesting things with which to play, and being placed when possible in a sitting position or sitting or standing against a hassock. A second test for Developmental Age was given after about a month (during which period the experimental group had received the treatment). It should be noted that the infants were not actually played *with,* but simply given the *chance* to play, plus being lifted and carried to and from their cribs. These youngsters made a highly significant gain in developmental age (about four times the rate they had shown before the study started). Unfortunately for science (but probably fortunately for the babies), the institution attendants apparently thought something to be emulated was going on and, the authors believed they observed, "sneaked in" some extra stimulation for the control children. Thus, the controls also gained, but considerably less (speaking in terms of statistical significance) than the experimental children.

Another study, Schaffer and Emerson (1964), was conducted by interviewing working-class mothers every four weeks during their babies' first year of life and again when the babies were 18 months old. Interviews are not the best source of data in the world, as will be pointed out in Chapter 2. But from their results, Schaffer and Emerson suggest that some of the large inter-infant variability in response to kinesthetic stimulation, including handling and stroking, may be constitutional: some babies, from birth, *like* cuddling, while others do not. This would certainly increase the variation in results of an experiment of kinesthesis which included handling, and thus make it more difficult to obtain significant results. A tendency (statistically not significant) also appeared for more girls than boys to like cuddling, at least as reported by their mothers. Of their fourteen girls, eleven were cuddlers; while of their fourteen boys, eight were cuddlers. This study must be viewed cautiously because of the small number of subjects, the dubious quality of data from maternal interviews, and the possibilities that girl babies either are preferred by mothers or are simply easier to get along with.

By 7 or 8 months of age many children sit alone and unsupported, and some can attain the sitting posture independently. A minority of babies is creeping or crawling; a few stand more or less alone. Reaching and grasping are rather well established; primitive efforts at self-feeding occur; an occasional child manages a cup precariously; and physical self-determination has progressed as dramatically as have reactions determined by the other sense modalities.

Throughout the first half year of life a majority of infants responds favorably to rocking and to relaxed cradling. Much modern psychological and pediatric advice favors the old-fashioned rocking chair or the cradle and encourages mothers to hold their children while they are being fed in order to simulate the breast-feeding situation as closely as possible. The tendency of many children to rock or hobbyhorse themselves to sleep is attributed by some to lack of sufficient contact and rocking on the part of parents in the very early days of infancy, although evidence on this point is far from final (Spitz, 1949). But the parent who takes such advice as an invitation to play constantly with the infant is likely to defeat the very purpose of the rocking, soothing movement. Such a child is kept in, or brought to, a state of fatigue and tension. Or, if the mother attempts to rock the child while she is tense herself, she is likely to increase his tension. Lipsitt (verbal communication, 1966) reports that infant preferences for rocking vary according to their activity level: highly active infants like rapid rocking (as judged by calming behavior); low activity level infants like a slower rate.

Erikson (1956), one of those who has thought deeply and creatively about the development of personality, believes that the sense of trust or security is developed during this first period of babyhood, and that frequent and relaxed bodily contact with the mother or mother-substitute is necessary for its development. Sullivan (in Mullahy, 1948), another creative thinker in the field, postulates a process of empathy, or a feeling with, that goes on in the baby as he has contact with the mother. Although no words need be spoken (and indeed, they would not be understood by the infant), the infant senses the mother's love for, acceptance of, and relaxation with him; or conversely, her displeasure, tension, and rejection. To date, no one knows precisely how to define or observe empathy, but it is a common observation that relaxed and accepting mothers are likely to have relaxed and amiable babies. Lakin (1957), whose study is reviewed more extensively in Chapter 3, provides evidence supporting such a conclusion. Certainly, the infant's kinesthetic sensibilities are very important in his interactions with his mother, father, other meaningful adults in his world and, indeed, with all aspects of his world.

PAIN

During his first few weeks of life infants seem to respond less directly and discriminatingly to pain than older children. Some experimenters believe that the baby is relatively insensitive to painful stimuli immediately after birth. Some theorize that the process of being born exhausts the baby's sense receptors, leaving him slow or lacking in response to all sensation and particularly to painful stimuli. Some have held that the brain centers for localization of pain stimuli are inadequately developed in infancy. The evidence on this score is by no means final. However, there is apparently less immediate reaction to pain on the part of the newborn than on the part of the older child. A single stimulus of a painful nature frequently produces no response, although normal infants respond to repeated painful stimuli by attempting to withdraw the part of the body that has been stimulated and by the massive, total type of response, including crying, which is so characteristic of their response to any strong stimulus. The capacity to respond to single painful stimulations is acquired rapidly. The literature on the sense of pain has been capably reviewed by Pratt (1954) and Zubek and Solberg (1954).

In another of the excellent Brown University studies, Kaye and Lipsitt (1964) established that there was a developmental decrease in electrotactual thresholds for infants from 1 through 4 days of life (that is, these babies rapidly became more sensitive to mild pain in the form of electric shock).

By the time the baby is 6 months old, the type of reaction he makes to pain depends considerably on the type of handling he has received from his parents. This effect is even more striking with older children. The parent who is frightened and reacts strongly to any pain the child may experience probably induces the child to show exaggerated emotional responses even to mild pain stimuli. The relatively relaxed parent who waits to see whether the child is genuinely hurt before he jumps is likely to have children who take alarm less easily. Here again, basic differences in reactivity probably affect the results of learning. The hyper-reactive child, handled calmly, will still, emotionally speaking, be more easily "wounded" than the passive, inactive baby who is handled in equally relaxed fashion.

Because pain may be an antecedent of anxiety, one of the most chronic and painful of human emotional ills, more study of its role in the developmental process is badly needed.

TEMPERATURE

The infant definitely responds to thermal stimulation, although it is difficult to separate temperature from sensations of touch, pressure, and pain. About the only pure heat stimulation possible is by radiant heat, but because the heat strikes a large area of the body, this type of stimulus makes localization difficult.

It is obvious that, for purposes of survival, organisms must respond to gross temperature changes. The human infant, who is in general helpless and ill equipped from the point of view of instincts or efficient physical patterns of reaction, conforms sufficiently to the biological laws of survival to make responses when necessary to maintain life, as in all cases of extreme sensory stimulation and variation. His patterns of response are crude, primitive, and of little use in themselves, but, by arousing responses from responsible adults, they result in protection, food, comfort, and love enough so that the infant survives. Responses to temperature follow this general rule.

Pratt (1954) has provided an excellent summary of neonatal reactions to thermal stimuli. It is clear that there is a response to temperature from birth, and it is probable that the fetus is capable of responding to temperature variations. Presumably there is a physiological zero or neutral point for all the senses, and certainly there is for temperature. At this temperature point a minimum of stimulation and incentive to activity is provided. Although no really systematic investigations of all the zones of the body have been made, this physiological neutral point ranges from 91° to 97° Fahrenheit for those body areas that have been studied. Adaptation, or getting used to temperatures occurs rapidly for infants, as it does for adults. We are all familiar with the rather quick adjustment to the bath that initially feels much too hot, or to the initially too-cold water of the swimming pool.

Nurseries are usually kept at high temperatures, and high temperatures are often recommended for the homes into which tiny infants are taken from the hospital. These recommended high temperatures make sense if one considers that the child has only recently come from the consistent temperature of his mother's body, about 100° Fahrenheit. Before birth, he has been accustomed neither to fluctuations in temperature nor to coolness, relative or absolute. When his postbirth surroundings approximate his body temperature, he reacts little, just as before birth. Where his environment differs sharply from his body temperature, he reacts strongly. To cold temperatures, the child shows withdrawing responses; he heightens his activity; he shudders, shivers, and scratches, this last being apparently a primitive device for removing the stimulation. When the temperature goes moderately above physiological neutral, babies have been observed to show seeking movements, although they react less to moderate upward shifts than to downward ones. Sucking is most vigorous for liquids above 100° Fahrenheit.

SENSORY STIMULATION AND GENERAL DEVELOPMENT

Many studies (see Chapter 3) show that babies are retarded in development when reared in institutions where there are many infants and few nurses. Development of reaching, grasping, so-called social behavior, smiling, and all types of coordinated sensory-muscular behavior lags behind that shown by babies reared either in their own or in foster homes. There is also evidence indicating that babies in an institutional setting cry far more than do babies living in a household (Aldrich *et al.*, 1945, 1946).

Some authors believe that nursery-reared babies languish because they do not receive consistent mothering. Spitz (1945), for example, presents a dramatic and appalling picture of high death rate, an almost vegetable-like and irreversible slowness in the rate of neuromuscular-intellectual growth, and emotional maladjustment as being characteristic of babies in nursery wards. Although his methods have been scathingly criticized (Pinneau, 1955), other evidence (see, for instance, Goldfarb, 1945) bears out the notion that mass rearing of infants slows their development in several respects, and suggests that the infant who is abnormally reared—who has not had some "tender loving care"—may suffer severe emotional impoverishment.

Hebb (1949, 1955) speaks less emotionally but equally convincingly of the need for rich perceptual stimulation in earliest infancy. Drawing on his own theories and research, as well as on the work of his students and colleagues, he concludes that the human infant is an exceedingly slow-learning organism compared with infants of other species. Hebb accepts the point taken for granted by many physiologists and neurologists: that the human brain is relatively undifferentiated and equipotential when compared with that of other species. To oversimplify, this means that there is little instinctual direction for babies: they behave as they learn to behave, not as their instincts or their genetically laid-down brain patterns direct them.

Hebb believes that in the first few months of the baby's life, learning is by trial and error: it is inefficient, slow, and passive in the sense that it depends for its occurrence entirely on the stimulation that is offered. Hence, if there is no stimulation, no learning takes place. Neurologically speaking, the first few months of the baby's life are spent in laying down "cell assemblies." These are the basic, relatively simple neural connections that result in the integration of the sense modalities and provide the basis for such responses as blinking, grasping, responding to a touch on the face by sucking, and for perceptions of form, color, and contrast.

If a rich foundation of such cell assemblies is not laid in the first few months of life, Hebb reasons, it may never be laid at all, and interference with, or slowed development of, higher perceptual-intellectual-emotional functions may result. His views receive support from experiments (as by Thompson and Heron, 1954) in which animals deprived of sensory stimulation in infancy show deficient intellectual behavior in their adult life. Less clear-cut evidence (Melzack, 1954; Melzack and Scott, 1957; and Melzack and Thompson, 1956) indicates that immature social and emotional adjustment is also characteristic of these animals.

According to Hebb, once cell assemblies are established, higher-order phase sequences begin to operate, making possible the insightful, symbolic behavior that we consider typical of intellectual human functioning. By implication, the more bountiful the supply of cell assemblies, the higher the order of functioning of the higher processes mediated by the phase sequences. As Hebb himself states, his postulated neurophysiology is speculative, although it does not violate known laws. His thinking, which is congruent with research studies of infants reared in deprived circumstances as well as with the results of animal research, suggests that a rich supply of sensory stimulation is essential for the child in the first year or so of his life as well as later.

Some regard the retardation that unquestionably takes place when infants are reared in institutions with small staffs as a function of lack of mothering; others think of it as a form of stimulus deprivation (it is toward such a hypothesis that Casler (1965 a, b) leans and which his studies are designed to test). In recent years, the results of research in this area have reached the ears of almost all infant institution administrators. One result is that the infant institution has almost become a thing of the past. When such institutions are necessary, as is the case of the one Casler describes, the administration and staff may actually overwhelm the baby with stimulating, swinging to the opposite extreme of deprivation in their fear of blighting their charges' development.

One of the best summaries and critical analyses of the literature in this area was written by Casler (1961). The author recommends that anyone interested in the problem of maternal deprivation or its alternative theoretical explanation, sensory deprivation, should read the Casler monograph carefully.

The reader should also become acquainted with H. F. Harlow's work with monkeys (Harlow, 1959a or b). This work has been so widely popularized in the published studies by Harlow and his associates and in semiprofessional and popular books, journals, magazines, and newspapers that it is not treated in any detail in this book since it is (1) known to almost every layman and (2) does not treat human infants. Harlow's major conclusion (in the eyes of the present author) is that monkeys for proper adult adjustment need at least something more than straight stimulation: they need the sort of stimulation that comes from social interaction. His results suggest that it doesn't make much difference whether this stimulation comes from their mothers or mother substitutes, or from other monkeys of roughly the same age, although peers seem to provide something essential not given by mothers, and mothers something unavailable from peers.

Piaget's Sensorimotor Stages

INTRODUCTION

Piaget is difficult to read, understand, and summarize. But clear and (it is generally agreed) adequate treatment of Piaget's theories such as J. McV. Hunt's (1961) and Flavell's (1963), have now appeared and, perhaps at least partly as a consequence of such treatments, Piaget has become *very* fashionable indeed. For example, the 1966 *Annual Review of Psychology* (Farnsworth, McNemar, and McNemar) discusses him in one way or another in four of its seventeen chapters: In the chapter on developmental psychology, about 3 percent of the thirty-six plus pages are devoted to cognition and Piaget. This section summarizes no fewer than eleven studies derived from Piaget's theories, and mentions two reviews of his work that have appeared in the time span covered by the chapter. In the chapter, "Cognitive Functions" (Van de Geer and Jaspars), four articles are mentioned and the authors regret, in explaining their choice of topics to and not to cover, that "Even then we have had to make some hard decisions. One of them is that we shall disregard the work of Piaget . . . ." (p. 149). He is again twice cited in the chapters on perceptual learning and psycholinguistics. It should be added that the author has made only a hurried statistical count of the 1966 *Review*. If anything, the figures he gives above *under-* rather than *over-*numerate the scholarly works coming either directly from Piaget and his colleagues or derived from his theories during the time covered by the *Review*.

Piaget has much to offer, even though he presents formidable reading. He was either partially ignored or vigorously rejected in the late 1930s, 1940s, and most of the 1950s, possibly because the average American psychologist either does not read French, or reads it too poorly to wade through Piaget's difficult prose and the dense thicket of ideas. A more likely reason is that this was a period of stark empiricism for child psychology: if you can't count it, it isn't any good! By the 1950s, the data accumulated by child psychologists had grown so numerous (and many of the data were very good indeed) that they required being put in order. The only satisfactory way the author knows to organize masses of data (or to generate new and imaginative data) is through a theory. Piaget is an engaging theorist: vague, inconsistent, original and even brilliant, witty, dogmatic, infinitely flexible—all at the same time. All theories have grown in popularity with child psychologists since the 1950s, but Piaget's has probably shown the most spectacular growth spurt. He has provided a valuable service by literally spawning theories from which to derive research, although it is difficult to pin Piaget down tightly enough to make a rigorous test of many of the things he says.

Finally, theories, like most other things, go by waves: unheard of one day, the next day and for a time they sweep the country. If they are good—if they prove really useful—they remain permanently, if anything can be said to be permanent. This is true, or at least has been for many years and still is, of such very different behavior theories as Freud's and Hull's. Over the years, they have changed greatly, but they have been tough and durable and the changes have not altered their cores. But the theory (or part-theory) that all stuttering results from a confusion in brain dominance, so popular in the 1930s, is extinct in the 1960s. It generated some useful data, they were incorporated into the literature and more general theories of stuttering. If Piaget is *really* good, he is here to stay. If his theories are not useful, they at least will have generated some research. Some of it has been, is, and will be good, some mediocre, and some poor. The good research will be helpful, the mediocre research not entirely useless, and the poor will be remembered only by its authors.

Piaget will be discussed in several sections of this book. The only part of his work that belongs logically to this chapter is his theory of the sensorimotor stages that characterize infancy. These stages are not theory in the true sense of the word, but instead are vivid, imaginative, and provocative descriptions. In the author's eyes, they have two *very* useful potentials, and he will capitalize on them: first, knowing what Piaget has to say about the sensorimotor stages makes one regard an infant more imaginatively. With Piaget's ideas in mind, we can look at our or others' infants with new eyes, try out new things, generate ideas for new stimuli and experiences. Babies, in other words, become more interesting to us and almost automatically we become better parents or caretakers. Second, child psychologists, pediatricians, and others who work with babies badly need better tests of infant development, particularly in the problem solving or intellectual area, than we now have. The author believes that Piaget's sensorimotor stages provide many clues to help develop such tests and therefore will point out some of these clues.

It would appear that Piaget based his ideas of six sensorimotor stages partially and probably entirely on observations of his own three children, Lucienne, Jacqueline, and Laurent. He was not content simply to let them grow and develop: from his fertile mind came many techniques for testing and stimulating them. It might be said that he observed *and* manipulated, thus enriching their infancies. Their development, as reported, was more advanced than the norms (the average ages at which babies do such and such a thing, as reaching for new objects) that have been well developed by professionals. in the United States, and there is no reason to think that Swiss babies are *ipso facto* more advanced than American babies. Of course, Piaget's children not only had unusually enriched environments; they also had unusually good genes, so to speak.

STAGE 1: EXERCISING THE READY-MADE
SENSORIMOTOR SCHEMATA[4]

By "exercising the ready-made sensorimotor schemata," Piaget means just what he says. A *schema,* in general, refers to the senses, nerves, and muscles involved in a given piece of behavior. For instance, there is a schema involved in sucking, as a set of muscles, nerves, taste buds, swallowing reactions. Stage 1, then, consists of using the equipment the baby is born with. He sucks, he cries, he waves his arms and legs, he belches. The *more* he does these things, the *better* he does them: for example, he is less groping, more sure of himself, more efficient habits are formed. In the process of performing these simple acts, people and things are in turn feeding him new stimuli and giving him a wide variety of new experiences. Each of the sense modalities described earlier is getting a workout—stimuli are impinging on and he is using all his sense modalities from his eyes and so on to pain and temperature receptors. He is both learning and maturing steadily and constantly.

This stage extends from birth to around 1 month of age. As may be inferred from the summaries of development of the different sense modalities given earlier in this chapter, environment in all likelihood affects the child even at this tender age: an environment absolutely barren of stimuli would probably prolong stage 1; one too rich in stimuli might overwhelm the infant, interfering with the orderly development of this stage. But for most babies, enough stimulation is provided even in the most barren homes that the infant goes through stage 1 in an orderly, automatic-seeming way.

The reader should note carefully as he goes through the material on Piaget's stages, how well they fit with Hebb's (1949, 1955) thinking, particularly the things Hebb has to say about cell assemblies and phase sequences. As far as the author knows, these two men worked independently of each other, at least Hebb (1949) does not mention Piaget in his author index. Piaget's stage 1 could almost be called Hebb's "cell assembly stage" if Hebb used such terms. Progressively, from Piaget's stages 2 through 6, we see the sort of process provocatively described by Hebb

---

[4] J. McV. Hunt's (1961) terms are used for Piaget's six sensorimotor stages.

under the broad heading of *phase sequence:* for example, short cutting, substitution of symbols for actions, learning by "insight," increased spontaneity, elaboration, and originality of behavior.

STAGE 2: PRIMARY CIRCULAR REACTIONS

The baby now begins to put individual or simple schemata together into more complex systems. First, he *varies* his simple schemata. Next, he *combines* schemata: for example, he looks or clutches while he sucks and he begins to suck anything he can grasp. Illustrations of these primary circular reactions can be found by the reader if he returns to the descriptions of development of the different sense modalities. For instance, the baby turns his head as well as tracks a moving object with his eyes; he tries to find the source of a sound. Piaget says this stage goes from about 1 to about $4\frac{1}{2}$ months of age. The present author believes this stage is more susceptible than stage 1 to environmental stimuli, as a very barren environment, lacking in interaction with people, will begin to slow up a baby seriously as he progresses through stage 2. "Almost any old household" will no longer do as it conceivably could in stage 1, since a fairly rich set of opportunities to learn must be provided, or beginning retardation may occur. During this age period, for example, it has been almost universally found that babies reared in traditional institutions where they receive few stimuli and have few contacts with adults begin to fall behind children in normal homes in all aspects of their development.

STAGE 3: SECONDARY CIRCULAR REACTIONS

This stage, according to Piaget, extends from about $4\frac{1}{2}$ to about 8 or 9 months. During stages 1 and 2, the baby has been for the most part a responder: if his stomach contractions pain him, he begins to yell; if someone touches him on his cheek, he turns (unless he is asleep or completely full of food) toward the touch. In stage 3, he begins to be an initiator: he is no longer the passive receiver of his environment; he reaches out, figuratively speaking, to manage it—to affect it, as well as be affected by it. Chance motions are incorporated into already established schemata, and single schema are combined.

It should be stated that these stages are not as separate—not as discrete—as either Piaget or the present author make them sound. They overlap and run together. For most babies, there will be some stage 2 behaviors in stage 1, and some stage 1 types of behavior may persist as long as to stage 3.

In stage 3, the baby begins to do such things as look for objects that have disappeared, suggesting for the first time memory and cognizance of things other than self. He anticipates his own acts or the acts of others.

He may be screaming with hunger one second, then become as quiet as a lamb when his mother enters the room. He *anticipates* that she is going to take care of him and, in a primal way, knows that crying will no longer serve his purposes. He'd better quiet down so as to be ready to eat. It might be said that he is partially in the phase sequence stage described by Hebb: he is short-cutting, he is using elementary symbols. He is probably also laying the foundation for future socialization, although Piaget does not mention this aspect of development in his description of stage 3: human beings begin to be something you can trust or distrust. An elementary sort of "love" begins. He reacts differently to strangers than family. As we have seen in the section on "Vision," he has already learned by about three months (while he was in stage 3) to distinguish between a human face and a colored picture of the same face. During stage 3, he watches *himself* act, and becomes intensely interested in his own body (particularly his hands and feet). He experiments constantly to see what he can do with them.

In this stage, there is no question in the author's mind but that opportunity to learn plays a crucial part in normal development. While babies can still be overwhelmed by stimuli, probably more are deprived of than are surfeited by stimuli sufficient to enrich and speed them through stage 3. Traditional institution-reared babies are seriously retarded by the age at which Piaget believes stage 3 "ends." If our tests were refined enough, the author believes we would begin to find real differences in adaptive, problem solving sorts of behavior between "good" and "bad" homes. A good home is considered one where there are many things to play with, and much friendly, playful interaction between adults and older children and the baby in addition to routine caring for the infant's needs. A bad home is one where little else than routine care is offered the baby.

It is important to distinguish between *intrinsic* and *extrinsic* stimuli. An intrinsic stimulus is one the baby provides for himself, such as watching or playing with his own hands. An extrinsic stimulus is one that comes from someone else: a peek-a-boo game with his mother, the offer of a toy, parental baby talk (which, while some experts disapprove of it, seems to encourage babies to develop their own language behavior—babbles, coos, and gurgles). A good home provides many extrinsic stimuli which encourage the baby in experimental behavior of his own (make him more curious, more active and, perhaps, more intelligent). A poor home leaves him to his own devices most of the time. Of course, all babies need some peace and quiet during their waking hours as well as when they are asleep.

We begin to get some cues about possible intelligence test items from the behaviors described in stages 2 and 3. Given Piaget's detailed descriptions of his own three children and applying some of his and Hebb's insights, we come up with ideas for a number of possible tests: any task that tests anticipation, ideas of permanence of objects (such as searching for things that have disappeared). Any demonstration of anticipation, planning, purpose, or deliberate imitation is evidence of "problem solving behavior" of a simple sort. Items built to measure such behavior seem to the author more likely to predict later intelligence than the items typical of most infant developmental tests now available. Stages 4, 5, and 6, as described by Piaget, also offer many ideas that, if transformed into test items, would make better developmental test batteries than now exist.

STAGE 4: COORDINATION OF SECONDARY SCHEMATA

Here the baby begins actively to try to reach his own goals: he works tirelessly to try to get to something he wants. He is a great imitator. Something resembling true social behavior sets in (Piaget considers that this stage goes from about 8 or 9 months to 11 or 12 months). He plays games. The baby "realizes" that such and such an act of his will bring about such and such a consequence. He tries to overcome obstacles and circumvent barriers (he will, for example, work persistently to bring a stick to himself through the uprights of his crib, trying the stick first this way, then that way). Previous behavior was accidental whereas this is purposeful.

Needless to say, the author believes that social interaction and rich extrinsic stimulation continue to be invaluable in helping the baby with stage 4, and is convinced that babies from poor homes, as defined above, will lag far behind babies from good homes; while babies from traditional institutions (see, for example, the discussion of Dennis' and Sayegh's 1965 paper) are seriously retarded. Dennis and Sayegh give a vivid, unquestionably accurate, and pathetic picture of the retardation of babies in the institution where they conducted their study.

By this stage, of course, almost all normal babies are crawling, half or more of them are pulling themselves to a standing position; many are holding onto low tables and "crab-legging" themselves around them (with, of course, many a bump in the process). A few of them are walking and, by the end of stage 4, about half of them, particularly girl babies, have a true word or so in their vocabularies.

STAGE 5: TERTIARY CIRCULAR REACTIONS

Piaget gives this stage a wide, loosely defined time range of beginning and ending: it begins at about 11 or 12 months and goes to about 18 months and possibly 2 years, thus overlapping in its later months with stage 6.

There is not much to add in talking about these stages: the baby or, from 14 months or so, the so-called runabout, simply does more of the same things we saw the crude beginnings of in stage 2 and which we began to see in more elaborate form in stage 4. Curiosity mushrooms. While this may drive the baby's caretaker crazy—"He is into everything!" is a common maternal complaint—it is probably one of the best foundations for later life a child can have. A more detailed discussion of this issue is presented later. For the time being, let us only say that the more stimuli that have been appropriately (probably including lovingly) fed to a baby, the more curious he is and the more stimulation he craves. This, then, is the crude beginning of intellectual curiosity which later becomes so important for learning in school—or anywhere else. Old schemata are varied, and the new is tried for its own sake: emphasis is on the *means*.

Anything new interests the child, although his interest may take the form of fright. During the early months of stage 5, he pays little attention to objects that are *completely* outside his experience, in the sense that he has never encountered anything even remotely resembling them, although later in this stage he will manifest such interest and many babies do so even earlier.

During this period, even our present, rather crude tests of infant development begin to show differences in developmental age (including intelligence) between children from lower-lower class homes, where babies and small children are likely to get minimum attention, and children from middle-class homes, where mothers, fathers, and older brothers and sisters do more playing and interacting with the infant-child. The author does not know whether this idea has been tested, but he predicts that the lower-lower class child of this age (and certainly the child reared in a conventional institution) will be much less curious than the middle-class child.

The infant-child begins to try to get others to do things for him that he cannot do for himself, or that he enjoys (such as pat-a-cake). Speech development may taper off (the evidence is not altogether clear on this) as the child consolidates his skill at walking and exploiting all the wonderful possibilities (some of them horribly dangerous) that this new ability opens up to him. Notions of causation become clearer; it is more obvious that he knows that things—objects—are permanent; and so on.

STAGE 6: INTERNALIZATION OF SENSORIMOTOR SCHEMATA

Piaget places this stage between about 18 months to 2 years of age. The child begins to operate more and more by symbols, becomes better and better at problem solving, his vocabulary mushrooms, he hunts for things that have been hidden, and remembers where he has put things, or where things are kept. He makes detours. He *internalizes,* although on a motor basis. He imitates constantly. He can occasionally conjure up the cause because of his knowledge of the effects. One of the author's children, for example, toward the end of this stage, came each morning to his bed with the demand, "Daddy, put on glasses. Wake up." The author believes this is an example of real understanding of causation: he is extremely near-sighted, and is not ready to face any aspect of his world in the morning until he has put on his spectacles. This child was verbalizing what she had observed: "*If* daddy puts on his glasses, *then* I'll get some attention from him." Conversely, without glasses, she could expect no satisfaction from her father.

The child will also imitate past actions of others. He, has, in other words, changed from infancy to childhood—from a little animal, in a sense, to a human being.

It seems fitting to end this lengthy chapter with this transition to "human-ness," as betokened by Piaget's Stage 6.

Summary

This chapter has stressed the impact of culture, interacting with the child's sense organs and other physical attributes, on the development of the human organism.

Culture, although organized in a bewildering number of ways, is defined as the major institutional and social patterns followed by a larger or smaller, but definable, group of persons. Families, themselves subcultures, transmit to their children the broad patterns of the culture of which they form a part. Considerable cultural differences exist as a function of social class.

Culture may affect a mother's physical condition during pregnancy, and her condition, in turn, affects the development of the fetus she is carrying. For example, maternal stress may be related to physical and emotional adjustment in infancy; certain types of infection during pregnancy may damage the fetus.

Since the culture cannot influence a child unless it impinges on him through his sense organs, this chapter has presented a brief summary of sensory equipment and development. With respect to vision, sensitivity to light, as judged by pupillary reflexes, is present at birth, but the first really functional use of vision—focusing on a source of light—does not appear until about 4 weeks. From that time, visual efficiency develops rapidly.

Hearing may not be present for a few days after birth, probably because of the presence of amniotic fluid in the ear. However, auditory sensory equipment is structurally complete in the newborn. Ability to localize sound appears at about 20 weeks.

Little is known about the development of the sense of smell, but it does not appear to function at birth. The infant's taste receptors do function in early infancy, and the acuity of taste seems to diminish through life.

The other sense modalities are touch (pressure or contact, and movement or kinesthesis); pain; and temperature.

In general, response to sensory stimulation progresses from crude and massive reactions to cumulative stimulation toward precise, adaptive reactions to discrete stimuli. By the time a normal child is 6 months old he shows much purposeful, adaptive behavior; is social within the limits of his powers; demonstrates complex learning; exhibits such idiosyncracies as taste preferences; and is ordinarily rather well attuned to his complicated environment.

Studies of infants reared in institutional settings strongly suggest that the intellectual and emotional development of such babies is seriously impaired. These findings have been explained in terms of inadequate and inconsistent mothering and, more recently, by a theory relating mature intellectual and perhaps emotional functioning to the richness and variety of sensory stimulation in infancy.

Piaget's six stages of sensorimotor development were summarized and illustrated, and implications drawn for child-rearing.

One must, to make sense of a child, view his behavior from different points of view. The points of view suggested were: A. School achievement-academic aptitude, or intelligence; B. Personal-social-emotional; and C. Physical-motor (including body build). Teachers are likely to stress A; social workers, psychiatrists, clinical psychologists, and others of the health-welfare professions are likely to pay over much attention to B; while physical educators or physicians may concentrate on C while neglecting A and B. But the child is *not* made up of neat categories: he is a *whole* human being, from the day he is born until he reaches adolescence or, for that matter, until the day he dies. Every aspect of each of his characteristics and functions interacts with and is inseparable from every other one.

This interaction has been stressed throughout the chapter: the environment not only affects the child, but he affects the environment. A hyperactive little boy may produce distracted, even "bad" parents who, had they been given a sweet little girl, would have been "good" parents.

The stimuli the world "feeds into" the child cause him to respond, thus provoking changes in his environment which in turn feeds him back new stimuli. Short of *overwhelming* very young children with too much stimulation (a fairly rare phenomenon), the more appropriate and appropriately administered stimulation a baby receives from the world, the more he reacts to it, and the "hungrier"—the more curious—for stimulation he becomes. This, in turn, very likely leads to more and more efficient problem solving behavior and intellectual curiosity on his part.

Methods and Problems in the Study of Child-Rearing Practices

CHAPTER 2

I n the preceding chapter, stress was laid on the crucial influence of culture and learning on children's development. During the formative preschool years this influence, which makes its impact on the child's sense organs and nervous system, is brought to bear primarily by his parents. Of course, parental influence continues to play a major role in the lives of older children, but in more diluted form.

Central, then, to an understanding of development in the early years of childhood is a study of child-rearing practices: their types and their effects.

A great volume of literature has been provided by professionals in child development in an attempt to meet the need posed by parental insecurity. Parents in the United States are probably insecure because they have been told by everyone from judges and clergymen to child psychologists and social workers that "the *parent* makes the child," and "as the twig is bent, so the tree grows." The author made the point in Chapter 1 that a family is a two-way street: parents affect their children, but their children also affect them. The inconsistency of the advice given by the experts has caused many to reject all authorities. Others, including some of the experts themselves, have concluded that little good evidence about the effects of child-rearing practices exists and, in consequence, have maintained that efforts to educate and guide parents are futile.

As with most human matters, the truth probably lies somewhere between the optimism of the early or more extreme child-development experts (or parent-family educators) and the pessimism of the more conservative or of those who have come more recently into the field. Admittedly, the record of the experts is not a happy one. At least two survey articles show that childcare recommendations have moved full circle between about 1890 and 1950 (Stendler, 1950; Vincent, 1951). In many respects, advice about infant care today adheres more closely to the practices of our grandmothers and great-grandmothers than to the lines of thought of the early behaviorists. But to the many, including the author of this volume, who assume that cultural and family factors are crucial in the development of personality and in social and intellectual functioning, the study of parent-child relations should nevertheless be one of the principal preoccupations of educators, pediatricians, psychiatrists, psychologists, social workers, and other professionals in human development and functioning.

Chapter 3 presents a detailed survey of the research literature on child-rearing practices. Regrettably, few solid conclusions can be drawn from these studies. A major reason for this state of affairs is that many, perhaps most, of them are weak methodologically. This chapter is devoted largely to an exploration of weaknesses often found in such research. The motives for presenting such a critique are two: (1) Critically alert, the student of child development will be less gullible in his reading and listening; and (2) possessed of general information about methodological pitfalls, he may be more precise, objective, and orderly in his own observations and research.

Dimensions of Research in Child Development

Spiker has suggested that every research study in the area of child development may be described in terms of its position on four dimensions, each forming a continuum ranging between two extremes. Although some of these dimensions may vary together, there is no logical necessity for them to do so. The four dimensions are: (1) normative-explanatory; (2) ahistorical-historical; (3) naturalistic-manipulative; (4) atheoretical-theoretical.

A continuum is simply something that goes from one extreme to another. Very few children, for example, can be classified as "completely without aggression." On the other hand (the other end of the continuum), very few if any children are completely aggressive: that is, react aggressively to everything that happens to them. A few very seriously, emotionally disturbed children may behave in such a way, but they are few indeed. The child without aggression is probably equally disturbed. Most children (or adolescents or adults) fall somewhere between the ends or poles of a continuum. Some children are relatively unaggressive, some children are relatively aggressive and, by definition, most of them are in the middle part of the population. They will "get tough" if they are provoked or unfairly treated, they will fight for their rights, but usually they are reasonable sorts of people.

To illustrate Figure 2.1, choosing the third item, *naturalistic* versus *manipulative,* let us move into the research area. At the naturalistic extreme of the continuum, we have as perhaps the prime example the work of traditional cultural anthropologists: they study their peoples,

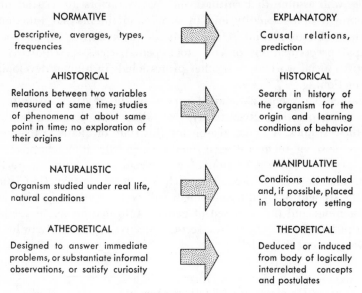

NORMATIVE

Descriptive, averages, types, frequencies

EXPLANATORY

Causal relations, prediction

AHISTORICAL

Relations between two variables measured at same time; studies of phenomena at about same point in time; no exploration of their origins

HISTORICAL

Search in history of the organism for the origin and learning conditions of behavior

NATURALISTIC

Organism studied under real life, natural conditions

MANIPULATIVE

Conditions controlled and, if possible, placed in laboratory setting

ATHEORETICAL

Designed to answer immediate problems, or substantiate informal observations, or satisfy curiosity

THEORETICAL

Deduced or induced from body of logically interrelated concepts and postulates

Figure 2.1   Four dimensions of studies in child development.

whether in Samoa or Kansas, in a natural setting and do not themselves exert any influence on the population. They simply "look to see" and take notes. Of course, their very presence alters the natural setting to some degree but, after the group they are observing is familiar with them, the group goes back to behaving completely or almost completely naturally.

Observers, for example, have little influence on a classroom of children accustomed to having teachers-in-training in the room, sitting in chairs, taking notes. The author was both an observer and a group leader in the famous Lewin, Lippitt, and White studies of authoritarian-*laissez faire*-democratic group management (1939). This study involved ten children at a time, and about twenty observers. The physical circumstances in which the study was conducted were in a large, third floor attic of an old academic building on the University of Iowa campus. The observers made their notes in moderate twilight concealed from the children only by a waist-high burlap cloth barrier: they could easily be seen by any child at any time. During certain phases of the study, it was required that the group leaders leave the boys to see how they would behave when alone. One activity of the experimental subjects involved making papier-maché masks, a messy operation involving soaking newspapers in water. There was no plumbing in the attic, so that to dispose of the water the boys had to leave the attic and travel some distance to pour it down the custodian's sink. During one such period of leader absence and with several pails of water to dispose of, the group agreed to dump the water out of the window. Their reason for so doing was expressed by one or two of them as "Why go all the way down the hall to pour the water out? Let's just dump it out the window. Nobody's watching." But twenty or so adults were sitting there in plain sight! In other words, it *is* possible for a good anthropologist to observe his subjects in natural behavior in their natural setting if he, in a manner of speaking, makes himself a part of the scenery.

A purely manipulative study involves bringing a subject into a laboratory, giving him a carefully defined treatment, and recording (mechanically or otherwise) his response to the treatment.

Somewhere toward the middle of the continuum—more toward the naturalistic than the manipulative side of the mean or average—is a study the author is engaged in. This study takes advantage of a decision on the part of a school system to try a combination of team teaching (manipulation) plus ability grouping to study what happens to children's patterns of friendship-rejection. This moderately manipulated group is compared with the next year's group (all sixth-graders) which, for administrative reasons, was moved back into the conventional homeroom or naturalistic situation.

A study can also be a mixture of types as, for instance in studies of the influence of water fluoridization on dental caries (tooth decay): it is *manipulative* in the sense that something has been added to the water that children drink; it is *normative* in the sense that its effectiveness is judged by the number of tooth cavities per child before fluorine was added to the water compared with the number of cavities per child after fluorine was added. Some studies of lung cancer as affected by smoking are another example of mixtures of continua and types illustrated in Figure 2.1. The *norms* (the most recent ones reported at the time of writing show that more women smokers than women nonsmokers have lung cancer) are assumed by the experts to have some *explanatory* value with reference to lung cancer.

NORMATIVE-EXPLANATORY

A major (perhaps the major) goal of early workers in child development was to describe the behavior and characteristics of the developing human organism—hopefully, from conception on. Many of the research findings discussed in the previous chapter are normative (for example, the average baby localizes sound at about 20 weeks, whereas he fixates on a source of light at 4 weeks). Normative studies of child-rearing practices often seek to gather such information as average time of weaning, method of weaning, number of mothers who breast feed, or time and method of initiating toilet training.

Collection of such norms can be helpful. A pediatrician becomes concerned if his small patient is not fixating light at, say, 8 weeks. A teacher, knowing that the average IQ of her class is 85, will pitch her instruction lower than if she knows it is 115, thus accommodating a majority of her class but not each individual. If the average mother begins toilet training at 11 months, one suspects that mothers who differ greatly from the average (who start at 6 weeks or 3 years, for instance) may have special effects on their children.

In the explanatory approach to research, an attempt is made to go beyond the compiling of frequencies and averages. Such an approach concerns itself less with the average time of starting toilet training (for instance) and more with the effect on children's later development of differences in the time of beginning toilet training; or with the motives and intentions of the mother who differs greatly from the average (or adheres closely to it, for that matter).

Research at the explanatory rather than the normative end of this methodological continuum seems more likely to contribute to an understanding of human development, although the establishing of accurate norms may be an essential first step in explanation. Good norms help us "restrict the range of our best guesses." The teacher who knows that the average IQ of her class is low will be less likely to err in her teaching level than the teacher without such information. The author of a second-grade reading text finds it useful, even necessary, to know how extensive and difficult a vocabulary the average child in the second grade can master. He must know the frequency with which English words are used, so that the child can master early those he most needs in order to comprehend what he reads.

But norms are not explanations. They do not enable us to predict the development of an individual child, nor do they help us, except in the sense of the preceding paragraph, to guide him. It is reassuring to the parent of a 14-month-old who is just beginning to walk to know that the average child walks at this age, but disturbing and without implications for guidance to the parent whose child is not walking four months later. Norms are, however, frequently taken for explanation, even by those who should know better. A parent, querying a child-development speaker, asks why her daughter, previously such a good child, has become naughty and now always says "No" rather than "Yes." The speaker asks the age of the child; the mother answers, "Twenty months," and the speaker says, "Oh, that is the time when negativism reaches its peak in girls." Both mother and speaker seem relieved, and each apparently believes that something has been explained. However, the fact is not the explanation. The full explanation is an accounting of how or why the fact came to be.

AHISTORICAL-HISTORICAL

There are two types of ahistorical research. The first type poses a question that, illustratively, might be: Are children less resistant during dental work when their mothers remain in the waiting room than they are when their mothers accompany them to the dentist's chair? In a hypothetical study to answer this question, the investigator might form two groups of children: an experimental group, whose mothers remain in the waiting room; and a control group, whose mothers go with them into the dentist's office. The two groups should be about the same in age and number; they should include similar numbers of only, first, and second or later children; the mothers should be of about the same educational level (or social class); and so on. If there is less crying and resistance in the experimental than in the control group, the investigator concludes that, for children like those he studied, dental work will be done more efficiently if mothers remain in the waiting room. But, in the ahistorical approach, the research worker does not concern himself with factors in the history of mother-child relations that might account for the difference between the two groups; nor does he ask how the history of the child who cries and resists with his mother absent differs from that of the child who makes no resistance.

The second type of ahistorical research measures two variables at more or less the same time and relates them to each other. For example, an investigator wishes to find the relation between mothers' and children's intelligence. As close in time as possible, he administers intelligence tests to a number of mothers and children. He finds that there is a tendency for the brightest mothers to have the brightest children, and vice versa, and concludes that mothers' intelligence is positively correlated with their children's intelligence. But he does not seek to determine why some bright mothers have children who are not bright (did they, for example, read less to their children when they were little? has the home been a quarrelsome one? and so on).

The historical approach, as can be seen, has something in common with the explanatory approach, and holds that the experiences an individual has had in the past determine the kind of person he is at the moment, how he perceives his current environment, and therefore what he will do in the present situation.

A true historical approach to many of the pressing questions in parent-child relations involves longitudinal (long-time) study of large numbers of children and their parents. But such studies are so complex and difficult, as well as expensive, that almost no individuals and few research centers can undertake them. Not least among the difficulties is maintaining the cooperation of a representative or typical sample of families year after year.

Many investigators attempt to reconstruct the child's history by interviewing his mother, or mother and father. Inquiries are typically made about the circumstances of birth, feeding, weaning, discipline, and so on. This approach might be called the semihistorical approach, and is typified by the Sears, Maccoby, and Levin (1957) study mentioned in the preceding chapter.

NATURALISTIC-MANIPULATIVE

In the naturalistic approach, the subject is studied in his natural setting; manipulative research, essentially, is laboratory research, in which the experimenter exerts controls in order to study in as pure a form as possible the phenomenon in which he is interested. In this sense, astronomy is a naturalistic, physics predominantly a manipulative science. An observational study of the child in his own home or in free play in a preschool setting is naturalistic; a study of the difference in his performance on a test when his mother is present, compared with his performance when a female stranger is in the room, would be manipulative.

The bulk of research in child development has been and continues to be naturalistic, although the tendency toward experimental work with children is growing. The manipulative approach is much superior to the naturalistic in precision. However, some think it is limited in the contribution it can make to knowledge of human development because of the difficulty of reducing pressing human problems such as sibling rivalry, mother fixation, classroom learning, or dependency, to dimensions that can be studied in the laboratory.

ATHEORETICAL-THEORETICAL

In the early days of child development, investigators tended to be atheoretical, even antitheoretical, in their approach to child behavior. Many considered theory sheer speculation, and wished simply to gather facts. But as the facts accumulated, the need for integration became obvious to more and more child psychologists, and theory itself became more objective and empirically grounded. Today few deny the usefulness of scientific theory. However, many practical problems not derived from or related in any close fashion to theory continue to demand and receive attention.

Methodological Problems

The remainder of this chapter treats two major types of problem that beset the scientific investigation of child-rearing practices. The first type is methodological, and pertains to the design and carrying out of empirical research. The second type of problem is theoretical, and pertains to the development of an adequate framework within which fruitful research can be carried out.

The following seven difficulties are among the most frequent in research on child-rearing practices, although they characterize other types of psychological, psychiatric, and sociological research as well: (1) contamination; (2) reconstruction through retrospection; (3) faulty logic; (4) poor definition of concepts; (5) direct influence of the investigator; (6) problems of sampling; (7) unsound generalization.

The research summaries and evaluations in Chapter 3 illustrate some of these faults in detail.

CONTAMINATION

The most frequent type of contamination occurs when the investigator knows the predicted nature of the relation between an independent and a dependent variable and has control over the measurement of both. The less objective and quantifiable the measurement of the variables (ratings or judgments based on interviews are notably subjective and difficult to quantify satisfactorily), the more likely contamination is to occur.

A typical piece of research, unless it seeks simply to describe children in terms of their height, weight, intelligence, or reading ability, is designed to test the relation between an independent (or, speaking loosely, causal) variable and a dependent, or effect variable. Depending on the kinds of questions being asked, the same factor may function as either an independent or a dependent variable. For example, in a study of the effect of lack of mothering on intellectual functioning, intellectual functioning is the dependent variable. In a study seeking to establish whether intelligence is related to superior school work, on the other hand, intellectual functioning serves as the independent variable.

As has been said, the possibility of contaminating research results always exists when the person collecting the data is aware of the predicted relation between the independent and the dependent variable. For example, one influential hypothesis about asthma, derived from psychoanalytic theory, holds that asthma occurs in children whose mothers have rejected yet overprotected them. It is maintained that such children are frustrated criers: they want to cry, but dare not for fear of losing their mothers' love. Hence they turn their crying in on themselves, producing the strangling, acute shortness of breath and difficulty in breathing that characterize asthmatic children.

In a test of this hypothesis, the dependent variable is the presence or absence of asthma. Since the criteria for asthma are fairly clear, asthmatic children can be readily distinguished from nonasthmatic children. But the question of whether or not a mother rejects her child is to a considerable degree a matter of the investigator's judgment. This judgment is most frequently based on interviews with or observation of the mother. If an investigator holds a strong theoretical bias (for purposes of this illustration, either toward or against psychoanalytic theory), and at the same time knows which mothers have asthmatic and which healthy children, his questions to the mothers of asthmatics may, quite unintentionally, be slanted either to pick up (for the pro-bias) or conceal (for the anti-bias) signs of rejection; and he may be differentially alert to signs of overprotection in mothers of asthmatics and healthy children. Similar possibilities for contamination exist when the subjects are aware of the relationship being studied.

The danger of contamination may also be present in studies not concerned with causal relationships whenever the investigator holds certain expectations about results. For example, in studies of threshold measurement (the lowest intensity of a stimulus that can be perceived), it has been found that the experimenter's expectations concerning the location of the threshold can influence his methods and hence the point at which it is actually found.

Studies involving individual testing of intelligence may contain a similar type of bias. If a child is known to be or suspected to be of high intelligence, borderline performances on an item may be scored as passed; for a child judged to be of lower intelligence, they may be scored as failed. In experimental studies of learning, children are extremely sensitive to variations of expression on the experimenter's face, or to differential cues springing from the apparatus. When systematic variations are present, learning guided by them, rather than according to the goal of the experiment, may be responsible for the child's performance. Rosenthal (1965) is conducting interesting studies showing contamination (probably through experimenters' bias) for research on both animals and humans, including very carefully thought out and executed manipulative experiments.

RECONSTRUCTION THROUGH RETROSPECTION

The technique of reconstruction through retrospection is widely (and often necessarily) used in studies of the effects of child-rearing practices. For example, an investigator may conduct a study of the personalities of sixth graders. He is interested in how some of the aspects of personality he has studied are related to the child-rearing practices used with his subjects. He constructs a questionnaire for mothers to fill out, or interviews the mothers about how the experimental subjects were fed as infants—whether or not feeding was scheduled, when and how the subjects were weaned, when and how they were toilet-trained, and so on. He relates these reported practices to the characteristics of the children he has studied and concludes that such and such a practice has such and such an effect on personality, or that infant-training practices do not affect the personality of intermediate school-aged children.

A number of factors, of which forgetting is an important one, force us to regard such retrospective data with skepticism. For parents who have several children, memories about the development of one child blend with memories of the growth of others. Forgetting is also selective: parents are likely to remember the pleasant things about their children's development and forget the unpleasant ones. An experience of the author's illustrates this point: a friend with a new baby inquired rather desperately when the author's children had begun to sleep through the night. The confident answer, "At around 2 months," was given. Later, to assure accuracy, he checked the baby books kept for the children in the family, and found that his statement had been glaringly false: none of the three had slept through the night consistently until he was about 14 weeks old.

Finally, a lack of frankness often accompanies reports of child-rearing practices. Most parents have had exposure to people who have told them how babies should be reared. On the other hand, no parent has done with his children precisely as he believes he should have. People try to put themselves in the most favorable light. Hence, parents' reports about how they reared their children are likely to be slanted to some degree in the direction they believe they should have done it, or in the direction they think the expert questioner believes they should have done it.

For reasons such as these, it is difficult to know how much reliance to place on research findings based on methods involving retrospection. Robbins (1963) among others, documents this point with data.

FAULTY LOGIC

Another characteristic of research in this area, faulty logic, particularly fallacious causal inference, is regrettably frequent. Research illustrations provided in the section on contamination are, in this sense, instances of faulty logic. In a study of different toilet-training practices (Holway, 1949), some mothers were rated as strict, others as permissive, or tolerant. The children's fantasy play was then studied. That of children strictly toilet-trained was considered to indicate that they were more disturbed, less happy, than those permissively trained, and this difference was attributed to the training. The possibility was ignored that strict toilet training may be associated with other restrictive child-rearing practices, and that it may have been any one of the other practices, or all of them together, that produced the fantasy differences. Furthermore, it is possible that neither strict toilet training nor general restrictiveness was associated with disturbed fantasy play, but that the children with disturbed fantasy were harder to handle than other children, so that the mothers were driven into restrictiveness by the characteristics of their children. As has been pointed out repeatedly, child-rearing is a two-way street.

POOR DEFINITION OF CONCEPTS

The results of scientific study are dependable to the degree that an investigator has spelled out what he means and what he has done. Both the specification of the concept and its measurement determine the clarity of scientific definition.

Every scientific investigation must make use of concepts—abstractions from observed events. Some concepts are quite close to the phenomena they represent (for example, concepts such as house or car). Most of the concepts used in child-rearing studies, however, are abstractions at a higher level, much less easily related to events in the concrete world. Examples of such concepts are maladjustment, dependency, aggression, overprotection.

The concepts used by an investigator must be defined both in abstract terms, so that insofar as possible they mean the same thing to the reader or listener and to the originator; and in terms of the operations (measurements) defining them in the particular study. These operational or experimental definitions are adequate to the extent that they are satisfactory behavioral indicators of the concepts they are intended to represent. Without a clear conceptual definition, an adequate and useful operational definition is impossible.[1]

It should be ovious that concepts vary enormously in the degree to which they can be clearly defined and reliably measured. When a definition means the same thing to two people, when it includes a clear-cut method of measurement, and when measurements can be made repeatedly by the same person or by different people with the same results, clarity of definition exists.

Studies in the area of child-rearing frequently fail to satisfy these requirements. For example, Rank (1929) has advanced the hypothesis

---

[1] Bergmann (1951) may be consulted for further discussion of this subject.

that maladjustments in children (and adults) may be due in part to birth trauma, the pain and shock of the birth process. Ruja (1948) reasoned that this hypothesis could be tested by determining whether infants who had had difficult births showed greater maladjustment than infants who had had relatively easy births. His criterion (behavioral indicator) for a difficult birth was the length of the mother's labor, as judged from her "in labor" admission to the hospital until the time of delivery. His criterion for maladjustment of the infant was the amount of time the child spent crying. The first criterion is open to criticism because, from the infant's point of view, it may be that precipitate, hurried labor is harder (more traumatic) than prolonged, gradual delivery. The second criterion is unsatisfactory because the most profoundly traumatized or damaged baby may be the one who lacks the energy to cry.

Ruja, not surprisingly, found no relationship between length of labor and amount of crying. However, because of his faulty translation of concepts into observable events, we cannot say that he has disproved or even offered convincing evidence against the hypothesis concerning birth trauma. Psychological literature abounds with evidence of equally poor definition.

DIRECT INFLUENCE OF INVESTIGATOR
UPON HIS RESEARCH RESULTS

Another problem frequently encountered in research on human relations, particularly if it involves child-rearing practices, is that the investigator himself affects the results of the study he is conducting. One of the potentially most profitable methods of studying children is to make repeated or continuing studies of the same child as he grows up. Such studies, known as longitudinal studies, have given us valuable information concerning the development of intelligence and the rate and pattern of physical growth. These are examples of topics on which the influence of the investigator is relatively small, and for which we have valid and reliable techniques of measurement. But longitudinal studies have thrown little light on the effects of child-rearing practices or on the question of how personality develops. There are two major reasons for this. First, it is difficult to ask meaningful (conceptually clear) questions about personality development. What, for example, is meant by adjustment? dependency? maternal rejection? Second, the investigator and the things he stands for and does influence the very child-rearing practices that are being studied.

The average person who does research with children has a real and special regard for them. If he sees them developing in a fashion that he knows is likely to lead to maladjustment, it is almost impossible for him to behave in a coldly dispassionate, purely scientific fashion. He must do something to help. But his behavior, though well-intentioned, distorts his results. The study becomes not a study of parent-child relations and their effects upon personality, but a study of parent-child-expert relations. Whenever the investigator, for extrascientific motives—no matter how good these are—directly affects the relations he is studying, the study he produces becomes different from what he originally intended.

The phenomenon of experimenter influence has been clearly demonstrated in the Hawthorne studies of the effects of different kinds of working conditions on the productivity of factory workers (see Homans, 1958). Regardless of the kinds of change introduced, and regardless of whether these changes were in the direction of better or poorer physical working conditions, the productivity of the experimental group continued to increase. The effect of physical working conditions was overshadowed by the effect of other changes: the workers' awareness of taking part in an experiment; their being set apart as a special small group; their altered relations with supervisory personnel. These social and attitudinal variables, indirectly related to the experiment itself, obscured the effect of the factors the experiment was initially designed to investigate. Something very similar seems likely to occur in longitudinal studies of personality, where, over the years, the investigator has continued an intimate interaction with the parents and children who form the core of the study.

As has been inferred, research workers may have not only direct but indirect influence on the population they are studying. A study by Dennis and Sayegh (1965) was discussed briefly in Chapter 1 under the heading of *kinesthesis*. The reader may recall that Dennis and Sayegh picked a group of experimental infants averaging a little less than one year old as their experimental subjects, and gave them an hour a day of new experience for fifteen weeks. *But* the attendants in the Beirut, Lebanon institution where both experimental and control children lived, sensed that *something* was going on. The attendants probably did not know exactly what, but seemed to think it involved extra attention to babies. One can conjecture that their reasoning went something like this: the experts are doing something extra with five of our babies. This must mean we are doing something wrong. Let's change it. Let's do something different with the babies these experts are *not* working with. So the attendants (or so Dennis and Sayegh suspected) provided extra experience for the controls. (It may be remembered that it was remarked "unfortunately for science but probably fortunately for the babies . . . .") The attendants' change in treatment of the control babies was probably responsible for their also showing accelerated changes in developmental age, and thus clouded the scientific value of the Dennis and Sayegh study. This illustrates *indirect influence of experimenter upon study outcome*.

PROBLEMS OF SAMPLING

The problems of sampling range from the practical difficulties of obtaining human subjects to the question of making generalizations from the population studied to other populations.

Practical difficulties in obtaining subjects result, for example, in our knowing little about child-rearing practices in lower-class homes; such parents usually do not understand nor are they interested in research. On the other hand, because of the availability of students in college psychology classes and of white rats, much of psychological fact and theory is based on the study of such populations.

Central to the problem of making sound generalizations from a study is the nature of the population on which it was based. Biased samples limit generalization. The basic definition of a biased sample is this: The measured sample fails to represent, and thus to predict, the sample it was originally supposed to predict. Bias is essentially a matter of systematic variation of some type, as opposed to random, or chance, variation.

Since it is almost impossible to work with a total population, or universe, a subsection of the population (a sample) must be selected for study. In a random sample, each member of the total population being considered has an equal chance of being selected as a member of the sample, or of being assigned to some particular method of study or experimental treatment in the total research program. The reason for randomizing selection is that if, and only if, a sample is random can the laws of mathematical probability be applied to findings based on that sample, and any sort of confident generalization applied to the population from which it was drawn.

The problem of the biased sample has been central, most markedly in the normative research approach. It is virtually impossible, from a practical point of view, to avoid a biased sample. For example, in studying the height and weight of 6-year-olds, a typical procedure is to enlist the cooperation of the public schools of a city, or several cities, so that all, or a random, or a representative sample of 6-year-olds can be measured during the shortest possible period of time. But such an apparently comprehensive sample will be biased because some 6-year-olds will be absent from school during the time of the study, perhaps because they are ill. If a large enough group of 6-year-olds is included in the study, the research worker will find a fairly good cross section and number of illnesses. In general, the children who are ill at any given time include many who, because of chronic illness, miss more days of school than their healthier classmates, and who are also thinner and shorter than children of normal health. Hence, we obtain a group that averages somewhat taller and heavier than the universe (which would include all 6-year-olds in the population).

In addition to the 6-year-olds ordinarily in regular attendance at school, but absent on the day of weighing and measuring, there are other 6-year-old children who never attend public school. Such children may have been born crippled or physically or mentally handicapped in some other way. They, like the chronically ill, will be found to weigh less and to be shorter than the group of 6-year-olds regularly attending school. Their absence will further bias the sample in the direction of producing norms (that is, averages and the range from the shortest or lightest to the tallest or heaviest child) that show 6-year-olds to be taller and heavier than they would be if all 6-year-olds were measured. Finally, some children will refuse to cooperate, or their parents will decline permission for them to be measured.

Results from such a study, then, do not pertain to "Kansas City, Missouri, 6-year-olds," but to "cooperative Kansas City, Missouri, 6-year-olds in attendance at public school at the time height and weight were determined."

Occasionally, another type of bias is introduced by an investigator. He formulates a hypothesis, designs a method to test it, secures the co-operation of subjects, and collects his data. The data fall in the direction of his prediction, but the results are not clear enough to reach statistical significance. He looks at his individual cases, and sees that most of them have behaved as he predicted they would; but a minority has not, thus reducing the over-all effect he hoped to show. He checks with this minority and finds that each one had "seen through" the purpose of his experiment. He concludes that "seeing through" his plan has kept these subjects from behaving according to prediction, and discards their results, leaving the average behavior of the remaining subjects striking enough to support his hypothesis statistically. But he has not checked to see whether, among them, there are some who had also "seen through" the experiment. He has, in other words, systematically altered his final sample from that he originally studied. This investigator would not have erred if he had included in his original research plan a check for "seeing through," with the initial declared intention of discarding the results obtained from all subjects who "saw through" the experiment.

Still another type of bias results from substituting volunteers for persons originally scheduled to take part in a study or experiment. If a research worker plans to study the attitudes of working mothers toward disciplining their children, he might, for example, secure the cooperation of the management of a large plant. From the personnel records of women working in the plant he obtains information about the ages of the women employees, the number of children each has, their average education, and so on. Because of the large numbers involved, it is not feasible for him to study all the women, so he constructs a representative sample: a certain proportion of women with one child, or with two or more; so many with children under school age, so many with children in elementary school; so many over 40 years of age; so many widowed, and so on. He then selects from the files names of women that will satisfy these requirements of a representative sample, and approaches them to ask their cooperation. Most are willing to serve as subjects, but some are not. He then calls for volunteers, picking from them women who match the characteristics of those who have refused; or continues to go through the files, finding women with characteristics that match the refusers, until he has rounded out a sample fitting his original specifications.

In doing this, he has biased his sample. The "volunteers" differ from the refusers on the important dimension of cooperativeness. It may be that cooperators, compared with refusers, are more sympathetic toward psychological research, better informed about recommendations for "good" discipline, and hence different in their ways of disciplining their children. Such a bias consequently influences the soundness of the conclusions about the universe (here, the total population of mothers working in the plant). Kinsey (1948) has often been criticized because of volunteer bias (it is suspected that his volunteers either were sexier, or claimed they were, than a truly random sample would have been).

Biased samples, then, are those that do not predict the sample they were originally intended to predict, although stratified samples help in overcoming bias. A stratified sample is a population selection based on known characteristics of the total population. But, generally, bias most frequently results from one of three processes: failure to measure all of the intended sample; elimination of subjects without previous specification of the conditions under which this will be done; and substitution of one type of subject for another.

UNSOUND GENERALIZATION

The three most common types of unsound generalization are:

1. Writing or speaking as though findings were more significant or clear-cut than they are.

2. Applying findings gathered in one situation to circumstances different in essential characteristics.

3. Applying findings from one population to another differing in basic dimensions.

Hypothetical examples of these are, for the first: using the well-established, moderately high correlation between the intelligence of mothers and their children as though it indicated that every child of a bright mother was himself bright, and vice versa.

An example of the second type of unsound generalization is the assumption that, because a child behaved inflexibly in an experimental situation (for example, failed to change his approach as the type of arithmetic problem presented to him changed), he will act rigidly in a wide variety of real-life situations.

An illustration of the third type of unsound generalization is the assumption that the height and weight of the "cooperative Kansas City, Missouri, 6-year-olds attending public school," mentioned previously, provide an adequate basis for judging normal height and weight of 6-year-olds in Tahiti.

Generalization, then, should be made according to the scientific certainty of the original findings, to situations having as much as possible in common with the original research setting, and to populations as similar as possible to the research population from which the findings were obtained. The more closely these conditions are met, the sounder the generalization.

Increasing confidence can be placed in a finding if it has been replicated. If a relation between a certain type of reward and speed of learning has been demonstrated for white rats, monkeys, 3-year-olds in Arizona and New York, eighth-graders in Minnesota, and college sophomores in California, one can be more confident in saying that it is a general truth or law than if this relation had been demonstrated for only one of these populations. However, one would still hesitate to say that it held for adult Australian aborigines.

Research workers in child development frequently overgeneralize, or generalize imprecisely, and advisers of parents and teachers err in this direction even more often than research workers themselves. For example, it is generally held that praise is better than punishment as a method of motivating children's learning. Yet, strictly speaking, this generalization is imprecise, because praise and punishment have seldom, if ever, been compared for their effect on precisely the same behavior. In teaching a child traffic safety, for example, one does not compare the results of praising him for standing on the curb and looking both ways before crossing the street with punishing him for the same behavior. A test in this situation would be to compare the speed with which he learned to use discretion in crossing streets under conditions (1) of being punished for darting into the street and (2) of being rewarded for staying on the curb until he had looked both ways. Still a third test, making for greater precision of generalization, would be (3) to train a group of children by praise for correct responses and punishment or criticism for mistakes. With such evidence, it could then be said that praise was preferable to punishment, or that a combination of both was better than either alone, in achieving the training goal.

The logical consequences of praise or reward and punishment alone, or a combination of the two, are often not recognized: praise, in effect, tells a child only what he *can* do; punishment tells him only what he *cannot* do; but a combination of the two (used almost automatically as a common-sense technique by most parents, teachers, and others who deal with children, as well as by children toward those who deal with them) tells a child *both* what he can and cannot do. The prediction follows that a child handled with a combination of reward and punishment will learn faster and perhaps more flexibly (or at least across a broader range of possibilities) than a child trained entirely either by praise or by punishment.

Serious overgeneralization has also resulted from studies of children's eating. Davis (1939) found that children who were given their free choice of a variety of simple, nutritious foods tended, on the whole, to choose foods that were good for them. Although one day they might eat only one item, and on the next go on a binge of eating another, over a long period of time they voluntarily selected a well-balanced diet. As a result, a whole generation of parents has been advised to "leave your children alone. They will automatically choose diets that are good for them." Such advice overlooks the fact that the children in the study were offered alternatives only among foods that were simple, essentially good for them— such as eggs, bananas, and simple cereals—and available at every meal; whereas the typical modern child includes among his alternative foods such items as chocolate candy, varieties of pie, and bleached-flour bread. Anyone who has watched children growing up cannot help wondering whether their own choices might not result in a diet composed almost entirely of white bread, candy, pop of various sorts, and chocolate milk.

Statistical and Measurement Considerations

Without some grasp of measurement and statistical concepts, and with no appreciation of common research faults such as those discussed in the preceding section (particularly *unsound generalization*), a reader is lost if he ventures into primary sources (original research articles), or tries intelligently to follow the research summarized and discussed in the rest of the book. In fact, he may already have been lost at times as he read Chapter 1.

CORRELATION

A correlation coefficient is an expression of the relation between one thing and another—the degree to which two things vary together. The correlation between height and weight in a sample of fifty young men can be illustrated as follows. First, array the men in order of their height, with the shortest man to the left, the tallest man to the right. Put a card over each man's head indicating his weight. Observation will show a tendency for the shorter men to be lighter, the taller men heavier. There will be a number of men who are heavier than those taller than they, and vice versa. But, for the group as a whole, greater height will go with greater weight. In other words, height and weight will covary—will be positively correlated with each other.

Correlation coefficients, theoretically, can range from perfect positive ($+1.00$) to perfect negative (-1.00). The condition of a perfect positive correlation would be met if, in our illustration, the tallest man was the heaviest, the next tallest the next heavy, and so on down the line to the shortest and the lightest man. The more interchange in weight status between men of different height (as, the third from the shortest man is found to be the third from the heaviest), the lower the correlation. If there is no covariance between height and weight, but simply a chance relation, the correlation is zero. If the shortest man were the heaviest, the next shortest man the next heavy, and so on, until the tallest man was revealed to be the lightest, the condition for a perfect negative correlation would be fulfilled.

PREDICTION THROUGH CORRELATION

The principal purpose in calculating a correlation coefficient (r) is to predict one variable from another. Knowledge of a man's height is more useful if it also helps us to predict his weight than if it gives us no information about him other than how tall he is. Correlations are likely to lead to deceptive inferences about causality: if two things are correlated with each other, it is tempting to say that one "causes" the other. Correctly, we should assume only that they are related, but should also be encouraged to look for the reasons for the relation. In general, tall men are heavier than short men for the rather elementary reason that they have more bones to cover and coordinate with muscle and fat. There is simply more to them. But their height did not cause their weight.

A simple calculation is useful in appraising the predictive value of a correlation coefficient. It is easy (but incorrect) to assume that the rather high correlation of .70 between a test of reading achievement and intelligence for fourth-graders means that all the brighter children read better than those less bright. This correlation indicates a substantial relation between reading and intelligence. Hence, knowledge of the children's intelligence helps us predict their standing in reading ability among other children of their age. But the relation is by no means a perfect one. To determine how much of the total variance of reading (all the factors that influence, or determine, reading skill) is accounted for by intelligence, one multiplies the correlation between the two by itself: .70 × .70 is equal to .49. Translated, this means that 49 percent of the variance of reading in our sample of fourth-graders is accounted for by the children's intelligence. To put it in other words, the .70 correlation between intelligence and reading accounts for 49 percent of the possible range of factors that enters into making a perfect prediction of where a child stands in his reading group. But 51 percent of the variance remains unaccounted for when we know only the intelligence-test scores of a group of children. Of this unaccounted for 51 percent of the variance, the amount of practice children have had is responsible for some; some is due to parents' intelligence; some can be accounted for by the number of books in the home libraries, some by motivation, some by study efficiency, some by the acuity and coordination of vision, and so on.

The average correlation of about .50 that has been found between the intelligence of parents and children indicates that only 25 percent of the variance of children's intelligence can be accounted for by the brightness of their parents. A correlation of .20 between children's strength and their speed of response means that only 4 percent of the variance of speed of response is accounted for by strength, leaving 96 percent to be predicted from knowledge of other factors.

Much faulty generalization results from failure to calculate how much of the variance of one variable is due to another with which it is correlated. A correlation of .70 looks reassuringly high, but still leaves us with 51 percent of the variance unaccounted for.

The correlation of about .50 that is usually found between the intelligence of children and their parents is often used in ways that are detrimental both to children and their parents: A teacher assumes that because daddy is a doctor and mommy is a lawyer, Junior Number One is bound to be bright. It isn't necessarily so, and the teacher's overexpectations for Junior may do him real harm. On the other hand, the same teacher is equally likely to assume that because daddy holds down an unskilled job, and both daddy and mommy finished the sixth grade only, it follows that Junior Number Two is pretty unlikely to be a profound scholar. The teacher *expects* Junior to do badly. Children, as will be discussed later, tend to behave as influential adults *expect* them to behave; hence, Junior Number Two may do poorly in school, not because he is stupid, but because he is *expected* to do poorly. Of course, poor school achievement is seldom if ever this simply explained, but teacher expectations play an important part in how a child performs. One of the best illustrations of the effects on a child of how the teacher expects him to behave (not only academically but socially) is given in Claude Brown's description of his elementary and secondary school days in his autobiography, *Manchild in the Promised Land* (1965). Academically, he performed wretchedly (nor was his social behavior by any means impeccable) in elementary school years. Eventually, teachers, their eyes unclouded by knowledge of or prejudice about relations between intelligence or behavior and family status, perceived that Claude Brown was a bright and (potentially) a good boy (in the sense of his possibly eventually becoming a good citizen). He satisfied both sets of teachers/caretakers: for those who expected him to behave stupidly and undesirably, he behaved stupidly and became a proficient delinquent. Later (but gradually and with a good many temporary slips backward) he was equally obliging to those who expected him to behave intelligently in the scholastic sense and constructively as a citizen. At the time he wrote his book, he was a college graduate with further educational ambitions and, even by stringent criteria, a good citizen.

Our Junior Number One—the son of the doctor father and lawyer mother—can also be injured by teacher overexpectations. If he simply *cannot* do advanced work, it is not only pointless to expect him to, but also damaging to him: the fact that he has disappointed a set of teachers, his parents, and his brothers and sisters leaves him, at best, psychologically scarred. A sophisticated search for a nonprofessional career for him, guiding him toward it, and helping his family accept it will, in all likelihood, make both a happier and a more constructive Junior than a simple set of high academic achievement expectations based on the fact that his mother and father are extremely intelligent and well-educated.

SOME GENERAL MEASUREMENT CONCEPTS

A *concept* is the general term for the class of behavior you are reading about or which the author of a research paper has studied. Illustrative concepts have been given in the section immediately preceding this: others are frustration, regression, anxiety, curiosity, and so on.

A *population* is the group the author has studied and on which he reports: it may consist of 27 hooded rats, 8 babies 4 days old, 10,000 Chicago fifth-grade children, or 100 fathers and mothers of first-graders.

A *normal distribution* is one that lies between the ends of a continuum, and is shaped approximately like a bell. Figure 2.2 illustrates a normal distribution.

It can be seen from Figure 2.2 that there are few (perhaps only one from a large population) at either End A or End B of the continuum. Most people (or cases, or subjects) fall between the ends. To use height as an illustration: very few ninth-grade boys are only 5 feet tall (End A of the continuum); an equally small number is 7 feet tall (End B of the continuum). The average American ninth-grade boy is about 5 feet 5 or 6 inches tall. This figure is arrived at by, hypothetically, measuring all ninth-grade American boys, adding their heights together, and

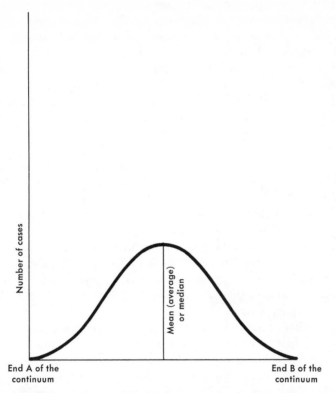

Figure 2.2   The diagram of a normal distribution.

dividing by the total number of boys who have been measured. You will, for reasons that have been discussed, arrive at a figure somewhat too great: chronically ill, seriously retarded, many lower-lower-class boys who have had poor nutrition, hence are not as tall as they may have been with better diets, will not be attending school.

In a normal distribution, as indicated in Figure 2.2, the *mean*, or average, and the *median*, or midpoint, are the same. By median is meant that point in the distribution above and below which exactly one half of the population falls. Means and medians are different from each other when your distribution is *skewed* or abnormal. If we compute the average annual income of five men picked at random from the street, we may obtain figures as follows: $3000, $4000, $5000, $6000, and $1,000,000. Our mean, in this case, is $203,600. It is ridiculous to assume from the data we have collected that the average American male earns more than $200,000 per year. By chance, we have secured a *biased* sample.

In such a case, the *median*, or midpoint, probably gives a more accurate or at least a more meaningful picture of the true state of affairs in the United States: the median is $5000 and our sample includes two men who earn more and two who earn less than this. Income and education figures for developing countries are often more meaningfully represented by medians than means: in such countries, there are typically a few very wealthy and a few very highly educated men and women, but a great mass who are desperately poor and/or illiterate. Including those who fall at or near End B of the continuum in Figure 2.2 (the very wealthy, the exceptionally well-educated) makes our mean misleadingly high.

Authors frequently speak of relatively *heterogeneous* or *homogeneous* populations. By heterogeneous, they mean that the population includes great differences among its members: in other words, Ends A and B of the continuum in Figure 2.2 are widely separated. In a homogeneous population, all the members are relatively similar to each other: the ends of the continuum are close together. A population including children from ages 3 to 13, boys and girls, Negro, Puerto Rican, and Appalachian in nature, with some of the children coming from very poor and others from very wealthy homes would be more heterogeneous for almost any conceivable dimension than a population of fifth-grade boys in a rural Illinois elementary school.

When authors talk of their results having high *variance*, they mean that some children changed not at all, or perhaps actually regressed, while others changed a great deal. For low variance, changes tend to be similar in amount and in the same direction. Variance is often expressed as the *standard deviation* (S.D.). The standard deviation is a statistical term—a figure that is used to indicate how variable a population or set of results is. About two-thirds of a population is included in the portion of the curve drawn in Figure 2.2 that falls between a score or measurement one standard deviation below the mean, and a score or measurement one standard deviation above the mean.

When the reader moves to primary sources, he encounters a number of specific statistical terms, such as Type I analyses of variance, F-ratios, chi-squares, *taus*, *W*'s and a host of others. Without having studied statistics, it is impossible for him to make sense of these. He must simply take the author on faith (most editors have checked to see that the authors' statistical procedures are legitimate). But, as has been pointed out, he should—indeed must—know in an elementary sort of way what *levels of statistical significance* or *confidence* mean.

LEVEL OF STATISTICAL CONFIDENCE

The central task of science is to discover lawfulness in its subject matter. Child development seeks to determine lawfulness in human structure, growth, and function. Statistics are among the tools used to demonstrate lawfulness. Among other tasks we assign to statistics is that of providing us with an estimate of the confidence we can place in our findings. We are particularly interested in whether we can assume that they happened for reasons other than chance.

Ordinarily, we speak with "confidence" of results that are statistically significant. In this volume, statistical significance refers to any result at or below the .05 (or 5 percent) level of confidence. Such a figure (which may also be referred to as P for probability, $P = .05$) indicates that the results to which it refers are of such magnitude that they would occur by chance only five times in a hundred. The .01 ($P = .01$) level of confidence tells us that results like ours would be expected through chance once in one-hundred times; the .001 level of confidence once in a thousand times.

In our earlier example, a correlation of .70 was postulated between intelligence and reading achievement for sixty children in two fourth-grade classrooms. To establish the significance or level of confidence for this correlation, we can consult a table or go through certain computations. Either of these procedures shows it to be significant at less than the .001 level. That is, a correlation of this magnitude, based on a population of this size, would be expected to occur by chance fewer than once in a thousand times.

For another illustration, suppose that the investigator's purpose is to test the effectiveness of an accelerated reading program. By a process of random selection, half the children in four classes of fourth-graders are assigned to an experimental group. The remaining children constitute a control group. The purpose of the study is to see whether the experimental children can be significantly advanced in reading skill over children remaining in the regular reading program by supplying individual instructions and enriched reading materials. Some safeguard must be introduced, however, so that it can be said that any superiority they show is due to the reading program, and not to the Hawthorne effect (improvement in performance as a result of taking part in an experiment). This safeguard is introduced by giving the control children an amount of individual attention equal to that given the experimental youngsters, but social rather than instructional in nature; and supplying them with attractive materials that differ in content from those regularly used, but are at the same level of difficulty. Otherwise, the experiences of the two groups are the same.

The children are tested for reading achievement before and after the study. The experimental (accelerated) group does not differ from the control group at the beginning of the study, but has gained a full grade level at its end, while the control group has gained only a half year. Statistical computations relating to this differential gain result in a numerical expression of sufficient size to have happened by chance only once in a hundred times. In practice, we proceed from this indication of lawfulness to the conclusion that the accelerated reading program was responsible for the difference in experimental and control group gains.

Faulty generalization often results from overconfidence in expressions of statistical significance, such as placing too much faith in a single experiment or study that shows significance at the .05 or .01 level. Less often, insufficient, hence faulty, generalization is made because of skepticism about the level of confidence of a finding.

This can become confusing, even to a rather sophisticated reader. In the Dennis and Sayegh (1965) study, the experimental subjects gained significantly in developmental age (at the .03 level). This means that there are but 3 chances in 100 that such gains could have happened by chance alone. In other words, there are 97 chances in 100 that the enriched experiences given the five experimental babies were associated with and probably caused by the treatment administered to them by the experimenters. It is difficult to secure a result significant at this level with such a small number of subjects. One's chances of obtaining statistical significance increase the bigger his sample is. But Dennis' and Sayegh's control group also increased more rapidly in developmental age than would have been expected during the experiment (the authors are vague about the exact level of significance of the gain). We are told only that "the gains of the control group were smaller . . . . By the sign test, which was used in the case of the experimental group, the change in rate of gain of the control group has a very low level of significance" (p. 88). We are left with the understanding that the experimental group of five babies improved significantly more than the control group of eight babies. But we are not given data sufficient to decide for ourselves (it should be added that the present author is sympathetic to the Dennis and Sayegh point of view) whether or not there was *really* a statistically significant difference between the children given the extra hour of experience each day for fifteen days and those who did not have this experience.

It is for such reasons that the author has decided to treat the important question of *how to go about reading a primary source*. A primary source is an article that reports original data, talks about it, analyzes it, formulates results, arrives at conclusions, and sometimes makes recommendations for action based on it. Needless to say, this is a procedure the author has found useful.

First, you read the article either because it interests you or it is assigned to you in a class. The reading procedure does not differ in either case.

Second, read the summary. What does the author say he has said? In at least half the summaries of primary source articles, the reader probably cannot tell, either because the author has not bothered to prepare an adequate summary or because he wants to make the summary ambiguous and unrevealing, so the reader must go ahead to read the entire article to find out what it is about.

Third, read the hypotheses. What is it the author is investigating; what questions is he trying to answer? Often, the author's hypotheses are backed by considerable theory. When they are, read backward to see what the theory is, because often the author has repeated his hypotheses one or more times as he discussed the theory that led up to them. If the article has scientific merit, its author has also provided the reader with the logic that led to the hypotheses.

Fourth, move to the method. It has already been mentioned that there are general concepts—for example, dependency or aggression or under-achievement. By this stage in reading, you will have discovered what general concept it is the author has in mind. It has also been previously pointed out that a concept, a general term, must be "brought down to earth." If an author is talking about underachievement in the sixth grade, exactly how does he bring this general concept down to earth? To him, is an underachiever a child who is in the bottom one-fifth of the class, or below the average according to teachers' marks? Or according to nationally standardized tests? There can be a great difference here. We know that teachers favor girls over boys when awarding grades, probably because girls are better behaved and the principal frowns on a teacher if she does not maintain good discipline. Thus, because girls give her less trouble than boys, she has something of a "halo" effect about girls. They are well-behaved, thus they must be bright, thus they should get good marks. Standardized tests are more objective. Few if any important differences in results from such tests are consistently found between boys and girls. Thus, the author who uses standardized tests as his measure of underachievement has done a scientifically more acceptable job of anchoring the general concept of underachievement than the research worker who uses teachers' marks. Which is a better definition of under-achievement: the bottom one-fifth of the class, or all the children who fall below the average of the class? The question cannot be answered so simply. The children's academic aptitude or intelligence must also be taken into consideration, since intelligence is related both to teachers' marks and to performance on achievement tests. The author who chooses a method something like this has behaved soundly. Using the correlation technique to predict what standing in class each child *hypothetically* should have in terms of his intelligence compared with the rest of the class, he chooses as underachievers those who fall markedly below their *ability* as far as their performance is concerned.

Fifth, note what the nature is of the population the author has studied. Is it European, Australian, French, United States? If the last, is it from a lower-class area in New York City, or an upper-middle class suburb of St. Louis, or rural? If the author has not told you this, he has not given you enough information for you to make an adequate judgment about his study. Is the population one of boys, girls, or half-and-half? This can make a tremendous difference and, again, if the author has not given you this information, you cannot make your own judgment about the merits of his study or the worth of his conclusions.

Sixth, move on to the author's *results* section. Look first at the tables to see what the author has found out. Only later go on to see what the author says about his tables. Often the tables and the text disagree. If they do disagree, the author has not been completely honest.

Seventh, if he includes one, read the author's *discussion* section. Here an author is at liberty to speculate about what his results mean: he is not completely bound by his data; he can ponder about why they do not fit his hypotheses, or why they do. He is free to consider where his results may lead, what relation they bear to other research, where he made his mistakes (if any), what were the strong points of his article, and propose needed new research, either for himself or someone else.

Eighth, and finally (the ideal way to read an article is with a pen or pencil in hand, underlining and making marginal notes), go back over the underlinings and comments you have made to formulate your over-all impression of the article, make a judgment of its worth, check the author for consistency or inconsistency, and so on.

The Development of a Theoretical Framework

The discussion so far has emphasized the methodological problems encountered by studies of the effects of child-rearing. But if they are to make their most effective contribution to knowledge in a given field, empirical studies must have a close and continuing relation with theory in that field. Theory, even if fragmentary, serves to guide research by pointing to areas in which meaningful relations are likely to be found and enhances the meaning of specific findings by relating them to more general concepts and principles. Research, on the other hand, serves to test existing theories and to provide a basis for their modification or for the development of new theories.

At a minimum, the theoretical framework within which fruitful investigations of child-rearing practices can be carried out must specify two dimensions: (1) the areas or stages of child development upon which parental behavior has a significant impact; (2) the types or characteristics of parental behavior that significantly influence development. In this section we shall consider, first, certain approaches to the definition of developmental stages, and, second, some of the attempts to isolate significant characteristics of parental behavior.

DIMENSIONS OF HUMAN DEVELOPMENT

Almost all authors in the field of human development who have thought
deeply about the matter have developed ideas about the most meaningful
developmental dimensions. Many have arrived at a conception of developmental stages. To some, these stages are chronological divisions. Gesell
(see, Gesell *et al.*, 1940), for example, appears to regard age as the most
important developmental dimension, and refers to types of behavior that
characterize the 2-year-old or the 12-year-old. He regards development as
a wavelike phenomenon, in which a period of integration and social
harmony is followed by a period of increasing disintegration until a
relatively disintegrated, socially inharmonious trough is reached. This,
in turn, is followed by periods of steadily increasing integration until
another peak is reached. This wavelike process ends only with maturity.

Gesell's theories leave little room for the constructive contribution
of environment: to Gesell, a child is *born* to be what he is born to be.
About the only effect his environment has on him is to keep him from
realizing his potential. But *potential* itself cannot be increased.

Carl Rogers (1951), best known for his theories and research in nondirective psychotherapy, seems to regard environment in much the same
way as Gesell: it can retard and it can prevent the child or adult from
actualizing himself. Implicit in Rogers is the notion that, while environment can retard or deform, it cannot increase potential.

Erikson (1956) is a *neoanalyst:* his theories derive from Freud but are
much more oriented toward learning and socialization than Freud's
traditional psychoanalysis. For that reason, while the present author
believes Erikson is one of the most provocative thinkers about human
development now living, treatment of his theory is delayed until the
sections on socialization later in this volume.

Other theories of development are implicit in some of the learning
theories, discussed in Chapter 4 of this book.

Two representative theories have been selected for very brief discussion in this chapter: the classical psychoanalytic theory of Sigmund
Freud and the neoanalytic theory of Harry Stack Sullivan.

Many have gone beyond the straightforward chronological conception
of stages and, like Freud (1933, 1938), take note of how at different age
levels different organ systems and their satisfactions are predominant
(for instance, during the first year of life, the mouth and eating). Freud
believes that predominance of a given organ system, interacting with
parental treatment of the child during its dominance (for example, style
of feeding the child), plays a major role in forming personality.

Still others (as Sullivan) talk not so much of the genetically or biologically determined dominance of different organ systems, but of the

child's maturing capacities—his ability to "understand" his environment. Others, perhaps because of the difficulty of measuring or evaluating developmental stages, resort to universal categories of socialization (such as feeding, toilet training, and so on) and, in effect, do not consider stages of development as such.

The next few pages describe some of these theoretical frames of reference in greater detail.

THE DEVELOPMENTAL STAGES OF FREUD

Freud was one of the first to consider in any dynamic way how the early life of the infant shaped his later personality. Well-grounded in biology, Freud believed that the influences of learning in infancy upon the developing organism profoundly affected the well-being or ill-being of the older child and adult. More than any other scholar, he is responsible for currently accepted ideas that all behavior is caused, none is random or meaningless; and that, to understand later behavior, we must understand development in infancy and early childhood.

The roots of personality, for Freud, were biological. Personality was shaped through the interaction between learning and the three vital organ systems of orality and eating, anality and elimination, and genitality and (eventual) procreation. These organ systems and processes he related to infantile sexuality.

The oral system is, of course, dominant during the first year of life. The child's first experiences with satisfaction and discomfort, and with kindly or unsatisfying human relations, come through his mouth and the feeding process. Deprived of food or otherwise harshly treated, the infant is overwhelmed by fear and anxiety. Throughout his life, he must devote an undue portion of his psychological energy to defending against such anxiety and insecurity. In other words, he is "fixated" at the oral stage and, unless fortuitous circumstances intervene, continues to be handicapped by the problems engendered during this early developmental period. The type of the adult orally fixated, because of deprivation, is one who is miserly, arrogant, aggressive and impatient, competitive, suspicious, depressed, and cynical.

Relaxed and generous, but not overindulgent, feeding is thought to produce childhood and adult personalities characterized by cooperative, peaceful, friendly, optimistic, and sharing-and-giving traits. When oral overprotectiveness exists and there is a lack of parental encouragement to move into later developmental or psychosexual stages, or when conditions during later developmental stages are unduly harsh or unrewarding, the child may become orally fixated in quite a different way. Feelings of unrealistic security and self-confidence are common; the individual is rashly trusting of others, at the same time expecting them to do everything for him. By way of contrast, the orally deprived baby becomes prematurely dependent on himself (self-sufficient), but is at the same time insecure and uncertain. Thus, he is later forced into unwilling and untrusting dependent behavior. In this sense, similar personality traits (dependence) may have sharply contrasting origins, just as very different-appearing behaviors may have similar origins.

After, but overlapping with, the dominance of the oral-eating system comes pre-eminence of the anal-eliminative system. Ordinarily, during this period (from about a year or 18 months to around 4 years), the child is asked to submit his will to that of his parents: to forego his own pleasure and accede to the demands of society. During this stage, he learns the rudiments of control: to withhold (for example, to be continent) and, voluntarily, to give (as to have his bowel movement, or to void, at the right time and in the right place).

The anal character (fixation at the anal stage) may, according to Freud, result from too early or too strict and harsh toilet training. Such a personality is characterized by excessive orderliness, parsimoniousness, and obstinacy; although if the child never "knuckles down" to parental training, adult traits of wastefulness, unpunctuality, extravagance, and vacillation may presumably occur. The necessary adult trait of dependence (and all of us must be able to handle dependency, since we are all dependent on others) develops either naturally or abnormally during the oral stage. The equally necessary trait of autonomy (loosely, self-determination or self-will) is thought to develop or be blunted during the anal developmental stage. Too strict toilet training is thought by some to inhibit the natural exploratory interest of the child; to cause him to be filled with shame, so that he is likely to regress to the oral, dependent stage and fail to develop self-confidence and independent problem-solving behavior.

Hypothetically, anal fixation, like oral fixation, can occur either through deprivation or through overgratification. A situation in which much affection accompanies complete accession to the child's demands, without imposition of limits, might constitute such overindulgence. If fixation due to indulgence occurred, one might speculate that the personality would include all-encompassing self-confidence, insensitivity to the needs of others, and extreme social dominance. However, at least two facts combine to produce fixation through excessive limits rather than through overindulgence. The first is that necessary limits on behavior have to be set for children of this age to protect them from bodily harm; second, even though their parents may be overindulgent, children early start bumping into limits set by their playmates and adults other than their parents.

During the phallic stage (between about $3\frac{1}{2}$ and 5 or $5\frac{1}{2}$ years of age) the child becomes entranced with his own power as well as his own body.

Here again, according to Freudian theory, too harsh and restrictive treatment may impair self-confidence, curiosity, and ambition, and produce anxiety about the body and its natural functions, particularly in the area of sexual behavior.

Fixation at this stage through overgratification is unlikely in our culture, since discouragement of childhood sexuality is almost universal. Even the child handled indulgently by his parents will encounter taboos through his friends and their mothers, and through other adults in his world.

Of central importance in Freud's theory of personality development is his account of the Oedipus complex and its possible outcomes. If normal development is to occur, boys must renounce an intense relationship they have presumably felt with their mothers, and girls must do the same with their fathers. The resolution of the Oedipal conflict, which is assumed to occur between 5 and 6 or 7 years of age, ushers in the child's identification with the parent of the same sex. When the Oedipus complex is successfully resolved, the little boy presumably takes a natural, easy, proud attitude toward his maleness, the little girl toward her femaleness. When, for one reason or another (such as unduly harsh, rejecting, or overprotective parents of either sex), the Oedipus complex is not resolved, the child may identify with the parent of the opposite sex to the detriment of his own later development. Cases in point are those who are homosexual, sexually impotent, or frigid. Again, as with the oral stage, similar behavior may have very different origins; one girl may conceivably become homosexual because of a strong, tender mother, a weak father; another because her father was harsh and rejecting but to a lesser degree than her mother.

Following the resolution of the Oedipus complex, it is thought that the child represses his infantile sexuality and the primitive fantasies connected with the organ systems of orality and anality. This repression marks the beginning of the latency period, characterized by reality orientation and lack of sexuality. Adolescence, which begins with genital maturity, re-evokes many of the infantile fantasies and conflicts. But, if these have been handled relatively well by the parents and other meaningful adults, the child moves fairly easily into natural heterosexual maturity, and is able to give as well as receive love.

Freud's conception of the stages of psychosexual development has been roundly criticized by many. It derives more from listening to adults talk about their own children than from consistent observation of children, although the correspondence of the stages to stages of physical growth is obvious.

The first three of Freud's stages—oral, anal, and phallic—lend themselves easily to a social-learning analysis of personality, since they involve organ systems subjected to training by all cultures. It is toward the

Oedipus complex that heaviest professional criticism has been directed, pointed particularly at Freud's postulation of its universality. Although the Oedipus complex is understandable in the context of the European or United States home, particularly the middle-class home, it seems less concordant with family structure in other cultures, such as those in which multiple mothering is practiced.

Freud theorized that, at about 5 or 6 years, boys renounce incestuous thoughts of their mothers because of a combination of two circumstances: first, fear of all the all-powerful father and the damage he may do to them (fear of castration); and, second, love for the father, which enables them to identify with him. But how does the first of these, a perception of the all powerful, potentially dangerous father, develop in cultures where the father is a mild and tangential adjunct of the family and the mother or a maternal uncle is the undisputed head? Boys do grow up in such cultures, and there is no evidence to indicate that they are any more mother-fixated or less masculine than boys in a standard United States culture. If anything they appear to have fewer sexual problems. If boys reared in these cultures do develop such perceptions of the father (and there is not solid evidence that they do), it almost becomes necessary for psychologists to subscribe to a biologically determined theory of personality, in which learning plays a relatively slight role.

Regardless of the criticism that has been leveled against Freud, no one else has come up with developmental dimensions that represent a substantial improvement over his ideas. His genetic theory of psychosexual development has made two profound contributions to our thinking about personality formation: first, that all behavior is caused, hence lawful, and that search for the causes is the central task of psychology; second, that the mind and emotions do not operate in a vacuum, but develop and function in the context of the individual's biological and physiological structure and function.

Freud has been criticized for mysticism and imprecision; but perhaps the two most pertinent criticisms are (1) what many believe to be an overemphasis on the influence of biological, organic needs on personality, even though great weight is given to the interaction of learning with these organic needs; and (2) the difficulty, at present, of making independent estimates or measures of the strength of organic drives in infants and young children, or of mapping the learning process as it goes on in infancy and early childhood. For example, we can infer the strength of the infantile oral drive and the way it was handled only from the behavior of older children and adults coupled at best (except in longitudinal studies) with retrospective maternal accounts of child-rearing practices. Drives and learning conditions that are measured in retrospect or by inference from the behavior they presumably help to explain are not scientifically very useful. To date, attempts to make the necessary independent measures of "constitutional strength" of the organic drives have been unsuccessful; hence their explanatory and predictive power is slight. As we shall see in Chapter 3, studies of child-rearing practices have not, so far, contributed definitive information.

A NEOPSYCHOANALYTIC POINT OF VIEW

Sullivan (1947, 1953), whose theoretical orientation differs from Freud's in several decisive respects, approaches the problem of developmental stages in a different manner. Whereas Freud's stages are primarily determined by physical maturational processes, Sullivan's have a much more intimate relation to the interaction the child as a developing self has with other people in his environment. Freud's stress is on the demands the child's organ systems make on the world in which he lives, and on the results of interference with (or overgratification of) these demands. Sullivan emphasizes the child's way of perceiving the world and adapting to it, and concerns himself less than Freud with stages of growth (although these are not neglected).

The key concepts in Sullivan's theory of personality development are euphoria, tension, and dependence. Absolute euphoria may be equated with total equilibrium of the organism; absolute tension with the maximum possible deviation from euphoria. Sullivan further distinguishes between the tension of (organic) needs, which is reduced by their (specific) satisfaction, and the tension of anxiety, which, in contrast with that of needs, is nonspecific, is interpersonal, and is reduced by the feeling of security.

The earliest experience of the infant presumably consists of undifferentiated states of comfort (equilibrium, euphoria) and discomfort (disequilibrium, tension). That is, the infant is not aware of hunger, thirst, or cold as such; he has not yet learned to identify the specific satisfactions that will reduce his state of tension. Further and of crucial importance to Sullivan's theory, the infant is totally dependent on the ministrations of another person to satisfy his needs.

Gradually, as a result of repeated alternations of tension and tension reduction, certain kinds of learning take place. The infant learns that certain objects or activities will alleviate certain kinds of discomfort: he stops crying at the sight of the nipple or the bottle instead of waiting until the nipple reaches his mouth. At the same time, he is learning something even more important: that his discomfort is generally alleviated fairly quickly, or that it is not. Out of his early, relatively undifferentiated, preverbal experiences concerning his needs and their satisfaction, there develop certain generalized expectations—what, from the point of view of the adult, might be called attitudes of trust or distrust, security or insecurity.

It should be noted here that Sullivan attaches far less significance to the simple failure to satisfy the infant's needs (for example, because the mother is temporarily absent) than he does to their unwitting frustration through anxiety in a situation where satisfaction would normally be expected to occur. Anxiety is initially induced in the infant by anxiety (which need not be related specifically to the mother-child interaction) in the mother, through a process Sullivan terms empathy. By this he means nothing outside the realm of sensory perception, but simply a feeling based on extremely subtle cues. Once the infant has experienced the highly unpleasant emotion of anxiety, however, this emotion becomes of central importance in his subsequent behavior.

Sullivan hypothesizes that the infant learns to make certain very important differentiations based on anxiety. There is first the differentiation (personification) of the good (need-satisfying) mother from the bad (anxiety-evoking) mother. Later comes the differentiation (personification) of good-me ("me" rewarded by the tenderness of the good mother), bad-me ("me" punished by the anxiety-evoking mother), and not-me ("me" overwhelmed by intense, sudden anxiety). In other words, the rudiments of what will later be the self-concept, according to Sullivan, develops from the reflected appraisals of significant others in the child's life.

What is particularly important for Sullivan's theory is that these differentiations—the earliest associations of anxiety with certain behaviors and situations involving the self and other people—are made long before language can define with any accuracy or precision exactly what it is that is anxiety-provoking, what it is that is "bad," what it is that is to be avoided. The combination of utter dependence and relatively unclear and uninformed perception, in other words, produces a situation in which the possibilities for distortion are enormous. The creeping infant stopped by a sharp "No" from his mother has no notion that he is about to bump into a table; that atop the table is a lamp; that if the table is bumped, the lamp will fall; that if it falls, the lamp will break; or that, if it breaks, this will matter to anyone, and so on. These "reasonable," cause-and-effect learnings come much later, long after any number of "unreasonable" learnings may have occurred.

The significance of one of the developmental schemes used by Sullivan—his analysis of experience into three modes—becomes apparent in the light of this view of how learning proceeds. The prototaxic is the earliest mode of experiencing the world. The infant "knows" only momentary states; he distinguishes dimly, if at all, between his body and what lies outside; his experience is undifferentiated, without definite limits. The second mode of experience identified by Sullivan is the parataxic. The infant begins to differentiate among his experiences and to attach meanings to them. But these meanings are not logically related, and many of them are highly special and unique to him (autistic). When one's meanings are common or shared (when chair means chair to him consistently, just as it does to all those with whom he comes in contact), these meanings are said to be consensually validated, and experience is said to be occurring in the syntaxic mode. Syntaxic meanings follow reality and logic as we think of them. Note the very different way in which Piaget (see Chapter 1, this book) describes basically similar phenomena.

It seems clear that the same child-rearing practices and parental behavior in general will have a very different impact on learning, including the learning involved in the development of personality, in each of these three modes. And although the age of the individual is to some extent related to his predominant mode of perception, the three modes are not mutually exclusive, nor are they ever altogether "outgrown."

In a further search for meaningful dimensions of personality development, Sullivan, like many others, resorted to a temporal sequence, although to him the nature of the interpersonal relations of the child and his capacity for different complexities and types of social relations at different levels is of more concern than chronological age or neurophysical maturity. Sullivan says that infancy becomes childhood "as soon as the infant has picked up a vocal trick, saying perhaps 'ma' and getting tremendous response from the significant adult, without any idea of precisely what has happened but catching on the second time it happens" (1947, p. 8). In other words, infancy ends and childhood begins as soon as the rudiments of language are acquired.

Childhood continues up to the time when the child can get on fairly well with his peers; the juvenile era begins when playmates are badly needed and are in most ways preferred to adults. The eruption, due to maturation, of a need for an intimate relation with another person of comparable status marks the beginning of preadolescence, a relatively brief period which ends with puberty. Adolescence is marked by a shift of interest from a person of one's own sex to one of the opposite sex, and by the patterning of adult sexual activity. At adulthood one is able, for the first time, to establish a love relationship in which the other person is almost as important as oneself.

The significance of these developmental epochs lies in the fact that each begins with new (interpersonal) needs and new (interpersonal) relationships, and each therefore to some extent affords an opportunity for new and more appropriate learnings:

> It is in general true that, as one passes over one of these more-or-less determinable thresholds of a developmental era, everything that has gone before becomes reasonably open to influence; this is true even in the organization of the self-system, which, as I suppose

I cannot stress too much, is remarkably inclined to maintain its direction. The changes which take place at the thresholds of the developmental eras . . . are far-reaching; they touch upon much of what has already been acquired as personality, often making it somewhat acutely inadequate . . . for the sudden new expanding of the personal horizon. Thus the beginning phase of a developmental era may considerably affect those inappropriate aspects of personality which emerge from what the person has undergone up to then.[2]

The theory of personality development outlined by Sullivan is essentially one of social learning. This social-learning frame of reference is one to which we shall return again and again throughout the book, for it is the point of convergence of a variety of theoretical strands and empirical facts.

OTHER APPROACHES TO THE DEFINITION
OF DEVELOPMENTAL STAGES

Chronological divisions have been adopted by a substantial proportion of United States child psychologists and educators but few, if any, have attempted the psychological plus chronological division used by Sullivan. Child psychology texts typically include sections on infancy, which is variously defined as consisting of the first 6 months to the first 2 years; early childhood, a stage ordinarily extending from the runabout period (about 18 months) to school age; the early school years (kindergarten or first grade through third grade); the intermediate school years (fourth through sixth grades); adolescence (beginning at the age of puberty and extending, according to some authors, to the age of about 24); and maturity, which follows adolescence.

Some authors, for example Whiting and Child (1953); Sears, Maccoby, and Levin (1957); and Heinstein (1966), in effect do not try to formulate developmental stages at all but concentrate on those organ-need and behavioral areas in which every society, if it is to function, must guide (socialize) its young. The first three areas of socialization postulated by these writers correspond to the Freudian sequence of organ systems and needs: (1) feeding and weaning, (2) elimination training, and (3) sex training. Although the authors mentioned above have been much influenced by psychoanalytic thought, their emphasis is more on learning as it affects functioning than on organ needs as they affect (or interact with)

2 Reprinted with permission from the William Alanson White Psychiatric Foundation and W. W. Norton and Company, from Sullivan, H. S.: *Interpersonal Theory of Psychiatry*. New York: W. W. Norton, 1953.

learning. For their fourth and fifth universal training areas, they move from organ systems and functions to emotional expression: (4) aggression training, and (5) dependency training.[3]

The summaries of research presented in Chapter 3 follow this latter pattern. Taken up in turn are studies concerning feeding and weaning, toilet training, sex training, and training the expression of aggressive and dependency feelings.

Up to this point, discussion has centered around the dimensions of child development. But meaningful categories for looking at and analyzing parental behavior as it impinges upon these dimensions must also be found.

THE SEARS, MACCOBY, AND LEVIN STUDY

Sears, Maccoby, and Levin performed a factor analysis of ratings and judgments based on a large number of interviews about child-rearing practices with mothers of 5-year-old children. Their study resulted in the identification of eight factors that appeared to underlie a wide variety of discrete parental behaviors.

Factor analysis is a procedure for determining which of a large number of items (or, in this case, types of behavior) are statistically related to one another. In other words, it is a statistical procedure for grouping discrete items. The analyst then attempts to find a descriptive name for the factor that he believes the items of a particular group have in common. Of the forty-four scales of maternal behavior devised by Sears, Maccoby, and Levin, sixteen appeared to be related to each other in such a fashion as to form the first factor, the common element of which could plausibly be called permissiveness-restrictiveness. Stated so that they define the strict, or nonpermissive, end of the scale, these maternal behaviors (as judged from the mothers' verbal descriptive and not from actual observation) are: high restrictions on play in the house and with furniture, and on making noise; high demands and standards for good table manners, being neat and orderly, and being obedient; strict toilet training and strict and rejective response to dependency; much emphasis on doing well in school; frequent use of physical punishment and severe punishment for aggression toward parents; low permissiveness for aggression toward parents, between siblings, or toward other children; low permissiveness for nudity, immodesty, masturbation, or sex play with other children.

The second factor identified by Sears, Maccoby, and Levin includes

---

[3] For Freud, the type of training necessary in these two areas, and its outcome, is viewed almost as a by-product, or inevitable consequence, of training in the first three psychosexual stages.

ten types of items that the mothers reported about themselves, and was labeled general family adjustment. Stated so that they define the high, or "good," end of the scale, these items are: the mother reports high self-esteem, gives a high evaluation of the father, is very satisfied with her current life situation, is not anxious about her ability to rear children. She was delighted when she became pregnant with the child who was the subject of the study, as was the father. She reports no disagreements with the father about child-rearing, enjoyed an affectionate interaction with the child when he was a baby, as did the father, and says she has no difficulty following through on her disciplinary actions.

The third factor was called warmth of mother-child relationship. The six items constituting this factor, stated so that they define warm relationships, are: the mother has much affectionate interaction with the child, is warmly demonstrative to the child, finds ample time to play with him, accepts his dependency cheerfully, praises the child for good table manners, and leans heavily on reasoning as a method of training.

The fourth factor, responsible child-training orientation, includes some of the items from previous scales. Its nine related items are: mother has high self-esteem; places high demands on the child for neatness and orderliness; enforces strict regulations on play in the house and with furniture; insists upon good table manners and strict obedience; uses much praise for good table manners and "playing nicely." To obtain obedience, she uses a combination of withdrawing privileges and offering many tangible rewards. Concerning a mother who scores high on this factor, the authors "get the impression that she keeps her attention rather continuously (and mainly pleasantly) directed toward the child, viewing him as a person who must be taught many things" (Sears, Maccoby, and Levin, 1957, p. 475).

The fifth factor identified in the study was aggressiveness and punitiveness. Mothers scoring high on the items related to this factor showed high demands for aggression toward other children and high permissiveness for such aggression. They themselves used much physical punishment and were severe in their punishment when the child was aggressive toward them. Needless to say, they were markedly nonpermissive about their child's aggression toward them.

The sixth factor was labeled by the author, perception of husband. Fathers who scored high were reported by their wives to be displeased when the wife became pregnant, to assume chief responsibility for child-rearing policies, and to be very permissive about the child's aggression toward other children.

The seventh and final purely statistical factor has been called orientation toward child's physical well-being. Health and safety practices predominate, and the mother who scored high tended to use scheduled feedings for the child as a baby; to demand good table manners, including eating everything on the plate; to be strict about bedtime; and to be firm about the child's wandering about the neighborhood. Such a mother was also likely to be anxious about her child-rearing ability.

Another pattern, less easily identified statistically but related to most of the seven statistical factors, also appeared from the mothers' interviews. This was the pattern of control or discipline used by the mother. Control techniques appeared to fall into two categories, one considered by the authors to be love-oriented, the other object-oriented. The love-oriented mother was likely to use praise as a method of reward, and to "withdraw" love as punishment. The object-oriented mother was more likely to use tangible rewards for good behavior on the part of her child (to bribe?) and to punish him either by physical discipline or by deprivation of privileges.

These factors (seven statistical and one "clinical") in child-rearing represent the thinking and research of one team of highly skilled and experienced investigators. Like the author of this volume, they believe that social learning (primarily, learning from the parents in the early years of childhood) is paramount in the development of personality. This learning results from environmental experiences impinging upon the child as he passes through various developmental stages. To discover the "how" of this process is perhaps the single most important function of child psychology. This "how" can never be discovered until dimensions are formulated for child-rearing practices and for child development which are clear (that is, which other people can understand and determine in the same fashion as the original investigators) and useful (related to significant aspects of the development of children). Eight child-rearing factors interacting with five developmental aspects (feeding and weaning, elimination, sex, dependency, and aggression) constitute Sears, Maccoby, and Levin's analysis of the major parental-practice variables as they are applied in the five most important child-training areas. Heinstein (1966) uses a rather similar approach.

THE SEWELL, MUSSEN, AND HARRIS STUDY

Sewell, Mussen, and Harris (1955) have studied child-rearing practices using methods similar to those of Sears, Maccoby, and Levin. First they interviewed a large sample of mothers of 5-year-olds and 6-year-olds. From these interviews they made ratings and judgments about child-rearing practices and then performed a factor analysis of their results.

The children studied by Sewell, Mussen, and Harris were 5-year-old and 6-year-old rural youngsters from Wisconsin, whereas those studied by Sears, Maccoby, and Levin were 5-year-old suburban youngsters from the East Coast. Sewell, Mussen, and Harris probably used more direct interviewing techniques (phrased their questions more pointedly) than did the Sears group. They secured information about thirty-eight aspects of child-rearing and also attempted to tap some parental attitudes and practices.

On the whole, Sewell, Mussen, and Harris found lower relationships among the different items of behavior subsumed under their factor headings than did Sears, Maccoby, and Levin. The seven factors that emerged from this study were: (1) practices generally considered to reflect permissiveness in early feeding situations; (2) permissive toilet-training practices (these two factors appear to be related to Sears, Maccoby, and Levin's first factor of "permissiveness-restrictiveness"); (3) practices involving much activity of the parent with the child (conceivably overlapping to some degree with "warmth of mother-child relationship"); (4) nonpunitive treatment of behavior (possibly related to "permissiveness-restrictiveness" but not correlated with factors 1 and 2 in the Sewell study); (5) practices making for early independence; (6) practices reflecting casual attitudes of the parents in a number of situations: bowel training, napping, eating, mischievousness; (7) noninsistent reactions on the part of the parent.

The biggest overlap, then, between Sewell, Mussen, and Harris and Sears, Maccoby, and Levin is their agreement that at least one very important variable in child-rearing practices is the degree of permissiveness or strictness that a mother shows toward her children.

Sewell, Mussen, and Harris believe that they failed to find any true common denominator of different child-rearing practices, such as a general "acceptance or rejection of the child," or even consistency from one area of child-rearing to another. Some of their conclusions neatly illustrate this point. For example, parents who were permissive in feeding practices were quite active with their children and treated them casually, but punished for misbehavior. Parents who did not punish the child for misbehavior were not particularly likely to be permissive in early feeding or toilet training, nor did they participate in much activity with the child, but they also tended to treat their child casually. Again, parents who said they encouraged early independence of their child did not treat him casually and did engage in much activity with him. Common sense would say that the child most likely to become independent was the one who was treated casually and whose parents engaged in relatively little activity with him.

It should be mentioned again that these findings are based on what parents report they do with their children. It is not known whether they actually behave as they say they do, nor is it known whether the children are as their parents describe them (this information was not provided in the Sears, Maccoby, and Levin study; no descriptions of the children's behavior are provided by Sewell, Mussen, and Harris). This matter of adequacy of mothers' retrospective reports has been studied for example, by Mednick and Shaffer (1963); and Lillian Robbins (1963). Their studies are discussed in the next chapter.

THE CRANDALL AND PRESTON STUDY

A third and final study to be reported here used statistical techniques other than factor analysis in a similar effort to get at meaningful dimensions of child-rearing practices. Crandall and Preston (1955), working with a smaller number of mothers whose children differed widely in age, but also using interview techniques, reported four major dimensions of maternal behavior. Their first major cluster they named affection. This cluster consists of rather highly interrelated maternal tendencies toward expressing affection, rapport (a close, friendly, mutually understanding relationship), approval of the child's behavior, and much contact between mother and child. It can be seen that this cluster of items has a similarity to the factor identified by Sears, Maccoby, and Levin as "warmth of mother-child relationship," and to the third factor isolated by Sewell, Mussen, and Harris, which relates to the amount of activity shared by parent and child.

Crandall and Preston's second cluster is labeled protective. The items included are babying, protectiveness, solicitousness, and child-centeredness. This cluster has no apparent relationship to any of the Sears clusters; it may be more or less opposite (hence logically related) to the factors of casualness and encouraging of independence identified by Sewell, Mussen, and Harris.

The third cluster of items found to be highly interrelated by Crandall and Preston they called coactive control. By this they mean, roughly, democratic control. Parents who scored high in this cluster justified their policies of handling their children to the children, endorsed and used democratic policies, were very ready with explanations, and were quite understanding of their children. No close resemblance to any of the Sears factors is obvious; there may be some resemblance to the Sewell factor of noninsistence, although the resemblance is not close. (The two most important items in the noninsistence factor are: father does not insist that child obey without question; mother does not insist that child obey without question.)

Crandall and Preston's fourth cluster they named coercive control. This cluster includes items indicating that the mother was very quick in enforcing either her demands or her suggestions, and was quite severe in her penalties. The similarity of this factor to several of the factors identified by the two studies discussed previously is obvious.

Summary

The purpose of this chapter on methodology is to make students in the field critically more alert. It contains material designed to improve their observations and research concerning child development and child-rearing practices.

Research in the area of child-rearing practices and child development in general can be schematized as varying along four dimensions: (1) normative-explanatory; (2) ahistorical-historical; (3) naturalistic-manipulative; and (4) atheoretical-theoretical. Although these dimensions are logically independent, there is a tendency for them to vary together, and each forms a continuum.

Seven major defects of research in the general area of child development, including child-rearing practices, are: contamination, reconstruction through retrospection, faulty logic, poor definition of concepts, direct influence of the investigator upon his results, sampling deficiencies, and unsound generalization.

Unsound generalization is often related to uninformed use of statistical concepts. Some basic concepts are correlation (a measure of relatedness), prediction through correlation, and level of confidence. Familiarity with these concepts is necessary to an understanding of research summaries given later in the text.

A recommended pattern for reading a "primary source"—an original research article—was given: summary, hypotheses, theory, method, nature of population, results, discussion, and overview.

To be most useful, empirical studies should have theoretical relevance. A body of theory consists of concepts and a set of propositions stating the relations between them, these propositions being subject to empirical verification. The function of theoretical categories (concepts) is to direct attention to those areas of the field in which significant relationships are likely to be found. At a minimum, then, theory in the field of child development must specify (1) the important dimensions of child development and (2) the crucial elements of child-rearing practices.

Freud postulated a sequence of organ needs and need-satisfactions, rooted in biology, as most relevant to personality development. Different organ systems predominate at different times in the child's life, and their effect on later personality is determined by the way infants are handled during the predominance of each system. The three systems with which Freud concerned himself are (1) oral-feeding, (2) anal-elimination, and (3) genital-sexual.

Sullivan, more than Freud, stressed infantile and childhood cognition and adaptation. He postulated three modes of experiencing the world; the prototaxic, the parataxic, and the syntaxic; and seven age epochs (important to him more because of the social phenomena that character-ize them than because of the chronological age variable alone): infancy; childhood; the juvenile era; preadolescence; early adolescence; late ado-lescence; and, of course, maturity.

Sullivan's concepts seem more susceptible of clear definition and trans-lation into operational terms than Freud's, although Freud's psychoana-lytic theories have elicited more attention and stimulated more research.

Other authors do not concern themselves with developmental stages as such but concentrate on areas of training common to all cultures. Most often agreed on are training in feeding and weaning, elimination, sex, aggression, and dependency. The next chapter is organized accord-ing to this framework, which stresses the learning of the human organism rather than his biological needs.

There is no general agreement on the important elements of child-rearing practices, but the findings of three representative studies indicate that the following may be significant variables: permissiveness-strictness, autocratic-democratic practices, punitive-nonpunitive discipline, warmth-coldness of parental attitudes and practices, casual-ignoring behavior toward the child, and stress on promoting independence as opposed to encouraging dependence on the parents.

Child-Rearing Practices

The preceding chapters have introduced the concept of culture and mapped the sensory equipment through which culture impinges on the child. Many authors have analyzed the stages through which the child passes, postulating that the culture makes a different impact on the child during each stage. There is no close agreement about the characteristics or even the dimensions of these stages, although all agree that the beginning years of life are crucially important and that, during them, development is profoundly shaped by the treatment the baby and young child receives from his parents.

The material in this chapter is organized according to a social-learning analysis of child training, principally because independent definitions have not yet been formulated for the stages of development that such authors as Freud and Sullivan have set forth. Studies concerning feeding and weaning, toilet training, sex, aggression, and dependency are discussed in that order. The effects of deprivation and over-all parental attitudes, including general techniques of control and training, are also treated.

It is often impossible to draw solid conclusions about child-rearing practices in a given area, since the studies may be too few in number, poorly designed, contradictory in their results, or all three. But, when possible, conclusions and applications of research are presented.

The goals of this chapter are, first, to summarize the facts concerning child-rearing practices and the *effects* of these practices when such effects have been studied and second, to give a rather detailed introduction to research, its evaluation, and the process of drawing from it conclusions and suggestions for practice.

Frank (1965) has written a review article concerning what we have learned from studies of family influences on human development (his particular focus is on psychopathology, but the critical points he makes concern normal as well as abnormal development). Frank's article is refreshing but probably hypercritical. Essentially, he makes the point that nothing has ever been found out, in any really solid sense, from our studies of how child-rearing practices, attitudes, and so on, affect the personalities of children. This, he believes, is true despite our universal professional assumption (stated in the first paragraph of this chapter) that family life, perhaps particularly in the preschool years, is crucial in shaping later development. Some supporting evidence for this assumption was given in Chapter 1 of this book.

As the author has struggled through the studies summarized in this chapter, he has often been tempted to conclude, as the reader may also do as he reads the studies, that Frank is completely correct, at least on the face of it. But, on the basis of our actual contact as parents, teachers, and professional workers both with individual children and groups of children, we "know in our hearts" that Frank is wrong: children's lives and adjustment *do* vary according to their families' treatment of them. These variations may be temporary—a function of some family crisis or improvement of family condition—or they may be long enduring. But Frank states that his review of the research of the last forty years has turned up no solid evidence that family practices affect child personality. "No factors were found in the parent-child interaction of schizophrenics, neurotics, or those with behavior disorders which could be identified as unique to them or which could distinguish one group from the other, or any of the groups from the families of the controls" (p. 191).

Frank gives a number of reasons for his pessimistic conclusions. The author, while not as pessimistic as Frank, agrees with his criticisms of the field, as he has said both directly and by implication in the methodological criticisms presented in Chapter 2.

Frank, for example, points out that a major problem in research on child development as a function of the family is that "human behavior is a very complicated event, determined by many factors, and not clearly understood out of the context in which it occurs, and, in this regard, not everyone reacts in like manner to similar life experiences" (p. 198).

He makes some of the criticisms that the present author will make later about studies based on data affected by parent recall, accuracy of interview reports, and other methods available to us for studying children and their families. He puts strong emphasis on investigator bias, as the present author did in Chapter 1.

Focusing on pathology as he does, Frank neglects some of the "hard data" dealing with influence of child-rearing practices on concepts like intelligence. These data will be taken up in later chapters. In the present author's judgment, he also underestimates the so-called Duke studies of the family backgrounds of schizophrenics. These will be discussed later in this chapter. His review also neglects relevant animal research.

But his article is useful. It makes us examine thoughtfully some of our basic assumptions and this is probably always a good thing.

With this rather pessimistic introduction, we shall now turn to the actual studies in the field. No systematic attempt has been made to bring everything up to date, in the sense of including all recent studies in the area, as the number of papers written in the years since the first edition of this book is enormous, their quality (as a group) has not improved noticeably, and general conclusions remain about the same as they were when the first edition was published in 1961.

A certain perspective is useful to introduce the bulk of this chapter. The present history is loose, but the following ways of looking at child-rearing practices have been useful to the author and, according to their statements, his students.

PRIMORDIAL CHILD-REARING

The earliest philosophy of child-rearing, if it can be called a philosophy, was primordial, pragmatic, and directed toward self-survival and family-survival: the father of the family (which typically included as many "wives" as could be collected) hunted, fought off enemies, and kept a thoughtful eye on his sons, particularly as they reached puberty. When they became a sexual-aggressive threat to him, he fought them and drove them off, until he grew too old and tired or some son sufficiently old and strong drove him off. The expelled son usually managed to find a family of his own. The old, tired father became an isolate, and eventually died of age, weakness, illness, starvation, or a combination of such factors. The wives bred, bore, suckled and nurtured children and the old man, and helped out the headman in crises. No fuss was made about their child-bearing: if the family was on the march, particularly in hostile territory, the mother stopped beside the trail, had her baby, and caught up with the group or she and her infant were likely to perish.

Man eventually became "civilized." Plato, in *The Republic,* thought of youth as eminently teachable, at least the boy child from an aristo-cratic family. Plato's notions of child-rearing were intellectual: bring the boy to be a man of the most sophisticated and knowledgeable type, willing and able to bring his education and talents to the service of his State.

Rousseau set forth a philosophy of child-rearing that shook up the aristocratic society of his time (1712–1778). Let the child mature in total freedom (until around pubescence). Then begin his education. Self-actualized, he is ready for effective teaching and learning and will become the sort of person who will create a good society because he himself is good. Rousseau has contributed in obvious and implicit ways to modern theories of child-rearing. In the following sections of this and other chapters, the reader can see the influence Rousseau had on man's thinking.

In the Victorian era children, boys *or* girls, were thought of as minia-ture adults. Their role was to be seen but not heard, to be obedient, to be little ladies or little gentlemen (including the dual code of behavior that boys could be sexy, girls could not). Pared to the bone, the Victorian theory of child-rearing was genetic-constitutional: if, from his parents' point-of-view, a child turned out well, he "takes after us." If he turned out ill, then "He takes after Uncle Ned or Aunt Elizabeth or 'his father's' family."

Carl Rogers and Gesell have something in common with Rousseau: society blunts children. To become the best possible adults, they should be accepted as they are and educated "according to their individual natures."

Social learning theory, perhaps among the above "theories of child-rearing," has most in common with Plato (although, more than Plato, it takes into account emotional as well as cognitive learning): man cannot only be optimized, but his "potential can be stretched" by the learning experiences with which he is provided.

This section is necessarily fragmentary, but it illustrates the smorgasbord of child-rearing theories from which any child caretaker may choose, from the almost instinctively directed primordial herd to the human product shaped almost entirely by his learning opportunities.

WEST PAKISTAN

Another logical addition to the introductory section of this chapter which may give the reader a more practical slant in his approach to it involves illustrations of cross cultural theories and practices of child-rearing. The present author was fortunate to spend the early 1960s in West Pakistan, and equally fortunate in being able to travel widely over that interesting country. He came to know life in the villages and, rather by accident, came to know a wider sample of upper- and upper-middle class Pakistani families than does the average non-Pakistani.[1]

The following sections present observations about child-rearing methods and goals for these two classes of family: the villagers, most of whom by our standards would be classed as lower-lower class agricultural; and the upper and upper-middle classes.

The villagers are permissive with their young children in at least four of the areas to be covered in this chapter: oral, or eating; anal, or toilet training; dependency; and aggression. The same is true of the lower and lower-lower-class residents of the big cities (the author knew Lahore best, but was relatively well acquainted with Abbotabad, Peshawar, and Rawalpindi). Sex and sex training are probably exceptions,

[1] This opportunity, deeply appreciated by the author, came about through Zafar Omer, M.D., with whom the author had close and warm professional and personal interactions.

particularly for girls: West Pakistan is more than 90 percent Moslem, religion is the core of the culture and, if anything, Islam is even more Puritanical about sex practices than the other major monotheistic religions, Judaism and Christianity.

There is a sharper cleavage between the sexes than is found in the United States. In Pakistan the girls and women, mothers and daughters, cleave together as do boys and men and fathers and sons. As soon as the daughter is old enough, she begins to work with her mother at the traditional woman's chores, learn, and talk with, her mother. The boy goes to the fields with his father. Clearer sex-role models and much more opportunity for day in and day out interaction are provided than is true in contemporary American society, except perhaps for the least modernized farms. Farming is a rapidly disappearing way of life in the United States. For example, currently, only 4 percent of the income of Indiana, commonly thought of as an agricultural state, comes from farming; and successful farms are no longer functions of father and son working manually together and in close personal contact and mutual endeavor but, rather, have the impersonality and mechanization of a factory.

One of the author's impressions of Pakistani lower-class child-rearing practices is that both men and women "have more fun with their little children" than we do in the United States. The difference between Pakistani adolescent boys and men and their American or British counterparts in the ability to relate relaxedly with babies and very small children is apparent to even the most casual observer.

Upper-class families, according to the author's observations, fall into one of two camps (the division, of course, is by no means that clear and there is much overlapping). The first is the traditional or Indo-Pakistani way of life: the old ways are observed. The child is turned over to an *ayah* (nurse) at birth, and reared almost exclusively by her until, with increasing size and independence, he takes an increasing part in family life. Thus, his upbringing is lower-lower class (*ayahs* possess very low status in the culture). The *ayah* is at the child's beck and call and her job (which may be literally a matter of life or death to her and her own children) depends on the pleasure of the child. An *ayah* may be (and often is) summarily dismissed on the basis of the complaint of a 2-year-old. Of necessity, then, the *ayah* indulges the child inordinately. His every wish is granted. Consequences of this for later "internalization of control and development of conscience" are discussed in this book's chapter on identification and conscience. To anticipate later content (speculatively), the child, particularly the male child, "regards the world as his oyster." Does this perhaps lead to the spectacular lack of conscientious and responsible leadership we often see in the governments of countries where children are so reared? Possessing rudimentary consciences, overweening self-confidence, and never having known anything but maximum indulgence, do they fail to develop the sense of democracy, freedom of speech, and incorruptibility of public and private practice that are hypothetically part of the so-called Puritan ethic (which is certainly by no means universal, it must be added in fairness, among United States or British citizens and their leaders)?

There are fewer dramatic contrasts in child-rearing among the so-called Westernized Pakistani. Their orientation is typically upper-class British and their behavior with their children (except for delegating to others a larger proportion of responsibility than is typical even among very wealthy American and probably British families) is not greatly different from that found in American families.

THE SOVIET

Bronfenbrenner (1962) has written interestingly on the basis of his observations of Soviet methods of character education. Briefly, he proposes that research should be conducted on its influences. What does it do to a child's cognitive style and his personality to have his education consistently and constantly linked to a dogmatic set of national goals? We experience no such phenomena in the democracies, thus have no idea what happens to children so reared. But, for enlightened self-interest (and intellectual curiosity) if nothing else, we need to know what this does to Soviet Union children, or to Communist-reared children in continental China. If we knew, we might not agree, but we should be able to communicate better.

Practical Applications　One more point should be made here. Readers, particularly those who deal with older children, often ask, "What earthly significance does it have for me to know how the child with whom I am working was treated in his infancy and preschool years?" The question can only be answered anecdotally since, as has been made abundantly clear above, we have few clear data about the effects of families and child-rearing practices during the child's early years on his later personality. A child was brought to the author and one of his colleagues for speech evaluation. At five, his speech was unintelligible. Detailed observation plus tests that did not require verbal interaction indicated that the child was of at least average and perhaps superior intelligence. General knowledge, based principally on "soft" or clinical data prompted the professional workers to ask, "Who looked after this child during his first 8 or 9 months of life?" The mother said that her career had demanded that she work during this time, and that she had turned the baby over to an older "very respectable" woman with several preschool and school-aged children, all of whom had turned out or seemed to be turning out well. The inference was obvious: this older woman, busy with her own children and chores, had never "talked" to the child in question: he had experienced a minimum of cooing, baby talk, and other verbal interactions with adults during this period when prespeech development occurs. His mother could not remember that he had ever "babbled,"—and babbling apparently leads to later clear speech.

Recommendations to his mother and kindergarten teacher were that he be rewarded (with a cracker, a small marshmallow, or some other tangible reward) each time he spoke intelligibly. Another recommendation was that the mother encourage after-school and week-end visits with children who spoke clearly: the child placed a high value on social contact with other children, particularly boys. It was obvious that his guests would not respond to him if he did not speak clearly to them. The average classroom teacher, of course, cannot go around popping a small cracker in a child's mouth every time he does what she wants him to. But this particular kindergarten was small and informal, so the recommendations were feasible. In Chapter 4, it is pointed out how teachers of older children in more formal settings can use similar "administration of reward" techniques.

Feeding

CHOICE OF AND SUCCESS AT BREAST FEEDING

One of the first decisions the mother must make about her baby is if she will breast-feed him or use some artificial method. A major study to which this chapter makes repeated reference has been done by Sears, Maccoby, and Levin (1957). Of the 379 mothers of 5-year-olds whose interviews make up the data, 39 percent had breast-fed the child who was the subject of the study. In the majority of the cases, the child had been breast-fed for less than three months.

The Sears, Maccoby, and Levin children were from the east coast, and the interviewers were reconstructing their histories from interviews with their mothers when the children were 5 years old. Heinstein (1966) studied a carefully selected sample of California (Bay Area) and statewide children, interviewing the mothers when their children were considerably younger than 5 years. He finds, as do Sears, Maccoby, and Levin, that the majority of mothers breast-feed their children for less than three months, although almost half of them try it for at least a time. He also gives some evidence that his mothers' reports possessed a moderate degree of accuracy.

It seems logical that the decision to breast-feed may be linked with other decisions about "closeness" to or "intimacy" with the baby. It may be that women who desire both to breast-feed and to be in intimate contact with their new baby are more "motherly" than those who do not. In one interesting study (Klatskin, Lethin, and Jackson, 1950), it was predicted that a choice to breast-feed would be associated with a choice to "room in" with the baby. Under the rooming-in plan, the baby is placed in the mother's hospital room almost from birth, and she assumes all the care for him that she can. In the conventional nursery plan, new babies are kept in the hospital nursery and brought to their mothers for feeding at regular intervals. Nurses assume care for the babies other than feeding.

Klatskin, Lethin, and Jackson interviewed 1251 mothers about their rooming-in and feeding preferences *prior* to the birth of their babies. These mothers were all from low-income groups, although many of them were the wives of college students and medical interns and residents, so that their education was higher than would be predicted from knowing their husbands' incomes.

In the total group, 53 percent chose to breast-feed, 40 percent to bottle-feed, and the rest were undecided.

The difference of 14 percent between the Sears, Maccoby, and Levin data for breast feeding and the Klatskin, Lethin, and Jackson data may plausibly be attributed to the period of the child's life about which the mother was queried: in the Sears study, mothers *remembered* what they had *actually done;* in the second study, mothers predicted what they *intended* to do. In addition, the mothers in the Klatskin study had been officially encouraged by the hospital staff both to breast-feed and to room in.

Rooming-in was chosen by 54 percent of the mothers. Thirty-one percent preferred the hospital nursery, and 15 percent were undecided at the time of the interview. As predicted, choice of rooming-in was positively associated with choice of breast feeding. This association is shown in Table 3.1.

Of the mothers who preferred the rooming-in plan, with all its attendant intimacy with the baby, almost two thirds (64 percent) chose breast feeding, which also demands close and intimate contact with the infant. Of those who preferred the hospital nursery, only about a third chose breast feeding, while three fifths selected bottle feeding (35 percent and 60 percent, respectively). The "undecided" mothers were intermediate. About half of them selected breast, the other half bottle feeding (47 percent and 43 percent, respectively). This association of infant-care preference and feeding choice is highly significant, P being less than .001.

There are other interesting trends in the data: The group that chose rooming-in had the fewest babies and the biggest percentage of first-born babies. The members of the rooming-in group were also, on the average, the best-educated and were married to husbands at higher occupational

levels. It is often popularly suggested that mothers of Southern European national origins and Negro mothers are more "motherly" than
women from old United States families or than mothers whose national
origins are British or Northwest European. In this study, there was a
tendency (not statistically significant) in the opposite direction. More of
the latter group preferred rooming-in; more mothers who were Negro
or could trace their origins to Southern Europe preferred the nursery.

Table 3.1   *Relationship Between Preferred Plan for Infant Care Following
Birth and Mothers' Choice of Method of Feeding the Baby.*

	BABY-CARE PLAN					
	ROOMING-IN		HOSPITAL NURSERY		UNDECIDED	
FEEDING METHOD	NO.	PERCENT	NO.	PERCENT	NO.	PERCENT
Breast	438	64	138	35	83	47
Bottle	194	29	235	60	76	43
Undecided	49	7	21	5	17	10
Total	681	100	394	100	176	100

ADAPTED WITH PERMISSION OF C. D. MAY, EDITOR, *Pediatrics,* AND ETHELYN
H. KLATSKIN, FROM KLATSKIN, LETHIN, AND JACKSON (1950).

However, this difference is probably due to educational differences that
undoubtedly existed between the two groups. No differences in "motherliness" were found for different religious groups.

Another study (Newton and Newton, 1950) relates maternal attitudes
toward breast feeding to actual success at breast feeding. In this study
ninety-one mothers who had given natural birth to normal babies were
interviewed about their feelings toward breast feeding. Trained judges
sorted the expressed attitudes into three categories: positive, doubtful,
and negative. The mothers were then observed to see how much milk
they were giving the babies, and how much milk they actually had
available. They were then classified as successful, unsuccessful, or abortive breast-feeders. The first group included mothers whose babies required no supplemental feeding after the fourth day of life; mothers
were classified as unsuccessful if, after the fourth day of life, their babies
required supplemental feedings; and as abortive feeders if they gave
up breast feeding entirely before they left the hospital.

Of the ninety-one mothers, fifty-one were classified as showing positive
attitudes toward breast feeding. Of these fifty-one, 74 percent were successful in breast feeding their babies. Only 2 percent (one mother) fell
into the category of an abortive breast-feeder. Twenty-three mothers

expressed negative attitudes toward breast feeding, and of them only 26 percent were successful breast-feeders. Thirty percent were included in the abortive bracket. The seventeen mothers who had doubtful attitudes about breast feeding included 35 percent who succeeded at it; half of them (47 percent) were unsuccessful; a fifth (18 percent) were abortive feeders.

Mothers with positive attitudes gave their babies an average of 59 grams of milk at each fourth-day feeding; mothers with doubtful attitudes, 42 grams; and mothers with negative attitudes supplied only 35 grams of milk per fourth day feeding. The authors of the study report that there were no real differences between the three attitude groups in the amount of milk actually available for the babies; and that such factors as experience with previous children and experience of actually putting the baby to the breast did not affect their results.

Adams (1959) administered a personality test and interviews to two groups of mothers, one group composed of thirty-five women who had chosen to breast-feed, the other of twenty-three who had chosen to bottle-feed. All were in the last trimester (three months) of pregnancy, and the groups were well-matched on a sizable number of factors.

A number of significant differences appeared between the groups. Mothers choosing to use the bottle were, as a group, more dependent, more rejecting of the child, and more dissatisfied with their own sex role. They also showed more signs of psychosexual disturbance. They seemed more maladjusted in areas concerned with eating, sucking, and elimination; manifested more sibling rivalry and guilt feelings; and were more preoccupied with themselves. More signs of penis envy (broadly speaking, jealousy of men) were shown by the group choosing to breast-feed.

These judgments were made on the basis of interviews and the analysis of responses to the Blacky test, a projective instrument revolving around a family of four dogs: the parents; Blacky, who is of indeterminate sex; and a younger brother (or sister) of Blacky. The person taking the test is asked to tell stories about pictures involving various members of the family.

Although there was considerable overlapping between the two groups of subjects, the tentative conclusion drawn from the study was that mothers choosing to breast-feed show a somewhat more secure and mature set of attitudes than those choosing to bottle-feed.

From these studies, all based in part on the interview method—and some of the dangers inherent in this method have been discussed—the following tentative conclusions emerge: half or fewer of the mothers studied actually breast-feed their babies; positive attitudes toward breast feeding seem to be associated with success at it and with other types of intimate mother-baby relations. Mothers choosing breast feeding show certain personality characteristics judged to indicate greater maturity than mothers choosing to bottle-feed. However, this last conclusion is based on a rather small group of mothers—fifty-eight in all.

THE SCHEDULING OF INFANT FEEDING

Another choice that a mother must make early in the baby's life concerns his feeding schedule. Shall it be the traditional rigid schedule, with a feeding every three or four hours; or shall it be a self-demand schedule, in which the baby is fed whenever he appears to be hungry? Traditional pediatrics has favored the former practice; modern pediatrics leans more toward the self-demand schedule.

Perhaps the most convincing evidence favoring self-demand schedules is afforded by a study (Aldrich and Hewitt, 1947) of 668 demand-fed babies up to their first birthday. The babies eventually set up realistic-appearing programs for themselves, although early in infancy they ate more frequently than the conventional every four hours. About 70 percent of them had switched to an adult-type schedule of three meals per day by the time they were 10 months of age. At 1 year of age, they averaged 29.4 inches in height and weighed 21.8 pounds, figures that compare favorably with generally accepted standards. At this age, fewer than 1 percent of them were severe feeding problems, although an additional 7 percent were somewhat resistant to eating and required coaxing.

Other studies of individual children and of twins (as Simsarian and McLendon, 1945; Trainham, Pilafian, and Kraft, 1954) also support the idea of self-demand schedules. A subfinding in a comprehensive study (Williams and Scott, 1953), which will be discussed in more detail later, indicates that children who have more rigid feeding schedules are less active in their first and second years than children fed more flexibly. But in this study, mothers who scheduled feedings strictly also engaged in a wide range of other restrictive practices, so that it is difficult to evaluate the influence of strict feeding schedules apart from the influence of other factors.

At a common-sense level, anyone who has watched new babies thoughtfully has reached the conclusion that they are highly variable and unstable creatures. Most moderately relaxed parents probably find it easier on their nervous systems to follow a self-demand feeding schedule, since ordinarily there will be less total crying under such a system than when careful schedules are enforced. However, if parents are over-solicitous and tense, self-demand feeding may be accompanied by over-stimulation of the child to the point of interfering with his easy development. Currently, on the basis of the facts available, we can conclude only that self-demand feeding seems to do the baby no harm in terms of the characteristics that have been studied.

In countries where refrigeration is inadequate, babies are breast-fed, either by nurses or their mothers, or else they die. Biologically, this is the way to do it. Breast feeding styles vary in the United States. Some studies report that mothers from lower socioeconomic classes are more likely to breast-feed than those from higher socioeconomic classes (as Heinstein, 1966, for California mothers). Different results come from other studies. The whole question of scheduling of feeding seems to have disappeared in the past few years (there seem to be no recent studies concerning it). Certainly, in the relatively nonindustrialized countries best known to the present author (India and Pakistan), scheduling is not thought about; the baby is breast-fed when he is unhappy. If this does not calm the baby, his mother looks elsewhere for his source of discomfort. The author has made no formal study of infant behavior in these countries, but has simply looked with a rather well-experienced eye. It does not appear that the happiness or relaxation of Indian-Pakistani babies is either more or less than those observed or the formally reported samples of United States babies. Of course, many of the subcontinental babies observed obtained little satisfaction from nursing: their mothers had little milk to offer them.

Speculatively, as said earlier in the chapter, unscheduled universal breast feeding affects babies' fathers as well as their mothers. Pakistani-Indian men seem to be more relaxed with young children than their American or British (industrialized society) counterparts. Whether this is part of a general way of life or not is a testable hypothesis.

Prothro (1960) offers anthropological data generally supporting the present author's point of view.

CUP FEEDING

Some years ago, there was much discussion of cup feeding babies. The literature was interesting. However, the topic (or practice), like that of scheduling, seems no longer to interest research workers. At least, the present author has found no more references to cup feeding in recent literature than to scheduling. The literature was interesting, however, and is summarized below.

This type of feeding, quite revolutionary, has been advocated and used: feeding the baby by cup from birth. Two types of study of this procedure have been conducted, only one of which (Fredeen, 1948) is relevant to this section. The reported weight gain for prematurely born babies fed by cup and by other methods is presented in Table 3.2.

Table 3.2 shows rather clearly the advantages of this type of feeding for premature babies, who are short on energy at birth. Other advantages claimed for this method of feeding are that the mother must of necessity have close, warm, personal contact with the baby as he is being fed: that is, there is no way to feed by cup without holding the baby. Such bodily

Table 3.2   *Average Weight Gain, in Grams Per Day, of Premature Babies of Different Birth Weights, Some of Whom Were Cup-Fed, Others Conventionally Fed.*

	CUP-FED BABIES		OTHER THAN CUP-FED BABIES	
BIRTH WEIGHT OF PREMATURE INFANTS	NUMBER OF INFANTS	AVERAGE GAIN IN WEIGHT PER DAY	NUMBER OF INFANTS	AVERAGE GAIN IN WEIGHT PER DAY
Less than 1.5 kg.	8	21.5 g.	4	19.7 g.
1.5 to 2.0	41	22.2	12	17.4
2.0 to 2.5	22	16.7	11	9.2

ADAPTED WITH PERMISSION OF C. D. MAY, EDITOR, *Pediatrics*, AND R. C. FREDEEN, FROM FREDEEN (1948).

contact is believed by most authorities to help babies' normal development. Bottles, on the other hand, can be given by means of holders. Cup feeding is thought also to be excellent for babies with disorders such as harelip and cleft palate. Apparently cup-fed babies suffer less frequently from ear disorders (which may be aggravated by sucking).

STYLE OF FEEDING AND THUMB-SUCKING

The third major feeding decision that a mother must arrive at, after making up her mind whether to feed by breast or artificially and how or if to schedule, concerns the total sucking time the baby shall have. Shall he be fed rapidly or slowly? This decision, of course, can be made more easily by the mother who chooses bottle feeding, where deliberate regulation of the speed of securing food is possible.

Some psychoanalytic writers, most notably David Levy (1934) contend that sucking is an instinct that *demands* gratification. If enough satisfaction is not given by sucking for food, then gratification will be secured through thumb-sucking, blanket-sucking, or some other type of nonnutritive sucking. Levy observed calves, some of which had suckled from the cow, others fed from the pail, and concluded that the latter did much more sucking than the former at the ears of other calves. He then separated a litter of six puppies, feeding three of them from slow-flowing, three from fast-flowing bottles. The latter showed more nonnutritive sucking than the former. Much ado has been made over these six dogs, who may well have influenced the handling of more babies than any other six dogs in history.

Kunst (1948) observed thumb- and finger-sucking in 143 orphanage babies. She concluded that such sucking increases steadily as time passes after the baby has been fed, regardless of whether he is asleep or awake. Extranutritive sucking was most marked one and a half or two hours after meals. The less rich the formula, the more sucking of the thumb. Evaporated-milk formulas produced less nonnutritive sucking than other formulas. Babies often begin to thumb- or finger-suck soon after birth, and the frequency of such behavior increases rapidly in the first 3 months, stays about the same until 6 months, then declines to 10 months. Teething babies are more likely to do it than babies who are not teething, and boys more likely to than girls.

Thumb-sucking[2] seems to be normal, at least in the sense that a very large proportion of children practice it. Klackenberg (1949) found half of a population of 259 babies sucking their thumbs at 1 year of age, and Brazelton (1956) reports that almost 90 percent of a group of seventy rather superior babies were thumb-suckers at some time during their first year, although by 1 year of age, only four of them continued to suck their hands except when they were under stress.

If sucking is a learned or partially learned response rather than an instinct or inborn drive, then babies with more practice at sucking should do more and more vigorous nutritive or nonnutritive sucking than babies with less sucking practice. Specifically, learning theory predicts that cup-fed babies will be least likely to do either strong extranutritive sucking; bottle-fed babies and breast-fed babies will do more; and breast-fed babies may well do the most.

Several studies have tested this differential prediction. The first (Davis *et al.*, 1948) divided sixty babies into three equal groups, one cup-fed, one bottle-fed, and one breast-fed during the first 10 days of life. Learning theory was supported to a moderate degree: breast-fed babies showed stronger sucking responses than the other two groups, although cup-fed and bottle-fed babies did not differ from each other. Sears and Wise (1950) studied eighty normal children from 2 to 3 months to 7 years 10 months of age to see how they had been fed, how long they had been sucking-fed, how severely they had been weaned, and what some of the differential effects had been. Some of these babies had been cup-fed from birth, more of them from about 2 weeks of age. They were classified as early-, middle-, and late-weaned according to the total amount of sucking feeding they had received. According to instinctual-psychoanalytic theory, it would be expected that the group weaned earliest would be most frus-

---

2 The definition of a "thumb-sucker" is complex. Does it apply to a child who at any time sucks his thumb, even though this may be mild sucking for a few minutes before going to sleep or when tired? Or does it apply rather to the child who exerts strong thrusting pressure on lips, teeth, and palate for (for example) four hours a day? Lack of clear definition is partly responsible for our failure to have a clear answer to questions about the relation between thumb-sucking and adjustment, or thumb-sucking and dental malformation.

trated by weaning and would most frequently be thumb-suckers. In fact, the reverse was found. The tendency for the late-weaned to be rated most frustrated was statistically significant when they were compared with the other two groups. Although differences in frequency of thumb-sucking were not significant among the three groups, they were in the direction opposite to that predicted by instinct theory. The actual frequency of thumb-sucking was greatest, not in the *early,* but in the *late-weaned* group. Suddenness of weaning was related to the amount of frustrated behavior the child showed. Those more suddenly weaned were more frustrated by weaning.

Another careful experiment (Brodbeck, 1950) shows that intensity of sucking goes *down* during periods when very young babies (in their first 8 days of life) are cup-fed, *up* when they are required to exert strong sucking pressure to get their food. Those who obtained the most food for their efforts were also the strongest suckers.

A husband-wife team (Blau and Blau, 1955) used as their subject for study only one baby, who was alternated on nipples that required much and little effort to secure milk. On the free-flowing nipple, this baby required fewer feedings per day, took more food, went to sleep sooner after feeding, cried less, did less nonnutritive sucking, and was less active after and between feedings. He also did less regurgitating.

Yarrow (1954) followed sixty-six children, twenty-eight boys and thirty-eight girls, for a number of years. Almost two thirds of the children (64 percent) were reported to be thumb-suckers at some time or another during the period of study. Somewhat more girls (66 percent) than boys (54 percent) had been thumb-suckers, and half of the thumb-suckers were still sucking their thumbs at the age of 4 years. Almost all (90 percent) who had at any time sucked their thumbs started before 6 months of age, and almost two thirds of them (63 percent) had begun before the age of 3 months. Three fourths of the children had stopped thumb-sucking by 6 years of age (perhaps as a result of teasing on the part of schoolmates), but some still persisted at 8 years of age. The duration and severity of the thumb-sucking had no relation to whether the child had been breast- or bottle-fed or to the age at which he had been weaned. However, there seemed to be a relation in babyhood (1 to 6 months of age) between thumb-sucking and length of time the child was allowed to suck at feedings. Those who were allowed to suck longer were less frequently thumb-suckers.

Three studies (Johnson, 1939; and Lewis, 1930 and 1931) relate to the effect of thumb-sucking on dental structure. The general conclusions are that thumb-sucking has a deleterious effect on bites that are already out of line, little or none on "good" bites. It is also suggested that although the structure of the baby teeth is altered by thumb-sucking, no effect is produced on the permanent teeth if the child stops sucking his thumb by the time the permanent teeth begin to come in (ordinarily during the seventh year).

From the time of Freud, thumb-sucking has been considered a neurotic symptom in children, a sign of fixation at the oral psychosexual stage, hence of immaturity and dependency. This has been more a matter of opinion than of fact. In the one study of the subject known to the author (Honzik, 1948) an effort was made to study the personalities of thumb-suckers as opposed to those who had not sucked their thumbs. Thumb-sucking was more intense and more frequent among children from homes rated happier, and whose parents were better educated. Thumb-sucking little girls actually grew into young women who, according to the Rorschach Ink-Blot Test of Personality, were better adjusted in the sense that they more easily accepted their role as women. There was no difference in the young-adult adjustment of the group of boys who had and who had not sucked their thumbs in childhood. This difference in frequency of thumb-sucking according to socioeconomic status and happiness of parents is probably due to the type of control techniques used. Better-educated and happier parents may discipline less harshly, hence be less likely to "break" their children of thumb-sucking.

In summary, then, there is no clear-cut evidence about the relation between thumb-sucking and style or length of feedings. Thumb-sucking is a frequent, even a normal, phase of development, which may provide real relaxation and peace to the baby or small child. Such evidence as exists indicates that it is not a neurotic symptom. There is no convincing evidence, either, that moderate thumb-sucking has any effect on permanent tooth structure or jaw alignment.

GENERAL MATERNAL REACTIONS, FEEDING, AND COLIC

The general "emotional climate" of the feeding situation may be more important than whether a child is breast- or bottle-fed, weaned early or late, or allowed to suck for a long or a short period of time. Brody (1956) and Escalona (personal communication) have stated that the best over-all indication of a mother-baby relationship is provided by watching how the mother feeds her baby. Escalona (1945) has also published informal observations of the feeding relationship between babies 10 days to 2 years of age who were placed in the nursery of a women's penal institution, and their mothers and mother-substitutes. Among the tentative conclusions she reached was that the mothers and mother-substitutes were tense and used the babies as emotional outlets for themselves. She especially noted ten babies under 1 month of age who refused the breast as a means of getting food. Of their ten mothers, she described nine as being very tense. When six of these mothers were given superficial psychotherapy, the child's eating improved. She also noted that as mother-figures were changed for fifteen babies, the babies changed their preference from orange to tomato juice or vice versa according to the preference of the mother-figure. According to Escalona, the babies' eating behavior correlated with the institutional atmosphere. Even small disturbances were reflected in the babies' adjustment.

A study by Stewart *et al.* (1954), done more formally than the one just described, used as its data maternal interviews and observations of mothers interacting with their babies during two-hour clinic visits. A total of ten boy babies and eight girl babies and their mothers (and, to a lesser degree, their fathers) were used as subjects. Eight babies were characterized by the authors as excessive criers ("colicky"). *Excessive crying* was defined as "episodic crying in the first three months of life after 2 weeks of age, over a period of at least 2 weeks, occurring at least once a day, lasting not less than 90 minutes and not related to obvious physical discomfort" (p. 688). This is indeed a great deal of crying, as anyone who has lived around a small baby knows. The mothers of these babies were characterized as ambivalent about their woman-mother role, as quite dependent, and as feeling some rivalry with their children or their husbands. It was concluded that they either openly neglected the babies or overcompensated by fussing with them and giving them excessive attention. Fathers of excessively crying babies were described as passive individuals who gave little real support to their wives.

A contrasting group of six babies was defined as low criers, or "very good" babies. Mothers of such babies were described as welcoming children as a fulfillment of their femininity. They were relaxed and happy. For them, motherhood was a method of getting desirable attention and support; the babies' fathers were able to give this support and themselves accepted their paternity and masculinity with little conflict. Compared with the mothers of the excessive criers, the mothers of the low criers met their babies' needs for both stimulation and food much more realistically. Crying differences between the two groups of babies did not begin to show until after about 2 weeks of age. By the time they were 6 weeks old, the low criers ordinarily stopped crying when adults appeared (perhaps as a matter of confidence and trust), whereas excessive criers intensified their wails when adults appeared.

An ingenious study by Lakin (1957) sought to determine personality differences between mothers of colicky babies (corresponding to the excessive criers discussed immediately above) and noncolicky babies. Lakin secured the cooperation of two rather well-matched groups of twenty mothers each, one with "good" babies, the other with "colicky" babies. The groups of mothers differed in age, with the mothers of the colicky being older (this is a serious flaw in the study) but similar in education. All were relatively well-educated; their husbands had high occupational status; and the ages and birth weights of the babies were similar for the two groups.

Lakin hypothesized that colic is due to a disturbance in the mother-child relationship. Specifically, he predicted that the mothers of colicky babies (1) would themselves have experienced poorer parent-child relationships, (2) would have had more conflict within themselves over their role acceptance (that is, would have more difficulty accepting themselves as women, wives, and mothers), (3) would be more concerned and worried about whether they were adequate as females, (4) would be less happily adjusted to their marriages, and (5) would in general be less motherly than the mothers of the low-crying babies. In the main, his data supported all hypotheses.

Lakin used a large number of techniques to test these hypotheses. He also carried out a long interview covering various aspects of child-rearing, marital adjustment, and so on. Among his interesting subsidiary findings were the following: The mothers of the colicky babies were more pessimistic than the other group—that is, they remembered fewer positive statements from a passage containing both positive and negative statements. They also more frequently drew pictures of mothers *with babies* in a figure-drawing test. Lakin points out that this fits in with the findings of other studies, in which professionally less secure people more frequently drew figures equipped with the "tools of their trade" (apparently, in an effort to reassure themselves by using props).

To an overwhelming degree such routine factors as the babies' diets, birth weight, specific type of feeding, length of labor, allergy history, and so on, failed to differentiate between the two groups of mothers. Although probably no more interview-history items than would be expected to appear by chance were significant, those that did discriminate appear logical. For example, compared with the control group, mothers of colicky babies stopped working earlier in their pregnancies, stopped sexual intercourse sooner, experienced more symptoms that are considered to involve emotional components both during and antecedent to their pregnancy, more frequently described themselves as habitually tense and nervous, and more frequently asked their mothers to come to help them out at the time the babies were born. There was a nonsignificant tendency for them to regard their husbands as being of little help with the baby. More of them had been depressed after the baby's birth, and (understandably, perhaps, in view of the colic) they felt more nervous and tense when the baby cried, had more trouble trying to interpret the crying, and believed that they were more tense and anxious in handling their babies. There was no difference between the groups in planned versus surprise babies, either in their intention to breast- or bottle-feed or their desire to have more children.

The three studies described in this section—one an informal, clinical study, one an elaborate and formal investigation, and one falling some-where between—suggest that, at the very least, babies' eating, as well as "how their food sits with them," is affected by tension on the part of the mother. This tension is probably communicated to them to some important degree during feeding and is certainly added to by the child's tension and crying.

BEHAVIORAL CONSEQUENCES OF STYLE OF FEEDING

The discussion so far has centered principally on the connection between different types of feeding and the child's concurrent adjustment. Psycho-analytic theory predicts that the consequences of different ways of han-dling children's oral needs persist indefinitely. Learning theory, although it makes a less certain prediction about the permanent effects of a specific method of feeding or weaning, agrees that there may well be long-lasting consequences.

As will be seen, widely different and flatly contradictory findings have come from the feeding-weaning studies. Those that have obtained results indicating major effects will be presented and evaluated first, followed by those indicating that there are few if any effects on personality.

STUDIES INDICATING MAJOR EFFECTS

In the first of the representative positive-effect studies (Holway, 1949), eight boys and nine girls, aged 3 years 3 months to 5 years 4 months were observed in a doll-play situation, and their play-fantasy behavior was recorded and analyzed. Their feeding and toilet-training histories were obtained from their mothers and rated. An unfavorable rating was given when the mother followed an exact feeding schedule; a favorable one when she allowed a complete self-demand schedule. A favorable rating was given for the longest breast-feeding time, an unfavorable one for the shortest; the mother's attitude or feeling tone toward the feeding schedule was also rated.

From the children's play, a measure of the amount of "reality" play (presumably "good") was obtained. Holway then separated the seventeen children into two groups according to the type of feeding schedule used. Of their total observed play time, the five "self-regulating feeders" spent 97 minutes in what she called reality play, whereas the more rigidly scheduled children, twelve in number, spent only 37 minutes in such play. This difference between the two groups was highly significant. The first group spent an average of only 3.4 minutes in "unrealistic fantasy play" with the dolls, whereas schedule-fed children averaged 47.7 minutes in such play. This difference is again highly significant statistically. Inferentially, the tendency of the demand-fed children to indulge in realistic fantasy play testifies to their good mental health—their ability to face reality—and the trend toward unrealistic or escapist fantasy of the scheduled babies indicates their need to "escape reality."

One of the most extensive studies of the effects of type of feeding on later physical development was published by Hoefer and Hardy (1929). This study included 383 children from 7 to 13 years of age, classified in different groups according to whether or not they had been breast-fed or artificially fed and the length of time they had been exclusively breast-fed. Hoefer and Hardy concluded that the artificially fed ranked in general physical development below all the breast-fed groups, and that the optimal period of breast feeding was from 4 to 9 months. A greater number of artificially fed than breast-fed children was classed as undernourished, although the two groups did not differ in height. The artificially fed seemed also to have been more susceptible to childhood diseases, and were slightly but significantly lower in intelligence and educational attainment. On the average, they had begun to talk later. This is an old study, and artificial feeding of babies may have been less adequate nutritionally than it now is.

Another study of this type was published ten years later in 1939, and used as subjects British children who had come to a general clinic and whose fathers' occupations ranged "from the small shopkeeper, policeman, and publican to the casual dock labourer and street peddler" and who were "in general, honest, straightforward, self-respecting" (Rogerson and Rogerson, 1939, pp. 1, 164). Interviews were conducted with those responsible for or intimately familiar with the life history of the child when the children were about 7 years old. All subjects had been seen at the clinic for at least six months and had started attending before they were 6 months old.

The children were classified into groups according to whether they had been entirely breast-fed by their mothers up until the time solid food was introduced (a group of sixty-two children called the group without feeding difficulties), or whether artificial feeding had been introduced (a group numbering forty-seven referred to as those with feeding difficulties). These two groups differed considerably in some important respects, although each included about the same number of boys and girls and the same number of children who had been delivered instrumentally. The mothers' ages were also similar, as was the age at which solid food had been introduced (about 31 weeks for both groups). But the so-called feeding-difficulty group included a higher percentage of premature and first-born children.

In infancy, the two groups did not differ from each other in restlessness, but a rough evaluation of general health showed 48 percent of the no-difficulty group in good health, compared with only 30 percent of the feeding-difficulty group. Only 2 percent of the former group were described as in poor general health, whereas 15 percent of the latter group were so classified. This group also averaged more visits to the clinic for health questions.

At the age of about 7, the group that had been entirely breast-fed in infancy tended (not statistically significantly) to have poorer appetites, according to their mothers' statements. There was no difference between the groups in the percentage of children who had sleep disturbances. A tendency existed for the feeding-difficulty group to have been enuretic (day or night wetters), nervous, to have shown fears at school ages, and to have done less well in school. Where a younger brother or sister had been born into the family, more of the feeding-difficulty than of the completely breast-fed group had shown jealousy.

This study was performed on a non-United States population. In addition, all the mothers had been urged to breast-feed. Finally, the feeding-difficulty group included more premature babies (who are hard to get started in life and who frequently suffer from parental overprotectiveness) and more first babies (who may also be victims of parental anxiety and inexperience). In other words, the differences between the two groups may well have been due to factors other than style of feeding. Infant feeding formulas were probably also less adequate then than now.

In another study (Maslow and Szilagyi-Kessler, 1946), college students were asked to take a test designed to measure their psychological security or insecurity. They then obtained from their mothers information about their breast-feeding history. Results showed that those who were breast-fed for less than 3 months, who were entirely bottle-fed, or who had been breast-fed for longer than 9 months were more secure than those who had been breast-fed from 3 to 9 months.

Many of the mothers of these students had come to the United States from national and cultural areas where prolonged breast feeding was the normal thing to do. The authors of this study reasoned that those mothers who could do so easily and comfortably tended to breast-feed for long periods, and that mothers who for some realistic reason could breast-feed for only a very short period of time or not at all felt guilty and made up for their "failure" by giving extra attention to their children. On the other hand, they suspected that mothers who breast-fed for a medium amount of time were self-consciously trying to fit in with the United States culture, in which long breast feeding was unfashionable. Such mothers were therefore less relaxed and easy with their children. In other words, Maslow and Szilagyi-Kessler attribute their observed differences between groups less to style of feeding than to mothers' attitudes toward it.

The theoretical position of Whiting and Child (1953) is the increasingly popular one of attempting to translate psychoanalytic concepts into social-learning terms, with the intent of making the learning system more dynamic and the psychoanalytic system more precise.

Whiting and Child have worked with cultural anthropological material gathered from more than fifty different cultures and have attempted to determine how various child-rearing practices affected behavior of children growing up in different societies. The phases of child-rearing that they believe are *universal* and hence both crucial and treatable by scientific method are oral, anal, sexual, dependence, and aggression. The variables of parental behavior with which they concern themselves are *initial indulgence* (the degree to which parents in a culture are generous and permissive) and its opposite, *initial anxiety* (the degree to which the child presumably experiences deprivation or hardship); *socialization anxiety* (the firmness, severity, or punitiveness, for example, that is typically connected with toilet training, dependence and aggression training, and so on; they hold that the less severe and intense the training, the less the socialization anxiety will be); and *age of socialization*. It can to some degree be assumed that late beginning of socialization is related to permissive socialization and thus to less socialization anxiety. Such an assumption, however, does not hold for all societies or all people in a given society. Prothro (1960) generally supports their findings.

Whiting and Child find, as did Sewell, Mussen, and Harris (1955), that there is little relation between the way a society handles one of these phases of child-training and the way it handles another. A given society may be indulgent in one area, severe in another; may socialize firmly in one, mildly in another; may start training a child almost at birth in one area but indefinitely delay training in another.

One of the hypotheses advanced by Whiting and Child is that the amount of anxiety a culture induces in one of the child-rearing areas (for example, the oral—feeding and weaning) will be reflected in the way it accounts for illness. For example, they predicted that a society that was rigid and depriving in its feeding practices would be more likely than an indulgent society to attribute illness to things that are eaten or drunk. This prediction was supported for the societies they studied: those societies with the strictest infant-feeding practices were also those most likely to attribute illness to eating or drinking some malign substance.

Again, Whiting and Child reasoned that if a society has given a child extensive and progressive satisfaction in one of the training areas, it is likely to believe that relief of illness will occur by means of treatment of that type. There is a tendency for those societies with the most initial oral indulgence (easy feeding-weaning practices) to believe that some sort of oral therapy (for example, seemingly magical foods or liquids) will cure the disease.

Whiting and Child also looked for the presence of "guilt" in the cultures they studied. *Guilt may be defined as feelings or emotions with which a person punishes himself, even though there is no likelihood that what he has done will be found out by anyone else.* In other words, there must be the development of a conscience before there can be guilt. The operational definition of guilt used by Whiting and Child was the following: The people in a culture are capable of guilt, or have developed guilt as a method of self-control, in proportion to the degree to which people in the culture who are sick are blamed for their illness. A substantial correlation of —.42 was found between age of weaning and presence of guilt as defined by Whiting and Child. This means that the later the customary age of weaning children, the less likely they are to endorse the "guilty" belief that the sick are responsible for their conditions—or, to put it another way, early and harsh oral socialization practices are associated with strong feelings of guilt.

Psychoanalytic theory predicts that deprivation during the oral stage results in a distrust of other people. This prediction was supported by Whiting and Child's data: oral socialization anxiety was significantly correlated with ratings of fearfulness of human beings and with "over-all fear of others." The correlations were significant, but not high (.29 and .27, respectively). They support the notion that oral deprivation, including severe weaning practices, reduces trust in other people.

Whiting and Child, then, may be said to provide support for the psychoanalytic ideas of the importance for later personality development of child-rearing practices during the first, or oral year. Severe treatment is associated with guilt and fearfulness, as they define it; permissive treatment with trust.

Goldman (1948, 1951) has attempted to relate weaning practices to personality type. The first step in her study consisted in defining an "oral optimistic personality" and an "oral pessimistic personality." The "oral optimists" had traits of general cheerfulness and hopefulness. They were positively interested in external events and people, had generous inclinations toward protecting the weak and needy, were sociable, unaggressive, moderately ambitious, and welcomed new things and experiences rather than clinging to the old. "Oral pessimists" were generally unhopeful and sour, and were passive-receptive in their attitudes toward life. They were socially aloof and withdrawn, and uninclined to be helpful or protective toward others. They appeared to be selfishly independent and self-sufficient.

From the group of forty-seven men and sixty-eight women from whom these two personality descriptions had been derived, she selected the twenty who seemed most purely to be oral optimists and the twenty who could most clearly be described as oral pessimists, and obtained their feeding histories from their mothers. She decided that the age of 4 months was a critical time for weaning from the breast, and then compared the scores on her test of oral optimism and pessimism for those who had been weaned before and after this time. She found a highly significant difference in pessimism scores for the two groups—the early-weaned scored +.14 on oral pessimism, those weaned later, —.19. This difference is significant at less than the .01 level. When she compared the group weaned before 4 months of age with a group who had been "excessively breast-fed" (for longer than 9 months), the difference was from a $+.14$ to a $-.35$ score on pessimism.

Many traditional psychoanalytic writers have suggested that early-weaned babies will develop frustrated, impatient, and orally aggressive personalities. Goldman's findings suggest, rather, that the tendency is for early weaning to produce pessimism, passivity, aloofness, and self-centeredness.

STUDIES INDICATING FEW EFFECTS

One large study of feeding practices and behavior (Peterson and Spano, 1941) deals with 126 Ohio children and their mothers who had been followed for a number of years for research purposes. Fairly reliable data about infant-feeding practices were routinely gathered, and a great deal of information was available about the children included in the study. However, absolutely no significant results emerged; all relationships were low, almost all were statistically nonsignificant, and many were in a direction opposite to psychoanalytic predictions. To illustrate, there was a tendency for those children breast-fed longest to be *less* affectionate, cheerful, confident, and kind, and *more* resistant and socially apprehensive. But they were also less aggressive, cruel, jealous, and quarrelsome. Ratings of the mother's acceptance or rejection of the child were not related to her feeding practices. Indeed, the correlations with ratings of such factors as child-centeredness, solicitousness, restrictiveness, and severity of discipline were low and frequently opposite to what might have been expected.

Two studies (Sewell, 1952; Sewell and Mussen, 1952) have been published dealing with the population of 162 Wisconsin farm children of 5 to 6 years of age discussed in Chapter 2. No relationships were discovered between any type of infant-training practice and later personality or behavior of the children.

One study in which college students were given a security-insecurity test, the results of which were related to their breast-feeding histories, was summarized previously. A similar study of college students at the University of Wisconsin (Thurston and Mussen, 1951) revealed absolutely no differences in the predicted direction between those permissively and those rigidly fed.

One of the most ambitious studies of child-rearing practices is the study by Sears, Maccoby, and Levin (1957) already referred to in Chapter 2. Three hundred seventy-nine mothers of 5-year-old children were intensively interviewed concerning their child-rearing practices, and they were also asked to describe the behavior of these youngsters. The mothers who were interviewed are considered to be reasonably representative of an urban population. All lived in two large East Coast suburbs. They were for the most part members of the middle class and possibly the upper-lower class.

This volume contains the most extensive body of data concerning mothers' dealings with their children from birth to the age of 5. It should be remembered, however, that the children's behavior is reported *as described by the mothers, not as actually observed* by the authors of the book.

The children were all enrolled in a public-school kindergarten. No mothers of children in parochial schools were used as subjects, and selection of mothers was made so that there would be equal numbers of boys, girls, only, first, middle, and youngest children in the sample. All cases where either the wife or the husband was foreign-born, where husband and wife were not living together, where the child in question was not natural-born, was a twin, or was in some fashion handicapped, were also excluded.

Feelings of pleasure or displeasure over the pregnancy, the degree of warmth in the mother-child relationship, and feelings of competence or inadequacy concerning child care were not related to mothers' decision about breast feeding. The only variable that was significantly related to a decision about breast feeding was "sex permissiveness" (that is, the mother's tolerance about her child's sex behavior). Mothers who were not sex-permissive were less likely to breast-feed. It is likely, the authors point out, that such attitudes are related to the mother's personal modesty.

Breast feeding or its lack had no effect on such child behaviors (as described by the mothers) as aggression, conscience, dependence, feeding problems, bed-wetting, or disturbance over toilet training.

As far as the scheduling of feeding was concerned, nearly half of the mothers (48 percent) were relatively relaxed. They partially or completely followed the infant's rhythm and made no real effort to impose a schedule on him. But about a fifth (22 percent) followed fairly rigid or inflexible feeding schedules. Those mothers who appeared to be most anxious about child-rearing were the mothers who followed their pediatrician's advice most closely. Since, at the time of these babies' birth, scheduling was frequently recommended, the scheduling mothers were also those most anxious about child care and rearing. According to the mothers' reports, type of scheduling and weaning did not affect the personalities of the children at 5 years.

About two thirds of the mothers began weaning before their child was 11 months old, and most of them finished the process within about four months. Babies whose weaning was started latest were most quickly weaned. Fifteen percent of the babies were not weaned by 2 years of age.

There was some tendency for late, severely, *or* very permissively weaned children to show upset more frequently than early, gently, but decisively weaned babies. However, nearly as many babies weaned between 5 and 8 months showed upset as did babies weaned after they were 16 months old (30 percent and 35 percent respectively).

Fifty-five percent of the mothers reported that their children had only very mild or no feeding problems. More than a sixth (17 percent) reported considerable or severe feeding problems. The presence or absence of such problems was not related to whether a child had been breast-fed, scheduled or fed by self-demand, or to his age at weaning, but accompanied such behaviors or reactions of the mother as the following: severe toilet training, strong suppression of the child's aggression toward his parents, being negative toward or rejecting the child's dependency (resenting clinging or attention demands), using much physical punishment, and manifesting little warmth toward the child.

In other words, these mothers' reports of their children's behavior do not demonstrate effects on personality of infant feeding and weaning practices as such, but suggest instead that feeding problems may be associated with general restrictiveness on the part of the mother.

WHAT, THEN, OF FEEDING PRACTICES?

How can this section on the effects of early feeding practices on later personality be summarized? What, if any, advice can be given to parents?

At least two authors have taken a thoughtful look at the type of advice that has been given to parents during approximately the last half century, up to about 1950 (Vincent, 1951; Wolfenstein, 1953). The record of the experts, whether they were medical or nonmedical in affiliation, is not a cheering one, or at least not a consistent one. For example, in 1920, 100 percent of the articles on the subject recommended *tight* feeding schedules; but in 1948, 100 percent of them recommended *self-demand* schedules. Other recommendations, though they did not make this full a cycle, were extremely variable from one time to another. There is some evidence that this "expert" advice slowly affects child-care practices of the general population (Brim, 1959; Bronfenbrenner, 1959).

A review of the representative literature, such as given on the preceding pages, shows that the actual evidence for what is "good" and what is "bad" is neither consistent nor conclusive. The author is inclined to shrug his shoulders about recommendations for child-rearing practices in the feeding area. The best conclusion about the specifics of feeding seems to be that mothers who are well-meaning and who try relaxedly to do what they sincerely believe is best for their children—particularly when this is in harmony with the cultural ways of the community with which they are most closely associated—obtain the best results with their children. Such evidence as we have indicates that feeding disturbances, though less related to specific methods of feeding a baby, are tied in with many aspects of mothers' and fathers' adjustment, personality, attitudes, and tension or relaxation with their children.

In making recommendations to caretakers of children, whether they are their teachers, parents, Scoutmasters, Sunday School teachers, or other, an author must keep several things in mind. The general theory for making such recommendations has been developed earlier, most specifically in Chapter 2, where the major problems in child development research were discussed, and a brief summary of two theories of development was given. Frank (1965) whose critical review was mentioned at the beginning of this chapter, also (implicitly) has worthwhile things to say about how one formulates recommendations to child-caretakers.

For example, both Frank and the present author have pointed out that different children respond differently to what, for an impartial observer, look like identical or very similar situations. In Chapter 1, in the discussion of Freudian theory, it was mentioned that there are great differences from one child to another in, for example, his oral drive or his level of activity. Such things must be kept in mind when any practical recommendation is made.

The children and their mothers who have been subjects of the studies reviewed in the *feeding* section of this book are all different from each other: They constitute an extremely *heterogeneous* population (see the section on *measurement terms,* Chapter 2, this book). In addition to forming a heterogeneous population, most of them react differently to similar situations.

Where does this leave the child's caretaker, particularly the caretaker of the older children such as classroom teachers? First, they should be well informed about the background of every child in their classes. Second, they should know what *probabilistic thinking* is. Probabilistic thinking is a willingness and ability on a person's part to think of many possible explanations for a child's (or a group's) behavior, and to devise many possible treatments to make such behavior more satisfactory if, in the first place, it is not acceptable in terms of classroom achievement, behavior, or the child's own personal happiness. If a certain treatment does not work, give it up and try another one (this process is the foundation of the scientific method).

For example, if there is any truth at all in Freud's theories about the effects of generous, nonscheduled nursing or, in this culture, bottle feeding of babies, then according to Freud we may expect that the child nourished supergenerously without any limits, will himself be extremely optimistic, generous, giving, perhaps overly self-confident, and probably rather self-centered. If the teacher/caretaker/therapist knows this about the child's history, he or she can take constructive guidance steps with the child. The completely optimistic, generous, giving but self-centered, overly self-confident individual is at a considerable handicap in a culture such as ours. Our culture operates in terms of enlightened self-interest, which includes the ability to perceive accurately what are the needs of one's peers (his classmates), his caretakers, his superiors. If we have not trained a child to operate according to the principles of enlightened self-interest, we have failed him. Complete optimism—the "Pollyanna" attitude—is out-of-line with our culture. While we want a child to be generally cheerful and trusting, blind optimism and trust are not useful techniques with which to face a complex, industrial society, whether one is 4 or 40 years old. If so, he would be a veritable Simple Simon.

The caretaker of such a child has at least one theory at his disposal; and that is Freud's theory, whether it is right or wrong (as the preceding section points out, it is supported by at least some fairly respectable data, such as Goldman and Goldman-Eisler, 1948, 1951). Give the theory a try. Look for yourself to see if it seems to apply to the child in question. If it does, use the opportunities for counseling available even to caretakers (teachers) of large groups of children to do something about it: devise procedures to show the child that blind optimism, complete, unselfinterested generosity, unlimited self-confidence often cause him to "fall flat on his face." Do not make these procedures extreme. If you use common sense and a plan, you may help the child considerably. You probably will not damage him at all if "he has been that way since infancy." There is a horrifying anecdote about a cynical father with a seemingly overly-trusting and optimistic son. When the child was about 4, the father told him: "Stand on the edge of the table. Jump! I'll catch you." The child jumped, the father deliberately failed to catch him, and the child landed with a painful thud on the floor. The father's comment was, "That'll teach you that people are not to be trusted."

The present author *certainly* does not have in mind such a recommendation. But sensible procedures designed to help a child learn that the world is no bed of roses are useful to the child and, *if* they are sensible, they are going to do him no harm. Children are "pretty tough." If the plan does not work, go on to the next plan you have in mind.

An insightful reader can devise other procedures to help children who, for example, are overly pessimistic, anxious, full of fear, or convinced they will fail at anything they undertake.

Finally, to conclude this section on feeding, readers should try for themselves to devise practical remedial procedures that apply to each of the other childhood treatment techniques and their possible derivatives summarized in this chapter: *toileting, sex, dependency,* and *aggression.*

Toilet Training

Although toilet training has been a matter of consideration and necessity in all cultures since the dawn of civilization, and although reams of speculative and "clinical" material have been written on the subject, the number of careful studies of just what mothers and fathers do, how it works, and what, if anything, happens to the child as a result of it is small.

Sears, Maccoby, and Levin (1957) provide a good picture of how toilet training is actually carried on in twentieth-century United States. A summary of their data and of some of their tentative conclusions about the effects of toilet training is given below.

Modern child-development specialists ordinarily encourage mothers to postpone bowel training until some time in the second year, when the child has fairly complete postural control, can voluntarily control his sphincters, and can be expected to learn to make some signal about his needs. But the average age at which the mothers in the Sears, Maccoby, and Levin study began bowel training was 11 months. The average age of completing it was 18 months. Thus, the training procedure on the average required seven months, although some mothers managed it in a few weeks and others took as long as eighteen months. Almost half (47 percent) of the mothers started toilet training before their children were 9 months old; fewer than 8 percent waited to begin until the second half of their child's second year. The children whose training was begun late learned most quickly.

Heinstein's (1966) mothers were more patient: only 43 percent of them had started bowel training by the time their children were 18 months old.

As a group, the Sears, Maccoby, and Levin mothers who were rated high in anxiety about sex started bowel training earlier than mothers more relaxed about sex, although the differences between the groups were not striking. The early-middle period of beginning bowel training (that is, from 5 to 15 months) produced the least emotional upset (as described by the mothers) on the part of the children.

Sears, Maccoby, and Levin worked out a 5-point rating of severity of toilet training. When ratings of 1 or 2 are considered mild ("child more or less trained himself . . . mild disapproval for some late accidents"), more than half (52 percent) of the mothers were characterized as mild in their training methods. When ratings of 4 and 5 are considered severe ("mother clearly shows disapproval; child may be left on toilet for fairly lengthy periods; . . . child punished severely for deviations; mother angry and emotional over them"), almost a fifth (18 percent) of the mothers were characterized as severe in their methods.

A number of other attitudes and practices were associated with severity of toilet training. Mothers who trained severely also put relatively great pressure on their children to use good table manners, be neat and orderly, be careful around the house and with furniture, keep quiet, and do well in school. They were more likely than lenient mothers to use physical punishment and deprivation of privileges, and reasoned less with their children.

In other words, Sears and his colleagues suggest, "toilet training" is not an isolated factor, but is accompanied by a whole set of other child-rearing practices affecting many phases of the child's social and sexual behavior. If this is true, it is impossible to single out toilet training as a determiner of personality. We must say that whatever is discovered concerning the relation between child behavior or personality and toilet training results from something more general—perhaps the Sears, Maccoby, and Levin factor of permissiveness-restrictiveness.

As their mothers described them, the severely toilet-trained children were more disturbed by training than those who were trained mildly. The sizable correlation of .47 between severity of training and children's emotional upset was one of the highest correlations obtained in the study. However, the degree of warmth the mothers injected into the process was also an important variable, so that mothers who were warm in their attitudes but severe in their training produced fewer emotional upsets in conjunction with toilet training than mothers who were relatively cold and severe (23 percent and 48 percent, respectively).

More than half of Heinstein's (1966) California mothers reported that their babies had completed bowel training by 30 months of age. The average age was 22 months. Girls were faster than boys. The older the babies were when bowel training started, the faster they learned bowel control.

The problem of their child's learning to sleep dry at night is a major one for parents. The mothers included in Sears, Maccoby, and Levin's study most frequently trained their children by getting them up at night to go to the bathroom, and many of them attempted to limit the amount of late-afternoon and evening liquids. Many used more severe methods, such as making the children wash out their pajamas or bedclothes. Many mothers offered rewards for night-dryness. Almost half the mothers (44 percent) reported that their children were dry at night by the time they were 2. Four fifths of the children were night-dry by the time the study was conducted, leaving a fifth still having an occasional or frequent night accident at the age of 5 or 6. Children tended either to be bed-wetters or to have feeding problems, not both.

The age of beginning bladder training made no difference in the age at which the children gained full bladder control, but mothers who had high anxiety about sex *and* were relatively cold and undemonstrative toward the child *and* used severe toilet-training procedures were, as the authors say, "most efficient for producing prolonged bed-wetting" (p. 131). Warm, permissive mothers with anxiety about sex got their children dry at night earliest. This relation is an intriguing one. An area of behavior that is extremely important to the mother, but about which she is punitive and cold, may be one in which the child refuses to conform, thus expressing his rebellion and resentment. Is this *his* way of "training" or punishing his mother? When the behavior is extremely important to the mother, *but* she is gentle and warm in her insistence on conformity, the child "compliments" or rewards her by taking note of her wishes, and doing as she wants him to.

Bed-wetting was not affected by severity of weaning, scheduled or self-demand feeding, or mothers' responsiveness to their children's crying. Such things as high demands for care with furniture and walls, strict requirements that the child stay in his own yard, demands for quick obedience, and pressure for good table manners and good performance in school also had no relation to bed-wetting.

Psychoanalytic theory maintains that bed-wetting is a child's way of getting back at or punishing his mother. The Sears, Maccoby, and Levin findings offer some support for this point of view, since there was some correlation between over-all severity of punishment and bed-wetting, particularly when the former was combined with a cold, rejecting manner toward the child.

Toilet-training practices in many different cultures were studied by Whiting and Child (1953). They found that anal indulgence and permissiveness were negatively but insignificantly related to a society's tendency to give anal-excremental explanations for illness. Anal socialization anxiety was not related to any of the factors they studied, but the progressive satisfaction given to the child in the toilet-training area (the degree to which he has "never given any trouble about it") was negatively related to a culture's use of excremental materials in warding off or curing illness. Whiting and Child found no relation between age of toilet training and fear and distrust of others.

The Whiting and Child findings about toilet training thus revealed less than their findings about feeding and weaning. Their principal result is tentative support of relatedness between permissive toilet training and lack of superstition about bodily wastes.

The Davis and Havighurst study (1946) reports an average age of obtaining bladder control of about 21 months; about 50 percent of the children they studied had achieved complete bladder control by 18 months. Sears and his colleagues report that a fifth of their mothers were quite severe in their training for bladder control. They state that 28 percent of the children in their study suffered emotional upset during bowel training, but give no similar figures for bladder training. However, about a third of the youngsters in the Sears study were still wetting their beds at 3 years of age or later.

There is little question in the minds of most of those who routinely gather data from mothers concerning their young children, particularly their sons, that the published norms for toilet training do not accurately represent the truth, particularly for bladder control. Both wetting and soiling are deplored in our culture, and parents have been made to think that delay in continence invariably represents both faulty child-adjustment and improper child-rearing practices. Hence, the pressure to report children as dry and clean at an early age is great.

Going as far afield as Australia, we find another study (Bostock, 1951) suggesting that breast feeding is unrelated to later enuresis, but that severity of toilet training is strongly related to it, as it is to acceptance of the child: unwanted children tend to receive more rigid training than accepted children. The congruence between these results and those of Sears, Maccoby, and Levin is immediately evident. McCandless and Heye (1951), using as subjects two different groups of children in a university nursery school, also found that maternal attitudes of acceptance, lateness of starting bladder training, and speed of achieving bladder control were linked to each other.

In the previously mentioned study by Williams and Scott (1953) of factors that are related to rapid as opposed to slow motor development, rigid toilet training (like rigid feeding scheduling) was associated with relatively slow motor development. A list of other factors that were associated with motor retardation reads very much like Sears, Maccoby, and Levin's list of factors associated with rigid toilet training. Children who were relatively retarded in motor development were weaned earlier, trained earlier, handled more punitively, and were more restricted in play space and experimentation; they had less bodily contact and time with others, and were less frequently breast-fed and for a shorter time.

Williams and Scott used as subjects Negro babies from two socioeconomic classes. The children more retarded in motor development were from the upper-class group of parents, who were also more generally restrictive in their child-rearing practices. Motor retardation or acceleration was judged from scores on an infant "intelligence" test—hence the somewhat surprising finding that those children who, according to confident prediction, will later score higher in IQ tests are in infancy less accelerated on a measure of development that stresses motor skills. In turn, slow development of motor skills is associated with relatively restrictive methods of child-rearing, which characterize parents from higher rather than lower socioeconomic classes and include relatively depriving or severe weaning and toilet-training practices.

Conclusions about toilet training are, for the most part, more clear-cut than those for feeding and weaning. This may be because children are older and hence better able to learn when toilet training is begun.

Studies of toilet training do not in any consistent way support psycho-analytic theory, but they suggest that psychoanalysts are correct in emphasizing the importance of toilet-training practices on later development. United States mothers, as we have seen, start toilet training earlier than the "experts" advise although Heinstein's (1966) mothers were closer to the recommended age for starting training than Sears', Maccoby's, and Levin's (1957) mothers. The earlier toilet training is started the longer it takes to complete. The more severe the training, the more upset the child is by it. Rigid toilet training, in conjunction with a number of other practices that might be called restrictive, also seems to slow down motor development in infancy.

Mothers high in anxiety about sex start toilet training earlier than mothers who are more relaxed about sex. The most successful mothers in early training for night-dryness are high in sex anxiety but use mild training procedures and show much warmth to their children. The least successful mothers also have high sex anxiety, but combine with it severe training procedures and relatively cold attitudes and emotions toward their children. In a study of primitive cultures, little relation was found between anality and cultural folkways.

Finally, and probably most important, the rigidity with which toilet training is carried out is related to a number of other child-rearing practices, almost all of which may be thought of either as restrictive or as indicative of insecurity and low self-esteem on the part of the mother. For this reason, we cannot say definitely that toilet training alone is important in shaping a child's personality; but we can say that it is one of a number of indicators of the mother's relationship with her child, and that all of these taken together have important and probably durable effects on personality.

The reader should refer back to the section on toilet training in this chapter for procedures for formulating treatment recommendations for older children who have had different types of toilet training.

Sex Training

CHILDHOOD SEXUALITY

Chapter 2 introduced the concept of infantile sexuality proposed by Freud—a sexuality, or libidinous gratification associated with the predominant oral, anal, and genital organ systems. Mishandled, the child may be condemned to a lifelong, neurotic attempt to make up for what has happened to him during these stages. Mishandling may occur either through deprivation and trauma or through overgratification.

Freud's views about infantile sexuality provoked strong emotional reactions and a storm of controversy. Unfortunately, his postulations have not been subjected to rigorous experimental test, and the great volume of material that has been written on the subject of sex in childhood is not often related to substantial or sound research. Most research in the area has been clinical. Purely anecdotal material also abounds. The conclusions of this section are therefore based more on clinical experience than on solid research.

Kinsey *et al.* (1948, 1953) tell us much about human sexual behavior but, about children, almost all that we learn is that they are interested in sex, experience orgasms earlier than is commonly thought and, from early childhood, show much more interest and participation in sexual behavior than the average adult guesses (or remembers).

In the United States, sexuality in children is currently much discussed in PTA groups and by "experts," but it still remains a matter of considerable discomfort to mothers and fathers. They appear to handle it by repressing or suppressing it, rather than by an intelligent use of learning principles.

GOALS AND PRACTICES OF SEX TRAINING

The most comprehensive and the soundest survey of child-rearing practices in the area of sexual behavior known to the author is provided by Sears, Maccoby, and Levin (1957). These authors state that there are four goals of childhood sex training in the United States. The first (apparently universal in all modern cultures) is to inculcate the taboo against incest; the second by no means universal although probably characteristic of industrialized and monotheistic cultures, is training against masturbation (training that almost universally breaks down at adolescence, particularly for boys); the third is to teach the child to avoid sex play with other children; the fourth is to control information: "Information control . . . is one of the methods by which adults attempt to induce the growing child to postpone sex gratification and limit sex activities in the early years" (p. 182).

Sears, Maccoby, and Levin point out that there are substitute gratifications for things the child gives up as he is weaned and toilet trained: solid foods are found to be tasteful and pleasant; parents' reward one for cleaning one's plate; being dry and clean have their virtues. But for sex, there are no substitutes until the time of adolescence. This leaves mothers with no possibility of *guidance* through substitute rewards; they can only *inhibit* sexual behavior. To do this, they predominantly try to prevent stimulation (for example, supervise play carefully, dress children in loose, nonbinding clothing, observe modesty in the home); distract the child (for example, by changing activity if children seem to be getting "sexy"); "borrow sanctions" (such as telling the child addicted to nudity that he will catch cold, or telling him, as he manipulates his genitals, that he will hurt himself); avoid labels (for example, by using euphemisms for the genitals); and control information (most frequently by elaborate subterfuges such as "I found you under a rosebush").

Much control of sex is accomplished through training for modesty. Sears, Maccoby, and Levin, queried their 379 mothers about how permissive they were about their children's going around indoors without clothes, and how severe was the pressure they exerted toward indoor modesty. Again using the two highest of 5-point rating scales to define permissiveness (little or no restraint on nudity, for example), about one third (36 percent) of the mothers were permissive. Almost half (44 percent) fell at the other end of the scale, believing that the "child must be clothed at all times," or being only very slightly permissive. On the other hand, the mothers were not very severe in enforcing their scruples about modesty. If mild pressure is defined as their doing nothing more drastic than teasing or gently remonstrating about nudity, then three fifths (61 percent) of the mothers used mild pressure only. If severe pressure is defined as scolding, warning, punishing, and becoming angry and emotional, only 7 percent of the mothers used severe pressure.

Children "playing with themselves" elicited considerable emotional reaction from the mothers. Fewer than a fifth (18 percent) felt "that a certain amount is to be expected," or that "it's natural, just curiosity"; while one half (49 percent) considered it wrong or harmful or "might not do anything if it happened just once, but wouldn't like it." As with nudity, however, they did not back up their strong opinions with strong action, since 45 percent of them used mild or no pressure against masturbation, and only a twentieth were classified as using severe pressure against masturbation.

The picture of permissiveness about sex play among children is similar. Fewer than a sixth (16 percent) of the mothers believed in permissiveness, and almost three fifths (57 percent) of them expressed firm attitudes against it. But again, opinions were not backed up by strong action. Almost half (46 percent) of the mothers said that so far as they knew, no incidents had occurred. When mothers mentioned that such incidents had occurred, 45 percent had been quite permissive in their actions, and only 13 percent had behaved severely and forbiddingly. Interestingly enough, more mothers who were rated high on their tendency to keep a close check on their children *did not know* of sex-play incidents.

Even though the mothers seemed to "talk loudly and carry a little stick" concerning children's sexual behavior, there was a high correlation between mothers' disapproval of a certain behavior and their taking definite steps to prevent it. The correlation between permissiveness and pressure was —.75 (that is, mothers who were not permissive about a given type of behavior *did* punish when it occurred).

The mothers in this study who were not permissive about sex permitted relatively little aggression toward parents on the part of their children. They were more likely than permissive mothers to toilet-train their children severely, keep a close watch on their whereabouts, use physical punishment fairly often, and be strict about noise, table manners, and care of household property. They were also relatively cold emotionally toward their children, did not like it when the children clung to them or made attention demands, and put much emphasis on their daughters being feminine, their sons masculine. In other words, these mothers fell toward the restrictive extreme of Sears, Maccoby, and Levin's behavioral factor of permissiveness-restrictiveness.

Whiting and Child (1953), in their cross-cultural study of child-rearing practices, found no relationship between sex training and explanations of disease. However, in the small number of societies they studied that were very permissive toward childhood sexuality, there were also recommendations for sexual activity as a method of *getting over* illness. In cultures where sexual behavior was severely inhibited, there were moderate tendencies not to use and even to avoid or abjure sexual types of therapy for disease. A high negative correlation (—.74) existed between the age at which training in sexual inhibition was begun and the development of guilt in the members of a society. Severe inhibition was also somewhat associated with fear of other human beings.

These two studies provide almost all the available data about sex training and its correlates. From them, we see that maternal permissiveness in the sexual area correlates with general permissiveness. United States mothers who have been studied seem to have generally negative attitudes toward children's sexual behavior, but they do not exercise very strong open pressure against it (perhaps because they themselves are guilty, uneasy, and uninformed in the area). When they punish, they punish the things they disapprove of. In a cross-cultural study, societies in which children's sexual behavior was indulged tended also to be those where sexual behaviors were considered therapeutic for disease. The same study demonstrated that early sex training was associated with the development of guilt (as defined), for which conscience is assumed to be a necessary foundation.

Clinical evidence and hypotheses about the effects of sex training abound, suggesting that both harsh and restrictive sex training and overly permissive training, including overexposure to sexual information and experiences, may leave the child sexually disturbed. Chapter 10 includes material, more of it theoretical than factual, on sexual development and the consequences for adult behavior of direct and indirect sex training.

The lack of solid data in this area is obvious and regrettable. There are, in the United States, strong sanctions against conducting research on sexual behavior at any age level, but particularly with children. However, any college counselor, any psychiatrist, can testify to the fact that a certain amount of sexual disturbance accompanies or underlies almost every psychological disability. The sex-based neuroses of our culture can be alleviated and prevented only when facts about the development of sexual behavior are more fully known and when the relations between different types of experience and training and later personality development and adjustment have been more fully explored. Children's caretakers, by implication, should be particularly thoughtful and careful about how they handle their charges' sex-type behavior.

Dependency Training

There are reasonably adequate studies of childhood dependency, but the early training of dependency behavior (positive and encouraging, or negative and discouraging) has been little studied by people other than those mentioned in the two preceding sections: Sears, Maccoby, and Levin (1957) and Whiting and Child (1953). These authors, following Freud's leads, have also contributed much to theories of dependency and its relation to socialization; but the details of this treatment more properly belong in the later chapter on social and emotional development.

Dependency is ordinarily not troublesome behavior. Usually, it flatters us to have people depend on us. Perhaps this is why the area is relatively neglected by research people. Aggression, as will be seen in the next section, bothers people and has received much research attention: "The squeaking wheel gets the grease."

Sears, Maccoby, and Levin devote a thirty-eight-page chapter to the topic of dependency, using the material they gleaned from their interviews with 379 suburban mothers of 5-year-olds. It must be said again that judgments about the children's behavior were made from what the mothers said about the children, rather than from observation of what the children actually did. Such judgments are bound to be frail reeds. The mother who rejects dependency behavior may see the occasionally whining child as very dependent indeed; whereas the mother who craves a child "who is always a baby and needs me" may perceive the same child as almost rejectingly independent. However, the Sears, Maccoby, and Levin data are at least as good and perhaps the best in the area and must be summarized here.

Almost equal proportions of the mothers perceived their children as, first, very slightly or almost not at all dependent (35 percent), and quite dependent or showing a great deal of dependent behavior (37 percent). More than half of the mothers reported that their 5-year-olds did not cling to them, follow them, or seek to be near them; while about a tenth (8 per cent) reported a great deal of this behavior. A fourth of the mothers reported that at one time or another their children had gone through a very dependent stage. Almost two thirds (62 percent) of the children at the time of the study put up no objection to their mothers' going out or leaving them with someone else (only 5 percent rather consistently raised a fuss about this). Only children were slightly but significantly more dependent than children with brothers or sisters. The latter seemed able to turn to their sibs for company.

Dependency behavior at 5 years of age had no relationship to the warmth the mother had given earlier, when the child was a baby, nor to breast or bottle feeding, nor to age of beginning or ending weaning. Neither did other infantile frustrations result in dependency at age 5, although they had frequently done so concurrently. The mothers ranged from being quite unresponsive to their babies' crying (16 percent) to quite responsive (usually or always picking up the baby immediately), with almost half falling in this reponse category. Such responsiveness had no relation with later dependency. Nor did early brief separation experiences seem to affect dependency at the age of 5.

The mothers ranged from low permissiveness toward dependency behavior (37 percent) to high permissiveness (30 percent). Two fifths (41 percent) of the mothers occasionally or never rewarded dependency; a fourth (23 percent) of them often or almost always did. A fourth were almost never irritated by dependency behavior, whereas more than one third (36 percent) were often irritable and punishing when the child hung and clung to them. As might be expected, these three tendencies—to be permissive, to reward, and not to be irritated—were positively interrelated one with the other.

When the mother had an accepting and tolerant attitude toward the child's dependent behavior, she was also likely to be affectionately warm toward him, gentle in toilet training, high in sex permissiveness, unlikely to use physical punishment for dependent behaviors, and tolerant when he was angry and aggressive toward his parents. She also manifested high esteem for herself and her husband. Irritable scolding and pulling away from dependent behaviors increased their frequency, according to the mothers' reports; and the most dependent children of all belonged to mothers who irritably rejected dependency demands for a time but eventually gave in to them, thus rewarding the child. This finding fits well with the results of experimental learning studies on partial reinforcement (see Chapter 4).

The cross-cultural material of Whiting and Child (1953) indicates that there is a relation within cultures between the tendency to be orally indulgent (permissive and generous suckling and late weaning) and to indulge dependency behavior. According to Whiting and Child, cultures that accorded high indulgence to children's dependency behaviors were not cultures in which illness was explained as being due to dependency. These authors also found that when an "avoidance therapy" is defined as isolating the patient or removing him from the home during his illness, there is a clear and positive relation between socialization anxiety for dependency and the tendency of a society to use avoidance therapy—that is, societies that discourage dependency also use illness therapy that involves isolating the patient or removing him from the home.

Whiting and Child found a moderate negative relation between the age at which independence training was begun and the degree to which the people of a society were judged to possess guilt. It will be remembered that these authors' definition of guilt for a society was the degree to which a patient was held responsible for his own illness.

In Chapter 2 and the introductory sections of Chapter 3, suggestions were made as to why the entire research area of family child-rearing practices and resultant child behaviors and characteristics is such a "mishmash." For example, Prothro (1960), who in his studies used the same data employed by Whiting and Child, arrives at different conclusions (if the reader has forgotten, he should look back at the discussion in Chapter 2 of general versus specific concepts: "dependence" is a general concept! Dependent on whom, at what age, under what circumstances, in what fashion, as a boy or as a girl?). It is not surprising that findings in the area do not jibe with each other. Perhaps no two investigators define dependence in the same way.

In any event, Prothro, among a number of other rather important things, says (he is talking about the relation between bowel training and later dependent-independent behavior) that some cultures begin toilet training early, evoke much anxiety about it, but begin serious independence training late (relatively) in the child's life. The opposite is true of other cultures. This apparent discrepancy (according to Freudian and other more recent theory) actually may have a practical, common-sense explanation. Much independence training, as Prothro points out, consists of leaving a child to his own resources. If a 2-year-old can set his own toileting pattern, along with it he may develop independence: as he goes out to have his bowel movement or to urinate, he stops to play and he may, because of the situation, be forced to learn to protect himself. These things develop his independence.

Geography may play a big role in this: the child in a respectable middle-class part of town is reported by neighbors to his mother if he urinates or defecates in public. In snow-covered Hunza, with every house built on the side of a Himalayan cliff and snow-covered half the year, mothers must (to keep their children alive), supervise them closely. They cannot toilet on their own and in so doing, possibly develop habits of free play and self-protection that are associated with independent behavior. But a Navajo or a Bedouin mother, in country where there are few wild animals and relatively little chance of getting lost, can give her child considerable freedom of choice in handling his eliminative needs. The country in which he lives is sparsely settled and dry: hence his productions bother no one particularly; and he can roam for quite a distance without losing sight of his hogan or tent and so experience the adventures that accompany roaming. He may thus become more independent.

While there are other studies in the area, to conclude this subsection, the author has chosen one by Waldrop and Bell (1965) and one by Mueller (1966). Waldrop and Bell find that male 2- and 3-year-old preschool-attending children are more snuggly, nuzzly, and generally dependent on their teachers when they come from big families of high density. By high density, the authors mean that the children in the family are close together in age.

Mueller illustrates a confusion that runs all the way through psychological-sociological data and discussions of emotional characteristics and behaviors as they differ for boys and girls. Mueller used college students as his subjects, asking them how they perceived their parents' characteristics. He found no significant results for girls (we shall see more of this[3]). But for his boys, those lowest in dependency scores perceived *both* their parents as being *strong* persons (speaking psychologically). The *most* independent boys perceived their fathers both as *strong* and *passive:* the father had plenty of power but kept quiet about it, thus leaving the boy free to develop his own independent ways, but all the time being sure the father could rescue him if necessary. Mueller has other interesting results that will be summarized in other sections of this volume. Mueller's young women subjects showed similar tendencies but not at an acceptable level of statistical significance.

Finally, in a study of the same general type as Mueller's, both Winder and Rau (1962) find that their most dependent late adolescent male subjects saw their mothers as high in anxiety and rejecting, and their fathers as low in self-esteem (opposite to Mueller's *powerful* but *passive* fathers).

To summarize this section, the majority of 5-year-olds in the Sears, Maccoby, and Levin study were reported by their mothers to be sturdily

---

[3] The chapter on sex-typing and identification in this book illustrates more clearly than any other portion the fact that we now have some plausible theories about the development of boys, but are much more unsure (perhaps men have always been bewildered by girls and women) about the developmental laws for girls. Is it because we have relatively few women psychologists-sociologists working in the area? Do boys grow up differently from girls in both obvious and subtle ways, the latter of which we have not begun to fathom?

independent youngsters. A mother's indulgence of dependency in her child was related, although not strongly, to a number of other permissive and warm behaviors on her part. Mothers who were irritated by dependency behavior yet eventually yielded to it believed they had the most dependent children. Only children were slightly more dependent than children with brothers and sisters. However, the mothers' descriptions of their children's dependency are particularly suspect, since they are liable to distortion by the mother's attitudes toward dependency.

The cross-cultural findings of Whiting and Child show a relation between oral and dependency indulgence, whereas Sears, Maccoby, and Levin find almost no relation between dependency and other infant-rearing practices. According to Whiting and Child, cultures that indulge dependency do not use dependency explanations of illness; cultures in which high socialization anxiety exists for dependency use "avoidance therapies" for disease. The age at which training for independence was started was found to be negatively related to guilt in a culture. Others working from the same data obtain different results. Geography-climate probably produce some of these apparent contradictions.

Boys (aged 2 and 3) from big families where children are close together are unusually dependent on their women teachers; and very independent young men perceive their fathers as both *strong* (powerful psychologically) and *passive*.

Aggression Training

THE NATURE OF CHILDHOOD AGGRESSION

Sears, Maccoby, and Levin (1957) have an excellent chapter on aggression in childhood and the methods by which mothers cope with and attempt to socialize it in their children. Of the 379 mothers they studied, every mother at one time or another had been forced to cope with angry outbursts or quarreling on the part of her children, and almost all mothers (95 percent) reported instances of strong aggression directed by the child against his parents. Among United States mainland children in nursery school, one study (McCandless, Balsbaugh and Bennett, 1958) reports that some sort of conflict, ranging from fairly mild to violent, occurs during free play about every 5 minutes for boys, about every 7 or 8 minutes for girls. Hawaiian nursery-school children show similar patterns, although they do not quarrel as frequently (about every 8 minutes for boys, every 10 minutes for girls).

Aggression in childhood, then, seems to be universal. As Sears, Maccoby, and Levin (and many others) point out, the aggressive child is the angry child, and an angry child is not a happy child. He is likely to provoke retaliation on the part of those toward whom his anger is directed, and this in turn makes him even angrier and more aggressive. In recent years, there has been a tendency (particularly among well-educated middle-class parents) to believe that suppressing a child is bad for him and that repressing aggression and feelings of hate will lead the child to build up still more anger and hate so that he either becomes neurotic or displaces his rage to other and innocent victims. They argue that it is all right for the child to express aggression toward his parents —that it is usually the parents who frustrate and hence anger the child and that it is better, more direct, and "healthier" for the child to express anger directly against the source of his frustrations. Thus his anger is "drained off."

There are at least two reasons to question these assumptions. The first is that there is little place in civilized, cooperative living for direct and primitive expression of aggression, when aggression is thought of as either physical or verbal attack. Certain "disguised" verbal aggression, such as gossip or "frankness" are condoned to a greater degree than physical attack or direct verbal abuse, but even gossip and frankness that conceal hostility are more likely to produce complications in human relations than to oil the wheels of social interaction. Second, learning theory predicts that the expression of aggression and its consequent momentary tension-relief strengthens rather than weakens the tendency to behave aggressively. There is evidence (Feshbach, 1956; Mallick and McCandless, 1966) to support this prediction. Nor does evidence (as, Mussen and Naylor, 1954; Purcell, 1956; Smith and Coleman, 1956) indicate that behaving aggressively reduces tendencies to be aggressive. If anything, these studies suggest that the opposite is true. Children and young adults with crude fantasies of aggression have been found to be more openly aggressive in their behavior than those whose aggressive fantasies are muted or contain elements indicating that the person is as concerned with the dangerous consequences of his aggression as he is with the aggression itself. In other words, aggressive fantasy *may suggest* or stimulate aggressive behavior, rather than drain off the motive to behave aggressively.

Four other representative studies support the points of view that catharsis (expression) of aggression does not reduce but rather may increase aggressive behavior; and that there are effective ways to divert children's open aggression. Today, we incline to think open aggression in a society like ours is more likely to create a vicious circle for the child than to relax and comfort him—make him well-adjusted. To list the studies alphabetically:

Bandura (1965) finds that 42- to 71-month-old boys and girls are likely to imitate aggressive behavior exhibited by a model. There is surprisingly little sex difference in aggression (we have been taught that girls are "sugar and spice and everything nice"), although the girls in this study were more likely immediately to "bottle up" their aggression if they saw punishment inflicted on the person they were imitating.

Gordon and Smith (1965) find that young children (3 to 4 years old, boys and girls) move from more to less aggression in two permissive situations if they have, between the two experimental sessions, been told a story about a lonely dog looking for something-someone to play with— an "affiliation arousing" story.

Mallick and McCandless (1966) find as did Bandura, that girls (in this case, third graders) are just as aggressive as boys *if they are assured no one is going to find out about it* (this is an important point). Like Gordon and Smith, they found that if the behavior of an older child (a sixth-grader who had frustrated them in a series of tasks they had been assigned) was explained sensibly to them, they became less aggressive. But if they were allowed to express aggression, either verbally or physically, between the initial and final test (frustration was interposed between the first and second tests) they showed more rather than less aggression.

Finally, Rosenbaum and Stanners (1961) found (they worked with college students) that their subjects with *low* self-esteem were more likely to react aggressively in aggression-provoking situations than subjects *high* in self-esteem.

These four studies fit together neatly: expression of aggression does *not* reduce aggressive behavior, but seems more likely to increase it; children imitate aggressive behavior from adult "models." Girls are as likely to be aggressive as boys if they have good reason to think no one will know about it. (Perhaps this is why, when girls and women gossip maliciously, they say, "Be sure not to tell a soul!") People (or at least, late adolescent boys) low in self-esteem (possibly insecure) are more likely to react aggressively when threatened than boys of the same age and general characteristics high in self-esteem.

On the other hand, case histories gathered by psychiatrists, social workers, and psychologists, as well as social experiences that we all have had, indicate that bottled-up hate which cannot be recognized, or constructively drained off, is painful, even destructive, to the person. It may be that an honest recognition and acceptance of feelings is one of the most important facets of good adjustment. Normal people do become angry periodically, but the well-adjusted person is usually able to recognize and accept his anger. He has enough control over his impulses and sufficient personal flexibility to make constructive (or, at least, not destructive) use of his anger. Our society permits and rewards such possible disguises of aggression as competitiveness, ambition, standing up for one's rights, and being "righteously indignant" over needs for social reform. The literature about aggression, as well as ordinary social observation, clearly suggests that children's aggression cannot safely be so thoroughly squelched that they become milk-toasts. On the other hand, blind acting out of aggression through physical violence and verbal tirades is socially destructive. Channeled in one way, aggression helps to build society; in another way, to destroy it. For such reasons as these, it is vital that we work to understand the means by which it can be constructively socialized.

EFFECTS OF AGGRESSION TRAINING

One of the earlier studies of aggressive behavior in nursery-school children (Appel, 1942) analyzes 641 different aggressive episodes involving 252 individuals. Property was involved more than any other factor, although there were many instances of unprovoked hostility. The older children were more persistent than the younger in their hostile behavior. Adult techniques varied widely in effectiveness. Most effective in stopping an aggressive episode was teacher diversion, which terminated hostility 93 percent of the time. Separating the children was slightly less effective, and arbitrary decisions on the part of the nursery-school teacher were quite ineffective. Interpreting the wishes and feelings of one child to another worked surprisingly well considering the age of the children, which ranged from about 2 to 4. Explaining property rights and suggesting solutions worked in about two thirds of the cases of conflict; very ineffective were such techniques as disapproving, moralizing, failure to understand, having children "talk it over," or being unsympathetic. When the adult was unsure of himself or his course of action, he was also unsuccessful in terminating conflicts.

Gordon and Smith's and Mallick and McCandless' more recent results fit well with Appel's findings.

Appel, after studying individual children, believes that their aggression may spring from either too much or too little discipline at home, from jealousy of their brothers or sisters, from excessive parental standards, or from home tensions.

Pauline Sears (1951) has studied some of the conditions that accompany fantasy aggression in children from about 3 to 5 years of age. As would be expected, she found that boys were more frequently and violently physically aggressive in their fantasy play than girls; but that the girls more frequently showed aggression through scolding and mischief, so that the hurt was mental rather than physical. Boys were much more hostile to a "father" doll than were girls. Children who were oldest in a family manifested less fantasy aggression than younger and only children, possibly because they had been subjected to more pressure from their parents against being rough with younger brothers and sisters. The pattern of fantasy aggression for boys whose fathers had been away from home for long periods of time was more like that of girls; they were markedly less aggressive than boys whose fathers had been home consistently. No such effect was observed for girls whose fathers had been separated from the family.

. The pattern of child-rearing that produces the most aggressive children, as revealed by the research of Sears, Maccoby, and Levin (1957), is one where the parents disapprove of aggression and, when it occurs, punish it with physical aggression of their own or threaten the child. This "counter-attack" on the part of the parent, though it may work for the moment, appears to generate still more hostility on the part of the child, which eventually breaks out (see Bandura, this book). Sears, Maccoby, and Levin point out that the parent who uses physical punishment is providing for his child a model of aggressive, destructive behavior that the child is likely to copy, either then or later. But highly aggressive children are also produced by homes in which the mother is permissive of the child's outbursts, whether or not they are directed against her. Where mothers were both permissive and physically punishing, they were most likely to produce highly aggressive children. Least-aggressive children apparently come from homes where aggression is disapproved of and is stopped, but where techniques other than physical punishment are used to stop it. The studies reported above of techniques used successfully and unsuccessfully to lessen aggression fit well with these conclusions.

In their cross-cultural study, Whiting and Child (1953) report that the more aggression is indulged (that is, the more the child is allowed to attain satisfaction through being aggressive), the less likely the society is to explain illness as some function of aggressive behavior; but the more severe the socialization anxiety about aggression (the more firmly a society stamps out aggression in its children), the more likely the society is to explain illness as a function of aggression. Finally, these authors demonstrate that the less the initial indulgence and the more the socialization anxiety for aggressive behavior, the more the people in the culture show an over-all fear of others.

Nakamura (1959) asked seventy-eight undergraduate women to prepare autobiographical workbooks while taking a course in the psychology of adjustment. He was interested in whether they considered their childhood discipline to have been positive or negative. Discipline was rated as *positive* if the subjects said they would use the same disciplinary techniques on their own children. Discipline was judged to be *negative* when the girls stressed physical punishment or the psychological hurtfulness of their parents' methods of discipline and rejected using the same sort of discipline for their own children. Nakamura hypothesized that overprotective parents would so impress their daughters with their power that the girls would be relatively unable to express hostility or criticism directly toward the parents, but would instead displace it to other people. He also predicted that positively disciplined girls would direct less criticism toward their parents than negatively disciplined girls. Both predictions were supported by his analysis of the autobiographies.

Parenthetically, the author has said that there are relatively few studies of dependent behavior in children. The dependent child is the good child—at times, he may annoy the teacher/caretaker, but he "minds," and he gives the adult responsible for him a sense of power and satisfaction. Aggressive children are "a different breed of cat." They irritate their families (in this book, it has been pointed out repeatedly that family life is a two-way street: parents do things to their children, and children do things to their parents; the same principle applies to teachers and children in classrooms). People may criticize a parent *mildly* for having a dependent child. But they criticize him *vigorously* if he has an aggressive child. The term, "A little terror," is commonly used in our society.

A few representative studies, fitting relatively well with those summarized above are discussed below, in more detail:

Byrne (1964) mailed questionnaires about their child-rearing attitudes and practices to mothers of college students. He also carefully measured characteristics of the students, finding that "repressors"—those who run away from or avoid things—tend to come from homes characterized either by their mothers or the students as permissive and accepting. The fathers and mothers were on cordial terms with each other, and the mothers were consistent and had good personal self-esteem. These young people—the repressors (an unfortunate term)—in other words, were not looking for trouble: they were optimistic, overlooked personal slights, wore no chips on their shoulders. Sensitizers (those who met situations "head on," who were alert to threat and who thus could be presumed to be more aggressive) came from restrictive and rejective homes. The subjects themselves were doubtful about their ability to be good parents, their mothers were inconsistent in practice and low in self-esteem, and the parents had poor relations with each other.

Hoffman (1960) reports that the mothers he studied who were unqualifiedly autocratic (that is, absolutistic, giving no explanations) had children who, at nursery school age, were hostile toward other children and their teachers. Hoffman believes that these children behaved in this way *because* their parents treated them as they did, not because they were born that way and goes ahead to make the interesting and clinically plausible statement that the mothers, perhaps behaved the way they did because their husbands put them into a role that demanded it. There are, unfortunately, problems with Hoffman's design and sample. Sears (1961) followed up the 379 5-year-old children, who have been so often mentioned in this chapter (Sears, Maccoby, and Levin, 1957), when they were 13 years old. His findings are so mixed and inconclusive (probably because of such methodological difficulties as were discussed in Chapter 2) that they cannot be summarized here.

Kagan (1958) finds that aggressive boys (6 to 10 years old) fantasied their parents as "angry people," and in turn felt angry toward their parents. Children in families where the "mother is boss" were less aggressive than when "Dad wears the pants," and these less aggressive boys reported they were more likely to mind the mother than the father (perhaps such boys are destined to become teachers' pets).

McCord, McCord, and Howard (1961) analyzing data from case histories of boys who were delinquent in various ways (in contrast to Byrne, who made careful experimental definitions of his repressing-sensitizing subjects), conclude that aggressive boys have been reared by parents who were heavy punishers, rejecters, poor supervisors of their sons' behavior, and were themselves deviant and often in intense conflict with each other. Conclusions from this study fit well with other studies summarized in this section, particularly Byrne's. Byrne used entirely different and careful experimental methods with his college students. Parenthetically, when results of studies concerning themselves with different age groups and different samples, studied in different ways, arrive at compatible conclusions, one becomes more confident about trends suggested by the studies.

The next few studies concern children's attitudes toward their treatment by their parents. The reader should relate them to the section immediately preceding.

Pikas (who does not say what percentage of boys or what percentage of girls constituted his sample—and in this confusing area, this is a methodological error), studied a large number of 11- to 15-year-olds living in Sweden. His results are consonant with results in the United States. This should be expected since the most logical characterization of a culture, at least for the present author, is not "primitive," versus "complex" or Eastern versus Western, but is instead *industrialized* compared with *industrializing* compared with *nonindustrialized*. Sweden, by anyone's definition, is an industrialized culture. Pikas' youngsters, in terms of aggressive impulses, were analyzed according to their reactions to either concrete (do thus and so—such as washing the dishes because I said so) directions from their parents or abstract (choose the profession of law as your career because it offers an interesting sample of human behavior—the words are the author's, not Pikas').

Even his youngest subjects responded better to rational—reasoning, abstract—techniques of control. The brighter the child was, the less he liked being flatly told what to do and the older he grew the less he preferred this technique. Incidentally to the purposes of this book, Pikas found that the altruistic—helping others—professions became more popular choices for older children and that intelligent children preferred them more than less intelligent children. The more the parents exercised rational control—reasoning at an abstract level—the more likely were their children to choose professions that, hypothetically, help mankind.

Roff (1961) offers another cue to *predict,* but not *explain* aggressive behavior. He followed the military careers of a number of boys who, during their elementary school years, had been referred to a child guidance clinic. His criterion, or definition, of aggressive behavior was commission of acts which had led to "other than honorable discharge" from the service, or to sixty or more days AWOL or disciplinary confinement while in the service.

Certainly, aggressive behavior is a serious social-personal-economic problem. The United States Children's Bureau, judging from 1964 data reported in 1966, estimates that one of every nine American youngsters will find himself in juvenile court before he is 18.

Roff's study is carefully controlled: he compared these young men with boys of similar intellectual level who had also been referred to the clinic (the next comparable case history number in the clinic's cumulative files), but who had made the rank of sergeant or better and accumulated no service demerits. The title of Roff's article describes its purpose: "Childhood social interactions and young adult bad conduct." He finds a historical difference between his good and bad service adjustment young man that is very significant: the "bad" young men, during their elementary school years, had poor relations with their peers—other children in their classes; the "good" young men had good relations with their peers. Lesser (1958) finds that overly aggressive boys are unpopular.

Menlove (1965) suggests that adopted children are more likely than nonadopted children to be aggressive. Menlove's study prompts the author to say some things that, to his knowledge, have no basis in solid facts or data: members of the human welfare professions (such as psychiatrists, clinical psychologists, social workers) almost seem to accept as an article of faith that adopted children have more problems than one's own children. This may be true in a statistical sense—as has been said, there are no sound data one way or another about the issue—but the author believes that, if such differences exist, they have little or nothing to do with the genetics-constitutions of the adopted children but rather to the attitudes and learning opportunities (particularly opportunities for emotional learning) provided by the foster parents. For some irrational reason—perhaps our middle-class or perhaps simply universal human beliefs and values—do parents who cannot have children in some way regard themselves as inferior to those who can? Even the most casual examination of population statistics demonstrates clearly that the ability to breed—to have one's own children—is associated with no other known socially desirable characteristic. If anything, the opposite is true: there seems to be a tendency for those less "fit" from an economic and perhaps a genetic point of view to have more babies than their more prosperous and intelligent counterparts. The whole issue belongs, the author believes, to the complex and ill-explored area of human emotions and self-concepts: its explanation (if the psychiatrists-clinical psychologists-social workers are correct) must eventually come from studies, not of people's intelligent and rational but their "gut level" behavior.

Matsushima (1962) finds that elementary school boys who score low on his test of emotional control are also impulsive and aggressive in their classes. He took these boys from their classrooms and set them to work in an experimental session which involved their working on a tedious task in the absence of the investigator. The aggressive boys, much more often than the nonaggressive boys, abandoned their task soon after the experimenter left and played with more attractive things in the experimental room, while the nonaggressive boys stuck with the job they had been assigned.

To illustrate the disruption to orderly society that results from unbridled aggression, the Louisville-Courier Journal (March 9, 1966) headlined a UPI story from Indianapolis: "For hundreds of Arlington High School students, there was no bus at the corner yesterday." Twelve bus routes had had to be canceled because of "vandalism, rowdyism and uncleanliness" on the part of the school-age passengers. The president of the transit system is quoted as saying "When those buses come into the garage . . . , they look like they've been hauling cattle."

These buses do not serve slum neighborhoods: "About 900 students live in the affected area of about four square miles, which encompasses a fashionable residential neighborhood." The present author is reasonably sure that this situation is not unique to Indianapolis.

To conclude this section, a cautionary note is added. The present author frankly admits and makes no apologies for his preference for explanations of human behavior that depend on *learning in a social context;* on the other hand, he knows that babies are *born* different. Anyone who has been the parent to more than one child or who has spent as much as a half hour observing the behavior of babies a few minutes to a few hours old knows that they are different from each other. Their differences, taking into consideration all the variables of difficult or easy maternal pregnancies and deliveries, surely cannot be accidental: they must have something to do with the babies' constitutional and presumably inherited predispositions: some babies cry a great deal, others are placid; some wiggle all over their bassinets while others are quiet even when awake.

The study of human genetics is perhaps even less well-advanced than the study of human behavior. Each is a new science. To document a differing point of view, it is necessary to resort to studies of animal behavior, where there is good knowledge of and control over heredity and learning opportunities. Two studies have been selected to illustrate the point. The first is Lindzey, Lykken, and Winston's (1960). They worked with four different, highly inbred strains of mice and administered to each of the different strains at four days of age (young, even for a mouse) a loud, high pitched, auditory stimulus. As "older child mice" (24 days) there were significant differences among the four groups in timidity (the opposite dimension to aggression). These differences lasted until the mice were adult (100 days).

Weir and DeFries (1964) offer similar evidence, also for mice. They put pregnant mice under stress. The offspring of the calm mother mice (the study was carefully conducted and controlled) as "child mice" were less bold (aggressive), presumably because of the treatment of their mothers, than would have been predicted. The behavior of the offspring of the timid mice were bolder than the control groups—thus bolder than would have been predicted.

Parenthetically, the study of animals offers interesting guidelines to those who work with humans. For one thing, we can study the influence of genetics among animals. We often cannot do this in any very scientifically rigorous way with humans. We can also control the environments of animals to a degree impossible for human subjects. On the other hand, mice, rats, and monkeys cannot talk and, if they use symbols—abstractions—at all, they do so to a limited degree. In other words, we obtain clues about human behavior from studying animals, but we are not at all certain that we can transfer our carefully established evidence about animals directly to humans, upon whom we can only perform less well-controlled genetic-environmental management studies.

Studies of children's fantasy play have generally shown that a second session of fantasy play in the company of a permissive adult reveals more aggression than the first. This increase in aggression has generally been attributed to the child's increased feeling of freedom to do what he wished to do. Some investigators (as Siegel and Kohn, 1959) believe that the determinants of children's aggression in any situation are a combination of the child's own need to be aggressive, his evaluation of and attitude toward aggression, the attitudes and values of other people in the situation, and his assessment of the likelihood of counteraggression on the part of others (particularly adults). These authors assume that our society consistently disapproves of open aggression. For this reason, they think, a child will construe an adult's *permissiveness* about aggression as actual *encouragement*.

As a partial test of their thinking, they took a number of pairs of boys and exposed half the pairs to two sessions of fantasy play in the presence of an unintrusive but friendly adult, the other half of the pairs to two sessions of fantasy play with no adult present. Every pair exposed to the adult-absent condition showed a drop in the amount of aggression from Session I to Session II, while two thirds of the pairs with the adult present showed more aggression in Session II. However, the over-all amount of aggression was approximately the same under the two conditions.

An alternative theory to account for these results is the following: Children are accustomed to having their parents assume considerable responsibility for their behavior, and this attitude toward their parents generalizes to other adults. The children with the permissive adult present felt "safe." That is, they could increase their aggressive play, feeling that if things got out of hand, the adult would "take over." The children with the adult absent, on the other hand, had to be responsible for the consequences of their own behavior, hence had to move from Session I to Session II in the direction of increasing aggression control. From this study, it cannot be said with any confidence which is the more appropriate explanation of the findings.

This aggression subsection, which includes a number of unusually well-conducted studies and thus lends itself better to a coherent set of conclusions than some of the other sections, leads first to the conclusion that aggressive behavior is not only "normal" but probably universal. Some animal studies suggest a genetic or constitutional basis for aggression. Observation of children shows that they differ widely in activity level, and it is quite possible that high-activity level children (perhaps because they are more often frustrated) may also be high-aggression children.

In our society, aggression is "circular." The child is aggressive, his parent or teacher retaliates, the child is further angered and frustrated and thus more aggressive, and so on. There seem few positive virtues attached to open, naked aggression in a cooperative culture. Aggressive young adults have been found to be unpopular as children, and over-aggressive children are also unpopular.

Boys usually show more aggression both in fantasy and "real life" than girls but these sex differences, at least in open or direct aggressive behavior, diminish or disappear when girls are certain that their aggression will go undetected.

Children imitate or model upon aggressive adults: thus the finding is reasonable that arbitrary and unreasonable methods of control and high levels of physical punishment are associated with aggressive child (and adult) behavior. However, children apparently construe parent or caretaker permissiveness about aggression as approval and, when so handled, are likely to be more aggressive than the average. It is quite possible that children *want* adults to help them control their aggressive behavior.

Persons low in self-esteem are more likely to react aggressively than those high in self-esteem. The best, or at least the most effective, ways of handling aggressive behavior seem to be diversion; appeal to motives other than hostility (such as need for friendship); and rational, explanatory methods of child control.

Effects of Infantile and Early-Childhood Deprivation

MATERNAL DEPRIVATION

Through the ages, mankind has been sentimental about the love of a mother for her child. The general public makes the tacit assumption that such love is universal (despite much evidence to indicate that there are brutal and rejecting mothers, that *smother* in contrast to *mother* love exists, and that even the best of mothers becomes mightily annoyed with her offspring). The assumption is also made by the general public that children cannot grow up normally without mother love. This assumption was formulated forcefully by Freud, and at present is generally held as an article of faith by child-psychology and developmental personnel.

What effects does deprivation of mother love have upon a child? It is certainly not necessary for a child to grow up with his *natural* mother. But what of the child who, for one reason or another, is separated from his mother or his foster mother after he has come to know and love her? What of the child who grows up in a relatively impersonal institution? If separation from or absence of a mother-figure is damaging to normal personality development, is it so at some ages and not at others, or at all ages?

It is to such questions as these that the present section is addressed. The effects of institutional or intellectually very barren environments on the development of intelligence in both children and animals are discussed in Chapter 8. Here it suffices to say that the evidence from research with children suggests strongly that poor environments (including life in institutions) retard intellectual development; good environments capitalize on it, and may even facilitate it. For animals, where more extreme environmental alterations can be produced, the evidence is even more convincing: environments of isolation retard "intellectual" development, and this retardation is lasting.

But, while granting that intelligence is one aspect of personality, this chapter concerns itself with topics more conventionally related to emotional development and adjustment. One of the earliest papers concerning the effects on infants of living in institutions was published by Lowrey (1940). A psychiatrist, Lowrey became concerned about the psychological state of a group of children who were referred to him. These children, twenty-eight in number, had been placed in a "model" institution when they were (with one exception) from 2 weeks to 11 months of age. Their psychiatric referrals occurred when they were between 2 years 11 months and 4 years of age. Their histories revealed that after leaving the institution, where model medical care had been provided, they had caught more diseases than would be expected of the general population. They also showed a high incidence of speech retardation, with poor vocabularies and more than the usual number of speech defects. They were frequently negativistic and had temper tantrums; they gravitated toward solitary activities and showed a fear of material possessions and were very frequently hostile. Their IQ's were lower than would have been expected from their family backgrounds, only one having an IQ as high as 115 and one being as low as 52 (almost down to the upper limit of low-grade mental deficiency).

Lowrey concluded that infants should not be reared in institutions. If institutionalization is necessary, babies should be provided with intimate, continuing, consistent contact with at least one adult so that they can develop techniques of socialization and channel their emotions in such a way that they will be able to handle later family living.

One of the most assiduous of the workers who have attempted to answer the question, "What are the effects of growing up without any consistent mother-figure?" (that is, of living in an institution), is William Goldfarb. Alone or with co-workers, he has published a number of papers, of which the study summarized here is representative. In this study Goldfarb (1945) first reviews some of his previous studies of children at ages 7, 8½, and 12. Each of these earlier studies had included rather well-matched (although small) groups of children. One group of children had lived in an institution until they were about 3 years old and had then gone to foster homes. The other group, after a very brief period of time with their own families, had gone into and remained in foster homes. The over-all findings at all three ages were consistent with one another, although different methods were frequently used, and are in agreement that the institution-reared group showed "a profoundly deviate personality type characterized by (1) marked impoverishment, meagerness and lack of differentiation in all aspects of personality, and (2) marked passivity or apathy of personality" (p. 20). Goldfarb states:

> Institution children were less secure, more isolated from other people, and less able to enter into meaningful relationships. They also showed more frequent speech retardation, school deficiency and mental retardation . . . the institution children were more retarded mentally and were considerably more immature in perceptual reaction and in level of conceptual performance. They also more frequently showed problems such as restlessness, hyperactivity, inability to concentrate, lack of popularity with children, poor school

achievement, fearfulness and excessive craving for affection. They were shown by experiment and case history to be deficient in drive and to be marked by an unusual degree of apathy or emptiness of emotional response. (p. 19)[4]

In the 1945 study, two groups of fifteen children were studied. There were nine boys and six girls in each group. The first group (institution children) were admitted at an average age of $4\frac{1}{2}$ months to an infant institution, and stayed there for almost three years, being placed in foster homes, on the average, at a little past 3 years of age. They were tested a little while before being placed in foster homes and again seven months later. The other group of children (foster children) had always lived in their foster homes. They were equated with the institution children for age, sex, age at admission to care, and age at first and second testing. The true mothers of both groups were similar in national origin. The mothers of the institution children were of a higher occupational but not educational level, and the true fathers of the foster children were lower socioeconomically.

On the first and second tests the institution children averaged 68 and 76 IQ respectively. The foster children tested significantly higher: 96 and 102 on the first and second tests respectively. Language development tests were also used, and the foster children scored higher than the institution group in intelligibility, language organization, total language score, and vocabulary. The groups did not differ from each other in motor development nor, on the first test, on the Vineland test of social maturity. But on the second test (perhaps because of their difficulty in adjusting to foster homes) the institution children dropped in score from 100 to 89, whereas the foster children raised their social-maturity quotients from 103 to 109 from the first to the second test. A score of 100 on the Vineland is considered average for United States children. The difference between the two groups on the second test is statistically significant.

Goldfarb concludes from these studies that the foster children have better contact and relatedness with the external world; have more will to meet and reorganize experience with the external world; and are superior to the institution children in "the richness and maturational level of personality as expressed in imaginative and conceptual competence and even in the more primitive levels of perceptual reaction" (p. 30).

In another study, Goldfarb (1944) examined the records of forty children with continuous foster-home experience and forty who, from infancy, had lived in an infant institution for about three years. At the time of study, the two groups were 7 years 7 months and 7 years 8 months

---

[4] Reprinted with permission of C. B. Farrar, Editor, *American J. Psychiat.*, and W. Goldfarb, from Goldfarb (1945).

respectively. They were matched for sex, age, age of admission to care, and years of dependency. Only one of the first group had had to move from a foster home at any time because of unacceptable behavior, whereas twelve (30 percent) of the second, or institutional, group had been forced to move from one to three times for such reasons. Goldfarb states that the institutional children showed aggressive, hyperactive syndromes, peculiar or bizarre syndromes, or emotionally unresponsive syndromes.

Spitz (for example, 1945, 1946) has published a number of studies dealing with similar topics. He has found institution babies to be massively retarded in scores on a measure of infant adaptive reactions. Considering the fact that good medical care was provided in the institution he studied, there was an extremely high rate of death from all causes, including contagious diseases such as measles—which, although serious, do not frequently kill their victims. Spitz also reports that his institution babies were very retarded in motor development, even in such things as learning to sit alone, to walk, and so on (although Goldfarb's institution babies were reported to have normal motor development). Extreme lack of attention, Spitz believes, results in an infant disease called *marasmus,* which is literally a listless withering away into death. According to Spitz, babies separated in about the middle of their first year from their mothers suffer from depression and frequently go on to develop serious mental disease.

Spitz's studies have attracted wide attention. An initial phase of uncritical acceptance of the dramatic results he reported has been followed by increasingly critical reviews of his methods, data, and form of reporting, culminating in so devastating a series of critical articles and replies (Pinneau, 1955a, 1955b; Spitz, 1955) that there is currently a danger of throwing out the baby with the bath. Spitz's is by no means the only evidence we have to indicate that barren environments of all sorts, including large and impersonal infant hospitals and traditional orphanages for young children, blunt the development not only of the human organism but of simpler nonverbal organisms such as rats, mice, dogs, and monkeys. There is some evidence to indicate that these effects are very long-lasting, the evidence for animals being more convincing than that for humans. Spitz maintains that such damage is irreversible. The findings of other authors (as Pasamanick, 1946; Rheingold, 1956) seem to suggest that when the situation is altered, babies regain at least much of their lost ground. However, animal research indicates that prolonged and severe environmental deprivation early in the life of the organism produces lasting interference with both intellectual and emotional responses (see Chapter 8).

What may be involved here is a phenomenon known as *imprinting,* or critical periods, which have been observed with some species of animals.

In imprinting, if these animals do not have the opportunity to observe and practice behaviors typical of their species at an appropriate developmental phase (usually very early in their life), they seem never to acquire them but to behave, insofar as they are able, in a way similar to the species with which they had their earliest experiences. Beach and Jaynes (1954) present an interesting summary of research in this area. Gray (1957) has reviewed the literature concerning children reared in isolation, or in very deprived circumstances. He concludes that imprinting occurs with humans (a possibility that has intrigued many people), and that it is effective from about the sixth week to about the sixth month. The sixth week, he argues, is the time of first socialization. It is at about this time that babies begin to make elementary "social" responses, such as smiling, and can be conditioned (see Chapter 4) fairly stably. The sixth month is the approximate age when fear of strangers and animals begins. Such theories are interesting and should be followed up by research, but at the present time they remain speculative.

The *critical periods hypothesis* differs from imprinting in that it refers to less specific types of behavior, and acquiring this behavior over a longer period of time. While a goose may imprint (develop in very specific ways the attributes of his "foster parents") in one or a few days, a critical period refers to a span of time during which a more general class of behavior (intelligent behavior, for example) must be acquired. Traditional Freudians seem to consider the critical period for character-personality development as the first 5 or 6 years of life. As mentioned earlier in this chapter, evidence exists suggesting that a critical period for developing clear articulation is between about 3 and 8 months.

The present author is skeptical about the concept of imprinting as an explanation for behavior of such complicated organisms as humans, although there is no doubt that it occurs in neurologically simpler species. He is open-minded about the possible power of the critical periods hypothesis in explaining human development.

John Bowlby (1952), writing for the World Health Organization, made a survey of literature in the area of maternal deprivation and from it concluded that certainly before the age of 2, and probably before the age of 3, any severe deprivation of maternal care, whether this took the form of physical absence or psychological rejection, damaged the personality development of the child. Testing this prediction four years later (Bowlby *et al.*, 1956), he studied the adjustment of a group of forty-one boys and nineteen girls who had been separated from their families for periods ranging from a little less than five months to more than two years, at various ages up to 4 years, because of pulmonary tuberculosis. About half of them experienced separation from their families before the age of 2 years. Since there were from forty to sixty children in residence at a time, the sanatorium had not provided them with substitute-mothering. These children were compared by Bowlby and his colleagues with a group of nonseparated controls who were in the same classes in school. At the time of the study the children were between 7 and 13 years of age.

There were few significant differences between the separated and the nonseparated children either in intelligence or in teachers' ratings of their adjustment, although on all scores the sanatorium children showed up less well than the nonseparated youngsters. For example, the average IQ of the sanatorium children was 107, that of the controls, 110. Those children who had been institutionalized before the age of 2 had an average IQ of 102, whereas those who had gone in after 2 averaged 110. This difference is significant statistically, but it is not of great practical importance.

A few of the teachers' ratings differentiated significantly between the two groups. The sanatorium children did more day-dreaming, showed less initiative, and got overexcited and rough in their play. Their attention was more likely to wander. They were also timid about competition, or seemed not to care how they compared with other children.

This study cannot be said to support Bowlby's earlier conclusions strongly, although where differences between groups were found, they favored children growing up consistently in one family.

In one study (Beres and Obers, 1950), thirty-eight young people were studied psychiatrically sixteen to eighteen years after they had been discharged from an infant hospital. They had originally been placed there when they were from 2 weeks to 23 months of age, and had remained in the hospital until they were from 18 months to $4\frac{1}{2}$ years old. Twenty of them were judged to have personal difficulties of an extreme sort, including mental retardation, psychosis, and neurosis, although eighteen were apparently adequately adjusted. In view of the findings of Lowrey and Goldfarb, it is surprising to find almost half of the young people normal; on the other hand, considering the fact that the children were physically normal, the percentage of disturbance is high, being much above that in the general population.

A British report on 277 children separated from their families for any of a number of reasons and received into a diagnostic and treatment center after some form of public care (Lewis, 1954), states that 51 percent were severely disturbed and 36 percent mildly disturbed emotionally. Of children received into the center from their own homes, 44 percent were severely disturbed, 30 percent moderately disturbed. The percentages of children manifesting *some* disturbance, then, were 87 and 74, a difference which is statistically significant. Lewis makes a number of analyses in an attempt to determine if and at what age separation from the mother produces emotional maladjustment, and concludes that lasting separation before 2 is the only type of separation that can be shown to be deleterious in and of itself. Early separation, according to Lewis, is not noticeably related to what such authors as Goldfarb have called emotional coldness and apathy; the most frequent type of emotional disturbance shown by these children was overaggressiveness.

All the studies reviewed so far in this subsection support, at varying levels of confidence, the proposition that institutional living in infancy is damaging to the personality and intellect of the child. If institutional living is thought of as "isolation," studies of animals reared in isolation (as reported in Chapter 8) lead to the same conclusion.

But research is a complex matter, and one study in the area stands out in flat disagreement with the others. In fairness to readers it must be summarized, although it cannot be explained. Orgel (1941) studies sixteen children who apparently came from the same institution reported on by Lowrey, whose study was the first to be mentioned in this subsection. These youngsters had entered the institution soon after birth, and had gone to foster homes when they were between 3 and 4 years old. Orgel reports that twelve of them adjusted easily, with only minor difficulties. Two had trouble in their first placement, but adjusted easily in a second placement. Their adjustment problem, Orgel believes, was due to the foster parents' impatience. Two others had serious and long-enduring problems and "had to be treated through the environment of the foster home before they adjusted" (p. 372). Orgel concludes: "I could see no evidence of these children being unprepared for or unequal to the demands of a family setting. On the contrary, the great majority readily accepted and met the demands made upon them by the family settings, in spite of the almost constant interference of the majority of the natural parents" (pp. 372–373).

The subject of maternal deprivation is one of serious and justifiable concern to almost everyone from the "garden variety mother" to professional workers ranging from judges and other representatives of the law to workers in the health and welfare fields.

Several general treatments of the subject (as well as general child care) are available. Since they are easily accessible to the reader, no attempt is made here to summarize them. Alphabetically, good summaries and discussions have been provided by Ainsworth (1962), Caldwell (1964), Casler (1961), Clarke and Clarke (1960), Hoffman and Hoffman (1964), Nye and Hoffman (1963) who concern themselves with the employed mother, a condition which may or may not be an aspect of maternal deprivation, Waters and Crandall (1965) who emphasize social class and maternal behavior, but relate it to deprivation, and Yarrow (1961).

Casler's review is an example of clear methodological analysis and constructive criticism. He suggests that the ills so clearly presented by children without adequate mothering may have no relation to "mother love" at all, but to lack of adequate (and perhaps appropriate) sensory stimulation. Such a possibility was explored in the section on sensory development in Chapter 1. H. F. Harlow (for example, 1959a, 1959b) appears to agree that both *mother interaction* and *socialization with peers,* or other young monkeys, contribute to normal simian development.

A different type of "maternal deprivation" as well as father absence has been investigated, but without arriving at really clear-cut results. For example, Rabin (1959) and Spiro (1958) report on the adjustment of children living in Israeli *kibbutzim;* that is, "institutions" staffed generously with well-trained personnel—a well-trained *metapelet* or "housemother" is in charge—to provide child care so that the parents are free to go about the intensive work necessary to reclaim the harsh and long neglected face of Israel, particularly its agricultural face. Parents typically spend generous amounts of time daily with their children, and the children usually go home with them on nonwork days. Rabin reports that children living in *kibbutzim* regard their families more positively than those living at home. This is plausible: their interactions with their parents are all "fun." The *kibbutzim* personnel bears most of the brunt of the often harsh realities of day to day routines and training. *Kibbutzim*-living girls, compared with those living at home, showed less positive attitudes toward their fathers, while *kibbutzim* living boys, comparatively, were more positive toward their mothers. There were no differences in attitudes of the experimental (*kibbutzim*) and control boys toward their fathers, or girls to their mothers. The youngsters studied by Rabin ranged from about 9 to a little more than 11 years old.

Spiro presents observational data, rather rough from a scientific point of view. His conclusions are not firm—he reports many problems at all ages, but concludes that the children eventually turn out all right. The present author, however, was uneasy as he read Spiro's book: the children, particularly the little ones, seemed more disturbed and upset than groups of children of the same age the author knows and has known. They seem to develop a remarkably close affiliation with peers (which is not surprising). Assumption of roles of independence, helping others, fair play, and justice is apparently made by the typical *kibbutzim* child earlier than we find in United States children living in nuclear homes (with father, mother, brothers, and sisters).

Clarke and Clarke give a more sophisticated definition of deprivation than most authors. They refer to social isolation, cruelty and neglect, institutional upbringing, adverse child-rearing practices, and separation experiences in about that order of severity of influence on the child. An additional, general factor of socioeconomic and cultural deprivation, they believe, should be added to their list, probably second or third in importance. They mention sensory deprivation, but only in passing.

From his experience (based on a continuing series of studies now in progress at Indiana University under the direction of Walter L. Hodges, Boyd R. McCandless, and Howard H. Spicker), sensory deprivation in the sense of an insufficient amount or number of stimuli seldom exists in the homes of the psychosocially deprived, borderline intelligence 5-year-olds who form the subject population of the Hodges, McCandless, Spicker studies. Rather, the problem seems to be one of overwhelming but undifferentiated stimuli: too many people in too little space, TV sets blaring indiscriminately, lack of organized and orderly meal times, lack of opportunity to converse in depth or variety with either brothers and sisters, parents, or other adults, cluttered houses (there is too little space to put up things), and other such factors. Fitting in with this observation is a study by Kellmer, Pringle, and Bossio (1960), who find that effects of early and prolonged separation from parents and residence (in institutions for most of the children) showed up most dramatically in vocabulary and reading (these are language deficits, and we learn language only when we have the chance to practice it in a wide variety of reasonably well-organized settings). Their subjects were 8- to 14-year-old children. They also report more general maladjustment on the part of their separated than their fairly well-matched control (living at home) children.

In summary of this subsection, it must be noted that there is some conflicting evidence about what happens to babies as a result of separation from their mothers, if this separation results in their being placed in an institution of the traditional type. The bulk of the evidence supports the conclusion that such placement is emotionally and intellectually severely damaging to the child. Studies of animals reared in isolation, later to be reviewed, indicate that simpler organisms, too, suffer from lack of normal stimulation and interaction. Relatively prolonged ill effects are also suggested by most of the research on this topic. Whether such effects are due to separation from the mother as such is a moot point. They may result from lack of appropriate perceptual stimulation, and (at least for human babies) from lack of opportunity to learn dependency, to resolve it, and to channel emotions so as to live harmoniously with others.

When institutions *must* serve babies, pains should be taken to assure that environmental stimulation and close, intimate, and tender personal relations with adults are provided.

Infant and childhood deprivation is not a simple concept: it may refer, not simply to the lack of a mother, but to social isolation, cruelty and neglect, institutional upbringing, adverse child-rearing practices, separation practices, severe economic and cultural deprivation, and lack of or inappropriate stimulation.

Existing evidence also suggests early adoption for infants who are to go to foster parents. Lynch and Mertz (1955) summarize data for forty-five babies placed directly from nursing homes when they were between 7 and 20 days old. The results of such early placement were considered excellent. The mothers who were willing to release their babies early seemed to be more genuinely concerned about the welfare of their children than the mothers who opposed early release. The foster parents were delighted to obtain their babies early, and the babies themselves turned out well. The authors suggest that many so-called gray placements (that is, other than through an established social agency) result because the natural mothers do not want their babies in intermediate foster homes (or, presumably, infant institutions).

LACK OF FATHERING

Little research has been done on the interaction of fathers and their children. One reason for this is theoretical: the assumption is frequently made, implicitly or explicitly, that it is the mother who has the major effect on early personality development and the father's role is relatively unimportant. At best, this assumption is dubious: In many sections of modern United States society, fathers interact a great deal with their children from birth, and often share with mothers all phases of child care.

The second reason for the dearth of information about the role of fathering is that it is more difficult to get research cooperation from fathers. Because they work during the day, the research worker must do his work on evenings and week ends. Fathers are justifiably reluctant to devote their leisure time to being guinea pigs. It may also be that fathers are less interested than mothers in the area of child development, hence less willing to serve as research subjects.

However, research done by Lois Meek Stolz and co-workers (1954) includes fathers, mothers, and children as subjects. This team of workers was interested in the effects of paternal absence during babyhood on the later adjustment of children. They secured the cooperation of nineteen families in which the fathers had been away from home (in the armed services) at the time of the children's birth and for at least eleven months thereafter. The time away from the children following their birth ranged from eleven to thirty-three months. At the time the study was conducted, the "first-born children" on whom it concentrated were all at least of preschool age, and some were in the early years of elementary school (up to and including second grade). The attitudes, practices, and emotional adjustment of these fathers, mothers, and children were contrasted with fairly well-matched control groups of families from which the fathers had never been away for a substantial period of time after the children's birth.

According to this study, the war-separated fathers had looked forward with mixed feelings (including apprehension) to vocational rehabilitation after the war (all were college students at the time of the study), to earning a living and to being a husband, but few had planned their new relationships as fathers. Coming back into the home, they found themselves resenting the child who had "usurped" much of their wive's love and affection. The children themselves were frequently shy, distant, or resentful of the strange new man who had come into the home. The most frequent role played by the fathers was that of disciplinarian: their complaints were that the child was too dependent on the mother, not well-trained in routines, not "manly enough" (when the child was a boy). At the time the children were studied, the fathers were relating more naturally and easily to children who had been born into the family subsequent to their return than they were to their first-born children.

The children themselves showed some personality damage when compared with youngsters whose fathers had not been separated from them. An association with the fathers' absence rather than with other factors is suggested by the fact that there were no differences between the groups of children studied in such factors as conditions associated with pregnancy, labor, and childbirth; nor in child-rearing practices related to the children's organic needs. But the war-separated children had been harder to train in their routines, and were reported to have poorer relations with other children that the nonseparated youngsters. This factor of reported poor social relations was substantiated by the investigators through actual observation of the children in their social groups. It was observed, among other things, that the war-separated children were more likely to be fringers and onlookers. They were also observed to have greater difficulty in acting naturally and easily with such adults as their teachers; and they seemed to be in conflict between being extremely obedient, on the one hand, and openly defiant on the other. The war-separated youngsters were also believed to be more anxious, and to show more serious fears and more tension patterns. The boys seemed somewhat more distant emotionally from their fathers than the girls.

This study presents clearly a picture of difficulties occurring for both fathers and children as a result of the father's absence—difficulties that had not been resolved within the period of several years following the father's return to the home. The problems uncovered appeared to result from a complex family interaction that hinged upon the absence of the father; in other words, they were due more to complications in human relationships as a function of absence than to absence as such.

Lynn and Sawrey (1959) studied the effects of father absence in a population of Norwegian boys and girls. The fathers of half the group (twenty-one boys, nineteen girls) were sailors of officer rank who were away from home at least nine months of the year, often as much as two years at a time. These children, all in the second grade and between 8 years and 9 years 6 months of age, were matched with twenty boys and twenty girls whose fathers were consistently at home on such factors as whether they lived in town or in the country, mother's age, number of brothers and sisters, their own position in the family, teachers' ratings of intelligence, and father's status in the community. To be considered equal in prestige to a ship's officer, the fathers of the control group had to be at an occupational level involving supervision of others—for example, shop owners, high civil servants, or office managers.

Judgments about the children's adjustment to their peers and the boys' *compensatory masculinity* were made from interviews with the mother. A child was assumed to be compensating if, for example, a mother described her son as acting in an exaggeratedly masculine way, but also related instances of his behaving in a fashion more characteristic of girls than of boys.

The children were also given a Structured Doll Play test. In this test, dolls are placed in a series of typical family and age-mate situations. The child is told what the situation is, and is asked to resolve it through doll play. For instance, he is presented with a crib and a bed, and is told that the little boy has two places where he can sleep, and that either is all right. He is then asked to put the doll to sleep. After that, he is asked which of his parents will come in, and what will happen. On the basis of his resolution of a series of such situations, each child was given a score for maturity, frequency of father choice, reaction to separation (after separation, which parent was chosen to return to the doll figure—presumed to represent the child), and dependency.

In general, Lynn and Sawrey's five predictions were supported, usually quite clearly. More father-absent than father-present boys showed immaturity. The father-absent boys, presumed to be insecure in their identification with their fathers, showed stronger strivings toward such identification. More father-absent boys were judged to show compensatory masculinity, and to be less well-adjusted in their peer relations. Father absence produced few differences between the father-absent and the father-present girls, except that the father-absent girls, perhaps because threatened by the absence of one parent, showed more dependence on their mothers than the father-present girls. This was not true of the boys.

Another study (Bach, 1946), conducted with children between the ages of 6 and 10, shows that boys whose fathers had been away from home from one to three years behaved, in a doll-play situation, more like girls than boys whose fathers had been in the home consistently. In other words, a possible problem of appropriate sex-typing appeared.

Bach also found, among his twenty subjects, two boys and two girls whose mothers, during long interviews, were consistently derogatory in the picture they painted of their absent husbands. The mothers of two other boys and two other girls were as enthusiastic about their husbands as the first group was negative. When the doll-play behavior of these two groups of children was compared, the children of the negative mothers showed many more fantasies in which the father in the doll-play situation was aggressive to the doll children, and in which he was *generally* aggressive. On the other hand, they showed the doll children more often yearning for affection from the father than the children whose mothers talked favorably about their husbands. Bach, plausibly enough, believes that the attitudes of the mother influence the way the child thinks of his absent father. However, it is possible that the mother *and* the child see the father as he really is. The study offers no information on this latter interpretation.

Siegman (1966) used the technique of "anonymous confession" to uncover "delinquency" histories of a sizable group of first year medical students (a rather frank, honest, and realistic group, as far as the present author knows them). He found fifty-one whose fathers had been away from home for at least one year during their early childhood, when they were between 1 and 4 years of age; and compared them with a group of eighty-nine young men whose fathers had stayed consistently at home. Siegman found that objectionable behavior fell into two major categories: antisocial behavior and parental disobedience. For the latter, the young men whose fathers had stayed consistently at home did not differ from the young men whose fathers had been away for a long period: one group was as likely as the other to do such things as cheat on school examinations, defy their parents to their faces, and use profane and blasphemous speech. But, when antisocial behavior was involved— that is, the sort that is likely to get a youngster in *real* trouble—the father-absent boys were more delinquent than the father-present boys. The most significant items in Siegman's antisocial behavior scale were truancy from school, damaging or destroying private or public property, having premarital and extramarital sex relations, and theft of property or cash ranging from $2.00 to $50.00. Implications for the caretakers of children are obvious.

Siegman suggests that father-absent boys are more likely, perhaps because in their very early years they had no man to model (copy) but were expected to act like "little men," "young boys frequently show exaggerated masculine behavior, which in fact is no more than a reaction against a basic feminine identification" (p. 71). Boys with fathers absent are perhaps more likely to do this, as is also suggested by Lynn and Sawrey, than boys with fathers present. Siegman suggests that father-absent circumstances may lead the young boy to confuse "being good" with being feminine; to be masculine, he must be "bad." The present author agrees with Siegman when he says, "This 'masculine protest' theory of antisocial behavior leads to the prediction that all factors which tend to produce strong identification with the mother, and failure of early identification with the father, also tend to produce antisocial behavior" (p. 71). In other words, if dad is at home during his son's early childhood, he may get just as much lip from Junior as if he had been absent for a long time, but on the other hand Junior, with dad absent, is more likely to do something which, if he were caught, would result in serious (probably legal) trouble.

Carlsmith (1964) conducted an interesting study on the effects of father separation on patterns of boys' intelligence. Typically, we find that boys do better than girls on tests of "intelligence" involving math, but less well or at least no better on tests that emphasize verbal reasoning, vocabulary, and so on. She uses as her criterion of "maleness" *math score higher than verbal score.*

She worked with a number of different samples of high school and college youth (most of the college boys were from Harvard) and, with each sample and usually at a statistically satisfactory level of significance, found that boys whose fathers had been away from home during their childhood because they were in the service showed "feminine" patterns, while those whose fathers had remained regularly in the home showed "masculine" patterns. Her data indicate that the younger the boy was when his father left home and the longer the father stayed away, the more feminine was the boy's test pattern.

Martin Deutsch (personal communication, 1966) reports that, among the predominantly lower-lower social class families whose psychosocially deprived children he is studying, boys from families with the fathers present average about 8 points higher in IQ than boys from father-absent homes.

A study by Winch (1959) reported later in more detail, suggests that boys whose fathers have been absent are less vigorous—less "male"—in their courtship patterns than boys who have had consistent fathering.

From results of a series of studies being carried on by Hodges, McCandless, and Spicker mentioned previously, while they do not have final data at the time this book is being written, it seems obvious to them that their 5-year-olds who lack consistent father figures in the home almost desperately seek attention from any male they can find who gives them even so much as a nod. This appears to be much less typical of boys from intact families. Stephens (1961) asked social workers to characterize boys from families with and without fathers (those are rather anecdotal data). The fatherless boys were more often judged to be anxious about sex and to be more effeminate.

Nash (1965) has published an excellent survey of "The father in contemporary culture and current psychological literature." Like the present author, he concludes first, that fathers are "here to stay!" That is, fathers play a genuinely important role in the normal development of their children and probably one more important for their sons' than their daughters' development. Like the present author, Nash deplores the paucity of evidence in this important area of children's development and family living as well as the poor quality of much of the research that has been done. For example, fathers' behavior (as was true in the Sears, Maccoby, and Levin, 1957, study) is often, perhaps usually judged from interview with the mother *about* the father rather than directly from the father. This can be very misleading: some wives see their husbands through a rosy glow, while others take a very dim view of them. Nash also points out that "There is, indeed, evidence from studies of homosexuality to support a hypothesis that maternal affection, in the absence of strong psychological ties to the father, can actually have effects on the boy's development which are undesirable in terms of our culture" (p. 289). He also points out the sharp contrast of United States society "to certain primitive societies with a family cooperative economy, which have typically a way of child-rearing which emphasizes the father-son and mother-daughter relationships" (p. 292).

Research summarized earlier in this chapter in connection with the discussion of aggression (Pauline Sears, 1951) has demonstrated that preschool boys (3-, 4-, and 5-year-olds) whose fathers are absent from home show fantasy patterns that are different from those of boys whose fathers are with them: they are more girlish, less aggressive. It is of course possible, though none of the studies cited was designed to probe this relationship, that the effect of separation from the father varies according to the age at which the separation occurs.

Fathers' presence, then, seems to play an important role in the development of their children, particularly their sons. Children whose fathers had been away from home at the time of their birth and for about a year or more thereafter were less well-adjusted on a number of scores than children whose fathers had been consistently at home. This maladjustment appears to have been related to complex interactions between father, mother, and child after the father's return—the child feels threatened by the stranger; the father, expecting immediate love from the child, finds that he must "win" the youngster; and so on. The fantasy play of boys whose fathers were absent for prolonged periods during preschool or early school years has been found to be less masculine than that of boys whose fathers were not absent.

A study of Norwegian children whose fathers were away from home a large percentage of the time provides results closely in accord with those obtained for United States children: boys were affected more than girls; and, compared with boys whose fathers remained at home, boys were more immature and less secure in identification with their fathers. Some evidence suggests that "father-absent" children, particularly boys, suffer unusual difficulties in social relations with their peers.

The Personality Pattern of the Family

Becker *et al.* (1959) conducted one of the few studies that concern themselves with both fathers and mothers. They charted extensively the characteristics of the families of twenty-five children who were not in need of clinical services (for behavior problems) and of the families of thirty-two children who were in need of such services. The children were between 6 and 12 years of age at the time of the study. The parents were of Caucasian extraction, and were living together. The groups were quite well-matched on variables other than the children's adjustment.

Factor analysis of the data indicated that the maladjusted children fell into two major groups. For purposes of convenience, the authors labeled the first of these the "conduct problem" group, made up of children who manifested uncontrollable or highly aggressive behavior. The second group was called the "personality problem" group. Its members showed such symptoms as shyness, undue sensitiveness, and feelings of inferiority. Both labels, of course, reflect personality problems, but they are applied in accordance with a widely used classification of children with behavior disturbances: those who act out their unhappiness (conduct problems); and those who "take it out on themselves" (the personality-problem group). They might also be called the "attackers" and "withdrawers."

Becker and his colleagues found that the parents of the conduct-problem group, typically, were maladjusted and inclined to be arbitrary with their children, and were themselves likely to give vent violently and unpredictably to their emotions. The mother was likely to be active and tense, very free with suggestions, dictatorial, and thwarting. But the fathers, apparently rather withdrawn from the situation, tended not to enforce regulations. Such a situation, obviously, can easily become a vicious spiral: the mother frustrated by the father, becomes shriller and shriller; the father, frustrated by the mother, withdraws more and more; and the hapless child is left in the middle, with an antagonistic parent on the one hand and a nonsupportive and withdrawn one on the other.

For the group of children with personality problems, the role of the father appeared to be significantly more important than that of the mother. None of her behaviors was particularly related to such symptoms; but the fathers were revealed to be maladjusted and thwarting of the child.

The authors conclude their study with the following statement:

"The many important associations between father and child behavior lead to the conclusion that future research, and perhaps therapeutic practice, should *give more consideration to the role of the father in child development*" (p. 117).

Peterson *et al.* (1959) report an apparent extension of this study and summarize their findings as follows:

> Personality problems seem largely independent of maternal attitude, but related to dictatorial attitudes and a lack of genuine concern among fathers. Conduct problems are related chiefly to maladjustment among mothers and to democratic attitudes and heightened feelings of parental concern among fathers. Both parents appear overpermissive, and characterization of the fathers of children who present conduct problems as generally weak and ineffectual may not be far wide of the mark. Democratic qualities are esteemed in our culture, but when they are combined with laxity, unwillingness to issue orders, exaggerated concern for children, and a tendency to shelter them in the fact of day-to-day problems the seeds of conduct disorders may be sown. (p. 126)[5]

In another study (Liverant, 1959), personality-test data from forty-nine sets of Caucasian parents of children referred for psychiatric help were compared with the test data of forty-nine carefully matched parents of normal children. Most of the families were lower middle-class people.

On the personality test (the Minnesota Multiphasic Inventory, usually referred to as the MMPI), the fathers of the disturbed children showed up as more concerned with body complaints and illness; they were gloomier in their outlook on life, yet at the same time appeared to be less mature and more impulsive; and they were more tense and anxious. The mothers, too, were more impulsive and less mature, and more depressed and anxious. They laid blame on other people for their problems, were less honest, and were inclined to act out their aggressions and unconventional impulses.

Although these findings are based on a paper-and-pencil test and do not directly represent real-life behavior, they fit well enough with the results obtained by Becker and Peterson and their colleagues.

All three studies, then, suggest that disturbed fathers and mothers have disturbed children. Children who might be described as "attackers" have mothers who are dominating and demanding, fathers who are unusually lax and withdrawn. The mothers of "withdrawers" do not differ as a group from the mothers of nonproblem children, but their fathers

---

[5] Reprinted with permission of W. E. Martin, Editor, *Child Develpm.*, and D. R. Peterson, from Peterson *et al.* (1959).

appear to be more dominating and restrictive. There are some indications that, for boys at least, it is best to grow up in relatively low-conflict homes where the father is dominant.

There exists in the literature a group of studies concerning the child-hood family patterns of men who later became schizophrenic—perhaps the most serious of the emotional illnesses. As a group, these are known as the "Duke Studies," although most of the authors have now moved to other universities. The studies are, on the whole, among the best in the literature on family relations and personal adjustment. They are too numerous and detailed to summarize here. This book is also focused on normal child development, and is in no sense intended to be an abnormal or clinical psychology volume. However, it is appropriate to select one of the Duke Studies for review. While some nit-picking can be done, the virtues of the study so overwhelmingly overshadow its flaws that it will be taken as it is without adverse comment.

From the Duke studies, and used in the one discussed here (Farina, 1961), a pattern of good and poor premorbid adjustment of schizophrenic males emerged. In other words, some of the schizophrenics (good premorbids) had been married before they became ill, had had good social relations, their illness had come on them more suddenly, and their chances of recovery were better than apparently equally sick men with poor premorbid histories (not married, few friends, gradual onset of disease). Significantly more of the good than the poor premorbids had come from homes where the father was reported or observed to be dominant. Farina tested this hypothesis carefully in an ingenious experimental study (his article is fun to read because his procedures are clear and clever, they are fully enough reported that others can repeat them if they wish, and his reporting is clear and open).

With unusually closely matched mothers *and* fathers of good and poor premorbid schizophrenic men, and a control group of parents of men patients with tuberculosis (some have linked tuberculosis and schizophrenia; the tuberculous patients, like the schizophrenics, had been in a hospital and away from their families for some time; hence, this is a good choice of control group). For seven indices of parent dominance (such as, in a potentially controversial situation, whether the mother or the father spoke first, which one talked the most, which one yielded the point at issue), the father was more dominant. In four of the seven, the difference between the mother and father was statistically significant. The pattern was not particularly clear for the control parents: usually they fell somewhere between the good and premorbids and *if* it is better for normal male development for fathers to be dominant, then in each case they should logically have been more dominant than the good premorbid families. Farina also obtained nine indices of conflict between the parents. All nine of these showed more conflict between the parents of the bad than the good premorbids, although this difference reached a satisfactory level of statistical significance for only three indices. In eight of the nine indices, the parents of the tuberculous patients showed less conflict than either the good or bad premorbid schizophrenics' parents, and nine of the possible eighteen comparisons were statistically significant.

Summary

This chapter summarizes the literature on the effects of child-rearing practices in the five areas in which all parents, regardless of their cultural affiliation, interact with their children. The areas are (1) elimination and toilet training; (2) orality and feeding; (3) sex and sex training; (4) dependency and dependency training; and (5) aggression and aggression training.

Research in the area of child-rearing practices includes an undue proportion of all the faults of psychological literature discussed in Chapter 2. Another of the problems in studying child-rearing practices is the failure of many and perhaps most authors to realize that a family is a two-way street: the parent affects his child, but the child also affects his parent. The second of these effects has been all too seldom considered in the literature. Families are extremely complex and dynamic structures: one may include a widowed mother and an only son, another be the typical two parent family with their three children, and a third consist of economically deprived parents (or a single parent) struggling to rear ten or more children in crowded and harried circumstances.

Regardless of the age of the child, there are advantages to the caretaker's knowing something about theories of child development and knowing a great deal about the infant and preschool history of the child under his care. Theories may provide guidelines for effective management of children handled in specific ways. Thus, either the theory or the information about how children are reared before they enter school may be of real practical value.

Also, in the hope of pointing the reader in a practical direction, the general styles of child-rearing in lower- and upper-class West Pakistani families were described. The question was raised about the effects on cognitive style, personality, and character of children such as those in the U.S.S.R. whose education, from their earliest years, is inextricably intertwined with a relatively monolithic and single-minded political philosophy quite foreign to students in democratic societies.

No solid conclusions emerge from the studies of orality and feeding practices. The best generalization we can make is that the mother does best who does what she and the subculture to which she belongs believe is right for the child. We have no conclusive evidence about whether breast feeding, for a long or a short time, is better than bottle feeding; whether early weaning has advantages over late weaning; whether feeding from a cup is better than the sucking-type feeding. There *does* seem to be some indication that unscheduled feeding (that is, feeding the baby when he is hungry rather than according to a firmly fixed every-four-hour type of feeding) is at least easier than scheduled feeding and that babies not fed by schedules do at least as well and probably better than those fed according to rigid schedules. This matter was one of interest and dispute several years ago. Questions about it now seem largely to have disappeared from public interest. For reasons of convenience if not others, most babies are fed according to at least a modified self-demand (nonscheduled) pattern. Mothers with neurotic tendencies probably have more trouble with their children's eating than better-adjusted mothers.

Perhaps because babies are older, thus can "register" child-rearing effects in a more measurable way, the results for anality and toilet training are somewhat clearer than for orality and feeding. However, it is probable that it is not toilet training *per se* that makes a difference to a child, but a whole set of severe parental-child managing practices that accompanies harsh toilet training. The experts recommend that toilet training not be begun until the child can sit up (maintain postural control) and express his needs either by gesture or words. For the average child, this is sometime well along in his second year of life. American mothers, according to a 1965 to 1966 study, seem to be moving in their practices in the direction recommended by the experts. It is also fairly well-established that the earlier toilet training is begun, the longer training takes. Children are more upset by severe than gentle toilet training; and harsh toilet training and the stern general disciplinary practices that typically accompany it seem to slow children down in their motor development. Mothers most successful in toilet training their children tend to be anxious about sexual matters, but toilet-train mildly and give considerable warmth to their children. The least successful mothers are also anxious about sex, but are severe and cold toward their children.

We know almost nothing about sex training children in the United States and other countries. Mothers permissive in the sex area tend to be permissive in other areas of child-rearing. While mothers in the United States are nervous about sex training (surveys show that about two thirds of American families would like to turn over-all sex education to the schools), they do not seem to take many harsh measures about it. Most sex training seems to be accomplished by diversion and modesty training.

In regard to *dependency,* 5-year-olds in the American culture are generally rather independent youngsters. This varies from culture to culture, and is probably related to toilet training. In societies where the youngster can eliminate waste material anywhere in the wilderness, without causing any inconvenience to himself or others, he will gain independence. Accompanying this freedom will be the chance to play, explore, and perhaps learn to cope with danger. The most independent boys see their fathers as strong but passive. Independent males also see their mothers as strong—the family apparently presents a solid and effective front.

Aggression, probably because it is so much more conspicuous and troublesome (to caretakers and society at large) than dependency, receives more research attendance than dependency. Evidence about child-rearing circumstances is clearer for boys than girls. (However, recent research suggests that when girls believe that their aggression will not be discovered, they are about as aggressive as boys.) Insecure people seem more likely to react aggressively to situations than those who are sure of themselves. Aggressive behavior is best avoided by diversion, introducing motivations other than anger-aggression, and by rational explanation. It has also been argued that raw and open aggression in our society hurts both the individual and those involved in his aggression: the child is aggressive, others behave aggressively in return, he becomes more aggressive, and so on. Boys whose fathers have been away for extended periods during their runabout-preschool years report more antisocial behavior than those whose fathers have been consistently present.

The best summary of "effects of infantile and early-childhood deprivation" that can be made is that the literature has neglected the role of fathers and the total family constellation. Not enough research has been done on such factors as social isolation, too little and too much (particularly inappropriate) stimulation, institutional upbringing; when and if and at what age the child was separated from his parent(s), poverty and cultural deprivation, and cruelty and neglect. The literature is consensual that each of these factors is at least temporarily detrimental to the child's development.

Fathers have "come into their own" only in recent research. Freud (at least by implication) gave them little importance, as far as their influence on children in their preschool years was concerned. Freud seems to have been wrong. Little boys suffer from prolonged absence of their fathers more than little girls. With their father gone for some time during these formative years, boys are likely to behave either in feminine or overly and inappropriately masculine (tough) ways. If their mothers mediate a good image of the absent father, this effect may be minimal (evidence on this point is scarce). Father-absent boys seem also to be more anxious and concerned about sex than father-present boys.

It is superfluous to add to this summary the conclusions from the literature that "disordered" families produce disordered children.

Learning
and Motivation

CHAPTER 4

The premise of this volume is that the processes fundamental for explaining human behavior are *learning* and *motivation*. The two cannot be separated from each other. Theories of learning are complex and, relative to other areas of psychology, well-developed. The research literature is vast. For such reasons, this chapter is schematic; it is intended neither as a survey nor a synthesis, but as a guideline laid out to clarify earlier and later sections of the book.

Many intriguing questions are raised in preceding and following chapters. Why, and through what mechanisms, does the sense of smell enter strongly into many emotionally charged behaviors, such as those labeled sexual: Literature on *classical conditioning* makes suggestions concerning this. What are the mechanisms through which deprivation in infancy slows intellectual development in human and animal babies? Ideas concerning *learning* to *learn* are relevant here. Why do studies on toilet training present clearer conclusions than those done with younger babies concerning feeding and weaning practices? Research on *verbal mediation* suggests the reasons. Why do children in some sections of the United States decline in intelligence as they grow older, and why are children of some socioeconomic strata less intelligent than those from other strata? Research dealing with the *effect of reward on learning* contributes suggestive answers to these questions.

This chapter, then, contains a schematic outline of concepts that underlie the development of human personality and intellect. These principles should be applied retrospectively to the literature on child-rearing practices and their effects and should be kept in mind as research on intelligence, physical growth, and socialization, sex-typing and iden-tification, is introduced. For each of these topics, the principles of learn-ing provide useful ideas for organizing research findings, instituting new research and, in a practical way, guiding children's development.

Any person who works with children should, ideally, have thorough training in learning theory and research. Lacking such training, he should do as much reading in the area as possible. Most good general psychology textbooks include a treatment of learning. As a supplement to this chapter, the beginning student might, for example, read the chapters on learning in Kimble (1956). Kimble's treatment is simple, but comprehensive. Mednick (1964) has also given us a short, easily read, sound treatment of learning.

Maturation and Learning

DEFINITIONS OF MATURATION AND LEARNING

Although learning has been stressed throughout the discussion of material to this point, no attempt has been made to define it, nor have general principles been provided by which it may be understood. Growth (for example, changing in height and weight) does not involve learning but relates, rather, to the concept of maturation. By *maturation* is meant development of the organism as a function of time, or age; maturation refers to neuro-physiological-biochemical changes from conception to death. Chapter 1 should have made it clear that, at least in a sense, *learning* opportunities may accelerate what has traditionally been thought of as "pure" maturation. The fetus is more mature than the embryo; the 18-month-old is more mature than the newborn baby; the 14-year-old more mature than the 6-year-old.

Increased height, weight, and strength, then, are in part the result of maturation (time and nutrition). But organizing these maturational phenomena so that performances previously impossible for the child can be accomplished involves *learning*. A baby sits alone partly because he has grown or matured. His head, in proportion to his torso and legs, is smaller; his back muscles, in consequence of both maturation and exercise, are stronger. As he has grown, he has practiced constantly. He has reared up from his stomach, using his arms as props; he has practiced balancing his head; he has used his legs. While lying on his back, he has tried to pull himself up by his hands and arms. Presently, he puts these separate learned skills together and a new behavior, the effect partly of learning, partly of maturation, results; he sits up alone.

Learning, then, involves the acquisition of new skills, such as sitting up, talking, walking, or dropping one of two toys in order to pick up a third that is more interesting. It also includes acquiring new meanings. Nothing will long prevent the 2-month-old from screaming when he is hungry, except the nipple in his mouth. But the 6-month-old will quiet for a few moments at the sound of his mother's voice, or the sight of her preparing his bottle. As the bottle approaches him, he stops crying and reaches for it. The 3-year-old will calm, when he is in the mood, for a considerable period of time because of his parents' statement that dinner will be ready in about ten minutes. These new meanings are themselves skills of a concept-formation type: they are methods of understanding and manipulating the environment and oneself. They lead not only to learning to do new things, but to learning *not* to do old things: not to behave in ways that lead to pain or disapproval. Tendencies to approach the stove, for instance, disappear early, although it is a rare child who does not get burned at least once before he learns to keep away.

Child and adult lives are full of such learning: to *do* things and *not* to do things; to *approach* or master, and to *avoid*. Learning, then, refers to the acquisition of new skills, meanings, and orientations, including avoidances and simple *not doing* what one has once done.[1]

Perhaps as good a definition of learning as any other is the following: *Learning* is a change in performance as a function of practice (see McGeoch and Irion, 1952). It should be remembered that learning not to do can be just as positive a "performance" as learning to do. Behavior effects due to fatigue are not learning, although they may affect learning.

How does learning differ from performance? Learning can be considered as something that goes on, or exists, inside the skin of the human or animal. So defined, it is not available for measurement. Reduction in the amount of reward given for a task often results in reducing the efficiency of *performance* (reduces output). However, this need not eliminate *knowledge* of what is correct. In this volume, learning and performance are considered as closely related to each other, although it is granted that they are not identical.

ROLE OF MATURATION AND LEARNING IN BEHAVIOR

Much research has been done to determine the relative contribution of maturation and learning to human development. *Maturity* is the *physical* readiness to learn, including both neurological and muscular maturity. One does not, for example, try to teach a 3-month-old how to walk, nor an 18-month-old how to read. They are not mature enough; they are not ready for the developmental tasks of walking and reading.

Research on the relative importance of maturation and learning has provided few facts of value to psychology, whether psychology is considered as a *science* or as a *method of understanding children*. The effects of maturation and learning cannot be separated from each other, any more than one can break up H_2O and still have water, or demonstrate that hydrogen is more important to water than oxygen. However, maturation-learning research has important implications for practice. If maturation is considered paramount (and much traditional treatment

---

1 This kind of learning should be distinguished from fatigue, which may be thought of as not doing something or doing it more slowly because one is *tired*.

gives it such importance), the role of learning is minimized; if learning is considered paramount, the role of maturation is neglected. Because of these practical implications, the traditional logically rather pointless research dealing with maturation *versus* learning should be discussed.

Few if any 3-month-old infants, regardless of the opportunity given them to practice, can sit alone, because they have not reached the necessary level of maturity. Their heads are disproportionately large and heavy compared with their torsos; their neck muscles are not yet strong enough to balance their heads; their back muscles are weak. But most normal 8-month-olds can sit alone, partly because of normal growth (maturity), partly because of practice, the rewarded result of which is learning. Spitz (1945) has shown that the 8-month-old, denied practice, does not sit by himself as a result of maturation in the partial absence of learning opportunity.

Dennis (1940) reports that Hopi Indian infants from the American Southwest who are confined to cradle boards learn to walk, when eventually given the opportunity, as early as other Hopi infants who have been reared without cradle boards. Since the latter, presumably, have had more opportunity for exercise and practice, Dennis concludes that maturation is more important than learning in motor development.

This research must be examined critically. Even the cradle-boarded Hopi infant has used *some* musculature (cradle boards include kicking room). He has been taken out of the cradle board at intervals for cleaning; and, because of the way he is carried, he has had much experience in balancing his head and using his arms and shoulders. He has seen other children walking and may have built up imitative tendencies, so that he is as ready to go, when he is released from the cradle board, as is the hypothetically more experienced unconfined baby. Indeed, the baby reared in the cradle board may have had more opportunity to observe the world around him than his ostensibly freer peer, since the cradle board makes it easy for his mother to take him with her wherever she goes. He has also had more experience with vertical posture. Because of his confinement, he may have developed more motivation to get out on his own than the baby whose activity drives have presumably been less blocked. Seldom or never having been separated from his mother, he may be psychologically more secure, hence more ready to strike out on his own. Even in this interesting piece of research, then, there has been no conclusive testing of the independent effects of maturation and learning on the development of a skill. Dennis has later changed his mind (Dennis and Sayegh, 1965), probably as a result of his work in an infant institution in Lebanon. He concludes, at least implicitly, that if infants cannot practice (learn), "maturation" is retarded (see Chapter 1, this book).

Several experiments (for example those of Gesell and Thompson,

1929; Hilgard, 1932) have sought to depict effects of maturation as distinguished from learning, using as subjects identical twin girls, *T* (for trained) and *C* (for control). This method of study is known as the *method of co-twin control*. It involves giving one of a pair of identical twins a certain type of experience, and delaying training for the other member of the pair. Since identical twins have identical heredities, differences in their eventual performance are assumed to be due to learning. If no differences in performance result, the assumption is made that identical heredities have resulted in identical maturational processes, which override the effects of differential learning.

On a number of different tasks, such as stair-climbing and fastening button strips to buttonhole strips, twin *T* was exposed early to the task, while twin *C* was given training later. After a time, during which twin *C* was also allowed to practice, the performance of the two girls on the task was measured. Few, if any, differences were found, despite the fact that twin *C* had had much less total practice. In general, it was concluded that maturation was more important in development than learning. That some learning *did* occur is indicated by the fact that, for at least a short period of time, *T* was superior to *C*.

The design of these studies neglected the factor of motivation. By the time *C* started her practice, *T* may already have been bored with the task, while *C* was intensely interested. Rivalry may have entered the picture to some degree. Finally, no amount of practice on a task for which the child does not have the appropriate physical equipment and coordination will help him to master it.

Another well-known pair of twins, not identical, were Jimmy and Johnny. The psychologist who worked with them (McGraw, 1935) exposed one twin early to experiences such as tricycling; the other twin was given such opportunities much later. Then, as with twins *T* and *C*, differences in performance were measured. Again, after the control twin had had a relatively brief period of practice, negligible differences were found between the boys (although, obviously, the experimental twin had learned and had experienced temporary superiority over his sibling). McGraw also concluded that maturation was more important in development than learning.

Although the logical error of such studies has been pointed out, their conclusions have been interpreted as implying that one can minimize opportunities for children's learning, since maturation will take care of the developmental process. This interpretation ignores the fact that more subtle results of early and late teaching have been neglected in studies such as those cited. How, for example, were interpersonal relations between these two pairs of twins—*T* and *C*, and Jimmy and Johnny—affected? What may have been the effects of early exposure to routine tasks on twin *T*, whose sister, meanwhile, was going free? How did *C* react to having her sister *master* certain skills before she was allowed the opportunity even to *practice* them? McGraw's experimental twin was trained to master such exciting aspects of his environment (as tricycles) before the control twin. How did this affect Jimmy's and Johnny's self-concepts, and their relations with each other? The only bit of evidence we have about later personality differences is Gesell and Thompson's report (1941) on the personalities of twins *T* and *C* at adolescence: *C* seemed to be more creative and flexible; *T* more methodical, less imaginative, perhaps more practical.

Today, discussion of maturation versus learning, or heredity versus environment is a little like beating a dead horse: all modern scholars realize that the two are intertwined and that (for humans, at least, with all the controls we must exercise in our research) their differential effects can never be clearly separated.

Some current books on child development give the classical but limited maturation-learning studies much attention and promulgate firm conclusions that, in the present author's judgment, are not firmly grounded on recent research. It is for this reason that he devotes more attention to their discussion in this and later chapters on intelligence than he thinks is necessary, except for practical (not scholarly) reasons.

Conditioned Responses

THE CLASSICAL CONDITIONED RESPONSE

It is widely accepted, and will be accepted here, that the simplest—perhaps the most primitive—form of learning is the *classical conditioned response*. The assumption is made that many of our automatic, persistent, emotion-laden responses, such as elation in spring and depression in February, develop through classical conditioning.

The first formal laboratory demonstration of the classical conditioned response was made by Pavlov, a Russian physiologist. He showed that, after a bell had been presented repeatedly in conjunction with food, dogs responded to the bell presented alone in about the same manner as to food. Response to the bell alone was considered to be the *conditioned response* (CR), and the bell was called the *conditioned stimulus* (CS). Since, at the beginning of training, sight (and perhaps smell) of the food produced a salivating response, food was called the *unconditioned stimulus* (US); and the response (in Pavlov's early work, the measure of response was the amount of saliva excreted) was designated as the *unconditioned response* (UR).

Figure 4.1 schematizes the presentation of the conditioned stimulus (CS), illustrates its temporal relation to the unconditioned stimulus

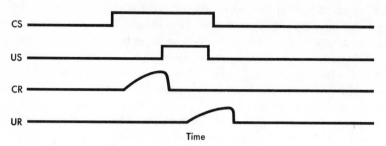

Figure 4.1 A schematic representation of the classical conditioned-response experiment. Time is represented along the horizontal lines. Departures from the horizontal line represent the presentation of conditioned and unconditioned stimuli and the occurrence of conditioned and unconditioned responses.

(US), shows that the unconditioned response (UR) follows the US temporally and that, following training, the very similar conditioned response (CR) occurs (but earlier than the UR).

Research on classical conditioning with humans is less complete than with animals, but for both circumstances favorable to developing conditioned responses seem to be the following, all of which are schematized in Figure 4.1: CS sets on before US is presented, and continues very briefly (a fraction of a second) after US ceases. At the beginning of conditioning, US is already associated with UR, and almost invariably produces it (food elicits salivation in dogs; electric shock is reacted to by withdrawal). US may be thought of as providing motivation: food appeals to the hungry animal; electric shock is painful, and the tendency is to withdraw from it. US is always presented whether or not UR (or CR—the distinction between them is difficult to make) results.

CR, once established, is likely to differ from UR, although it is designed to accomplish the same purpose (obtaining food, escaping shock). CR appears sooner after the onset of CS than does (or did) UR. Finally, CS loses its power to evoke CR unless it is occasionally coupled with *primary reinforcement* (in this illustration, food or shock). The "loss of power to evoke" is called *extinction*, and is probably related to forgetting.

The graphic pattern by which a conditioned response is usually considered to be acquired and extinguished is shown in Figure 4.2.

The ordinate of Figure 4.2 represents the percentage of trials on which CS elicits CR. Since one of the characteristics of CR is that it precedes UR in time, it is an *anticipatory response*. The most common measure of conditioning is the counting of anticipatory responses, although some measures such as salivation do not lend themselves readily to this procedure. CS can also be presented without US to see whether

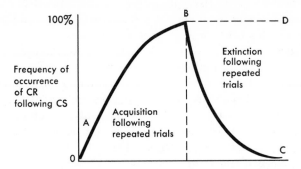

Figure 4.2 Typical pattern of growth (acquisition) and extinction of a classical conditioned response.

it evokes CR; but in this case, each test is also an extinction trial, so that acquisition is slowed.

As can be seen from Figure 4.2, learning hypothetically begins at zero. That is, the bell alone does not originally result in salivation (or, in the case of shock, withdrawal). Gradually, CS acquires power to elicit CR, as shown by the section of the curve between points A and B. The horizontal line, or abscissa, of Figure 4.2 represents the amount of practice that has been given. At point B, learning levels off or reaches its *asymptote,* usually at less than the 100 percent level of the power of CS to elicit CR. At point B in Figure 4.2 the experimenter stops presenting US with CS. Gradually the power of CS to elicit CR disappears (as a function of such extinction trials). Presumably, the experimental subject begins to stop regarding CS as a signal that food is in the offing. Finally, at point C in Figure 4.2, CS fails altogether to elicit CR, and *extinction* of the conditioned response is said to have occurred. The rising curve between points A and B represents the process of acquiring the conditioned response. The curve for extinction is an approximate inverted mirror image of the curve for acquisition.

It is not necessary, either for humans or for animals, to present CS without US to produce extinction. Presentation or adventitious occurrence of stimuli similar to CS, hence having much the same effect, may accomplish the same purpose. In children and adults, but not animals, verbal or other symbolic representations of CS may also result in extinction. The mental rehearsal of a painful experience may, for example, partially reduce its potency.[2] This is another illustration of concept formation.

[2] When conditioning starts from zero, the shape of the acquisition and extinction curves is usually considered to be S-shaped. The question of shape is important in developing further theory, but does not concern us here.

Some evidence (Estes, 1944) indicates that an animal must have experiences with CS and its attendant CR in the absence of US (the primary reinforcer) for CS to lose its power. The same thing may hold for children *before they acquire symbols* (which they can use to rehearse, thus to extinguish conditioning). In the absence of practice, the persistence of conditioned responses in very young infants for as long as seven months has been noted. Thus, one might speculate that if a conditioned response is established and the experimental subject subsequently goes for a long period of time without again experiencing CS-CR, then CS may indefinitely preserve its power to elicit CR. This is illustrated by the dashes between B and D in Figure 4.2.

This interpretation has interesting implications for the practical handling of children, pointing out as it does for the need to practice *unlearning* (extinguishing) maladaptive responses as well as *learning* adaptive ones. It is conceivable that stimuli associated with some trauma in infancy, if not re-experienced and adapted to, may years later evoke the same unfortunate emotional responses with which they were originally associated.

Such tentative theory gives a certain foundation to the advice that children be allowed to express reactions such as fear and hate, even when these are inappropriate, so that they may be extinguished. In a warm, relatively permissive, democratic atmosphere the child feels free to exhibit a wide range of behaviors, "good" and "bad," helpful and harmful to him. His parent or teacher then has an opportunity to help him consolidate or acquire firmly the adequate or adaptive behaviors and to extinguish the inadequate or maladaptive ones. Without an active process of *unlearning,* it may be that the maladaptive behaviors and feeling persist indefinitely. Such reasoning at this stage of our knowledge is speculative, but it is plausible and potentially useful educationally.

Classical conditioning appears to be an automatic process, and seems to depend neither on insight nor on more than the most elementary nervous system or intelligence. Indeed, there is some evidence (Munn, 1954) to indicate that it is difficult to produce classical conditioning in older children and adults, particularly when UR is subject to their voluntary control (as is true of responses involved in hand or finger withdrawal from an electric shock). Some have interpreted this resistance to classical conditioning on the part of older children and adults as distaste for being placed in a situation where they must learn against their will: they fight against learning. Perhaps, also, one must possess language if he is to resist classical conditioning. An older child has available cues that he can put into words immediately, saying, in effect, "The shock has stopped (or is intermittent). Why should I bother to respond to it?" Through such a mental set or intent or development of a concept, he can inhibit *voluntary* responses, although classical con-

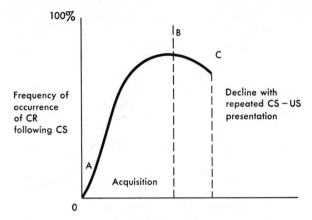

Figure 4.3 A schematic representation of the decline in power of CS to elicit CR when CS and US are paired together after learning has been established.

ditioning of *involuntary responses,* such as the eye-blink, is easily accomplished with both adults and children.

Evidence is clear that conditioning occurs early in life. Munn's summary (1954) indicates that sucking, blinking, limb withdrawal, respiration, crying, general activity, galvanic skin response (electrical conductivity of the skin), and fear reactions can, during infancy, be conditioned to tactile, visual, and auditory stimuli. However, a baby must be hungry (drive or motive must be present) before conditioning of the sucking reaction is possible. Newborn infants can be and have been conditioned, although their reactions often lack stability. Research from many places (see particularly the Brown University Studies, mostly published in the 1960s, by Lipsitt and others) consolidate our conclusions that much infant learning, including classical conditioning, occurs in the first few days of life. Some of these studies are discussed in Chapter 1. Conditioned responses in older infants are usually more stable than those of the newborn. Such responses have been maintained over periods ranging up to seven months. Spontaneous recovery (temporary reappearance of CR) occurs following partial extinction training. The curve of extinction for conditioned responses (particularly feeding, which has been studied most) approximates a mirror image of the acquisition curve. Finally, continued presentation of CS and US together, after conditioning has been established, may result in a decrease in the frequency of CR.

This last point requires more explanation. The decrease in frequency of CR following repeated presentations of the paired stimuli US and CS is represented in Figure 4.3. This figure is analogous to Figure 4.2.

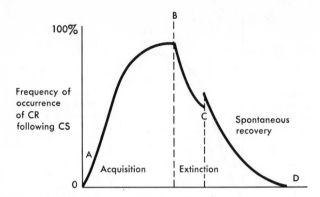

Figure 4.4   A schematic representation of spontaneous recovery during extinction training.

The percentage of test trials on which CS produces CR is represented by the curve between points A and B. The decrease of which Munn speaks is represented by the curve from points B to C. By the time point C has been reached, a considerable decrease in frequency of eliciting CR by CS has occurred despite the fact that CS has been followed in every case by US. Why should this drop occur? Why does CS lose its power even when it continues to be associated with reward?

At least two factors are necessary to explain this. In some instances the reason may be reduction in drive. If a small amount of food (US) is given for each learning trial, the animal or infant becomes less hungry with each trial. We know that eliciting CR depends on drive or motivation, such as hunger. Hence, the lower the drive, the less likely the response is to occur. Even when the drive or motive is pain avoidance, and US is electric shock, reduction of drive through repeated trials may occur because the individual in the experiment becomes adapted (or accustomed, or relatively insensitive) to shock of the intensity being used in the experiment.

A second factor that may help to reduce the power of CS to elicit CR is fatigue. The more times a subject practices a response, the more fatigue accumulates and detracts from the likelihood or probability of the occurrence of the response. This fatigue factor is probably largely responsible for Munn's conclusion above concerning spontaneous recovery (see Figure 4.4).

Figure 4.4 is partially familiar. The curve between points A and B represents acquisition of the conditioned response, and the curve between B and C represents the beginning of extinction as we have seen it in Figure 4.2. However, extinction training has been interrupted by a rest period at point C. On the resumption of extinction training after rest, the frequency of CR in response to CS increases temporarily, although the continuation of extinction training reduces it to approximately zero power at point D. This increase in power at point C is probably due to the fact that fatigue has been dissipated, leaving CR with a greater probability of occurrence than immediately before rest. Many have had the experience of changing from a car with a standard gear shift to one with an automatic shift or *vice versa,* as stick shifts, particularly on foreign cars, are once again somewhat popular. At the beginning, driving the new car is accompanied by almost automatic manipulation with the left foot and leg to find the clutch that is not there. At the end of the first long practice session, the clutch-pushing reaction is almost extinguished. But after a night of rest the reaction comes back again, although not as strongly as at first. This reappearance after partial extinction is known as *spontaneous recovery.* Old ways of doing things are always cropping up in our everyday life. Spontaneous recovery is at least partly responsible. Many children's errors in school-work are due to this.

Although studies of classical conditioning with human infants and children have been less extensive and less rigorously controlled than the experiments with animals (the Brown University Studies, see Lipsitt and co-workers, are probably an exception in terms of excellent controls), they indicate that conditioning in infancy and early childhood follows approximately the same patterns and laws as it does with animals. Many of the responses of older children and adults also seem, at least superficially, to belong to this *family*[3] of the conditioned response, with all its primitive, automatic, preverbal associations. Our disgust at the sight or smell of vomit or feces is not an intellectual but a frequently violent, somatic, apparently automatic response. It seems plausible that the sight and smell, for instance, of vomit (CS) have been associated in early childhood with the stimuli of nausea (US) and the UR of vomiting. Our adult reactions of disgust and even gagging or vomiting are the persistent conditioned responses that have resulted.

More pleasing behaviors may be thought of in a similar way. For the adult brought up in a temperate climate, the smell or sight of a flowering apple orchard (CS) evokes responses of relaxation, pleasure, and well-being (CR's). As a child, he may have associated the smell of apple blossoms with warmth, space, and fresh air (complex sorts of US), and the unconditioned responses of muscular freedom and comfort. Even in an urban flat in February, the odor of apple blossoms may evoke some of the pleasant responses associated with spring. It may be hazarded that many of the responses such as those associated with smells, tastes, half-caught vistas or faces of strangers belong logically, although in complex fashion, to the family of the classical conditioned response. Much adver-

---

[3] Speaking of "classical and instrumental conditioning families" is loose, or popular, talk. Pure scientists will not accept such terms.

Figure 4.5   Sequence of instrumental conditioning.

tising is based on the evocation of such old CS-CR connections; and much social usage (for example, the use of perfumes) depends on their existence.

Of course, in these illustrations, hundreds of separate conditioned stimuli and responses exist, but the over-all process appears to belong in the classical conditioned-response category.

INSTRUMENTAL CONDITIONING

A second, superficially more complicated, type of learning is called *instrumental conditioning.* In one of the simplest forms of instrumental conditioning, an animal—typically, a white rat—is confined in a cage with a trip bar. Pushing this trip bar provides a pellet of food for the animal.

In instrumental conditioning or learning an animal or a child does *one* thing to accomplish *another.* In the case cited above, he pushes a bar to receive a pellet of food. The pushing of the bar is the conditioned response (CR); the food he obtains is the unconditioned stimulus (US). Eating the food (or salivating in its presence) is the unconditioned response (UR). The bar itself, plus his own internal sensations, is the conditioned stimulus (CS) and the animal's learning task is to utilize this stimulus as a sign that if CR is performed, US will present itself and UR can occur. Figure 4.5 diagrams this process.

The learning (or establishing the conditioned response) seems to occur by trial and error. CR occurs first by chance during the time when, for example, the white rat is exploring the box into which he has been placed. However, it is common practice to attract his attention to the bar by smearing it with food. This is equivalent to giving a child instructions on how to proceed in a task, and is designed to shorten the learning process by orienting the subject properly to the work at hand.

A *gradient of reinforcement* appears to operate in learning, so that the behavior most relevant to securing the reward or escaping the punishment is most reinforced. In the first stages of learning, this applies to behavior made in closest proximity to delivery of US and performing UR. In the case of the rat, the responses most relevant to US-UR are to remain in the vicinity of the trip bar and to manipulate it (particularly the latter).

Reinforced less strongly or not at all is behavior that is far distant in time or space from the US-UR event, such as exploring the side of the cage opposite the bar. Probably the subportions of the larger response that originally tripped the bar are more strongly and precisely reinforced (in part because they require less effort) than the gross original response. For example, it might be that the rat originally tripped the bar by climbing on it, but eventually his behavior is streamlined so that he trips it, with minimal exertion, with his paws.

A young rat the author recently observed had just begun to learn to toss a ping pong ball (almost as big as she was) into a basket about 8 inches from where the food pellet, which was her reward, was delivered. Her learning was talented, thus unusual: her delivery of the ping pong ball was done by fancy left hook. She was still rather mixed up between her method (means—CR) and her goal (US-UR—eating the food pellet). After making a successful basket, she was as likely to explore the basket and the ping pong ball as she was to go directly to the food delivering machine.

With more practice, she will undoubtedly stop making her fancy left-hook shot in favor of a simpler method of putting the ping-pong ball through the hoop. She will no longer stay around the basket or the ping-pong ball after a successful shot, but go in a beeline to her pellet of food. In other words, she will streamline her behavior as a function of the *selective* function of drive discussed later in the drive-motivation section of this chapter. Her behavior illustrates some things about children and adults: in new learning situations, we are not quite sure which is means (CR) and which is end (US-UR or goal). We often become so interested in the technique (CR) that at least for a time we lose sight of the goal (US-UR). The present author may be unduly cynical, but he thinks something of the kind has happened in the area of modern mathematics—the technique has become more important than the goal of easy, rapid, and accurate manipulation of numbers.

After an animal has learned the initial conditioned response—bar-pushing—he can be taught to acquire still other refinements of learning, such as to push on the bar only when a light is shining or a bell ringing. This is accomplished by rewarding him (giving him food) when he pushes the bar while the light shines or the bell rings, and not rewarding him for pushing the bar at any other time. This type of learning is one form of *discrimination learning*.

Differences between classical and instrumental conditioning are obvious. CS is present at all times in the example of instrumental conditioning given above, and the animal is free to approach or ignore it as he wishes. This gives him more control over the situation than is afforded in classical conditioning, since he can determine the interval (amount of time) between CS and CR-US-UR. The frequency and number of responses or trials and the time between them are also up to him rather than the experimenter. US (food) results *only* when CR (bar-pushing) occurs; CR resembles UR little or not at all; and the CR-UR sequence is not forced as in classical conditioning.

With so many variables open to control by the subject, it is obvious that classical conditioning is somewhat more efficient as a highly controlled demonstration of learning; but that instrumental conditioning is a valuable technique for the study of motivation in addition to learning.

It is possible, at the risk of overgeneralizing, to move from the simple situation of the rat in the cage to the more complex behavior of human beings, from instrumental *conditioning* to the more complex case of instrumental *learning*, which has much in common with it.

Let us assume a small boy, Tommy, aged $3\frac{1}{2}$ years. This small boy attends a nursery school, in the yard of which is a tree that includes a tempting fork 4 feet off the ground, in which Tommy wishes to sit. This tempting fork may be thought of as the unconditioned stimulus; sitting in it, as the unconditioned response. But there is no direct way to reach the fork: it is too high; the tree trunk is too thick for Tommy to climb. A conditioned response is called for to help him achieve US and obtain satisfaction from UR. He sees a ladder (CS) on the other side of the tree and climbs it (CR), reaches the tree fork, sits in it, and looks around him like a prince on high (UR).

Such behavior, though made up of multitudinous conditioned responses, both classical and instrumental, follows the pattern of the instrumental conditioned response. Because of its complexity, however, it is better referred to as *instrumental learning*. Most of our daily behaviors have arisen in this fashion: we use forks or chopsticks in order to *eat,* good manners and flattery in order to *secure warm responses* from others, and work in order to earn the salary to *pay our rent.* In other words, instrumental learning has a goal-oriented or purposive nature apparently lacking in classical conditioning, or behaviors that belong in the classical-conditioning category. It, rather than classical conditioning, is probably the foundation of cognitive styles, concept formation, and most human learning.

Stimulus Generalization

PRIMARY STIMULUS GENERALIZATION

The simplest form of transfer of training consists of the application of a response or set of responses originally evoked by one stimulus to another

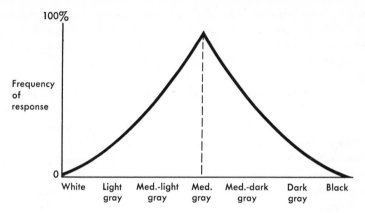

Figure 4.6 A schematic representation of primary stimulus generalization.

stimulus or stimuli. If a person is trained to push a telegraph key upon the presentation of a medium gray stimulus and a slightly lighter or darker gray stimulus is presented to him, he is likely to press the telegraph key. But if a white stimulus or a black one is presented, there is less likelihood of his responding. Such *generalization* is due to the physical similarity of the stimuli and, in a sense, is a function of the subject's "confusion" (failure to discriminate) about what is and what is not the stimulus to which he has been trained.

Figure 4.6 is a schematic representation of the *primary generalization* gradient. It shows that response probability is greatest for stimuli much like the one used in training and decreases steadily with decreasing similarity of the test stimulus to the original.

The generalization model shown in Figure 4.6 is negatively decelerating in both directions from the stimulus for which training was given (that is, the curve descends in a shallow concave shape from the peak response to the original stimulus). As is true of learning curves, there is disagreement about the shape of the generalization curve, or gradient. Although this disagreement has implications for complex psychological theory, it does not concern us here. The actual shape of the generalization curve probably varies according to the method used to test for generalization; the amount of training that has been given on the "correct" stimulus (apparently, the greater the training, the wider the generalization); the intensity of the stimulus (the more intense the stimulus, the wider the generalization); very possibly the type of stimulus (the shape of the curve from medium to bright stimuli may differ from that for medium to dim stimuli, for example; or the shape of the curve for colors may conceivably differ from that for sounds, lights, and so on).

There are some not entirely consistent data showing that younger children generalize more widely than older ones (Mednick and Lehtinen, 1957). This finding has an interesting, although frankly speculative, bearing on the notion that childhood experiences (learnings) have more widespread effects than similar experiences or learnings at a later age.

GENERALIZATION TO COMMON ELEMENTS

If one has been trained to press a telegraph key to an outline of a square with three sides drawn in red and one in black, it might be predicted that the same response is more likely to occur with another square having two sides or one side drawn in red than with one all four of whose sides are black. In other words, the more elements complex stimuli have in common, the more likely it is that the same response will be made to them. Our hypothetical subject will probably also be more likely to respond to a circle drawn half in red, half in black, than to an all-black circle.

This type of generalization has not been much studied, but the gradient of generalization from an original stimulus to one having *many* elements in common with it, then to another with a *moderate* number of elements in common, and to another with *few* common elements, would probably resemble that in Figure 4.6.

SECONDARY GENERALIZATION

Secondary generalization refers to the process involved in making similar responses to stimuli that, objectively (in terms of primary stimulus characteristics), are different from each other. Such words as *gorgeous, pretty, beautiful, winsome, lissome, attractive* all convey, at least to the masculine reader, the notion of a girl who has substantial "social stimulus value." But these words have little in common with each other in terms of *primary* stimulus generalization. Their similarity is *learned* whereas, for all practical purposes, primary stimulus generalization can be considered innate.

Secondary generalization is a particularly useful concept in understanding human behavior. Independently, or in combination with primary generalization, it appears to underlie the ability to transfer learning in one situation to another that may, in terms of objective characteristics, be very different. The principle of secondary generalization is basic to our generalizations, principles, and classifications, providing guidelines for cognitive, planned behavior, and a foundation for cognitive styles and concept formation. It will be more fully developed in the next chapter.

The secondary stimulus generalization gradient probably resembles

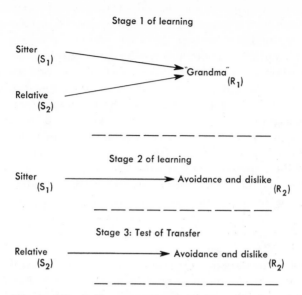

Figure 4.7 A diagrammatic illustration of a case of verbally mediated generalization, exemplifying an account in the adjacent text.

that in Figure 4.6; but instead of physical stimuli (such as a range of stimuli from white to black), *meanings* are the basis for generalization. Mule, for example, is more similar to *horse* than *chicken*.

MEDIATED STIMULUS GENERALIZATION

At a colloquial level, *mediated generalization* can be defined as secondary generalization in action. When two concepts, or words, or any other stimuli have acquired, through training, the capacity to evoke a common response, and another response is then learned to the first of them the second, although never directly trained or "attached" to the new response, will tend to evoke it (see Figure 4.7) when a test is made.

An anecdote that illustrates the real-life importance of mediated generalization concerns a small boy left with an elderly baby-sitter, who insisted that he call her "Grandma." She was a pleasant-appearing, bespectacled gray-haired woman, who proved to be an unsuccessful baby-sitter. By the time his parents came home, the child was bitterly unhappy.

A month or so later, the little boy's glamorous and youthful-looking grandmother, whom he had not seen for some years and had forgotten, came to visit and was introduced to him as "Grandma." His reactions were chilly. Indeed, it was days before he would make a friendly gesture toward her or respond to one offered by her. The process responsible was, of course, verbally mediated generalization. To one lady, who had given him a bad time, he had learned to apply the term "Grandma." "Grandma," applied to another lady who came into his home, mediated to him the whole complex of unhappy associations he had had to the first grandma, and produced the same responses of dislike and avoidance.

In other words, although he had never had unpleasant experiences with his real grandmother, the experience with the baby-sitter who insisted on being called "Grandma" transferred, through learned meanings, to his real grandmother. The concept "Grandma" included two ladies; and the sentiments and reactions learned to the sitter (S_1) transferred via words and their associations to the real grandma (S_2) in the absence of his knowing anything directly, either positive or negative, about her.

The child who has learned that a bad, punishing, rejecting parent is "Boss," and who has also learned that teachers are "bosses," may transfer, via verbal mediation, the negative and frightened feelings he has toward his parents to the first teacher he encounters. Parents—particularly, it seems, punitive ones—often assist destructive verbal mediation by such preparation for school as this: "Just wait until you get to school! The teacher will whip you into shape!" This process is as important in formal or cognitive learning including concept formation, as in the emotional type of learning discussed above.

Verbal mediation has much in common with Hebb's phase sequences, and Piaget's sensorimotor developmental stages 2 through 6, as discussed in Chapter 1.

Discrimination Learning

ESTABLISHING DISCRIMINATIONS

In the preceding section it was noted that a child or adult trained to react to medium gray will respond, less often but still frequently, to medium-light or medium-dark gray. Such imprecise reactions (or generalizations) are likely to cause trouble in real life when the reaction is supposed to be to the correct thing *only*, not to something resembling it, however close the resemblance may be. Precise reaction calls for *discrimination* between what is correct and what is similar but incorrect. This too is part of effective concept formation.

In a simple case of discrimination learning, the subject is given a reward or reinforcement when he reacts to the correct stimulus—for purposes of illustration, medium gray. This reinforcement may consist of such things as money, a piece of candy, or praise. But when the closely similar stimulus of medium-light gray is responded to, no reinforcement, or punishment, or a delayed reinforcement (reinforcement distant in time from the response) is provided. Thus, approach-positive tendencies are built up to medium gray; and avoidance-negative tendencies to medium-light gray. The gradient of generalization, in other words, steepens: In Figure 4.6, for example, it would no longer extend from medium to medium-light gray, but only to medium grays so close together that they were beyond the limits of perceptual differentiation for the subject.

Such learning is easiest to establish when medium gray and medium-light gray are presented together (simultaneous discrimination); probably harder when they are presented one after the other; and still harder when, for example, an adult or child is asked to respond by pressing the left-hand telegraph key when the medium-gray member of the stimulus pair is presented on the right, but the right-hand key when medium-light gray is presented on the left. This last case is called *successive discrimination,* and is the sort that children are required to make constantly in the earlier stages of reading when, for example, they are expected to respond one way to *s-a-w,* and another to *w-a-s;* one way to *l-a-d,* and another to *l-a-p,* and so on. Much practice is necessary in such cases before the complex stimulus, *l-a-d,* comes to be identified by the child as *"el-a-the one with the loop on the left and the line sticking up in the air,"* and is differentiated from the other complex stimulus, *l-a-p,* *"El-a-the one with the loop on the right and the line sticking down."* Only after such stimulus compoundings and differentiations have been patiently established, through endless teacher and parent reinforcements of "Yes, right," and "No, wrong," does the quick, effortless comprehension of *l-a-d* as *lad,* and *l-a-p* as *lap,* occur. It is fairly easy to learn to discriminate *d's* presented simultaneously with *p's; d's* presented with *b's* are less easily discriminated because of their greater similarity; and the appropriate function of these letters in successively presented words is discriminated least easily of all. Much reading readiness training ignores such basic processes entirely: what, for the psychosocially deprived child, lies behind such teaching-learning?

In the first place, a psychosocially disadvantaged child entering first grade almost certainly knows none of his letters, particularly those that look as much alike as *d* and *b* or *p* and *q* (primary stimulus generalization). In other words, he does not have the foundation even for *beginning* to establish discriminations since, in the first place he does not know what discriminations *should* be established. Often he does not know the difference between up and down and usually does not know the difference between right and left. He is likely to be totally lost in distinguishing *was* from *saw,* even though he may know what the words mean. He is at even more of a loss with such words as *lad* and *lap,* since he not only does not know anything about the letters that go into them but he probably also does not know what they mean (possibly he knows what a *lap* is, although he is less likely to have been much held in one than a middle-class child).

Where do we start with him in discrimination learning—a necessary foundation for the later discrimination and concept formation that go into reading? Do we start with the alphabet? No—we start with ideas of left and right, up and down, circular and straight—the "near" *cell assemblies* of which Hebb speaks, or the *secondary circular reactions or coordinations* or *coordination of the secondary schemata* to which Piaget refers (if the reader does not remember these terms, he should refer again to Chapter 1).

We should help him with these discriminations through every sensory medium he can use appropriately: his eyes, in the sense of using them up and down, right and left, for black and white, red and green; his ears —tell him about them and have him talk about them; his kinesthesis— tracing as he uses his eyes up and down and to register different colors. We can't handily have him "taste" or "smell" letters or concepts of up and down but we can certainly have him see, hear, and "feel" them. Only when a sound groundwork of elementary meaning is established can the abstractions of letters, letters combined into words, and words combined into reading be accomplished. Work with numbers follows similar concept formation principles. Such techniques, at different levels of abstraction, seem appropriate for all children, privileged or deprived.

ACQUIRED DISTINCTIVENESS OF CUES

Secondary and mediated generalization involve the learning of similarities between and common reactions to two things that are not necessarily similar but "serve the same general purpose." *Acquired distinctiveness of cues* enables one to act *differentially* in situations that have considerable objective similarity to each other but call for differential behavior.

To the small child, a nickel and a dime are perceptually quite similar to each other, yet it is sensible for a child offered a choice between them to choose the former. Preteaching that *this* coin is a nickel and *this* one a dime, until the child has learned to attach the names appropriately, gives these objectively rather similar stimuli extra stimulus differentiation—makes them, cognitively, more *unlike* each other than they originally were because they have acquired added meanings or verbal stimulus properties. Thus, the appropriate discrimination or choice is facilitated in a later learning situation in which the child is expected to choose the more valuable, but smaller, coin. Children with such pretraining learn faster than those without it.

Pretraining of this kind is one of the factors in reading readiness. The child who has been taught that $d = dee,$ while $b = bee,$ will be more ready to discriminate between *gab* and *gad* than the child who has not learned this. The child who has clearly learned that left is left, and right is right, and that in the United States one reads from left to right, will differentiate between *saw* and *was* more easily than the youngster who does not know his directions.

In other words, any addition of differentiating cues to objectively similar stimuli makes them more unlike and hence, later, more easily discriminated from each other. Acquired equivalence of cues is the basis of concepts of induction or generalization; acquired distinctiveness of cues is the basis, in a sense, for deduction and differentiation.

TRANSPOSITION

The discrimination theory discussed indicates that coming to choose or prefer one stimulus rather than another that originally had equal value results from having received rewards for choosing the first and no-reward, punishment, or a delayed reward for choosing the second. If *a* is correct, *b* is incorrect, and if the child is confronted with both at the same time he says, in effect, to himself, "Approach *a,* avoid *b.*" If they are presented one at a time, he says "Approach" to *a,* "Avoid" to *b.* In the successive discrimination situation (such as learning the difference, in standard reading training, between a *b* and a *d*), he learns, "If *b,* then not *duh,* but *buh;* but if *d,* then *duh,* not *buh.*" This is analogous to training the rat to approach left and avoid right for the white stimulus; and to go right and avoid left for the black.

But experimental psychology as well as real life frequently requires relative or relational rather than absolute choices. Let us suppose that a subject, *without specification of the principle,* is trained to choose the larger of two squares. Then he is presented with two different squares, the *larger* of them being the same size as the *smaller* of the two to which he has been trained. At least as often as not, and usually more often, a *relational* choice (according to the principle or concept "larger," rather than according to an absolute property of the stimulus—its size) is correct. Making such relational choices is called *transposition.*

Transposition can be predicted by learning theory, although the prediction is based on theories too complex to be presented here. This theory leads to the prediction that, if a very young child has been trained to choose the smaller of two squares, one of 100 and the other of 85 square inches, he is more likely to transpose if his alternatives on a test trial are close in size to the original—for example, 75 and 60 square inches—than if they are very different from the original—for example, 30 and 15 square inches.

However, when children are old enough to have learned the concepts "smaller" and "larger," transposition or relational choice occurs regardless of the difference of the test-stimulus pair from the training pair. In this case, it may be said that verbal mediation has taken place. Examples of research demonstrating transposition have been provided by Kuenne

(1946), and Spiker, Gerjuoy, and Shepard (1956). Words—language—are usually the foundations for concepts, mediating principles, generalizations, insights, strategies, and plans.

LEARNING TO LEARN

For higher animals and children, problem-solving ability seems to increase with increasing practice, even though each new problem may be different from its predecessor (see, for instance, Harlow, 1949). This tendency is roughly analogous to mediated generalization, but what is transferred is a "problem-solving set" rather than a technique for solving a particular problem. This issue is discussed in more detail in Chapter 7. Such a "set" results in progressive efficiency in problem-solving, even where the problems have little in common. It is a general way of approaching life which is held to be desirable, and a major goal of child-rearing and education.

Learning to learn may also be called "nonspecific transfer of training." It refers to a child's acquiring a method of solving problems. A planful, observing, organizing child ordinarily learns almost anything faster than one who learns by rote or trial and error (see House and Zeaman, 1962).

The practical principle to be abstracted is obvious: give children formulae or plans or strategies. Teach them to work and think in such ways. Even though these may be wrong, they provide him with a systematic way to approach any problem, new or old, and they appear to increase his efficiency. To the present author, this principle is the core of "cognitive styles" and "concept formation." As has been mentioned, most human strategies consist (at least as far as the school room is concerned) of plans-formulated-in-words. But one has only to watch a good quarterback or a good basketball player to know that strategies can also consist at least partly of "motor plans." A basketball player may be completely unable to communicate verbally why he executed a brilliant strategic play, although probably somewhere words (*implicit* language, at least) entered into his strategy.

If the child has been taught the observing-strategic, learning-to-learn approach, he also learns to try a new strategy (a new generalization or plan) if the old one does not work. This is perhaps the reason why even a wrong plan is better than no plan at all.

Drive or Motivation

It has already been mentioned that organisms do not learn unless some *motive* or *drive* exists. A drive or motive performs one or more of three functions (Farber, 1955): it *energizes* or *sensitizes, selects,* and *directs.* Drives are frequently classified as *primary* and *secondary.* A *primary drive* is considered to be one related to the biological needs that must be satisfied if life and the species are to be preserved. Hunger, thirst, and sex are illustrations of such biological drives. *Secondary drives* have been learned, presumably in the course of satisfying primary drives. Dependency and a need for mastery are illustrations of secondary drives, and aggression and anxiety may also belong to this category.

ENERGIZING AND SENSITIZING
FUNCTIONS OF DRIVE[4]

When a drive *energizes,* it puts the organism into a state of heightened activity "designed" to encounter maximal stimulation in the "hope" of finding stimuli that will reduce the drive. When the drive acts as a *sensitizer,* stimuli pertinent to reducing the drive are more likely to be perceived than when the drive is not operating: their perceptual *threshold* is lowered. Of course, some learning must have preceded before a motive can sensitize a person to a stimulus: he must have learned that the stimulus is related to or will help to satisfy his drive.

In the beginning of an organism's life, the energizing function of drive is entirely, or at least partially, unlearned. This function may be illustrated by an example taken from the behavior of a 2-week-old baby. If we first begin to observe him an hour after he has been fed and changed, we find him very relaxed, breathing evenly and deeply. His hands, arms, legs, neck, and head—indeed, his whole body—are still, almost limp. Observed at the second hour after feeding, he remains relaxed, but occasionally clenches and unclenches his hands. This motion is not an intense one. As we watch him during the third hour after feeding, we see his hands grow more active; he "flutters" with them. Presently, he makes motions with his arms; his head turns; his mouth purses; he moves his feet and legs. Then, as the third hour draws to a close, he is in motion "all over." He moves his head restlessly; arms and hands and legs move; his color heightens. Then his eyes open and, after a moment of adaptation to the light, his body comes to even more vigorous motion. He vocalizes, whimpers, cries—first plaintively, then vociferously, with total body action and deeply flushed features accompanying the crying. Every parent recognizes the symptoms: the baby is hungry. The only thing that will stop this feverish activity for more than a few seconds is food. The intensity of the baby's hunger drive is directly proportional to his "time of deprivation" (the amount of time that has gone by since he was last fed).

[4] This discussion of the threefold function of drive is based on an analysis originally made by Melton (1950).

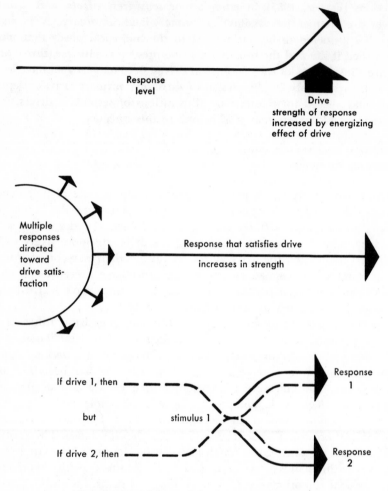

Figure 4.8   Schema of the functions of drive.

Thus drive, in its energizing sense, has put the baby's whole body in motion so that he may make contact with a maximal range of stimulation in the "hope" that one of the stimuli encountered by his many responses will reduce his drive or satisfy him (in this case, supply him with the breast or bottle). The responses of sucking and head-turning to the bottle are the ones that eventually put him in touch with the nipple.

The sensitizing function of drive is similarly adaptive. When drive energizes, the organism is more active and presumably more likely to encounter drive-reducing stimuli. The sensitizing function of drive depends more on learning than the energizing function. All of the processes discussed earlier in the chapter may well have contributed to this sensitizing function: in some cases, it has been affected by classical conditioning, in others by instrumental learning. Generalization operates, in that stimuli like those that earlier satisfied the drive are now perceived as worth exploring, while those that are clearly different from the original stimuli are ignored.

The added alertness that goes with the sensitizing function of drive puts the organism (child) in touch with the stimuli appropriate for satisfying whatever drive is operating.

At three o'clock in the afternoon, the 3-year-old may run happily through the kitchen a dozen times, at no time attending to any of the stimuli it provides. But at four-thirty or five o'clock, a trip through the kitchen is suddenly halted; he stops, cries, "I'm hungry," and begins to yank at the cupboard where he knows the cookies are, or the drawer where the bread and crackers are kept. He is suffering from "time of deprivation." His heightened hunger drive makes him more sensitive to stimuli that earlier had made no impression on him: the cupboards and drawers where cookies, bread, and crackers are kept.

Adults may work cheerfully all morning in a room close to a restaurant kitchen or bakery, at no time noticing the odors. But at eleven-thirty, the smell stimuli suddenly impinge on them and they begin to feel ravenously hungry. This, too, is an example of the sensitizing function of drive.

Social or learned drives or motives may work in a similar manner. Preschool children who have been deprived of adult attention for a brief period of time will achieve more in an apparent attempt to gain attention (or satisfy their heightened dependency needs) than preschoolers not so deprived (see, for example, Hartup, 1958). This result is analogous to the energizing function of drive. The young child in an institution reacts with exaggeration to the smallest attention of the visiting adult— perhaps an illustration of the sensitizing function of drive. For children of any age, *curiosity* has a sensitizing and an energizing function: they work harder if they are curious, and they are more sensitive to intellectual stimulation of all sorts (the reader may wish to refer back to the "sensory development" sections of Chapter 1, where speculations were made about the development of curiosity).

THE SELECTIVE FUNCTION OF DRIVE

The baby discussed above who becomes progressively more restless with the passage of time since his last feeding exhibits, in his most excited state, a number of different behaviors. He (1) cries; (2) thrashes with his arms and legs; (3) agitates his torso; (4) rolls his head; (5) intersperses crying with sucking movements; (6) agitates his legs. When the bottle is between his lips, all these movements except sucking diminish or disappear. As he grows a little older, the touch of the bottle or breast on face terminates all these responses except an adaptive head-turning in the direction of the nipple, seeking motions with his lips, and eventual sucking responses. Still later, the mere sight of the bottle ends the random behavior and causes him to get ready for the nipple. In other words, the reward (food) that reduces the drive helps the baby to *select* appropriate or facilitating responses: first sucking, then seeking, and, later, grasping.

The rat and the trip bar that provided the illustration of instrumental conditioning also illustrate the operation of the selective function of drive. The rat's original reactions to the CS (the trip bar) may have included nibbling at it, jumping over it, sniffing it, creeping under it, and, finally, tripping it quite by accident as he climbs on it. Having received a piece of food immediately after depressing the bar, he soon prefers the vicinity of the bar to other parts of the cage; an increase in the tendency to react to the bar by climbing on it, rather than sniffing it or going under it, will come later; and, finally, from the numerous responses involved in climbing, the more efficient response of pushing with one or both front paws will be selected as the method of responding to the bar. The "basketball playing" rat described previously in this chapter, with further training and reward, will soon drop her fancy left hook.

All our learning involves *selecting* and *fixing*, through reinforcement, some responses and *eliminating* or *extinguishing* others. For our purposes, reinforcement may be said to strengthen the tendency for a given stimulus to evoke a given response; the most usual reinforcement occurs because the response that was made reduced the drive that was associated with or produced the stimulus in the first place. However, there appear to be instances of reinforcements provided by increased rather than reduced drive (as, for example, in sexual fantasy without orgasm). In any event, it is here assumed that reinforcement is provided, if not by drive *reduction,* at least by some type of drive *satisfaction.*

An adult, seeking a certain right-hand turnoff in a strange city, consults a city map before he begins his trip. He makes mental approximations of distances, and fixes certain landmarks in his mind. As he reaches the first of these landmarks, he begins to drive more slowly and with more hesitation. He strains to read street signs well before he reaches them. He becomes mildly anxious. At last, he succeeds in making the appropriate right turn. On his second trip over the same route, many of his earlier behaviors have been eliminated. He is less anxious; he strains less to anticipate street signs; his hesitations are fewer. He moves later to the slow, right-hand lane of traffic. At the same time, some responses have become selected or strengthened: he recognizes the hospital that stands in the block before the necessary right turn. At sight of it, he smoothly and confidently moves into place for his turn. For school children, so it is with reading, number work, and their other school activities.

This function of drive, then, is the one that helps to eliminate maladaptive or inefficient responses; and assists in establishing efficient, instrumental ways of behaving. Teachers can use it to help children learn-to-learn.

THE DIRECTIVE FUNCTION OF DRIVE

The energizing function of drive is probably innate, serving the biological economy by increasing the probability of the organism's coming into contact with stimuli that will reduce the drive and thus enabling it to survive. More learning accompanies the sensitizing than the energizing function, but it too is directed toward survival. The selective function of drive is synonymous with learning, in the sense that it results in greater efficiency in satisfying drive. The directive function is learned—it is a *cue* function. For one drive plus a given stimulus, one type of behavior is appropriate; for another drive and the *same* stimulus, another behavior is chosen. This function of drive enables the individual to choose one of two or more behaviors already potentially available to him, each of which is equally appropriate to the stimulus (when "stimulus" is considered only as an objective event or thing). The drive *provides information* to the individual about how he should behave: it is, itself, an informative stimulus.

By way of illustration, let us consider 3-year-old Sally. Sally has been up very late on Tuesday night, and awakens to go to nursery school on Wednesday somewhat the worse for wear. She arrives, passes the nurse's inspection, and enters the playroom. She sees a blue blanket in the doll corner (the stimulus) and approaches it. Her drive (avoidance of the unpleasant symptoms of fatigue), coupled with the blanket, suggests to her that she pick up the blanket, take it to a cot, and lie down with it to rest. The drive, in other words, interacts with the objective stimulus and directs her behavior. But on Wednesday night Sally goes to bed early, and arrives at school rested and bursting with energy. Her drive is for exploration and play; this drive couples in an informational or cue fashion with the same blue blanket in the same doll corner. But this time, the information it gives leads to using the blanket as one prop in a lively game of housekeeping in which she plays the role of mother, and recruits several other children to play the parts of brothers, sisters, father, and baby.

In the same fashion, the lonely adult may welcome a large, formal social function; on the other hand, after a week filled with social activities, the notion of attending a similar function may be repugnant. Or, after moving to a strange city with accompanying mild or severe loneliness, the mental stimuli of friends or relatives prompt voluminous letterwriting; after six months, when new friends have been made, the same mental stimuli may prompt only the grudging reaction: "Oh, I should write to Uncle Herbert, but I don't really want to!" The kitchen smells that were so hunger-arousing before lunch may be mildly unpleasant after a heavy meal. In each case, different drives coupled with the same objective stimuli have directed the individual to choose very different responses from among those available to him.

The same general stimulus, "teacher," may evoke very different types and intensities of behavior from a child. Teacher A, who is firm, warm, and competent (but still only a subheading under the stimulus generalization, "teacher") may secure from a child efficient effort and hard work. Teacher B, indecisive, vague, and ill-prepared, possibly harsh and unfair, may produce the opposite behavior from the same child: he day dreams, or sulks, or misbehaves, and accomplishes little as far as his major task—school learning—is concerned.

Reward and Learning

Although it is not accepted by all that a drive must be reduced if learning is to occur, it is granted that learning typically occurs when drive is reduced. The agent or thing that reduces the drive is commonly referred to as the *reward*. There may be cases where more stimulation or greater drive is sought (see, for example, Hebb, 1955, and J. S. Brown, 1955). In such a situation, increased stimulation or drive may be thought of as the reward. In any event, reward, coupled with drive usually results in learning.

The aspects of reward considered to bear most directly on learning are its *amount, consistency,* and *immediacy.* A reward, of course, must be *relevant* to the drive associated with the activity that results in obtaining it before learning will occur. To the full but sleepy infant, more food is not a reward; nor are soda crackers to the extremely thirsty child. The delinquent is not interested in the approval of the community pastor; and to the shy, plain, but bright girl, another A will be less rewarding than being asked to go to the movies with a boy of her age.

It has often been stated (as, for example, by Mussen and Conger, 1956) that learning is directly proportional to the amount, immediacy, and consistency of reward. According to this principle, the greater the reward, the sooner it follows the action designed to obtain it, and the more consistently it occurs, the higher the level of learning will be. There is some question about the accuracy of these conclusions.

At the present stage of research knowledge, it seems more accurate to say that *speedier* learning is likely to occur with large, immediate, and consistent rewards; but that small, somewhat delayed, and inconsistent rewards eventually produce about the same *level* of learning.

There is evidence to indicate that behavior acquired through inconsistent reward (more commonly known as *partial reinforcement*) reaches its asymptote (its peak) more slowly than under consistent-reward conditions. But such behavior is more resistant to extinction and remains longer in the individual's behavior repertory. One tentative explanation for this fact is that the partially reinforced animal or child "continues to hope." He has had the experience of efforts sometimes being rewarded, sometimes not, so that extinction training is a less radical alteration for him than it is for the animal or child who has had consistent reinforcement (see, for example, Crum, Brown, and Bitterman, 1951; Hake, Grant, and Hornseth, 1951; Jenkins and Stanley, 1950; and Lauer and Estes, 1955). Knowledge concerning the role of partial reinforcement, "hope" or expectancy, and extinction is incomplete at present. Although most of the research has been done with animals, the phenomena also seem to characterize children (see Bijou, 1957; Rosenblum, 1956).

Human life is so complex, the relations between parents and children and teachers and children so varied, that it is fortunate that children seem to be able to learn, and learn well, from small, often delayed, and necessarily inconsistent rewards. Their *own symbolic behavior* (their saying to themselves, "I did OK!") often seems to constitute the only reward they get for many performances, yet they learn. On the face of it, complete consistency is impossible between caretaker and child, if for no other reason than that the parent or teacher is not always with the child. No teacher can give every one of the twenty-five or more children in her class a reward, even a word of approbation, every time he does something praiseworthy; nor can she administer punishment (reproof, correction, or criticism) every time he does something not praiseworthy. She has too many other children to deal with, and she cannot guide the child in every detail of his academic or personal learning during the school day.

To be completely honest about it, no contemporary psychologist is comfortable when he writes anything conclusive and definite about reward and its effects on behavior. It was comforting to the present author to hear one of the world's recognized experts on reinforcement theory (the effects of rewards and punishments), William K. Estes, admit in an address given in 1966 that, while he was certain about reward-reinforcement and its effects in the 1940s, he knew less about it after studying it for more than twenty years than he *thought* he did when he was a humble graduate student.

However, from a practical point of view, the conclusions and suggested applications given by the present author in this section seem to work relatively well, although reinforcement theory is vague; nor are all the dimensions of *what* reward works *when,* if indeed it works at all, definitely known.

SKINNER AND REWARD REINFORCEMENT

Skinner (1938, 1948) and his students give us provocative ideas about reinforcement, both of reward and punishment. Skinner maintains that he is not a theorist though it would appear that he is and that his theory is deceptively simple. Skinner's theory can be summarized very briefly: an organism (pigeon, rat, child, adult) arrives at any given type of behavior through a series of progressive approximations that work (that is, that secure what the organism is looking for). By *progressive approximations* is meant the same thing that was talked about earlier in this chapter under the heading of the *selective function of drive.* When the organism's behavior works, it is consolidated more and more efficiently into his response or behavior repertoire. When it does not work, it is dropped.

To produce the sort of behavior you want in a child, you first define it carefully. Then you observe the child carefully until you see him behave in some way that resembles *your* goal for him (not necessarily his goal for himself). As soon as he "emits" this behavior, give him a reward. Punish (usually ignore) undesirable behavior. Your observation can by no means be casual: you must find out, as you observe, what is important (valuable) and unimportant for the child. Allowing him to obtain the things he wants is positively reinforcing (rewarding). Denying them to him is negatively reinforcing (punishing). Your own discovery depends on your skill as an observer-detective.

Keep on rewarding him *immediately* for any behavior that resembles what you desire and presently, if you have been accurate in determining what is important to him, he will behave as you want him to.

Skinner's system works not only in the laboratory but in the home or the classroom. A fifth-grade teacher (a mobile young woman who moved rapidly around the room, teaching and talking as she moved) once asked the author what in the world she was to do with a child who was so completely withdrawn from anything that went on in the class that she had begun to wonder if he was autistic (seriously emotionally ill in the sense of almost complete withdrawal from people). The author followed Skinner's "recipe" and went, armed with a pencil and a lined pad, to observe the child who for our purposes we shall call William. William was *indeed* withdrawn. He seemed to attend to nothing except (by inference) something private, going on only *within himself.* But as the observation proceeded (for a full half day) a pattern emerged. The teacher was not only mobile, but often called on children by name and gave them a brisk pat as she moved by their seats. Whenever she called William by name, or patted him, or looked directly into his eyes, he paid attention for a fleeting moment. The author's recommendation was simple and easy for this particular teacher to follow. The recommendation was that she call William by name more frequently, fix his eyes with hers whenever possible, and give him her typical brisk pat as often as she could without seeming to favor him unduly. When his attention was thus obtained, even for a half second, she was to follow up with a question or comment, addressed to him (but applicable to the class or a relevant subpart of it) and concerning the topic under consideration. If William responded correctly, or even half-sensibly, she was to give more reward. She put this plan into action and within about six weeks William was attending to class proceedings approximately 50 percent of the time (average for a fifth-grader) in contrast to the near 0 percent attention he had given earlier.

As has been mentioned, Hodges, McCandless, and Spicker are carrying on an extended series of studies with psychosocially disadvantaged 5-year-olds of low intelligence. As one part of their classroom management, they use Skinnerian techniques. Each child is carefully observed, best guesses are made as to what is important and what is valueless to him, and when his behavior approximates the class goals, he is *immediately* rewarded (a small cracker or marshmallow is popped into his mouth, as a child is chronically hungry; *but* as this is done and so as to teach each child that people as well as food are important, he is told, "Good boy," or "Good girl"—which is a form of classical conditioning). The results are remarkable. By midyear, a typical group of fifteen such children no longer requires many tangible (food) rewards, but responds to a friendly smile or a word of praise. Their social and school-oriented behavior is almost incredibly improved. It must be mentioned that these Skinnerian techniques of reward are only one part of the total treatment of the children. Punishment for most of the children, who like to be in the group, is typically "time out" (isolation). However, any child is allowed to reenter the group whenever he decides he can again behave acceptably.

What a parent or teacher thinks of as punishment may actually be reward (or *vice versa*). The author was observing a class of 5-year-olds. He happened to know each child well and had in fact made Skinnerian-type observations on each child for research-curriculum purposes. During a story time, when all children were supposed to be sitting around the teacher listening to a story, a boy named Johnny took off his shoe and tossed it into a far corner of the room, thus effectively disturbing the group. The teacher firmly sent him after the shoe, and when he returned to the reading circle she pulled him close with her arm around him. As far as the teacher was concerned, this was no gesture of affection: it was meant as restraining-type punishment. But previous observation of Johnny had revealed clearly that one of his major goals in life was to be physically close to his beloved teacher, regardless of how he got there. Hence, what was punishment according to the teacher's perception was the height of reward for Johnny and was much more likely to result in more rather than less future group-disruptive behavior on his part. The teacher was accomplishing the *opposite* of her goal.

Skinner's "theory" has many virtues. It makes keener observers of teachers and other professional workers; it develops their own problem solving approaches as to what will and what will not work with a given child. It makes them more sharply and accurately aware of children's individual differences. It makes them more aware of *their own* behavior. They may find, for example, that they are inadvertently and unconsciously rewarding and thus consolidating the very behavior they wish to eliminate as with Johnny above, or failing to reward approximations of the behavior they wish the child to develop. Finally, in most cases, they become better caretakers (parents *or* teachers). However, the initial observation and planning are time consuming, and there is usually at least one child in a group for whom no plan can be developed or, if developed, it does not work.

GAGNE AND CONTROL
OF THE EXTERNAL EVENTS OF INSTRUCTION

Gagne (1965) has worthwhile things to say about learning, particularly in practical situations such as homes or classrooms.[5] Gagne proposes that four basic conditions of learning must be fulfilled if instruction (home *or* school, although Gagne is talking about school) is to be effective. These are: (1) stimulation, (2) response, (3) assessment and feedback, and (4) transfer.

Stimulation includes the motivational value of instructional strategies and materials (the reader should note how well this corresponds to Skinnerian "detective work"). In considering stimulation, first the internal state of the learner must be determined (his attitudinal factors, his background experience) and second, the external events of instruction must be arranged. These external events of instruction (Skinner's reinforcements that shape responses) control the stimulus situation and include such things as directions and instructions; giving information about expected outcomes; helping children become familiar with and organize learning materials; relating new to old material; and guiding forward new discovery (learning to learn).

[5] The author is indebted to Ellis Evans for help in the treatment of this topic, as well as for many ideas for supplements to the book.

Response, of course, refers to what the learner *does.* Ideally, we should help him make useful and meaningful responses. We also want him to make his responses publicly rather than to himself alone, both for his own good and the good of his associates, as well as to help us evaluate or assess his status and progress.

Assessment and feedback consist of much more than standard report cards and formal examinations. To be useful, feedback from assessment should follow the principles of reward: the more immediate, informative, positive, motivating, and unthreatening it is, the better.

Transfer has been discussed earlier in the chapter. It refers to the generalizability and breadth of applicability of what has been learned. Both vertical and lateral transfer are possible: vertical transfer can be loosely defined as "additional insights in depth," while lateral transfer means application of knowledge in as great a variety of new situations as can be devised by the parent or teacher and child working together.

Summary

One of the most striking and exciting things about children is that they *learn.* Learning is a change in performance as a function of practice, although this definition ignores the difference between performance— that which is *manifested* or *public*—and learning. The latter may consist of knowing better or knowing how, but not demonstrating it. Since this latter type of learning is not and cannot be subject to measurement, the author makes no distinction between performance and learning, but concerns himself essentially with performance as it *reflects* learning.

Maturation (roughly, growth and development) and learning cannot be separated in the development of a child, any more than we can separate H_2O and still have water. Nor can their relative importance be assessed, since both are essential, hence all-important.

For babies, learning is likely to be slow, and to advance through a process of trial and error. Many aspects of it are almost automatic, as in classical conditioning, during which a new stimulus comes to evoke a response already present. Instrumental learning, more goal-directed, results in the child's being able to use tools to accomplish his ends. These tools may be words or behaviors.

Primary and secondary generalization play a major role in human learning. If a response is learned to one stimulus, the same response is likely to be evoked by other stimuli similar to it along dimensions of physical likeness (primary generalization) or meaning (secondary generalization). Transposition is akin to secondary generalization, and is the name applied to the ability of older children and adults to respond, in general, to the *relations between things* rather than to their absolute properties. Relational response is ordinarily more adaptive than absolute response, and underlies our ability to make generalizations.

Although it is important and useful to respond to life in terms of general laws, accurate discriminations are also necessary. Secondary generalization, transposition, and mediated generalization allow the older child and adult to behave according to generalized abstractions; but acquired distinctiveness of cues enables them to make the fine distinctions that are equally necessary. These are fundamental to concept formation.

Drive and motivation can be separated from learning no more than learning can be separated from maturation. There are three major functions of drive: (1) the energizing and sensitizing function, which, by increasing the organism's activity, increases his chances of encountering the stimuli necessary to reduce his drive and also makes him more alert to appropriate stimuli; (2) the selective function, which helps him to slough off behavior irrelevant to satisfying his motive, thus making him more efficient; and (3) the directive function which, following considerable learning, enables him to act adaptively to the same stimuli under different drives, or different strengths of drive.

Reward, typically, results in strengthening (or establishing) the rewarded behavior. Although large, immediate, and consistent rewards may result in *speedier* learning, approximately the same *level* of learning appears to be reached with small, delayed, and inconsistent reward (or punishment).

Special Factors in Human Learning

The preceding chapter contained an abbreviated discussion of some of the basic principles of learning. These principles mesh fairly well with the general point of view developed by the Yale-Iowa, or Hullian, theory of learning. This theory is by no means accepted by all psychologists, but it is relatively complete and has demonstrated its usefulness in predicting and understanding many aspects of human behavior. Its proponents believe most of its principles apply both to humans and animals, although much of the research on which it is based has used animals, not humans as subjects.[1]

The most important psychological difference between the human being and other animals is that the human possesses a rich symbolic system, the most conspicuous aspect of which is speech. Speech makes possible an infinite variety of symbolization; using it, one can plan ahead, or practice a task unofficially by thinking about a previous practice session. Speech makes insight possible, and provides substitute or fantasy satisfactions for primary needs. All of these functions of symbols make the study of human learning much trickier than animal learning, and there are those who believe that the understanding of human learning will require a theoretical system entirely different from one developed for animals.

The following sections treat a number of tentative principles, some of which have been considered by learning theorists, others not. Many of the ideas presented are frankly speculative since little, if any, research has been done concerning them.

---

[1] Animals are much used in psychological research because they are easier to work with than humans. The experimenter does not have to plead with them to cooperate. They can be studied without interrupting their schoolwork. One does not run the risk of "hurting their feelings." They do not confide to other potential subjects the purpose and procedure of the experiment. Their living circumstances can be controlled. They act naturally, and do not attempt to hide their feelings, or behave as they think you *want* them to behave, and so on.

Expectancies and Probability

Consciously or unconsciously, we appear to behave as we do partly in terms of probability "estimates." No one with the slightest common sense darts across the street at an unlighted intersection if the chances are as low as 50–50 that he will reach the other side in one piece. Seldom do we make a formal estimate of probability under such circumstances, but we do usually wait until it appears that the nearest moving vehicle is far enough away so that chances of a safe crossing stand at about 100 to 1. We vary our odds according to our needs, however. If we are about to be late for an extremely important appointment, we will take more chances in crossing the street than if we are heading back to the office or to class with a time leeway of ten minutes. We might predict that the urgency or importance of the goal we are seeking will affect the risk we accept concerning the route to that goal: we will take more chances for an urgent goal or a big reward than for a small reward or a goal to which we are relatively indifferent.

The urgency of his goals will push an insecure child into behavior with a low probability of success: he will take great chances with his physical safety to impress his peers. Showing-off and daredevil behavior are perhaps attempts to obtain such goals. The bully, who usually chooses "safe" or high-probability behavior as represented by "picking on" smaller and younger children will, when cornered, actually fight with someone as big and skillful as he to avoid losing face. His prestige is very valuable to him, so that he will risk much to maintain it. When safe routes are shut off, he will make the risky choice of fighting someone who may win.

Other things being equal, however, if there are several different procedures an individual can use to achieve his goal, he will take the one he estimates to have the highest probability of success. Interesting treatments of the theoretical role of expectancy are provided by such authors as Brunswik (1951), Lewin (1935), Rotter (1954), and Tolman (1932), who present and treat in detail ideas relating to those above. Piaget also has much to say about probability.

Motivation for one type of activity (goal) over another also depends to a substantial degree on the relative expectancy of success. The slow-learning child in a classroom full of normal and bright children estimates his chances of competing with his classmates at 0 to 100. Hence he does not try to accomplish even as much as he is able to, but chooses instead to be a troublemaker. The nearsighted, scrawny junior-high student sees no chance of experiencing success at basketball in competition with his huskier classmates. He does not even report for basketball practice, but seeks his satisfaction in getting good grades, or in daydreaming.

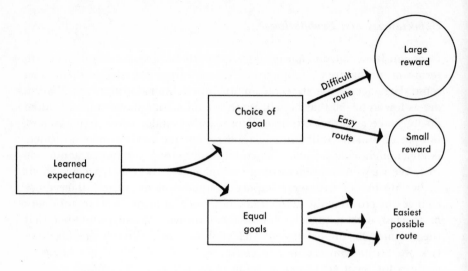

Figure 5.1   Expectancies determine the route of behavior.

A set of expectancies may be accurate with reference to the setting in which it has been learned, yet be both discouraging and maladjustive. If the slow-learning child of the previous illustration who judges quite accurately that he cannot compete with his peers generalizes this notion to the point where he does not compete even with himself and does not make *any* intellectual effort, then he seriously handicaps himself as far as his future success is concerned. When characteristics of children are compared with biased norms (standards), expectancies of limited accuracy may be developed that are seriously maladaptive. The girl who is as attractive as the average, but who grows up with three sisters who are raving beauties, may predict with a high level of personal certainty that she is homely and will never be able to catch a husband. She may generalize or extend this feeling to such a degree that she makes no effort to get along with boys. She may even snub them. Perhaps without knowing it, she is defending herself: "If I freeze them out first, they will have no chance to rebuff and hurt me." In such a case, obviously, she is causing her own expectancies to come true, thus reinforcing or proving them correct. But from an outsider's point of view, she could compete quite adequately in the "courtship market" were she able to relax and be self-confident in her behavior. The boy of average intelligence who grows up in a family of brilliant siblings may react similarly in the academic area, with a very similar result. He expects so definitely to fail that he *does* fail, and consequently proves to himself what he "knew" about himself all along. Such behavior might almost be called "self-fulfilling prophecies."

The author knows two boys (the Jones brothers, for our purposes). Each is unusually bright, attractive looking, big and strong for his age, and quick and agile. The principal difference between them is that they are two years apart in age—it has been found that this age difference produces maximum sibling rivalry (competition between brothers and sisters). As is known, each child must find his "place in the sun." Eddie, the elder Jones brother, has found his place in academics. As a fifth-grader, he is the teachers' joy. He *loves* to learn—anything, anytime, anywhere; and he works hard and efficiently at his learning. From the first grade, he has topped his classes. Tom, the second, apparently felt that the Jones brothers' place in the academic sun was already taken by Eddie and that his probability of success there was negligible, at least compared with Eddie's. While Eddie is a better-than-average athlete, his heart is not really in it. This, because Eddie was not a competitor, is where Tom chose to shine (and we can be sure Tom did not deliberately or consciously say this to himself). As a third-grader, he makes a respectable "gentleman's B," but he does not work very hard and his interest in academics is no greater than the average third-grade boy who would rather be having fun than studying. Where *he* shines is in athletics. Unconsciously, he seems to have figured his probabilities of success there, at least as compared with Eddie's, as high. Just as Eddie is the classroom teacher's joy, so is Tom the physical education teacher's pride and delight. To him, athletics-sports are supreme and he is *very* good at them.

In such subtle ways, expectancies and probabilities are planned, rehearsed, fulfilled, and incorporated into ways of life.

Nunally, Duchnowski, and Parker (1965) illustrate this process neatly in an experiment with second-grade boys and girls. They coined three nonsense syllables: *zoj, myv,* and *gyq.* The children were then presented a spin-wheel game. Under conditions of *reward* (for *zoj,* for example), the children received two pennies every time the pointer on the spin-wheel stopped at *zoj.* Under conditions of *punishment,* the children lost a penny every time the pointer stopped on *zoj.* Under neutral conditions, nothing happened. Later careful checking showed that the children under *zoj*-equals-reward preferred it (attributed more desirable qualities to it) than to *myv* or *gyq.* Under conditions of punishment, *myv* or *gyq* were significantly preferred to *zoj.* Neutral conditions produced no differences in preference. The children were also shown the three nonsense syllables placed so each child could determine for himself by pressing a switch how long he looked at them. Under conditions where *zoj* had been rewarded, the children looked significantly longer at it than at *myv* or *gyq.*

A later game involved giving a child fourteen chances to find a quarter (twenty-five cents) in one of twenty-one boxes identical except that seven of them had *zoj* printed on their tops, seven *myv,* and seven *gyq.* The children significantly more often looked for the reward in the *zoj* than in the *myv* or *gyq* boxes: in other words, *zoj* had not only become "better" and more attractive to them, but they had given it an expectancy—a probability—of bringing them good luck.

But unrealistic positive expectancies (which may also be based on biased samples) may lead to difficulties. The girl of somewhat above-average ability who goes to a school with low standards and is the brightest child in her class may develop a set of expectancies predicting success for herself as a lawyer or doctor or physicist. When she moves from high school to college, the falseness of her expectancies may be disastrously revealed. For the first time in her life she does badly. She has had no experience in dealing with academic failure or mediocrity, and accordingly she suffers deeply. The overprotected small child, going to public school for the first time and finding that he is not "king of the universe," may likewise experience great difficulty in his adjustment.

Expectancies such as those we have discussed are obviously learned. They are based partly on the information an individual has, or *thinks* he has, about an immediate situation. In the case of crossing the street, or entering a busy highway, he looks right and left, sees how many cars there are and what their distance from him is, and judges how rapidly they are moving. Depending on the information thus gathered and evaluated, he remains where he is or moves out. This, of course, is all done in terms of previous learning. One who has grown up crossing streets and driving in San Francisco or New York can assess his chances in heavy traffic accurately. One who has grown up on a ranch in Nevada man be confused and frightened.

Current expectancies, then, reflect previous learning. If a child has always been punished for being aggressive and has thus been defeated, his expectancy of success in handling a new situation by being aggressive will be low (Rotter, 1954). If, on the other hand, he has repeatedly succeeded by acting in an aggressive fashion, his expectancy of success for aggressive behavior in a new situation will be high.

Rotter has also proposed that the effectiveness of a reward depends at least in part on the expectancy held for a given undertaking. If an individual has a low expectancy of success for behaving in a certain fashion, yet succeeds, the value or strength of reinforcement through success may be great. This may be related to partial reinforcement, as discussed in Chapter 4. After a chain of failures, a success is striking, hence particularly reinforcing. The shy girl who tries to flirt for the first time and finds that boys flock around her will have her flirting behavior strongly reinforced. The timid boy who suddenly finds that, by speaking up and being aggressive, he can get his way, will have such behavior much strengthened. Maturity, in many senses of the term, depends on such revelations. The adolescent who has always thought of herself or himself as gawky and unattractive overhears someone say, "What an attractive girl she has grown to be!" or "Isn't he getting to be a strapping young man?" will have his expectancies altered radically. The saying, "Nothing succeeds like success," may be based on such an alteration of expectancies.

Failure may operate in a similar way. Criticism or failure may serve as an excellent motivating device for the bright and able child yet discourage and handicap the child who is already doing poorly; whereas reward does not do very much "extra" for the bright and successful but motivates the unsuccessful child highly. Rotter's notions fit well here. The bright child expects to succeed, hence success and praise do not surprise him or raise him to new levels of performance. He does not expect to fail or be criticized; hence, when such things happen to him, the effect is great. The punishment, as it were, is so severe that he redoubles his efforts to avoid encountering it again. The failing child expects failure and criticism, hence it has little effect on him except to confirm his beliefs and reduce his effort. But an experience of praise or reward is so striking and sweet that he works doubly hard to encounter such a state of affairs again.

Charlesworth (1965) reports two well-conducted studies, too elaborate to report here in detail, that seem to support the idea that surprise engenders curiosity and that "disconfirmation of expectancy" (if it is not too threatening) causes a youngster to increase his efforts to find out the principle (to reduce his "cognitive dissonance," a concept that will be discussed later). Charlesworth tricked children ranging in age from 37 months through third grade. Those who had been tricked (that is, who were sure how his game was going to turn out and startled when it turned out differently) were delighted and kept at the game much longer and worked harder than children not surprised. Mild frustration *could* be involved here and we know that frustration increases drive, thus strength of response. But the apparent pleasure the children took in being tricked does not seem to fit the frustration-drive theory. Incidentally, Charlesworth's results are sharply different from Piaget's predictions that "failure of assimilation" (in this case, correct prediction of outcome of the game) is a manifestation of failure.

One of Charlesworth's conclusions is worth quoting, both in connection with this section on probability learning and a section later in this chapter on curiosity, as well as other material in the book on motivation and academic achievement: "The role of surprise then would seem to be important in cognitive development, since it almost invariably accompanies the nonconfirmation of an expected event and can serve to signal the need for a necessary adjustment to take place in the cognitive apparatus." Later, Charlesworth says that possibly surprise resulting from nonconfirmation "raises the general drive level above that normally characteristic of the subject (which) . . . may accelerate learning and hence increase the strength of the newly acquired habit" (p. 1185).

Another ingenious experiment (Spector, 1956) also related to the propositions discussed above has been done with young men in a simulated military situation. Thirty-six teams of four men each were placed in a situation where their performance on a group task presumably had a direct effect on whether they would be promoted from corporal to sergeant. Half the groups were told that three out of the four men in the group would be promoted (high expectancy for promotion); half were told that only one of the four men would be promoted (low expectancy). These groups were then halved again, all the men in half the groups (regardless of previous information) being promoted, all the men in the other half of the groups failing to receive promotion.

After having completed two tasks and receiving or failing to receive promotion, the men were asked questions designed to tap their morale. These questions dealt with such factors as the attractiveness of the group for its members, satisfaction with the two tasks that had been assigned to the group, evaluation of the group's productivity, and so forth. A composite score of morale was made up from the answers to these questions.

From the highest to the lowest morale score, the results follow in orderly progression: men with low expectancy who received promotions reported the highest morale; men with high expectancy who were promoted came next; men with low expectancy who were not promoted were third; while men with high expectancy who were not promoted suffered the most damage to morale. The average morale scores for the different groups were in many cases not greatly different from each other, but their arrangement in the order obtained could happen by chance only once in twenty-four times. The actual fact of promotion or nonpromotion, however, had a greater over-all effect on morale than did high or low expectancy.[2]

On the surface of it, the results of the Charlesworth study, where children were delighted with *surprise* (nonconfirmation of expectancy), and the Spector study, where *confirmation* of expectancy (particularly expectancy of success) appeared to be rewarding, seem incompatible with each other. The difference lies in the consequences to the individual of confirmation or disconfirmation of expectancy: Charlesworth's children were playing a game; no penalty was attached to nonconfirmation.

---

[2] This experiment must be criticized on one score: men whose internal expectancies did not conform with the instructions given them by the experimenter (men who were skeptical or who kept their own previous expectancies) were excluded from the analysis of results that reached statistical significance—an illustration of one of the research faults discussed in Chapter 2.

Spector's young men were playing for keeps, so to speak, and nonconfirmation was punishing. This raises interesting questions about the role of ego involvement and tangible and intangible rewards, among others, on the effects of results and their similarity to or difference from expectancy: where one is uninvolved, when the results do not really matter, is surprise or nonconfirmation (as Charlesworth suggests) pleasurable and motivating; where one is involved and the consequences are serious, is negative nonconfirmation demoralizing? The author knows of no studies where such important questions have been answered; but their answers should hold important implications for such things as motivation, school learning, and morale, as well as many other aspects of human behavior.

The usefulness of an expectancy in guiding behavior depends upon the *completeness* and *accuracy* of the information possessed by the individual. The information which the urban 3-year-old has about busy streets is perhaps as complete as that of the 10-year-old, but it is less accurate. Hence we leave the 10-year-old reasonably free to move around unsupervised, but keep a watchful eye on the 3-year-old in all potentially dangerous situations. The girl of average good looks who has grown up in a family of beautiful sisters has neither complete nor accurate information about her own expectancies. We have seen how these expectancies govern her behavior so that they are confirmed. The friendly and gregarious 8-year-old who has had an overwhelming majority of experiences of being liked and accepted by strangers enters a new school with a broad grin and an open and friendly interest in his new classmates. They are flattered, relax, and soon accept him, thus confirming his expectancies. The occasional social failure he may have causes him, in terms of this theory, to redouble his efforts to be accepted.

Expectancy-probability theory has interesting implications for parental or teacher (caretaker) under- or overprotection. When do we allow our sons or pupils to have scout knives, or to swim unsupervised, or to go alone for a walk in the neighboring woods, or to ride alone from one city to another on the plane? Each caretaker makes his own judgment: a rough rule-of-thumb of common-sense protectiveness is probably the caretaker's judgment that the child can undertake the venture with about eight or nine chances out of ten of emerging from it relatively unscathed. Underprotective or casually rejecting caretakers lower the ratio, overprotective caretakers raise it (and the latter will always worry, no matter what the probability limits they set for safety).

PIAGET, EXPECTANCIES, AND PROBABILITY

Piaget's facile mind has covered many aspects of the development of the child's sensorimotor, mental, and moral processes. His treatment of sensorimotor development up to the age of about 2 years was summarized in Chapter 1. Piaget, as was suggested in Chapter 1, is not really a theorist in the strict sense of the word, but an acute *observer,* describer and classifier, often given to dogmatic conclusions and carelessness in research methods.

Among the aspects of child development he has considered are expectancy and probability. Three major stages in the development of expectancy-probability occur:

1. Preoperational (approximately ages 3 through 6 years), where the child is influenced in his behavior by irrelevant factors, such as continuity in space and time, or color. He does not distinguish possibility from necessity nor does he respond to the unequal relative proportions in an experiment. He has no sense of "lawfulness."

2. Concrete-operational (approximately ages 7 through 10 years), when he first separates that which is necessary from that which is simply possible. He acquires the idea that there are multiple possibilities, and develops notions of probability. He finds out that his reasoning is not always reliable, and begins to distinguish between certainty, probability, possibility, and simple chance determination.

3. Formal-operational (beginning at about age 11 years), only in this stage does he begin truly to master the concept of probability. This stage ends with its complete mastery. The child acquires such abstract mental or conceptual abilities as combinations, permutations, and proportions. It goes without saying that some individuals progress only incompletely through all three stages.

The present author has selected two of the many studies testing Piaget's notions of expectancy and probability. Both experiments correct the procedural faults so commonly found in Piaget's work. The more elaborate study (Davies, 1965) shows that children progress from nursery school through 9 years of age much as Piaget suggested they do. Whether they do this because of some maturational process, as Piaget intimates, or whether this occurs because of increased experience, particularly practice with and mastery of language and thought, Davies does not say. Davies' subjects were taken from midwestern public nursery schools, kindergartens, and public schools, and included equal numbers of boys and girls.

That developmental progress with age occurs is about Davies' only agreement with Piaget. Children of nursery school ages clearly demonstrate by their behavior in choice situations (they responded by pressing levers so that language and verbal formulation of rules were not required) that they had practical working expectancies or probability estimates. They *expected* to get a red marble from a jar which contained four red to each white marble, and a white marble from a jar that contained four white to each red marble.

As would be expected because of language proficiency alone, Davies' subjects could *demonstrate* mastery of the concept of probability before they could put it in words, but by age 8, *all* her subjects could formulate their probabilities-expectancies in words. Piaget apparently does not believe this possible until after about age 11. Piaget reported that boys were better in dealing with probabilities-expectancies than girls. Davies found no sex differences, although her girls were nonsignificantly better on the average than her boys (as would be expected if language mastery is the crucial factor, as girls are commonly found to mature faster than boys in language).

Goldberg (1966) in an equally well-controlled but less elaborate study, found that Piaget had penalized his children by failing to reward them for correct choices, by using words they did not understand, and by failing to control for color preference and attention in his tests. When these factors were controlled, thus giving the child the opportunity to use his "native intellectual power" (if there is any such thing) so as to make decisions, she found her late 3- to early 5-year-olds much superior in probabilistic thinking than Piaget would have predicted.

In other words—and we shall see this in other careful studies of Piaget's theories or descriptions—Piaget is not always found to be correct when he is carefully tested and, while he is currently very popular, his place in history is by no means settled. However, he has been useful in spurring us on to do useful and informative studies that otherwise might not have been done. His ages seem to be older for given stages than found in the United States, probably because of his population or methods or both.

Weir (1967) approaches the problem from a learning point of view. When his 9-year-olds were provided with a memory aid—a verbal mediation—they responded so as to get the greatest possible return from their efforts, although his 5-year-olds had not yet uniformly reached that stage. Weir never "paid off" his subjects for correct performances more than 66 percent of the time. Providing a memory aid to adults did not affect their performance: presumably, they had already built in their memory aids by having already learned to mediate and shortcut or operate in terms of probability principles. Weir also points out that his 9-year-olds did not *verbalize* their behavior, but they used environmental cues (ratio of payoffs) to determine their behavior.

Spiker, Gerjuoy, and Shepard (1956) also have found it possible to teach very young children the concept, middle-sized, using nonsense syllables conditioned to the middle-sized training stimuli.

Curiosity

Many people who have worked with higher mammals, such as monkeys and chimpanzees, or with children, have been struck by the tendency of such subjects to be curious. Even when well-fed, not thirsty, and, as nearly as can be ascertained, generally comfortable or in equilibrium, such subjects constantly explore their environment. Some investigators have postulated a *curiosity drive* to account for this behavior; others talk of an *activity drive*. Hebb (1955) may have in mind a phenomenon such as this when he speaks of the organism's seeking an optimal stimulation level. It is difficult to see how the so-called primary drives (thirst, hunger, need for elimination, and so on) produce such common behavior as we see in the warm, dry, recently fed baby who kicks, chews, and bangs his rattle, waves his hands in a dance just for fun, and is never still for a moment while he is awake.

Some studies present evidence suggesting that curiosity is a drive, possessing the properties of energizing and sensitizing, selecting, and directing behavior. In one of these (Montgomery and Segall, 1955), rats learned to discriminate between black and white when the reward for a correct choice was the opportunity to run for one minute in a situation new to them. In another (Montgomery, 1955), it was found that tame rats who had been handled preferred "risky" open elevated runways; whereas wild rats, presumably more uneasy in the whole experimental situation, chose "safe" enclosed runways. Curiosity, operating as a drive, was thought to be responsible for both sets of results, and it was proposed that curiosity and fear are antagonistic drives, with fear inhibiting curiosity.

Glanzer (1958) has published an excellent theoretical review of the literature on curiosity and stimulus satiation, in which he suggests that an organism requires a certain amount of information or stimulation per unit of time. If enough information is not present in the organism's environment, it will be actively sought. If too much stimulation is present, the organism tries to reduce the amount. In animals, this may take the form of freezing, avoidance, and even seizure. It has already been suggested (Chapter 1) that the human infant may seek to reduce stimulation by sleeping, although this avoidance or reduction phenomenon has not been studied as such in humans, and that his curiosity develops under conditions where there is appropriately given generous stimulation.

Glanzer sets up a postulate that, if correct, has profound implications for early child-rearing. He suggests that an organism's requirements for information are set by its past experience. If a high flow of information has been directed at it in the past, it will have high requirements later (be highly curious). Coming from an impoverished informational environment, a low requirement or standard will be established. This postulate suggests differential effects of early and late experience— new information is predicted to have more effect on changing the organism's standard and therefore its behavior if given earlier rather than later in life. There is considerable direct and indirect evidence to support this prediction, with respect to both animal and human problem-solving behavior (intelligence). This material is presented in considerable detail in Chapters 7 and 8.

In explaining and predicting human behavior, a distinction is often made between primary and secondary drives. *Primary* drives refer to the universal, usually physiological, drives such as hunger and thirst; whereas *secondary* drives are thought to be learned. Examples of drives usually considered to be secondary or learned are dependency, love and affection, and so on. The question has been raised whether certain drives, particularly curiosity, anxiety, and aggression, are primary or secondary drives (indeed, as will be pointed out a little later, the question has been raised whether they are drives at all). Such a classification is not of great practical significance, since in either case a drive operates in about the same way. Furthermore, our culture seems to provide opportunities for *all* its members to learn and receive repeated reinforcement for curiosity, aggression, and anxiety, thus satisfying the criterion of universality which a postulated drive should have if it is to be widely useful in explaining behavior.

There is a certain logical appeal, on the other hand, to considering curiosity as a well-established "habit of responding," or a well-learned and probably universally learned set of expectancies. Very early in the life of any higher organism, its own activities have resulted in reward: by wriggling closer to the mother, mammals have found warmth; by sucking, they have found nourishment; by pawing and grasping, they have secured food more easily. A general learning might be postulated, functioning almost like a trait: "Something occurs following moving around and trying out things." This "something" may be good or it may be painful, but the probabilities are that, at least for children of solid-type families, curiosity results more often in reward than in punishment. It is to be hoped that the average parent rewards curiosity more often than he punishes it by answering questions, purchasing new toys, and so on.

It might be postulated that secure children, who experience reward more frequently than punishment, will be more curious than children for whom the ratio is reversed. However, the principle of partial reinforcement may also apply to curiosity: even if curiosity is rewarded only occasionally, it will be reinforced as a response system (the needs it serves will be satisfied, hence it will be consolidated), thus functioning in the practical sense much like a drive. Nor is it inconceivable for curiosity to develop when the learning history of the child includes a preponderance of punishments over rewards. In such a case, a portion of the motive or drive producing curious behavior would be anxiety. In effect, one had best be curious and learn about his environment in order to avoid the pain inherent in it. Curious behavior would then serve to reduce both anxiety and curiosity. However, Penney (1965) working with fourth-, fifth-, and sixth-graders, finds that both the boys and girls in his study who were high in anxiety scored low (were less curious) on his curiosity test (the median correlation was about —.35). Other studies suggest the same thing (as Mendel, 1965).

For humans, confirmation of expectancies, quite without other reward, may also be reinforcing. Things happen to the curious child. Even though they are apparently neutral in a reward sense, the mere confirmation of his expectancies is rewarding to him. There is no question that being able to say "I was right," without any other reward, is satisfying, hence rewarding, to older children and adults. Observation leads us to believe that younger children and even infants are also gratified by being right. The game of peek-a-boo may have as part of its reward the constant confirmation of expectancies: "Mamma is still here, and I am still here." The endless glee resulting from opening, closing, and reopening a jack-in-the-box is perhaps another illustration of the rewarding nature of confirmation of expectancies and of surprise. The morning ritual of checking for all the dolls, or looking to see whether the cat is in his accustomed place (without any apparent interest in playing with or petting the cat), may also illustrate this expectancy-confirming phenomenon. Confirmation of expectancies may thus be security-giving although, as Charlesworth (discussed in the previous section) has shown us, in a game situation, surprise—(disconfirmation of expectancy)—seems to please children and arouse their curiosity.

For our present purposes, curiosity is considered to be a drive or motive. Montgomery and his co-workers seem to have demonstrated that reducing curiosity results in learning in lower animals; observation indicates that curiosity exists in very young infants. Montgomery's research indicates that responses motivated by fear appear to inhibit or prevent curious responses, and the inhibition of *overt* curiosity about taboo subjects, such as sex, is a phenomenon familiar in our culture. Ordinarily, as children move into the elementary-school years, they ask other children, not their parents and teachers, about sex. Yet curiosity about sex persists.

Whether drive or habit, or a mixture of both, curiosity plays a basic role in human learning. It seems desirable to reinforce the behaviors that reduce or satisfy it, but *at the level at which it exists in the child.* An anecdote about the son of an astronomer is in order. The boy asked his mother about the planet Mars. "Why don't you ask your father?" she said. "He's the expert." The son's reply was, "Yes, but I don't want to know that much."

It is possible that mild frustration and partial reinforcement will result in stronger curiosity than consistent reward. Answers that come too easily are less rewarding than answers that require more effort. But consistent punishment of curious behavior, or indifference toward and failure to reward the responses designed to reduce curiosity, may either distort its expression and the means by which it is satisfied (as, in the sexual area, by "Peeping Tom" behavior), or result in apathy and resignation. The apathetic, bland acceptance of things as they are that has been reported as characteristic of institutionalized and extremely poor children may be due to the failure of their environment to reinforce curiosity behavior. One author (Hofstaetter, 1954) reports that most of our standard judgments of intelligence up to about 20 months of age are based on a factor he calls *sensorimotor alertness* which is a term embracing behaviors that seem closely related to curiosity. The important idea that an information-rich environment in very early childhood results in the need for more stimulation (in more curiosity) at later stages of development should not be neglected in research on child-rearing.

This section on curiosity has been based more on speculation and research with animals than on research with children, although some studies of the effect on babies of novelty were summarized in the sensorimotor section of Chapter 1. Recent years have seen a rise in the amount of research on curiosity, possibly because people have begun to realize how fundamental it is to learning, language development, concept formation, and social development. The present author has selected (almost at random) four of the many studies demonstrating that novelty appeals to children of different ages, the forms in which they show their curiosity, and some of the conditions (aside from Charlesworth's surprise-in-games) that produce maximum curiosity.

The first of these studies (Greene, 1964) gave children one of two choices: choosing an envelope of the correct color rewarded the child by an enclosed picture; choosing the incorrect color envelope yielded only a blank piece of paper. In a second phase of the study, an envelope of still a third color (the novel stimulus) was added, and the child was asked to make his choice. Greene's children ranged in age from about $3\frac{1}{2}$ to $5\frac{1}{2}$ years. Regardless of whether they had been successful or unsuccessful on their first choice, significantly more children chose the new or novel envelope, although fewer of those who had been correct did so than of those who had been wrong. She also reports that still older children (up through fifth grade) are more likely to shift to new or novel stimuli after they have been right in their first choice. In other words, they have done it, they have been successful, and they want to move on to something new.

Mendel (1965) studied boys and girls about the same age as Greene's subjects. Her study is exceptionally carefully done. She used such toys as a foreign flag, a knight on a horse, a miniature old-fashioned horse-drawn bus, and an old-fashioned wooden fishing boat. Of the sixteen toys, some were very familiar, others totally unfamiliar, while still others were intermediate. The younger half of her group (about $3\frac{1}{2}$ to $4\frac{1}{2}$ years old) did not respond differentially to novelty, but the older half strongly preferred the more novel or unfamiliar toys. Boys were more predisposed to like novel toys than girls (a finding that fits in well with a widely accepted idea that girls are trained to be traditional, obedient, responsible, and conservative and thus, as women and mothers, to serve as a brake on too rapid changes in a culture). Her last conclusion agrees with Penney's, although she used different aged subjects (hers were younger) and different techniques for measuring anxiety (teacher ratings rather than a test): the less anxious a child was, regardless of sex, the more he preferred the novel toys.

Berlyne (see Berlyne and Frommer, 1966) has interesting theories about curiosity. To him question-asking is one form of *epistemic* behavior. Epistemic behavior is motivated primarily by epistemic curiosity. Epistemic curiosity, in turn, is aroused (Berlyne considers curiosity a drive) by conceptual conflict arising from such things as "novelty, surprisingness, complexity, incongruity, and power to induce subjective uncertainty" (p. 178). Note how closely Berlyne and Charlesworth agree on the function of game-type surprise.

Berlyne and Frommer worked with boys and girls from Canadian kindergartens, first grades, third grades, and fifth and sixth grades in two separate studies reported together. They told the children stories, showed them pictures, and combined stories and pictures. The children were invited to ask questions following each stimulus presentation.

Questions demanding explanation occurred seldom if ever before about the fifth grade, and were most frequent in connection with surprising magic tricks. Surprising items in general evoked the most explanatory and specific questions. The authors conclude that "with increasing age, sensitivity to gaps in information increases, and questions are more precisely aimed at information that can relieve uncertainty most effectively" (p. 188).

Finally, Turner and Wright (1965) investigated some of the conditions that blunted or enhanced curiosity. Their study is practically a model for research of its type, although it is too elaborate to summarize fully in the available space and is somewhat oversimplified here. They, like Berlyne and Frommer, report two experiments. One of their groups is made up of nursery school children from about 4 to 5 years of age, the other of 6- to 8-year-olds. They used such toys as plastic tennis rackets with a ball attached, power operated robots, guns with rubber darts, jigsaw puzzles, and four-way periscopes. The experimenter gave one of several different treatments for each child (after having the child rate the toys in order of his preference), then left the room for five minutes to observe the child through a one-way mirror; returned, and asked the child to rate the toys again.

The conditions that decreased toy preference (interest in, or curiosity about) were (1) removal, where the experimenter sneaked the toy out with no explanation; (2) removal with the statement "I'm taking the toy and you can never play with it again," coupled with actually taking the toy; (3) mild threat as, "I'm going to leave the room for a minute or two. Don't play with this one while I'm gone." (Does such a mild instruction suggest that the adult is relatively uninterested in the toy?).

Conditions that increased preference were (1) taking the toy out *but* returning it, having promised that it could be played with when the experimenter returned; (2) "I'm taking the toy out to fix it—it's dusty and not working right" (perhaps indicating to the child that it is an important toy to the adult); (3) strong threat as, "Don't play with this toy while I'm gone—it would be very naughty and you can never play with any of the toys again!", perhaps indicating to the child that the adult values the toy highly, and also appealing to a tendency often attributed to human nature to see the grass on the other side of the fence as greener.

Houston and Mednick (1963) worked with college undergraduates rather than children so their interesting study will be mentioned only briefly. But they found their creative University of Michigan students showed much more interest in novelty (new things, curiosity) than those they judged as noncreative. The interested reader should look at their paper because of the ingenious research methods Houston and Mednick devised and used.

From these studies, the reader should be able to adduce a number of general principles and specific techniques for arousing interest: new things are more interesting than old things; temporary disappearance with some assurance of eventual reappearance arouses interest; the child is more interested in things that seem to be of more value to the adult; surprises arouse curiosity and explanatory questions, particularly among older children; anxious children are less curious than more secure children; and boys (perhaps bolder) are more interested in the new and novel than girls.

It is pathetic to see how schools fail to capitalize on research like the studies above. The average teacher does not introduce gimmicks; the same dusty appurtenances stay on bulletin boards or walls for weeks and months at a time; routines are followed as invariably, dully, and without surprise as one sheep follows another, for the daily schedule never changes; the social science class is always conducted the same way; nobody is ever tricked.

The anxious and fearful child is ignored. Studies such as Penney's and Mendel's may give clues explaining findings from the Yale studies of children's anxiety, in which it is generally shown that anxiety interferes *progressively* with school learning from first through fifth grade (see, for example, Hill and Sarason, 1966). Anxious children are less curious, they ask fewer explanatory, fact-finding questions, they are less likely to explore new and different things. In other words, their anxiety limits the range of their inquiry-exploration. The general topic of anxiety will be more fully discussed later in this book.

How about trying something like this: at the peak of a class's interest in a subtopic, drop it, only to bring it out again a day or two later, thus still further intensifying interest, inquiry, and presumably deepening knowledge. The author's more conservative colleagues may mutter at about this point something negative about "teaching by gimmicks!" If a gimmick works, why not use it?

Nor is such behavior unique to schools. The home lives of many children are as stabilized and curiosity-stifling as any situation described immediately above.

What the author has said about teaching and child-rearing applies equally to such things as psychotherapy. Psychotherapists tend to belong to "schools." Some are Freudian, some Rogerian, some Skinnerian. A single therapeutic technique, used day after day with a patient (or client, as some counseling and guidance and clinical psychology workers call him) can become immensely dull. Rogers (for example 1951), in his earlier formulations of nondirective therapy, advocated that the therapist be passive and confine himself to reflection of feelings. Rogers, a master therapist, was (and is) able to vary this method. But his slavish and less discerning disciples, fearful lest they convey approval or disapproval, or anything other than simple acceptance, are likely to limit themselves to reflection, not of feeling but of content. (The term feeling does not differ much from what a psychoanalyst or learning theorist calls "interpretation.") The nondirective school of therapists came to be called by the irreverent the "mm-hmm" school.

Any technique, carried to the extreme, is more likely to put both patient and therapist to sleep than it is to cure the patient. In other words, surprises, new techniques, unusual variations, verbal shocks, walks in the park, sharp disapproval or strong approval, or frank revelations of the therapist's own point of view (usually withheld according to the principles of conventional theories of therapy) may all be useful variations in the therapeutic process.

Finally, we may grow less curious with age, perhaps because we know more (or *think* we do), possibly because we are tired.

Schools often operate in other ways to stifle children's curiosity, or fail to arouse it. Lower-class children from large families with working mothers tend to be treated by their parents in ways that make them apathetic, passive, and dull. "Be good! Be quiet! Get out of my way! Don't bother me!" Schools *continue to reward such behavior:* such children are *not discipline problems* (incidentally, while they are being good, they are also not learning). It has also been found (and this will be discussed later in more detail) that highly creative children—those who are always looking for or manufacturing the new and surprising, or asking the offbeat question—are not very popular with teachers. They are a nuisance, they disrupt the class routine, they don't go for the pat and superficial answer.

While such authors as Berlyne and Frommer, and Charlesworth find surprise and nonconfirmation of expectancy pleasing in a game-like setting (the child is not playing with anything very important "for keeps"), Spector finds that young men whose expectancies for something important are disconfirmed are demoralized. This, the present author suspects, often happens to bright children entering first grade and perhaps kindergarten: they come to school expecting to be *taught to read.* Instead, a deadly dull and often long-lasting period of "readiness" is inflicted on them. At one time, the State of California had a mandatory period of readiness for all children, regardless of their level of ability or pretraining. Reading is *important* to such children, they expect reading, and disconfirmation of their expectancies is as likely to be demoralizing to them as it was to Spector's young men. Such children, too, are "playing for keeps." Of course, many and probably most children need "reading readiness" before beginning in dead earnest the complex process of learning to read.

LANGUAGE AND CONCEPT FORMATION

Books have been written on the topic of language and concept formation, linguistics is a full-fledged science, speech and reading are the tools of our civilization. All this the author admits. But the "royal treatment" should be saved for an educational, not a child, psychology book.

Oversimplifying brutally, the rudiments of language begin with the baby's first cry, as discussed in Chapters 1 and 4. This vocalization is reinforced by attention coupled with the mother's presence. Somewhere around 3 to 9 months, the baby begins to couple his voice with his mother's presence: he babbles, this substitutes for mother, and is steadily refined and varied. Through the selective function of drive, nonsensical babbling eventually becomes meaningful words. These words serve to help the child to acquire distinctiveness and equivalence of cues and to mediate: to shortcut and, in a primitive way, to reason. The more practice the child has, the more language he knows, the more he is *rewarded* for thinking and shortcutting (forming specific and general concepts or principles), the better at such things he will be. *Concept formation,* to the present author, is simply a term for verbal mediation ranging from the very simple to the very complex and, for humans, formation of concepts rests predominantly on language.

Language is, of course, much more than the use of the human's sound-making apparatus. It originates there, but its foundations are multiply sensorimotor. The interaction and interdependence of language, thought, and concept formation and all of the receptors (senses) and effectors (the child's motoric) were stressed throughout the latter sections of Chapter 1. A child who has had a wide range of kinesthetic experiences, both as receiver and actor, should become a better reader and thinker than the child who has been scanted in this respect. The more you have seen, the better you should be able to talk, think, and form concepts about your experiences. To illustrate, Eskimos' very lives depend on snow. They touch it, see it, fall into it, dig their way out of it, judge whether it is hard-packed or soft, and so on. Conceptually, so the linguists tell us, they are much richer than the average American adult (or child) in their conceptualization of snow. They have multiple and refined words and formal concepts for it in their language and thought. The lower forty-nine states have many fewer: along the Eastern Seaboard and westward to the Rockies, we talk about wet snow, slippery snow, deep snow, light snow, and that is about it. Snow is a blessing to children, gardeners, farmers, and designers of Christmas cards. It is an inconvenience to the rest of us in the ordinary course of our lives. Hence, we are conceptually poor with reference to it. The word itself perhaps does not exist in languages originating in the tropics: a bright, verbally highly superior 3-year-old friend of the authors moved from San Francisco (definitely not the tropics, of course) to the Eastern Seaboard, awoke one morning to see his first snowfall, and cried out to his parents: "Come look! What is it? Is it flowers? Is it fog? Or is it like Christmas cards?" In the author's judgment, Piaget could have picked up some principle from this simple illustration.

It has also been pointed out in Chapters 1 and 4 that mediational processes are not necessarily verbal. Presumably, all the potentialities the child or adult possesses can serve as mediators. But, in our culture, verbal mediation is probably the type most often used. This poses one of the major problems in the education of the deaf, who have their primary source of language formation—hearing—cut off.

While the material presented above represents the present author's simplified view about the foundations of language, thought, and concept formation, he respects such authors as Piaget. Piaget, among others, has given us potentially useful suggestions for pinpointing development in these areas, even though much of his own research has been careless. Illustrations of how he has spurred "hard-nosed" experimentalists to investigate concept formation and thinking are presented below. Since it is impossible in the space available in this book to make even a sound random selection of studies in this field, the author has selected a few that were prompted by Piaget in one way or another, and presents them, hoping to move the reader to read more deeply in the field. Piaget, as some of the authors of the studies summarized below mention, can be fitted into more clearly and precisely formulated learning theory without resorting to Procrustean methods.

Kagan and Henker (1966) make pertinent criticisms of Piaget's theories of cognition (language-concept formation and use of concepts): they mention that "as usual varied stages of organization are proposed, and the dominant theme is that classification operations neither arise directly from language nor require language as a central explanatory factor in their development" (p. 24). The present author disagrees with such thinking of Piaget's, as Kagan and Henker also seem to, at least implicitly.

It was mentioned earlier that some of Piaget's results were affected by his asking children questions in words they did not understand, and presenting them with boring experimental tasks. Piaget and his co-workers also seem to assume that impulsivity, curiosity, task involvement, and question comprehension are equally present in children of all ages. This assumption is not tenable. In the preceding section on curiosity, we saw that results very different from Piaget's findings were secured when such factors were experimentally controlled. His work seems to under- rather than overestimate the abilities of children perhaps (as stated earlier) because of his methods and/or population.

One of the studies the author has selected for brief review was done by Jahoda (1964) to test Piaget's belief that few if any 9-year-olds can grasp the idea that they are simultaneously members of a city and a country. They are not capable of double classification.

Jahoda worked with 6- to 11-year-old Scottish children born in Glasgow, and asked them such questions as "Are you Scottish? Are you British?" If a child answered "Yes" to both questions, he was asked to explain how he could be two things at once. Jahoda found that many children younger than 10 or 11 (the age Piaget sets for grasp of the city-state-national concept) clearly understand the concepts involved. Piaget's stages simply did not hold up. Jahoda criticizes Piaget's thinking and methods because his criteria are ambiguous, for invalidly assuming that development of necessity inevitably proceeds from comprehension of *spatial* (which Piaget seems to equate with *geographical*) to *national;* and says that Piaget's results are due as much to children's failures to comprehend the language used in asking them questions as to inability to form concepts of "nationality."

Piaget also talks of conservation (for example, a chunk of plasticene will weigh the same regardless of the shape into which it is molded), and argues that the concept of conservation is developed first for mass, next for weight, and third for volume. Before about 5, Piaget believes, the child is "perceptually bound" and logic takes second place (that is, the world is flat because it looks flat, a misconception that, as we know, was held for millennia by adults as well as by children until exploration, or experience, scientific method, and logic demonstrated that the world is *really* round-ish). From sometime between 5 and 7 years, logic begins to take over.

Halpern (1965) carefully separated from a group of 236 suburban upper-middle-income pupils, twenty children (10 boys, 10 girls) who approached problems either empirically—"according to how it looks"— or deductively. The empirical group, given the weight conservation problem (such as molding plasticene chunk into different shapes, then being asked about the weight) gave such answers as "They weigh the same because they look the same," or "This is big like that." The deductive group used explanations that directly or indirectly referred to previous events in the test series, such as "You showed me they weighed the same." There were no sex differences, within her narrow age range there were no age differences, and the deductive group made significantly fewer errors than the empirical group. Her study is only one more piece of evidence supporting the present author's contention that the best teaching procedure is the one that instructs the child to *think about* or mediate what he observes: the principle, in a sense, is more important than the fact.

Wallach and Sprott (1964) investigated number conservation—the hypothesis that "young children do not recognize that amount of matter, number of objects, and other properties remain unchanged with variations of form and arrangement" (p. 1057). The authors succinctly summarize their findings for middle-class public school children from about $6\frac{1}{2}$ to about $7\frac{1}{2}$ years old by saying that "number conservation was induced in first-grade children by giving them experience with the reversibility of rearrangements which they regard as implying changes in number" (p. 1057). The first-graders were able to transfer their learning to new sets of objects. They also "preserved" or were able to use the new, more accurate, and efficient concept several weeks later, and overrode suggestions by the experimenter to the contrary. There were tremendous differences between Wallach and Sprott's trained and untrained groups.

Here again, we find Piaget's notion of relatively fixed stages untenable, and children, given proper circumstances and training, able to incorporate and maintain (even when prestige figures suggest the opposite) concepts at ages much earlier than Piaget believes possible.

Jensen and Rohwer (1965) find that children who are instructed to make up a sentence including two objects they are shown simultaneously learn a series of such pairs much more rapidly than children not so trained. They refer to this process as *syntactical mediation*. They worked with children from 5 to 17 years of age, carefully matched on IQ and socioeconomic status. The children were bright since the average IQ was 119, where 100 is considered the national average. The mediation instructions practically wiped out age differences in speed of learning after the age of 8 years, although high school youngsters apparently did not need instructions to mediate: they had learned through experience that this was the most efficient way to operate.

Huttenlocher (1964) found as would be predicted that younger children did better in concept formation involving fewer sequences, and that the ability to handle more and more logical steps increased with age from her youngest group of boys and girls (first-graders) to her oldest group (eleventh-graders). The most effective teaching procedure in her study was training a child by giving him first a negative then, second, a positive illustration of the principle. Successive negative sequences presented the children with the most difficult learning situation. This is consistent with reasoning advanced in Chapter 4 by the present author: Huttenlocher's most effective teaching sequence told a child first what he could *not* and second what he *could* do so as to proceed effectively. Older children, presumably doing more spontaneous mediating, were less affected by the sequence of training than younger children. This fits well with Jensen's and Rohwer's findings, summarized in the preceding paragraph.

Koffsky (1966) has reanalyzed Piaget and presents what to the author seems a more reasonable eleven-step description of how children learn to make classifications ranging from simple equivalence to complicated classifications of "inclusion" involving elaborate combinations of "some, all, none."

Rossi and Rossi (1965) find children able to cluster (group objects into categories) as soon as they are able to talk. Even their 2-year-olds tended to remember large numbers of stimuli by putting them into categories, even though they probably could not have given the experimenters the names of the categories they used (in this case, fruits, toys, clothing, and eating utensils). This provides still another example of the underestimation Piaget makes of children's abilities, which is probably due to his faulty research techniques. Children begin to remember things in the order they were presented (serial learning) later than they remember them by clustering. Indeed, serial learning seems to be a phenomenon setting in (at least for Rossi and Rossi's sample) after about 4 years of age.

Finally, as far as this series of representative, Piaget-inspired studies goes, Neale (1966) postulated that emotionally disturbed children, because of less effective and accurate social interaction during their lives, will be more egocentric than carefully matched normal and noninstitutionalized children. His subjects ranged from 7 to 11 years, and his hypothesis was supported. His test was one used by Piaget. The measure of egocentrism was the number of different views of a mountain scene a child could encompass in addition to the view with which he was personally presented (in other words, the less you can adopt others' points of view, the more egocentric you are).

To summarize this admittedly incomplete section, Piaget has spurred research workers to get down to the job of finding out how children learn and form concepts. Few studies support him totally, but most suggest improvements in investigative techniques, and provide us with useful information. None of the studies obtains results that cannot easily be fitted into relatively clear, simple, and straightforward learning theory. The reader should also recheck the probability expectancy section to note the Weir (in press, 1967) and the Spiker, Gerjuoy, and Shepard (1956) papers.

Fixation

Not all human behavior is adaptive and rational. All of us have learned and persist in ways of behaving that range from being inappropriate and ineffective to disrupting our general well-being. The girl with such a fear of insects that even a fly fills her with acute discomfort and anxiety is not behaving rationally. Her behavior will not ruin her life, but it will be consistently inconvenient, embarrassing, and uncomfortable for her and, if her reactions are noticeable, for those around her. The adolescent whose sexual impulses are uncontrollably channeled into voyeurism, on the other hand, runs the risk of public disgrace and humiliation, and repeatedly places himself in a situation of serious personal danger. Yet he repeats his potentially ruinous behavior over and over again, even after he has been caught, beaten, and legally punished.

There are two common conceptions of fixation. The first, and more general one, refers to the forming of a very strong habit or association. The second, perhaps as widely used, is the Freudian, which refers specifically to either an arrest of libido at an immature stage of development (see Chapters 2 and 3) or its strong attachment to early and inappropriate love objects.

The present treatment of fixation regards it as a strong and persistent response which occurs regardless of whether it is appropriate or inappropriate, and even in the face of observable or predictable punishment. The assumption is that this fixated response is somehow rewarding in terms of tension reduction (or optimum tension). Such a conception of fixation seems to offer a model for Freudian theories of fixation. At least, it fits well with the Freudian defense mechanisms—postulated to reduce anxiety—which spring at least in part from fixation. The present conceptual treatment of fixation was suggested quite directly by Freud to account for the persistence of neurotic symptoms (and presumably those that serve more effectively as well). His treatment of fixation and the defense mechanisms has been further developed by such representatives of learning theory as Dollard and Miller (1950), R. R. Sears (1951), and Whiting and Child (1953).[3]

Because of its nature and frequency, it is important to try to understand fixation. Alcoholism, for example, can be thought of as a fixation. Estimates are that there are as many as 5 million persons in the United States who are "problem drinkers." Men and women who persist in overeating despite their physician's well-based warning that they are "eating their way into the grave" may also be thought of as fixated on eating. The tendency to overeat is certainly one of the major health problems in the United States.

To develop a hypothesis of how a fixation is established, let us take the case of a small boy, Tommy, aged 16 months. Tommy is a toddler, not very steady on his feet. One day, before his parents can prevent it, the neighbor's bouncy terrier jumps at him, knocks him down, and stands over his face, breathing hotly at him and barking excitedly. Tommy screams convulsively, is very difficult to comfort, calms eventually, but goes into hysterics the next time he sees the dog. He also reacts with terror whenever he sees *any* dog. This terror generalizes to the tired old cat his parents own, and presently he shows acute fright reactions to all animals—even to the ducks at the zoo, to which he has previously enjoyed feeding stale bread. Such reactions go on for months; Tommy begins to have nightmares about animals, and no amount of reassurance, explanation, derision, or even punishment helps him.

What has happened to Tommy? First, he is demonstrating very wide primary stimulus generalization (see Chapter 4). The beginning of this behavior can be thought of as belonging to the family of the classical conditioned response, with the dog the conditioned stimulus, the sensations of being knocked down the unconditioned stimulus, the resulting pain and fear the unconditioned response, and the later fear, crying, and avoidance, the conditioned response.

Since this experience was an extremely *traumatic* or frightening one, it is possible that conditioning or more properly learning, could occur in one trial. Figure 5.2 demonstrates the observable, or overt, aspects of the first stage of the conditioning process. Figure 5.3 illustrates what may be happening "inside" Tommy.

The next stage of the fixation may be represented as it is in Figure 5.4. Here CS (the dog) arouses anxiety besides causing Tommy to be afraid, to cry, and to run away. *His being afraid, crying, and running*

---

[3] The conditioning paradigm for fixation has been developed in about this form by I. E. Farber (personal communication).

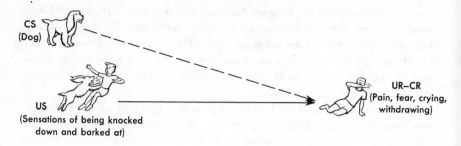

Figure 5.2   First stage in acquiring a fixation.

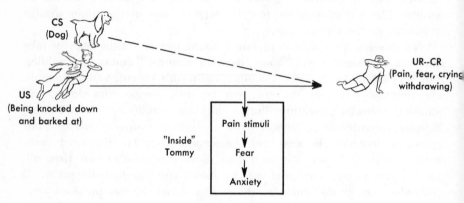

Figure 5.3   Internal aspects of the first stage of fixation.

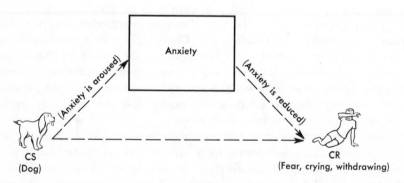

Figure 5.4   A diagrammatic representation of established fixation.

away reduced his anxiety—an anxiety rooted in his early, preverbal history. Hence punishment, such as scolding or derision, the meaning of which he has learned later, and which arouses either fear or shame, does not eliminate his hysterical behavior. Nor does comfort help greatly, since it (like scolding and derision) ordinarily occurs after the child has already reduced his anxiety in good part by crying and running away. For these reasons, the scolding, derision, and comfort do not become associated in a meaningful fashion with anxiety reduction. Since it is commonly assumed that anxiety is one of the most intolerable drives, anything that reduces it is heavily rewarded or reinforced, hence likely to be well-learned and extremely persistent.

Not only primary but also secondary stimulus generalization occur in this situation, so that instead of reacting hysterically *only* to the dog that frightened him, Tommy reacts similarly to all dogs, cats, and to many or most other animals.

The hypothetical case of the compulsive overeater is somewhat more complex than the illustration above. Let us create a fictitious adolescent, Mary, who is a pretty girl but very overweight which causes boys as well as girls to shy away from her and poke fun at her. Physical examinations show nothing medically wrong with Mary; she could slim down if she would simply eat less. But, despite parental and medical urging and ostracism by her peers, she continues to eat "senselessly." Instead of slimming down, she grows even fatter. For Mary, going back to Figure 5.3, food may be thought of as the conditioned stimulus. Pain associated with hunger, perhaps as a result of rigid infant scheduling, is the unconditioned stimulus; and eating is the unconditioned-conditioned response that eliminates the hunger pains. If Mary's early hunger experiences have been painful enough, they may have evoked great anxiety, so that food (as the CS) evokes anxiety and eating reduces it.

Through stimulus generalization, other anxiety-arousing stimuli may become conditioned stimuli for eating. Due to their similarity to the anxiety associated with eating, these new anxieties may in turn come to be reduced by eating. Since eating also satisfies the primary drive of hunger, it is a doubly reinforced response: Mary eats both to live and to keep herself from being anxious. In the face of such satisfactions, Mary foregoes popularity, parental approval, and good physical health.

Conditions under which fixation could conceivably be produced are listed and discussed below. In the present state of our research knowledge these are frankly speculative. But it seems reasonable that a response is likely to be fixated if one or several of the following conditions exist:

1. A fixation depends on trauma or overlearning.

2. To be fixated, a response must satisfy a need (in the sense that this has been discussed).

3. Responses that require relatively little effort are more likely to be fixated than those that require great effort.

4. Responses that have been acquired and are maintained under conditions of partial reinforcement are most likely to be fixated.

5. It can be predicted, but less confidently, that the greater the reinforcement for a response, the more likely the response is to be fixated.[4] Two reasons may be advanced for this prediction. First, let us think of the *likelihood that a response will occur* as a product of the amount of drive or need attached to it and the amount of previous learning that has occurred for it. Hence, if we have two competing responses of the same strength—one, for example, of avoiding a stimulus, the other of approaching it—the one with the greater drive or motive is more likely to occur and under appropriate circumstances, to be reinforced.

For example, 2-year-old Billy has been taught not to "raid the refrigerator." This habit (H) has a strength of 10, let us say. In combination with such a habit, Billy has a need or drive (D) of 10 to maintain the love and affection of his mother. The strength of his refrigerator-avoidance response, then, is $D \times H$, or 100. Billy, however, has also learned to look to the refrigerator for food, and this habit has a strength of 10. If his hunger drive is low (5, for example), the two competing behaviors of raiding the refrigerator as opposed to "minding his mother" have respective excitatory potentials, or "likelihoods-of-occurring," that may be represented by the figures 50 and 100; Billy therefore avoids the refrigerator. The hungrier he gets, the stronger the drive that combines with the habit of refrigerator-raiding. When his hunger drive reaches a strength of 12, we see him moving in on the refrigerator. The "excitatory potential" for that response is now 12×10, or 120, and can compete successfully with his refrigerator-avoiding behavior, which has a strength of only 100. When both responses are at the same level (100 for both approach and avoidance), we may think of Billy as being in *conflict*. The greater the excitatory potential of the two matched responses, the greater the conflict may be (Brown and Farber, 1951). That is, if Billy is *very* attached to or afraid of his mother, and also very hungry, his conflict may be stronger than if he is only moderately attached to or afraid of his mother, and moderately hungry. It should be added that this account is oversimplified and ignores, for example, the fact that increased hunger drive may combine, not only with refrigerator-opening responses, but also with other responses.

Regardless of the level of his drive or habit, if Billy raids the refrig-

---

[4] As mentioned in Chapter 4, psychologists still have much to learn about the effects of reinforcement. The effects on *behavior* of amount of reinforcement is a particularly unclear part of reinforcement theory.

erator and gets away with it, his habit of doing so will be somewhat strengthened (reinforced). Habits accompanying the competing motive (regard for, or fear of, his mother) are not reinforced in this setting— hence lose in *relative* strength.

The second reason great reinforcement may be more likely to produce fixation than moderate reinforcement is that *the amount of reward has some bearing on the speed of learning.* Again using Billy and the refrigerator as an illustration, if Billy is *extremely* hungry, the *single* reinforcement of his refrigerator-raiding may have, for example, a value of 5 in increasing the habit, thus bringing its strength up to 15, comfortably (or uncomfortably for his mother) above his avoidance-habit strength of 10. But if he is more restless and bored than hungry, the increase in habit strength from a *single* refrigerator-opening response may be negligible, so that there is little or no resulting difference in the habit strength of refrigerator-raiding, as opposed to mother-minding. In other words, a response made under high drive may increase in strength much more rapidly each time it is made than one made under low drive.

Related to the effect of amount of reinforcement on fixation is the effect of strong reinforcement in a strange situation, or when a child is under stress. It may be that strange situations arouse anxiety, and that anxiety adds to whatever motivation already exists. An event that reduces the anxiety and *other motives* may provide extra reinforcement for the response that brought about the event or is associated with it. A strong punishment in such a situation may, in similar fashion, reinforce whatever responses result in escape from punishment.

There is also some evidence to indicate that wider stimulus generalization occurs under circumstances of anxiety. One study (Levy and McCandless, 1952) indicates that subjects who were administered electric shock in a situation about which they had no information later expected more frequent shocks than those who had been shocked but had (or thought they had) information about the experimental circumstances. Evidence (Mednick and Lehtinen, 1957) indicates that younger children show wider stimulus generalization than older ones, from which we can possibly infer that children generalize more widely than adults. If this is true, some basis is provided for arguing that the same experience may have more widespread effects on children than on adults.

Approach-Avoidance, Conflict, and Displacement

APPROACH-AVOIDANCE GRADIENTS

The idea of approach-avoidance has already been introduced as we talked about Billy and his refrigerator-opening behavior. Hunger com-

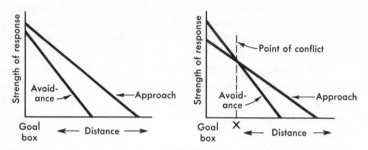

Figure 5.5   A schematic representation of approach-avoidance tendencies.

bining with habit (previous learning) cause him to approach; but love for and need of his mother in combination with habit cause him to avoid. Lewin (1935) has discussed what he calls positive and negative valence (attraction-repulsion), and has hypothesized that negative valence lasts a shorter time and extends a shorter distance from the goal than does positive valence. Miller (1951), working with similar concepts, postulated *approach-avoidance gradients.* Experimental work by Miller and his students (for example, Murray and Berkun, 1955), as well as that of such workers as Judson Brown, has lent factual support to these ideas.

Taking a simple case, let us say that a white rat has been both shocked and fed in a goal box. In him will have been built up tendencies both to approach and to avoid the goal box. See Figure 5.5. A demonstrates the "spread" of the two gradients of approach-avoidance tendencies in terms of space from the goal box.

It will be noted that in both *A* and *B* of Figure 5.5 the avoidance gradient is steeper (extends less far from the goal box) than the approach gradient. For Figure 5.5 *A,* the avoidance gradient is not so high as the approach gradient, although at the goal box they are close together. It might be predicted that our white rat will move more slowly as the distance between the approach and avoidance gradients grows less, but that he will nonetheless proceed to the goal box and eat. Such a pattern probably characterizes Billy when his hunger reaches the level at which he is ready to override his mother's prohibitions.

But in Figure 5.5 *B,* the avoidance gradient at the goal box (or, in Billy's case, the refrigerator) is higher than the approach gradient. In the case of the white rat, this may be either because he is not very hungry or because he has been shocked more often or more intensely than he has been fed. In Billy's case, the same things might be postulated—that is, either he is not very hungry, or he has only recently been punished by his mother for refrigerator-raiding, or he is in a particularly dependent state so that he needs his mother very much. Billy also possesses language, and can increase his hunger by thinking about food, or his avoidance behavior by thinking about his mother. Thus, it is harder to predict his than a rat's behavior: we do not know what is going on in his mind. What goes on there may affect either approach or avoidance behavior, or both.

CONFLICT

Since the avoidance gradient is steeper than the one for approach, Billy and the white rat are free to move to point X in Figure 5.5 *B,* although again it is predicted that they will move toward refrigerator or goal box more slowly as they approach it. At X, *conflict occurs and they are immobilized.* In other words, conflict can be defined as the place or time when *approach equals avoidance* in strength. This conflict may be resolved by time: as they hover at point X, they become hungrier. *Thoughts* of food (symbolic behavior) may serve almost instantaneously to increase Billy's hunger. For the nonthinking rat, presumably only *time* will accomplish this purpose. As their hunger drive increases, excitatory potential for approach is raised until the approach gradient is higher than the avoidance gradient and they move toward food. On the other hand, ideas of Billy's mother may enter his mind and raise his avoidance gradient to the point where conflict is removed by his leaving the entire situation. He "gets away from temptation."

The process of learning to read or of going to school at all, also illustrates approach-avoidance behavior. The good teacher is friendly and approachable; she "rules" with affection, kindness, and reward rather than with sarcasm and coldness. She attempts to understand each child in order to keep his anxieties and fears at a relatively low level and appropriate to the child's task rather than inappropriate. Some anxiety, when attached to appropriate, efficient responses, actually may result in their being more frequently made, hence reinforced. Thus, she strives to keep pupils' avoidance gradients low. By the same token, she tries to tie in her teaching with experiences from the children's own lives. She chooses textbooks that are suitably written, attractively put together, and interesting. In this fashion, she tries to raise pupils' motivation for learning, and this motivation in turn raises the approach gradient.

At the same time, teachers and parents are setting up different approach-avoidance gradients for activities that are detrimental to school learning. They praise (help to heighten approach gradients) when children do well in school. They typically criticize or punish when school success is low—that is, they set up avoidance gradients for pursuits that are incompatible with school success, such as dawdling, playing truant, daydreaming, and so on. There are social-class differences in the degree to which parents support the school (aid it in raising school-learning approach gradients; cooperate with it in discouraging behavior that may run counter to good school performance, such as regular school attendance, cooperation and courtesy in the classroom, and so forth). Middle- and upper-class parents support the schools strongly; lower-class parents do so to a lesser degree.

Actually, many subcultures actively oppose schooling, at least beyond a certain point. For years, the state of Iowa has been waging legal battle with the Amish, who want "their own people" teaching their children and believe that education beyond the eighth grade disrupts the "Amish way of life." Since they want their own people teaching, but their own people are not highly educated, it follows that Iowa cannot certify either the teachers or the schools; yet the law requires all normal children to attend state-accredited schools until a certain age.

For many youngsters, particularly boys, being a good scholar means being the teacher's pet which in turn leads to ostracism by his male peers. What on the surface looks like a reward from the teacher is actually a punishment when seen in the total meaningful context of the child's life. Urban gang psychology is essentially antischool (see, for example, Claude Brown, 1965). Observation and evidence (see Chapter 14) support such a point of view indirectly, and indicate that lower-class children do relatively less well in school than, for example, middle-class children. Many factors, of course, enter here; and this rather serious social problem is discussed in more detail in Chapter 14.

DISPLACEMENT

Conflict has been defined as the state of an organism when affected by *equally strong approach and avoidance tendencies* toward a stimulus or goal. As has been pointed out, the organism may react with *immobility*. A child may *reason* through the conflict, thus *resolving* it, or may eventually approach because, as a function of delay, increase in drive occurs. The opposite may also happen: if avoidance tendencies increase sharply, the individual may simply *leave the situation* where conflict has occurred.

Ways of *avoiding* conflict and of avoiding or diminishing the anxiety associated with it also exist. Freud postulated a variety of defense mechanisms, such as repression, reaction formation and projection, and regression. One of the most important of these is *displacement*. Displacement seems most likely to occur when the original goal cannot be reached and when other goals, more or less similar to the original one, are available. Displacement is a *clinical* term, suggested by Freud. It is now thought that it is at least partially explainable by the *laboratory* term, generalization, which was discussed in Chapter 4. Miller (1948) and Dollard and Miller (1950) have given close attention to the concept of displacement, have related it to generalization and shown how it may be used as an important explanatory device for certain kinds of human behavior.

The girl angry with her teacher may *displace* her hostility so that she is saucy to her mother or, if she fears her mother or loves her so much that she cannot bring herself to be rude, she may abuse her younger brother. *Compensation* appears to be a special case of displacement: the boy who is shy, isolated, and inadequate in athletics may displace earlier efforts to excel physically onto his academic studies; or the boy inadequate academically may concentrate on becoming a star athlete or a school rowdy.

Miller (1948) discusses the assumptions that must be made before displacement can be used precisely in predicting human behavior. He states:

> Five assumptions are needed to deduce the tendency for displacement to occur in situations in which the direct response to the original stimulus is prevented by conflict. These are: (1) that the direct response to the original stimulus generalizes to other similar stimuli, with the amount of generalization becoming smaller the less similar the stimuli; (2) that the response which conflicts with the occurrence of the direct response to the original stimulus also generalizes to other similar stimuli, becoming weaker the less similar the stimuli; (3) that the gradient of generalization of the conflicting response falls off more steeply with dissimilarity than does that of the original response which it inhibits; (4) that when two or more incompatible responses are simultaneously excited, the one with the greatest net strength will be the one which will occur; and (5) that the net strength of a response will be its strength minus that of any response incompatible with it which is excited at the same time. . . . In addition to these assumptions, two more will be useful in dealing with other aspects of the problem. One of these is (6) that an increase in the drive involved in either type of gradient will raise the over-all height of that gradient. . . . The final assumption is (7) that gradients of generalization approximate the form of negative growth curves. (pp. 167–168)[5]

Granted these assumptions, most of which have been discussed earlier in this chapter, it is apparent that one stimulus can serve instead of another, one response take the place of another, substitute goals can be used and, at least to some degree, gratification of some needs can be made to serve others.

---

[5] Reprinted with permission of the American Psychological Association and N. E. Miller, from Miller (1948).

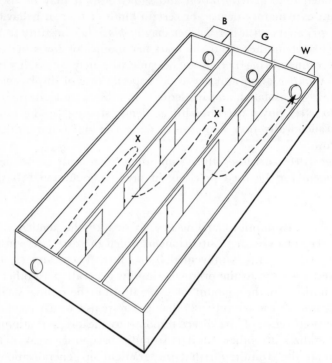

Figure 5.6 A representation of the Murray-Berkun
(1955) maze and a hypothetical goal path followed by a
rat showing displacement.

An animal experiment by Murray and Berkun (1955) illustrates this
process. Rats were placed in a three-alley maze, one alley being black,
one gray, and one white. Windows were cut in the walls between alleys
to allow the animals to move from one to the other, as in Figure 5.6. The
rats were first trained to seek food in the black(B alley and goal box.
After they had learned this, they were shocked in the black goal box
until they had learned to avoid it. Previously they had explored all three
alleys; but during training the alley windows had remained closed. On
a test, the windows were opened. The dotted line in Figure 5.6 shows a
typical rat's "path to the goal." At spot X in alley B, the rat comes into
conflict (his approach gradient is crossed by his avoidance gradient). The
rat retreats and passes through the window into the gray alley (G),
similar to but different from the one in which he had been fed and
shocked. At point X he again reaches the conflict point and retreats to
the white alley (W). Here, in this very different alley, his approach
gradient is stronger. He goes all the way to the goal box and obtains
food. He has "displaced" one goal with another.

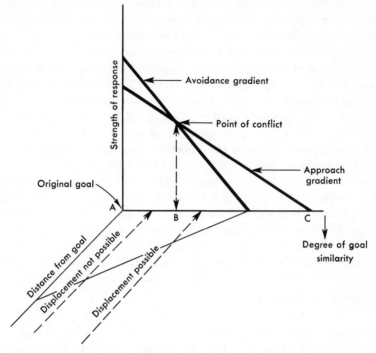

Figure 5.7   A schematic representation of how displacement occurs as a function of conflict. (Adapted with permission of the American Psychological Association and E. J. Murray, from Murray and Berkun, 1955.)

One might call this process substitution when it is "conscious." For example, little children learn to argue rather than to hit with sticks or to kick; to ask for food from the refrigerator rather than to "snitch" it, and so forth. In displacement, presumably, the process occurs without the individual's being aware of the fact that he is displacing. Because of its clinical origin, many reserve the term *displacement* for socially and personally maladaptive behavior. The term *sublimation* can be applied to "truly happy" displacement of libidinal drives. For instance, it might be said that the good nurse "sublimates" her own dependency needs; they become transformed into a desire to care for others. *Compensation* as described above is another case of displacement. Its social-personal utility (or mental-hygiene value) seems to fall between sublimation and displacement. The assumptions used to explain displacement in learning terms seem equally plausible for compensation and sublimation.

Figure 5.7 is a schematic three-dimensional representation of displacement. The horizontal axis from A to B represents goals that are moderately close to the original goal (located at point A). Instead of goals, stimuli, responses, or drives could be arranged along this axis in similar fashion.[6] For simplicity in writing, "goals" will be used in this section, although any of the other terms could be substituted.

The goals between A and B are unavailable to the human or animal because they lie in an area where the avoidance gradient is higher than the approach gradient. The approach and avoidance gradients intersect at the point indicated, since the slope of the avoidance gradient is steeper than that of the approach gradient. The goals between B and C on the horizontal axis can be approached along the "displacement possible" arrow since, from point B, the approach gradient is higher than the avoidance gradient. Presumably, the goal as close as possible to A will be the one selected for displacement. To the extent that the substitute goal is similar to the original goal (satisfies the same or a related need), the displacement is successful—tension is reduced. When these conditions of similarity or "mutual" satisfaction do not exist, or are at a low level, the displacement is not successful. Thirst goals, for example, cannot be satisfied by hunger goals; or sex goals by dominance goals.

TREATMENT OR THERAPY

Displacement, particularly when it is persistent, can be thought of as a special case of fixation. What can be done about both fixations and displacements, particularly when they are very damaging to the individual?

Simple maturity, the learning that accompanies it, and resultant changes in self-confidence and self-concept often help. It is unlikely that runabout Tommy will continue all his life to fear dogs. Although anxiety and fear responses seem to be extinguished very slowly, they eventually weaken. The world is full of friendly dogs; little boys are endlessly curious; eventually it is likely that Tommy's approach tendency for dogs will become stronger than his avoidance tendency. If his new experiences with dogs are pleasant, approach tendencies will grow even stronger. As Tommy grows older, he also learns that it is "sissy" to show fear, so that he acquires "an avoidance tendency for his avoidance tendency" and, to show his bravery, goes up to dogs and pats them. Because he is unhurt, his approach tendency is further strengthened, his avoidance tendency further weakened.

Finally, as Tommy grows older, words mean more to him, and he understands better the connection between his fear and the event in his

---

[6] The interested student should consult Murray and Berkun (1955) for a detailed study of their animal experiment, suggested applications of their analysis to a psychotherapy case, and a schematic representation of their theory of displacement.

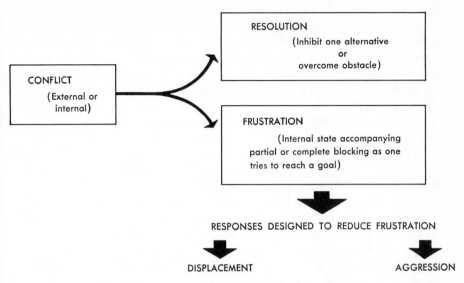

Figure 5.8   Various ways of handling frustration.

earlier childhood particularly if people older and wiser (hopefully) talk to him about this event in his childhood. It may be that the universal child request to "Tell me about when I was a little boy/girl" is motivated by the child's trying to understand himself. The fascination for children of their own "baby books" (a middle-class phenomenon) where parents have written about the baby, his language, and motor development, and have pasted in pictures, may belong to the same *my childish behavior* category of "I am trying to understand myself." Such understanding, or "insight," seems to reduce avoidance tendencies and to permit new learning to take place. The child's increased size, strength, speed, and coordination also combine to make situations less threatening than when he was a runabout. Once his fear of one dog has been reduced, the generalization gradient works in reverse, so that unreasoning fear of *all* dogs is reduced.

This suggests a therapy for Tommy, and, by implication, for fixations in general. One recommendation is that parents acquire an old, tired dog, who is thoroughly accustomed to small children, and bring him into the home without any attempt to force Tommy into having traffic with him. Then, with comfort afforded to Tommy for whatever panic reaction he may have when he sees the dog, and repeated reassurances and explanations about dogs, "let nature take its course." The constant recurrence of anxiety will be wearing to Tommy and weaken his excitatory potential for anxious responses. His parents' reassurances may weaken them still further and may also increase his approach tendencies (his interest) concerning the dog. Eventually he will reach the point where he can approach the dog. If the animal reacts in a friendly fashion or not at all, extinction begins to set in for the avoidance-response-to-dogs and the approach-response-to-dogs is reinforced. This extinction-of-fear behavior by the dog is the reason a "safe" animal should be acquired. If one is to work with the environment for therapeutic or training purposes, he needs to take precautions to see that the environment is going to fit the needs of the situation. In other words do not, in such a situation, get a small, bouncy puppy with sharp teeth.

The principles of therapy for fixations of all sorts are very similar to those that have been described above. The alcoholic drinks himself into a stupor, fatiguing himself with drinking and building up, for a time, an avoidance tendency for alcohol. For a few days or weeks he stays "on the wagon." The compulsive eater gets gas pains, or is warned by the doctor, or is shocked by the scale reading; he goes on a diet for a few days, weeks, or months. But such "self-therapies" seldom work for long. The fatigue, the nausea, the gas pains wear off—the avoidance gradient is reduced; the old approach tendencies reappear; and the individual returns to his self-destructive behavior.

Some fixations can apparently be broken by understanding how the family of conditioned stimuli first came to be attached to the family of unconditioned stimuli. Such understanding can perhaps be gained only through words and a precise pin-pointing of the original experience. With experiences occurring in infancy and before the acquisition of language (as appears to be true of experiences associated with alcoholism and compulsive overeating), such pin-pointing and understanding may be difficult or impossible. The antecedents of such fixations are, in addition, undoubtedly both severe and complex. It may be for these reasons that conventional "insight" therapy for alcoholism and overeating is so difficult and so seldom successful.

For alcoholics, at this time, the most successful therapy resembles very closely that illustrated by the case of Tommy, in which understanding and pin-pointing play a minor role. A powerful avoidance gradient for liquor must have been established, perhaps by the almost complete ruin of the person through drinking. The support, warmth, and inspiration of such an organization as Alcoholics Anonymous may help to establish a strong approach tendency for abstinence, which counteracts the residual approach tendency for alcohol. Being able always to call on a brother Alcoholic Anonymous for friendship and support is undoubtedly important in setting up such a tendency.

Another type of therapy can be mentioned here. This is Levy's *release therapy* (1939). It is apparently particularly successful with very young children (by whom, presumably, fixations have not been strongly over-learned) who have previously been well-adjusted or reasonably well-adjusted, but whose adjustment deteriorated after some specific trying experience or experiences (a serious fright, an illness of the mother, a new baby whom they have not been able to accept, or a hospital experience such as a tonsillectomy). Release therapy consists of placing such children in a play situation that duplicates or resembles the situation that is thought to have caused the trouble in the first place (the principle of generalization operates here). The therapist is warm and reassuring. Ordinarily, children soon show strong emotions of the type they presumably showed in the original situation. But a typical extinction process apparently occurs. The conditioned stimuli of the hospital setting, for example, evoke the conditioned responses of panic and fear, but nothing happens: the unconditioned stimulus (pain and shock) no longer occurs following the conditioned stimulus (the hospital setting). Instead, the child is reassured; simple explanations are given to him; and presently he "recovers." Here, of course, the original circumstances of learning are relatively simple and accurately known. Under such circumstances, therapy may be very effective.

One 3-year-old girl, well known to the author, was compelled to undergo a tonsillectomy. The experience was frightening, and the postoperative healing experience was painful. A week or so after the operation she regressed in her sleeping habits and was wet at night frequently. Ordinarily a sound sleeper, she began to awaken because of bad dreams and fears. She sucked her thumb compulsively, showed shyness and fear around strangers, and in general behaved in a fashion unlike her usual rather well-adjusted self.

One evening she asked that her bedtime story be the recounting of her hospital experience. She demanded to have every unpleasant detail— from entering the hospital, through getting into the hospital bed and having the ether mask applied, to awakening in fear from the anaesthetic —recounted to her. She demanded the story not once but a half-dozen times on this first occasion. The next night she again demanded the story repeatedly. This went on night after night, but with fewer repetitions being requested as time went by. In a week or ten days interest in the "story" had subsided, and during the same period her signs of maladjustment diminished and disappeared.

Although simple improvement in health probably accounted for much of this recovery, some seems to be explainable by the same principles of extinction and limited insight that we have applied to release therapy. For the child, the conditioned stimuli (the story of the operation) were constantly repeated without the occurrence of the unconditioned stimuli (the pain, fear sensations, nausea), so that the responses of anxiety, tension, and panic were extinguished. In addition, these conditioned stimuli were presented in a setting of security, with the child in her own bed, warm and safe. For such a child, with a fairly well-developed symbolic system, the scene of her original difficulties was, of course, evoked not literally but symbolically (see Chapter 4). Again, the pleasure children take in hearing stories—good and bad—of their babihood relates to this point.

Therapy cannot be dealt with in the easy fashion that has been used in the preceding paragraphs. The professionals who attempt to heal persons (infants, children, or adults) from their emotional difficulties are more confused than those who attempt to deal with physical illnesses. For some *physical* illnesses (as poliomyelitis, "old-fashioned" or nonvirus pneumonia) the medical doctor knows exactly what to do. For the former, he uses preventive measures, for the latter he uses therapeutic measures. Prevention and recovery rate are now exceptionally high for both illnesses. Cancer, however, remains a mystery.

Professional workers, particularly those in the medical and allied professions, psychologists, and social workers can usually recognize children who have problems, as can classroom teachers (although even today they are more likely to label the child who disrupts routines as a problem than the child who sits quietly in his corner of the room and says never a relevant word). For diagnosis of children's emotional and intellectual difficulties, psychologists are probably the best trained of the groups mentioned above, combining as theirs does scientific method and clinical skill. But psychologists and all the other professionals mentioned still grope for the means to move a child from mental illness to mental health. This area of practice, study, and research, is one of mankind's most serious problems.

To conclude this chapter on special factors in learning, it must be admitted that no current theory, whether derived from psychoanalytic or learning principles, is comprehensive or vital enough to encompass, explain, or guide the adult or child through states of despair, terror, tenderness, and dependence such as are constantly encountered. The child or adult whose defenses have broken down so that he is psychotic represents problems of adjustment and therapy that we only *begin* to understand. But only by patient application and testing, confirming and rejecting of hypotheses formulated as explicitly as possible, can we ever hope to understand, guide, or cure.

Summary

This chapter is not easy to summarize. It consists, at least in the author's thinking, of a series of vital concepts none of which fits completely neatly into a learning-theory framework, as did the concepts and research discussed in Chapter 4 of this book. But this set of concepts (and children's behaviors that relate to them) are the type any child or clinical psychologist, or psychiatrist or teacher or social worker or parent, meets every day. If the concepts and their associated behavior are always with us, then they must be discussed, although they cannot be tidily pigeonholed.

The chapter includes six major sections. The first section deals with expectancies and probabilities. These we learn. We behave according to our best expectations that the behavior we choose will be successful. If the chance of loss (as life, money, prestige) is great, if possible we wait for more favorable circumstances before we do anything. In other words, our behavior in terms of a *risk* factor is partly determined by our knowledge and commonsense, partly by what we need for personal reasons and how badly we need it.

The second major section of the chapter concerns *curiosity*. The author considers that it is a drive that underlies such things as school success, good relations with our friends, and even our level of effective intelligence. Schools, as currently organized, reward good, passive, noncurious children but penalize curious, questing, offbeat children. Middl class parents do a better job of teaching their children to be curious than lower-socioeconomic-class parents. Evidence exists that the more information that has been fed to children as infants and runabouts, the more they are likely to be curious (motivated) in school and other life settings. When children are "playing for keeps," surprises (disconfirmations of expectancy) may be demoralizing. In game-type situations, surprises, novelties, "gimmicks," all appear to be helpful teaching devices.

The third major section of the chapter concerns language and concept formation. Such behavior emerges naturally from children's ideas of probability, expectancy, and their curiosity about life. Piaget has stimulated considerable worthwhile research about language and concept formation, as well as probability and expectancy and curiosity. Though Piaget can be criticized for poor scientific methods, he is to be respected because of his heuristic (knowledge producing) influence. To the present author, language and concept formation are simply subcategories of general learning theory: the more experience a child has, and the more he has been taught to organize his knowledge into categories formed according to principles, the more effective a person he will become, whether he is a first-grader or a 90-year-old. The principle of learning how to learn, how to *induce* and *deduce,* is more important as far as the author is concerned than facts learned in isolation. Facts for facts' sake are typically useless. We must know how to integrate and use them.

The fourth major section of the chapter cannot be adequately summarized. It concerns fixation—such topics as addiction, and other self-defeating mechanisms were discussed. Fixations, even though they may be destructive to the child personally and socially, serve his purpose in that they reduce his anxiety. They limit him, as there is solid evidence that the anxious, fixated child is less curious, less bold, less active, thus allows himself less chance to learn and thus correct his own behavior, than the relaxed, unfixated child.

The fifth section of the chapter deals with approach-avoidance, conflict, and displacement. Toward most things, we have mixed tendencies: we want them, but getting them involves behavior that ranges all the way from being inconvenient to being disastrous. Regarding approach-avoidance, it can only be said that when a tendency to approach something is equal to the tendency to avoid it, conflict results. The stronger the needs (personal involvement) for approach as opposed to avoidance, the more intense the conflict. When a child experiences too many intense conflicts, he may break down.

As discussed in the final section of the chapter, it is found that child specialists do a reasonably good job of pinpointing *what* is wrong with a child (diagnosing), but they are still at the stumbling stage in their knowledge of how to change him from being maladjusted and unhappy to being happy and at ease with himself and others.

R. W. White (1959) wrote a "general" article that gives an excellent summary of many of the matters taken up in this chapter. His concluding sentence (p. 330) is particularly relevant: "Man's huge cortical association areas might have been a suicidal piece of specialization if they had come without a steady, persistent inclination toward interacting with the environment."

Earlier in his article, White says that there are many behaviors of humans (and animals) that cannot be conceptualized neatly as either primary or secondary drives. "This behavior includes visual exploration, grasping, crawling and walking, attention and perception, language and thinking, exploring novel objects and places, manipulating the surroundings, and producing effective changes in the environment" (p. 329).

White maintains that all these have a common biological (the present author would add the word, psychological) significance. Through them, the child learns to interact effectively with his environment. White chooses the word *competence* to summarize effectiveness of the behaviors described above. White, like the present author, thinks that competence comes, at least in large part, from early and later childhood playful and exploratory activities which are at the same time purposeful, selective, and persistent. Children who behave in such ways, White thinks, have "a feeling of efficacy."

The
Self-Concept

CHAPTER 6

As a child grows and develops, he learns, not only about the world about him and his place in it (the type of learning that has been stressed so far in this volume) but about himself. Such learning is intensely personal, is in large part private, is heavily symbolic and often illogical, and is of vital importance to both private happiness and public behavior.

Each person lives with *himself* and hence, to some degree, is always alone. No one can ever completely know the self of anyone else, although in the quest for understanding oneself and others there has developed much of human thought and philosophy, including psychology. Man has long held the hope of answering such questions as: Who am I? What am I? How did I come to be this way? And their logical consequence, the search for purpose: *Why* am I?

The psychological construct, the *self-concept,* connotes this area of essentially private experience and self-evaluation—essentially private even though it is in part translated into action by most of the things we say and do, by the attitudes we hold, and by the beliefs we express.

The beginnings of the self-concept have been little studied. Sullivan, some of whose thought was summarized in Chapter 2, considers the self-concept or self-dynamism central to human personality, and he has devoted much thought to it. From the learning point of view, the self-concept is the apex—the culmination—of all the social and personal experiences the child has had. Conditioning and instrumental learning, primary and secondary generalization, reward and punishment, motives and drives, expectancies and probabilities, conflicts, fixations, and displacements—all these processes and experiences play a part, first in distinguishing "others" from "me," later in an only partly articulate personal awareness and evaluation of "me," and finally in the mature "me," who may be cynical or trusting, happy or depressed, or self-confidently male or female.

All but very young children have formed some concept of themselves as people, and considerable study of the nature of the self-concept and its relation to behavior and adjustment has been made. A review of this literature forms the bulk of this chapter. Although the self-concept is highly complex, most of the research done to date has been concerned with a single dimension—the good-bad or positive-negative dimension. At the end of this chapter suggestions are made about some other characteristics of the self-concept that deserve attention but have been little studied, if at all.

The self-concept may be thought of as a *set of expectancies, plus evaluations of the areas or behaviors with reference to which these expectancies are held.* Thus, it is considered to be learned (see Chapters 4 and 5). Confining ourselves, for the moment, to the good-bad dimension of the self-concept, we may say that the total self-concept of an individual may vary from extremely poor or negative, to very good or positive. The over-all self-concept may be visualized as an algebraic total: if, in considering the many areas making up the self, *more,* and *more important,* areas are regarded as good than bad, then a positive self-concept can be inferred, and vice versa.

An Illustration of the Development of the Self-Concept

Let us examine a portion of the day of a rather bright and attractive $4\frac{1}{2}$-year-old girl, whose self-concept is as yet vaguely formed. Dimly, she knows that she is well-loved and attractive. Upon awakening, she goes to her parents' room, is patted and kissed and sent on her way to get dressed for nursery school. She achieves this but neglects to brush her hair. She is sent back and, upon her return, although still not well-brushed, is told, "How pretty you look."

Her first period at school is an out-of-doors one. Her concept of her physical proficiency is poor, since she is small for her age and not particularly agile or graceful. She protests to her teacher that she does not want to go out, but is sent along. She finds almost all the children who are present running faster than she can run and climbing higher than she can climb. Someone runs into her and knocks her down; she sobs, then goes to the safety of the sandbox and plays quietly, perhaps alone, for the remainder of this period. The next period is an indoor activity period, where the choice of activity is free. The girl knows, in a poorly articulated fashion, that she is proficient at several things, among them the morning's offerings of woodwork, clay work, and painting. She chooses woodwork, and in half an hour has produced an object of several pieces and many nails that is accepted by her peers as a fine jet plane. She is admired for this by her teachers.

The next period is "the circle," when all children group around the teacher for general demonstrations, discussion, and "sharing." The girl is a little ill at ease in large groups and has a soft voice. She sits in the circle, attempting, for security, to get as close to the teacher as she can. Her turn comes when the subject of jet planes arises; she eagerly extends her jet plane, but the big boy next to her with the big voice says, as he takes it from her, "See, she has the wheels too far back"; and the conversation and attention move on around the circle from her.

The rest of the morning is free; the weather is such that indoor equipment can be moved outside. She is verbal, imaginative, and proficient at dramatic play, so she takes several dolls, a carriage, and a baby bed outside and is soon the center and arbiter of a long and elaborate sequence of family play with three other girls and two boys. This lasts until she goes home.

Most of this girl's expectancies, rather soundly based on her credits and debits, have been confirmed on this particular morning: she has found parental love and admiration, has been defeated in large-muscle activity, has done well with finely coordinated small-muscle activity, has not excelled in the formal and competitive "circle," but has had a minor triumph in quiet, dramatic play.

Projecting into the future and oversimplifying, one might predict a generally positive self-concept for this girl. Her "failures" are not those that society regards as very serious for a girl; her successes are those that society holds to be desirable for females. We can almost see her as a young adult, looking prettily down her nose at gross motor activities— scorning tennis, for example; and, by this age, not being particularly affected if, when she is forced into a game of tennis, she does poorly. She may shun large, formal groups; speak up seldom in college classes, but do well on exams; and come vividly to life in individual creative enterprises and small informal groups. She may well be popular, a respected group member, but not a leader.

Nine years later, the author continues to know this child well. His predictions have been supported as she has developed. As a 13-year-old adolescent, she is popular, an indifferent student except when strong intellectual challenge is presented, despises all forms of formal physical education/competition, is well-liked by boys, continues to be so nervous when making a formal presentation (such as a poetry reading or extemporaneous speech in front of her class) that she spends days in preparation and rehearsal with any intimate who will listen, emerges from such presentations with excellent marks but consistent comments by teachers and peers to the effect that "You showed how nervous you were—don't let people see that your hands shake—your voice broke because of nervousness several times—I noticed you were sweating" and so on. How influential were the insensitive teacher and the big boy with the big voice in "sharing" when she was four? She exerts substantial influence in her class, but it is of the behind-the-scenes sort: the official class leaders find her rewarding to talk to, reflect her ideas (usually rather good ones), seldom give her credit, and such a situation is exactly what she wants. Once, nominated for class office, she demanded that her name be stricken from the ballot.

Admittedly, this child constitutes an N (number) of one, hence is not the substance of a good statistical paper, but the accuracy of prediction of her later development from observation and analysis of her 4-year-old behavior is rather precise.

Slowly, it can be assumed, the things at which one is more successful (by means of which he solves his life problems) become more important to him, with either positive or negative results. If these strata of his success are socially useful, he becomes a valued member of society; if socially neutral, a nonentity; if socially destructive, possibly a criminal. When a certain type of proficiency is either important to survival and fulfillment (such as adequate attractiveness to the other sex), or is highly regarded by society (such as being brave), then a perceived deficiency present in the self-concept is important and may contribute in a major fashion to the over-all self-image.

The self-concept, then, is a complex thing, and a function of the *importance* (or reward value) of its various facets and the *feeling*, positive or negative, about them.

For the girl in our example, by way of illustration, taking her at either 4 or 13 years old:

Imaginative play, positive self-concept, high value	+10
Large-muscle activity, negative self-concept, low value	−2
Formal group competition, negative self-concept, moderate value	−5
Individual creativity, positive self-moderate value	+6
Personal attractiveness, positive self-concept, high value	+10

Such a listing is obviously incomplete, and the assigning of numerical values an arbitrary device, but it permits us to represent schematically what is meant by "a generally positive self-concept."

Our illustration also suggests that the self-concept holds properties in common with drive (see Chapter 4), in that one *selects* some developmental, recreational, and avocational areas as a function of certain characteristics of the self-concept, and *rejects* others. Or, because of its *directive function,* one person will behave one way (for example, intellectually, through discussion), while another reacts to the same situation in quite another way (as aggressively through fighting). The girl in our illustration, given free choice, is likely to select individual or small-group informal activities where imagination can be exercised. One can see her, as she grows older, choosing drama before debate (which she has done). One cannot see her going out for girls' intramural sports. She is not likely to be very disturbed by the prospect of a boy-girl party, where her attractiveness will stand her in good stead (as it does at age 13). However, as noted in Chapter 5, a real defeat in small groups or a genuine success in a formal activity, such as debate, may change her self-concept much more than a failure at tennis or a success in sewing class would. She illustrates the self-fulfilling prophecy—she seeks those things where success is probable, avoids areas where she is likely to fail (see first part of Chapter 5).

Some authors (as Sullivan, 1947) conceive of the self-concept as a unit, but one made up of many, many facets in dynamic equilibrium. This balance, whether it results in a positive or a negative self-concept, they believe to be essential in the adjustment of the child or adult because it represents the safest and most satisfactory solution to his life situation that he can manage at a given time. Since any disturbance of it represents a threat to the individual's well-being, however precarious this well-being may be, changes in or attempts to change the self-concept will be rejected. Those who hold such a point of view seek to account in this manner for the seeming irrationality of some of the behavior of most people: Why does the objectively successful man continue to regard himself as stupid? Why does the bright and talented girl consistently go to pieces when she competes for a part in the school play? It is argued that such behavior is designed to protect or maintain the *status quo* of the self-concept.

This reasoning is plausible, but such conceptions as *fixation* and accompanying anxiety reduction, as discussed in Chapter 5, fit better with the theoretical position adopted here. For our purposes then, in recapitulation, we shall regard the self-concept as complex, made up of many facets, with each facet differing in importance, or reward value, from the others. Expectancies have been learned for each facet, so that the individual can predict success or failure in connection with behavior that pertains to a given facet. These expectancies have been acquired and can be changed according to the principles of learning previously discussed. The various aspects of the self-concept, in some senses, have properties similar to *drive:* to protect a good self-concept, we will strive hard (the energizing function) or will *select* those behaviors that preserve or enhance it. For example, if we are poor at sports we will drop sports; if good at talking, take up public speaking. We will also behave in ways that are congruent with our self-concept: the beautiful woman, coming into a new room, looks into the mirror; the homely one studies the pictures on the wall.

This introductory chapter section must include some other authors' judgments (for reasons unknown, the rate of research in self-concept appears to have declined in the 1960s). Admittedly (reasons for this statement are given later in the chapter) the field of "self" is a somewhat "sloppy" area in which to do research. But no one who works with children, adolescents, or adults, be he clinician, parent, or teacher, can avoid what we call (rather loosely) "self-theory." Each individual is here to stay, as far as he is concerned, and he wishes and needs to be regarded as a whole person.

Crowne and Stephens (1961) point out (this pertains to the next section of the chapter) that in their judgment about two thirds of the relevant findings in self-concept research are due to "social desirability." Youngsters, in other words, will admit good things, deny bad things about themselves. Crowne and Stephens go on to say that the whole research area suffers from three untenable assumptions: self-concept instruments *really* measure what they purport to measure (in other words, we all have a "self," and the tools for measuring it appeal to us, whether or not we are honest in our answers). Second, investigators seem to assume that all subjects see any given test the same way. This is patently ridiculous, as has been pointed out in·detail in Chapter 5. Third, and this criterion of Crowne and Stephens definitely pertains to the next section, items for self-concept scales have been selected in many, many ways, some of them weird and wonderful!

Lowe (1961) wonders if there is really anything at all to the "self-concept." Lowe points out that there are at least six notions of what the "self" is: (1) the self that knows—the "I" or Freud's ego; (2) the motivating self: I must do well because it is important to me. Again, this resembles Freud's ego. (3) The "humanistic, semireligious conception of the self as that which experiences itself" (p. 333). This, to the present author, is the eternal, essentially private aspect of self-concept research. (4) The organizer. The reader should look again at the discussion in the summary of Chapter 5 on competence. This version of self also corresponds to Freud's ideas of the ego, and is closely related in the present author's thinking to Lowe's first definition above. (5) The self can also be a pacifier: "An adjustment mechanism which seems to maintain congruence between the self and nonself" (p. 334). This again seems to fit with Freud, and blends well with the present author's thinking about self-concept. (6) Finally, the "self is the subjective voice of the culture, being purely a social agent. It is the self of both sociology and S-R (stimulus-response) psychology, for it sees behavioral responses solely in terms of social conditions or stimulus inputs" (p. 334).

Finally (and it cannot be summarized, as it is a full-length and well-done book), Wylie's (1961) work must be mentioned. No one seriously interested in self-concept research and theory can ignore this book.

Measurement of the Self-Concept

We have discussed the idea of the self-concept in some detail. But, to be useful in science, an idea must have an objective referent: there must be a method of measuring it, and a number of methods have been devised to measure or estimate the self-concept. None of them captures the idea in its entirety, but most seem to catch enough of it to demonstrate that the self-concept is an important personality variable.

All measurements of the self-concept include the idea of *desirability* and *undesirability*. Desirability may be evaluated by one investigator according to an abstract social norm: to be good, or to be pretty, or to be intelligent, is ordinarily something that society values positively; to be bad, to be ugly, or to be stupid is something that society thinks of as a negative quality. Other investigators assess desirability and undesirability in terms of the evaluations of the subjects themselves: for one girl, to be vivacious may be "good"; another may be indifferent to vivacity; for still another girl, this quality may have negative connotations. One boy may think of sophistication as something he wants and values; another may think of it as a sissy quality of which he wishes no part.

Measurements of self-concept vary, then, along the dimension of how values are attached. Some research workers use general social norms; others use the personal norms of the people they include in the study. In most measures of the self-concept, a number of terms, traits, values, or characteristics, presented to the subjects. Some research workers list adjectives such as *good, brave, beautiful, strong, honest,* and ask the subjects of their study to estimate the degree to which each term applies to them. Ordinarily, a rating of 1 means "Very much like me" or "Very characteristic of me"; while a rating of 5 carries with it the idea of "I am almost never like this" or "This is not at all like me." The adjectives listed above are characterized by the *social* notion of desirability. Another list might read, *vivacious, ambitious, nonchalant, sophisticated, self-contained.* Here, the social value of the words is less clear-cut. Some will think of *vivacity* as meaning alive, glancing, scintillating, whereas others will think of it as jittery, artificial, birdlike. To some, *ambitious* means hard-working, sober, wanting to advance. Others think of it as pushiness, disregarding the rights of others. As Crowne and Stephens say, no two people see a test in quite the same way. For such a list of adjectives, the subjects of any given study are ordinarily asked, as with the first list, to estimate the degree to which the adjective is characteristic of them; then, after they have gone through the list of adjectives, they are requested to estimate the degree to which the adjective is characteristic of them; next, after they have gone through the list of adjectives, they are requested to estimate the desirability of the quality they have just rated. Again, a rating of 1 for desirability ordinarily means that they think the quality is desirable; a rating of 5 indicates that they dislike and devaluate it.

Regardless of which system is used, every choice of every subject is given a positive, a neutral, or a negative value. Ordinarily, these are added algebraically, and the resulting figure is thought of as an "index of the self-concept."

There are many other ways of getting at the self-concept. Some investigators use lists of traits more elaborate than simple adjectives. Examples are: "I go out of my way to look after people who are in trouble; . . . I am particularly fond of animals; . . . I think poorly of people who get ahead by questionable methods." Again, the subject makes a rating of how characteristic of him the statement is, and of how desirable the trait is. Other investigators use paired but opposite adjectives, such as *warm and outgoing* versus *cool and self-contained; constantly on the go* versus *relaxed and a little lazy*. Such investigators may ask their subjects to check where they think they stand on a line drawn between the two adjectives of a pair. After such a series of checks, estimates of the value of the quality to the person are made.

Still other research workers ask their subjects simply to answer the question, "Who am I?" They use expert judges to help them classify the answers as indicating a positive or negative self-concept; or ask their subjects to go back over their answers and indicate with a plus all the answers they think are socially or personally desirable, with a 0 those they think are neutral, and with a minus those that are socially or personally undesirable.

Another common variation of the method is to have the subject do a "Q-sort." In this technique, a large number of statements or adjectives is given to the subject on separate slips of paper and he is asked to sort these slips on, for example, a seven-point scale. He is forced to distribute them according to a preordained quota system from those "least like him" to those "most like him." Of 100 such statements he is allowed to place only seven, for example, on the figure 1, meaning "most like me," and only seven on the figure 7, "least like me." In second and sixth positions, he may place twelve statements each; in third and fifth place, nineteen; and in the middle or fourth place, twenty-four statements. These statements may be judged positive or negative in terms of the abstract social norm by expert judges, or may be rated for desirability by each subject.

Another, less frequently used, method of measuring the self-concept consists of having the subjects respond to some projective technique, such as the Thematic Apperception Test. This test consists of a number of pictures. For each picture, the subject is asked to tell who the characters are, what has happened to them before, what is happening at the time the picture was taken, and what the outcome will be. Psychologically sophisticated judges then decide with whom the subject is most closely identified (who "stands for" the subject, or, according to psychological terminology, is the "hero"), and rate the attributes of this character in the story as positive, neutral, or negative. From these ratings, a judgment of the self-concept is made.

Some of these techniques, such as the Q-sort, are rather complicated to use with children, but variations of all of them have been used with children as well as adults. Compared with the number of adult studies, there are few studies of the self-concept in children. Those studies that have been done with children ordinarily use a simple technique of listing a series of adjectives or traits. They then ask the children to indicate whether these are "like them" or "unlike them." After this has been done, the request is made that the child indicate by a plus whether he thinks the quality is a "good" one; by a 0 whether he does not care one way or another; and by a minus if he does not like this aspect of himself. The "Who am I" technique has also been used with children old enough to write. Self-concept studies of children younger than about fourth-grade age are rare, since each child must be examined individually (because of reading and writing difficulties); and an individual examination in an area such as this is likely to affect the results. The child, alone with the adult, is likely to respond not according to the way he feels or believes, but in the way he thinks the adult wants him to feel or believe.

One of the first questions that must be asked of any measuring technique, or of any behavioral indicator of a concept, is: Are its results repeatable; are they stable over time? If not, one is forced to question either the measures or the long-run scientific usefulness of the concept. In general, measures of the self-concept have demonstrated moderate stability over time. To support this statement, one representative piece of research can be introduced. Engel (1959) tested a group of sixth- and eighth-graders on a self-concept measure; then, after two years, repeated the same test (a Q-sort). After certain legitimate corrections of her statistical techniques, she arrived at a correlation of .78 between the first and the second test. The younger children showed as high a level of stability as the older, and boys were no different from girls in stability. In other words, even in the presumably unstable period of adolescence, a self-concept measure accounts for a little more than 60 percent of the variance of a second measure made two years later.

The Self-Concept and Personal Adjustment

INTRODUCTION

Earlier in this chapter it was said that the self-concept, though essentially private, influences and is revealed by most of a person's behavior. If this is correct, then poor self-concepts should be reflected in other behavior that represents poor personal and social adjustment, and good self-concepts should be associated with good adjustment. The studies reviewed in this section indicate that the good-bad dimension of the self-concept is related to scores on anxiety tests as well as to more general measures of adjustment; to effectiveness in a group; and to self-honesty of a nonself-destructive sort. All the relations are in the expected direction: persons with good self-concepts are less anxious, are judged to be generally better adjusted, are more effective in groups, and are more honest with themselves and less defensive.

Three studies illustrate these points. First, Hassan and McCandless have found that strong, muscular, elementary school-aged boys tend (nonsignificantly) to be less anxious than fat or scrawny boys; are at least as "well-adjusted" as fat or scrawny boys; and are significantly more willing to admit mildly negative characteristics about themselves (this finding fits well with Taylor and Combs (1952) whose study is discussed later in the chapter). Ring, Lipinski, and Braginsky (1965), working with ninety-six women undergraduate students who were first, only, and later-borns, find their first born and only young women to be much alike and, when compared with girls who come later in their families, less confident about their self-ratings, more unreliable in rating themselves, and more likely to be "stimulus bound." That is, if their current situation is a happy one, their over-all estimate of themselves is good; if the current situation is bad, they take a gloomy over-all view (this fits well with the research of Irene Rosenthal (1963) who finds men more reliable reporters of their past histories than women). Ring and his co-workers also find their first-borns more likely to be anxious in ambiguous and possibly dangerous situations, and to seek more often than later borns to fit themselves into the group situation in which they find themselves at any given moment.

Reese (1961) worked with fourth-, sixth-, and eighth-grade upstate New York children. He found that girls generally reported higher self-esteem scores than boys. In general, children, both boys and girls, who "liked themselves" also liked others.

People seem to assign positive evaluations to those of their traits that have been approved by their parents. Other research indicates that specific patterns of child-rearing are associated with certain maladaptive types of self-concept, and that the self-concept (presumably affected by patterns of child-rearing) is significantly related to achievement in school. The studies reviewed in this section follow the topical order of this introductory statement.

THE SELF-CONCEPT AND ANXIETY

First, several studies of both children and college students indicate a relation between self-rejection, or negative self-concept, and measures of anxiety. In the first of these, Lipsitt (1958) asked a large number (about 300) of fourth-, fifth-, and sixth-grade boys and girls to indicate whether each of a series of adjectives was "very like them" or "very unlike them." They were then asked whether each of the traits was personally desirable or undesirable. This provided an over-all index of the good-bad dimension of their self-concepts. They also took an anxiety test. Children with poor self-concepts were more anxious at a statistically significant level (for both boys and girls) than children with good self-concepts.

The anxiety scale used (Castaneda, McCandless, and Palermo, 1956) appears to have a moderate degree of validity. Children who test high on it, when compared with children who test low, are less popular (McCandless, Castaneda, and Palermo, 1956); have more difficulty with conceptually complex learning tasks (Castaneda, Palermo, and McCandless, 1956; Palermo, Castaneda, and McCandless, 1956); and in at least some cases do less well with the more complicated school subjects (McCandless and Castaneda, 1956). These findings fit well with the later longitudinal study by Hill and Sarason (1966). Children referred for behavior problems test higher in anxiety than those not so referred (Rynerson, 1957); and Negro children in an area where racial role changes likely to produce tension are occurring test higher than their non-Negro peers (Palermo, 1959).

Another author, Coopersmith (1959), used this anxiety scale for a different sample of fifth- and sixth-grade children—102 in number—but used a *different* measure of self-concept. He found that children who had high self-esteem were significantly less anxious than those with low self-esteem. The youngsters with high self-esteem were also more popular (self-esteem and popularity correlated .37). The children were apparently rather accurate in their self-concepts, since teachers, in the main, judged the youngsters very much as they judged themselves. Coopersmith (1960) also reports that fifth- and sixth-graders who have high self-esteem (good self-concepts) recall (presumably so as to correct) their failures, while children with poor self-concepts suppress and deny them. Since a good self-concept probably goes along with low anxiety, Coopersmith's study is one more of a series (see Chapter 5) suggesting that high anxious children are less curious, hence poorer students, than low anxious children.

Such relations between self-concept and anxiety are not limited to children. For example, Mitchell (1959) measured the self-concepts of 100 freshmen and sophomore women students, and correlated their anxiety scores with the adequacy of their self-concepts. The resulting correlation coefficient was .41 and the better the self-concept, the less the anxiety.

It will be recalled from Chapter 2 that one's confidence in a generalization increases in proportion to the frequency with which similar results are obtained from different populations and from different but related instruments. In this regard then, rather convincing evidence exists relating poor self-concept to high anxiety, *as these are measured*.

Research done by Crandall and Bellugi (1954) will be discussed later in more detail, but should be mentioned here, because it provides still further evidence (based, in this instance, on a presumably rather sophisticated sample of juniors and seniors in a highly rated private liberal arts college) that good self-concept is related to good adjustment. This research introduces still another experimental sample, and a different measure of adjustment—the Incomplete Sentences Technique, which provides an indirect index of adjustment. The subject's "creative" endings to sentence stems (such as "My mother . . ." or "When I . . .") are given adjustment ratings by expert raters. In other words, this study adds still more confidence to the generalization that good self-concept is related to good behavioral adjustment.

EFFECTIVENESS IN GROUPS

The Mussen and Porter study (1959) bears on the question of the effectiveness in groups of people holding high or low esteem for themselves. This study used male volunteers from undergraduate psychology classes.

The young men highest in feelings of adequacy and with favorable rather than negative self-concepts were rated by other men who took part with them in free-wheeling, or leaderless, discussion groups as being generally *more* effective than those who expressed feelings of inadequacy and negative self-concepts. The criteria that the group members—all of whom were initially unacquainted with each other—used in making their judgment of group effectiveness were, among others: contributing the best ideas to the group, degree of activity in the group, amount of intellectual stimulation provided to other members of the group, adequacy in explaining their ideas and clarifying the ideas of others, most influential in the group, and most appealing in that the rater desired to become better acquainted with him.

This study supports the suggestion made above, that self-concepts *are* translated into action, and contributes further support to the finding that good self-concepts are related to generally adequate social functioning, including popularity.

A related study (Dittes, 1959) supports the Mussen and Porter conclusion: the self-esteem ratings of 104 male college freshmen were positively correlated with ratings of adequacy made by fellow group members (Dittes does not give the correlation). Some of Dittes' subjects were led to believe that they were rejected by the group, while others were given the impression that they were accepted, or that acceptance was likely. Not surprisingly, he found that "Persons made to feel well-accepted in a group found the group more attractive than did those made to feel poorly accepted" (p. 81). But an individual's rating of the *attractiveness of the accepting group* varied according to his self-concept, the group being rated significantly more attractive by those with low self-esteem. Dittes believes that low self-esteem should be considered indicative of a "strong need for acceptance." Remember that Ring and his co-workers found about the same result for their undergraduate young women. The implications of such studies in conjunction with others that have been summarized in this section is that, while people with poor self-concepts are less popular than those who have high esteem for themselves, and while they are generally rated as less effective in groups, they have a stronger need for groups and, if anything, overreact to group acceptance. It would be helpful, from an educational and therapeutic standpoint, to investigate the effect of group acceptance on the self-concept and adjustment of isolated people with low self-esteem. We apparently also most want to be liked by those we hold in highest esteem (Wurster, Bass, and Alcock, 1961).

ACCURACY OF THE SELF-CONCEPT

A rather subtle criticism can be applied to several of the studies reported in this section, particularly those that relate anxiety to self-concept. This criticism postulates that correlations are found between the two measures, not because there is *really* a relation between anxiety and poor self-concept, but because the method of measuring the two constructs ordinarily involves self-criticism (or its lack). To obtain a poor self-concept rating, an individual, when the usual techniques are employed, must say negative things about himself. Similarly, to get a high anxiety rating, he must admit to mildly derogatory or quite negative things about himself. Sample items from the Children's Manifest Anxiety Scale (Castaneda, McCandless, and Palermo, 1956) are: "It is hard for me to keep my mind on anything . . . I feel I have to be best in everything . . . I am secretly afraid of a lot of things . . . Often I have trouble getting my breath . . . My feelings get hurt easily when I am scolded." "Yes" answers to each of these statements are considered to indicate anxiety. Since this "admission phenomenon" (or willingness to be frank or self-critical) characterizes the self-concept test, the anxiety test, *and* the Incomplete Sentences Test, some had said that *it,* rather than a genuine relation between anxiety and self-concept, is responsible for the relations found.

This criticism would be less telling if it could be demonstrated that children judged as well-adjusted by some technique subject to the "admission phenomenon" are, on some other measure, more willing to admit derogatory things about themselves than children judged as maladjusted. That is, if the admission phenomenon results in their obtaining a favorable adjustment score on the personality test, it should operate to produce a low score on an instrument designed to elicit admissions of derogatory traits or feelings. If good personality scores result from the admission phenomenon, then its operation should assure that the "well-adjusted" will admit the fewest derogatory things about themselves.

Taylor and Combs (1952) provide the suggestion that such results as were summarized in this section are *not* due to the admission phenomenon. They used a sizable sample (202 in number) or rural sixth-grade boys and girls. Their hypothesis was the following: Well-adjusted children should be more accepting of unflattering things about themselves than poorly adjusted children. To test this hypothesis a personality test, the well-standardized California Test of Personality, was given. Analyses of girls and boys were made separately. By sex, they were broken into two groups, the well-adjusted (those who scored above the median, or that point above and below which exactly half the boys or girls fell), and the poorly adjusted (those who scored below the median). They were then asked to indicate whether such statements as the following did or did not characterize them: being lazy sometimes, talking back to mother sometimes, showing off in front of other children sometimes. Twenty such statements were included in this text. Note that such statements *are* admissions of foibles, but they do not suggest "real" self-rejection or self-dislike. The well-adjusted boys admitted an average of 9.2 such items, the poorly adjusted ones only 5.1; the well-adjusted girls admitted 8.4, the poorly adjusted girls only 5.8. Such behavior is probably a lack of defensiveness rather than self-rejection. The differences for both boys and girls were highly significant statistically; and hence, by inference, willingness to admit derogatory things about oneself is positively, not negatively, related to adjustment. Hassan and McCandless, in the study they are currently working on, obtain similar results. These findings suggest that the relation between poor self-concept and high anxiety may be genuine, rather than due to an admission phenomenon common to the two tests. If better-adjusted children are *more* likely to admit derogatory things about themselves than maladjusted children, then their scores on an anxiety test, incomplete sentences tests, and self-concept tests should *maximize* their poor adjustment scores. If maladjusted children are least likely to admit derogatory things, their poor adjustment scores should be *minimized* by their "No" answers to negative items and their "Yes" answers to positive items. In other words, the Taylor and Combs and Hassan and McCandless results suggest that relations obtained between anxiety and self-concept measures are, if anything, too low, but represent lack of defensiveness, not true "self-rejection."

The studies summarized immediately above suggest that honesty about oneself, which may also be thought of as accuracy, is an important aspect of the self-concept and may well be related to good adjustment. Chodorkoff (1954a) attempted to take account of accuracy of self-concept in an ingenious study using college men as subjects. The subjects did a Q-sort of themselves, and persons trained in clinical psychology used tests, items from their biographies, and other information to make the same Q-sort—that is, to state what characteristics were or were not applicable to them, and to what degree. If the subject's own Q-sort was very similar to that of the "experts," he was given a high rating on the factor of "accuracy of self-description." If the Q-sort of the subject was very different from that of the clinical psychologists, he got a low rating. The clinical psychologists also scored the subjects for general adjustment on the basis of various tests and information about their biographies. Another index of adjustment was taken from a standard personality test (the Rorschach Inkblot Test). In general, the more accurate the young men were in their self-descriptions, the better adjusted they were according to both indices.

One flaw of the study, of course, is that the clinical psychologists were using the same information to judge adjustment as that used to describe the young men in the first place. But still another test, *not* subject to this criticism, was utilized in the study—a test of defensiveness. It is commonly assumed in psychological literature that "defensiveness" represents poor adjustment. Defensiveness is frequently defined as the tendency to blot out of one's conscious mind, or deny, those things in his environment that are threatening or unpalatable.

Hill and Sarason (1966) find that young boys are more defensive than girls of the same age. Parenthetically, this is an interesting derivative of our culture: Girls can admit their feelings, worry, cry, express emotion, be dependent, but they must also be very "good." Boys can be "bad," but are supposed to be able to take care of their own feelings privately. May this be one reason why the average American woman lives four or more years longer than the average American man since she can "be herself," while he must, according to cultural dictates, cope alone with his feelings and emotions?

Coming back to Chodorkoff, he first dictated to his subjects a series of one-hundred words, to each of which they were asked to make some verbal response. Of these words, fifty were "emotional," and fifty "neutral." For each subject ten words judged to represent "personally relevant threatening stimuli" and ten neutral words were selected. These were then flashed before the subject repeatedly, starting with such short exposure times that the subject could not recognize them and increasing the exposure time until the word was recognized. A subject who recognized neutral words much more quickly than threatening words was considered to be defensive (was regarded as blocking out threatening stimuli), whereas a person whose reaction time for threatening and neutral words was approximately equal, or who recognized threatening words more quickly than neutral ones, was considered to be nondefensive. The men who were more accurate in their self-descriptions (self-concepts) showed less defensiveness than the men who were inaccurate. Surprisingly, the *most* accurate men actually recognized the threatening words more quickly than the neutral ones. Chodorkoff suggests quite plausibly that one aspect of good adjustment is the ability quickly to recognize threat (and, presumably, to deal effectively with it).

Three studies have used very different experimental populations (rural New York sixth-graders, Indiana elementary school boys, and University of Wisconsin undergraduate men) and very different methods (paper-and-pencil tests, and experimental techniques) in an effort to relate self-honesty or lack of defensiveness to good personal adjustment. All three studies secured results supporting the hypothesis when simple honesty, but not "deep self-rejection" was involved.

THE EFFECT OF CHILD-REARING PRACTICES

In line with the assumption that the self-concept is learned, it would be expected that one would develop a good self-concept without attendant anxiety about those of his traits that had been valued and rewarded by parents and other important persons during childhood, but would have a poor self-concept and marked anxiety about traits that had been punished, or had failed to receive reward. Child, Frank, and Storm (1956) attempted to check this hypothesis by asking male undergraduate students about how persons important in their childhood had reacted to such of their behaviors as competitiveness, aggression, mannerliness, and so on. The young men also indicated their own self-concepts and associated anxiety in these areas. The results of the study were not spectacular, but *did* lend support to the hypothesis.

Ausubel *et al.* (1954) include, in a study of the effect of parental attitudes on children's self-concept, some findings supporting the hypothesis that children's self-concepts develop according to the pattern of parents' rewards and punishments but that when this pattern stresses objective success rather than the needs of the developing child, unfortunate personality characteristics may develop.

These authors developed a scale they call "Extrinsic Valuation." By this, they mean that the parents show excessive concern about the child's school accomplishment and presumably view it as a factor that enhances their own status. Children of such parents see their parents as over-motivating them, as planning for their careers in grandiose terms, and as displaying their school and other achievements publicly to an excessive degree. Children who report their parents in such terms were themselves grandiose, according to their answers on a scale called "Could You Ever?"

In this scale, the forty 10-year-old boys and girls who were used as subjects of the study were asked eighty sex-appropriate questions dealing with their ability to achieve a number of goals which, in terms of probability of success, ranged from probable to highly improbable. Some of the questions concerned childhood achievements; others referred to what the child thought he could accomplish as an adult. "Grandiose" answers are those indicating that the child has an unrealistically ambitious or "cocky" notion of what he can do both in the present and in the future.

Children who saw their parents as valuing them extrinsically were also more persistent (probably to an unrealistic degree) in believing they could do well "the next time" on a task at which they were consistently failing. The children were rated by an arts-crafts teacher and by their classroom teachers for emotional maturity. Those who saw their parents as valuing them extrinsically emerged with less favorable ratings for emotional maturity than those who perceived their parents as valuing them for themselves alone. The authors defined maturity as consisting of two traits: (1) *executive independence* or not asking for help on a task they were physically able to do; and (2) *ability to postpone hedonistic gratification* or putting off an immediate reward for some future, desirable goal. The relations reported here are those that achieved a satisfactory level of statistical significance. In other words, youngsters who are loved for themselves alone seem to be better adjusted than those whose parents consider them as show-pieces. Of course, any normal parent, in addition to liking and loving his child, is also pleased to see him do well in life. Intrinsic and extrinsic valuation are not mutually exclusive.

SELF-CONCEPT AND SCHOOL ACHIEVEMENT

It can be predicted that poor self-concepts, implying as they so often do a lack of confidence in facing and mastering the environment, will accompany deficiency in one of the most vital of the child's areas of accomplishment—his performance in school.

The Coopersmith (1959) study of fifth- and sixth-grade children which has already been mentioned in this section supports this prediction. For the 102 children included in the study, a correlation of .36 was found between positive self-concept and school achievement. Hill and Sarason (1966) report similar findings. In fact, many studies discussed in Chapter 5 of this book relate to and support such a prediction.

Another research worker (Walsh, 1956) has interested herself in differences in self-concept between very bright boys (IQ above 120) who fell in the lowest quarter of their class in terms of academic achievement, and a group of carefully matched "adequate achievers" whose academic achievement was in the top half of their class. Twenty boys from the second through the fifth grade were included in each of these groups.

The Driscoll Playkit, consisting of a facsimile (floor plan) of a six-room house, toy furniture, and a doll family (father, mother, boy, girl, and baby), was used to elicit the boys' self-concepts. Nine incomplete stories were read to the boys, and they were asked to tell and play out the endings to the stories. They could make up a tenth story of their own in which anything they wanted could be made to happen. Judges inferred their self-concepts from their story-endings, making judgments about freedom of action; freedom and adequacy of emotional expression; feelings of belongingness (with their parents); response to environmental stimulation (whether the child used opportunities to gain direct satisfaction of his needs, conformed and obeyed without question, or saw his world as something he must defend himself against through such behaviors as rebellion, negativism, unreasoning opposition, and so forth); and sex-typing (as degree of normal "maleness").

There were extremely significant differences for three of these categories. The low achievers more markedly than the adequate achievers portrayed the boy doll or "hero" (from whose behavior their own self-concept was inferred) as being restricted, or not free to pursue his own interests and feelings, and as acting defensively. Results were statistically significant, but not as clear-cut, in the "belongingness" area. The low achievers more frequently depicted the boy doll as being isolated, criticized, or rejected.

This well-done study has obvious practical implications for education, suggesting as it does that children who have come to feel that their freedom is restricted, that they cannot pursue their own interests or express their feelings, that they cannot cope with their environment, that the world is "against them," and who do not feel close to their families, may express the conflicts so engendered by "rebellion" against the educational process—that is, by achieving far less than they are able to accomplish. For such children, active "emotional" education in addition to academic teaching may be necessary.

In this connection, Long and Henderson (1966), working in a Southern community, adopted the hypothesis that community conditions will affect the self-concepts and social concepts of Negro and white children differentially, to the disadvantage of the Negro child, and that these differential effects will manifest themselves in school. They worked with children from a rural area who were just beginning school: thirty-six Negro boys, thirty-six Negro girls, and seventy-two white children of the same age, grade, sex, and community were used as subjects. As might be expected, the Negro children (when compared with the white youngsters) were from a lower socioeconomic class, were of lower intelligence, had more brothers and sisters, and more frequently came from father-absent homes.

Compared with the white children, the Negro children had lower self-esteem, were less realistic in evaluating their skin color, were more identified both with their mothers and teachers (this probably means they were more dependent on adult female persons who loomed important in their lives), and less identified with their fathers. As will be seen in Chapter 11, this matter of identification with fathers, particularly for boys, is tremendously important in sex-typing, identification, and moral and conscience development.

When the group of Negro youngsters was considered separately, it was found that teachers made higher ratings of those who had higher self-esteem (they were judged as the relatively more mature members of their class); who were realistic in their estimate of their skin color (note how this conforms to evidence that a realistic self-concept tends to accompany good adjustment, as discussed later in this chapter); and who were more identified with the teacher (this last is perhaps an illustration of the halo effect: "I think well of those who think well (are dependent) of me").

As might be expected, those Negro children from father-present homes identified more highly with fathers than did children whose fathers had left the home.

Long and Henderson's results, because of the difference in social class between the Negro and white children, cannot be clearly ascribed to "Negro-ness." They may be due entirely to the effects of poverty and low social status, although it is probable that the discriminatory practices to which the Negro is subjected in the United States (more obvious in the rural South than elsewhere) contribute substantially to their findings, over and above the effects of social class.

In sum, then, the self-concept *does* appear to be related to school adjustment. Substantial evidence indicates that children and adults with poor self-concepts when compared with those who have more positive self-concepts, are more anxious and less well-adjusted generally, are less popular, are less effective in groups (although they value groups that accept them more highly), and are less honest about themselves (or more defensive). The pattern of parental rewards and punishments seems to affect the self-concept, and, quite certainly, the self-concepts of bright but underachieving youngsters are less positive than those of children who are doing as well as can be expected in school. Incidentally (this will be discussed in more detail later), children tend to mold their self-concepts according to the way they think their teachers regard them (the "mirror" self-concept). Payne and Farquhar (1962) have written an outstanding article that embodies this mirror-self-concept.

Discrepancy Between the Perceived Self and the Ideal Self

The studies reviewed in the previous section related self-concept—that is, how the person sees himself or how he evaluates himself with respect to certain characteristics or attributes—to various other measures of adjustment and effective functioning. This section concerns itself with a quality that might be called self-satisfaction or self-discontent. What does it mean if a person sees himself as being very similar to the person whom he would *ideally* like to be or, on the other hand, sees himself as much inferior to this idealized self?

The studies reviewed in this section are not in complete agreement. Generally, their results indicate that really sharp differences between one's perceived and ideal status are related to unhappiness; but they include suggestions that excessive self-satisfaction has its disadvantages and that a certain amount of restless discontent may act as constructive motivation. They also indicate that dissatisfaction with oneself may be related to *general* dissatisfaction "with life."

Many studies, in addition to asking subjects for *self-perceptions*, obtain an additional measure: the subject, after indicating how he feels about himself, is asked to go through the same set of items again and indicate how he would like to be *ideally*. Since almost all of us would like to be "better" than we are, the *ideal self* is invariably judged to be at least as good as and almost always better than the perceived self. The difference between the scores for the perceived self and the ideal self is the *discrepancy* score: to obtain it, the score of the perceived self is subtracted from the score representing the ideal self. The larger this *discrepancy* score, the more dissatisfied with himself the person is presumed to be.

Most studies of this topic have used adults as subjects. However, the findings contain implications for children, and there are a few studies in this area that have used children as subjects. In the first of these (Hanlon, Hofstaetter, and O'Connor, 1954), the subjects were seventy-eight boys who were juniors in a parochial school and who averaged 16.3 years of age. They were given the California Test of Personality, and asked to Q-sort 100 self-evaluating items both for their perceived self-concepts and for their ideal self-concepts. Their discrepancy score was then related to the over-all adjustment score on the California Test of Personality and to its subscales.

No particular relations were found between age or intelligence and self-ideal congruence, nor did the measures of adjustment show any particular relation to intelligence or age. But the correlation between total adjustment and discrepancy was a highly significant .70. Similar figures for the subscales of the California Test of Personality, and *P* (probability that the relationship could have occurred by chance) are given in Table 6.1. The relations found in this study between self-ideal discrepancy and personality adjustment are on the whole higher than those found in any other study in the literature.

Table 6.1   *Correlations Between Self-Ideal Discrepancy and Adjustment as Measured by the Subscales of the California Test of Personality.*

CALIFORNIA TEST OF PERSONALITY SUBSCALE	CORRELATION WITH SELF-IDEAL DISCREPANCY	P
Self-adjustment	.70[a]	.001
Self-reliance	.48	.001
Sense of Personal Worth	.50	.001
Sense of Freedom	.40	.001
Feeling of Belonging	.55	.001
Freedom from Withdrawal Symptoms	.56	.001
Freedom from Nervous Symptoms	.39	.001
Social Adjustment	.59	.001
Social Standards	.08	NS (nonsignificant)
Social Skills	.52	.001
Freedom from Antisocial Tendencies	.22	.05
Family Relations	.30	.01
School Relations	.45	.001
Community Relations	.50	.001

[a] These positive correlations mean that the *less* the discrepancy, the *better* the adjustment.
ADAPTED WITH PERMISSION OF THE AMERICAN PSYCHOLOGICAL ASSOCIATION AND T. E. HANLON, FROM HANLON, HOFSTAETTER, AND O'CONNOR (1954).

Bruce (1958) studies the self-ideal discrepancies of 184 sixth-grade children, drawn from eight sixth-grade classes. Compared with the children who had low self-ideal discrepancy scores, the self-dissatisfied youngsters were significantly more anxious on the Children's Manifest Anxiety Scale, and were rated by observers as being significantly less secure.

Mitchell (1959) obtained results that are similar to Bruce's results in a study of 100 college freshman and sophomore women. Among other data, Mitchell secured measures of self-ideal discrepancy and anxiety. His self-rejecting (high-discrepancy) women were more likely than the self-accepting (low-discrepancy) women to say such things about themselves as that they give up easily; are more sensitive than others; are less happy, less calm, and more restless; and that things pile up on them. They believe they are more distractible and high-strung, that life is a strain, and that they cannot live up to their parents' expectations for them. Mitchell found an over-all correlation of .41 between self-ideal discrepancy and anxiety (the greater the discrepancy, the higher the anxiety score). However, as a group, the self-rejecting women did as well in school as those who were self-accepting, and did not differ from them in intelligence.

Two other studies relate directly to self-ideal discrepancy but are in disagreement with each other. Both use college students rather than children as subjects. The fifty-six men and women subjects in the first study, by Block and Thomas (1955), Q-sorted eighty adjectives for the typical measures of perceived self and ideal self. The self-ideal discrepancies, referred to as "self-satisfaction" (where little discrepancy means high satisfaction), were then correlated with the subscales of the Minnesota Multiphasic Inventory (MMPI).

Several interesting findings resulted from the study, most of them fitting well with the results of the studies summarized in the preceding section which dealt with the "goodness" or "badness" of the self-concept. For example, the students with high discrepancy scores also obtained high scores on MMPI subtests thought to indicate tendencies to project and feel that "others are against you," and demonstrated tendencies toward morbid self-preoccupation. But on the other hand highly self-satisfied subjects scored rather high on a test of defensiveness (unwillingness to admit to undesirable traits), and denied "characteristics and feelings of an adverse and personally disparaging nature." An interesting and apparently useful scale called "Social Maintenance" has been constructed from a number of MMPI items. People with mental illness who "do well" on the scale have, for instance, been found to be better prospects for rehabilitation into society than those who score low. Self-satisfaction showed a negative relation with Social Maintenance score: the highly self-satisfied did "less well" than those who were more self-critical, although the correlation was not high (—.34).

The authors went one step further in their analysis, checking to see what the differences in type of self-criticism were between those who were *extremely satisfied* with themselves, those who were *moderately content* (the "Middles") and those who obtained high scores for *self-dissatisfaction*. They conclude that the highly self-satisfied emphasize "social appropriateness over interpersonal intimacy," and wish to control "their expressiveness and spontaneity," but at the same time be accepted and popular. "Their uneasiness with the affective life is stressed by their preference to be ideally less sentimental, less dependent, and less jealous than the Middles" (p. 258).

The highly dissatisfied group was made up of students who were judged by the authors to be "confused, overly introspective, despairing and with unrealistic, contradictory aspirations," and who were seeking

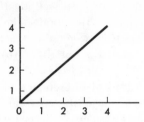 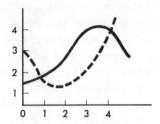

Figure 6.1   Graphs representing, from left to right, a linear and a curvilinear relationship.

"a feeling of personal integrity," whereas the Middles appeared "to be reasonable and accepting in their self-appraisals. They would like more of what they value and less of what makes them uncomfortable. They accept the ambiguity of emotions and are comfortable in their relations with others. They have their problems, certainly, but they neither despair nor deny" (p. 258).

This suggests what statisticians refer to as a *curvilinear relation* between self-satisfaction and adjustment, in contrast to the linear relationships implied by the other studies we have talked about. Figure 6.1 demonstrates these contrasting relationships.

The graph to the left in Figure 6.1 represents a linear relation. If we let the abscissa represent self-satisfaction, or congruence between perceived self and ideal self (0 meaning great, 4 meaning little discrepancy), and the ordinate represent adjustment from poor (0) to very good (4), then it follows from the graph that people with the least self-ideal congruence are least well-adjusted, those with the greatest congruence best adjusted. The solid line in the curvilinear graph to the right, representing the Block and Thomas results, tells a different story. Both high congruence and low congruence are related to poor adjustment, although those with high congruence between perceived self and ideal self are better adjusted than those with low congruence. Degrees of congruence represented in the middle (entries of 1, 2, and 3) are the best adjusted of the group. This curvilinear type of relation is a common one in studies of human behavior (for example, policies of excessive strictness and excessive leniency both seem to have undesirable effects on children's development).

In other words, the Block and Thomas study suggests a curvilinear relation between self-ideal discrepancy and adjustment; excessive self-satisfaction appears not to be the ideal human attribute, but too little self-satisfaction is also undesirable.

Another, somewhat similar study has been done by Chodorkoff (1954) using as subjects thirty college men. Here too there is found a curvilinear relation between adjustment and self-ideal congruence. But Chodorkoff's findings are in opposition to the results obtained by Block and Thomas. The curvilinear relation graphed by the dashed line at the right in Figure 6.1 represents Chodorkoff's findings. Both the high and the low self-satisfaction men received better adjustment ratings than those with moderate discrepancies.

There is no way to resolve these contradictory findings, and we can only say that they may have resulted from the different methods and the different populations used. Block and Thomas used men and women, Chodorkoff men only. Block and Thomas used a standardized, paper-and-pencil test to measure adjustment; Chodorkoff used primarily the Thematic Apperception Test and the Rorschach Inkblot Test of Personality as his basis for inferring adjustment. He and his colleagues based a rating of adjustment for each subject on the results of the two tests.

We can only conclude that the relation between self-satisfaction and adjustment is not a simple one. When does self-dissatisfaction cease to be a "desire to improve oneself" and becomes a serious handicap? There is a very real difference between the person who sees himself as being not perfect yet manages to live comfortably with himself as he is and the person who tortures himself with inferiority feelings and self-doubts. But, using the methods of measurement we have available, these two types of people could obtain identical self-satisfaction scores. Block and Thomas' analysis of differences in the ways people are dissatisfied with themselves may represent a method of getting at the answers to some of these questions. Additional measures, not simply of the number and type of self-dissatisfactions, but of their intensity and "ego value" or "reward value" also appear to be needed.

People who have used the Rorschach Inkblot Test in personality diagnosis have maintained that certain ways of responding to it indicate a tendency toward depression, and have developed methods of scoring the test responses for indicators of depression. One author (Bills, 1954) predicted that people with high self-ideal discrepancies would be more likely to be depressed than those with low discrepancies. He reasoned that "self-perceptions of a lack of unity within the personality or of a discrepancy between the perceptions of self and the ideal self should be disorganizational experiences leading to feelings of depression" (p. 135). Bills obtained two comparison groups, one with high and one with low self-ideal discrepancy, and tested to see whether more of the former than of the latter would respond in a "depressed" fashion. Using men and women undergraduate students, he found this to be true for five of the six Rorschach indicators he used. Results for the sixth indicator closely approached significance in the predicted direction.

A socially brighter picture of high self-ideal discrepancy is presented by Martire (1956), who worked with college men. His findings indicate that high self-ideal discrepancies are associated with high achievement motivation (which may be somewhat loosely called ambition, or desire to do well). This quality, of course, can have its drawbacks if it is too strongly present or if it exists in an area in which a person for one reason or another simply cannot succeed.

One implication of several of these studies is that individuals are in conflict about those traits for which their self-ideal discrepancies are the greatest. Cowen, Heilizer, and Axelrod (1955) used college freshmen to test this implication. It was predicted that new learning would be slowed up if it involved the names of traits or qualities on which there was a large self-ideal discrepancy (conflict). From the self-concept test of each subject the authors of the study picked six neutral words and the six adjectives on which he had shown the greatest self-ideal discrepancy. They then tested to determine the differential speed with which one-syllable nonsense words could be associated (a memory bond formed) with the conflict and the neutral words. They found that, on the average, it took about five more trials to build up an association between a conflict word and a nonsense syllable than between a nonsense syllable and a neutral word.

Another ingenious study (Friedman, 1955) demonstrates that normal young men show a rather close relation between perceived self and ideal self; that neurotics have far greater discrepancies (are more dissatisfied with themselves); but that paranoid schizophrenics do not differ from normals in self-satisfaction. Judges then "constructed" the self-concepts of the heroes of Thematic Apperception Test stories told by the men, using the same procedure by which perceived-self and ideal-self measures had been obtained directly from the men themselves. These Q-sorts were called the "Projected Self." The normal men and the neurotics projected themselves rather accurately; but the paranoid men projected with little or no accuracy. In other words, the normals were rather *self-accepting* and *projected* with moderate accuracy; the neurotics *did not like themselves* but were *accurate in their projection;* whereas the paranoids were *self-accepting* but *without accuracy of projection.* Achenbach and Zigler (1963), in a careful study of adults, find that those who are more socially competent have less self-ideal self-discrepancy. Their sample consisted of psychiatric patients. It has been pointed out that the more frequently we find similar results in very different populations, the more confidence we can put into the generalizations we may make. The very different Achenbach-Zigler populations lend confidence to the notion that a moderate self-ideal self-discrepancy is probably "better" than an extreme one.

Workers in the area of the self-concept have tended to confine themselves to the person as he *is* and as he *would like to be,* and to ignore the fact that a tendency to self-dissatisfaction or to self-satisfaction may perhaps spread out to all phases of life—may, in fact, be something akin to general pessimism or general optimism. Levy (1956) believed that this might be true. To test this hypothesis, he had college students, almost all of them men, do a Q-sort of 100 items to obtain a measure of perceived self. He developed another set of items referring to one's home town, and asked the same students to Q-sort them. Then the subjects did a *self-ideal* and a *home town-ideal* Q-sort. In general, the students who were dissatisfied with themselves were also dissatisfied with their home town, and vice versa. There was a highly significant correlation of .70 between the two sets of discrepancy scores. Levy wonders whether, rather than simply a self-ideal discrepancy related to personality adjustment, there may be a maladaptive tendency for some people *generally* to perceive the *actual* as very different from the *ideal:* in other words, a pessimism factor may exist in personality. Luckey (1960) reports findings that support this point. In a study of happily and unhappily married couples, one of the most pervasive characteristics of the unhappily marrieds was that they perceived not only themselves, but also their husbands or wives and mothers and fathers as rather cynical, depressed, begrudging people.

This topic of *discrepancy* between the perceived and the ideal self has been given separate treatment from the *self-concept* considered alone. There is some logical question about separating the two, since there are suggestions in the literature that the results obtained in self-ideal discrepancy studies would have been obtained as clearly and simply (or even more so) by employing a measure of perceived self only (for example, Lipsitt, 1958). Ideal-self scores elicited from a population tend to bunch together at the favorable end of the scale, whereas perceived-self scores are normally distributed. This fact means that the *discrepancy* score is almost perfectly correlated with the *perceived-self* score, so that little additional information is gained from calculating it. The hypothetical set of scores below illustrates this point:

Subject A's perceived-self-score is 20, his ideal-self-score, 30; his discrepancy score, 10.
Similar scores for subject B are 15 and 31; his discrepancy score is 16.
For subject C, the perceived-self-score is 10; the ideal-self-score, 30; and the discrepancy score, 20.

In other words, we learn just as much about these people by the simple procedure of giving and scoring a perceived-self-test as by adding the ideal-self-test and computing the discrepancy score; almost all the difference among the three discrepancy scores above was contributed by the *perceived-self-score.* However, even though such purely statistical considerations may have affected many self-ideal discrepancy studies, the study of self-acceptance and self-criticism continues to be important.

More sophisticated ways of obtaining measures both of perceived self and of ideal self will contribute to such research.

In summary, most research evidence indicates that people who are highly self-critical—that is, who show a large discrepancy between the way they actually see themselves and the way they would ideally like to be—are less well-adjusted than those who are at least moderately satisfied with themselves. Evidence indicates that highly self-critical children and adults are more anxious, more insecure, and possibly more cynical and depressed than self-accepting people. They *may* be more ambitious and driving, however. At least some evidence indicates that people experience conflict about the traits on which they have the greatest self-ideal discrepancy, and that this conflict is sharp enough to interfere with learning involving such areas. The evidence for a curvilinear relation between self-ideal discrepancy and adjustment is not clear, and there is some question whether the topic of self-ideal discrepancy is really different from the topic of positive and negative self-concepts.

Self-Concept and the Real Self

There is, of course, no way of knowing the "real" self. The closest approximation that can be made, in the current state of our knowledge, is to compare the statements of a person about himself with judgments of people who know him well. For understandable reasons, studies that compare the self-concept and the real self are infrequent: self-concept studies are easy to do on "captive" populations, such as a group of high-school students or college sophomores in an introductory psychology class. But to study the real self it is necessary to work with groups whose members know every other member well, and are willing to make the effort to cooperate with the research worker.

One of the few studies of "real" self and self-concept was done by Calvin and Holtzman (1953), using as subjects late adolescents (college men). These investigators elicited the cooperation of four fraternity groups, each member of which knew every other man well. In all, seventy-nine men cooperated. All were given the Minnesota Multiphasic Inventory (MMPI) in groups. They were then seen individually so that background information for each could be obtained and each could rank his buddies (including himself in his rankings) on traits of leadership, tolerance, adjustment, drive, tactfulness, and social understanding. The pooled ranks of every other man for a particular man constituted his score for "inferred self." If a man ranked himself higher than his buddies rated him, he was said to be "self-enhancing"; if he ranked himself lower, he was "self-depreciative." The closer to his buddies' pooled ranking his own ranking was, the more "insightful" he was considered to be.

Men considered by their buddies to be relatively well-adjusted had lower scores on the MMPI scales of depression, psychasthenia (morbid self-preoccupation) and schizophrenia; and also appeared to have traits that were more masculine than the men who were ranked as poorly adjusted. These correlations, while statistically significant, were not outstandingly high (in the high .20s and low .30s), but provide some evidence for the validity of some of the subscales of the MMPI. There were tendencies (correlations in the high .30s and low .40s) for men who were self-enhancing (who had better opinions of themselves than their buddies did) to score low on the depression, psychasthenia, and schizophrenia subscales of the MMPI, while self-depreciative men scored high, or in the poorly adjusted direction.

The authors of the study suggest that persons scoring high on these three scales "reflect a chronic state of marginal maladjustment including concern with one's self. Subjects who score high on the factor would tend to have difficulties in their social contacts, possibly by reason of their dissatisfactions, worry and disgruntlement, and their complaining and pessimistic attitude" (pp. 42–43). When the accuracy of the men's insight (the degree to which their rankings of themselves jibed with their buddies' rankings) was studied, it was found that men with more accurate insight had lower scores on the hysteria (attitudes of emotionality and immaturity) and psychopathic deviate (attitudes of social irresponsibility and delinquency) scales. They were also more masculine in their attitudes than men with less accurate insight. Such conclusions fit well with the conclusions reached by Friedman (1955) and Chodorkoff (1954a) who found that men who were more accurate in their self-descriptions tended to be less defensive.

In another study of young men in the Army (Howard, 1957), fifty-one men filled out a self-rating, and at least two of their buddies filled out the same rating for them. The discrepancy between their "real selves" (the buddy rating) and their own self-concept was then computed. It was found that the correlation between this discrepancy and their Army rating of delinquency was .56 (the greater the discrepancy, the greater the delinquency). When effects of intelligence were ruled out statistically, the correlation increased to .64. This again is evidence indicating that accuracy of self-perception is related to good adjustment, in the sense that well-adjusted people are less likely to be delinquent. This conclusion is interesting in the light of the Calvin and Holtzman findings that their inaccurately rating fraternity men had more emotional and less mature attitudes, and also scored higher on attitudes of social irresponsibility and delinquency than the men who rated themselves accurately. These findings also fit well with results obtained by Hassan and McCandless, and Taylor and Combs.

Coopersmith's (1959) study of fifth- and sixth-grade children has already been mentioned in the section on self-concept and adjustment. In addition to his data about the self-concept, he secured teacher judgments about the children (their "real selves"). Some of his subjects rated themselves high, others low, in self-concept. Although the youngsters were in general accurate (in the sense that the teachers agreed with their self-estimates), disagreements between child and teacher judgments occurred. From the total population of self- and teacher-judgments, Coopersmith secured a group of *high* self-esteem children whose teachers thought *poorly* of them (the high-low, or HL group), and another group of children who thought *poorly of themselves,* but who were *highly regarded* by their teachers (the low-high, of LH group). When these groups were compared, the children who were objectively successful, but who regarded themselves poorly (the LH's) were found to be more popular, better academic achievers although more self-critical, and more ambitious. These youngsters appear to "take it out on themselves," but are well-regarded by both teachers and peers, and are academically successful.

Coopersmith also selected two other groups for special study. In one of these, the good self-concept of the children agreed with the favorable "real self" teachers' rating. These youngsters comprised the high-high, or HH, group. Another group of children had poor self-concepts with which their teachers agreed (the low-low, or LL, group). The LL's were less popular, achieved less well, were more anxious, and held lower ideal concepts of themselves (yet, at the same time, were more self-critical) than the HH's.

In other words, humble yet successful children seemed to "do better" according to our United States criteria of success than less humble but equally favorably rated children, although at some personal price. Children who neither *thought* they were doing well nor *were* doing well, were relatively unidealistic about themselves yet, in their own eyes, failed even to meet their relatively low standards.

Two studies, then, suggest clearly that accuracy of self-estimate is associated with a number of other indices of good adjustment, although another study suggests that this relation is affected by whether the self-concept is *high and accurate,* or *low and accurate,* the former condition being more likely to accompany good adjustment. In the last study, self-depreciating children who were regarded by their teachers as successful were popular with their peers and academically successful, yet at the same time very self-critical.

Self-Acceptance and Acceptance of Others

The notion that people who are self-accepting are accepting of others has been frequently tested. This theory (Rogers, 1949) is of obvious practical importance, particularly to those who believe that personal maladjustment is socially learned. The maladjusted, self-rejecting person, if he also rejects others, is likely to be rejected by them in turn, with resulting exacerbation of his maladjustment. If, in counseling, the self-concept can be improved and if this improvement results in increased acceptance of and by other people, then a spiraling effect of "cure" or personal improvement will result: a "newly friendly" world will help along the counselor and the client.

Most studies of this specific topic indicate a clear and significant relation between acceptance of self and acceptance of others for both men and women, although actual popularity does not seem to be associated with either self-acceptance or acceptance of others. At least seven studies support the prediction that self-acceptance accompanies tolerance of and liking for others, thus suggesting that the self-accepting person sees the world as a friendlier and more benign place than the self-rejecting individual. These studies are so congruent in their results that they need only to be listed here: Berger (1951); Phillips (1951); McIntyre (1952); Crandall and Bellugi (1954); Omwake (1954); Fey (1955); and Levanway (1955). McIntyre and Fey also dealt with the relation between actual popularity and self-acceptance.

The one study (Zelen, 1955) in disagreement with these was done with sixth-grade children, but failed to separate the sexes in data analysis. Since at this age boys reject girls socially and girls boys, this failure to distinguish according to sex obscures the meaning of the study's findings.

Fey (1955) has made a rather refined analysis of his data, and his conclusions throw some additional light on the more general findings. He secured (1) measures of self-acceptance, (2) acceptance of others, (3) each subject's judgment of how well he was accepted by others, and (4) an estimate of actual acceptability, or popularity. His subjects were a presumably sophisticated group of fifty-eight third-year medical students, all or most of whom were probably men. His highly self-accepting (good self-concept) men were more accepting of others, and estimated their own popularity higher than did the less self-accepting men. But they were not *actually* any more popular. Men who were highly accepting of others estimated themselves as more popular than those who had little acceptance of others, but were not actually more popular (r, representing correlation, between acceptance of others and actual acceptance by others was .20, which does not reach statistical significance). Interestingly enough, there was no accuracy at all on the part of the men in estimating their popularity, the r between estimated acceptability and actual acceptability being .00.

Fey then split his subjects into groups of men who markedly overestimated their popularity (had self-enhancing tendencies) and men who markedly underestimated it (were self-derogatory). He found the latter group to be significantly more popular than the former, with an average of 6 friendly mentions each to the self-enhancers' 1.5. Fey believes that individuals who are very self-accepting but who reject others are possessed of "defensively organized" attitudes of superiority, are unperceptive of their actual group status, tend to disparage others, and are consequently rejected because they are threatening to the security of other people. But men who have low acceptance of themselves, together with high acceptance of others, are seen as nonthreatening, hence rewarding; and are well liked. The reader has probably noted that this result of Fey's is similar to Coopersmith's (1959) study, which used children of both sexes. Fey believes that the "prototypic well-adjusted person" (the one with high self-acceptance of others as well as himself) "may not appear to 'need' friendship or to repay it . . . his very psychological robustness is resented, or perhaps it is perceived and rejected as a Pollyanna-like façade" (p. 275).

To summarize, self-acceptance (a lack of cynicism about the self) seems to be associated with accepting other people. This indicates that the self-accepting person views the world as a friendlier place than the self-rejector. However, perhaps because of the complexity of social interaction (our tendency to conceal hostility and to exercise techniques of good manners and warmth toward people whether we like them or not), acceptance of others has not been found to be associated with actual popularity. It has been suggested that self-disparaging people, particularly those who are objectively successful, are better accepted socially than the "prototypic well-adjusted person," perhaps because they present no threat to and seek to please their friends.

Changes in Self-Concept

Change in self-concept is, of course, required by the process of maturing and is central to such activities as counseling, psychotherapy, and remedial teaching. Considering the importance of knowledge about development and change of the self-concept, it is surprising that little direct study has been made of these topics. Engel (1959) for example, has demonstrated that adolescents improve in self-concept over a two-year-period, without therapy or other special attempts to change their self-image. Of the group she studied, those with initially negative self-concepts improved the most, although youngsters with good self-concepts maintained their original status. Rogers and his students (Rogers and Dymond, 1954) have shown that adult self-concepts tend to improve with psychotherapy; indeed, they regard improvement in self-concept as an indicator of successful therapy.

The present discussion of the self-concept has been based on the assumption that it is learned. It seems logical to think that the self-concept, based as it is on attitudes and values held about the *self,* has much in common with general social attitudes and personal beliefs and values. Any theory or research, then, that relates to changing attitudes *should* have relevance for changes in the self-concept.

Festinger (1957) has developed a provocative theory about attitudes and their change, from which have come interesting studies of children and college students. His theory is very briefly presented below, and the assumption (admittedly speculative) is made that it applies to self-concept as well as to more general and more objective (or thing-centered) attitude changes. Many ingenious experiments to test this theory have been carried out by Festinger and his students. Some of these are reviewed below. Following each review, and assuming underlying similarity of the principles governing self-attitude and general-attitude changes, theoretical extensions for the self-concept are formulated on the basis of the research results.

As with all theories, Festinger's has historical roots: He was one of Kurt Lewin's students; and Lewin (1935) laid the ground rules for his theory, just as he did for the Neal Miller's theories of approach-avoidance that were treated in the preceding chapter. Like all people "who stick out their necks," Festinger has his critics. Chapanis and Chapanis (1964) belong to the critical school that throws out the baby with the bath. They say that "the experimental manipulations are usually so complex and the crucial variables so confounded that no valid conclusions can be drawn from the data" (p. 1), and add pessimistically that "fundamental methodological inadequacies in the analysis of results . . . vitiate the data" (p. 1). However, like the present author, they find the simplicity of the theory attractive, although, unlike him, they believe its simplicity makes it self-defeating.

The author regards Festinger in much the same way he thinks of Skinner (see Chapter 4). Skinner's thinking seems almost unduly simple, but his ideas work. So do Festinger's. Silverman (1964), replying to the Chapanis', comes to Festinger's defense, although Festinger and his students manage well on their own. The carefully done Turner and Wright (1965) study that was discussed in considerable detail in Chapter 5 fits as well with the theory as do the less recent studies summarized below.

Festinger maintains that when inconsistent perceptions are held by a person, either about himself or about his environment, he is placed in a state of tension, which Festinger calls psychological "dissonance." This is an uncomfortable state of affairs, which an individual attempts to alleviate or dissipate by bringing his cognitions closer together (reducing the ratio of inconsistent to consistent cognitions). Plausible evidence has been reviewed that indicates that individuals with high self-ideal discrepancies are uncomfortable people, who may be struggling to get their self-concepts and ideal self-concepts more in line with each other; and that improvement in self-concept is regarded at least by some as an indication of increased personal comfort and happiness. Certainly, much of counseling and psychotherapy has as a goal improvement in self-concept, reduction in self-ideal discrepancy, and reduction of confusion and conflict in self-concept.

The first of the studies to be reviewed here was done by Festinger and Carlsmith (1959). They have published an engaging report of research supporting the following hypotheses: (1) If a person is induced to do or say something that is contrary to his private opinion, he will change his opinion so as to bring it in line with what he has said or done. (2) The greater the pressure used to elicit his dissonant behavior (above the *minimum* required to elicit it), the less likely he is to change his opinion. In other words, the greater the pressure, the more likely it is that he will be able to divorce his behavior from his personal conviction.

These authors induced undergraduate college men through harmless and amusing deceits to report favorably to a putative next-in-line subject for the same experiment about an excruciatingly dull experimental session to which they had been subjected immediately prior to the report. Relative rankings of this dull task were secured (1) from a control group that had not been induced to make such a report; (2) from an experimental group that had been offered $1.00 per man to make such a report (the minimal-reward group); and (3) from a second experimental group (the maximal-reward group), each member of which was offered $20.00 to make the report.

The task they were ranking involved spending a half-hour putting twelve spools on a tray, emptying the tray, refilling it with spools, and so on, working at their own speed and using only one hand; then, for a second half-hour, working with a board that contained forty-eight square pegs, the task being to turn these one at a time a quarter-turn clockwise, then another quarter-turn, and so on, again using one hand and working at their own speed. It is difficult to imagine a more anesthetizing task.

In line with the hypotheses, the control group gave the task a mildly negative rating (one might say that it showed good manners); the minimal-reward group rated it as moderately enjoyable; and the maximal-reward group gave it a neutral rating. Subjects in the minimal-reward group also testified to their willingness to go through the procedure again, whereas the other two groups indicated reluctance.

This study suggests the following speculative prediction for self-concept change: If, through mild pressure or reward, an individual can be induced to do something contrary to his self-concept, he will alter his self-concept in the direction of his spoken opinion or overt action. If one who considered himself a poor speaker, for example, were in some low-pressure fashion induced to make a good speech, he might improve his conception of himself as a speaker. This prediction fits well with material in Chapter 5 that unexpected rewards may result in more alteration of expectancies than rewards that have been predicted.

In a second study, Cohen, Terry, and Jones (1959) gave one group of male college freshmen *an option* of listening or not listening to a propaganda session on a topic concerning which they held strongly opposing opinions. Another group was subjected to *strong pressure* to listen to the session. The low-pressure group moved almost four times as far as the high-pressure group in the direction of agreeing with the propaganda. The suggestion for self-concept change is obvious: One is more likely to induce an individual to make changes in his self-concept by nondirective, low-pressure methods than through high social pressure. This suggests that therapy voluntarily entered will be more successful than when entered involuntarily.

Brehm (1959) exposed adolescents to two sets of conditions, in one of which there were high social consequences (the young people's behavior was ostensibly to be reported to their parents); whereas in the other their behavior would remain secret. Brehm obtained like-dislike ratings from eighth-graders for thirty-four vegetables. Then an experimenter, posing as a nutrition research worker, asked the youngsters to take part in a food-testing program. The test, of course, was designed so that the vegetable each adolescent was asked to "test" was one he heartily disliked. He was told that he could eat it or not, as he wished. If he ate it, he would be given his choice of either two movie tickets or two records. For the *low-consequence* group, nothing more was said; but for the high-consequence group, the experimenter mentioned casually (when the youngsters had almost finished eating the dish of vegetables), "Oh I almost forgot to mention that one of the reports we plan to put out from this study will simply be a letter to the parents of each person who takes part, just indicating which vegetable that person ate" (p. 380). Mama, in other words, would know that he had consumed something which was "good" for him, but which he loathed.

After this tricky sequence, the subjects were asked to rate the thirty-four vegetables again. They were told in a permissive fashion that some people change their opinions, while others do not. The high-consequences group changed significantly more in their ranking of the previously disliked vegetable than the low-consequences group, although this latter group also gave higher ratings to the test vegetables after having tasted them.

Implications for self-concept change are obvious: If the behavior contrary to the self-concept is likely to be known by *important other people* (is going to become public), then the predicted self-concept change will be greater than if the consequences remain private.

Brehm and Cohen (1959), using sixth-graders as subjects, demonstrated that when a choice must be made between two highly *dissimilar* rewards (toys), the increase in preference rating for the chosen one, and the decrease in preference rating for the unchosen one, is greater than when the choice is made between two rather *similar* toys. The reasoning is that the subject sees himself as giving up more in the dissimilar than in the similar choice situation, so that more dissonance is produced and more change of opinion results. These sixth-grade children also changed more in favor of the chosen and against the unchosen toy when they were required to choose among four rather than two alternative items. The assumption is that having to give up three things produces more dissonance than having to give up one. These results suggest the "sour grapes" phenomenon.

Speculative predictions for self-concept change are more difficult to make from this study than from the first three summarized in this section, but the following might be hazarded: Let us take, for example, a boy who has entered junior-high school when, for the first time clear choices of activity must be made, some being sacrificed so that others may be pursued. He has equally strong and equally valued conceptions of himself as an athlete and as a scholar, but must choose between two activities: debate and basketball. He chooses debate. It can be predicted that he will sharply devalue the importance of basketball and possibly of all sports; but will sharply upgrade the importance of debate and other types of intellectual activity. The actual *direction* of his conception of himself as an athlete may not shift, but the *value* to him of this facet of his self-concept will change in a negative direction. Conversely, the value of intellectual activities will become greater, and the importance of the intellectual facet of his self-concept will increase. Less marked changes will occur if he has to choose between, say, swimming and basketball or the Science Club and debate. More marked changes will occur if he has to choose one of many activities than if he has to choose between only two.

In summary, one may predict from the Festinger dissonance theory that the self-concept will change in the direction of overt behavior relating to it. Change will be greater if the behavior is induced by low pressure or accompanies a high degree of freedom of choice; and if the behavior is likely to have tangible consequences (that is, if it is expected to become known by people important to the subject). Shifts in the importance or value of facets of the self-concept will occur when the individual is forced to choose behavior that relates to one facet but excludes another. These shifts will be to the advantage of the facet to which the chosen behavior is relevant.

Other Qualities of the Self-Concept

To this point, the discussion of the self-concept has followed the research literature rather closely. Research in this area has concerned itself almost exclusively with one aspect or quality of the self-concept: its positive or negative balance. Suggestions of other qualities of the self-concept that merit more consideration and research than have been given them are listed below.

1. Complexity and breadth. It can be assumed that normal adults have more complex and broader self-concepts than children; and that highly intelligent and cultured adults have more complex and broader self-concepts than, for example, adults of borderline intelligence, little education, and a narrow range of experiences. The person who lives only for his work can be expected to have a narrower self-concept than an individual with a great variety of interests and activities. The married man and father must develop facets of his self-concept for which the bachelor has no need.

2. Congruency and accuracy. The self-concept should conform to the actual life situation of the individual. Some research on this topic has been reviewed. There are many occasions or periods during the developmental process when the self-concept is out of line with actuality. For example, the author has known many early-maturing children who, as far as their physiques were concerned, were full-fledged adults and who were reacted to by teachers and others as though they were substantially older than they really were, yet who still carried conceptions of themselves as children. On occasion serious although usually temporary maladjustments have resulted for some of these young people.

Also common in our culture is the middle-aged individual who still carries with him a self-concept of the dashing blade or winsome belle of 21. One of the problems of old age is failure to change the self-concept to fit failing health, diminished strength and endurance, and brittle bones. Wheelchairs are full of old ladies who broke their hips because of their misconceptions that they could still scramble up a stepladder to change a light bulb.

As has been mentioned, many successful people still maintain the self-concept of shy, inadequate adolescence. Less frequent, probably, is the example of the essentially inadequate individual who sees himself as a powerful and successful figure. Much psychotherapy and counseling has as its goal an increase in reality of the self-concept.

3. *Clarity or articulateness.* Highly self-aware or inner-directed people perhaps have clearer and more articulate although not necessarily more accurate or positive self-concepts than those who are extroverted or outer-directed. It is also possible that highly verbal individuals have clearer or at least more articulate self-concepts than relatively nonverbal persons.

4. *Consistency.* Many maladjusted children and adults carry within them contradictory and conflicting self-concepts. The self-concept of the bully will usually be found to include incompatible facets of insecurity and fright on the one hand, and hostility, aggression, and combativeness on the other hand. It has been suggested that the Don Juan sees himself both as a sexually inadequate individual but one whom women find irresistible.

The stability of the self-concept is related to consistency. An extreme example of instability of self-concept is provided by the manic-depressive psychotic. In the manic phase, he may see himself as gregarious, charming, powerful, successful, and leading "the good life." Depressed, he regards himself as worthless, the world as bleak and gray, and things so hopeless that often he attempts suicide, and sometimes succeeds.

Certainly, self-assurance varies to some degree with success and failure, good times, and hard times. But this veering, for a well-adjusted person, should not be extreme to an unrealistic degree.

5. *Flexibility.* The notion of flexibility is of course somewhat related to both congruency and accuracy as well as consistency, but it includes something more: the ability to change roles and shift from one appropriate self-concept to another as occasion demands it. When he comes home from the office, a man should be flexible enough to drop the concept and role of a successful or driving manager of men and to assume instead the role of husband and father.

Flexibility is also somewhat related to the notion of complexity. When mature an individual should have varied self-concepts: in one situation, he may need to see himself as a leader and be able to adopt the appropriate role; whereas in another the self-concept and behavior of follower may be required. Adults must usually change from a high degree of personal freedom and independence to breadwinning or housewifery and parenthood; from parents of preschoolers to parents of adolescents; from the family circle to the social circle and back again; from the security of the at-home routine to the excitement and unfamiliarity of the vacation; or from an intimate circle of friends to occasions when they are the only strangers.

6. Still another dimension of the self-concept that appears to have been neglected in the literature, although considerable research is now accumulating, can be tentatively called *self-acceptance*. There are some who can regard themselves accurately, who can face the fact that they are not all they would like to be (that there is substantial discrepancy between their actual and ideal selves), yet who live happily and constructively with this awareness. There are others who are in constant turmoil because they are not what they think they should be. It may be that this latter type of uncomfortable adjustment acts as a drive or motive to spur such people on. Ambition may, in part, have such a base.

These, undoubtedly, are only *some* of the qualities of the self-concept that are worth investigating, but a chapter on the self-concept would not be complete without mentioning them.

Summary

The assumption this chapter makes is that the self-concept is learned, and can best be visualized as a set of expectancies plus evaluations of the areas or behaviors concerning which these expectancies are held.

Most of the research that has been done on the self-concept has concerned its "good-bad," or positive-negative, dimension. Items (usually some form of questionnaire) designed to measure this dimension are either selected because they have consensual social value (positive *or* negative) or are rated personally by the individual being measured.

The considerable body of research on traits, attitudes, behaviors, and various qualities associated with the self-concept indicates that good self-concepts are associated with such desirable characteristics as low anxiety and generally good adjustment, curiosity, popularity, and effectiveness in group relations but relative independence from the group (that is, close group affiliation seems less important to people with positive self-concepts than to people with negative self-concepts). Those with good self-concepts seem more honest with themselves than individuals with poor self-concepts, and appear to be less defensive.

Parental attitudes shape the self-concept and children whose parents value them "extrinsically" (that is, for what they *do* rather than what they *are*) seem to be grandiose in their self-conceptions, less mature, and unrealistically persistent—even rigid—in certain attitudes pertaining to the self. Underachievers in school have poorer self-concepts than normal achievers and reflect feelings of undue restriction on their freedom, of defensiveness, and of loneliness.

A related but not necessarily independent type of self-concept research concerns itself with the discrepancy between the actual and the ideal self. This area is labeled as "not necessarily independent" because of indications in the literature that the amount of self-ideal discrepancy is a function more of the positive-negative variation of the self-concept than of variations in the ideal self. Generally speaking, the greater the self-ideal discrepancy, the less adequate the adjustment, according to a variety of criteria. The responses of those with high self-ideal *discrepancies* seem quite similar to those of subjects in other studies that have taken account only of the good-bad dimension of the self-concept.

In studies where the self-concept was compared with ratings of the individual made by others, those who were more "accurate" in their self-perceptions received scores on personality tests indicating good adjustment and less often manifested delinquent tendencies. But, the effect of accuracy varies according to whether the self-concept is *good* and accurate, or *poor* and accurate. Good-accurate self-concepts are more closely associated with good adjustment than poor-accurate ones. Children who are inaccurate in their self-concepts, in that they regard themselves poorly but are rated by their teachers as successful, are popular and academically successful, yet self-critical.

Self-acceptance appears to be related to acceptance of others, although not to actual popularity. Those who are self-rejecting but who accept others, are rated as more popular than highly self-accepting men who are not highly *other*-accepting.

Although self-concept change has not been intensively investigated, the Festinger theory of dissonance (built around more objective attitudes than those that characterize the self) suggests a number of predictions about how such change takes place. This theory states that individuals holding inconsistent perceptions about themselves or their environment will attempt to eliminate the tension aroused by this inconsistency by bringing their conflicting perceptions closer together. The following speculative predictions were made from research suggested by this theory: The self-concept will change in the direction of overt behavior that relates to it; low social pressure for change will result in more change than high pressure; when the behavior is expected to have real-life consequences, more change will result than when no consequences are expected; shifts of value in facets of the self-concept will occur when an individual is forced to choose behavior that relates to and supports one facet, but excludes another. This theory has been strongly criticized and defended in the literature, but continues to be useful.

Finally, several aspects of the self-concept other than the positive-negative dimension which are important and need research were discussed. These aspects are: complexity and breadth, congruency and accuracy, clarity, consistency, flexibility, and self-acceptance.

Intelligence: Measurement and Educational Practices

One of the major achievements of the science of psychology is the measurement of intelligence. Although much controversy surrounds the theory and assessment of intelligence, the research literature on this topic is perhaps as solid as any in the entire field.

Because much highly specialized research relating to intelligence has been done, two chapters are devoted to a review of pertinent findings. This method of treatment should not be taken as implying that intelligence is independent of other developmental phenomena. It is, of course, *interdependent,* influencing and influenced by almost all other aspects of development.

Definitions

Many volumes have been written on intelligence, and attempts to define it are legion. These attempts range from stating that "intelligence is what intelligence tests measure" to such definitions as "intelligence is the ability to do abstract thinking."

Some early (Thorndike *et al.*, 1926) as well as recent (Ferguson, 1954, 1956) workers in theory and measurement of intelligence have argued that there are many intelligences, or that intelligence is made up of a number of pure or "primary" factors, each relatively independent of the others. Thurstone and Thurstone (1950) have devised tests for children and adults that purport to measure a number of these primary factors, such as ability to deal with spatial concepts, number ability, word fluency, and vocabulary. Guilford (1966) believes in a factorial intelligence.

Spearman (1927), a pioneer in work with the concept of intelligence, held that there was a general, or *g*, factor that influenced all intelligent or sentient behavior; and that there were many special, or *s*, factors, some of which were heavily dependent on *g* (number ability, for example), whereas others were relatively independent (for example, music or motor ability). Still other authors speak of verbal ability and performance ability (as Wechsler, 1944).

RECENT THEORETICAL DEVELOPMENTS

There has been relatively little recent theoretical concern with intelligence. Ferguson (1954), surveying the scene, states:

> At present no systematic theory, capable of generating fruitful hypotheses about behavior, lies behind the study of human ability. Current approaches are largely empirical. . . . The concept of intelligence . . . is no longer a useful scientific concept except as subsuming some defined set of clearly distinguishable abilities. (p. 95)

After this somewhat negative pronouncement, Ferguson develops a theory of intelligence that is more a learning than a genetic theory and has perhaps been indirectly prompted by Hebb (1949). Ferguson believes that ability, or intelligence, as tested by our current intelligence tests, is made up of correlated types of overlearning. Overlearning, in interaction with an individual's biological heritage, has resulted in these separate abilities (which, when grouped, are called intelligence) reaching their asymptotes. That is, regardless of how much an individual tries, he will become no more proficient in performing such tasks; nor regardless of how their practice is neglected, will efficiency in performing them decline much with time. Ferguson would say that a score on an intelligence test is highly useful in predicting success in school simply because the overlearned skills represented by an intelligence quotient have substantial transfer to the types of learning an individual must master in school.

Ferguson maintains that those abilities essential for satisfactory adjustment to a culture increase regularly as a child grows older, up to perhaps age 17; those abilities that are not necessary for adjustment to a culture fail to increase at the same rate, and indeed may not increase at all. By this reasoning he accounts for the differences in measured intelligence between people who live in different countries, or in rural rather than urban areas, or in institutions rather than homes, or in circumstances of cultural isolation rather than cultural intercommunication, or in one social class rather than another. Representative studies bearing on such cultural factors will be taken up in more detail in the next chapter. But further to illustrate Ferguson's provocative point of view, let us anticipate later material by saying that there is substantial evidence that children growing up in culturally isolated rural areas (for example, the mountains of eastern Tennessee) show a progressive *decrease* in intelligence as measured by standard intelligence tests: older brothers and sisters have a materially lower IQ than younger brothers and sisters.

Ferguson would explain this by saying that the skills measured by a standard American test of intelligence are simply not very important in adapting to existence in the Tennessee mountains; hence, they decline with age.

One interesting study (Havighurst and Hilkevitch, 1944) indicates that a sample of ninety-two Hopi Indian children, relatively remote from the standard United States culture, scored substantially higher on a performance (nonverbal) type of intelligence test than Indian children living closer to the standard culture. Indeed, with a mean IQ[1] of 115, they scored substantially higher than the group of white children on which the test had been standardized. They also tested much higher than a group of twenty-nine Shiprock Navaho children, whose average score was 96, despite the fact that the Hopi youngsters were "much less acculturated." However, the twenty-one most isolated of the Hopi children—an Old Oraibi group—averaged 105 IQ, whereas the rest of the "more progressive . . . more subject to white influence . . . group averaged 117 IQ" (p. 430).

It might be conjectured, according to Ferguson's point of view, that the elaborate tribal organization and ritual, high artistic level, well-developed architectural abilities, and complete dependency on an environment so hostile that survival demands it be studied in exquisite and painstaking detail, all helped to develop high performance skills. The artistically and architecturally less proficient Navahos who are, on the whole, herders rather than farmers may have less opportunity to develop the skills measured by this intelligence test. The same thing may be true of the standardization group of Midwestern children, who lived in moderately comfortable, undemanding surroundings.

In this connection, Ferguson's statement applies: "Presumably children reared in different environments, which demand different types of learning at different ages, develop different patterns of ability" (1954, p. 99). Ferguson also hypothesizes that different abilities may be required at different stages of learning a task. "An individual might possess the ability to improve rapidly in the early stages of learning, but might lack the abilities necessary to attain high proficiency at the stage of high habituation or overlearning" (1954, p. 2). Most of us, that is, can learn the elements of playing the piano; few of us, regardless of how we practice, can become good enough to be concert pianists. Evidence exists to support this point of view. One study of young men (cited by Ferguson, 1956) indicates that in the early stages of learning a visual-motor task, the rate of learning depended most heavily on spatial and verbal

---

[1] The intelligence quotient is obtained from a measurement of the child's mental age. Mental age is then divided by chronological age, and the result multiplied by 100 to remove decimals. For example, a child tested on his tenth birthday and found to have a mental age of 10 will obtain an IQ of 100, which is considered to be average.

abilities. Those who could best manipulate spatial concepts, those who were superior in verbal ability, picked up the beginning essentials of the task most rapidly. However, eventual mastery—a highly superior finished performance—depended more on speed of reaction time and the rate at which the individual moved. Another study (Ritchie, Aeschliman, and Pierce, 1950) used rats as subjects, and found that the first stages of learning depended heavily on the animal's visual discrimination ability, whereas perfecting the maze learning was a function of the animal's ability to utilize motor and kinesthetic cues.

Bayley (1955), who has conducted longitudinal studies of the development of intelligence in United States children, comes to a conclusion in part similar to Ferguson's. Bayley states:

> I see no reason why we should continue to think of intelligence as an integrated (or simple) entity or capacity which grows throughout childhood by steady accretions. . . . Intelligence appears to me, rather, to be a dynamic succession of developing functions, with the more advanced or complex functions in the hierarchy depending on the prior maturing of earlier simpler ones (given, of course, normal conditions of care). (p. 807)

Ferguson's approach seems to consider intelligence as a single factor —an overlearned ability to solve problems. Bayley, on the other hand, speaks in the paragraph immediately above of "a dynamic succession of developing functions. . . ." Nor does anything, actually, that Ferguson says indicate that "overlearned habits" are simple merely because they are habits.

In other words, the previous section on definitions does no violence to a concept of intellectual simplicity or complexity, nor is violence done to either conception by Guilford (1966), who regards intelligence as problem-solving ability, but one made up of many, many factors—to be exact, 120 factorial cells. Guilford has made perhaps the most significant and far-reaching theoretical contributions to intelligence theory of anyone who has worked in the field since Ferguson wrote in 1954 and 1956.

He considers that the following components, some of them structure, some content, some operations, some products, make up intelligence or intelligent behavior. His approach to the structure of intellect (SI, as he calls it) may be schematized as a cube, sectioned in one direction by five *operations,* in another direction by six *products,* and in the third by four *contents,* for a total of 5 by 6 by 4, or 120 cells, each containing an operation, a product, and a content.

Guilford's Operations These are cognition (knowing or perceiving), memory (remembering, the things we can recall), divergent production (the production of originals), convergent production (the logical induction or deduction from possession of a relatively complete set of knowledge according to logical procedures), and evaluation, or screening, in which the worthwhileness of the product is judged.

Guilford's Products   These are units (such as single memories or events), classes (or groups), relations (connections between units or classes), transformations (alterations in relations), and implications (results of combinations, transformations, and so on). These definitions are the present author's, not Guilford's.

Guilford's Contents   These may be figural (actual representations or "images"), symbolic (such as the printed word as it stands for something), semantic (such as the rules of grammar or representation), or behavioral (actions, which may in turn be symbolic, as in gestures).

Guilford has for many years been trying to single out the factors and their assortment that fit into the 120 cells he hypothesizes. At the time of his 1966 publication, he believed that he had 75 cells fitted by eighty abilities (at times, two or three abilities fit into a single cell, such as cognitions of rhythms, which are kinesthetic-spatial, and melodies, which are auditory, into a cognitive or memory cell).

Guilford, unlike the Thurstones, has not devised an elaborate series of tests for predicting intellectual function as it applies to success at discrete undertakings, although he plans to do so and has ventured into the field of mathematics performance prediction. He also rejects the notion of *g*, but thinks different kinds of information come into experience at different times, and development in handling them progresses at different rates (a position similar to Bayley's). He points out that figural and behavioral information are present from or almost from birth, whereas symbolic or semantic information comes much later. "The early differentiations of abilities," he says (p. 23) "must mean that the brain develops naturally different ways of processing the various products of information, as it develops different mechanisms for the five kinds of operations."

The cognitive abilities for dealing with behavioral information, six in number, according to Guilford, are equivalent to social intelligence, such as has been postulated by Thorndike. Guilford also believes there is tremendous importance in the sheer acquisition of information, as has been stressed in Chapters 1, 4, and 5. Only through environmental exposure can information be acquired by an organism.

Guilford thinks that input into his structure of intellect (SI) comes both from the environment and the soma, or body, the latter being of both motivational and emotional types, and from the brain as well as the internal receptors. Filtering or screening occurs, shutting off some sorts of input, facilitating other types. Filtering, in other words, is much like the more traditional term attention. The organism is always evaluating, checking and self-correcting. Such checking is not the final stage of problem solving, but occurs throughout the entire process. "Awareness that a problem exists and identification or structuring of the problem are cognitive operations . . . during which . . . there is dependence on memory storage and there is evaluation of cognized information. In the effort to cognize the problem, there may be a seeking for new input information" (p. 25).

Guilford thinks that the factorial structure of intellect may well be complex from birth, a conclusion with which Stott and Ball (1965) agree. They believe that "definitely intellectual" items for testing intelligence can be devised for earliest infancy (Piaget would agree; see Chapter 1). Others (such as Garrett and Spearman as discussed by Guilford) seem to believe that early intelligence is simpler or more unitary, becoming more complex and differentiated with age. Still another position, and the correct one, for all the present author or perhaps anyone else knows, is presented by Leinert and Crott (1964) who believe that they have "shown that the structure of intelligence exhibits a trend toward differentiation from childhood to adolescence and toward integration from adolescence to adulthood (differentiation-integration hypothesis)" (p. 163).

INTELLIGENCE AS PROBLEM-SOLVING ABILITY

By and large, the concern of this book is with United States children who are normal, live in relatively average situations, and go to regular schools. For such a group, it is perhaps most practical to think of intelligence as *problem-solving ability*.

Such an ability must be considered complex, not simple, as has been stated. Problem-solving involves concentration, speed, and depth or power, among other things. One type of problem may involve numbers, another spatial or geometric concepts, another only the use of words. One man may be an "intelligent" safe-cracker, yet unable to grasp algebra or foreign languages. A brilliant author may be "stupid" if he tries to become a farmer or woodsman or mechanic. There does, however, appear to be a moderate relationship between different types of problem-solving ability. The efficient safe-cracker, had he been socially oriented and more conventionally motivated, could probably have made an excellent mechanic.

Approaches to Measurement

There are many different types of intelligence tests, and many different versions of each type. The *Sixth Mental Measurements Yearbook* (Buros, 1965), for instance, includes reviews of 130 different intelligence tests, or instruments allied to intelligence tests. Such tests are most simply classified according to (1) the age group for which they are suitable and (2) their type. There are tests suitable for measuring intelligence (or something presumed to be akin to it) in infants, preschool-aged children, children of elementary-school age, adolescents, and adults (including certain extremely difficult instruments designed to measure the intelligence of the most superior adult). There are tests that must be given individually, whereas others are intended as group instruments. There are tests of so-called verbal intelligence (such as verbal reasoning analogies: "*Good* is to *bad* as *love* is to . . . ." and vocabulary tests), and there are performance tests. These latter do not involve the use of words in responding, although probably subjects guide their behavior by thoughts expressed to themselves in words. Examples of such tests are: solving paper mazes by drawing a trace through them with a pencil; fitting together individual pieces to make more complex forms; and replacing missing pieces into a picture from which they have been cut. There are tests, or individual items within tests, that tap speed (the faster the individual works, the higher his score); power (problems range from very simple to extremely difficult, but for which no speed limit is set); and breadth (for instance, range of vocabulary or information). The most commonly agreed-on two factors of intelligence are verbal and performance.

Binet, with whom intelligence-testing may be said to have begun, was trying to solve a practical problem: How can we predict whether a child will succeed or fail in school? At present, intelligence tests accomplish this goal fairly satisfactorily. When a child is successful, as compared with other children of the same age and culture, at dealing with certain problems—such as defining words; repeating a list of numbers from memory after the examiner has said them aloud; figuring out the answers to such questions as "What makes a windmill turn?"; judging how a piece of paper that has been cut when it was folded will look when it is unfolded—he is classified as bright. Other things being equal, when his IQ is high, he will do well in school. Doing poorly on such tasks in comparison with other children results in a low IQ, which usually means that a child will do poorly in school.[2]

Intelligence tests predict best for groups of children in elementary school, and predict less adequately the higher up the academic ladder we go. Almost all American children attend elementary school; they are exposed to a relatively homogeneous curriculum; and usually they have only one teacher, except for special subjects such as music, art, and recreation. In junior high school, prediction is typically made more difficult by the platoon system, in which different teachers teach different

---

[2] The school curriculum, of course, is itself a complex matter. A child who stands very high in reading ability may be relatively poor in arithmetic, although ordinarily he will do better than the average of his class.

subjects. A math teacher, for example, may be very efficient in getting the best achievement from almost every child, whereas the social studies teacher may get the most from her favorites but have a discouraging effect on other but perhaps equally able children. Such factors reduce the accuracy of prediction. High school presents further complexities: some children take part-time jobs and some take easy curriculums or electives while others take more difficult ones. Some let their grades go, spending all their time in extracurricular activities or in pursuit of the opposite sex. A whole group—the slow learners—who could be diagnosed very accurately by intelligence tests, have dropped out of school or been placed in special vocational schools.

In college, motivation and study efficiency affect success almost as much as intelligence. There is no one to enforce study hours; hence the student who finds it difficult to plan ahead will almost certainly have academic trouble, regardless of how bright he is. There is a wide range of electives—some easy, some difficult. Ordinarily, only the relatively bright go to college in the first place, so that again the "easy-to-predict" lower-intelligence group is no longer present. In college, then, intelligence-test scores predict actual achievement even less accurately than they do in high school.

Finally, few enter professional and graduate schools without possessing very high intellectual ability, so that the success or failure of graduate students is perhaps due even more to temperament, interest, efficient studying, and motivation than it is to intelligence as such. Testing experts continue to struggle with the creation of intelligence tests that will permit accurate predictions about success in law, medical, or engineering school as well as the other learned professions. They are also searching for measures of aptitudes ranging from mechanical skills to the qualities required for making good as a banker.

Predictions about how a student will do in professional training can be made with some success for high-school students. Accuracy of prediction is greater still for students of college age. But as yet there is no way to pick out the potentially successful engineer or nurse during the elementary-school years, although general intellectual ability can be measured rather accurately by the time a child is $2\frac{1}{2}$ to 3 or 4 years of age. That is, a moderate degree of accuracy has been achieved in predicting how well a child will do in school, but forecasting his specific intellectual and performance strengths and weaknesses is still a psychological frontier.

Infant Intelligence Tests

The most widely used intelligence tests, or developmental schedules, for infants (children up to approximately 2 years of age) are the Cattell (1940), Gesell (Gesell and Amatruda, 1941), Kuhlmann (1939), and

Northwestern (Gilliland, 1949). To anyone who knows infants, it is obvious that finding test items that tap what we have called problem-solving ability at so early an age level is difficult, if not impossible. A *problem* involves a *goal* for the individual being tested, the *route* to which is not clear. The goals of the very young infant (younger than about 6 months) are quite primitive: he wants to be full, dry, warm and, when awake, "seeking." But he has no direct methods of reaching these goals; he is dependent upon adults for his achievement. How, then, can we devise an intelligence scale for infants?

The builders of such scales have used as items sensorimotor responses to changes in the environment, behaviors that indicate social responsiveness, and relatively primitive problem-solving activities. Examples of these are, respectively: turning the head in the direction of a bell or light, smiling in response to the smile and/or verbalization of an adult, and dropping one of two cubes or toys to take a third different one.

The Bayley infant tests, used in a national study of infant development, will, upon their release to the psychological public, undoubtedly become the most widely used tests in the field. At the time of writing, their use is confined to research. Bayley (1965) has reported findings based on her battery for a very large sampling (1409 infants, aged 1 to 15 months, representative of families according to the 1960 United States census in terms of social, ethnic, and other groups). From this preliminary report, the test battery appears very promising.

Additionally, it is possible, as was suggested in Chapter 1, to devise better infant tests than have so far been devised. Language in infancy (for example crying, babbling, diversity of speech sounds) has been insufficiently explored as a predictor of later intelligence. For example, Karelitz *et al.* (1964) report a correlation between outburst frequency in infants' crying when they were 4 to 10 days old and Stanford-Binet IQ at the age of 3 years of a surprisingly high .45. Piaget has many suggestions for items of a problem-solving type for infants, and Stott and Ball (1965) believe that there already occur in existing infant intelligence tests "definitely intellectual" items that are likely to be better predictors than at present suspected.

All tests of infants are, of course, individual. In a careful analysis of tests given over the years to children who took part in a longitudinal study, Hofstaetter (1954) concludes that the major element tapped by the items that make up infant intelligence tests is "sensorimotor alertness." A child who is advanced in a sensorimotor way earns a high score on the tests; a child who is retarded earns a low score. But the nature neither of the test items nor of measurable intelligence in infancy (the two are related, and it is difficult to say which is which) changes with increasing age, so that this factor of sensorimotor alertness plays little part in intelligence-test items designed for children older than about 40 months.

The findings that have resulted from studies of infant intelligence tests are easily summarized:

1. Grossly mentally defective babies can be distinguished from normals.

2. Babies who live in institutions score lower than children in homes with true or foster parents.

3. Some authors (as Spitz, 1945, 1946) maintain that institution-reared children never recover from their retardation; others (Pasamanick, 1946) indicate that when the environment becomes richer, or more nearly normal, infants recover the lost ground, at least to some degree. However, no studies clearly resolve this important issue. Studies done with animals throw some light on this point; they will be reviewed in the next chapter.

4. Scores on intelligence tests given to children younger than 18 months have at best a low relation to the scores they earn later on more conventional, problem-solving types of intelligence tests. Some controversy persists regarding this point. A representative study supporting the conclusion was done by Cavanaugh *et al.* (1957), in which the Cattell was used for children through 24 months of age, the Stanford-Binet for older children. (This was a longitudinal study, the maximum number of children compared at any two ages being 191, the minimum 34.) But Knobloch and Pasamanick (1960) report studies obtaining correlations of .50 to .75 between tests given in infancy (apparently at about 40 weeks) and tests given at the age of 3 years.

5. When other factors are controlled, socioeconomic status and race have no influence on infant test scores (see, for example, Pasamanick, 1946; Knobloch and Pasamanick, 1960; and Bayley, 1965).

6. In the hands of a sensitive and well-trained tester, infant intelligence tests can reveal a baby's specific disabilities, such as deficiency in social responsiveness, vision, hearing, and so on. In other words, like a physical examination, they provide a moderately good picture of the child as he is.

7. Babies tested when they appear to be in a good mood test about the same on a later test, whereas those who were thought by the examiner to be disturbed or other than normal at the time of one testing score substantially higher when they are tested later (Gallagher, 1953).

8. Scores for the same baby on different tests agree poorly with each other, since there are consistently large differences in *average* quotients from one test to another. Individual scores also fail to show a high correlation from one test to another (Harms, 1957). That is, a baby may stand toward the top of his comparison group on one infant intelligence test, but toward the bottom on another.

Probably the most important of these findings is that infant intelligence tests *can* and *do* reflect environmental deprivation. It will be recalled that Hebb (1949) would predict such an effect, and one can venture the guess that he would consider such retardation permanent. But for the broad normal range of babies, infant tests do *not* predict later intelligence in any really useful sense. The child who scores 180 on a Cattell Infant Test may score 105 on a Stanford-Binet given when he is 6 years old; the child who scores 90 on a Kuhlmann may score 130 on a later Wechsler Intelligence Scale for Children. Socioeconomic class is related to intelligence at all later age levels; it shows no relation to intelligence as measured before about 18 months of age, nor does parental intelligence have any relation to babies' test scores. But certain regularities or irregularities of development *do* show up on the tests when they are skillfully used.

We are left with the conclusion that infant intelligence tests do not make the same highly useful predictions as intelligence tests given at a later age. On the other hand, no one expects a physical examination at 6 *months* to guarantee that a child will be healthy at 6 *years*. Why should an infant intelligence test necessarily be expected to predict that the "bright" baby will be a bright 6-year-old? If the test tells us that the baby is progressing normally, it has accomplished a purpose. If it points out to us certain remediable lags in development, it has been valuable.

Despite this, there is a fundamental flaw in infant intelligence testing, at least when compared with the physician's physical examination of the infant: the latter "gets at" or is presumed to reveal a condition of "wellness" or good health and to an unknown degree actually reflects good health; whereas infant intelligence tests, except within the very broad limits discussed in the summary above, do not adequately reflect intelligence. The difference, of course, is more qualitative than quantitative.

Preschool-Age Tests

Tests for children up to about 5 years of age are also given individually. They may be both verbal and performance tests. That is, some items require purely verbal responses; others, such as fitting together a jigsaw puzzle or form board, do not require the child to use words. Examples of verbal items at the preschool-age level are: asking the child to identify toy objects, such as miniature cars, dogs, and dishes; or pictured objects, such as birds or ships.[3] Performance items for young preschoolers (about 2 years of age) are building a low tower from one-inch cubes; fitting three simple geometrical forms cut from wood back into their recesses on a rectangular piece of wood. An item partly verbal yet also requiring performance is to identify different parts of the body by pointing to them upon request.

Such items approach the concept of problem solving that we consider to be the core of intelligence, yet they are very simple and involve reasoning, testing, and rejecting different problem solutions, and so on, to only a limited degree. Hofstaetter's study (1954) of tests given repeatedly to the same children concludes that for youngsters from about 20 to 40 months of age, intelligence-test items are characterized by a factor that may be called *persistence*. This factor, he thinks, may be a "tendency to act in accordance with an established set rather than upon interfering stimulation" (p. 162).

From one point of view, persistence is the opposite of sensorimotor alertness (the tendency to react to whatever stimulation comes along). Persistence means that attention is given to one stimulus until an appropriate response can be made. This formulation makes good common sense. We cannot respond to the environment unless we can attend quickly and efficiently to many aspects of it, but we cannot begin to cope with any aspect until we can concentrate long enough on it to make a suitable response. Persistence, in other words, is defined more by the goal than by the stimulus.

Bruner (1966) has recently published a discussion of the development of mental abilities that is somewhat broader, but not contrary to Hofstaetter's. Like Hofstaetter, Bruner (p. 71) believes that "The first stages are relatively manipulative, marked by highly unstable and single-track attention. Knowing is principally how to do, and there is minimum reflection . . . ." The first system "is through manipulation and action." This characterizes infancy and the early preschool years during which "you must get the perceptual field organized around your person as center before you can impose other, less egocentric axes upon it" (p. 72).

Bruner's second broad stage, corresponding to the later preschool and early elementary-school years is characterized by "internal representation," or "perceptual organization and imagery"; while the third stage is not reached, Bruner believes, until around adolescence. It is a function of the highest development of language and problem solving through symbolic behavior. Bruner likens these three stages to mastering

3 Actual test items included in the more common standardized tests are not given here, but illustrations are derived from them.

the major tool systems man must use to link himself to his environment effectively: the first for the hand, the second for the distance receptors, and the third the reflective or thinking.

PREDICTIVE EFFICIENCY OF PRESCHOOL TESTS

As we have indicated earlier, one of the values of an intelligence test is the degree to which it predicts later intelligence-test scores of a child or group of children. Predictions of this kind are valuable for such problems as placing children in ability groups, deciding whether or not to let an underage child into kindergarten, or making diagnoses of mental retardation and special-class placement. Infant intelligence tests, we have seen, do *not* predict later intellectual status well, although they have certain values of their own. How successful in predicting later intelligence are tests of preschool-aged children?

As might be expected, the older the child is, the more accurate his intelligence-test score is and the better is the prediction that can be made of his young-adult intelligence level. In the Berkeley Growth Study (Bayley, 1949), "young adulthood" was thought of as 18 years of age. This ambitious study followed a group of children from birth to age 18. Intelligence tests given the children at 6 months of age actually had a slight, although statistically insignificant, *negative* relationship with intelligence as measured at 18 years. Tests given at 1 year of age showed about a .25 correlation with intelligence measured in young adulthood; by 2 and 3 years of age the correlation had moved to about .50 (thus accounting for 25 percent of the variance); for tests given at age 4, the correlation was in the high .60s, rising to the middle .70s for tests given at age 5, 6 and 7. In other words, tests given in the early preschool years predict later intellectual development moderately well, although extreme individual variations in mental growth can and do occur from the preschool ages to maturity. The accuracy of prediction for tests given in the preschool years increases sharply as the age of the child increases, particularly up to about 5 years of age.

The correlations obtained in this same Berkeley study from another but less intensively studied group of children were lower than those given above. For this group, the correlation figure between tests given at age 2 and again at age 18 was about .30; for tests at ages 3 and 4 and again at age 18, about .40; for tests at ages 5 and 18, .55; and for tests given at 6 and 18 years of age, about .60. The difference between these two groups is probably due to the fact that the examiners knew the children in the more intensively studied group better, and the children were more at ease in the testing situation; hence the test results were more accurate and the prediction better.

This divergence highlights the fact that a major reason for poor prediction from preschool tests may be the circumstances of testing. To possess scientific value, any measurement technique must have *high repeatability*. Repeatability is reduced when circumstances of error and random variation enter into test results. Examples of conditions that may produce random variations in scores are tenseness, fatigue, and illness on the part of children; and different degrees of relaxation, expertness, familiarity with the child, and warmth on the part of the examiner. It is likely that the sex of the examiner also affects children differentially (Harms and Spiker, 1959). Young children are easily made insecure; their language is not necessarily clear; their attention span is short and they easily grow fatigued. One teacher of testing asks his students: "What would be your diagnosis if, while observing a test being given to a 3-year-old by a rather experienced tester with whose techniques you could discover no major fault, you noted that the child squirmed, was easily distracted, glanced continually around the room, and seemed constantly to be retreating from the test?" He states that his typical student believes that the child is insecure and is attempting to avoid the issue of the test. His question then is: "Have you thought that maybe the child needs to go to the bathroom?"

Anything that can be done to reduce or explain the variability of individual test fluctuations is likely to be to the advantage of the child —thus the value of attaching a "clinical protocol" to intelligence test results, regardless of whether given during infancy or adulthood. The clinical protocol describes the conditions of testing, the general condition of the person being tested, special conditions, and so on. Such a protocol helps the reader to better understand the test results and arrive more accurately at any action based on them; and test results are *very* frequently followed by action, such as special class placement, admission to school, and so on.

Three separate tests given to the same child may illustrate this point: as a $3\frac{1}{2}$-year-old, the child was tested one morning while fresh in familiar surroundings by an examiner well known to her, who was very warm and leisured in her approach. The child's IQ was 163. On the basis of the test results, recommendation was made and followed for advanced placement in a 4-year-old kindergarten class.

One and one-half years later, the child was re-examined by a brusque, business-like examiner who was rather bored by the whole process of test administration, in noisy circumstances off the main playroom of the kindergarten in which the child was then enrolled. Additionally, the child had been taken by her parents to her first symphony concert the night before, and was extremely tired. The test result yielded an IQ of 120, on the basis of which it was recommended that, since the child was underage and the class in which she was enrolled averaged highly superior in IQ, she be retained for a second year in kindergarten. Fortunately, this recommendation was not followed, partly because of the earlier test results. The child throughout all later schooling behaved much more in line with predictions based on the 163 than on the 120 IQ, and serious adjustment problems might well have resulted had the second examiner's recommendations been followed. A third test was given to the child under routine circumstances when she was in fourth grade, where she tested 150. This illustration is meant to reveal both the extreme fluctuations in intelligence quotient a child may show, some of the factors that produce these fluctuations, and some of the consequences (good and bad) of taking action on the basis of a single intelligence test, particularly one given in early childhood when the child is more at the mercy of his environment than in later years.

Despite the relatively large correlations reported above between preschool and young-adult tests, the authors of one study (Honzik, MacFarlane, and Allen, 1948), involving 252 children who had repeatedly taken intelligence tests between the ages of 21 months and 18 years (further data from the Berkeley Growth Study), conclude that between the ages of 6 and 18 years almost 60 percent of the subjects changed 20 or more points. Some children moved rather consistently upward or downward as much as 50 points in score, and their changes tended to be in the direction of the intellectual level of their families. Special circumstances in their life history affected some but not other children.

PREDICTIVE EFFICIENCY OF DIFFERENT TYPES OF ITEMS

For the most widely used test, the Stanford-Binet, items involving memory and the use of words are more effective in predicting later intelligence (correlate more highly with later IQ's) than items involving numbers, or not involving words (Bradway, 1945). However, the differences are not of great practical significance. But another careful study, done with a different preschool test (Goodenough and Maurer, 1942), reaches the opposite conclusion, so that the question of what type of item best predicts later intelligence remains open.

Some support is given to the first set of results by a study (Catalano and McCarthy, 1954) done with a rather small number (twenty-three) of institutionalized children between 6 and 18 months of age. The speech of these children was studied, and correlations were calculated between speech and Stanford-Binet intelligence tests administered when they were between 3 and $4\frac{1}{2}$ years of age. All the correlations were positive, and some were quite high (for example, a .45 correlation was found between IQ and the number of different kinds of consonants the child had used during infancy). However, because of the small number and special type of children included, this study, though promising, can be thought of only as an exploratory one. Karelitz et al., in the study of prediction of 3-year-old intelligence from infant crying mentioned above, also support this point.

Intelligence Tests for Elementary-School Children, Adolescents, and Adults

As soon as children reach an age when they can follow instructions, inhibit distractibility, and use a pencil, group intelligence tests can be used. The overwhelming majority of intelligence (or general aptitude) tests that are given are of the group type, although individual tests must be used with infants and preschoolers and are sometimes given to older children and adults as well.

Tests for school children and adults fall into the same general categories as those for preschool children: *verbal* and *nonverbal* or verbal and quantitative. On verbal tests, older children may be asked to define words, ranging from such simple ones as *letter* to such complex ones as *indefatigable;* or to unscramble sentences against a time limit—being allowed, for example, one minute to make sense out of the following: TOWN LITTLE FOLLOWED THE TO DOG ME. Adults and older adolescents, in a test of concentration and memory, may be asked to repeat as many as nine digits read monotonously by the examiner at the rate of one per second; or to give in reverse order as many as seven or eight digits read in the same fashion. Analogies of different levels of difficulty are a popular test item. A relatively simple example is: "*Sharp* is to *blunt* as *tall* is to . . . ?" Riddle-like situations are presented. The child is asked to read a passage against a time and an error limit, and to give back as many ideas as he can from the passage.

Performance items consist of such things as assembling elaborate form-board or jigsaw-puzzle tasks against a time limit; of running elaborate paper-and-pencil mazes; or of planning a route of search for an object lost in a field. These are commonly said to be nonverbal, or performance, tasks. Several authors (as Sarason, 1953) have pointed out that this is probably not an accurate description, and have maintained that most Americans from early childhood on will give verbal tags to the tasks on which they are working, even though they do not say the words aloud. This is undoubtedly the verbal mediation discussed in Chapter 4, used consciously as a tool. On a maze, for example, they may say to themselves, "A left turn—no, there's a blind alley—better try a right turn." In other words, there is no clear distinction between verbal and performance intelligence-test items, although certainly factors of efficiency, speed, and spatial relationships enter into the latter that do not enter into the former. A survey of the literature indicates that there is a median correlation between verbal and performance intelligence-test quotients of about .65. In other words, there is a clear tendency for those who do well on one type of test to do well on the other; but, in prediction, one accounts for only a little more than 40 percent of the variance of the other. Rather than performance items, some group tests concentrate on use of numbers, both in computation and reasoning problems. Such tests are usually referred to as quantitative (Q) as contrasted with verbal (V) tests of intelligence.

There is scattered evidence in the literature that children of average or near-average *verbal* IQ, whose *performance-test quotients* are much higher, may have reading difficulties more often than would be suspected from their verbal IQ alone. Children from lower-class homes are likely to have verbal quotients equal to or lower than performance quotients, whereas the opposite is true for children from middle-class homes. There is also evidence to indicate that delinquents are likely to have performance quotients higher than their verbal quotients. Children or adults with brain damage apparently test lower on performance items than on verbal items. Although these findings hold for groups, they are of little practical importance in dealing with individuals.

According to Hofstaetter (1954), who has performed a factor analysis of longitudinal data from the Berkeley Growth Study, the common characteristic of intelligence-test items for older children is "what Freud has called 'provisional action' . . . or . . . the manipulation of symbols . . . the anticipation of future actions in the present" (p. 162). Again, this makes good common sense. First, we attend to the multifarious stimuli in the environment (sensorimotor alertness); next we concentrate long enough on one stimulus to make an adaptive response (persistence); and, finally, we integrate both the past and the present, at a symbolic level, in order to thread our way through the complexities of a problem (provisional action). Bruner's 1966 analysis fits well with Hofstaetter's.

Other things being equal, group tests probably predict school success better than individual tests, since they have more elements in common with school-learning tasks. Children ordinarily read and do arithmetic or spelling in groups. Hence a test taken in a group has more factors in common with the regular school situation than a test taken individually, where an alert examiner reassures the child and draws his very best from him. The anxious child will not do well in a group intelligence test, just as he will not do his best in a group reading or arithmetic session— hence the test score predicts his performance accurately (what he will do, not what he could ideally do). The calm, efficient child who likes competition does his best in both types of situation; hence either group- or individual-test scores predict his school performance accurately. The relation between anxiety and tested intelligence is discussed later.

A good school is, of course, interested in more than prediction of academic achievement. One common school aim is to help those with high potential but relatively low achievement. Here lies the value of the individual test: If a child scores 20 points higher on an individual than on a group test, yet his school performance is in line with his group-test score, the school psychologist or trained teacher infers that he has the capacity to do better than he is doing, and initiates action to make him a more efficient worker (attempts to bring his school performance in line with his score on the individual test). This effort may involve extra coaching, reassurance, counseling, working with the home, or a combination of such measures. A group test may predict quite adequately what the child with a severe reading difficulty is actually *doing* in school; but when his individual-test score is 30 points higher than his group-test score, the need for remedial reading is dramatically brought home.

Special Considerations in Using Intelligence Tests

Many teachers and school administrators are skeptical of the uses of intelligence tests, which have indeed been widely misused. One teacher came to the author with the lament that in her third-grade class she had an engaging and well-liked child from a foreign-language speaking home. Mike was doing well in school, according to her report, but she felt sorry for him because he was "feeble-minded." Further questioning elicited the fact that Mike had taken a group test in first grade, when he had had only the most elementary grasp of English. Inevitably, he had scored low, and had done poorly in school during his first year. As he learned English, his schoolwork improved, but the feeble-minded score remained on his record. At the suggestion of the author, he was retested on an individual test. His score was a superior 130 IQ.

Another teacher had counseled with the parents of a first-grader, alerting them (to their utter dismay) to the fact that their child, Maria, would never do well in school and, indeed, might be considered retarded. The middle-class parents accepted this, albeit reluctantly. The consulting psychologist to the school, while leafing through the group-test booklets for the first grade, noted that one child, Maria, had colored in the outlines of the test items rather than drawing lines from the criterion to the proper alternative. The type of test used was one where, for example, the child is asked to draw a line from the model in the left-hand margin of the page (perhaps the picture of a hen) to the one of several alternatives at the right that resembles the model (for example, to the hen among a pig, a rooster, a duck, and a pigeon).

When the test was discussed with her, Maria tearfully confessed that her mother had taught her it was naughty to "mess up" a paper with random lines, and that she had therefore tried to color all the correct responses, but that this had taken her so long that she had become hopelessly lost. The teacher, routinely grading the tests, had failed to catch the nuances of Maria's very neat coloring and had assigned her an exceptionally low score. Maria, assured that it was indeed all right for her to draw lines on the test, scored comfortably high upon retest. The mother, too, learned a lesson about setting too severe standards for her child.

Even experienced test users frequently forget that the best of tests, given under ideal circumstances, can make only a partial prediction of how well a child will do in school. In our search for precision and exactness, we often fail to realize that IQ's do not remain completely constant for any given child—that a child who tests high in first grade may be functioning at a very different level in the fifth grade. Such factors have led some to condemn tests entirely, thereby losing the substantial guidance they can contribute to education.

Opponents of intelligence tests are likely to say that "any teacher worth her salt knows how bright her children are without going through all that foolishness." Alexander (1953), among others, decided to test this statement. As his subjects he used 978 public-school pupils in grades three to eight, and their thirty-five teachers. Fifty percent of the teachers had completed 120 hours of college training, and their median teaching experience was twelve years. The study was done in about the middle of the second semester of the school year, so that each teacher had had ample opportunity to get to know the children.

Alexander asked each teacher to list the five pupils in her class who in her opinion were the most intelligent; and the five who were the least intelligent. They were then asked to list the five pupils who were working closest to their capacity and the five who were performing furthest below their capacity in the major academic areas as reading and arithmetic. All the pupils were then given tests for intelligence (or academic aptitude), and for actual academic achievement.

Alexander found that the teachers were accurate in picking the highest and the lowest IQ's for only a few more than half the cases (57 and 58 percent respectively). They picked only about one fourth of the highest and lowest achievers (in relation to their capacity). The tendency of the teachers was to rank as "achieving up to capacity" those children who stood toward the top of their particular class, disregarding factors of age. They operated in about the same fashion in picking the low achievers. But even allowing for the fact that they tended to judge in relation to their own classes, they were accurate in judging the high achievers only about two fifths of the time, and the low achievers only about one third of the time. In view of the fact that marks indicating absolute success or failure are still very widely assigned by teachers and accepted as gospel by children and their parents, such a finding indicates that a majority of children are being graded according to some factor other than their actual academic achievement, and that they receive ratings of brightness or dullness that may be completely at variance with their actual ability. The very bright, high-achieving, but young child would, under such circumstances, probably be graded lower than the older child who is working up to capacity, but who, because he is older, is doing *relatively* less well.

This subsection on using intelligence tests is not complete without at least some anticipation of the treatment of anxiety, particularly as it relates to test taking. Most of the studies on anxiety are taken up in Chapters 10 and 13 of this volume. However, anxiety is sufficiently related to intellectual functioning and intelligence testing that some mention of it should be made here. Two representative studies have been selected for brief summary and discussion.

Yamamoto and Davis (1966) were interested in the interactions between the types of instruction they gave to children before a test was taken, the children's scores on the Task Anxiety Scale for Children (see Hill and Sarason, 1966), and the children's tendency to be dependent on adults. They worked with 480 children from fourth, seventh, tenth, and twelfth grades from a large suburban midwestern school, using the Kuhlmann-Anderson group test of intelligence as their intelligence measure. They administered the tests under different sets of instructions, which according to their report, did not make a great deal of difference in the results (the instructions were for an intelligence test, an achievement test, a routine test, and the regular test instructions). The most significant finding from their study was that the more anxious children for all four types of instruction at every grade and for both sexes scored lower on the intelligence test than the less anxious children. The average or mean difference was 8.0 in favor of the less anxious children. The difference was highest for the oldest children, 16.43 for the twelfth-grade students who were told they were taking an intelligence test.

Hill and Sarason report similar results, but for younger children (through fifth grade). Not only do their more anxious children score lower in intelligence, but also in tests of proficiency in the regular school subjects. The older the children in their elaborate, longitudinal study, the greater was the interference from anxiety with both intelligence and achievement.

In other words, as has been suggested in Chapter 5 in the discussion on curiosity, anxiety interferes with all sorts of school related, intellectually related functions, ranging from question-asking and information-seeking, to question-answering as represented on intelligence and achievement tests.

The next section raises the question of culture free or culture fair intelligence tests. By their very name, they suggest that intelligence tests are not fair to all sections of the population, perhaps particularly to those who have been reared in very deprived circumstances in which, to use Bruner's words, there has been inadequate opportunity to learn the tools and techniques which put them into effective interaction with their environments.

The question of the ethics of intelligence (and other) testing is very much in the forefront at this time. It is being considered legislatively, the core group of testers (the members of the American Psychological Association) is much exercised, and at least one State (New York) has banned routinely given intelligence tests in favor of academic achievement tests. The testing of college students as one basis for draft deferment has raised cries of "Unfairness" and "Discrimination."

It is an oversimplification, although in the present author's judgment a legitimate one, to say that there is nothing more unethical about administering an intelligence test than there is about weighing a child. Of course, the test must be given and used by professionally trained personnel who know its legitimate uses, who are aware of its possible abuses, and who use its results cautiously. The information gained from each type of measurement can be used to help the child and guide him more effectively. But used unwisely, by the ill-trained, with the absolute faith put in the results that is granted by some—then, as in all human interactions, questions of violation of ethics can be raised. We have seen that an intelligence quotient can be affected by poor testers, by fatigue on the part of the person being tested, by unfavorable circumstances, by different types of motivation, such as anxiety. If these modifying variables are not taken account of in the use of the IQ that results from a test, then the test is not being used properly. If all the modifiers are allowed for, it does not seem legitimate to raise the question of ethics.

Culture-Free or Culture-Fair Intelligence Tests

Those who say that teachers will "peg" their children according to their IQ and discriminate against the low-scoring child while putting all their efforts and attention into working with the high-IQ child perhaps have a point. We have mentioned above that there is an almost universal tendency to look for the exact and tangible. An IQ score has a deceiving appearance of precision and unchangeability, and there is no doubt that many accept the IQ altogether too uncritically.

One articulate and influential group of critics of conventional intelligence tests (Eells et al., 1951) maintains that children of low socioeconomic class (children of working families) are discriminated against by our standard intelligence tests (as well as by our standard school curriculums, and for the same reasons). They say that intelligence tests abound in abstractions and verbal conventions that form part of the culture of middle- and upper-class children, but are foreign to lower-class children. For these latter children, this group of critics believes, the world is one of harsh reality and down-to-earthness. The future is an uncertain thing, so they live in the here-and-now. Abstractions will not buy bread nor win a fight in the street; hence they have neither much use for, nor familiarity with, the abstract, preferring the concrete and tangible. Eells and his colleagues believe that this factor of differential familiarity, rather than a "real" difference in intelligence, is responsible for the intellectual differences found between children from different socio-economic classes. Like the present author, they think of intelligence as being, in general, problem-solving ability.

In one elaborate study of this matter of "culture-free" intelligence tests, by Haggard (1954), conventional, abstract items were rewritten in familiar, concrete terms. Examples of the standard items and Haggard's revisions are given below:

Conventional Item	*Culture-Free Item*
Cub is to *bear* as *gosling* is to: fox, grouse, goose, rabbit, duck.	*Puppy* goes with *dog* like *kitten* goes with: fox, goose, cat, rabbit, duck.
A weighs less than *B; B* weighs less than *C;* therefore: *B* weighs more than *C; A*'s weight is equal to *B*'s and *C*'s; *A* weighs less than *C*.	Jim can hit harder than Bill. Bill can hit harder than Ted; so: Ted can hit harder than Bill; Bill can hit as hard as Jim and Ted; Jim can hit harder than Ted.

Haggard points out that the second, syllogistic type of item proved to be the most difficult for his lower-class subjects.

Haggard studied 671 children 10 to 12 years old in his carefully done study of how they would perform on the two types of test under several different conditions. Among his numerous hypotheses were the following: The lower-class children would do much better on the culture-free form of the test than on the conventional form; however, there would be little difference for the middle-class children; and practice and motivation would do the lower-class children much more good, particularly on the culture-free test, than the middle-class children. He also found that both the middle- and the lower-class children made much greater gains from one testing situation to another on the culture-free than on the standardized test, with some not clearly significant tendency for the lower-class youngsters to gain relatively more on the culture-free test than the middle-class children. Haggard was correct in hypothesizing that the lower-class boys and girls would do better on the culture-free than on the standard test; but the middle-class children also did better, so that class differences were just as marked on the culture-free as on the conventional test.

From the study emerged useful information that middle-class children enter testing situations better motivated than lower-class children. They also generalize training in test-taking better. Under optimal conditions, the differences in average test scores between social classes can be reduced, although they do not disappear. In other words, conditions of motivation and interest favoring the already relatively privileged middle-class children make the class differential in intelligence more pronounced than it "really is."

For years, studies of class differences in intelligence (see H. E. Jones, 1954) have demonstrated that lower-class children score lower than middle- or upper-class children. Proponents of culture-free intelligence tests have predicted that much of this difference would disappear if their test, rather than a conventional test, were used. But studies with the new type of test (Angelina and Shedd, 1955; and Rosenblum *et al.*, 1955) fail to substantiate this claim. Knief and Stroud (1959), for example, found that social class correlates .31 with one of the more widely used culture-free tests, and .30 with a conventional intelligence test.

Findley and McGuire (1957), accepting the point that lower-class children are handicapped in taking conventional intelligence tests because they do less well on abstractions than middle-class youngsters, predicted that for types of problems that are not frequently encountered in any sector of the culture (for which there has been *no* differential in opportunity for practice between social classes), lower-class children would do *better* than their test score would predict; but that prediction from test scores would be accurate for middle-class children. Specifically, they predicted that between groups of middle- and lower-class pupils matched for IQ on a conventional test there would be a difference in problem-solving performance favoring the lower-class youngsters. That is, Findley and McGuire reasoned that lower-class children are actually brighter than indicated by their test scores, whereas the quotients are accurate indices for the middle-class children.

To test this hypothesis, they devised a rather elaborate block-sorting test of abstracting ability that did not involve language ability and was unfamiliar to all the children. This test was administered to ninety-six children from grades three, six, and nine, half of whom were lower- and half middle-class, and who were matched in IQ as measured by a standard group test. Contrary to the expectations of advocates of the culture-free intelligence test, the middle-class children did better on this nonverbal test than the lower-class children.

There are also rather clear indications that culture-free intelligence tests predict school success less well than the more conventional tests. This is to be expected, since the conventional tests presumably have more "operations" in common with school learning, as it is now structured, than do the culture-free or culture-fair tests. Altus (1956) and Love and Beach (1957) have demonstrated this point convincingly.

However, critics of any position, instrument, or idea must take care not to throw out the baby with the bath. Haggard has demonstrated that improvements in motivation and practice in test-taking can be helpful to lower-class youngsters, and that the measured intellectual difference between lower- and middle-class youngsters can to some degree be lessened by using nonconventional tests and modifying testing techniques.

From the intelligence-test differences between social classes, we would expect differences in school progress, middle- and upper-class children being expected to do better schoolwork than lower-class children. The actual differences in academic achievement between social classes are even more dramatic than the differences in intellectual level. On the whole, lower-class children achieve less well in school than their intelligence tests predict they will, whereas middle- and upper-class children approach their academic potential more closely. This state of affairs is one of the most serious of American school problems, and is undoubtedly due in part to middle-class bias by teachers and to curriculums and textbook materials that are foreign to the experiences of lower-class youngsters. In questioning the efficiency of the culture-free intelligence test, we do not intend to maintain that the schools, including their psychological personnel, are doing the best they can with lower-class children. This problem will be discussed more fully in a later chapter.

Growth and Decline of Intelligence

Hundreds of studies have been conducted purporting to reveal the rate of growth, the time of leveling off, and the onset and rate of decay of all sorts of human behavior that can be roughly classified as "intelligent." Findings vary widely, so the conclusions set forth here (although they fall conservatively in the middle range of findings) can be disputed in terms of individual studies. Competent reviews of research in this area have been made by, among others, H. E. Jones (1954), G. G. Thompson (1952), and Zubek and Solberg (1954).

Intelligence appears to grow less rapidly with increasing age. This pattern produces the negatively accelerating growth curve illustrated in Figure 7.1, which represents intellectual growth from about $10\frac{1}{2}$ to

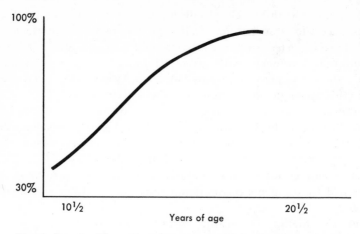

Figure 7.1   Intellectual growth from 10½ to 20½ years of age.
(Adapted with permission of the National Society for the Study
of Education and H. S. Conrad, from Jones and Conrad, 1944.)

20½ years of age. This figure is adapted from H. E. Jones and Conrad
(1944), who have drawn it to incorporate findings from three major
studies of the growth of intelligence.

Figure 7.1 reveals that somewhat more than 40 percent of mature
intellectual status has been reached by 10½ years of age, and that growth
from then on is progressively slower. No more "intellectual power" is
added after about 19½ years of age, although of course individuals can
add almost limitlessly to personal skills of all sorts. There is evidence to
indicate that intellectual growth continues longer for the bright and
superior and stops earlier for subjects of low intelligence (Gurvitz, 1951;
H. E. Jones, 1954; Miles, and Miles, 1932), although the most recent
evidence that has come to the author's attention (Bayley, 1955; Owens,
1953) indicates that intellectual development continues well into maturity for relatively retarded as well as intellectually superior persons.

Figure 7.2 presents a curve of intellectual growth that, from birth to
the late teens, is in the shape of a very shallow, steeply slanted S. This
means that during infancy and the early preschool years there is a
tendency toward positively accelerated growth (faster as the child gets
older). At school age, growth has become negatively accelerated (slower
year by year), as shown more clearly in Figure 7.1. And growth is very
gradual (Figure 7.2) from the late teens on. Earlier studies as reviewed by
Zubek and Solberg (1954), for example, have rather consistently indicated that intellectual performance begins to drop at about the mid-
twenties. This drop is minimal until a person reaches his forties. From
this age, there is a steady decrease in efficiency for most mental functions.
Tests that involve speed and, possibly, close attention or concentration

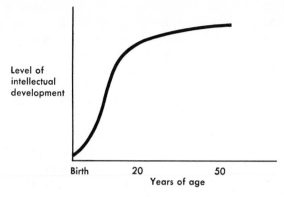

Figure 7.2 A hypothetical composite age curve representing the growth of intelligence from birth to the middle years. (Adapted with permission of the American Psychological Association and Nancy Bayley, from Bayley, 1955.)

seem to show decreasing scores earliest in life (in the mid-twenties or even earlier); scores on power tests decline later; and scores on a type of test that Zubek and Solberg have called "breadth tests," such as tests of vocabulary and information, show a negligible decline, and in some studies an increase. Some of the information provided by Bayley (1955) on the development of intelligence during the years of middle age comes from tests that might be called power-breadth tests. In other words, intelligence seems very durable.

Owens (1953) readministered the same test to 127 men after an interval of thirty or thirty-one years. These men had originally taken the tests as college freshmen, and, obviously, the second testing occurred when they were middle-aged and established.

The men whose cooperation Owens secured were not conspicuously different in general characteristics from those who refused to take part in the second test. He found that these mature men were significantly higher in total IQ than they had been as entering college freshmen. Their gains were most conspicuous in tests that presumably tap abilities called practical judgment, and on tests of synonym-antonyms, disarranged sentences, information, and analogies. Abilities to follow directions, handle arithmetic problems, and manage number series had stayed constant or decreased very slightly and not significantly. Men who were below 50 years of age in Owens' sample gained slightly more than those who were above 50, although both groups gained. Those who had completed the most college work gained more than those who had had less education; general science majors showed more upward movement than agriculture or engineering majors. Those who had moved from rural to urban settings during their life appeared to have gained more than those with other patterns of residence. Other characteristics, such as type of job held, income earned, physical exercise, marital status, number of children, and number of brothers and sisters showed no relationship to the amount of gain made by these men.

THEORIES ABOUT UNUSUAL PATTERNS OF INTELLECTUAL CHANGE

The section immediately preceding this has dealt with the regularities, or established patterns of intellectual growth and decline. The present, more theoretical, even speculative section, is designed to arouse interest and make suggestions about irregularities of change. It advances more questions than it answers.

First, it would seem (see the discussion of "Piaget's Sensorimotor Stages" in Chapter 1) that the more these developmental stages are facilitated in infancy, the more stimulation and more opportunity for primitive problem solving a child has during his first year or so of life, the more ready he will be later to process and use effectively the types of variable discussed by Hofstaetter, Guilford, and Bruner (see the "Definitions" section of the present chapter). Bruner (1966) actually speaks of the informational-habit stratum of early learning as "readiness," by which he does not mean such conventional things as readiness to learn to read or do numbers, but readiness involving receptivity and capability for later and more effective acquisition of things that are ordinarily thought of as intellectual skills.

In Chapters 1 and 5, it was suggested that, within normal limits, the more stimulation the young infant receives, the more it will demand as an older child; in other words, the more curious the child will be. It has also been pointed out in Chapter 5 that the more anxious the child, the less curious he is. One section in the present chapter links high anxiety with low IQ, as well as with low academic achievement. Denenberg (1964) hypothesizes, in an excellent review of animal infants which takes some account of human infants, that the greater the stimulation given the infant, the less its interfering emotionality later in life. Brownfield (1964) in an equally good review article, argues that barren infancies blight the growth of behaviors that can well be subsumed under the heading of intelligence. The whole literature on culturally deprived children (see Chapters 8 and 14) suggest that children who grow up in impoverished environments, particularly where there is little adaptive but much restrictive language, and few opportunities to explore but many opportunities for punishment and inhibition, do not reach the same intellectual levels as those from happier and richer, more stimulating environments. Not only do they not reach as high levels, but they begin intellectual decline earlier.

Other authors (Eagle, 1965; Munsinger and Kessen, 1964; and Kagan *et al.,* 1964) discuss cognitive styles and preferences and, by implication, at least, link certain styles and preferences with acceleration in intellectual change, others with deceleration.

Eagle, for example, studied five cognitive styles: (1) category width, or the ability to make fine discriminations; (2) field independence, or the ability to separate figures from ground, even though the two are confused in presentation; (3) tolerance of ambiguity, or the ability to tolerate unclear stimuli and to wait and make conclusions when the situation is uncertain; (4) semantic spontaneous flexibility, or the ability to produce widely diverse ideas when given the opportunity to do so; and (5) acquiescence to cognitive habit, or the inability to develop performance against the interfering effects of modes of behavior that have been strongly reinforced by the culture. Eagle predicted that individuals high in the first four of these five cognitive styles would be "IQ gainers," while these high in the fifth style, acquiescence to cognitive habit, would be "IQ losers." He worked with 267 eighth-grade students who had earlier been tested for intelligence when in the third and fourth grades and, while he did not emerge with dramatic results, found some of his hypotheses supported, at least to the degree that he could say that some types of cognitive style interfered moderately with intelligence gain, others facilitated it. His most striking result is that children very high in IQ in the third and fourth grade are either gainers or "stand-patters" as far as eighth-grade IQ is concerned, while those low in third- and fourth-grade IQ tend to lose by eighth grade. Perhaps the cognitive styles in which he is interested have already made their mark by the elementary school years, a point which is supported by such authors as Brownfield and Denenberg, who regard early intellectual and general stimulation as more important than later experience.

Kagan *et al.* (1964) present an elaborate series of studies of first-graders through fourth-graders in their study of information processing in children, with particular reference to analytic and reflective attitudes as opposed to impulsive and "off-the-cuff" methods of proceeding intellectually. Implicit but not explicit in their work is the suggestion that the more the child analyzes, the less he jumps to conclusions, the more likely is he to do well on tasks of an intellectual nature and thus to gain more rapidly than the impulsive child in IQ. Kagan's *impulsive* children (boys are more variable than girls) may be "high-drive" children (the energizing function of drive is discussed in Chapter 4). They may also be children who do not value intellectual goals highly; that is, such goals are not particularly important to them. Thus, they are willing to take many risks in their work (see "Expectancies and Probability," Chapter 5), since the outcome does not matter much to them. Mischel (1962) finds that impulsivity is associated with low mental age, low chronological age, and low IQ.

Like Kagan and his co-workers, Munsinger and Kessen (1964) imply but do not demonstrate that "reaching" (preference for difficult over easy tasks) is characteristic of those who will gain in IQ. However, Munsinger and Kessen's work is more clearly related to curiosity than to intelligence, and all their subjects were adolescents or adults.

Haan (1963) presents data for youngsters followed into adulthood suggesting that males who gain in IQ are happier or better adjusted than those who lose, and are also more masculine in their adjustment; while females who gain are less happily adjusted, but more masculine in adjustment than females who remain the same or lose.

Moss and Kagan (1961) find that boys are more likely than girls to gain in IQ, and that 6- to 10-year-olds who gain in IQ are those who are also highly achievement motivated in childhood.

Finally, R. Scott (1966) brings one more study into the literature demonstrating that children consistently exposed to poor environments lose in IQ, even though his subjects were beyond the so called critical periods of early childhood. He worked with first- through ninth-grade Negro boys and girls, whose median family income was about $4800 per year, whose parents averaged only ninth-grade educations, and who lived in poor neighborhoods.

Educational Practices and Intellectual Level

What are the responsibilities, and what special provisions exist, concerning the education of children at one or the other extreme of the intelligence distribution? A thoughtful observer is likely to conclude that American public schools do, on the whole, a fairly good job of "special education" (training children who are slow-learning, partially sighted or blind, partially hearing or deaf, cerebral-palsied, or with rheumatic hearts). It is true that these children are more adequately looked after in urban than in rural schools, and in states with large populations than in states with small populations. Special educators may be more successful than regular teachers because, in a sense, they always work in an emergency situation. They deal with relatively acute situations (working with nontypical children) that demand remediation. They are forced, by the very nature of the children with whom they deal, to pay attention to individual differences, probably more so than regular classroom teachers. They are able to do this because of the nature of their training and orientation and also because their classes are usually small. Probably more intensive and careful research has been done to assist them than is available to regular teachers. Their motives for going into the field of special education may also be such as to make them particularly oriented to children's needs and individual personalities. The author predicts that they are likely to lead the way in such necessary breakthrough school modifications as so-called compensatory or intervention education (see Chapter 14). This thoughtful observer probably will not be strongly dissatisfied with what the schools are doing for children in the middle ranges of intelligence—perhaps from 90 to 115 or 120 IQ. The schools are geared to the average child. But in our modern classrooms the prospect for the very superior child—from approximately 125 to 130 IQ and up—is less bright.

THE GIFTED

Intensive studies of the characteristics of bright and dull children have been made. As a group, the bright are taller, handsomer, stronger, healthier, show fewer behavior problems, are less likely to have cavities in their teeth, and do better work in school. Although a higher percentage of children from "good" families belong to the bright group than is true for families in the middle and lower classes, in terms of absolute numbers the majority of gifted children are middle-class, and vast numbers of children from lower-class families also classify as gifted. Children toward the lower end of the intellectual scale can be characterized in terms opposite to those we have used for the gifted: they are less popular, less healthy, do less well in school, and so on. But both the bright and the dull achieve below their capacity and the academic achievement of the bright in United States public schools is far lower than we would expect on the basis of their IQ.

Ketcham (1957) reports on a group of forty gifted boys as they progressed from 6 to 12 years of age, and from the first to the seventh grade. At age 7, for example, their mental age averaged 9 years, 3 months, but their over-all educational age only 7 years, 2 months. The same figures for forty-two gifted girls similarly followed were also 9 years, 3 months and 7 years, 2 months. At 12 years of age, the boys averaged 17 years, 11 months in mental age, and 15 years, 8 months in educational age; the girls, 17 years, 5 months in mental age, and 15 years in educational age. These youngsters were relatively accelerated in reading, lagged most markedly in arithmetic.

Paradoxically, this same tendency typifies public-school children at the opposite end of the intellectual spectrum. It is probable that the phenomenon of underachievement, occurring in two such different groups, has very different causes. The bright are victims of underexpectation and understimulation; the slow learners are victims of frustration, defeat, and overexpectation.

Historically and currently, United States schools have used the following techniques with the gifted: they are accelerated, segregated, admitted early to school (a special form of acceleration), or given an enriched curriculum.

It has been widely held that *acceleration* is bad for a child. Pushed ahead a grade or two, he may be with children of similar mental age, but will lag behind his classmates in physical maturity and social development. To some degree and in extreme cases, this is undoubtedly true. But discreet acceleration of children whose physical size and social maturity is in line with their intellectual ability and reading achievement appears to do them good rather than harm. In the United States the most extensive work with the intellectually gifted has been done by Terman and his associates (Terman and Oden, 1947). Terman has found that the most successful gifted adults were those accelerated a year or more in school. No social-emotional disadvantages seemed to result from this acceleration.

Worchester (1959) should be quoted in this context:

> It is interesting that, although acceleration has undoubtedly been used far more than any other method of providing for the rapid learner, and although there has been more research as to the outcomes of acceleration than there has been for any other method, and although almost all of the research has shown results favorable to acceleration with hardly any study showing negative values, still a large proportion of teachers and administrators will have little or none of it. (p. 1)

Worchester comments that acceleration is "a sort of daylight saving. We get the chores of the world done early in the day so that there may be more opportunity for the real joys of living a little later" (p. 3), and estimates that "if we got the top 3 percent of our gifted into their life work a year earlier, the country would have the advantage of some million years' additional use of its best brains, and it could probably find use for them. Only good effects, in general, have been found for up to two years of acceleration" (p. 4).

Segregation into special classes has often been tried for gifted children. Where research on the results has been carried out (Albers *et al.,* 1947; Ausubel, 1951; Bonsall, 1955; Carlson, 1947; and Havighurst *et al.,* 1955) positive results have usually been reported. Both teachers and children enjoy the classes, and the children typically accomplish twice as much or more schoolwork than in their regular class. But for reasons that are logically not very clear, segregation has been condemned as undemocratic. Is it not better for the very bright child to encounter stiff competition from his intellectual peers than to coast along with his regular class, always getting the top A yet never really having to work for it? Does the child third from the top bitterly resent having the two gifted children in his class removed to a special class? Probably not; when they were in the regular class, he could *never* be first, no matter how hard he worked. With them gone, he may often be tops.

United States schools segregate in many ways. The best contact athletes are segregated into football or basketball teams; the best musicians are segregated into glee clubs and bands. No one argues that this is particularly undemocratic (although many are concerned about a school tendency to produce observers rather than participants in the performing arts and sports). Why then do we argue that segregation of the intellectually gifted group is undemocratic?

Such segregation, of course, presents school administrators with very real problems. Many parents whose children are *not* gifted secretly or publicly believe that they *are,* and often exert strong pressure on school authorities to place their youngsters in classrooms for the gifted. Such pressures, when they come from influential citizens, are hard to counter. It can be surmised that many a school superintendent has abandoned the practice of segregated classes for the gifted with a sigh of relief.

If superior children are to be placed in special, segregated classes, this placement should of course be made only after full consideration of *all* the child's needs. A simple measure of IQ does not provide enough information. We must know how efficiently the child is using his IQ, obtain an estimate of his social maturity, find out how placement in a special class will affect his relations with friends, parents, brothers and sisters. All these things should be known and taken into account before placement is made. If they are, one might predict outstanding success for special classes.

A common United States practice in education for the gifted is *enrichment.* Ideally, every class should be small enough to permit the teacher both to plan for and attend to the individual needs of each child in the group. Every teacher should be trained so that she can make such plans efficiently. Every classroom should have, among its books and equipment, materials simple yet interesting enough to appeal to its slowest-learning child and give him some feeling of mastery and success, yet complicated and difficult enough to challenge the brightest youngster. This represents a surprisingly wide range of material. It is not at all uncommon, for example, for a fourth-grade class in an ordinary middle-class neighborhood to include some children who do not read at all—who are *literally* functioning at a kindergarten or early first-grade level—and other children who are achieving at a college-freshman level as far as reading is concerned, and as high as eighth- or ninth-grade level in number skills.

The average classroom does not include such a range of teaching aids, and its class enrollment is so large that even the most dedicated and skilled teacher lacks the time to do careful individual planning for any but the "problem" children in her class. Far too few teachers are thoroughly trained to do individual planning, aside from having to spend a disproportionate amount of time on the "squeaking wheels" of the class—the children in the bottom fourth or fifth academically, and those with behavior problems. Since, in general, the very bright are relatively self-sufficient, manage at least to do all right with their schoolwork, and rather infrequently present serious behavior problems, they tend to be neglected.

Even well-trained teachers can pick out only about half the children in their classes with extremely high IQ's. Reasons for this lie partly in the nature of teacher-training, and partly in the characteristics of United States children. For rather nebulous reasons, Americans distrust "egg-heads." It is not particularly fashionable to be "the best student in the class." More emphasis is put on being popular or good at games than on intellectual achievement. This may be true of boys even more frequently than it is of girls. Consequently, very bright children may "hide their light under a bushel" and simply do not try very hard. The present author has related elsewhere in a discussion of this topic (McCandless, 1957) an anecdote about an 11-year-old friend of his who, during her first five grades of school, had consistently been the best in her class in work with numbers. During the sixth grade her arithmetic standing plummeted to about the class median. Asked how this had happened, she shrugged and said, matter-of-factly, "Girls are just not *supposed* to be that good in arithmetic."

These points illustrate some of the difficulties confronting teachers when they try enrichment. They cannot enrich the program of a gifted child if they do not know who he is; if they must spend too much time on children who, for one reason or another, are school problems; if gifted children, for cultural reasons, are dragging their heels; or if the classroom does not include appropriate types and ranges of material.

Another method that has been tried with the very bright child is *early admission* to school. This is a special form of acceleration, and many of the same reservations have been expressed concerning it. Few of these reservations are buttressed by facts. One of the most ambitious studies of the question has been done by Hobson (1956), concerning children in the Brookline, Massachusetts, public schools. For twenty-five years preceding his evaluation, these schools had been admitting to kindergarten children with mental ages of 5 or more years, but who were as young, chronologically, as 4 years on October 1 of the year they entered school. Criteria in addition to IQ were employed in admitting such children.

Hobson's sample is impressively large. His subjects include 550 underage children and 3891 regularly admitted children (to whom he refers as "others"), all of whom graduated from the Brookline schools between 1946 and 1955. Included in his "others" group were many underage children who had transferred to Brookline from other schools. These children in general did better than their older classmates, although they did less well than the carefully screened early-admitted children who had begun school in Brookline. Some of the representative findings are listed below.

"Graduation with honors" from Brookline high school demands a solid A and B average for all subjects taken in the last two years of school. Hobson's underage boys exceeded the "other" boys in better than a 2:1 ratio of 18.75 percent to 8.43 percent. Corresponding figures for the girls were 25.46 percent and 15.04 percent.

A second criterion of school success was broader than graduation with honors. Election to Alpha Pi in the Brookline schools depends on the student's accumulation of points, one third of which come from participating in extra-curricular activities. Such items as election to class offices are included. Of the underage boys, about 13 percent received this honor; less than 6 percent of the "other" boys did. Corresponding figures for girls were 19 percent and 9 percent.

Hobson also studied two classes more intensively, obtaining about the same results as those given above. As a group, underage boys and girls averaged 18.8 extracurricular activities during their school years; the "other" group averaged only 12.1. The only category in which any possible disadvantage appeared for early admissions was boys' contact sports (such as football and basketball), where more of the "others" took part. But in other sports, such as tennis, the underage group was somewhat superior to the "others." Underage children were also more frequently accepted into serious, highly rated four-year colleges and universities.

This careful study offers a strong argument against those who say that moderate acceleration handicaps children in the areas of social and motor skills.

In justice to United States public education, it should be added that attitudes toward training the gifted are currently becoming more flexible, that the major methods of furthering their progress are being reevaluated, and that new adaptations of these major methods are being developed. For example, many school systems now have "enrichment" consultants; in many schools the first three or four years of school are ungraded, and children are allowed to progress through them as fast as they can master the work; and so on.

Intellectual giftedness, as studied in some of the most recent studies in the field, as well as the classical and older studies that have been mentioned earlier, seems to account more importantly than any other factor in academic achievement. Kwall and Lackner (1966) studied the effects of ability, popularity, and parent-child relations on school achievement, finding that ability was much more important than the other variables. However, ability coupled with teacher and peer ratings of high leadership and industry was more closely linked to achievement than ability alone. High ability children of well-educated mothers also did better than high ability children of less-educated mothers.

Lucite (1964) demonstrates that the very bright (he worked with sixth-graders) are less conforming than dull children, whether on easy or difficult tasks (this fits well with the section on "creativity" discussed later in this chapter); and Harter (1965) finds that very superior (130 or higher IQ) "learn to learn" more rapidly than average or dull children. The concept of learning to learn was introduced in Chapter 4 of this book: essentially, it refers to the ability to profit from past experience in approaching new problems efficiently.

OTHER EXCEPTIONAL CHILDREN

Segregation and highly specialized training are taken more or less for granted for other groups of exceptional children, such as the cerebral-palsied, deaf, and blind. There is some tendency, the full merits of which are not yet clear, to incorporate into regular classrooms all children who can possibly succeed. In one situation, blind children are provided with both intensive and extensive preschool experiences (to facilitate socialization); then, at an appropriate developmental age, are placed in the regular grades. Results are tentative, but encouraging. For the most part, however, such groups, including the low-grade mentally defective (below about 50 IQ), receive specialized and segregated training.

Controversy exists, however, about education for high-grade mentally defective and borderline children (with IQ's from about 50 to about 85), whose educational attainments by the middle of the elementary-school years are ordinarily below even the modest level that would be predicted from their IQ. Deceleration (failure to promote) and segregation have been the most frequent educational measures used by the public schools, at least in those systems where special procedures have been tried at all.

Convincing evidence exists (Goodlad, 1954; Sandin, 1944) that failure to promote a child is accompanied on his part by discouragement, progressive retardation, hostility (active or latent) toward the school, and symptoms of general maladjustment. But it is not clear whether this cluster of socially maladaptive behaviors and attitudes is the result of failure to promote or whether it accompanies the academic difficulties that lead to the child's not being promoted. In any event, the presence of large, physically mature, surly, older children (a majority of whom are usually boys from lower socioeconomic classes) in classes of younger boys and girls presents very real problems in the school situation. Probably a majority of United States schools now practice what is sometimes called "social promotion," that is, regardless of the child's academic achievement, an effort is made to keep him with his age group. The results of this practice are particularly striking (and troublesome) when a child moves from elementary to junior high school. Typically, at this time, a child changes from a class that revolves almost entirely around one teacher to a platoon system, where different teachers teach different subjects; formal academic requirements ordinarily become more stringent. Where, in the first six grades, a child may have been limping along, in the seventh grade he becomes immobilized, with severe accompanying disturbances of all sorts.

There is no easy way out of this dilemma. Speaking very tentatively and without solid conviction, the author favors special or segregated classes, placement in which is made on a broader basis than an IQ test. Segregation of the slow-learning has been vociferously attacked as undemocratic and out of line with the philosophy of "developing the whole child." Anyone who has observed in the public schools knows that there is discrimination against pupils in "opportunity rooms." Common parlance for such classes by school children is "dummy rooms," and certainly some school systems make them little more than baby-sitting arrangements. However, clever and devoted teachers can produce remarkable results. One teacher (E. McCandless, 1943), working for two successive years with slow-learning children newly admitted to an institution for borderline mentally defective problem children, produced an average academic gain of nearly three grade levels per year. Prior to their commitment to the institution, these children, who averaged about 13 years of age at the time of commitment, had averaged a gain of only about .3 grade levels per year. Most of them had attended the generally very adequate schools of Detroit, Michigan.

Since academic achievement tests were administered independently of the teacher, there was no contamination of results in this study. The techniques used were those of individual diagnosis, strong personal interest in and attention to each child, and moderate firmness, although disciplinary techniques appeared to be milder and more democratic than those prevailing in other classrooms in the institution.

One interesting but tragic study (G. O. Johnson, 1950) charts the academic progress and social acceptance of mentally retarded children (average IQ, about 64) in regular public-school classes. The picture is a hopeless one. During each year of school attendance, the youngsters fell further and further behind academically. First-graders lagged 4.7 months behind their classmates academically (for a combination of arithmetic and reading); second-graders 9.5 months; third-graders 12.7 months; fourth-graders 17.6 months; and fifth-graders 27.8 months! This picture of progressive frustration and defeat holds true despite the fact that the mentally retarded children averaged almost two years older than their normal classmates.

Although these children comprised less than 6 percent of the total group of children studied, 40 percent of the most rejected children in the twenty-five classes included in the research came from the mentally defective group. Other children characterized them by such phrases as "rough, mean, teases, bullies, fights, misbehaves in school, poor sports, cheats, is dirty, smells." Not only were they actively rejected, but few children named them as friends. In these classes, social acceptance mounted steadily with intellectual level, the low (below 59 IQ) mental defectives being less acceptable than the highs, the borderline children more accepted than either group, the normal children still better accepted, and the superior youngsters (above 130 IQ) having the highest acceptance and the lowest rejection scores as determined by votes of their classmates.

Even though the number of mentally defective children in this study is relatively small, the picture the study presents is brutally clear. The life of the slow-learning child in the regular class is a miserable one of academic failure, increasing in severity year by year and compounded by social rejection. It seems that he *could not be worse off* in a special class, either academically or socially, even though other children in the school called it the "dummy class." In the special class he is at least competing with other children of his own level, and can occasionally taste success. From a mental-hygiene point of view, it is perhaps better for him to have some victory and some acceptance from his peers, even though the majority of children derogate his class, than to be integrated but rejected.

In this section, we have reviewed the more common practices of United States public schools in educating special groups of children, particularly superior and slow-learning groups. Since relatively little definitive research has been done in this area, no definite conclusions about what practices are best can be drawn. The research that exists favors acceleration and segregation of the gifted, although such practices are not currently fashionable and considerable prejudice against them still exists. However, more flexibility and experimentation are being encouraged. The evidence is even less clear about deceleration (failing to promote) and segregation of slow-learning children. Both practices have drawbacks. The evidence we have surveyed indicates that mentally retarded children may be better off in special rooms than in regular classes, and that a number of socially maladaptive attitudes and behaviors characterize nonpromoted children. It is not clear whether these are the results of failure to promote or of general academic ineptitude and frustration.

CREATIVE CHILDREN

In the past several years, much research literature has accumulated concerning a special subgroup of gifted children, differing from the intellectually gifted, not because they are not also more than usually bright, but because they are divergent thinkers (see, for example, Guilford, 1966). Guilford defines creativity in terms of divergent thinking—unusual, or novel thought. He has suggested a number of tests to define this ability, which is one of the operations postulated for his structure of intellect (SI), as this was discussed in the Definitions section of the present chapter.

Attempts have been made, presumably since man first became interested in the process of creativity and originality, to isolate the factors that make children and adults creative, original, and innovators, whether this be in art, industry, or literature. Guilford and those who have followed him have taken specific steps to identify and measure creativity and originality, and it is with their somewhat controversial work that the present section largely concerns itself.

Golann (1963) has published a workmanlike review of the psychological studies of creativity, and it is suitable to begin this section with a discussion of his article. He employs Stein's definition of creativity as an acceptable definition: "Creativity is that process which results in a novel work that is accepted as tenable or useful or satisfying by a group at some point in time" (Golann, p. 551).

This definition obviously leaves those who are creative in literary and artistic areas in some difficulty, at least as far as recognition in their lifetime is concerned, since judgment of the satisfactoriness of their work is often not made until years after their deaths.

Golann (p. 549) also believes that "A higher level of creativity introduces some new element of meaning or some new order of significance while a lower level gives further development to an established body of meaning by initiating some advance in its use." Social transactions may also be judged along a creativity dimension.

Specific tasks to measure creativity have, for the most part, been suggested by Guilford and adopted, in whole or with modification, by other research workers. Typical tests of creativity are: stating defects in common implements or institutions; producing words that include a specified letter or combination of letters; producing, against a time limit, synonyms for stimulus words; naming objects that have specified attributes; listing in a given time as many uses as possible for common objects; elaborating shapes, making complex objects from one or two simple shapes, and so on. Creativity tests are usually divided into verbal and nonverbal, very much as intelligence tests are, and emphasis is usually on the quality produced rather than the quantity. Novelty is statistically identified: the more unusual a response, the more creative it is judged to be—hence, the term, divergent thinking. One criticism of the work of Guilford and his followers is that it includes little recognition of social desirability, but only of unusualness or uniqueness. Nor are subtests of creativity, particularly motor and verbal, highly related to each other.

Correlations between creativity as judged, for example, by art, science, mathematics, or literature teachers, and by tests have for the most part been rather low (see, for example, Klausmeier, Harris, and Ethnathios, 1962).

Perhaps the most ambitious studies of creativity, following the leads and testing techniques of Guilford, have been done by Getzels and Jackson (1962); and Torrance (1962, 1965). Getzels and Jackson used a highly atypical school from which to select their subjects, a procedure for which they have been widely criticized, probably justifiably. Their data typically consist of comparing youngsters from the highest 20 percent of their population in creativity, but the lowest 80 percent in conventionally measured intelligence, with those in the highest 20 percent of measured intelligence but the lowest 80 percent of creativity. Their subjects are usually adolescents. Representative findings are that IQ ceases to be an effective correlate of performance after IQ levels of between 120 and 130, creativity, originality, diligence, and motivation accounting for superior achievement from those IQ levels on up the scale. Other investigators, such as Cicirelli (1965) fail to find similar results, and believe that most of the variance of achievement, regardless of level of creativity, is due to the intelligence of the population on which the research is carried out. Nor does Torrance replicate Getzels and Jackson. In other words, this finding may be due to the special nature of Getzel and Jackson's school population, since the studies of Cicirelli and Torrance are, speaking generally, more conservative methodologically than Getzel and Jackson's.

Measures of creativity have typically been found to have rather low but positive correlations with conventional measures of intelligence (from about .15 to about .40, although figures above and below this have been reported; see Golann and Cicirelli).

Many studies, summarized by Golann, have been done of descriptions of children, youth, and adults who test as highly creative. The following are typical descriptions: original, imaginative, curious, enthusiastic, impulsive, less contented and conventional, assertive and authoritative, gloomy, loud, unstable, bitter, cool, dissatisfied, emotional, nonneurotic, reflective, do not mind disorder, and so on and so on. One might almost say, choose your word or phrase and it will apply to some creative person or another. However, enough of the adjectives and descriptions are of an order usually considered socially disruptive or nonconforming or unpleasant that Getzels and Jackson's finding that highly creative children are not popular with their teachers comes as no surprise to one reading the literature in the field. Their unwillingness to pattern themselves on models provided by authority figures may also help to account for the fact that teachers do not like them very well (Getzels and Jackson, 1960).

Getzels and Jackson (1960) think well of their creatives; however, they say that their highly creative youngsters have "the ability to produce new forms, to risk conjoining elements that are customarily thought of as independent and dissimilar" (p. 123). On the other hand, the high IQ, lower creativity subjects "possess to a high degree the ability, and perhaps the need, to focus on the usual, to be 'channeled and controlled' in the direction of the right answers, the socially accepted solution" (p. 123).

In other representative research, Houston and Mednick (1963), working with college students, find that the higher the creativity of their research subjects the higher the novelty of the stimuli they seek as rewards; in other words, the more curious they are. Fleming and Weintraub (1962) find that the higher children of fourth- to sixth-grade ages score on a test of rigidity, the less well they score on tests of creativity. Iscoe and Pierce-Jones (1964) working with 5- to 9-year-old white and Negro children, find the Negro children more creative than the white children, except at the kindergarten ages. They believe this is due to the inferior nature (cultural impoverishment) of the kindergarten their Negro children attended. All their subjects were from lower socioeconomic classes, although the whites were from a higher stratum and also tested higher in IQ than the Negroes.

In summary, the field of creativity seems to be well worth studying. Any method whereby the innovator and originator, particularly if his products are socially useful, can be identified and guided is well worth employing, and fully deserves study. There seems to be no question but what the creative are less conventional than equally or more intelligent but less creative children. Intelligence is probably much more closely related to academic achievement than creativity at any level of either intelligence or creativity. Creative children are, in all likelihood, uncomfortable children to their teachers, thus less well-accepted than more conventional children.

Summary

Psychological treatment of the concept of intelligence has been more successful in *practice* (that is, in the well-developed area of intelligence-testing) than in *theory*. This chapter views *learning* as playing a heavy, perhaps a preponderant, role in the development and maintenance of intelligence in the physically normal human being. The basic definition of intelligence adopted here is that it is *problem-solving ability*, but that this ability is complex, involving among other things concentration, speed, depth and power, and probably breadth.

The types of intelligence test most frequently employed vary along the dimension of *age* (infancy, preschool, childhood, adolescence, and adulthood), although items on some individual intelligence tests range in difficulty from those designed for preschool children to those designed for highly intelligent adults. Some intelligence tests must be administered *individually;* others can be administered to *groups.* There are *verbal* and *nonverbal* (or performance) intelligence tests. Some intelligence tests emphasize *power* (no time limit); others speed.

Test items used with children up to age 2 seem to have in common a factor of "sensorimotor alertness." The factor of "persistence," or goal-orientation, then enters; and after about 4 years of age, intelligence-test items seem to tap a factor of "provisional action," or symbolic, problem-solving ability. The stages of mental development perhaps go from manipulation (the hand), through distance receptors, to reflective thinking. Infant intelligence tests do not predict intelligence as well as it is measured on tests given to older children and adults, but they have certain legitimate and valuable uses. Grossly defective functioning can be detected; sensory deficit can often be picked up by skilled testers; and a good "here-and-now" picture of the infant's status can be obtained. By the time a child is about 3, fairly good predictions of later intelligence can be obtained by skilled testers who know the children well.

The most common, and probably the most useful, employment of intelligence tests is to predict school achievement. Such prediction is most accurate for the elementary grades, becoming less accurate as the child progresses through junior and senior high school, college, and graduate school. There are several reasons for decreasing accuracy in prediction. First, those who are clearly going to fail drop out of school as early as they are allowed to. Second, the further the child progresses in school, the less standardized is his curriculum, and the more his individual study efficiency and motivation affect his academic performance. Anxiety also seems to interfere with the measurement of intelligence, more for older than younger children.

Culture-fair or culture-free intelligence tests (those designed to minimize social class differences) predict academic performance less well than traditional tests, probably because they have less in common with the traditional curriculum. For the opposite reason, it may well be that the group tests predict school success better than individual tests. The question of whether intelligence tests are fair has caused some to consider intelligence testing unethical.

Intelligence seems to develop most rapidly during infancy and early childhood; probably about half of its potential is attained by about 10 years. Whereas it was formerly believed that growth in intelligence stopped at about 16 to 20 years of age, more recent studies indicate that intellectually superior populations are still gaining in intellectual power (as measured) in their 50s.

Boys are more likely than girls to gain in IQ, and children highly achievement motivated more likely to gain than those not so motivated. The bright are more likely to gain than the dull.

Creative children tend to be questioners. They are innovators, flexible, nonconforming, and tend to be less popular with their teachers than less deviating children.

The gifted and the slow-learning present special educational problems, and the former, particularly, have been relatively neglected in American schools until quite recently. The most frequent educational procedures used with the gifted are acceleration, including early school admission; segregation; and enrichment. The last-named, although currently the most popular, is not often practical in the harried modern public school.

Although segregation of the slow-learning into special classes has many aspects that are distasteful to democratically-minded Americans, evidence suggests that it may be less damaging to the children than the steady and progressive frustration and defeat they experience in regular classes. Deceleration (failing to promote) does not appear to benefit children but, particularly from the time of junior high school, "social promotions" also present serious problems. More attention clearly needs to be paid to "special education" for both the gifted and the slow-learning, as well, of course, as for all other categories of exceptional children.

Sources of Variation in Measured Intelligence

major, although only moderately profitable, psychological debate was carried on in the United States, during the thirties and forties of this century, concerning the question whether heredity or environment was more influential in determining the level of intelligence reached by a child. In the area of normal intellectual development, this controversy has for the most part been reduced to its common-sense merits. The debate is still being carried on, however, concerning the determinants of such disorders as simple mental deficiency (low intelligence without accompanying glandular or neurological disorder) and schizophrenia, the most serious and wide-spread of the mental diseases.

The Nature-Nurture Controversy

Anastasi and Foley (1948) have provided a sensible analysis of the dimensions of the heredity-environment problem. They maintain that the first approach should be to decide whether *structure* or *function* is being talked about; and then to ask further whether it is *hereditary* structure or function that is involved, or *environmental* structure or function.

Few argue with the fact that, under normal circumstances, the pattern of a child's physical growth and his eventual height, his tendency to be fat or thin, broad- or narrow-shouldered, brown- or blue-eyed, blond or brunette, is a matter of *structural* characteristics determined by *heredity*, although extreme nutritional deprivation or excess can greatly change the rating of body type (Shuttleworth, 1949) and may result in such alterations of structure as are produced by rickets. On the other hand, no one argues that heredity produced the change that occurs when an arm is crushed and must be amputated, or when a head injury or infantile case of whooping cough changes a previously normal child to one who is brain-damaged and mentally defective. These are obviously cases of *environmental* influence on *structure* which also results in changes in function.

Such diseases as Tay-Sachs disease (also called amaurotic idiocy) seem clearly to be *hereditary* interferences with *function* (with accompanying structural changes). In this disease, the previously normal child begins, most typically toward the middle of the first year of life, to show less muscular control, particularly of the head and neck; a cherry-red spot appears on the macula of the eye; muscular degeneration and blindness progress rapidly; and death ensues. Phenylpyruvic idiocy, or amentia, is another example of a genetically determined functional disorder. The diagnostic sign of the disease is the presence of phenylpyruvic acid in the urine. It may well be that the metabolic disorder which accompanies this condition affects nervous tissue (or the phenylpyruvic acid does), with resulting low-grade mental deficiency. Except for intellectual deficit and a fine muscular tremor, individuals so affected appear quite normal. They achieve puberty, and grow to average height and strength. This tragic disorder is no longer necessarily the "destroyer of brains" that it once was. Tests have been devised so that the presence of phenylpyruvic acid can be detected in very young infants, and the once inevitable deteriorative effect prevented by special diets.

Such functional-structural characteristics as near- or far-sightedness are probably partially determined by heredity. But no one has learned to read without being taught. This is a case of *environmentally* determined *function*. Some types of microcephaly (a type of mental deficiency in which the head is very small and "pointed") seem to result from such environmental factors as the mother's having had German measles or heavy pelvic x-ray irradiation during her early pregnancy, although in other types of microcephaly there is apparently a hereditary component (Tredgold, 1947). These are cases of environment affecting function, although in the case of microcephaly, structure is also altered.

Concerning such conditions as those described above, there is little argument between hereditarians and environmentalists. For other types of ability and disability, however, it is more difficult to get agreement about whether the classification should be one of *hereditary function* or *environmental function*. Intelligence is one such trait.

Clear-cut facts about the inheritance or acquisition of such complex traits as intelligence and personal adjustment are hard to come by, for about the same reasons as those discussed in connection with the maturation-learning controversy (see Chapter 4). An argument about relative importance is meaningless on similar grounds. When each of two conditions or states is required for the existence of a phenomenon, neither can be more important than the other. Heredity and environment begin to exert their influence at the time a child is conceived. They cannot meaningfully be separated from each other. As one geneticist, Stern (1956), has ably put it, the environment comprises "all that is not genic. It means the intra-uterine surroundings of the embryo and fetus, the food and climate which impinges on the child and adult, and the psychological and cultural influences of home, school and society in their complex reactions upon the personality" (p. 48).

Ordinarily, there is an interaction between heredity and environment —an interaction overlooked in the classical studies of the Jukes and the Kallikaks. In the latter family (Goddard, 1912), young Martin Kallikak founded two clans, the first by begetting an illegitimate male baby with a presumably mentally defective barmaid during Revolutionary times. The descendants of this child had remarkable records of criminality, mental deficiency, illegitimacy, and generally poor citizenship. But Kallikak's descendants by a later union with a woman of his own social and intellectual status had equally conspicuous records of success and good citizenship. Overlooked in reports of these families was the fact that the environments of the two father-related clans differed to an even greater extent than their heredities which, at least for the first generation following Martin, overlapped genetically by 50 percent. The children of intelligent, successful parents ordinarily grow up in security. They are well fed and well educated. The children of dull parents, who are typically rather unsuccessful in making their economic way through life, mature in a setting of deprivation, uncertainty, and depressed neighborhood conditions.

Human family histories are so fragmentary that accurate assessment of the attributes of ancestors is impossible, except in certain rare cases— for example, some royal families—and only partially so for them. (For example, intelligence tests have been in use only since the middle of the second decade of this century; and it is doubtful whether many royal children have been subjected to the Stanford-Binet.) Compared with most lower species of animals, the span between human generations is so great that any one scientific worker can ordinarily encompass no more than two generations in his professional life. Psychology and human genetics are new sciences, whose progress is so rapid that techniques useful for assessing one generation are outmoded by, and noncomparable with, techniques available for the second generation. As a matter of fact, techniques applicable in one *decade* are frequently outmoded by techniques developed in the second. This fact has added greatly to the difficulty of longitudinal research, particularly in the emotion-personality area.

An adequate study of heredity and environment necessitates control over mating as well as rather extreme manipulation of the environment.

In a Western European society such as ours, controlled mating is impossible. People marry whom they will. Manipulation to produce extreme environmental circumstances is, for good reasons, socially and legally impossible (for example, we cannot place the very superior 2-year-old of very privileged parents in a situation where he would have no contact with humans). Yet to study environment and heredity in any conclusive fashion, extreme manipulations of heredity (mating of one mentally defective and one very superior person, for example) and of environment are necessary. It is for such reasons as these that some of our best information in this area comes from studies of animals, in which it is possible to manipulate both the genetic pool and the surroundings. Some of these animal studies are reviewed later in the chapter. Some societies do provide for arranged marriages, often between first cousins and even closer relatives. The offspring of such marriages would be a valuable genetic research pool, but one which so far has not been exploited.

SIGNIFICANCE OF THE NATURE-NURTURE QUESTION

Even though it is *logically* unclear and scientific answers are difficult, if not impossible, the nature-nurture question is discussed here at some length. This question merits full discussion for several reasons, of which the least important is that it has been historically and is currently a matter of preoccupation in the study of child development. More important is the fact that heredity is heavily weighted in placing babies for adoption, and any information that we can obtain about contributions to the variance of human intelligence is important information.

There exist very real reservations, possibly but not clearly justified by evidence, about placing for adoption babies whose parents are mentally defective or borderline in intelligence, or who are psychotic and even neurotic. Yet the evidence for the inheritance of these traits is not clear-cut. Rather impressive evidence exists (Skeels and Harms, 1948; Skodak and Skeels, 1949; and Skeels, 1966) to show that, given a good environment, many children who might have become simple mental defectives had they stayed in their true homes, turn out to be perfectly normal in all respects when placed in good adoptive homes. Little or no evidence exists about the effects of adoptive placement on children of psychotics or neurotics.

When an issue intimately affects the lives of many children and in addition has numerous other broad social implications, this issue and the evidence with reference to it should be examined. Because the data currently available are inconclusive, few scientists today are willing to take an extreme position. One widely accepted viewpoint has been advanced by Stern (1956):

> The genetic endowment in respect to any one trait has been compared to a rubber band and the trait itself to the length which the rubber band assumes when it is stretched by outside forces. Different people initially may have been given different lengths of

unstretched endowment, but the natural forces of the environment may have stretched their expression to equal length, or led to differences in attained length sometimes corresponding to their innate differences and at other times in reverse of the relation. (p. 53)[1]

Relatively recent reviews of studies using human subjects and exploring the role of environment and heredity in intellectual development have been made by Hunt (1961), H. E. Jones (1954), McCandless (1952), and Pinneau and Jones (1955). No attempt to repeat these reviews will be made here. We will, however, try to summarize the findings concerning this issue under seven headings: (1) studies of adopted children; (2) studies using twins as subjects; (3) studies of the effects of institutional living and isolation on intellectual development; (4) investigations of the effects of preschool attendance; (5) research on the effects of socioeconomic class; (6) subcultural or simple mental deficiency; and (7) environmental influences on speech, including the relationship of intelligence and bilingualism.

Studies of Adopted Children

The first conclusion that can be drawn from a study of the literature concerning the intelligence of adopted children is that they are above the national average in IQ. Skodak and Skeel's study (1949) of a group of 100 adopted children tested at an average age of 13.5 years showed them to have an average IQ of 117 whereas, for the nation, the figure is 100. This same group, containing a number of children who later dropped out of the study, had tested 117 on their first test at the age of 2 years, 2 months. There were 180 children in this initial group. For the 152 who took a second test, average IQ was 112 at 4 years, 3 months; and for the 139 who took a third test, the average was 115 at 7 years of age.

Another study (Skeels and Harms, 1948) reports on the average IQ's of three groups of adopted youngsters, all of whose true parents were inferior in social history (mothers were mentally defective, or fathers were in the lowest possible occupational brackets—semi- or unskilled labor—or both). Most of these children were tested at about kindergarten age. One group of 87 tested 105.5; another group of 111 tested at an average of 110.3; a third group of 35 tested at 104 IQ. These findings are representative of what has been found in other studies.

There are at least three reasons for the above-average IQ's of adopted

1 Reprinted with permission of the Child Welfare League of America and C. Stern, from Stern, C.: *Hereditary factors affecting adoption. A study of adoption practices*, Volume 11. New York: Child Welfare League of America, 1956.

youngsters. The *first* is that all obviously retarded children are screened out before adoption so that there are few, if any, feeble-minded youngsters to pull down the average. The *second* is that adopted children, by definition, are badly wanted by their parents and consequently probably get more than an average amount of love, attention, and stimulation. *Finally*, since the majority of children are probably placed by social agencies, only the "better" homes are given babies for adoption.

Although intelligence scores of adopted children do not correlate highly, if at all, with the intelligence quotients or education of their foster parents, the average level of their intelligence is about the same as would be predicted for the true children of their foster parents.

The pioneering Skodak and Skeels study mentioned above found that the IQ's of adopted children averaged either 20 or 30 points higher than those of their true mothers. The difference in these figures is due to the fact that two different tests were used for the children. The authors took a sample of 180 children and followed them from the time they were placed in their adoptive homes, which in all cases was before the age of 6 months. Although not all the mothers had taken intelligence tests (63 had) there was a correlation of .44 between the IQ's of the true mothers and the IQ's of the children at the time the children were more than 13 years of age. Such a correlation, of course, accounts for less than one fifth of the variance in children's IQ (19 percent). One striking aspect of this study is the elevation of the children's IQ over that of their mothers. Whereas the mothers functioned, on the whole, at a borderline level, the children were significantly superior to the national average in intelligence.

This study has been severely criticized. It is maintained that the mothers were tested under disadvantageous conditions (fairly soon after they had had their babies, and ordinarily after they had decided to give them up). There is little doubt that these factors operated to lower the intelligence-test scores of the mothers as emotional upset, unusual conditions, and so on, certainly contribute to errors in measuring intelligence. But the biographies of these 63 mothers indicate that they were marginal social persons whereas the children, on the whole, were successful adolescents. Thirty-one percent of the children had IQ's higher than 99 percent of the true mothers. Seventy percent of the true mothers had IQ's below 95; only 16 percent of the children fell so low. Whereas 25 percent of the true mothers had IQ's below 75, only 4 percent of the children did. One evaluator of the study (Honzik, 1957) makes much of the correlation between the IQ's of the true mothers and the IQ's of the children, but partially ignores the fact that the children's intellectual functioning is a socially important level above that of the mothers.

The striking Skeels and Harms study (1948) concerns the intelligence of children whose true parents were socially disadvantaged. Skeels and

Harms studied three groups of adopted children. The mothers of the 87 children in the first group all had intelligence-test scores of less than 75. The putative fathers of the 111 children in the second group were at the lowest occupational levels (semi- and unskilled laborers). A third group of 35 children was made up of children whose mothers tested below 75 IQ *and* whose fathers were at the bottom of the socioeconomic ladder in terms of their occupation. About 80 percent of the children in this study were illegitimate.

The IQ's of these three groups of children were 105.5, 110.3, and 104 respectively. In other words, all three groups tested above the national average, yet their true parents were, at the very best, marginal members of society in terms of intelligence and occupation. The correlations between the intelligence of the three groups of children and their true mothers were, respectively, .23 (significant at the .05 level); .22 (just missing significance at the 0.5 level); and .12, a statistically insignificant figure. For none of the groups does the intelligence of the true mothers account for more than about 5 percent of the variance in children's intelligence.

These two studies plus Skeels' (1966) study indicate that placement in an adequate adoptive home before 6 months is extremely effective in raising the general level of intelligence of large groups of children, even though for the one group a statistically significant relation exists between the intelligence of the children and that of their true mothers. Although there is some tendency for the less bright of the adopted children to be the offspring of the less bright of the true mothers, and for the brighter to be the offspring of the brighter, their general intellectual functioning has been moved from the feeble-minded or border-line level of their true mothers (and presumably their fathers) to one that is above the average. They approximate, not the intellectual level of their true mothers and fathers, but that of their foster parents, even though there is no correlation between their intellectual status and their foster parents' educational level.

A study by Leahy (1935) shows little effect of adoption on intellectual level of children. But the true mothers and fathers of the children who were the subjects of this study were far superior to the true mothers and fathers of the children in the two studies just reviewed.

Studies of Twins

The relation between the intelligence of nontwin siblings (brothers and sisters), fraternal twins (born at the same time, but from different eggs), and identical twins (born at the same time, and from the same maternal egg) have also been studied. It has been argued that since both heredity and environment differ to a considerable degree for nontwin sibs, their IQ's should show the lowest resemblance. For fraternal twins, according to this line of reasoning, heredity differs but environment is very similar; hence their IQ's should show a higher relation than those of sibs. Identical twins, it has been hypothesized, have identical heredities *and* environments; hence the relation between their IQ's should be the highest of any of the groups.

It has been argued that if this predicted pattern of relationships is found, the case for heredity is strengthened. Such a pattern has been found: in general, the modal correlation between the IQ's of nontwin brothers and brothers, brothers and sisters, and sisters and sisters is about .50: for fraternal twins, correlations in the .60s and .70s have been established; and for identical twins, IQ correlations are in the .80s and .90s.

These findings do not, however, necessarily support the heredity argument. The difference in the correlations between nontwin sibs and fraternal twins may well be due to increased environmental similarity for the latter; but the difference in correlation between fraternal and identical twins is not necessarily attributable to the identical heredities of the latter. Identical twins, by definition, are of the same sex and extremely similar in appearance; few people can tell them apart. Of an identical twin pair, "John" is almost as frequently labeled "Jim" as he is by his own name. In other words, for identical twins, not only is the heredity the same, but the environment is much more likely to be similar than it is for fraternal twins. When identical twins are reared together, therefore, there is no way of telling whether the increased IQ correlation typically found is due to common heredities or common environments.

Although the number of subjects is small, a major study (Newman, Freeman, and Holzinger, 1937) of identical twins who were reared separately strongly suggests that the more widely different the environments in which they grew up, the more divergent their IQ's were likely to be. In one of the nineteen pairs studied, one girl had spent much time, during her early elementary years, in an isolated mountain setting where there were no schools, and had dropped out of school entirely when very young. Her twin sister had been adopted into a home where there was much emphasis on "getting ahead through education," and had been stimulated and even pushed, particularly by her foster mother. The Stanford-Binet of the first girl was 92 and that of the second 116, which is a difference of 24 points. The second girl was advanced in educational age over her sister by almost seven years. Of course, much of this difference was due to formal opportunity. The authors calculated a correlation between IQ differences and differences in judged educational opportunities for their subjects, and obtained a figure of .79 when Stanford-Binet IQ's were used as the expression of intelligence.

In other words, studies of twins suggest strongly that environment is of major importance in determining intelligence, but in no way discount the fact that heredity, too, plays an important part.

Institutional Living and Isolation

Most studies of the effects of isolation and institutional living (Goldfarb, 1945) show that IQ's of children so brought up are quite low. A few studies of dubious scientific merit concern children reared by animals. These children are reported to behave not like human beings but like animals. However, folklore plays more part than science in relaying the data about these children (Dennis, 1951); for example, we do not know whether they may not have been abandoned in the first place because they were feeble-minded.

Another study (Spitz, 1945, 1946) of children reared in an institution found that during the first year of life their average developmental quotient dropped from an initial level of 124 to 72, or from a classification of superior to one that could be considered defective. This study has been severely criticized (Pinneau, 1955) on the basis of its methods, and the criticisms are so severe and apparently well founded that no more than limited confidence can be placed in its results. However, more careful studies by Goldfarb (1945) and Ruth J. Levy (1947) obtained similar results, as did a study of Chinese infants (Hsü, 1946), in which it was found that the longer the infants had been in a baby ward, the lower their developmental quotient was likely to be. Spitz maintains that the effects of such deprivation are irreversible, and the evidence of Goldfard and Levy to some degree bears him out. Pasamanick (1946) found that baby-ward living had severely retarding effects, but implies that when the condition is remedied, the babies come back to normal. A study by Beres and Obers (1950) of 18-year-olds who had spent much of their early life in institutions indicates that a substantial number (about half) of them were normal emotionally (and presumably intellectually), Rheingold (1956) has demonstrated that one interested, around-the-clock "mother figure" can improve the social responsiveness of institutionalized infants.

Of course, there are institutions and institutions. Unpublished data (Harms, 1957) indicate that babies who are resident in a nutrition ward in which there are many nurses' aides and a warm, motherly chief nurse, who are fed in the laps of adults, and who have convalescent children running in and out of the ward, approach normal mental and emotional development even though many of their parents are of socially inferior stock.

Some of the studies mentioned above imply or state that the indisputable developmental retardation of infants brought up in baby wards where only routine attention is given by a large number of adults is due to the lack of a "significant and consistent mother figure" (see Chapter 1). It might also be suggested that this retardation is due simply to lack of adequate sensorimotor stimulation. But the questions of the factors responsible and the degree of irreversibility remain open. Speaking from a social-welfare point of view, enough evidence has accumulated to indicate that group living for babies, in a baby ward where only routine care is given, is sufficiently damaging (whether temporarily or permanently) to justify recommendations against such arrangements.

Effects of Nursery-School Attendance

Considerable controversy has attended research on the effects of nursery-school experience on intelligence. Consistent intelligence gains (approximating an average of $5\frac{1}{2}$ IQ points for six months' attendance) have been reported for children attending the State University of Iowa Laboratory Preschools (Wellman, 1945). For twenty-two groups of children tested with one or another form of the Binet test before and after five to fourteen months of attendance at nursery school, average IQ changes ranging from −0.6 to +10.1 points have been reported. Similar reports for six groups of children not attending nursery school indicate changes ranging from −4.5 to +0.8 IQ points on tests separated in time by five to ten months. The average IQ gain for all nursery-school children was +5.4; for the Iowa group, +5.5; for all children in the Iowa control groups, +0.7; for all children not attending nursery school, whether from Iowa or elsewhere, +1.1.

The Iowa studies show that these gains persist through time, and that the children's academic performance is rather consistently in line with the "new" rather than the "old" IQ's. The Iowa Preschools are heavily staffed (about one professionally trained teacher to every four or five children), and offer an emotionally supporting and intellectually stimulating program to the children enrolled. Children attend about three hours a day, five days a week. Although the children gain during the academic year, they do not gain over the summer holidays when they are not in school, despite the fact that on the average they come from rather superior homes. The occupations of a plurality of the fathers are professional and semiprofessional or managerial.

Two studies (Starkweather and Roberts, 1940; Wooley, 1925), widely separated in time, report gains in IQ by children attending nursery school at the Merrill-Palmer School in Detroit. Another study (Barrett and Koch, 1930) shows that orphan children placed in a nursery-school program in an institution where, concurrently, the entire living schedule for the children was psychologically improved, gained an average of about 21 IQ points over a period of six to nine months. Their carefully matched controls (children not attending nursery school) gained only about 5 points. In another institution (Skeels et al., 1938) where a nursery school was started without extensive accompanying institutional changes, children did not change in IQ as a result of nursery-school attendance, but their controls (children not attending nursery school) lost dramatically in IQ. The large average loss was, however, disproportionately due to the large IQ drops of certain of the children. This last study has been criticized on statistical grounds (McNemar, 1940), but re-analysis of its data by Wellman and Pegram (1944) has produced approximately the same results.

On the other hand, reports from nursery schools similar in type and presumed excellence, at such places as Western Reserve University (Anderson, 1940), Rhode Island College of Education (Bird, 1940), University of Minnesota (Goodenough and Maurer, 1940), University of California (H. E. Jones and Jorgensen, 1940), and Winnetka (Voas, 1940) do not show gains. A study (Frandsen and Barlow, 1940) of two groups of children, one of which attended nursery school at the Utah State Agricultural College and the second a WPA nursery school, showed borderline gains (3.34 IQ points in five-and-a-half months of attendance). Children who entered the relatively privileged Moosehart children's institution from relatively underprivileged homes when they were less than 6 years of age gained about $6\frac{1}{2}$ IQ points during their first four years of residence. Most of this gain, 5+ points, was made during their first year of residence (Reymert and Hinton, 1940).

For schools reporting IQ gains following nursery-school attendance, the gains have been greater than could be accounted for by practice effects. However, practice effects, greater experience with a variety of adults in many types of situations (and possibly, in the case of the Iowa nursery schools, with the testers themselves), increasing maturity and poise on the part of the children, and a possible halo effect, all may plausibly account for some of the gain.[2] Arguments have been presented (Wellman, 1940) to demonstrate that none of these factors operated in the pioneering Iowa studies. Tests had been routinely administered to the nursery-school children for years before an analysis was made that demonstrated they were gaining in IQ; practice effects can be thought

[2] A so-called halo effect may occur, for example, when the tester knows that a child is very bright and, almost unconsciously, rates borderline performance on an item as a pass. It also works in reverse: For a child who has previously tested low in IQ, borderline performance may be judged as a failure.

to be operating minimally when a child stays the same or loses in IQ from a spring to a fall test (the Iowa children averaged about a half-point loss over the summer months) yet gains from fall to spring; nursery-school children gained more than controls who had had the same number of tests, and so on.

A study in progress (Truax, 1966) provides some evidence that questions about examiner influence should not be given too much significance. Truax finds that children without siblings are the ones who gain in IQ in preschool. Those with brothers and sisters do not gain in IQ. Apparently, preschool provides children who have previously had little opportunity to play with other youngsters with intellectual stimulation not otherwise available to them. There is no reason to think that examiner influence would differentiate between only children and those with siblings.

One interesting study (Worbois, 1942) used as its subjects elementary-school children and tested the differential effects of attending a rural consolidated or a rural one-room school. The different populations studied were rather closely matched for all factors but the type of school attended. The study was carried on for two years. The first group of children reported on experienced their first year of school while the study was in progress. Children attending a rural one-room school gained an average of one IQ point (from 105 to 106); rural consolidated-school children gained 5 points (106 to 111). The difference in these gains was significant. A second group, whose first two years of school coincided with the period of the study, showed a 16-point gain for consolidated children (from an average of 105 to 121); the one-room children moved from 104 to 108. This difference is highly significant. A third group of youngsters had their second and third years of school during the experimental period. The consolidated children changed from 112 to 116; the one-room children from 105 to 103. This was the smallest of the groups, and the difference in changes did not quite reach significance. Worbois believes that differences in the teachers' training, together with the richness of experiences provided, accounted for these differential intelligence gains.

Recent years have seen a surge of interest in the effects of preschool or nursery-school attendance for so-called culturally deprived, or culturally disadvantaged children. Programs which pull children from depressed environments (such as the federally sponsored Head Start program) in order to give them enriched experience have become very common. Three representative studies in this area will be mentioned here: those of Deutsch (1962); Gray (1965); and Hodges, McCandless, and Spicker (1966). These studies can also be classified as environmental intervention studies. Deutsch and Gray have worked more with preschool aged children, while Hodges, McCandless, and Spicker have concentrated their efforts on 5-year-old children. Deutsch and Gray work with both parents and children in a so-called total push program, whereas Hodges, McCandless, and Spicker have concentrated on developing a diagnostically based curriculum to which the child is exposed without involving his parent(s). Their thesis is that a practical program is one that can be developed through the school, and that the total push, while perhaps desirable, is not practical due to its expense and shortage of personnel to staff it.

All three studies aim at increasing IQ, improving language, upgrading social skills, and developing academic type interests and skills on the part of the children. Provisions are also made to improve the child's emotional security. An implicit aim of all the studies is to make "the lower-lower-class child more like the middle-class child." If he can blend in, it is thought that he will be more successful, at least in the crucial area of school achievement.

The results of the studies are not completely analyzed: There is a tendency for the children to show initial gains far greater than those of the control group (average IQ gains of 15 to 20 points in one academic year for the experimental group are not uncommon). While this great difference has tended to lessen or disappear by second grade, there remains the fact that, at least in the early phases of the studies, the experimental groups were objectively better able to manage school related tasks than the controls, thus having at least a temporary but marked advantage.

Other authors are also interested in this problem. Goldstein and Chorost (1966) analyzed the school success of low socioeconomic class first-, second-, and third-grade children according to whether they had had preschool or kindergarten experiences. They used as criteria of success in elementary school intelligence scores, achievement test results, report card grades, and teacher ratings of behavior. Their conclusion is that either kindergarten or nursery preschool experience helps the school performance of low socioeconomic status children. This topic is discussed in more detail in Chapter 14.

To summarize, conclusions concerning the effects of nursery-school attendance on IQ are somewhat tentative. Evidence exists that children gain moderately in intelligence in many nursery schools, and that those who attend, on the whole, gain more than those who do not. But attendance at some nursery schools does not result in intellectual gains. Descriptions and personal observations of some of the nursery-school settings that we have discussed show no obvious differences between schools where gains occur and schools where they do not. Some aspects of the research work in this field probably operate to account artificially for part of the average gain.

Where information is available, it appears that the gains made in nursery school are permanent, and are positively correlated with later academic performance.

Effects of Social Class and Other Social Factors

A comprehensive review of research on social class and intelligence is provided by H. E. Jones (1954, pp. 645–659). The evidence for social-class differences in intelligence is very clear-cut; the evidence is also clear that environmental opportunities substantially influence intellectual development. The social implications of this finding are readily apparent. No sensible person denies the important influence of heredity on all phases of human development, but the precise degree to which it affects so complex a phenomenon as intelligence is unknown. Likewise, no sensible person denies the influence of environment, although questions about the extent of its contribution to intellectual development are not yet answered. But we can *do* something about environment, little or nothing about heredity. Consequently, detailed studies of the range and type of environmental effects, and courses of action built upon the results of such studies, are of utmost social importance.

Dozens of studies (see H. E. Jones, 1954) have been made of the resemblance in intelligence between parents and their offspring living in their own homes. Regardless of social class, level of parents' education or parental intelligence, the correlation between measures of parental social status and children's intelligence is about .50.[3] It is ordinarily a little lower than this for social class as measured, for example, by occupation; often a little higher when parental intelligence or educational level is used as a criterion. Some studies show that fathers' intelligence is more closely related to children's IQ than mothers'; other studies show the

---

[3] The correlation between parental social status and children's intelligence is remarkably stable. For studies of our highly complex human nature and behavior, a correlation of .50 is high, but accounts for only 25 percent of the variance in intelligence. Yet this 25 percent represents the *combination* of parental genes and the environment provided by the parents. We must look elsewhere—no one knows precisely where—to account for the other 75 percent of this variance. Studies of the intelligence of grandparents, aunts, uncles, and gread-grandparents may account for a larger share of the variance of children's intelligence than is usually considered likely. More sophisticated studies of motivation, personality, and *effective* environment should help still further in predicting children's intelligence. An *effective* environment is one the child actually experiences; an *objective* environment is the one the outside observer can see. The wealthy child, whose nursery is crammed with toys and books, may be said to have an intellectually stimulating *objective* environment; yet if his contacts with adults are confined to a nurse of borderline mentality, who is not literate enough to read him the books or interested enough to stimulate him in play with his toys, his *effective* environment is poor.

reverse. The safest conclusion is that both parents contribute about equally. Kagan and Moss (1959), for example, found that the median correlation between the IQ's of boys (measured at ages between 3 and 10) and their fathers was .39, and between boys and their mothers, .41. Fathers' IQ correlated .51 with girl children's IQ; mothers' IQ .48. Fathers' educational level had a median correlation of .24 with their boys' IQ, and .39 with that of their girls; mothers' educational level had a median correlation of .45 with sons' IQ; .57 with that of their girls. These findings suggest that mothers have more to do with the pattern of family stimulation, but that both parents (as would be expected) contribute equally to genetic endowment.

One of the more common ways of determining social class is by level of father's occupation. According to one occupational scale, Class I is made up of professional men (lawyers, conventionally educated ministers, physicians, and so on); Class VII comprises unskilled laboring men. The 1937 revision of the Stanford-Binet test (Terman and Merrill, 1937) provided norms for 831 children between $2\frac{1}{2}$ and 5 years of age, classified according to their social status. Class I children averaged 116 IQ; Class II children (whose fathers were semiprofessional and managerial) averaged 112; Class III (fathers clerical, skilled trades, and retail workers) averaged 108; Class IV (rural owners) averaged 99; Class V (semiskilled, minor clerical, and small business) averaged 104; Class VI (slightly skilled laborers) averaged 95; and Class VI (urban and rural day laborers) averaged 94. Similar results were obtained for other age levels up to the ages of 15 to 18.

This large study was somewhat unrepresentative of the national population, since rural and unskilled laboring groups were not fully represented. But here and in other studies, an average difference of about 20 IQ points was found between children of parents at the lowest and the highest social-class levels, regardless of the index used to measure social class.

Such a finding supports conclusively neither a hereditary nor an environmental point of view. It can be argued, probably legitimately but somewhat circularly, that people who "don't get ahead" are of inferior genetic stock, hence pass along a less adequate intellectual endowment to their children. That they provide less adequate intellectual stimulation is clear.

Our conclusion must be that the higher the socioeconomic class of the parents, the brighter, on the average, the children will be. One ambitious study has gathered together intelligence-test records of 45,000 children. fourth- through eighth-graders, from 455 schools in 310 communities in thirty-six of the then 48 United States (McGehee and Lewis, 1942). The upper 10 percent of these children were classified as superior; the lower 10 percent as retarded. Fathers' occupations were scaled from I (professional) through V (unskilled, day labor). Class I produced 2.4 times as many superior children as would be expected, whereas Class V produced only .3; in the mentally retarded group, Class I parents produced only .14 times as many retarded children as would be expected, whereas Class V produced more than 1.5 times as many as expected statistically. Yet, in terms of sheer *numbers,* Classes II, III and IV (as the authors call them, the "great middle class") produced more than four fifths of the total (84 percent) of superior children and about two thirds of the "retarded" children. It should be noted that this study included as its subjects only those children actually enrolled in public school. Children of extremely low intelligence were thus excluded. Some evidence exists (Halperin, 1946) to indicate that the higher socioeconomic classes produce more than their share of such children, perhaps because they can afford better medical care so that a larger proportion of severely handicapped children born to them survive.

In general, urban children do better on intelligence tests than rural children, although much of this difference in test quotients results from performance on certain types of items: urban children do better than rural children on verbal items. Yet, since much of the manifest functioning of intelligence in our society is verbal, this is an important difference. Several studies exist (see H. E. Jones, 1954; McCandless, 1952) which demonstrate that children who mature in depressed rural areas, where schools are poor and there is a minimum of stimulation, decline progressively in intelligence as they grow older. Studies of Tennessee mountain children reported by Wheeler (1942) demonstrate the effect of a barren environment on children's intellectual development, yet contrast current tendencies with the more depressing picture that existed ten years before he gathered his data. In 1930, 6-year-olds from this region tested an average 95 IQ. In 1940 they tested an average 103. Older children tested lower, both in 1930 and in 1940, than 6-year-olds, so that in 1930 16-year-olds averaged only 73.5 IQ; in 1940, an 80 IQ. Some of the difference in scores between older and younger children is undoubtedly due to reading deficiency on the part of the older ones, since for them reading has a greater effect on test scores than it does for 6-year-olds.

This study is representative of many which demonstrate that prolonged residence in a depressed socioeconomic-educational environment retards measured intelligence; and that, despite the warnings of geneticists, children tend to measure higher in intelligence from one decade to another. The tentative conclusion is that this increase in measured, functioning intelligence is the result of better schools for more people. Increased test sophistication, in an era where most children are exposed to tests from their early school years, may also have something to do with the results.

It has been demonstrated that Negro children from Louisiana measure higher in IQ the closer to New Orleans they dwell. Presumably, New Orleans has the best schools in the state, and the influence of the New Orleans school program diminishes with distance. Klineberg (1935), the author of this study, has also demonstrated that the longer Negro children from the South live in New York City and attend New York schools, the higher their IQ's will be. By the third emigree generation, they test about the same as their non-Negro peers, whereas genetically similar Negro children in the deep South test substantially lower than the national average. This difference shows up even for first-generation emigree children: those who have been in New York City for a short period of time test 81 IQ; those who have been there for two to three years test 84.5; and those who have lived there for longer than four years test 87 IQ. Klineberg offers some evidence to demonstrate that selective migration (the fact that the brighter Negroes move out of the South) is not responsible for this phenomenon. Certain of his more crucial findings have been independently found within a population of Negro emigree children in Philadelphia, Pennsylvania (Lee, 1951).

Knobloch and Pasamanick (1960) found no differences in infant intelligence-test scores between white and nonwhite babies at 40 weeks of age, but found that (for example) their language intelligence scores differed by 16 points at the age of 3, in favor of the white youngsters. The major reason for this difference, they believe is socioeconomic influence: the nonwhite youngsters have had fewer advantages and less stimulation.

Lesser, Fifer, and Clark (1965) have conducted an ambitious study of mental abilities of children, both in terms of their social class and their cultural origin. They worked with 6- and 7-year-olds, and studied the intellectual variables of verbal ability, reasoning, number ability, and space conceptualization. Their different cultural groups were Chinese, Jewish, Negro, and Puerto Rican, and the social classes they compared middle- and lower-class groups.

They found extremely significant results according to social class for each of the mental abilities they studied, with middle-class children doing better; but also found rather interesting cultural differences. For example, Jewish youngsters were significantly better than all other groups in verbal ability (this is determined with the effects of social class statistically controlled). Chinese ranked first in reasoning, Jewish first in numerical ability, while Jewish youngsters did least well in space conceptualization. Their Negro and Puerto Rican children generally fared less well than the Chinese and Jewish youngsters.

They also report sex differences, with the boys in their study doing better than the girls on verbal ability (most studies report the opposite), as well as on space conceptualization (a finding in line with most other studies in the literature).

Kent and Davis (1957), in a very different type of study, found that different types of parental discipline were associated with very different child IQ levels. They separated a sample of the parents of 213 children into the following four categories of family discipline:

1. *Demanding* parents, who "set high standards . . . which take the child's weakness too little into account . . . provide good opportunities for the child to learn, and the home is a stimulating one, but they expect him to conform to a model of what they think he should be. This model is inflexible and they are intolerant of any departure from it" (pp. 27–28).

2. *Overanxious* parents, who "tend to be ambitious for their child, but in particular . . . are ceaselessly anxious lest he fall short of what they expect. . . . Their model is inconstant, although it may be emphatic. Also, they tend to be inconsistent in their use of reward and punishment; they are sometimes indulgent and sometimes intolerant, because they are apprehensive and uncertain. They sap the child's confidence. . ." (p. 28).

3. *Normal* parents, who "are tolerant and patient, although firm . . . placidly enjoy each of their children and are affectionate toward them" (p. 28).

4. *Unconcerned* parents, who are content if their child keeps out of trouble and does not make demands on them, are haphazard and inconsistent in their use of punishment.

The authors report no particular relation between fathers' occupation and discipline category, although there was a slight but nonsignificant tendency for fathers in the overanxious class to be in the lowest occupational category.

Kent and Davis administered the Binet test of intelligence (among other tests) to these children, and found that the IQ's of the children of demanding parents averaged 124; of overanxious parents, 107; of normal parents, 110; and of unconcerned parents, 97. Tests of statistical significance showed the demanding parents' children to be significantly brighter, the unconcerned parents' children significantly less bright, than the children of "normal" parents.

In other words (although undoubtedly at a severe emotional cost), effectively "driving" and highly stimulating parents produce bright youngsters.

To summarize, socioeconomic class is indisputably related to intellectual level. How much of this relation is due to heredity and how much to differential learning opportunities is by no means clear. Educational opportunities apparently affect measured IQ: where children have better educational opportunities, either as a result of migration from a disadvantaged area, or because of the passage of time, or because of parental demands on them, average IQ's rise or are found to be higher than those of children under less favorable circumstances. The longer the residence of a child in a disadvantaged area, the lower his IQ is, on the average, likely to be. In one such area, differences of more than 20 IQ points have been reported in favor of 6-year-olds over 16-year-olds.

The Subcultural or Simple Mental Defective

We have already defined the group of simple mental defectives as neurologically and physically normal children testing below about 70 IQ on standard intelligence tests. Dressed in good clothes, and silent, they cannot be distinguished from normal children. Ordinarily, their IQ is not below 50, and the overwhelming majority come from the most disadvantaged of the social classes (Sarason, 1953). They comprise perhaps 2 percent of the American population—a relatively small percentage, but a tremendous number: more than 4 million persons if we use as our base a United States census of 200 million population. From their ranks comes a disproportionate number of relief, charity, delinquent, criminal, and promiscuous persons, although (see Charles, 1953) even in this marginal group a majority seems to be self-supporting and law-abiding.

Intimate experience with, and deep interest in, this group has earlier led the present author (McCandless, 1952, pp. 684–685) to formulate two hypotheses concerning the way in which subcultural mental deficiency develops:

First, the environment from which the subcultural mentally defective person comes is one providing minimal opportunity for the learning of skills subsumed under the term *intelligence.*

Second, the environment from which the subcultural mentally defective person comes is one in which he has had maximal opportunity to learn "self-defeating" techniques—expectancies of failure, absolute as opposed to relative thinking, concrete as opposed to abstract thinking, belief in his essential worthlessness, and so on. Ferguson's thinking (1954, 1956) is also relevant in this connection.

Study after study (see McCandless, 1952; Sarason, 1953) reveals the hopelessness of the environment from which such children come: stark poverty, parental abandonment, social humiliation, rejection and defeat; parental drunkenness, feeble-mindedness, and psychosis; school failure and rejection by peers, progressively increasing with age; malnutrition; cultural barrenness of the home; parental indifference to the child's educational progress and community success; poor health, bad teeth, retarded growth.

It has been demonstrated that a relatively simple and circumscribed experience of failure can prevent children from taking advantage of practice that, under ordinary circumstances, would improve their score on intelligence-test items (Lantz, 1945). Such failure had the greatest influence on items that test the "thinking process." It has also been demonstrated (Kendig and Richmond, 1940) that schizophrenics—the most seriously ill of the psychotics—do poorly on items involving motivation and concentration. Such people seem to have much in common with the "simple" mental defectives. If circumscribed experiences of failure and frustration can interfere so markedly with intellectual performance, it seems plausible that a lifetime of frustration will interfere far more. Such experiences characterize the lives of children and adults who belong to the group of subcultural mental defectives. In addition, of course, their lives are impoverished in terms of sheer cultural opportunities to learn.

Kephart (1940) has demonstrated that the longer simple defectives remained in their homes, the lower their IQ's were likely to be. Upon transfer to a relatively privileged institution, where there were about two employees to every seven children, the pattern of IQ change reversed itself, particularly during the first year of residence. However, it should be stated that many of the children were tested under conditions of stress before being admitted to the institution. This fact would accentuate the picture of their steadily dropping IQ while in the community and in their own homes, and exaggerate the gain they made while in the institution, where tests were given by highly skilled examiners under standard and relaxed conditions after the children had begun to feel at ease.

The influence of the environment varies, however, according to the type of child. Kephart and Strauss (1940), in a study of children at the Wayne County Training School, separated children who were brain-damaged from those who were neurologically normal, and checked the rate of mental growth they had shown before and after admission to the institution. They concluded that neurologically normal, mentally retarded children were more sensitive to environmental influence than children of about the same IQ who have suffered neurological damage.

In somewhat similar studies, Clarke and Clarke (1954, 1958, 1960) and Clarke, Clarke and Reiman (1958) report on the effects of extremely bad backgrounds as opposed to relatively favorable backgrounds on the later intelligence changes of mentally retarded persons committed to institutions (which, presumably, were more of a change for the better for the former or "bad background" than for the latter or "good background" group).

They rated the homes, considering "very bad ratings" as no fixed abode, no fit person in charge, home conditions bad, considerable neglect, irregular school attendance due to neglect, gross poverty, crime in home, child found begging, and so on.

Clarke and Clarke present a complex analysis of results, of which the following is typical: subjects coming from very bad homes, following institutionalization, gain an average of 11.1 IQ points in their first three years of institutional residence, while those from less pathologic homes gain only 4.5 points (this presumably represents a contrast effect). The influence of the new environment loses potency in the second three years of institutionalization, the gain for the "very bad home" group going down to 5.1, although their over-all six-year gain was 16.2 IQ points, a highly significant figure. During the second three years of institutionalization, the "good home group" gained 5.7 points, for a total six-year gain of 10.2 IQ points. The difference, although lessening with time, still favors those for whom the institution was, relatively speaking, a great improvement over their former circumstances.

Mundy (1957), in a study done in Britain, supplies evidence that the stimulation provided by community living results in more intellectual gain than residence in an institution for the mentally retarded. She matched twenty-eight mentally retarded women between 18 and 50 years of age who had left the institution with twenty-eight who remained, and found that, over about a two-year period, those residing in the community had gained about 11 points in IQ, whereas those who remained in the institution had gained only about 2 points.

How do subcultural mentally defective children function as adults? A number of studies, of which one by Charles (1953) is representative, indicate that although they do not do well, they do better than might be expected. Charles traced 127 children from an earlier study of opportunity-room children, all of whom had tested below 70 IQ (the average was about 60), and made as full an investigation as possible of them when they were between their mid-thirties and late forties. A disproportionate number—over 15 percent—of the group had died (twice as many as the national average; and of those dead, almost one third—mostly males—had died violently). More than one third had been entirely self-sufficient economically during their adult lives; fewer than half had had assistance from public relief funds. A smaller percentage than would be expected (on the basis of the national average) had married, although this was partly attributable to the fact that a number of the group were or had been institutionalized (about 18 percent either were in institutions for the mentally defective or psychotic, or had been institutionalized and then discharged). Those who had married averaged 2.03 children, a figure slightly lower than the national average. Those children of the original group who could be reached for testing (seventy-three in number) ranged in IQ from 50 to 138, with an average of 95.

Only two of these children were so retarded that they had to be institutionalized.

The divorce rate of the group was about the same as that for the nation; a greater percentage of the group than of the population as a whole lived in single-family houses; and over half of them owned or were buying their own homes (about the same as the national average). The men were, for the most part, laborers; the women housekeepers. Of the sample that could be reached, about 40 percent had been involved in some breach of the law. Twenty of the 127 were retested for IQ. When scores from the same test that had originally been used were averaged, the figure was 58 (about the same as the original score; but this particular test places adults at some disadvantage). A more modern and widely used test gave an average IQ of 81 for these twenty subjects. As is typical of subcultural mentally defective persons, an IQ based on verbal items was far inferior to one based on performance items (the respective IQ's were 72 and 88).

Miller (1965) has followed this group into its early 50s, and finds them, in middle age, still functioning intellectually, physically, and socially at a level far above the original expectation.

Levine and Dysinger (1964) believe that success in life outside the institution is a function of performance intelligence, those subjects with high performance IQ's, regardless of the pattern of their intelligence, doing better than those with low performance IQ's.

Another interesting study of prediction of success post-institutionalization was done by Krishef (1959). He finds that his subjects who rebelled against the institution (acted out or ran away) actually adjusted better to the community than those who were good inmates prior to parole. Simplicity of environment, according to Krishef, also plays a role in post-institutional adjustment: Adjustment is better in rural than urban settings.

Probably more mothers belonging to the group of subcultural mental defectives have illegitimate babies than is true for the general population. It is also likely that more of their babies are placed for adoption than the babies of mothers who are intellectually and economically more advantaged. Are such babies in turn mentally defective? We have already reviewed some evidence that this is not the case. The average of the children who could be tested in Charles' study approached normal IQ, and ranged as high as 138 IQ (very bright, or superior). In another study involving 312 children separated from their mothers before they were 4 years of age (Snygg, 1938), the children of the 98 mothers whose IQ's were less than 70 averaged 91 IQ (low normal), even though their foster-home placements were not in any sense ideal. The over-all correlation between the IQ's of children and their true mothers was .13, accounting for less than 2 percent of the variance.

Speer (1940) studied a group of children whose mothers' average IQ was 49. The IQ's of children separated from their mothers before they were 2 years of age were normal. The average for this small group of twelve children was 100.5. The average IQ for a group of sixteen children who stayed with their mothers until they were from 12 to 15 years of age was 53.

Another study (Stippich, 1940) reports the results from an investigation of children born to forty-eight mentally defective mothers with IQ averages between 60 and 63 (depending on which of three intelligence tests was used in computing IQ). All the mothers had been legally declared feeble-minded, and had been institutionalized. The children had been separated from their families before they were 1 year of age, and placed in boarding homes or institutions that offered less than ideal care for them. Even under such unfavorable circumstances, the children averaged 83 IQ at an average age of 5 years, or a minimum of 20 IQ points higher than their mothers. This study also included the similarly separated children of twenty-nine mothers whose IQ's averaged 102. These youngsters averaged 97 IQ. Since it has not usually been found that environments other than rigorously depriving ones (such as impersonal institutional life) affect children before the age of about 18 months, this study provides support for a genetic point of view. In similar but deprived environments, children of brighter mothers are brighter at the age of 5 than the offspring of duller mothers. Even so, the children of the mentally defective mothers were a good 20 points higher in IQ than their mothers.

This section has offered evidence indicating that the longer children live in very depressed environments (including homes where the mother is mentally defective), the lower their average IQ is likely to be. There are indications that environmental reversal can change this developmental direction, although some of the evidence is weak. Several studies report normality or near-normality for children of feeble-minded parents placed early in foster homes, and report that there is no practically significant relation between the IQ of the mother and that of their true children when these are separated from the mother early. The most pessimistic of the studies still reveals an upward differential of a full 20 points between the IQ's of the feeble-minded mothers and their children, even though the children had been less than optimally placed.

Language, Intelligence, and the Culture

Although our present tests of intelligence are very useful, they also have obvious defects, and their results are frequently misused. The definition of intelligence used in this book has been the rather traditional one of problem-solving ability. This ability, at least in conventional school programs, depends heavily on being able to handle abstractions; and these, in turn, are dealt with best by children who are high in verbal and number ability. Most of our current intelligence tests include many items involving these abilities. Of eight "primary abilities" separated by Thurstone, two have to do with words and word usage: the factor *V,* or verbal comprehension; and the factor *W,* or word fluency. Wechsler (1944), the author of probably the most widely used individual test of intelligence for adults and one of the more widely used tests for children, reports that scores from the vocabulary subtest of the total scale, composed (for the adult scale) of 42 words that the subject is asked to define, correlate .85 with the entire scale. Such a correlation accounts for almost three fourths of the variance of the full-scale IQ (72 percent). It has been pointed out that there is substantial evidence to indicate that performance (nonverbal) problems are solved better by those who give verbal labels to the tasks; it has been clearly demonstrated (Spiker, 1956) that children learn new tasks more efficiently when they have names for the elements of the process or for the pieces of equipment that must be manipulated successfully in order to demonstrate learning.

In other words, we are safe enough in saying that anything affecting the use of words probably has an effect on intelligence as we now measure it.

Vocabulary and general adequacy of speech vary by socioeconomic class. Speech is poorer in form and articulation, less in amount, more restrictive and less precise for children at lower socioeconomic levels than for those at higher social levels (see Irwin, 1948). The only glimmer of hope we have for predicting the later intelligence of children tested as infants lies, as has been pointed out, in measuring their speech sounds (Catalano and McCarthy, 1954). Children reared with scant adult attention, who are relatively isolated, or who live in institutions are retarded even more in their speech than in their general IQ level. This retardation has been shown to exist as early as 2 months of age. Children who, at elementary-school ages, test at the mentally retarded or borderline level started talking later than children who measure normal or bright. At least during the early years of their lives (presumably because they communicate primarily with each other, and depend to a lesser degree on adults), twins and triplets test lower in both speech and intelligence than singletons, although much of this ground is regained by school age. Their speech seems to be even more retarded than can be accounted for by their somewhat lower intelligence-test scores. Although the evidence is not entirely clear-cut, children who are bilingual during their preschool years—that is, typically, those whose homes use one language, while their schools use a different one—test lower than monoglots (speakers of one language). Although social class is involved, since children from such homes are rather more frequently from lower- than from upper-class homes, the effect seems greater than can be accounted for by social class alone.[4]

As we have seen, social class seems to be directly related to vocabulary level; yet children from some middle-class homes have been shown to have low vocabularies, while children from some lower-class homes have good vocabularies. One author (Milner, 1951) provides evidence indicating why there are such exceptions (at the same time presenting data to show that the child's language status and his socioeconomic status correlate somewhere between .78 and .86, depending on which of two statistical techniques is used).

The 21 high-scorers in Milner's study of forty-two Negro first-graders came from homes ranging from upper-lower to lower-upper, this latter being the highest social class included in the study. The high-scorers were distinguished as a group from the twenty-one low-scorers by such factors as eating breakfast and dinner with their families, and engaging in conversation during these times. Their parents tended to use verbal methods of discipline, whereas physical punishment was more characteristic of the low-scoring children. High-scorers more frequently were expected to look after their own possessions and/or room, and received more praise and affection from their parents. More high- than low-scorers had been exposed to baby-sitters; and they went to bed later, frequently as late as 10 at night. Low-scorers were "bribed" with small gifts of money more frequently than high-scorers. The high-scorers, as might be expected, possessed more books, and indicated that their mothers and fathers more frequently read to them. More low-scorers said they could not recall ever feeling "real happy," and were more infrequently able to recall instances or situations in which they had felt happy. Low-scorers more frequently possessed as reading material only funny books or schoolbooks.

Such factors as those listed above are, of course, strongly related to social class; but where there are variations in language ability within a social class, it seems plausible that such variables as parental conversation, attention, praise, and so on, could account for the differences between low- and high-scores.

The hypothesis just formulated is supported by a study of Irwin's (1960). Irwin secured the cooperation of a large group of mothers whose husbands were mostly skilled, semiskilled, and unskilled laborers. Ordinarily, such mothers do little reading to their children at any age, and almost certainly none in the first year or so of their babies' lives. Irwin persuaded fifty-five mothers to read aloud to their children for at least ten minutes a day from the time they were little more than babies

---

4 For a comprehensive review of this area, see McCarthy (1954).

(1-year-old). The participation in the study of another, control group of mothers, was elicited by offers to check on the development of their babies. Otherwise no change was made in the interaction between them and their children.

Irwin measured the youngsters' speech development regularly and found great differences in all phases of speech by the time the children were 20 months of age. The study is especially provocative when we consider the relations that have been found between speech and intelligence. Irwin reports the experimental mothers' amazement and chagrined amusement: "You asked us to read ten minutes a day," many exclaimed, "but I can't get away from that kid. He wants me to read to him all the time."

Once established during the preschool years, can a child's language level be changed? Since language is so closely related both to intelligence and to school achievement, the answer to this question is important. Dawe (1942) attempted to answer the query in a study that involved eleven pairs of children resident in an orphanage. When she began her study, the children ranged in age from 3 years, 7 months to 6 years, 10 months. Her experimental, or trained, children were very carefully matched with the control children for school group attended, sex, chronological and mental age, IQ, and vocabulary. All the children were going either to the orphanage nursery school or to kindergarten, and Dawe did her speech and language training on weekends for a total of ninety-two hours over a period of about seven and a half months.

At the beginning of her study, the experimental group averaged low-normal (IQ 80.6) as did her control group (IQ 81.5). The training consisted of help in understanding words and concepts, looking at and discussing pictures, and listening to poems and stories. Occasionally she took them on short excursions, although this proved to be difficult within the framework of the orphanage.

Dawe's experimental group of children gained an average of more than 14 points in IQ during the training period, whereas the controls dropped an average of 2 points. At the beginning of training, average IQ's of the two groups were almost identical. At the end of the study they differed enormously, not only on the test originally given to them but on another form of the test. Even on a performance test there was an average difference of 5.5 points in favor of the experimental children, although language presumably does not greatly affect success on such a test (an assumption which, as we have pointed out, is rather dubious). This latter difference, however, was not a significant one. Dawe's training did not include test-coaching, although her method of teaching may have helped the experimental children to approach more efficiently problems with elements similar to those included in intelligence tests.

Both groups of children gained in vocabulary, the experimentals $17\frac{1}{2}$

score points (words), the controls 10 score points. The experimentals gained significantly more than the controls. Information-test scores also increased significantly more for the experimental than for the control children. In addition, Dawe obtained measures of such factors as attentiveness and intellectual interest. Dramatic improvements in almost all aspects of these important traits occurred for the experimental group, but such measures were not available for the controls.

Animal Research

It has been pointed out that for practical reasons studies using humans as subjects cannot throw definitive light on the relative influence of environment (social learning) and heredity on the development of human intelligence, nor on any other complex psychological trait. The research worker cannot subject his human subjects to extreme environmental or hereditary variations; nor, indeed, can he exercise any very rigorous control over his subjects' environment or heredity. These considerations apply to a far lesser degree to research work done with animals.

It is unusual to include animal studies in a volume devoted to child development. We have done it here, however, because of the practical social importance of knowing to what degree the environment can modify the organism. We can make *no direct translation* or *application* to human beings of research results or theories based on animals; but *suggestions* about human development may, and frequently do, arise from such results. Further, if we make the reasonably tenable assumption that animals are simpler organisms and are more "genetically and instinctually bound" than man, then we can argue with some force that if environment affects an animal to some degree, it is not unlikely to affect the more complicated, self-determining, adaptable child or man to an even greater degree.

This section is not designed to include a comprehensive review of all environmental studies of animals, but selected studies will be reviewed and general conclusions drawn concerning the effects of early experiences on later development—emotional, social, and physical as well as intellectual. Most of these research studies have been suggested by the work of Hebb (1949, 1955), whose theories have already been discussed.

ISOLATION AND PROBLEM-SOLVING

One of the most elaborate experiments, although not the earliest in the series, was done by Thompson and Heron (1954). These authors used as subjects twenty-six Scottish terriers, all of them descendants of one litter, hence genetically quite similar to one another. Thirteen of the animals were reared as pets, in private homes or in the laboratories, from weaning time (at about 4 weeks of age) until they were about 8 months of age, when they were put in ordinary dog cages. During this period the dogs were exercised outdoors every day when the weather permitted, were fed well, and had a moderate amount of experience with humans.

Thirteen of their brothers, sisters, and cousins were reared very differently after weaning. Three conditions of isolation were imposed on them. Two dogs experienced *severe isolation,* spending all their time up to between 7 and 10 months of age in one of two types of rather small cages (30 by 40 by 60 inches). Every day they changed cages through a sliding door. One cage was kept in darkness, whereas light was allowed to enter the other; the dogs therefore spent every other day in the dark. Eight pups experienced *moderate restriction,* two to three of them per group living for 8 to 10 months in ordinary dog cages whose walls were cardboard-covered, so that they could not see out. Light came in from the top of the cage. They had contact with humans about ten minutes a day while the cages were cleaned. Three pups were *slightly restricted,* and lived for about 7 months in cages similar to those of the moderately restricted group, except that the cardboard was removed from the front and top of their cages. They thus had considerable perceptual experience, but only of the environment immediately outside their cage.

At the end of this "experimental treatment" period, the restricted animals were handled precisely as were the normally reared ones. The experimental animals were reported to be quite hyperactive after their release, and for the first few weeks to months demonstrated considerable sensorimotor disturbance: they bumped into things, had trouble with stairs and steps, and so on. After this time, however, they seemed normal enough. The experimental and control groups lived under similar conditions for somewhat more than a year after the end of the period of isolation. At this time, "intelligence" testing of the animals was begun.

Although very simple from an adult human point of view, these tests fit well enough with our definition of intelligence as problem-solving behavior. Six tests were given the animals, an orientation Test I and II, a barrier Test I and II, an attention test, and a maze test consisting of eighteen different arrangements of wire panels within a 17-foot square maze. These arrangements ranged from very simple to rather complex.

For the first orientation test the animal was placed in corner D of an 8-foot square, as shown in Figure 8.1. He was given ten trials on which he ran to food at corner A. All of the animals that were given this test—eight normals, three slightly restricted, five moderately restricted, and two severely restricted—easily acquired this habit in ten trials. After the habit had been learned and while the animal was watching, the food pan was switched 90° to corner C (to the left rather than to the

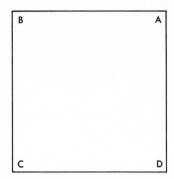

Figure 8.1   A diagram of the testing situation for
Thompson and Heron's orientation Tests I and II.

right of the dog). Attention was further brought to the food by banging
the pan on the floor and holding the food out so that the dog could see
it. Five trials were then run for all animals. The pan was then changed
to corner B, and another five runs were made by the animals; after this,
another trial from D to C was given; then two trials from D to A; and
a final trial using corner B as a starting point, requiring the animal to
move to corner A to get his food. An error was scored when a dog did
not go directly from his starting corner to the food.

The average number of correct trials out of fourteen tests was 13.7
for the normally reared (control) animals, but only 5.9 for the restricted
(experimental) dogs. The poorest of the control animals did better than
the best of the experimental group. The difference was highly significant,
P being less than .001. All the experimental animals continued to go to
corner A first before proceeding to the new position, although they were
eventually able to locate the food.

Orientation Test II was slightly more complicated. A starting box,
open on one side, was placed in the middle of the square so that its
opening faced wall AB, as shown in Figure 8.1. The animal went to food
located in corner A for ten trials; the box was then rotated to face in
turn walls BC, AD, and CD. One trial was given in each position. The
starting box was then rotated back to its first position for three trials.
After that the food was moved to corner B for one trial, and the dog,
before being placed in the starting box, was taken to it and allowed to
sniff it. For these seven test trials the control dogs averaged 5.1 correct
runs (that is, ran directly to the corner where the food had been placed
rather than to an incorrect corner); but the experimental animals averaged only 2.7 correct trials (P for this difference was again less than .001).
Only one of the experimental animals did better than the poorest control, doing as well as three other controls. The least efficient control dog
had experienced the shortest period of time living as a pet.

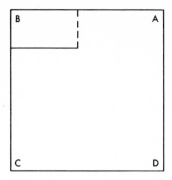

Figure 8.2 A diagram of the approximate arrangement for Thompson and Heron's barrier Tests I and II.

In barrier Test I, a chicken-wire barrier was extended at right angles from wall BC about two feet from corner B, as shown by the solid line in Figure 8.2. The food was placed behind it as the dog watched, and after he had had five trials of going from corner C to get the food before the barrier was put in place. A correct trial consisted of the dog's avoiding an error zone—that is, the dog was correct if he angled from corner C out past the end of the barrier and then went directly in to get the food. Control animals averaged 6.75 correct runs out of ten trials; experimental animals 2.4. This difference was significant at less than the .001 level. The experimental animals again manifested behavioral rigidity, frequently moving straight forward from corner C to the barrier, then circling it.

For barrier Test II an addition was made to the barrier, as represented by the dotted line in Figure 8.2. The animals were placed, one at a time, in this partial enclosure after having been allowed first to sniff the food outside the barrier. Time for reaching the food was measured for each trial. To get at the food, of course, the animals had to turn their backs on it, run through the opening, and around. The average time for the control animals was 29.4 seconds. The experimentals on the average required 72.1 seconds. This difference is significant at less than the .05 level, and there was only one case of overlap between the groups.

Another test was designed to measure the dogs' attention span. After they had learned to go immediately to the one of two doors behind which they had watched the experimenter place a pan of food, they were tested to determine how long they could "keep this in mind." That is to say, they were required to wait behind a door for periods of time ranging from 5 to 300 seconds before being allowed to run to the easily opened door behind which they had watched the placement of the food. Even without delay, six of the seven experimental dogs were never able to handle this problem, and the one successful dog solved the problem for a delay of only 25 seconds. The *least* apt of the five control animals tested handled a 50-second delay. These differences are obviously highly significant, indicating that deprivation interferes with attention span.

The final test given was the maze test. All dogs were given five easy trials to get them accustomed to the maze, then were given progressively more difficult problems. There were no group differences for the easy problems, and the average score for the control dogs was lowered by one pregnant female, who tired easily and gave up. Even when her scores were included, the controls averaged a total of 237 errors, whereas the experimentals made an average of 344 mistakes. This difference is significant at less than the .01 level. All dogs learned in a similar fashion: that is, both groups steadily improved in performance, and the learning curve showing the effects of practice was the same in shape for the two groups. At all points on the curve, however, the experimentals did less well than the controls.

This striking study has been reviewed in detail because it has so many implications concerning the influence of early stimulus or environmental deprivation on later problem-solving behavior. Dogs reared in isolation as puppies, even when given a long period (more than a year) of living in a relatively normal environment, clearly do less well than dogs reared as pets on a series of tasks that seem to involve a factor we could call intelligence.

It has been pointed out that we cannot apply animal research directly to humans. On the other hand, the implications of this study (done with higher mammals) are too striking to be completely ignored or dismissed. The authors describe the deficit of the dogs as "a lack of ability to discriminate relevant from irrelevant aspects of the environment, or to adapt to changes made in the experimental situation. There also seems to be some disturbance in the attention processes of the restricted animals" (p. 29). It will be remembered that Hofstaetter (1954), in an analysis of common factors in intelligence-test items for infants and preschoolers, found that the items thought to measure intelligent behavior before the age of speech are characterized by a factor he calls "sensorimotor alertness." This factor is of great importance up to 20 months of age. The major factor in intelligence-test items appropriate for children from about 20 to 40 months of age seems to be "persistence," or "a tendency to act in accordance with an established set rather than upon interfering stimulation" (p. 162). Certainly, the deficiencies of the restricted dogs in the Thompson and Heron study could be described by Hofstaetter's words. In fact, the two descriptions are almost interchangeable. Persistence certainly involves attention.

Results similar to those obtained by Thompson and Heron have also been obtained (see Bingham and Griffiths, 1952; Thompson, 1955) using rats as subjects and employing similar research techniques.

SPECIAL STIMULATION IN INFANCY

Other investigators have secured results congruent with those reported above. In one study (Gibson and Walk, 1956) rats were reared in identical surroundings and with identical treatment, except that on the walls of the experimental animals' cages hung pieces of black metal cut into the shapes of equilateral triangles and circles. The cages of the control animals had blank walls. For most of the white rats used in this study, hereditary influences were controlled by splitting litters, putting half of one litter in an experimental and half in a control group. At 90 days of age and without any "meaning" ever having been attached to circles or triangles, the animals were set to learn a discrimination problem involving these two geometric shapes. The rats exposed to the two stimuli proved far superior to the control group in learning the problem, the difference between groups being significant at much less than the .01 level.

Forgus (1956) has done several studies along the same general lines. One of these exposed groups of eleven baby rats to cutout forms—a circle, a triangle, a cross, and a square. The cages of the animals were blanked in, so that the forms were the conspicuous elements in the environment. These forms were placed on the walls of their cages as soon as their eyes had opened (at 16 days of age) and moved around from time to time to avoid direct association (meaning) between them and obtaining food and water. The forms were kept in cages until the rats were 41 days of age.

Another group of rats was similarly reared, except that the forms were not put into their cages until they were 41 days old, and were left there until the animals were 66 days of age. Appropriate groups of control animals (in most cases, members of the same litter as the experimental animals) were reared identically, except that they were not exposed to the forms.

The rats that had been exposed to the forms from infancy were placed in a discrimination situation similar to that in the Gibson and Walk (1956) study when they were 41 days of age. The animals used as controls for this group also started to learn the discrimination (between a triangle and a cross) at this age. Animals who had been exposed to the forms only from the time they were 41 days old, and their controls, began the discrimination problem when they were 66 days old. After the problem had been learned, the forms were rotated 90° to see how well the rats could generalize. Table 8.1 shows the results for the four different groups.

The figures of statistical significance for this table indicate clearly that an advantage accrues both in learning and in generalizing to the rats exposed early in life to the forms. They did better in learning and generalizing than rats who were exposed later in life, and the late-exposed rats in turn did better than rats never exposed to the forms

Table 8.1   *Number of Trials Required to Learn a Discrimination Problem by Rats Exposed to Forms Early and Later in Life, and Their Controls.*

	NUMBER OF TRIALS REQUIRED FOR LEARNING	NUMBER OF ERRORS MADE ON GENERALIZATION TEST
Forms in infancy	33.8	4.7
Forms at 41 days	39.4	11.1
Early controls	48.2	19.7
Late controls	46.5	19.6

PRINTED WITH PERMISSION OF J. BLACKBURN, *Canadian J. Psychol.*, FROM FORGUS (1956), WITH APPRECIATION TO THE UNIVERSITY OF TORONTO PRESS.

before discrimination-testing. The early and late controls showed no difference in their discrimination learning, although the animals tested later moved through each discrimination problem faster than those tested earlier; they seemed more confident or less fearful.

In another interesting study, Forgus (1954) reared rats in three different types of environment. Group I lived in a good-sized black-painted cage, in which a number of white objects, such as blocks, alleys, tunnels, elevated platforms, and inclined planes, were placed around the walls so that the animals had free access to them. Group II rats lived in a similar cage, but a clear plastic frame was placed so that they could see but not reach the playthings. Group III lived in small, black, unfurnished boxes.

On various tests, Forgus found that Group I and II animals moved around faster than Group III animals, were less emotional and frightened, and showed much more varied behavior. They were also much more efficient at a problem that involved insight. But where visual discrimination was necessary to solve a problem, Group II (the group that had looked but not manipulated) usually did somewhat better than Group I. Forgus reasoned that this was because Group II animals had spent their lives being able to do nothing *but look*. Consequently, when problem-solving depended on using their eyes, they would do better than animals reared like Group I, whereas Group I animals would do better than animals who grew up under conditions similar to those of Group II at problems demanding manipulation, and in situations involving no visual cues.

Forgus tested this reasoning in an experiment (1955b) in which his Group I and Group II animals were reared in the fashion just described. They then started discrimination learning in a maze that provided visual cues. These were removed before learning was complete; and the experiment was continued to see which group learned faster and made fewer errors. Group I, the "visuomotor" group, learned in an average of 19.5

trials, and made an average of 60.5 errors during the learning. But Group II (visual only) required an average of 26.6 trials, and made 83.1 errors on the average. These differences are statistically significant.

Forgus, with Luchins (Luchins and Forgus, 1955), has performed another experiment of the same general type. In this study the experimental animals were brought up in cages equipped with blocks, alleys, and elevated platforms, and were played with by humans for about an hour a day. The controls lived in a barren cage without much contact with people. Experimental tests showed that in a new situation the experimentals were much more confident: they moved around far more. They explored their environment more (a greater number of alternate routes to a goal was used by them than by the controls). They showed more insightful and efficient behavior in solving problems than the controls; and they showed that they could more rapidly drop an old method of problem-solving that had become inefficient.

Summary

It is difficult to assign differential responsibility to "heredity" and "environment" (or nature and nurture) for intellectual development. Since no organism can function without both a heredity and an environment, and since environment begins to exert its influence at least as early as conception, it is scientifically impractical to say that such and such a percentage of the variance in intelligence is accounted for by genes, and the remainder by environment. However, since the nature-nurture question arises urgently in practical matters (such as early adoption of children, or placement for adoption of children from inferior social stock), it is important to review what evidence we have concerning the respective contributions made to intellectual development by environment and heredity. Some relatively recent animal research gives more definitive information on the matter than does research with humans. Both nature and nurture can be more effectively controlled for animals than for humans, and the generation span for most animals is much shorter than that for humans. Selective breeding, impossible in scientific studies of humans, is acceptable for animals; and severe environmental manipulations that cannot be performed with humans are possible with animal populations. Animals, of course, are not verbal.

This chapter has reviewed research literature on eight major topics:

1. Research on adopted children indicates that they are on the whole brighter as a group than own or true children, probably for at least two reasons: severely retarded children are seldom placed for adoption; and adopted children are ordinarily sent to relatively superior homes, where they are very much wanted.

Children of socially inferior parents (whose mothers are feeble-minded or of borderline intelligence and/or whose fathers occupy a low socio-economic status), when placed in average and superior homes, are more intelligent than their true parents. Indeed, they approach the intellectual level of their foster parents, particularly when they are placed in adoptive homes very early. However, a positive correlation between the intelligence of foster children and that of their *true* parents has been found, although this correlation accounts for little of the variance in children's intelligence. Studies on this topic show that, when adoption occurs early, true parents' intelligence (or education) accounts for between 0 and 10 percent of the variance in the intelligence of their children. It is doubtful, however, whether the adopted children of very inferior parents will average as high in intelligence as adopted children whose parents are normal or superior in intelligence. The evidence on this point is not clear.

2. Studies of twins indicate that the correlation of intelligence for *identical* twins reared together is very high—in the .80s and .90s; for *fraternal* twins reared in the same home correlations are lower (usually in the .70s); and for *nontwin siblings* reared together, the correlations cluster around .50. The correlation between intelligence for identical twins reared *separately* is lower; and the more disparate the environments in which they have been reared, the less similar they are in intelligence. Some of the correlation in intelligence between identical twins may be due to the similarity of social stimuli they evoke.

3. Evidence concerning the effects of residence in conventional institutions on the development of very young children is quite clear: standard institutional living exerts (at least temporarily, and probably lastingly) retarding and disturbing influences on intellectual and emotional growth.

Children growing up in culturally isolated areas ordinarily test low on standard intelligence tests. When families migrate from such areas to urban centers, the longer the family's residence in the urban center, the higher the children's intelligence scores.

4. Nursery-school attendance has frequently been found to be associated with gains in tested intelligence, although some careful studies have failed to show such gains. Where nursery schools have been set up in institutions for orphaned or deprived children, attendance at nursery school appears to have arrested the drop in intelligence that is typical for children who reside in institutions. When the institutional regime has been concurrently improved, nursery-school and kindergarten attendance has been accompanied by significant gains in tested intelligence, particularly for culturally deprived children.

5. Socioeconomic class is definitely related to intellectual level: the lower the social class, the lower the intelligence according to conventional measures. Lower social class is also ordinarily accompanied by inferior opportunities for education and by less encouragement from parents for conventional intellectual achievement.

6. Subcultural mentally retarded children are those who are neurologically normal, but who usually test between about 50 and 70 IQ. Most such youngsters are born and mature in families from the very lowest socioeconomic group: their childhood is harsh; they receive little intellectual stimulation at home; they do poorly in school. On two counts, therefore, they might be expected to be low in intelligence. First, they have had little opportunity to learn the skills that make for adequate performance on intelligence tests; and second, they learn many self-defeating attitudes through their repeated experiences of defeat and failure. Even so, more of them succeed as adults than might be predicted from their childhood histories.

7. Language development during infancy has been shown to be more highly related to later tests of intelligence than any other measure of infant "intelligence." With adult attention, the language development of infants can be accelerated: for example, the more reading infants have been exposed to, the more advanced their language development is likely to be. Love-oriented techniques of child-rearing, and a home atmosphere characterized by relatively high intellectual stimulation, are typical of families whose children are accelerated in language, regardless of the social class from which they come.

8. Research using animals as subjects indicates that they are retarded in problem-solving ability as a result of having spent their early months in isolation, and that isolation also appears to distort their "emotional" and "social" development. Introducing specific perceptual cues into animals' infantile environment helps them use these cues in later learning and problem-solving. Such animals perform better than animals that have not previously encountered the stimuli, even though their histories have included no *specific* learning related to the cues.

Physical Growth and Motor Development

E very facet of social and personal development is affected by the body. The first, although by no means the most profound or important, impression a person makes on others in ordinary social living is likely to be based on his physiognomy and on his body and the way he handles it. Typically, one's first comments in attempting to describe a stranger concern his physical characteristics and his age: the dimensions most commonly used in such descriptions are height, weight, general body build, coloring, and attractiveness. Unusual and striking attributes of grace or awkwardness, thinness or obesity, apparent strength or weakness, and voice pitch are also likely to be mentioned.

An individual's conception of his body appears to be closely related to his self-concept. If he thinks well of himself, he is likely to be tolerant and accepting of his body; if he is self-rejecting, he rejects his body image (Laverne C. Johnson, 1956; Secord and Jourard, 1953). Self-rejection has been found to be associated with perceived parental rejection. This perceived rejection includes notions of being regarded as unattractive, or weak, or sickly by one's parents.

The nature of one's body and its functioning probably has much significance in the development of a pattern of interests, and possibly in selecting a vocation, although there is no conclusive evidence about this relationship. It is obvious that the weak and awkward boy will not, for example, become a professional athlete. His sturdy and graceful age-mate has before him a wider range of available interests, hobbies, and occupations. Bodies and faces that are markedly unattractive by cultural standards handicap their possessor in his social and heterosexual life, and create additional problems to be solved in an existence that, for most people, is already sufficiently complex.

For many years there has persisted in the United States the stereotyped notion that one type of growth or development occurs at the expense of other types. Commonplace are the clichés: "all brawn and no brain"; "beautiful but dumb"; "the mad genius"; and their like.

Much research has been done on the relation of physical growth to other variables. The conclusions are not particularly helpful for guiding a particular child, although the generalization that "all good things cluster together" has been generally borne out. A large group of children selected because they are far above average in intelligence, will be found to be heavier, handsomer, healthier, stronger, and better coordinated, as compared with another large group of the same age and sex distribution selected because they are far below average in intelligence. However, many of these relations are the result, not of intelligence, but of social status. The bright children come from wealthier homes, which provide them with better nutrition, better schooling, and more chances for constructive physical exercise. Although height and weight may correlate better than .60 with intelligence, intelligence and motor coordination are unlikely to show a correlation higher than the low .20s.

Developmental Norms

The first step in any field of scientific endeavor is to make such descriptions and quantifications of its data and to establish *norms* based on them. Norms, of course, do not explain either growth or behavior, but they are useful in locating extremes and in charting the progress of both the normal and the atypical child.

The word *normal,* when used to describe a child, refers to one or more of his characteristics that, quantitatively, fall close to the middle of the distribution of such characteristics for a sizable and presumably representative sample of children of his age and ethnic group. *Normal,* then, means "average." It does not imply optimal or ideal, although the word often has this latter connotation. That this connotation can lead to fallacy is well illustrated by research concerning pubescence. The *average* boy reaches sexual maturity, as judged by the appearance of coarse, kinky pubic hair, some time around 14 years of age. But studies by Ames (1957), Mary Cover Jones (1957), and Mussen and Jones (1957), for example, indicate rather clearly that the *early*-maturing boy has social and psychological advantages over the late-maturer (and probably over the average-maturer). These advantages may be partially lost in middle age (Mary C. Jones, 1965). The evidence is less clear for girls. These studies will be discussed in more detail later in this chapter.

To a degree, norms restrict the range of best guesses that we must make constantly in our practical dealings with children. Since complete data about any phase of the development of children do not exist, such "best guesses" are necessary; children must be reared, taught, and counseled. Take, for example, the professional worker in a children's psychological clinic. One of his first and most important tasks is to locate the factors that have contributed to a child's problems. If the child comes from a typical middle-class family and neighborhood and his IQ measures 108, then the chances are slight that intelligence as such contributes significantly to his problem. But if his IQ is 85, the suspicion immediately arises that intelligence is an important factor. The same considerations may be applied to physical growth and motor development. Extreme deviations may be influential in producing poor adjustment or, as in the case of unusual beauty and symmetry for girls or great strength and co-ordination for boys, may aid greatly in social and personal development.

Many workers in physical growth use the term *norm* not in the sense of a statistical average but as defining the range of acceptable variation. The reader should be alert to discover the sense in which the word is being used.

Principles of Physical Growth and Motor Development

Certain general principles (each of which has significant exceptions) have emerged from research on physical growth and motor development. Two of these generalizations concern developmental direction.

The first, or *cephalocaudal,* principle refers to the fact that growth and motor development proceed, in general, from the head to the tail end of the human organism. At birth, the part of the body that most closely approximates adult size is the head; the legs least closely approximate adult size. The first effective motor control is exerted over the major muscles that lift the head from a surface when the baby is in a prone position. Later, arm, shoulder, and abdominal muscles are used so that the baby lifts his torso. Only later still are leg and thigh muscles employed so that the pelvis can be lifted clear of the surface on which the baby lies.

An adult built along the lines of a baby would be a top-heavy monstrosity. The baby's crown-rump height is approximately 60 percent of his total height; the adult's height equals only about 50 percent of his standing height.

There are exceptions to the cephalocaudal principle. For example, during the fifth and sixth weeks following conception, the fetus grows an external tail. This decreases in length during the seventh and eighth weeks, and by the time of birth has become the coccyx (end of the spine). It is also true that the baby is only somewhat less adroit in reaching and holding with his feet than with his hands. Many 6-month-olds hold the bottle efficiently between their feet as they feed themselves, but manipulation with the feet rapidly becomes less effective after the child begins to use them in the "heavy duty" of walking.

The second, or *proximodistal,* principle refers to the fact that growth and motor development proceed from the axis of the body outward to the periphery. This principle can be vividly demonstrated. The baby's early reaching is accomplished by gross movements from the shoulder. The arm and hand are used, not flexibly, but as a unit. Only well along in his first year does the baby make independent finger movements, or oppose his thumb and his finger.

The third principle is that of progression from *general* to *specific action* patterns, and from *general gross* to *specific refined control*. There has been considerable argument, some of it heated, about whether development proceeds from the general to the specific, from the specific to the general, or whether it occurs in both directions. The best conclusion that can be drawn is that the most obvious or conspicuous development is from the general to the specific, but that development in the opposite direction also occurs, and that the processes complement each other.

The infant, pricked with a pin, reacts all over his body: he cries, kicks, and thrashes with his arms. But at 6 months, he reacts much more specifically and adaptively: he may cry, but he also withdraws efficiently if withdrawal is possible. Early grasping attempts have their fulcrum at the shoulder, are crude, and involve much heaving, puffing, and grunting. By a year of age or earlier, the baby manipulates cubes and pellets with well-coordinated movements of the wrist, and with the thumb in opposition to the fingers, which operate individually or work in unison. There is minimal involvement of other bodily parts, except for the coordination of his head and eyes with what he is doing with his hands.

However, it is obvious that many discrete neural connections and specific areas of muscle growth have occurred before even the grossest motor activity is possible. In other words, the argument about the direction of motor development has little practical value; although, from the observer's point of view, the most obvious development proceeds from general to specific.

Increasingly effective *motor chaining* or *motor serial learning* also occurs. This development parallels the other types of learning that have been discussed. By *motor chaining* is meant simply that the child becomes more efficient in any motor activity he practices. Inappropriate muscle sequences drop out, and those that remain become smoother and more effective in accomplishing their purposes.

A striking illustration of the chaining process is the difference in walking between the average 18-month-old and the average 2-year-old. The former "walks all over," and he walks for the sake of walking; for the latter walking is relatively efficient and automatic and, rather than being perceived as a goal in itself, serves simply as a means of getting the child to the place where he wants to go.

In the development of highly complex motor skills, all the processes of learning and development that have been discussed occur, and in many different sequences. An accomplished Spanish dancer, for example, has moved in his or her performance from relatively crude, gross movements to refined and at first partially independent movements with the feet, legs, arms, and hands. Chaining of responses has occurred. But

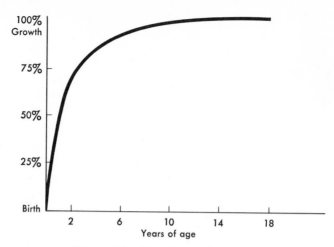

Figure 9.1   Neural growth pattern.

eventually, the separate skills, movements, and postures must be integrated—changed from specific back to the general (but a very different "general"). Only then is the performance "convincing," or "good." Such a process is necessary for all complex motor skills, including superior athletic performance as seen in boxing, swimming, or tennis.

Patterns of Physical Growth

At least three broad postnatal growth curves have been identified. The first may be called the *neural curve*. This curve, which includes growth trends of the head, the brain, the spinal cord, and the eye, is illustrated in Figure 9.1. Neural growth is rapid during infancy, changing rather abruptly to a much slower rate during early childhood.

The second pattern of growth might be called the sexual or *reproductive*. Figure 9.2 illustrates the development of the primary sex characteristics—genitals, ovaries, and testes. The secondary sex characteristics—breasts, body and facial hair—follow a similar pattern of development. There is a slight increment in early infancy, but almost no change between late infancy and late childhood. A striking increase in rate of growth occurs before and around puberty, followed by a slower gain that tapers off in and during adolescence, although testes continue to grow until the middle twenties.

The third growth pattern is the one most obvious to the casual observer of the child. It may be called the *somatic* pattern, and includes such easily observable characteristics as length of arms and legs, girth of chest and abdomen, weight and height, the surface area of the body,

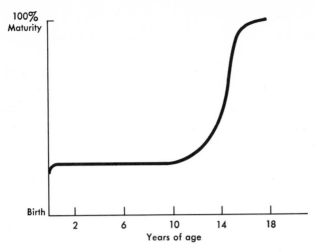

Figure 9.2   The development of primary sex characteristics.

and width of shoulders and hips. Some of the internal organs, such as the liver and kidneys, also grow according to this pattern, which is illustrated in Figure 9.3.

As can be seen from Figure 9.3, the rate of growth is rapid (following a brief initial decline, probably in weight only) during infancy. During childhood, the rate of growth is moderately slow. Around pubescence (and earlier for girls than boys by approximately a year), there is moder-

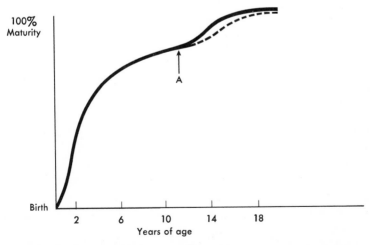

Figure 9.3   The general growth curve for the more obvious body dimension of some of the major internal organs. From point A, the solid line represents girls' growth; the dotted line, boys'.

ately rapid gain, followed by a slow year-by-year increase in later adolescence.

Factors That Modify Physical Growth

Preoccupation with modifiers of physical growth is characteristic of parents. "How can I make my child gain (or lose) weight? Is there anything I can do so that he will be taller (or shorter)? Is he gaining at about the right rate?" These are questions the pediatrician and nutritionist face constantly, and they concern matters in which not only parents but scientists have a legitimate interest.

Answers to such questions are by no means complete. Today, United States infants gain in weight and height much more rapidly than a generation ago. This may be the result of vitamin-enriched diets, or to the earlier addition of solid food or, as far as anyone knows, to mutation or increased atmospheric radiation. Young people achieve their maximal height as much as two years earlier than they did two or three generations ago (although the average height of old American stock at full maturity is not greatly different—perhaps a half inch—from what it was in 1900). This maximal height is reached now by the age of 16 (girls) or 18 (boys), whereas formerly girls kept growing until they were about 18 or 19, boys until they were about 21. This trend, however, seems to be changing in recent years, and children are taller than their parents.

Research on the factors that modify physical growth is incomplete and results are inconclusive. A certain adequate level of vitamins in the diet is necessary for normal growth, but there is little agreement whether a child partaking of an average United States diet is getting enough vitamins or too many. There is no question that a variety of foods—calciums and other minerals, starches, proteins, and fats—is essential, but there is not full consensus about the proper proportion of these food types. Some advise starting the infant early on solids, others suggest keeping him on milk until the second half of his first year.

Few generalizations about growth modifiers can be made. It is agreed that children need sunlight, sufficient sleep, fresh air, exercise, and varied diets made up of milk, fruits, vegetables, and meats. Beyond these recommendations, little can be said.

Anatomical Changes

Meredith (1957) lists various categories of physical change that are of interest to the student of physical growth. His clear and useful classification is the one that is presented here.

CHANGES IN KIND

Life starts with change in *kind*. The union between sperm and ovum produces a new entity, the zygote. This simple structure is modified during prenatal life to include blood cells and bone cells, muscle tissue and adipose tissue, nervous system and skeletal system, and limb segments. In the second month of prenatal life an external tail begins to grow. A few weeks later it disappears. Most of the cartilaginous portions of the skeleton of the baby and the preschool child change to the bone of the older child and adult. The bones of the aged are more brittle than those of the young. All of these changes are examples of changes in kind.

CHANGES IN NUMBER

During adolescence, the number of bone masses drops from around 350 to fewer than 220, principally because of epiphyseal union. The 5-year-old has in his head from 48 to 52 teeth in one or another stage of development, but by the time he is 15 he has ordinarily lost 20 deciduous (temporary) teeth. With increasing age, more teeth are likely to be lost, the wisdom teeth typically going first either because of decay or because the jaws cannot accommodate them.

Hair Changes   This section is included here for completeness, although it concerns adolescents rather than children. It *does* illustrate very striking types of growth change—of pattern, number, and texture.

There are striking development and sex differences in hairiness. For the male, hair around the genitals begins to proliferate, darken, and change in texture during adolescence (on the average, at 13 to 15 years), until by the time of the middle or late teens, the adult type of relatively thick, coarse, and curly pubic hair surrounds the genitals and covers a large portion of the groin region. Most frequently, distribution is roughly triangular with the apex of the triangle extending toward the navel. The appearance of axillary hair (coarse and curly hair in the armpits) follows the appearance of pubic hair. Next comes thickening and coarsening of facial hair, and the adolescent boy begins to shave. The growth is first noticeable on the upper lip. It extends outward and upward and downward with time until, in his middle twenties, the average male is bearded over his lower and lateral face and the upper throat region. Last in the maturational sequence is mature hair type and distribution on the extremities. Thicker, longer, and coarser hair begins to show on the lower legs, extending upward with time toward the crotch and buttocks and on the lower arm, developing progressively toward the elbow in one direction and the back of the hand and finger joints in the other. For a substantial portion of the male population, similar coarse hair begins to develop around the nipples, extending in area until, by the middle twenties, the entire chest is hairy, and there is extensive coverage of the upper back and shoulders. Many males, however, develop little or no chest hair. Body hairiness appears to be genetically determined.

At about the time pubic, axillary, and facial hair has reached its maximal density and distribution for the male, the inverse process begins at the top of his head. By the time they are 30, many men have conspicuously receding hairlines, and some are partially bald. This loss of hair is a continuous process which seems to be genetically determined, and (to the chagrin of many) is apparently irreversible.

There are conspicuous ethnic differences among males in the distribution and quantity of bodily and facial hair. If ethnic groups are divided (such a grouping is, of course, very rough) into the Caucasoid, the Negroid, and the Mongoloid, bodily hairiness decreases in the same order, with Caucasoid the hairiest and Mongoloids the least hairy. As adult males, the last group, typically, will have thin beards, relatively narrowly circumscribed pubic hair, comparatively little hair on lower arms and legs, and essentially hairless chests.

There is no known relationship between sexual function and hair distribution, despite the popular stereotype of the virile and hairy-chested male. But there is, among white United States males, a certain amount of positive value attached to the possession of abundant bodily and facial hair. Slow or negligible development of bodily hair may pose a certain adjustment problem for boys, analogous to but probably milder than the problems created by delayed pubescence.

Ethnic differences among females are less marked than among males, although the differences that exist are similar in direction to those for the various male populations mentioned. There are conspicuous sex differences in the values attached to bodily hair in many cultures, certainly in that of the United States. The manufacture and distribution of depilatories—agents for removing hair from the arms, underarms, legs, and face—is, in the United States, a huge business, whose purchasing public is overwhelmingly feminine.

The pattern of hair change for girls around and following pubescence is similar to that for boys, although less striking. First, as with boys, longer and coarser hair that later becomes curly begins to appear around the genitals. This hair extends laterally and upward, and eventually assumes the distribution of an inverted triangle, but one whose area is confined to the genital region rather than, as with the male, extending upward toward the navel. Soon after the appearance of the first pubic hair, as with boys, axillary hair develops. Some girls also develop marked facial hairiness, which follows the same, although a less striking, pattern as that for boys. The hair of the lower legs and arms becomes thicker.

longer, and coarser, although only rarely to any degree approximating that of the typical male. The development of face, arm, and leg hair may be a matter of shame, embarrassment, and anxiety for girls, particularly if its development is sufficient to be conspicuous. Ordinarily, the female develops very little or no chest-breast hair.

Women's hair also thins with age, although not as conspicuously as that of men. However, in old age, many women have quite thin hair on top. Following menopause, women are likely to be troubled by increased growth of facial hair similar in type to, but not as striking as, the adolescent growth of facial hair in boys.

CHANGES IN SIZE

Most lay people, when they consider physical growth, think primarily of changes in size, particularly in height and weight. Such changes are perhaps the most conspicuous and dramatic instances of growth, but constitute only one of its aspects.

There are periods of positive growth (or gain), of negative growth (decrease), and of little or no change in either direction. For example, the ligaments from the testes to the floor of the scrotum increase in length from 3 to 6 months of prenatal life; in the seventh prenatal month, these ligaments shorten by 50 percent; and by the time of birth they have shortened another 25 percent.

For the first few days after conception there is no change in the size of the zygote. Following birth, almost all babies lose some of their birth weight. From around 20 to 30 years, there is a minuscule change in standing or sitting height, but height decreases steadily, although not rapidly, during the mature years and old age. Height actually decreases between a quarter and a half inch from the time of getting out of bed in the morning to the time of retiring again at night, but this loss in height is recovered again by morning.

The thymus gland (presumably a regulator of growth) increases in weight almost to puberty, then declines strikingly in size. For both sexes, the genitals remain at approximately their infantile size until shortly before pubescence (11 or 12 for girls, 13 to 14 for boys). At this time and through middle adolescence begins a dramatic growth process—one that is often embarrassing, particularly for boys, who fear that their larger penis will show through their clothing (although they are, in actuality, usually very proud of this indication of their manhood). The typical sex-driven adolescent boy is frequently tormented by fear of betraying that he has an erection, which at this stage of development is frequently precipitated, often unpredictably, by casual environmental stimuli or fantasy. Penis length ordinarily reaches its maximum at about 17 or 18 years, although the testes increases in volume until in the middle twenties.

Girls begin to bud around adolescence, and their breasts increase rapidly in size until, usually at 17 or 18, they reach a stage of development that may be considered mature. When her breasts first begin to grow, the girl is likely to be as embarrassed by her new bosom, as the boy is by his larger penis. Later, however, deficiency in this area will cause her as much agony as is caused the boy by undersized or underdeveloped genitals. However, with increasing age, breasts change in shape, becoming more pendulous. Pregnancy and nursing also produce marked changes in the size and shape of the breasts.

It has earlier been pointed out, and illustrated in Figure 9.3, that the curve for height and weight gain shows a rapid increase in infancy, a much slower gain in childhood, another rapid increase a year or two before pubescence, and, in later adolescence, a slow year-by-year gain. Maximal height for boys is reached as much as two years earlier than it was fifty or sixty years ago—ordinarily, by the time the boy is 18 or 19.

The same trend is followed by girls, who today usually reach their mature height by about 17 years of age, whereas their grandmothers were probably still growing at 18 or 19. However, we do not have as much information about the growth of females fifty and sixty years ago as we do for males, since much of the information about the latter group was obtained from men entering military service.

A popular conception exists that each generation in the United States is taller than the preceding one. What actual gain there is in mature size is slight. Meredith estimates (personal communication) that in the United States it has not been more than a half inch, if that, since the latter part of the nineteenth century. But there are striking differences in the rate of growth in height and the age at which mature height is reached. All during childhood, children are taller today than formerly, but maximal height is also attained earlier. Recent studies, however, seem to modify this conclusion—1966 youth *are* taller than their parents.

The average mature white man in the United States is about 5 feet 8 inches tall; the average mature white woman about 5 feet 3 inches. Height, given adequate nutrition and normal health, is partially or completely determined by heredity, and shows marked ethnic differences. In the United States there is little, if any, difference in the height norms for Negroes and whites, although probably more members of the Negro population have faulty or insufficient nutrition. The Mexican-American population is, on the whole, slighter and shorter than the "Anglo" population in the same area, although again a portion of this difference is probably due to nutritional factors. Those of Oriental origin, although substantially taller—probably by an inch or two—than their progenitors, are as a group shorter and slighter than the white population (Greulich, 1957). The subsections of the population whose parents and grandparents came from Europe will usually be found to be taller and heavier, on the average, than their parents and grandparents; but, for all practical purposes, they merge into the general population. Those of North European and British Isles national origin are, on the average, taller than those from South Europe (Meredith, 1939).

The growth curve for weight is about the same shape as that for height. The fat-rumped, relatively narrow-shouldered boy of 11 to 13 may take some comfort from the fact that for boys, shoulder width increases somewhat more rapidly than hip width, so that his adult proportions will be somewhat closer to the ideal adult figure than his present ones.

The weight curve, unlike the height curve, does not reach an asymptote in the late teens. Typically, weight increase continues into and frequently beyond the "sagging forties." As one passes middle age, this trend is usually reversed; the old are relatively thin. Overweight is a major problem in many societies in which the food supply is more than sufficient to provide for bodily needs. In the United States it is probably one of the most serious health problems. Chronic obesity based on over-eating seems to have deep roots in emotional maladjustment; clinical reports indicate that it is almost as hard to "cure" as alcoholism, and indeed, "Fatties Anonymous" clubs have been organized. Many children seek security in eating, and food-based obesity is considered the symptom of a serious emotional problem when found in children.

Weight, like height, is principally determined by heredity under constant environmental conditions; but, more than height, it is subject to environmental manipulation. A regime of proper nutrition and appropriate exercise will keep most children and adults relatively trim. However, equivalent amounts of food affect different individuals differently. One may burst at the seams with weight gain; another, on the same rations, maintains a constant weight. Exercise amount is probably the factor most responsible for weight—nervous, high activity level people burn up calories that would otherwise go onto waistlines.

CHANGES IN SHAPE

We have already referred to the changes in proportion from infancy to and following adolescence. Prenatal changes in shape are even more dramatic than they will be at any time after birth. Avey (1954), for example, shows that at the end of week 2 following fertilization, the embryo is shield-like in shape, but a month later is cylindroid and strongly bent.

The preschool child, whether boy or girl, is potbellied. During the first few years after pubescence, the typical boy has a concave abdomen. In his early twenties, this concavity begins to fill out, and from 30 on he is likely to be fighting the battle of the bulge, or else passively surrendering to it. His feminine counterpart will have been more curvilinear than he since puberty, and she too will have problems of sagging and bulging where she does not want to. Childbearing to some degree makes her problems more serious than those of the male.

Around adolescence, sex differences in proportion become more marked. For both boys and girls, the winged shoulder blades of childhood pull in so that backs are flatter transversely. As has been mentioned, pot-bellies recede. Boys' shoulder width increases somewhat more rapidly than their hip width, giving them an approximation of the narrow inverted triangle that is the ideal, although rarely attained, masculine figure. The opposition is true for girls, whose bodies are assuming the proportions that will fit them for easiest childbearing.

With the advent of teeth and the loss of baby fat, the shape of the face has more and more approximated a long oval, and the jaw has become more pronounced. When the teeth are lost, the face again becomes more compressed.

CHANGES IN POSITION

Changes in position are not as immediately striking after birth as some of the other changes that have been described, although they are dramatic indeed during fetal development. The most obvious position changes in postnatal life involve the teeth. It has been mentioned that at 5 the child has between 48 and 52 teeth at one or another stage of development. In the process of acquiring his permanent teeth, two sets of teeth—the deciduous and the permanent—have moved upward or downward, depending on which jaw they are in, and have otherwise extensively changed their position.

At birth, the big toe is more widely spaced from the others than it will later be; and has been even more widely separated earlier. For most boys, the testes have descended from the abdomen to the scrotum before birth, although for some this process, either naturally or through surgery, follows birth. In the course of its development, the stomach moves from a vertical to a transverse position. The ribs change from a forward to a lateral Venetian blind position, and from open to closed.

CHANGES IN PIGMENTATION

The hair of many babies is relatively dark; but is replaced by blond hair which, during later childhood and maturity (to the despair of many women) darkens, and then, in middle or old age, changes to gray. Like the hair, the skin progressively darkens, but the iris of the eyes is likely to become lighter because of the resorption of pigment granules.

CHANGES IN TEXTURE

Changes in texture are striking and easily observable. The older preschool child has lost his baby fat and no longer has the "sponge-rubber" feel of the 6-month-old infant, whose fatty tissue is easily compressible. The postadolescent girl "feels" different from the preadolescent, having, as she does, a greater percentage of fatty tissue than formerly. The postadolescent boy, on the other hand, has more muscle and less fat in his tissues than before adolescence. His muscles are harder. The bones of the aged are more brittle than those of the young adult. From the time of early maturity, the skin progressively loses its elasticity, so that crow's-feet and wrinkles develop. The pubic and axillary hair of adolescence and maturity is very different in texture from the down it replaced.

Changes in Function

To this point, we have been discussing anatomical changes. But changes in physical and physiological function are of equal importance. Such changes seem to have influenced Freud in setting up the psychosexual stages that constitute so important a part of his theory of personality.

THE MOUTH

The little baby (up to 7 or 8 months) is essentially a passive receiver as far as the mouth and feeding are concerned. He has no teeth. His most effective motor function is sucking. But between 6 and 8 months, for most babies, teeth begin to erupt and the mouth can be used for something else than sucking. Indeed, as teeth irritate the gums, the baby begins to mouth and chew; and when teeth actually appear, nipping and biting are added to his behavior repertory. Among the Sioux, according to Erikson (1945), the addition of biting behavior results in a sharp change in the baby's relationship with his mother: where, previously, he had been enveloped in love and permissiveness, now, when he bites while feeding, he is thumped resoundingly on the head. This is his first experience of outside interference with his pleasure, and Erikson wonders whether this frustration, coming as it does so sharply after a history of great indulgence, may not be the root of the capacity for fury that characterized the Sioux as a warrior. This change occurs at the time that Freud postulates a change from oral eroticism to oral sadism. The parallel is easy to see—from sucking to biting.

THE SPHINCTERS

A second change in function results from an interaction between maturation and the learning-teaching environment in which the child lives.
The sphincters that control the elimination of urine and feces operate
involuntarily during the first year of life. Voluntary, predictable control
over them is difficult to establish before about 18 months at the earliest,
with control often not being accomplished by 2 years. Even in adulthood,
under conditions of stress or extreme visceral tension, sphincter control
may be lost; and the loss of this control is a frequent accompaniment of
severe emotional disturbance and the diseases of old age.

POSTURE AND LOCOMOTION

Between 7 and 8 months, the neck, trunk, abdominal, back, and leg
muscles become sufficiently strong to permit the body to function in a
sitting position. This landmark is important to the child. He can voluntarily make his world assume an entirely new perspective; things that he
could not see before except when someone lifted or carried him are now
visible at will.

A little later, still new coordinations and strengths are achieved, and
he can crawl and later creep to a desired object from the spot where he
espied it. By 10 or 11 months the baby, with constant practice, has reached
the stage where he can pull himself to an upright position by using the
side of his playpen, a chair, or the coffee table. Many babies learn to pull
themselves erect before they know how to get down again, and the inexperienced parent is frequently concerned by his baby's tendency to pull
himself erect, stand for a time, scream inexplicably, then calm when replaced in a sitting position. In a little while, the baby goes through the
same sequence. This pattern disappears when the child learns to lower
himself. Soon after standing the child edges around his support, and some
time between about 12 and 15 months sets off alone, walking independently.

Again, one can appreciate the importance of these landmarks in motor
development only if he attempts to put himself in the position of the
baby. Just as the world does not look the same from a lying-down and a
sitting-up position, so it looks different from a sitting and a standing
position. The object across the room has an entirely different meaning
if it can be crawled or crept to, even though this is an effortful undertaking. It has a different meaning still if it can be walked or run toward.
The world is thus rendered infinitely smaller and more accessible to the
infant.

The upright position is one of mankind's greatest developmental advantages, almost rivaling the ability to use symbolic behavior. It frees the hands, which in turn are uniquely structured to allow man to oppose his thumb and fingers for refined manipulation and exploration. In the phylogenetic sense, it may be speculated that the upright position made finger-thumb opposition possible; and that this in turn enabled man to gain a refined control over his environment impossible for any other species: with hands freed, and thumb and fingers working pincer-wise, it became possible to manufacture implements and weapons, to build fire, and to make shelter. It is conceivable that as he mastered more and more of his environment, man began to experience the need for labeling its complexities so that, slowly, gestures, symbols, and words developed.

LATERALITY

During the first year, many babies are ambidextrous. But by the second year, a majority of them have developed a preference for one hand over the other; and by the end of the preschool period, about nine out of ten United States children have established a clear preference for the right hand. This preference does not, however, necessarily extend to all functions. A person may eat with his left hand, write with his right, yet shovel snow left-handedly. The left-hander may bat a ball right-handed, or vice versa. Nor does right-handedness imply the dominance of the right eye, the right foot, and so on.

There is no well-established theory about laterality. The cerebral-dominance theory, once widely accepted, is now considered at best speculative and at worst wrong. This theory said that if the left side of the brain were dominant, the individual would, for example, be right-handed; whereas if the right hemisphere of the brain were dominant, he would be left-handed. Implicit in this theory was the idea that damage would be done to the child if his preferred handedness were changed. Many authors have attributed stuttering and reading and writing difficulties (particularly reversals, mirror images, and so on) to forced change in handedness.

If indeed such problems accompany a handedness change, it now appears more likely that they are a function of the way the child was taught to change rather than of the change itself. Our society is a dextral, or right-handed, rather than a sinistral, or left-handed one, and has gone through periods when left-handedness has attributed to it "sinister" implications. The very derivation of *sinister*, coming from the Latin *sinister* (meaning left), testifies to this association. An adult can get some notion of what it means to a child to have his handedness arbitrarily and peremptorily changed if he forces himself to spend a half hour writing with his unpreferred hand and, at the same time, imagines some authority figure standing over him supervising, enforcing, and criticizing.

It is likely that heredity has something to do with handedness, although the evidence is scanty. Social learning, including direct imitation, probably plays at least as great a part. Some have maintained that adopting a left-handed preference is a sign of negativism.

The advice that might be given to parents concerning handedness is this: In a mild way, encourage children to be right-handed, since there are advantages to this in terms of using classroom chairs, tools, sporting goods, and so on.

Encourage right-handedness by handing the young child the things he wants in his right hand. If he persists strongly in left-handedness, let him alone. However, make sure that he learns the correct orientation skills for left-handed people. Such tutelage will avoid, for example, the crabbed and roundabout way of writing that many left-handers develop.

REPRODUCTIVE ORGANS AND SEXUAL BEHAVIOR

This section on changes of function would not be complete without a discussion of changes in use of the reproductive organs, even though this material chronologically belongs with adolescence. In this case, and because so many children of elementary-school age are physically mature, the adolescent material seems appropriate.

Intricate developmental patterns bring the human organism to maturity. Sexual maturity is delayed until most physical and muscular growth has occurred. Then physical growth slows and stops, while the primary and secondary sex characteristics develop rapidly to their mature status.

Although the male baby and the little boy have experienced penis erections, only after pubescence can the true reproductive function be performed: erection and ejaculation of mature semen containing sperm. However, even from infancy, both boy and girl babies appear to be capable of experiencing either orgasm or orgasm-like states.

For the girl, entry into pubescence is marked by the onset of menstruation: the sloughing off of the nutritive tissue that accompanies ovulation, which occurs approximately monthly during the years of her reproductive potential. For some time following the first period, her menstrual cycles are likely to be irregular. For most girls a period of sterility, lasting for a year or two, apparently follows the first menstruation, although this period is highly variable from individual to individual (Montagu, 1946). It might be speculated that this state of affairs serves a useful purpose in helping to ensure full bodily growth before assumption of the tasks of pregnancy and motherhood.

It is not definitely known whether such a period of sterility follows pubescence for boys. In general, it is more difficult to establish criteria of sexual maturation for the boy than for the girl, since the "crossing over" is much less dramatic and much more due to culture: that is, a boy, because of morality, may delay masturbation for years, whereas the time of menstruation cannot be changed. According to Kinsey, Pomeroy, and Martin (1948), the middle and late teens—a time when, in our culture, free sexual activity is not generally permitted—mark the period of greatest sexual drive and potency for boys.

The overwhelming majority of boys—probably almost 100 percent in our culture—explore sex actively, to the degree of achieving orgasm, before marriage. Kinsey estimates that 95 percent of boys have experienced orgasm by age 15. Cultural sanctions are more relaxed for the male than for the female. Kinsey *et al.* (1948, 1953) report that the male sex drive is more urgent and, compared with that of the female, can be more easily aroused by fantasy, pictures, and other symbols. The male sex organ is also more visible and easily available for manipulation. Even without manipulation, seminal pressures produce tumescence (erection) in sleep, so that following pubescence most boys experience occasional or frequent orgasms during the night. These are known popularly as "wet dreams," which occur at a set time, regardless of the boy's desires. They may be speeded, of course, as in the case of a boy who sleeps on his stomach, thus applying pressure to his genitals. Generally, however, wet dreams occur directly in response to the male system of hydraulic pressure, when and only when the hydraulics have built up to the point of ejaculation.

Girls less frequently experience orgasm before marriage although, according to Kinsey and his associates, almost two thirds of them have done so. Spontaneous orgasms are less likely to occur for girls than for boys: between the ages of 16 and 20, 91 percent of boys report such experiences, whereas only 7 percent of women do. Masturbation to orgasm (or climax) is less frequent for girls than for boys, the respective percentages being about 25 and 99. However, the *proportion* of orgasms due to masturbation is about the same for the two sexes.

Premarital intercourse is likewise less frequent for girls and women than for men, with about 50 percent of girls entering marriage as virgins. For boys, depending on their educational level, between 2 percent (for the lowest educational level) and 33 percent (for the best educated) enter marriage without having experienced intercourse. Premarital sex activity varies sharply according to social class. Middle-class males are considerably more inhibited than those of the lower class. The nature of sex activity also varies according to social class: premarital sexual activity for middle-class boys and girls is more likely to be solitary and to consist of masturbation, whereas lower-class youngsters are more likely to experiment socially and with a partner of the opposite sex. Extramarital sex seems, on the other hand, to continue later in life for the middle- than for the lower-class person, particularly the male. Early-maturing males tend to be more active sexually (in all types of sex activity) than late-maturers, but the same trend does not hold for women. At the time of

Kinsey's survey (the 1940s, for the most part), the sex activity of younger women seemed to be substantially greater than that reported by older women, whereas very little change since the 1900s was manifested by men.

In line with other sexual activities, the male of the species is more likely to explore homosexuality actively. Kinsey et al. (1953, pp. 474–475) report that an accumulative incidence of homosexual responses had ultimately reached 28 percent for the female population he studied, with 13 percent having had overt homosexual contacts to the point of orgasm. The same figures for men were 50 percent and 37 percent. The women had also engaged in homosexual contact for shorter periods of time, and more frequently than men had had only one or two partners.

Some of the figures reported by Kinsey and his colleagues (1948, 1953) indicate that more lower- than middle-class males have had homosexual experiences, although the trends are not clear. The opposite is true for women, for obvious social reasons: the middle-class female is more likely to be a career woman and/or to remain a spinster, and to be sexually inhibited. Heterosexual courting starts earlier and is more vigorous in the lower-class group. Supervision of heterosexual contacts is closer for the middle-class girl, and the boy who courts her is likely to be less aggressive than the boy who courts the lower-class girl. All of these factors result in relatively greater opportunity for, and pressure toward, sex activity with other women than is true for the lower-class girl. The class difference in homosexual incidence for males (if it does exist) may, of course, be due simply to the greater freedom of social-sexual expression of all types that seems to characterize the lower class, and not to any difference in degree of heterosexual orientation.

The curve of sexual desire for the male changes steadily, declining from its peak in the middle and late teens to a fairly low but long-persisting level in the mid-fifties. A highly variable "male menopause" in the fifties or sixties has been postulated by many, but is not well documented by research; and there are many evidences of full-fledged sexual and reproductive activity on the part of males in advanced old age. The notion of the dangerous forties, particularly for middle-class males, appears to have some validity: the male, his virility flagging and his wife fading, seeks one last fling. This phenomenon is of course psychological and social, and may characterize only societies such as ours, which, besides being youth-centered, are organized on principles of monogamy and sexual restraint.

The course of development of female sexuality (Kinsey et al., 1953) is quite different from that for men. The young girl rather typically is "not awakened," and, indeed, many girls feel no conscious sex desire until after their first complete heterosexual experiences. For many women, sex desire is highest preceding and following menstruation (Landis and Landis, 1957). The average woman experiences a rise in her sexual appetite, following its typically low level in the teens, which often continues into and beyond the middle forties. These trends produce complications in the relations between the sexes: the enthusiastic young bridegroom or suitor encounters a relatively cool partner; the tired middle-aged husband may prove singularly frustrating to his eager spouse. Although the capacity for reproduction ceases following female menopause, a substantial amount of interest in sex remains, often into old age.

Although Kinsey, who has been quoted frequently in this section, has gathered more data concerning human sexual behavior than any other investigator, it is possible that his data may overstate the case. All of his subjects were volunteers, who differ in many systematic ways from a randomly selected population. At least one study (Maslow and Sakoda, 1952) indicates that women volunteers are likely to have unorthodox attitudes toward sexual behavior, and may either indulge or profess to indulge in more sexual activities than nonvolunteers.

Physical Factors and Personality

It has already been mentioned that between the ages of 11 and 13 girls are, on the average, taller and heavier than boys. Also, most girls reach physical maturity, although not necessarily "official" pubescence, earlier than most boys by about two years. The problems associated with this differential rate of maturity are obvious to anyone who visits a sixth-, seventh-, eighth-, or ninth-grade classroom, or who knows children in this age range. Whereas many of the girls are interested in dating and dancing, their male peers are frequently a head shorter than they, physically immature, and markedly uninterested in things heterosexual. The girl is thus reduced to going out with boys who chronologically are considerably older than she; or the boy is forced into the company of someone larger and more mature than he. This maturational difference has occasioned some to propose that girls should start school earlier than boys. Although there is merit to this suggestion, it is impractical for obvious reasons.

THE EFFECT OF EARLY PHYSICAL MATURITY ON BOYS

Research workers at the University of California (Mary Cover Jones and Bayley, 1950; Mussen and Jones, 1957; and Mary Cover Jones, 1957) have investigated the consequences of early and late physical maturing for boys, and H. E. Jones (1949) and Mary Cover Jones and Mussen (1958) have reported results for early- and late-maturing girls. These workers report on data from a longitudinal study of California children, some of whom are still participating in their middle forties.

The Jones and Bayley study (1950) uses skeletal age, as judged from x-rays of the long bones of the hand and the knee, as its criterion of physical maturity. From a group of ninety boys who were studied for an average of about four and a half years, the sixteen most consistently accelerated and the sixteen most consistently retarded were studied intensively by means of observations and ratings both by professional adults and by the boys' buddies. See Figure 9.4 for illustration.

At the age of 14, ratings of physical maturity made from nude photographs showed almost no overlap between the two groups. The physically accelerated boys were taller, heavier, showed more advanced pubic hair, and had larger genitals. From 13 to 15 years of age the physically retarded boys tended to be long-legged, of slender build, and relatively weak during the period when they lagged most markedly behind in size. The retarded boys were rated by adults as lower in physical attractiveness, less masculine, less well groomed, and more animated and eager ("childish"). They sought attention more, were more affected and less matter-of-fact, and were tenser. However, they did not differ from the more advanced group in ratings of popularity, leadership, prestige, poise, assurance, cheerfulness, or social effect on the group. They were considered to be less mature in a heterosexual social situation.

When rated by their buddies, the physically retarded boys showed up about the same as when rated by adults, but the differences between them and the physically advanced group were less marked. Buddies estimated the physically retarded to be more restless, talkative, and bossy. They believed that they were more attention-seeking and less inclined to have assurance in class. Their buddies regarded them as less popular, and as less likely to be leaders. They were also rated as less likely to have older friends, as being shorter on a sense of humor about themselves, and as having a less attractive general appearance.

The Mussen and Jones study (1957) uses data taken from the Thematic Apperception Test, given to seventeen late-maturers and sixteen early-maturers when they were 17 years of age. In this test, the subject is shown a series of pictures and is asked to tell a story about each one: who the characters are, what has happened, and how it comes out. From the story he tells, a number of judgments (sometimes of dubious validity) can be made. As has been mentioned in Chapter 6, psychologists assume that the story-teller (the subject) projects his own needs and ideas onto the central character of the story he tells (the hero). This hero's actions, then, are assumed to be those that the story-teller sees as reasonable or desirable for himself. The hero's motives and needs are assumed to be those of the subject of the investigation. The TAT is one of the most useful measures of personality—Lindzey and co-workers (1952, 1955, 1956, and 1958), for example, have contributed evidence to show that it is, within broad limits, valid—although care should be taken not to overgeneralize from it.

In the Mussen and Jones study, it was found that more of the late-

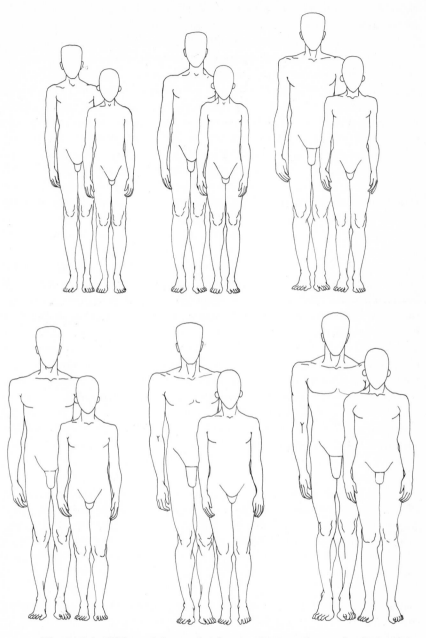

Figure 9.4 Differential growth of an early maturing and a late maturing boy. Drawings represent the boys' statuses at yearly intervals from 11½ to 16½ years of age. (Adapted from Shuttleworth, 1949.)

than of the early-maturers used TAT themes such as the following: the hero (with whom the boy presumably identified) was described in negative terms (for instance, as being an imbecile, a weakling, or a fanatic); the hero is rejected, scorned, or disapproved of by parents or by the authorities; the hero leaves home and/or defies his parents; the hero falls in love, or has a romance; the hero is helped, encouraged, or given something by someone other than his parents. One other theme came close to distinguishing significantly between the two groups: More of the late-maturers described the hero as feeling helpless and seeking aid or sympathy.

These patterns cluster sensibly together, and allow us to make tentative inferences about certain tendencies of this group of physically retarded boys. They are more likely than physically advanced boys to possess negative or derogatory self-concepts; they seem to blame their parents for their status, although perhaps not consciously; and they feel relatively weak, alone, and helpless. Hence, they seek assistance and affiliation.

The physically advanced group more frequently than the retarded group told stories in which the hero was aggressive in a physical and asocial fashion. They also tended somewhat more frequently to say that the picture elicited in them no thoughts or feelings. Here, perhaps, is an indication of self-confidence—an assurance that they can get away with aggressive behavior if they feel that way; and a tendency to be rather matter-of-fact, or unimaginative, as was observed by the raters in the Jones and Bayley study discussed above.

There were no differences between the two groups of boys in the number who told stories in which the hero is prevented by his parents from doing something he wants to; in which he establishes good relations with his parents; attempts to gain a high goal or do something creditable; or seeks fame and/or high prestige status. In other words, we can infer, very tentatively, that although the physically retarded boys bear somewhat more hostility toward their parents, they have, when compared with the physically advanced boys, an equal amount of positive feeling; and that the two groups subscribe equally to the cultural notion of the successful, occupationally climbing, bold man.

BODY BUILD AND PERSONALITY IN BOYS AND MEN

For thousands of years, philosophers and physicians and, more recently, anthropologists and other scientists have speculated (and done research) on relations between body build, function, constitution, and temperament. Efforts to classify body type apparently date back at least to Hippocrates (460?–377? B.C.). Tucker and Lessa (1940) state: "It is a curious and perhaps significant fact that 2500 years ago Hippocrates said that there are two roots of human beings, the long thins and the short thicks. Almost all simple classifications of type since that time have nearly the same basis, despite variety of nomenclature and detail of description" (p. 419). Kretschmer (1925) used a somewhat similar classification of body type in his controversial but influential hypotheses about the relations of body build to temperament and mental illness (for example, that long lean people, if they succumb to mental disease, will become schizophrenics; short blocky people will become manic-depressives).

In their scholarly review, Tucker and Lessa include a bibliography of 334 items, a large number of which refer to body build or constitution and temperament.

Sheldon has received much attention for his work in the area of body build and temperament. Sheldon and his colleagues (1940, 1942) have interested themselves in methods of characterizing body build and relating it to personality. One of his works (1949) takes an extreme position, and is endorsed by few; and the statistical assumptions of his whole technique of classifying or describing body build have been strongly and tellingly criticized (Hammond, 1957; Humphreys, 1957; Meredith, 1940). However, his work has had so much impact that this text would not be complete without a brief description of it.

Sheldon has worked mostly with college-age students—that is, people in late adolescence. His data are ordinarily nude front, side, and back photographs, and he has worked more with male than with female subjects. Each photograph is rated from 1 (having very little of) to 7 (having very much of) on three dimensions: endomorphy, mesomorphy, and ectomorphy. The barrel-chested, big-bellied individual would receive a high *endomorph* rating; the muscular, broad-shouldered, narrow-hipped, rather big-boned individual would be rated high on *mesomorphy;* the long and lean individual, whose external body surface is large in relation to his weight, would obtain a high rating on *ectomorphy.* Figure 9.5 consists of line drawings illustrating these patterns at $11\frac{1}{2}$ years and Figure 9.6 shows the same boys three and a half years later.

Each photograph is given three ratings: a 7–3–1 would describe an almost impossibly pure case of endomorphy; a 1–3–7 an equally improbable example of ectomorphy. Sheldon also rates on *dysplasia* (bodily disharmony), *gynandromorphy* (bisexuality), *texture,* and *hirsutism* (hairiness).

One ingenious study (Brodsky, 1954) suggests that there *are* differential social reactions to characteristic body builds. Brodsky prepared five 15-inch silhouettes of males, representing: (1) extreme endomorph; (2) endomesomorph; (3) mesomorph; (4) ectomesomorph; and (5) ectomorph. He also constructed a questionnaire containing such items as the following: Which one of this group of five men is most aggressive? Which one of this group of five men is least aggressive?

To secure divergent research populations, Brodsky recruited seventy-

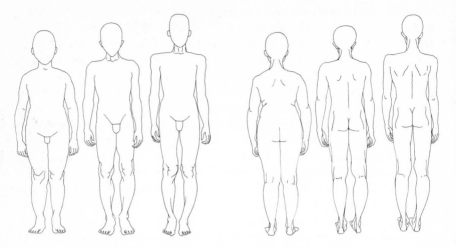

Figure 9.5 Front and rear views, reading from the left, of an endomorph, a mesomorph, and an ectomorph boy, about 11½ years of age. (Adapted from Shuttleworth, 1949.)

five male medical and dental college students from Howard University, all or almost all of whom would be expected to be Negro; and fifty male college students from George Washington University, all presumably white. The questionnaire was given to the men in groups numbering no

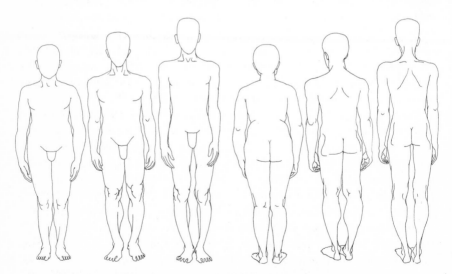

Figure 9.6 The three boys shown in Figure 9.5, in the same order from left to right, at 15 years of age. (Adapted from Shuttleworth, 1949.)

more than five. There were no important differences in the way the two samples of respondents answered, so Brodsky pooled his groups. This homogeneity in opinion of superficially quite different groups of men lends weight to the notion of a "cultural stereotype," or characteristic way of regarding body build.

The various traits were usually assigned by the respondents to the "pure" silhouettes—the endomorph, mesomorph, and ectomorph. Those assigned to the given silhouette by a third or more of the respondents are listed below.

More than one third of the respondents labeled the *endomorph* silhouette as representing the man who eats the most, eats the most often, will make the worst soldier, will make the poorest athlete, will be the poorest professor of philosophy, can endure pain the least well, will make the least successful military leader, will be least likely to be chosen leader, will make the poorest university president, will be the least aggressive, will drink the most, will be least preferred as a personal friend (but, ironically, would have many friends), will make the poorest doctor, and will put his own interests before those of others.

This picture is an almost consistently negative one, and one of social delinquency. If there is any truth to the notion that a person behaves as he is expected to behave, a dismal picture of the direction of personality growth of the endomorph is presented by this study.

The *mesomorph* fares as favorably as the endomorph does unfavorably: the respondents said that he would make the best athlete, the most successful military leader, and the best soldier. They chose him as the man who would assume leadership, as well as the man who would be elected as leader. He was judged not to smoke at all, and to be self-sufficient, in the sense of needing friends the least. However, he was most preferred as a friend, and was judged to have many friends. Respondents also said that he would be the most aggressive, would endure pain the best, would never have a nervous breakdown, and would drink the least.

The stereotype of the *ectomorph* is far less socially desirable than that of the mesomorph, but in general more favorable than that of the endomorph. The ectomorph was judged to be the most likely to have a nervous breakdown before the age of 30, to eat the least, and the least often, to smoke three packs of cigarettes a day, to be least self-sufficient, in the sense of needing friends the most (but, unfortunately, was judged to have the fewest friends), to hold his liquor the worst, to make a poor father, and, as a military leader, to be likely to sacrifice his men with the greatest emotional distress. He is the socially acceptable neurotic.

This study illustrates that there may be certain characteristic ways of reacting to different types of male physique, and that the pattern of reaction is such as to favor the mesomorph. In this context, it should be mentioned that Jones' early-maturers, best adjusted according to her criteria, were more mesomorphic in average body build than her late-maturers.

These relationships remain only suggestions until more research has been done, but *provocative* suggestions they are. The following studies are derivatives.

Walker (1962) has made an elaborate study of children's body build and their presumably associated behavior as judged by nursery school teachers' ratings. Like Sheldon, he used nude photographs of the children as the basis for judging whether they were mesomorphic, endomorphic, or ectomorphic. After elaborate statistical treatment, he secured reliabilities of rating of around .75 for his 2-, 3-, and 4-year-old children, ranging from .71 for the 2-year-olds to .81 for the threes. Boys were more negativistic about having nude photographs taken than were girls.

Walker's premises were that preschool children show important associations between physique and particular behavior, with girls being steered by mesomorphic body builds into social behavior, boys into physical, gross-motor activity. "In particular, variations in physical energy, in bodily effectiveness for assertive or dominating behavior, and in bodily sensitivity appear as important mediating links between physique structure and general behavior" (p. 79).

Girls exceeded boys in rated endomorphy; boys exceeded in mesomorphy but less in ectomorphy, and were more variable. The correlations between ectomorphy and endomorphy were so high (—.87 for boys, —.84 for girls) as to suggest that a two-factor analysis (into mesomorphy and ectomorphy or endomarphy) would have been more suitable than a three-factor analysis.

For simplicity, only those correlations significant at the .01 level or below are reported for these children's relations between body build and behavior: Walker's endomorphs were self-assertive and revengeful, which is reminiscent of the traits attributed to them in the Staffieri study reported immediately below, where delinquent behaviors are considered to characterize endomorphs. His mesomorphs were easily angered, leaders in play, quarrelsome, ambitious, daring, taking chances, self-assertive, energetic, noisy, boyish in interests, revengeful, and self-confident. Again, with the exception of being quarrelsome and revengeful, these boys sound like the all-American boys described as the social stereotype for mesomorphs in the Staffieri paper, where it was found that "mesomorphs were all things to all boys."

Walker's ectomorph boys were described as the introverts—the non-objectionable neurotics—that Staffieri found in his social stereotype paper. They were not self-assertive, not noisy, not boyish in interests, not daring, not social in play, not a leader in play, do not attack others, not inconsiderate or unkind, not revengeful, daydream a lot, not self-reliant, not energetic.

Walker found almost no such relations for girls, with the exception of the fact that endomorphic girls recover easily from upsets, and mesomorphic girls attack others.

In other words, Walker uncovers considerable evidence for boys, although it is by an elaborate statistical system of ratings of body build and behavior, thus not as reliable as it might be, between body build and behavior, with endomorphs behaving in a generally delinquent fashion, mesomorphs in an assertive but socially acceptable boyish fashion, and ectomorphs in a withdrawn but "nice fashion."

His correlations, when he moves to an analysis of clusters rather than single variables, present very much the same picture.

Staffieri (1967; also Staffieri and McCandless, 1966) worked with boys aged 4 years through 10 years of age. He separated his subjects according to ectomorphy, using an index developed in England which is more objective—less subject to ratings from nude photographs—than the Sheldon methods. The index he used was:

$$\frac{\text{Height in inches}}{\sqrt[3]{\text{Weight in pounds}}}$$

In other words, his criterion groups of boys were long lean boys compared with short thick boys. He asked these boys to attribute a series of adjectives to three 15-inch silhouettes, one set of silhouettes representing adult meso-, endo-, and ectomorphs, and another set of silhouettes representing child figures that were mesomorphic, ectomorphic, and endomorphic. He found a remarkably similar tendency at all age levels, in his study of social stereotypes of body image in children, for the endomorphic silhouettes, whether of adults or children, to be described as socially offensive and delinquent, his mesomorphic silhouettes as boyishly (or manlike) aggressive, outgoing, active, a leader, and so on; and his ectomorphic silhouettes as retiring, nervous, shy—adjectives that betoken a nonobjectionable introvert or neurotic.

The youngsters were also given the chance to choose which silhouette they would like to look like, and overwhelmingly picked the mesomorph as first choice. They were also asked to choose the silhouette that looked most like them, and did so with considerable accuracy. This leads to the following conclusions: children (boys aged 4 through 10 years of age) know what their body build is actually like; they describe unfavorably, and in a socially rejecting way, silhouettes that are short and thick (endomorphs), as social introverts silhouettes that are long and lean (ectomorphs), and as boyishly desirable, leaders, and so on, silhouettes that are muscular and sturdy (mesomorphs). This leads to the conclusion that many boys, probably because of reasons of social stereotyping, reject their own body builds. Staffieri also found that ectomorphs and mesomorphs were chosen as the most popular by their peers, leading to the tentative conclusion that endomorphs are unpopular, reject their body image, and know that they are unpopular, which has many implications for personal adjustment.

Washburn's study (1962) moves beyond the pre- and elementary school age levels, as he worked with 16-year-old boys. He found, using the Parnell index for ectomorphy, that his short thick boys were considerably higher than his long lean boys in the self-concept variables involving manipulation of the external environment to attain approval as symbolized by social status. That is, these boys were more confident that they would manipulate their environments to suit themselves than were the long lean boys. There was a triple interaction here: it was hypothesized that the families of the extremely active, shortest thickest boys had worked on them to make them more withdrawn as far as environmental interactions were concerned, while the families of the longest leanest boys had worked on them to be more environmentally and socially aggressive. The variable of body build was found to be considerably more important for this factor of social conquest than the variable of family conflict. The boys with high family conflict were not affected as far as environmental mastery was concerned, while those with short thick body builds were "masters of their environment."

Cortés and Gatti (1965) worked with high school senior boys, college girls, and adult male prisoners. For all three groups, although only the boys are reported here, they found that mesomorphs rated themselves significantly more often as confident, energetic, adventurous, and enterprising, endomorphs as kind, relaxed, warm, and soft-hearted (related to Staffieri's rating of lazy), and ectomorphs as detached, shy, reserved, and tense, which again fits well with Staffieri's ratings of the socially acceptable neurotic.

Cortés and Gatti used indices of physical growth to give them much more reliable indices than Sheldon's. Ectomorphy was rated by:

$$\frac{\text{Height in inches}}{\sqrt[3]{\text{Weight in pounds}}}$$

Endomorphy (a predominance of the organs derived from the endodermic embryological layer of the soft, round, circular, fat physiques) was rated from subcutaneous fat in three sites of the body. These young people were referred to as the circular type. The mesomorphs, or triangular body builds (organs come from the mesodermic embryological layer which is more often found in strong, hard, athletic, muscular physiques), were rated by measuring certain bones and muscles of the arms and legs, while the ectomorphs, or linears, were derived from the height in inches divided by the cube root of weight in pounds index given above.

Cortés and Gatti's results are remarkably in line with Walker, Staffieri, and Washburn, and lead us to think that "there must be something here."

THE ADVANTAGES TO THE MALE OF EARLY
PHYSICAL MATURATION AND STRONG BODY BUILD

It has already been noted (Mary Cover Jones and Bayley, 1950) that adult raters give more favorable ratings to early- than to late-maturing boys, and that their peers esteem early-maturers somewhat more highly (although other research does not give strong support to this conclusion). It is not unlikely that positions of leadership are allocated earlier by adults to such 14-year-old boys. Hence, if expectations in any way govern development, the boys will develop into more responsible and mature people, more socially self-confident than late-maturers.

Certainly, there is a period of years during junior high school when the early-maturers excel at athletics because of their superior height, weight, and strength. Athletic prowess, for boys, is a matter of tremendous prestige. At maturity they do not, as a group, lose their status as far as height, weight, and musculature are concerned, and may as individuals remain burlier than average- and late-maturers (although within the group their adult height is distributed much like that of the male population as a whole).

It must be remembered that the vital capacity of these boys—the amount of oxygen per unit of time that the body can utilize—lags behind their more obvious physical capacity. In other words, although they may appear very grown-up, they have not reached adult stamina, nor will they do so for two or three years after they have achieved maximal height and adult weight. Stolz and Stolz (1951), in this connection, cite the case history of Ben, a boy tall and rugged for his years, who was placed early in competitive athletics but was not able to perform, and consequently lost much prestige. This failure appeared to be due to his lag in vital capacity—he simply could not gulp in and utilize the large amounts of air needed for persistence in hard physical activity.

Early-maturing 14-year-old boys possess a clear heterosexual advantage for a period of several years, maturing as they do at about the same time as the girls in their classes. Consequently, their drives and interests are relatively well matched with those of their feminine age-mates, and they are able to take out their girls without the embarrassment of being the shorter and slighter member of the pair.

Late-maturing 14-year-old boys, on the other hand, although for the most part they catch up in height and weight with their early-maturing peers, undergo a long period of social disadvantage during an important formative period of their lives. During this time, they are likely to be perceived and treated as relatively immature and irresponsible, are at a disadvantage in athletics, and are biologically unready for, and hopelessly outclassed in, courtship competition. As Kinsey has pointed out, early-maturing boys not only precede late-maturers as far as initial sexual experience is concerned, but they establish a regular pattern for sexual satisfaction much earlier and, for many years, retain a higher rate of sexual output than late-maturers. This pattern may produce considerable conflict for early-maturers during adolescence (before sexual activity is condoned), but its net effects should be positive, including as they do an important and enduring source of satisfaction and a contribution to a self-concept of sexual adequacy and virility. Such a self-concept should also favor satisfactory and appropriate sex-role identification (see discussion of this topic in the following chapter).

When body build is concerned, there is an apparently clear superiority in adjustment and social stereotype for mesomorph (triangular) boys over endomorphic (circular) or ectomorphic (linear) boys. The former, at the preschool levels, have been characterized as more boyish, energetic, adventuresome, and so on, while the endomorphs are aggressive and revengeful. The ectomorphs are seen as socially unobjectionable, withdrawn, and shy. In a study of social stereotypes, endomorphs are seen as socially undesirable, mesomorphs as highly desirable, and ectomorphs as neurotic and introverted. Children recognize their own body type and, presumably, the endomorphs and ectomorphs reject it. Endomorphs are not accepted socially as well as mesomorphs and ectomorphs. Another study of high school seniors shows that the short thick boys are self-willed and energetic, and in a high dominance relationship over their environment, whereas the ectomorphs are much more environmentally withdrawn. Still another study shows that these are the actual self-perceptions of these body builds.

PHYSICAL MATURATION, BODY BUILD,
AND ADJUSTMENT IN GIRLS AND WOMEN

These adolescent data for girls are given in the interests of complete and consistent coverage. Fewer data exist for girls than for boys concerning the relationship between body build and temperament, and between time of sexual maturity and later personality. H. E. Jones (1949) has made many provocative suggestions concerning these relationships. He has suggested, for example, that for girls in our society, early development is disadvantageous, late physical maturing advantageous—a pattern opposite to that for boys, but resulting from similar general social principles. There is some tendency for early-maturing girls to be stockier, later in their development, than their late-maturing sisters. In our culture, the stocky figure is not the fashionable one. The social gap between the early-maturing girl and the boys in her class is of course striking—a span of important years goes by before there is any boy of her age who is tall enough so that she can appear in public with him without feeling conspicuous. Sexual maturity attained while psychologically immature may engender confusion, conflict, and uncertainty. The early-maturing girl may be driven beyond her depth in courtship, dating boys substantially older and more sophisticated than she, with attendant social-sexual complications. H. E. Jones (1949) has reported that late-maturing girls were judged by adult observers to have attained higher prestige, and to show more leadership, than early-maturers. They were also rated as having greater social-stimulus value. Mary Cover Jones and Mussen (1958) state that, over a three-year period of time, late-maturing girls were more frequently mentioned in the high-school paper, and were elected to more offices in extra-curricular activities. However, an analysis of TAT stories told by these girls at the age of 17 revealed few differences between early- and late-maturers (only two out of twenty differences were statistically significant). If anything, on this measure of "fantasy," the early-maturers showed more characteristics believed to be favorable than the late-maturing group.

TRAIT STATUS AND PERSONAL CONCERN

Earlier in this chapter mention was made of the intimate relation between self-concept and attitude toward one's own body. It was also pointed out that a healthy, well-proportioned, strong, and graceful body undoubtedly aids, although it does not necessarily accompany, good emotional development and adjustment, whereas graceless and unattractive bodies often make personal adjustment more difficult.

The advantages, particularly to boys, of early physical maturity have been discussed. It has been pointed out that, by men at least, mesomorphic body build is more favorably regarded than endo- or ectomorphic structure, and is associated with masculine stereotypes and actual traits and self-concepts.

It is probable that most children, particularly before and during adolescence, worry considerably about the development of their primary and secondary sex characteristics. Schonfeld (1950), for example, believes that inadequate masculine physique (including delay of puberty, small sex organs, or deficiency in secondary sex characteristics) can be a matter of considerable concern to boys and result in serious personality conflicts or psychosomatic complaints (physical ailments often considered to be psychological in their origin). His report is based on a population of 256 boys seen by him, who had expressed concern over their physical development, or whose parents had been worried about it. Most of these boys, he found, were normal in the sense that their development fell within the limits of normal variability.

Schonfeld has reported very good success in treating these boys. Thirty-five percent of them were adequately taken care of simply by reassurance, and the majority of the rest profited from re-education, psychotherapy, and in some cases, hormonal treatment.

Angelino and Mech (1955) report that girls, too, worry about their physical development. Most of their worries center on the possibility that deviant height and weight development will interfere with, or complicate, their social and emotional life.

There is no question that children should receive more information than most of them are now given about the ways their bodies grow and are likely to grow. Few youngsters (or, for that matter, their parents) understand the wide variability in physical growth and the onset of pubescence. One boy, at 14, began to have nightmares and to lose weight. He became moody and depressed, was insolent to his parents whereas previously he had been a model boy, withdrew from his former circle of school friends, and showed deterioration of a previously highly superior academic performance. This boy was a somewhat late-maturing youngster who was, in addition, one year advanced academically, so that at 14 he was in a grade where he was the youngest by almost a year, and where some boys were almost 17 years of age.

On the basis of professional advice, his parents decided to leave, where he could find it, a little volume prepared by Shuttleworth (1949) which, by means of pictures and easily understandable text, portrays the great variability in reaching pubescence. The boy's natural curiosity led him into the volume and, almost as if by magic, his symptoms of conflict disappeared. A few months later he talked with his parents about his earlier conflicts and worries, and told them how obtaining factual information on the basis of which he could peg his own physical development, compare it with that of his older friends, and predict its course, had alleviated his concerns. Not all adolescent worries, of course, can be so easily dissipated.

Many adolescent worries are quite unrealistic, as, to some degree, were this boy's. Although objectively inadequate physical development can lead to conflict and disturbance, conflict and disturbance can also be tied, in symptomatic fashion, to perfectly adequate and normal physical development. A well-developed but insecure girl can (and many have been known to) blame her lack of social success on the fact that she is "too fat" or "too busty," when in reality she has excellent proportions. A normally sturdy, muscular boy can, in an almost neurotic fashion, think of himself as skinny, or an attractive but stocky boy can believe he is fat.

Motor Development

The author of the present book is not so much interested in physical and motor development per se, even though their study is a legitimate and necessary area of scientific study, as he is in the relations of physical and motor development for the infant and child in their relations to the world around them. For that reason, little has been given by way of norms for physical development, and norms and details (from the strictly motoric point of view) will be equally sparingly used in this brief section on motor development. For the student interested in a more detailed and normative treatment of motor development, such sources as Thompson (1962) will prove valuable.

Of more interest to the present author are the so-called physical and motor landmarks—those stages of development which result in a sharply changed relation of the child to his environment. Most of them may be loosely grouped under the heading of antigravity postures: the strengths and skills the infant and child develop to counteract the force of gravity which would bind them to one spot, flat on the surface of the earth. Speaking teleologically, it seems as though the ultimate goal of physical-motor development is to make the human organism as independent of gravity as is possible within the limitations of the human body. In other words, physical and motor development normally progress so that the organism is maximally mobile and self-propelling.

The most dramatic of the physical and motor landmarks (with the exception of pubescence) occur for normal children in their first 18 months to 2 years of life. From birth, the infant can move his arms and legs against gravity, but for a time his head and trunk are bound by it—thus his voluntary perceptual field is sharply limited. The first "victory against gravity" occurs in the first month of life when, while lying on his stomach, the infant can lift his chin and make primitive side-to-side movements of his head, thus widening his perceptual field.

The next major landmark, arrived at through the processes of maturation, learning, and coordination of fractional skills in an infinitely complex fashion, is the ability to get his chest and head away from the horizontal—off the floor or crib mattress, partly by the use of the back and stomach muscles and eventually with the help of the leverage of the arms. These skills are typically developed between 2 months and about $3\frac{1}{2}$ months. Again, the child's perceptual field is sharply increased over what has been available to him before.

During the next two or three months, another dramatic, perceptually broadening skill has been mastered—the abilities to move from belly to back, or from back to belly. These skills, coupled with the ability to hold the head steady and move it forward, backward, and sidewise, give the child a 360 degree command of his environment hitherto available to him only as someone lifted or turned him.

Soon after comes his first voluntary mastery of the world from a vertical rather than a horizontal point of view. At about 7 months, he is able to obtain and sustain for increasing amounts of time the sitting position. This gives him a new perspective on distance. It is, interestingly enough, often a time of excessive irritability as the child sees further than he has seen before, and perceives things at a distance that, through experience or because of curiosity or both, he values. But he cannot reach them. He is space bound and seems often to experience intense frustration and anger over his inability to reach that which he desires.

However, creeping and crawling follow soon after voluntary sitting, so that he can progress (by about 8 to 10 months of age) from where he is to where he wants to be. This is a major triumph over gravity, opening up to the infant an entirely new world, and putting to an end the period of frustration over seeing but being unable to obtain. That his perceptual possibilities are vastly increased thereby goes without saying.

Coordinate with his mastery of the antigravity postures comes increased ability to manipulate the aspects of the environment he can reach. Some time between about 32 and 52 weeks he develops a behavior essentially as uniquely human as speech: thumb-finger opposition. With an efficiency paralleled by no other organism, he can bring these objects that are graspable and liftable close to him to mouth, turn, smell, feel, and otherwise manipulate. Another perceptual curtain is lifted.

At about 11 months, gravity is still further defeated as he becomes able to pull himself to a standing position and soon thereafter to embody the beginnings of walking by moving crabwise, while holding on, around the edges of tables. A new dimension of height is added to his perceptual fare.

In another two or three months, he can stand alone, not holding on to anything; and by about 13 or 14 months, the average baby is walking. Posturally, he has become a human!

He is running by the time he is 2. For some time preceding this, if given the chance to practice, he has been able to manipulate stairs. By 3, if given the opportunity, he has mastered the lever and he can tricycle. In other words, the fundaments of motor and physical development have been mastered. Coupled with his activity drive, his curiosity, the period from about 15 months to about $2\frac{1}{2}$ years is a time of parental concern and anxiety, as well as pride. The child can get almost anywhere, obtain almost anything (all to the enrichening of his perceptual-cognitive life) but, once obtained, he has no sense about its use. He does not know the dangers of chewing the matches he can now reach, nor does he know that the now available knife is a lethal weapon. Constant supervision is necessary, and endless patience is demanded. The wise and patient mother can make the runabout years unbelievably rewarding and enriching. The too fearful or restrictive mother can blunt and distort the child's entire relation with his environment, while the negligent mother runs the risk of having her child involved in dangerous, even fatal accidents.

During this time, from about 6 months of age when the first tooth erupts, the child has become a biting and chewing rather than a mouthing and gumming organism. For United States children, biting and chewing have replaced sucking by 2 years of age or earlier. The teeth are not only the tools for new methods of securing sustenance, but are powerful weapons of defense. Along with toilet training, one of the earliest limitations and controls a child must learn is that against biting as a means of aggression—a lesson many children find it hard to master.

Summary

The human body, the way it is handled, and general physical appearance are fundamentally linked to social living, self-concepts, and very possibly choice of vocation. Charting how the body grows and develops is an important task assumed by scholars in child development and physical anthropology. One major goal of such scholars is to describe and establish the norms, or general characteristics, of physical growth and body build and function. These norms do not *explain,* but they assist in establishing a range of acceptable variation, which is useful both psychologically and physically.

A second task assumed by research workers in the field of physical growth is to uncover general principles of development. To date, the cephalocaudal (head to tail) and proximodistal (center axis to periphery) principles of development hold up well for both physical growth and motor development. The third principle is that of development from general to specific action patterns. This principle has aroused considerable argument; the best conclusion that can be drawn is that, whereas the most conspicuous development is from the general to the specific, development in the other direction also occurs: the processes are complementary.

Different parts of the body grow according to different patterns. The *neural* pattern is one of rapid increase during infancy and slow gains during later childhood and adolescence; the *sexual* pattern is one of little change (long latency) up to somewhat before the time of adolescence (12 or 13 years for boys, 11 or 12 for girls). At this time the primary and secondary sex characteristics "mushroom," usually reaching mature development in five or six years. The *somatic* pattern (including changes in height and weight) is one of rapid growth in infancy, moderately rapid growth in childhood, a spurt preceding pubescence, and a tapering off from the middle to the late teens.

Other scientific goals in the study of physical growth include determining the factors that modify physical growth, and their relation to growth, health, stamina, and so on at all age levels. For example, how does growth vary from season to season, or from one climate to another? Does excessively rapid growth in infancy exert a positive or deleterious effect on the health of adolescents and adults, and so on. Another goal is to determine the relation between physical growth and other aspects of development: How are patterns of growth related to strength and speed, or to intelligence?

Physical growth, by definition, involves change. The seven varieties of anatomical change that have been most studied are the following:

1. Changes in kind. The zygote is very different in kind from the sperm and egg that make it up; pubic is very different from childhood down.

2. Changes in number. At 5, the child has 48 to 52 teeth in one stage of development or another; by adolescence, 20 deciduous (baby) teeth have been lost; by late adolescence one or more third molars (the wisdom teeth) have often been lost; and by old age it is common to have lost all of one's teeth.

3. Changes in size. The child steadily increases in height, for example, to 18 years or so, but in middle and old age height actually decreases; the primary sex characteristics develop very slowly during childhood, but increase dramatically in size before, during, and for a time after puberty.

4. Changes in shape. The proportions of the adolescent are very different from those of the baby; the chest becomes broader and flatter during childhood, more circular again after middle age.

5. Changes in position. Elbows and knees at first project outward from the sides of the body—later the knees rotate toward the front, the elbows toward the back; feet move from paralleling the axis of the lower leg toward the perpendicular.

6. Changes in pigmentation. Hair usually grows darker during childhood and ordinarily grays in middle and old age; skin darkens in middle age.

7. Changes in texture. Muscles harden, particularly for males dur-

ing and after adolescence; in middle and old age, bones become brittle and skin loses its elasticity.

Changes in function also occur. The mouth becomes less an instrument of sucking, more an instrument of biting, chewing, and vocalizing; the sphincters come under voluntary control; legs are used for walking. The penis acquires the function of ejaculation.

Babies seem to be divided about evenly as far as "natural" hand preference is concerned; but by about their second year, 90 percent or more of them have chosen or been trained to right-handedness. When it is possible to develop a right-handed preference without undue pressure on the infant, this should be done; our culture is *dextral,* and it is obviously more convenient to be right-handed.

Sexual behavior varies greatly according to social class; and men seem to indulge more in sex, including its fantasy aspects, than women. Overt sexual behavior seems to be more "social" among those with less education (they tend more to *mutual* sex behavior, less to such solitary sex behavior as masturbation). Almost all boys and men have masturbated to orgasm, and most have experienced intercourse before marriage; whereas about 50 percent of women enter marriage as virgins, and only about one fourth of them have masturbated. Women's sex desires reach their maximum later than those of men, and these trends may produce complications in the relations between the sexes.

Attainment of physical maturity is an important landmark in our culture. It comes at a time when the child is changing in many ways. Indeed, social change for young people in their early teens is as dramatic as physical change, and the two are closely linked in their dynamics and their results.

For boys, almost all the consequences of early physical maturity—immediately and for fifteen or more years thereafter—appear to be fortunate. Early exposure to opportunities for leadership, the prestige they enjoy in athletics during this important and formative period, the closing of the social gap between them and girls of their own age—all seem to give them a "start" that is better than that enjoyed by the late-maturing boy.

For girls, the evidence concerning the effects of differential physical maturity is unclear. Temporarily, early maturity may be to their advantage, but long-lasting positive correlates of early maturity have not been revealed.

There is no convincing evidence that body build is associated with personality, although one interesting study indicates that if there are correlations between personality and body build, social mediation could account for them. In United States culture, the mesomorphic (muscular) body build is regarded far more favorably than the ectomorphic (long

414   PHYSICAL GROWTH AND MOTOR DEVELOPMENT

and lean), which in turn meets with more approval than the endomorphic (stocky). If social expectancies have an influence on personality, the positive expectancies held for the mesomorph should influence him favorably, whereas the negative expectancies for the mesomorph may have deleterious effects. This study has led to several others, indicating that mesomorphs (triangular body builds) are more "boyish" than endomorphs (circulars) who are seen as fat, lazy, and socially undesirable; whereas ectomorphs (linears) are seen as socially acceptable introverts. Boys recognize their own body builds and ectomorphs and endomorphs presumably reject it.

Finally, the physical-motor landmarks are: head control, torso control, rolling over, sitting alone, creeping, standing, walking, running, tricycling, biting instead of sucking, and thumb-finger opposition.

Social and Emotional Development

The preceding chapters have been written taking for granted that the phenomena with which they deal exist in a social setting and are accompanied by emotions: child-rearing practices are social in nature and more often than not are determined by and responded to with emotions. Human learning is mostly done in a social setting, and the motives for learning are in large part social and emotional in nature. The self-concept is but one way of viewing how a person organizes himself as a social and emotional being; intelligence, as discussed in Chapters 7 and 8, is heavily socially determined, its expression and function may be facilitated or interfered with by emotion, and may be used in manipulating social situations and expressing or controlling emotions. Physical-motor development, while not socially determined, has an important effect on the social interactions of the person, and it may be that certain types of physical constitution are associated with special types of emotional adjustment, although the evidence is not clear.

For these reasons, it is appropriate to take up the theory and substantive research that bear directly on social and emotional development. For purposes of convenience, these topics are combined in this chapter. As will be seen, research and theory are more complete and sophisticated for social than they are for emotional development, where the science of human behavior is still quite primitive.

Social Development

The term *socialization,* as the psychologist uses it, refers to a wide range of behaviors and processes. We say that a child has begun to be socialized when he first responds to other people (usually, his parents) by some recognizable, consistent, and predictable sign that they are meaningful stimuli for him. Some say that the first real sign of socialization is the smile (Gray, 1957), which typically appears as a response to the father or mother around the age of 6 to 8 weeks. The following are other early signs of socialization: The child stops crying when he sees his mother; laughs at the sight of his parents; plays peek-a-boo; waves "bye-bye"; pulls at his mother to indicate his need for help when he cannot reach something he wants; gestures, pulls, or attempts to climb the adult to show that he wants to be held; cries when his parent leaves him; acts differently with strangers than with his parents or intimates.

These are all *social responses.* Socialization, however, implies not only social responsiveness but also *social* (and, ultimately, personal) *controls:* the child stops doing something when his mother says, "No, no," or does something he does not want to do when he is asked by her to do it. As he grows older, he can often be heard saying "no, no" to himself as he reaches for the forbidden ashtray or figurine, even when his parent is absent. The time comes when he signifies that he has to go to the toilet, and later he inhibits urination or defecation for considerable periods until he can be helped or can go independently to the toilet. As he grows still older, he will eat only his share of the brownies his mother has baked, saving their share for older brothers and sisters away at school. He may bring home to parents and siblings a portion of the birthday cake he has been offered at a party. Eventually, he postpones some of his own immediate gratification to do things that may be rewarding only in the far-distant future: he relinquishes basketball after school to do his homework or practice the piano; he saves money from baby-sitting or a paper route to apply it to a family vacation or a later college education.

First, then, comes social *response;* later come social and impulse *control.*[1]

The Agents of Socialization and Their Goals

Socialization implies not only an object—the child—but an agent, at first, ordinarily, the parents. It is thought that socialization (in the sense of control) will not occur at all until and unless the parents, *in and of themselves,* become reinforcers or rewarders to the child. If this parental role is lacking, social response will also be severely retarded. Typical parents acquire reward value (or reinforcement properties) by giving the child routine but tender physical care: the baby is fed, washed, dressed, bathed, put to bed; and this is done not coldly and mechanically, but with coos, pats, kisses, and lullabies. It has been demonstrated (Rheingold, 1956) that early infant routines accompanied by social stimulation, including bodily contact, produce more socially responsive babies than routines carried out coolly and efficiently, but impersonally and quickly.

---

[1] In sociology, the term *socialization* is ordinarily restricted to the second meaning, "adopting society's rules of behavior."

Babies handled in the latter fashion speed up in their rate of social development when the type of treatment is changed to one of tender, loving care, and quickly learn social responsiveness. Rheingold, Gewirtz, and Ross (1959) have also demonstrated that a baby can quickly be conditioned to make social responses and to increase them in frequency when an adult responds socially to the baby's vocal responses.

Once the child is responding socially, it becomes necessary to train or channel his responses so that they are acceptable to his parents, brothers and sisters, and society at large. "Bye-bye" and "peek-a-boo" are well-regarded in 1-year-olds, but inappropriate in this form for kindergarten. Wet diapers are all right at age 1, but frowned on at age 4. Crying for food is appropriate behavior in the 9-month-old but not in the fifth-grader. More and more control and direction of behavior are demanded of the child from the time he first begins to make social responses until he becomes a civilized, law-abiding, relatively unselfish adult.

The process of social control and adaptability starts with the child's interactions with his parents and family, and continues with his playmates, relatives, and teachers. These socializing agents must provide a pattern of reward, acceptance, permissiveness, and punishment that enables the child to gain law- and amenity-abiding adulthood yet remain or become relatively secure, calm, happy, appropriately masculine or feminine, and vocationally self-sustaining.

According to Erikson (1956), the socialization process consists of eight phases—the "eight stages of man." Erikson has been deeply influenced by Freud, but he also adopts a strong social point of view in his account of personality development. His eight stages of man were formulated, not through experimental work, but through wide-ranging experience in psychotherapy, including extensive experience with children and adolescents from low- as well as upper- and middle-social classes. These stages are linked less than Freud's to organ systems, and more to the types of learning that go on at different age levels. Each stage is regarded by Erikson as a "psychosocial crisis," which arises and demands resolution before the next stage can be satisfactorily negotiated. These stages are conceived in an almost architectural sense: satisfactory learning and resolution of each crisis is necessary if the child is to manage the next and subsequent ones satisfactorily, just as the foundation of a house is essential to the first floor, which in turn must be structurally sound to support the second story, and so on.

For Erikson, the eight stages of development are the following:

1. Learning trust versus mistrust. Chronologically, this is the period of infancy—the first one or two years. The child, well-handled, nurtured, and loved, develops trust and security and a basic optimism (see Chapter

3). Badly handled, he becomes insecure and mistrustful.[2] Freud, it will be recalled, refers to this as the oral phase, and Sullivan believes that, during it, learning is empathic.

2. Learning autonomy versus shame. The second psychosocial crisis, Erikson believes, occurs during early childhood, probably between about 18 months or 2 years and $3\frac{1}{2}$ to 4 years of age. It coincides generally with Freud's anal stages and, in our culture, is the period when one of the most obvious "learning of control"—toilet training—is being acquired. The "well-parented" child emerges from this stage sure of himself, elated with his newfound control, and proud rather than ashamed. Autonomy is not, however, entirely synonymous with assured self-possession, initiative, and independence but, at least for children in the early part of this psychosocial crisis, includes stormy self-will, tantrums, stubbornness, and negativism. For example, one sees many 2-year-olds resolutely folding their arms to prevent their mothers from holding their hands as they cross the street. Also, "The sound of NO rings through the house" or the grocery store.

3. Learning initiative versus guilt. Erikson believes that this third psychosocial crisis occurs during what he calls the "play age," or the later preschool years (from about $3\frac{1}{2}$ to, in the United States culture, entry into formal school). During it, the healthily developing child learns to imagine, to broaden his skills through active play of all sorts, including fantasy; to cooperate with others; to lead as well as to follow. Immobilized by guilt, he is fearful; hangs on the fringes of groups; continues to depend unduly on adults; and is restricted both in the development of play skills and in imagination. This stage seems to combine Freud's phallic and Oedipal stages.

4. Industry versus inferiority. Erikson believes that the fourth psychosocial crisis is handled, for better or worse, during what he calls the "school age," presumably up to and possibly including some of junior high school. Here the child learns to master the more formal skills of life: relating with peers according to rules; progressing from free play to play that may be elaborately structured by rules and may demand formal teamwork, such as baseball; mastering social studies, reading, arithmetic. Homework is a necessity, and the need for self-discipline increases yearly. The child who, because of his successive and successful resolutions of earlier psychosocial crises, is trusting, autonomous, and full of initiative will learn easily enough to be industrious; but the mistrusting child will doubt the future; the shame- and guilt-filled child will experience defeat and inferiority. This stage corresponds to Freud's latency period.

---

[2] In this connection, it may be profitable to return to the discussion of Sullivan's theories in Chapter 2.

5. *Learning identity versus identity diffusion.* During the fifth psychosocial crisis (adolescence, from about 13 or 14 to about 20) the child, now an adolescent, learns how to answer satisfactorily and happily the question of "Who am I?" But even the best-adjusted of adolescents experiences some identity diffusion: most boys and probably most girls experiment with minor delinquency; rebellion flourishes; self-doubts flood the youngster, and so on.

Erikson believes that during successful early adolescence, mature time perspective is developed; the young person acquires self-certainty as opposed to self-consciousness and self-doubt. He comes to experiment with different—usually constructive—roles rather than adopting a "negative identity" (such as delinquency). He actually anticipates achievement, and *achieves,* rather than being "paralyzed" by feelings of inferiority or by an inadequate time perspective. In later adolescence, clear sexual identity—manhood or womanhood—is established. The adolescent seeks leadership (someone to inspire him), and gradually develops a set of ideals (socially congruent and desirable, in the case of the successful adolescent). Erikson believes that, in our culture, adolescence affords a "psychosocial moratorium," particularly for middle- and upper-class American children. They do not yet have to "play for keeps," but can experiment, trying various roles, and thus hopefully find the one most suitable for them.

6. *Learning intimacy versus isolation.* The successful young adult, for the first time, can experience true intimacy—the sort of intimacy that makes possible a good marriage or a genuine and enduring friendship.

7. *Learning generativity versus self-absorption.* In adulthood, the psychosocial crisis demands generativity, both in the sense of marriage and parenthood, and in the sense of working productively and creatively.

8. *Integrity versus despair.* If the other seven psychosocial crises have been successfully resolved, the mature adult develops the peak of adjustment: integrity. He trusts, he is independent and dares to essay the new. He works hard, has found a well-defined role in life, and has developed a self-concept with which he is happy. He can be intimate without strain, guilt, regret, or lack of realism; and he is proud of what he creates—his children, his work, or his hobbies. If one or more of the earlier psychosocial crises have not been resolved, he may view himself and his life with disgust and despair.

These eight stages of man, or the psychosocial crises, are plausible and insightful descriptions of how personality develops. But at present they are descriptions only. We possess at best rudimentary and tentative knowledge of just what sort of environment will result, for example, in traits of trust versus distrust, or clear personal identity versus diffusion.

Helping the child through the various stages and the positive learnings that should accompany them is a complex and difficult task, as any worried parent or teacher knows. Search for the best way of accomplishing this task accounts for much of the research in the field of child development, particularly research such as that summarized and discussed in Chapters 3 and 6.

Socialization, then, is a learning-teaching process that, when successful, results in the human organism's moving from its infant state of helpless but total egocentricity to its ideal adult state of sensible conformity coupled with independent creativity.

PATTERNS OF PARENTAL REINFORCEMENT AND SOCIALIZATION

Moving satisfactorily through Erikson's eight stages of man obviously requires guidance, and it is logical that, at least during the first four stages, this guidance must come primarily from the family in terms of its patterns of treating the infant and small child.

Essentially, there are two ways of giving guidance to the child—the first through psychologically or love or intangibly rewarded methods; the second through physical, or concrete reward methods. The threat of the withdrawal of love comes of necessity early, as will be pointed out below, to the infant. His bottle cannot be given to him the moment he demands it. He must be isolated because he is naughty. He craves activity, but must remain for a few minutes longer in his bassinet or crib. The infant sees these deprivations as threatening to his security, as a loss of parental love. Later, he will come to modify his behavior so as to prevent this loss of love.

More sophisticated forms of threat of loss of love are denying the child the caress he seeks, or the smile he craves, or the word of praise he wishes.

Thing-oriented techniques of control range from inflicting physical punishment on the infant or child when he is "bad" to denying him food or treats, to bribing him for good grades or good behavior.

Love-oriented techniques of control tend to manage the child through demonstrating to him that intangibles, including the attention of other people, are important. They teach him self-control because he anticipates loss of love—punishment that he himself has brought on. Thing-oriented techniques of control teach him to be afraid of the tangible, even brutal punishment of others, and teach him shame—the need to be good because someone will hurt you or catch you. The former is control through guilt or conscience or the superego, and corresponds to moral development. The second is control through shame—behaving because someone will catch you. Guilt may be paralyzing if too omnipresent and strong, while shame, to inhibit the person, depends on "moral policemen" everywhere. Obviously, guilt is the more socially efficient of the methods of social control, working as it does in the absence of adults or policemen.

POSITIVE AND NEGATIVE REINFORCEMENT

These techniques of control may be applied in positive ways: mommy loves you because you do so and so; or negative ways through threat: mommy will not love you if you do not do so and so; or bribery, mommy will give you thus and so if you do so and so; or threat, again: mommy will spank you if you do so and so. These are known as positive and negative patterns of reinforcement, the former rewarding, and the latter punishing.

Other things being equal, it is almost certain that a child learns faster if he receives both positive and negative reinforcement. Positive reinforcement tells him what he may and should do, and negative reinforcement tells him what he may not and should not do. Thus, if he receives both types of reinforcement, he is more fully informed than if he receives only one.

These principles are well-illustrated in the work of Hartup, Moore, and Sager (1963), who show that little boys are taught to act in sex-appropriate ways by being rewarded for behaving in masculine ways and seeking out masculine toys, yet punished when they do girlish things or seek girlish toys. Girls, on the other hand, are rewarded when they seek girlish things, including toys, but are ignored when they behave in boyish ways, seek boyish toys, or act like tomboys. As would be predicted, boys learn sex typing earlier and more efficiently than girls. This finding is in line with other data presented by Brown (1958).

PATTERNS OF REINFORCEMENT

When reinforcement is administered immediately, consistently, and generously, whether it be positive or negative in type, learning apparently precedes more rapidly than when reinforcement is delayed, is inconsistent, or is meager and grudging. This last point is by no means clear (Mednick, 1964), and falls under the heading of amount of reinforcement. It may be that this is relative: a child will build to such and such a level of behavior under moderate reinforcement, and increase markedly if reinforcement is increased from that level, or decrease in efficiency and regularity of behavior if the schedule of reinforcement is reduced. The answer to these points is not known at this time, although it is believed that inconsistent or partial reinforcement, of the type necessary in the complex human domain, builds up more permanent learning (refer back to Chapter 4). No teacher or parent can possibly know all the good things a child does in order to reward him immediately, consistently, and generously. Hence, partial reinforcement. The partially reinforced child keeps hoping (for positive reward) or dreading (for negative reward), thus holds on to already established patterns of response longer than the consistently rewarded child.

PARENTAL POWER

All reinforcements are administered from a basis of power. Mischel (1958), and other studies of boys from fatherless homes (see, for example, Deutsch, 1962; Lynn and Sawrey, 1959; and Sears, 1951) show that boys brought up in father-present homes are more aggressive, at least in fantasy, than boys brought up with the father absent. Mischel shows that such father-present boys are more trusting (refer back to Erikson), and are more willing to delay an immediate but smaller reward for a delayed but larger reward. Mischel also demonstrates other advantages, at least in efficiency, of control through guilt: the older and brighter the child, the more he is willing to delay reward. If he has been reared lovingly, he will modify his behavior more when rewarded; if harshly, more when punished (Baxter, Lerner, and Miller, 1965). The experimental study from which this generalization is drawn was done using young volunteer men who were college students. Moulton *et al.* (1966), also working with young college men, showed that the more powerful *and* loving parent is more likely to produce sons who control themselves by means of their consciences; and boys from homes where the father is powerful and loving are better sex-typed (more fundamentally masculine: see Chapter 11) than when the mother is the more powerful-loving figure. Grusec (1966), in a well-conducted study of kindergarten-aged boys and girls, adds further solid evidence that highly rewarding (loving) adults are more likely than nonrewarding adults to cause children to criticize themselves (rather than, for example, blame others), particularly when "withdrawal of reward" techniques were used (either of a reward or punishment nature).

Wolowitz (1965) presents a diagram of the sources of power through which reinforcement is administered to children. The first type of power, easily perceived by the infant and small child, is physical power, of the type that lifts and soothes, by both father and mother. Later, the father becomes more possessed of it, according to the perceptions of the child, particularly the lower-class father, where physical labor is the common method of earning a living, is more likely to be seen as possessing physical power than the middle-class parent, and fathers are seen as possessing more power than mothers.

This may be disillusioning to the child, and damage his identification process as he comes to learn, as in the case of the lower-class father, that physical power is the least esteemed source of power, and that power through social and economic influence, or through wisdom and knowledge is more highly esteemed.

The second source of power is sexual: the child comes to see his parent as a sexually potent figure. This perception, Freud notwithstanding, probably does not come early, not until the child has built a perceptual and language basis for the perception of sexual power. If the father is seen only as a source of brute sexuality, the mother as a source only of primitive fecundity, the child's sex modeling may be sharply distorted. This is what often seems to happen to children, particularly those from the lower classes. Fathers ("Uncle Henry's") are present only to domineer and breed. What this does to a child's masculine model is probably very serious, where brutal maleness (masculine protest, in a sense) is seen as the only possible masculine model. This appears particularly likely to happen in father-absent homes, especially where promiscuity is present, and may characterize minority groups such as the lower-class Negro family where fathers are often absent and when those present are exaggerated sexual figures.

The third source of power is wisdom, or omniscience. This source of power, too, is somewhat subtle, and is seen by the child only when he is older. In our anti-intellectual society, wisdom and knowledge may never be seen as sources of power, although they certainly are to the curious, questing child.

The fourth source of power is social influence: Whom do your parents know? Whom can they invite to their house? Who invites them to their house? This source of power, like wisdom, tips the scales in the direction of middle-class parents whose wisdom and social influence are relatively great just as their fourth source of power, economic influence, is great. Papa may not be big and strong, but he knows a lot, important people invite him, and he brings home a large weekly paycheck. It is for such reasons that middle-class children are probably more amenable to the control techniques of their parents since their parents possess more power.

The ratio of positive and negative reinforcement against the background of power is also an important phenomenon. When physical strength accompanies punishment, but wisdom accompanies reward, the child's modeling or imitation is likely to be with wisdom. Other things being equal, it is probably true that all social learning (see Mussen and Distler, 1959) is more efficient, or at least more predictable, when the ratio of reward exceeds that of punishment.

Consistency in the use of power is also important. The consistently handled child learns how to modify his behavior so as to obtain what he wants and avoid what he wishes to avoid. Docility, in other words, can be rewarding.

TYPES AND URGENCY OF THE SOCIALIZATION PROBLEM

Adequate socialization is perhaps the human being's most important single accomplishment. An occasional total social misfit achieves, albeit unhappily, the status of genius; but the vast majority of socially maladjusted people lead lives that are miserable for them and produce misery for their fellow men. Wars reflect the ultimate failure of socialization of groups; psychosis, delinquency, narcotic or alcohol addiction, psychopathy and crime, homosexuality, possibly certain types of mental deficiency, and neurosis are extreme examples of failure in socialization by individuals. Tragically, in a nation with perhaps the most advanced natural science and technology in the world, we have at present only the most rudimentary science of socialization. In United States society the frequency of such failures of individual socialization as those listed above is as high as, or higher than, that of other Western European, Eastern, or "primitive" cultures. We lead, for example, in our rates of delinquency, crime, and divorce; and are well toward the front in our incidence of drug and alcohol addiction, psychosis and neurosis, and sexual aberration (perhaps only because we have the best statistical and census facilities).

The terrible social urgency of these various problems, plus the likelihood that failures of socialization originate in early childhood, is the reason this book gives such diligent attention to the admittedly very incomplete data about socialization. Some have said that all psychology is social psychology, and perhaps this should be the case.

The discussion of socialization follows logically from the content of the last several chapters. A basic assumption accepted here is that socialization occurs as a result of the learning process, as this has been described in Chapters 4 and 5. Neither the innate evil nor the innate good of man is assumed; only his almost infinite malleability through learning. Much social learning is clearly conscious: children learn not to walk on the tulip bed because their parents have said frequently, consistently, and emphatically that this is not to be done, and because they themselves can see the damage to the flowers which they, as well as their parents, enjoy. More subtle and complex learnings occur through a combination of tutelage, maturity, and personal intellectual effort.

A 5-year-old announced one day that she had begun to enjoy her kindergarten rest time, except when Ellen, a "fighting friend" of hers, got to sit on the teacher's lap. "This," she stated with annoyance, "is just not fair!" Her mother asked, "What *would* be fair?" With little hesitation she said, "It would be fair if I got to sit on her lap first." After a minute of thought, she added, "But David (her good friend) ought to have a turn, too. Then me again." A long pause followed, then the beginning of insight: "But maybe all the other kids feel like I do— maybe they all want to sit on Miss Rickard's lap. Maybe they don't think it's fair when I get to."

Still more subtly, perhaps unconsciously, other social learnings occur. Learning to dislike the odor and sight of urine or feces is probably not conscious learning, but is picked up from subtle parental cues. Indeed, as has been pointed out, it is likely that many of the learnings that belong to the family of the classical conditioned response are unconscious, yet we know that they are strikingly effective.

There is little reasonable question that large individual differences exist in the ease with which children are socialized, although there is not much acceptable *scientific* evidence about individual differences in socializability. Today the "bad seed" idea of genetic transmission of psychopathic and criminal personality is not accepted; nor is it by any means clear that there is an important relation between genetics and most mental illness or even the majority of cases of mental deficiency. But there are strong suggestions of subtle interactions between constitution and environment that make it harder for some children than for others to grow into reasonable, controlled adults. Research by Sontag (1941), for example, suggests that children born following certain types of difficult pregnancy are more active, impulsive, and irritable than children whose mothers have had uneventful pregnancies. Observations and individual case histories accumulated during some of the longitudinal studies of development (Ames, 1957; Mary Cover Jones, 1957; Mussen and Jones, 1957) suggest that interactions between the social and physical environment and physique, time of reaching physical maturity, and activity level may produce very different effects on personality.

The life of a placid girl baby born as an only child to tired, middle-aged parents will, for example, be very different from that of a hyperactive, impulsive little boy born to the same parents. But if the phlegmatic little girl were born to a youthful couple whose way of life included strenuous activity from early morning until late at night, the consequences for her personality would almost certainly be very different. Late physical maturity can be much more traumatic for a boy with an early-maturing brother only a year younger than he than for a boy with *no* younger brothers or brothers *much* younger than he or brothers who are also late-maturers. And so it goes.

Birth order, for example, has obvious and subtle influences on children. The literature for firstborns, for example, reveals that they are bossy (see, for example, Sutton-Smith and Rosenberg, 1966; Hilton, 1966; and Oberlander and Jenkin, 1966), having had as their first childhood experiences the repertoire of being the older, more dominant child. They are also apparently more bound to their parents because of having been reared more according to love-oriented techniques, with a longer period of verbal and loving interaction with the parents. Thus, they are more intelligent, more suggestible, more likely to volunteer for unpleasant tasks (perhaps to operate according to guilt), more conforming, and more likely to behave in ways calculated to assure them social-emotional returns in terms of love and affection.

All the considerations and circumstances described in the previous chapters apply to socialization. Socialization depends, first of all, on sensorimotor stimulation. Intelligence certainly plays a major role. The child of low intelligence is by definition less sensitive to the complex environmental cues that can guide his socialization. The extremely bright child may be so much more perceptive than his age-mates that his very acuity puts him out of touch with them, thus complicating his process of socialization.

The child whose parents differ markedly from their community may also have special socialization problems. The permissively reared child in a strict, conforming neighborhood may constantly run afoul of neighborhood parents other than his own, and be rejected by his community playmates because of his freedom of action. Members of minority groups, whether ethnic or religious, experience peculiar complexities in socialization, as do children whose parents belong to a socioeconomic level diverging sharply from that of the rest of their neighborhood.

The Socialization Process

PRESSURES TOWARD SOCIALIZATION

Every society has developed sanctions concerning the behavior of its members. The most nearly universal one is directed toward control of sexual behavior: all known contemporary societies include rigid incest taboos. Every organized society must have prohibitions concerning aggression. Such prohibitions range from forbidding physical combat among preschoolers to prohibiting murder. Rules, formal and informal, exist in all societies for the protection of property. Certain minimal standards of parental conduct toward children are ordinarily prescribed. Some nations have state religions; others, such as the United States, have informal sanctions that encourage but do not require the individual to profess and practice religious belief.

In other words, through implicit and explicit codes, most of which have a moral, or right-wrong overtone, societies set up standards of behavior for their members. Great latitude may be granted the individual in some societies, relatively little in others; and a specific society may vary widely in permissiveness from one time to another. Freedom of political thought and action in a democracy is, for example, usually curtailed during a time of war and the period of readjustment following war. The penalties for deviation from acceptable conduct vary widely: the death sentence for murder is common in Western European civilizations; but the middle-class mother who breast-feeds her baby beyond 18 months is only gossiped about. Random heterosexual activity by young males, although against formal canons of law and Judeo-Christian religious teaching, is winked at and even envied; the same sexual activity on the part of a girl may result in her being firmly, albeit informally, ostracized.

In short, the political-religious organization of any organized society blends with, influences, and is influenced by the informal sanctions of that society in defining correct conduct for its members and in setting up the methods by which parents and the community guide and direct children's conformity to social norms. For example, our society has quite clear expectations about dependency, sex, and aggressive behavior on the part of children and adults of different ages and sexes. It also says that parents should not use brutal punishment on their children or neglect them in obvious ways. It is assumed that parents should love and protect their children, and set good examples for them. Yet our culture is in many ways contradictory: the obedient, conforming, sexless *ideal* 9-year-old boy is expected to become the independent, enterprising, adequately masculine *ideal* 21-year-old who welcomes his chance to serve in the armed forces. Many things that are taught children must be unlearned by them before they become successful adults.

SOCIALIZATION THEORIES

The development of any individual depends upon how he sees and reacts to the socializing forces of the culture of which he is a member. How does the whole process look to the child? Society prescribes the sort of a man or woman he is to grow into, and lays down certain rules to guide his parents and teachers. But what are the forces and perceptions *within him,* as an individual, that cause him to respond in one way or another to these forces *on the outside?*

There are two broad theoretical orientations to the socialization process. The first is represented by both psychoanalytic and social-learning theory. Each of these subscribes to the idea that the adult end-product is a direct function of the teaching forces of the family and the environment as the child perceives them and as they affect him. If these forces are benign, the resulting human product is a happy one; if malign, the net result is unfortunate. The organism is thought of as shaped by its experiences. It becomes good or bad as these experiences are good or bad. Psychoanalytic or Freudian theory places more emphasis than social-learning theory on certain critical developmental stages, during which certain prescribed types of experience have a maximum of effect, and somewhat discounts the influence on emotional or personality development of learning experiences after the ages of 5 to 7. Social-learning theory tends more to regard the human being as modifiable at any age. However, the influence attributed by each theory to *learning* is enormous.

The second broad strand of socialization theory holds that the forces of growth and development within the organism are essentially creative. If the child is *accepted*, if his developmental needs are not blocked by society, he will grow into a happy, creative, socialized individual. Such a theory does not discount the effect of learning, particularly when it is imposed in a negative, restrictive, and frustrating fashion. It simply argues that, given moderately constructive circumstances, the organism is self-directing, and that its self-direction is intrinsically constructive. Active teaching is assigned a lesser role in such theory than in Freudian or social-learning theory. The essential condition in the child's environment is acceptance. If that condition is met, everything will work out well. This theory was perhaps first enunciated in modern times by Jean Jacques Rousseau in *Emile*. Such contemporary theorists as Rogers (1951), Maslow (1954), and Gesell (1954) hold this viewpoint in common, although they differ in many of their derivations from it and their reasons for adopting it.

The difference between these two broad theories can perhaps be made clearer by an analogy from horticulture. The first theory would heartily endorse the principle, "As the twig is bent, so shall the tree grow." A good environment of proper soil, light, water, and fertilizer would be recommended. But active pruning, shaping, grafting, and cross-fertilizing would also be practiced. The second theory would also argue for an environment of proper soil, light, water, and perhaps fertilizer. But it would take the position that nature knows best how the tree is to grow. Pruning, shaping, grafting, and cross-fertilizing are to be left to the natural course of events plus the innate nature of the organism. There is a difference between the two theories (they are brutally simplified here) along the activity-passivity dimension, with *more* and *less* teaching activity, respectively, being regarded as "desirable" by the first and the second theory.

According to the first theory, the child will become social, altruistic, self-confident, or what have you, to the degree that he learns he must adapt himself to others in order to have his own needs gratified. The ease of this process, and the cost of it to the individual, will depend on the skill of the teacher and the appropriateness and effectiveness of the teaching process. According to the second theory, the germs of adequate adaptation or socialization are present in all people, and will come to soundest maturity in a benign and accepting but rather passive environment. It is probable that of the three theorists mentioned in connection with the second position, Gesell places more emphasis on inborn constitution and heredity than Rogers; that is, Gesell would not say that, given a suitable environment, everyone will turn out all right.

It is not known which of these two theories about socialization and development is correct—or whether, indeed, either of them is. Each places a heavy burden on those responsible for the environmental aspect of socialization—the first, or "learning," theory perhaps more than the second, or "developmental," theory. Both, with the possible exception of Freud as a representative of the first and of Gesell as a representative of the second, are optimistic. There are cross-overs between representatives of the two theories: Freudian theory seems almost to assume the "innate asociality of man," in the sense that the selfish, hedonistic, libidinous infant must be transformed into the altruistic and pleasure-postponing adult. Social-learning theory makes no assumptions about this issue, but postulates that altruism and pleasure-postponement are learned rather than innate. Freud, like Gesell, places heavy emphasis on universal, developmental-maturational sequences in growth, but does not put Gesell's emphasis on heredity as a determinant of individual differences.

LEARNING THAT OTHER PEOPLE ARE NECESSARY

Freud has spoken of the socialization process as a change from the *pleasure principle* of immediate need-gratification (characteristic of the very young child and infant) to the *reality principle,* which presumably govern the much older child and adult. This change seems to begin when the child realizes that his own gratification depends on the cooperation of other, older, stronger, and more proficient people, usually his parents. If he offends them by his own impulsiveness and "selfishness," then they in turn can keep gratification from him. At first it is likely that he conforms to their desires only to ensure that his own are met. Only later —often not until well into adolescence—does he begin genuinely to consider the needs of others because of an altruistic, "highly socialized" pleasure that he takes in seeing them happy.

The foundation of socialization is simply this: A socialized individual attaches importance and pays attention to people and the rules that have been developed to mold them into and keep them functioning as a society. If he is successfully socialized, he also rather *likes* people and has a generally positive attitude toward the majority of the rules of his society. Both introverts and extroverts can be thought of as being successfully socialized, since there is more than one method of successful socialization. The scientist or artist working alone in his laboratory or studio, and the insurance salesman, politician, or reporter who deals with dozens of people every day, are both socialized, although in different ways, to the degree that they direct or inhibit personal behavior in deference to people and social rules.

How is this regard for people and social rules developed? In discussing this question, the author has drawn most heavily on the work of Dollard and Miller (1950), Whiting and Child (1953), Bandura and Walters (1963), and Sears and his co-workers (Sears, Maccoby, and Levin, 1957). They in turn have been influenced by such theorists as Freud (1938) and Hull (1952), and have themselves been prolific in their research.

If a child is to learn to attach importance to people and rules, he must first attach *meaning* to them: to find out that they are useful, powerful, and associated with both rewards and punishments. The infant is helpless in satisfying his own needs. Without adults, he would die. Adults feed and warm and soothe and cleanse him. Soon, as a result of these ministrations, adults themselves come to have positive meaning for the baby; in the terminology of social-learning theory, they are perceived as "secondary rewards" or "reinforcements." The infant seeks them out not only to satisfy his *primary* needs, but also for themselves, to satisfy his newly developing *social* needs. As we have said, the smile that appears from 6 to 8 weeks of age is one of the first signs of socialization.

Evidence such as that presented in Chapters 1, 3, and 7 indicates that babies who have had little opportunity to interact with adults are seriously retarded and perhaps permanently blunted in socialization. We might also speculate on the consequences for socialization of *complete and consistent reward* in infancy. It is reasonable to suppose that those who have never been cold fail to appreciate warmth, and that those who have never been insecure or afraid attach relatively little importance to security and freedom from fear. The child, in other words, to become socialized, must first have experienced many warm and loving relations with adults; but he must also have learned the importance and value of these relations by having experienced at least their temporary loss.

In real life, this question is largely academic. There is no way to rear a baby so that he does not experience temporary and rather frequent loss of attention and love. Not the most diligent of mothers can always feed her baby the instant he becomes hungry. In even the most child-centered family, there are times during the child's early life when his parents are not there at the moment he needs them. The child probably sees such experiences as "abandonment" or "deprivation of love." They presumably result in enhancing his appreciation of love and attention, and increase the reward value that adults have for him.

In addition to the deprivations that must of practical necessity occur for all children, parents impose deliberate deprivations or other penalties on their children in order to produce the behavior the parent considers desirable, or to eliminate undesirable behavior. These deprivations range from "love-oriented" manipulations ("Mommy thinks it would be nice if you went to the potty," or "It makes mommy feel bad when you are a naughty boy") to object- or thing-oriented techniques. These in turn range widely, from depriving or threatening to deprive the child of some of his television time, or outdoor play, or allowance, through depriving him of physical comfort by spanking or slapping him. Corporal discipline and "punitiveness" are commonly placed under this heading of "thing-oriented" discipline.

Love-oriented techniques, although they may be vicious in their extreme form (the mother who, when only slightly thwarted, retreats to her room in tears to place a damp cloth over her eyes), seem to result in more dependable social control through the exercise of the child's own conscience than thing-oriented techniques (see, for example, Sears, Maccoby, and Levin, 1957; and Miller and Swanson, 1960). But research in this important area is very incomplete.

To become socialized, in short, a child must have learned that his parents and (through generalization) other people are important, and that he is dependent on them. Dependency, as a *theoretical construct,* should be distinguished from dependent *behavior.* In the first sense, it refers to the *reward characteristics of the parents and others,* which have presumably been developed through a combination of good mothering and fathering, coupled with anxiety about the loss of this parental nurturance. In the second and more common sense, it refers to the clinging, lap-sitting, affection- and assistance-seeking behavior usually referred to as dependent.

Those parents who have helped their child to acquire dependency (in the theoretical sense of the word) have provided a powerful tool for his later, more complicated socialization. If his parents, that is, are important and generally rewarding to him, then, through the process of generalization, other adults, children, and their rules also become important.

BASIC DRIVES AND PERSONALITY

As Freud and his followers, particularly Sullivan and Erikson, have recognized, the basic drives around which a child's dependency (and probably important aspects of his later personality) is organized are those that involve much interaction with adults. These are the drives he cannot satisfy himself, or whose expression he must alter to conform to adult standards.

The child can *breathe* on his own; no one tells him *how* to breathe; no one teaches him *to* breathe. Thus it is not likely that air hunger and breathing are extensively involved in personality development. On the other hand, the baby interacts constantly with adults in such matters as eating and cleanliness and, as he grows older, he must *change* his ways of eating and eliminating to conform to adult expectations. In our culture, he must also learn to inhibit or hide sex behavior or interest. These changes, suppressions, and concealments are all based on interaction, some of it usually unpleasant, with adults, and the expression of dependency and aggressive needs must themselves be altered with increasing age. Curiosity is undoubtedly another drive that enters powerfully into socialization.

It is plausible, then, that the drives most significantly related to early personality development and socialization are the hunger, eliminative, sex, and curiosity drives. Because these drives require the mediation of adults for their satisfaction, the child learns dependency; through deliberate or spontaneous manipulation of his dependency need he is taught elimination, sex, and aggression control, and his expression of the dependency need itself is changed. The same is true for curiosity, or the activity drive.

ALTERATIONS IN DEPENDENCY

Although early learning of dependency, in the theoretical sense, logically appears to be the foundation of socialization, dependent *behavior* must be sharply modified during the developmental process. The sort of dependency typically shown by the child between 1 and 2 years of age is inappropriate in the later preschool years. It is typical for the child of 2 to cling to his mother, to be shy with strangers, and openly to seek affection; but the child of 4 is expected to have modified this "babyish" behavior.

It has been found that, by the preschool years, children who are most dependent on adults are least popular with their age-mates (Marshall and McCandless, 1957; McCandless, Balsbaugh, and Bennett, 1958; and Marshall, 1960[3]). Interestingly enough, being dependent interferes more with girls' than with boys' popularity (McCandless and Marshall, 1957), probably because of differences in the type of dependency shown by boys and girls (Heathers, 1955; McCandless, Balsbaugh, and Bennett, 1958). The latter seem more frequently to employ what might be called *emotional* dependency; they cling to adults, apparently seeking reassurance and affection, or openly ask for affection. Boys do not differ greatly from girls in amount of over-all dependency, but the type they show is different. They are more likely to be *instrumentally* dependent: that is, to seek help in accomplishing the aims of their work and play. "Help me put the wheel on the truck . . . Where is the big plane we had yesterday? . . . Will you move this ladder for me?" These are dependency requests

3 Personal communication.

of the type made more frequently by boys than by girls, and they seem not to interfere with popularity.

Boys also appear to be more task-oriented than girls (McCandless, Balsbaugh, and Bennett, 1958). They will more often go to almost any length of compromise or combat to continue their activity, whereas preschool-age girls, when blocked or engaged in conflict themselves, ask the adult in the situation to settle it for them.

There is some indication that these different modes of dependency and different ways of making use of adults in conflict situations result from learning: mothers of daughters more frequently than mothers of sons intervene in their conflicts and help them work out solutions.

For reasons probably similar to those implied above (society condones and perhaps even approves dependency in girls, but condemns it in boys), dependent behavior has been found to be more consistent from childhood to adulthood for girls than for boys. Kagan and Moss (1960) have found rather substantial relations between dependent behavior in girls, as rated from their case histories at the age of about 7 and as rated independently by a second investigator from interviews when they were in their early twenties. There was no indication in the behavior of young adult men whether they had been highly independent or dependent in their seventh year. The authors attribute this difference to the effect of the culture. It is all right for girls to be dependent; hence they do not "disguise" their dependency as they move through later childhood and adolescence. The dependent boy, on the other hand, is "punished"; hence, whether he "feels" dependent or not, he assumes the cloak of independence.

Jakubczak and Walters (1959) have found that dependent 9-year-old boys are more suggestible than nondependent youngsters of the same age, and that they are swayed more by the opinions of adults than by the opinions of their peers. This finding suggests that the dependent youngsters were oriented more to adults than to their peers, and provides a possible clue about why dependent youngsters are less popular than nondependent ones.

Generally, in the preschool years, dependency and "seeking to do well at tasks," or achievement orientation, have been found to be negatively correlated. One study (Crandall, Preston, and Rabson, 1960) has found that the mothers of achievement-oriented 4- and 5-year-olds—presumably, nondependent children—reward their children when they seek *approval* and when they try to accomplish difficult tasks. The mothers' general affection and their pattern of reward when children sought emotional support or help, were unrelated to the children's achievement efforts, although it appears from the data in this study that those mothers who not only were affectionate but also rewarded their children's requests for help, emotional support, and approval may have been the mothers of children with the highest achievement orientation.

To some degree, a negative relation between dependent behavior and achievement orientation may be "built in." Achievement is usually defined as *independent* task-orientation, perseverance, and so on; hence, measures of dependency should be negatively correlated with it. But task-orientation which the child uses as a means of obtaining social reinforcers (approval, praise, affection) may well be positively related to dependency (Endsley[4]).

We have said that the behavioral manifestations of dependency must change with the age of the child—it is generally inappropriate for 8-year-olds to sit in the laps of their mothers in public. How does this change in behavior come about while the parent at the same time satisfies the child's "inner" need for dependency? There are five possible ways in which the change from immature dependent behavior to more mature independent behavior can occur. (1) The reward value of the parent is in some fashion reduced as the child grows older; or (2) the threat of the loss of love, which presumably intensifies theoretical (and behavioral) dependency, is reduced; or (3) the parents gradually transfer their rewards from dependent to independent behavior, yet continue to satisfy the drive for dependency; or (4) the reward value of peers increases; or (5) the child's increasing size, strength, and skill afford him increasingly frequent and wide-ranging opportunities to master his environment, thus reinforcing his independent and autonomous behaviors. Successful autonomous or independent behavior is probably strongly reinforcing, and is probably generalized widely, since it indicates to the child that he can now gain a given goal quite directly and *by himself.* In other words, he need no longer depend on a mediating agent whose behavior he cannot always predict. If independence succeeds in one area, the child will probably try to extend it to other areas.

It is most likely that (2), (3), (4), and (5) are the conditions that operate. With increasing ability to symbolize, to incorporate past experience by thinking about it, and to envision future experience, the child of consistent and loving parents comes to see that his parents have loved him in the past, love him *now,* and will presumably continue to love him in the *future.* Thus the fear of loss of love is reduced: the 8-year-old realizes, as the 3-year-old does not, that a baby-sitter for an evening does not signify parental desertion. Parents (as indicated by the Crandall, Preston, and Rabson study) may combine affection with reward for achievement, yet continue to accept and even reward immature requests for help and emotional support,[5] thus helping their children make the transition from the more immature dependent to the more mature achievement-oriented or independent behavior with a minimum of

[4] Manuscript in preparation.

[5] This conclusion from the Crandall, Preston, and Rabson study was reached from an inspection of their pattern of correlation coefficients, but not from a formal analysis of their data; nor is it among the conclusions presented by the authors.

sudden change and insecurity. It seems certain (from the research summarized above, and from observation) that peers become increasingly important to children, and that peers reinforce independent behavior, particularly that which does not obviously seek to elicit adult affection and support. Finally, with increasing age, strength, vocabulary, and so on, the child becomes more and more able to master his environment.

This section, then, indicates that a necessary condition for socialization—in the sense of both social response and social control—is learning that other people are necessary, and that one should therefore modify his behavior in accordance with their needs and wishes as well as his own. The fact that people are "important" can be thought of as theoretical dependency, and it is the lever society uses to mold the self-centered child into the considerate adult. Good mothering and fathering, plus anxiety about losing such a state of affairs, appear to be responsible for the development of dependency, so defined.

In the young child dependency is expressed in dependent *behavior;* but in our society the seeking of help, affection, and nurturance from adults must be transformed into independent, achievement-oriented behavior. This change is apparently accomplished by an increase in the importance of approval from peers; by a shift in parental approval from dependent to independent behavior, while at the same time the child is assured that he continues to be loved; and by the child's own ability to remember the past, understand the present, and predict the future. The obvious fact that increasing size, strength, and adaptability help the normal child to master more and more aspects of his environment also aids in acquiring independent behavior.

Mutual Interdependence of Social and Emotional Development

It is impossible to separate the topics of social and emotional development as, for its very existence, the former depends on the latter. When we speak of social interactions, we speak of emotionally loving and giving, or cold and withdrawn or grudging people. We go out toward the former, refrain from social interactions with the latter. Sympathy, as it were, begets social response of a positive sort, as does the "warm" smile, while the "angry frown" repels socialization, or stimulates aggression. The "cold shoulder" is responded to in kind. Hostility provokes hostility, friendship stimulates friendship, withdrawal begets withdrawal, approach leads to approach. Only through socialization—an analysis of the language of gesture and expression—are emotions even recognized, let alone responded to.

Some of the studies of emotion have used facial expressions as stimuli

(Schlosberg, 1954). It is considered that at least three dimensions are necessary to describe the emotions reflected in facial expressions. These involve activation (similar to the energizing function of drive described in Chapter 4); a continuum ranging from pleasant to unpleasant, and another involving attention (paying heed to the stimulus evoking the emotion to ignoring it). This last continuum should be further broken down into attention with a view to approach through to attention with a view to avoidance.

Another categorization of emotions sorts them on a three dimensional chart: emotions accompanied by pleasant approach, such as joy, love; emotions accompanied by unpleasant approach, such as anger; and emotions accompanied by unpleasant avoidance, such as fear. These again are all related both to the energizing and sensitizing functions of drive, as discussed in Chapter 4.

This drive state breaks down into moderate, pleasant or not unpleasant physiological concomitants, such as those characterizing elation, mild anxiety, and surprise, to mobilization of the whole emergency system of the organism, such as occur in anger and fear.

When the organism is mobilized for an emergency, the sympathetic aspects of the autonomic nervous system take over. Such mobilization may occur very quickly, but abates relatively slowly. For example, we will still show shock reactions for hours after a severe accident. When the organism is mobilized for an emergency, the pulse rate and blood pressure rise, thus increasing the efficiency of the circulatory system. Respiration rate also goes up so that individual can get and use as much oxygen as possible, and the inspiration/expiration breathing ratio increases. Adrenalin and sugar are released into the blood stream so as to provide for greater energy. The digestive tract is inhibited, in that muscular movements of the stomach and intestines decrease or stop. Accompanying this, salivation is decreased, producing the so-called dry mouth of the highly emotional person. Perspiration also increases to cool the "fevered body." This is all preparation for flight or fight but, oddly enough there is no distinction between the body's preparation for these two very different emotions, one an unpleasant approach, one an unpleasant avoidance emotion.

Emotions may be thought of as pleasant-integrative and unpleasant-disintegrative. The latter have been more studied in both children and adults, first because they have obvious physiological accompaniments and thus interest the physiological psychologist, even though he has not made much progress in distinguishing one violent emotion from another in terms of its physical accompaniments; second, because they are so disruptive of behavior and their study promises or at least relates to better human adjustment.

The activation dimension of emotion, as has been mentioned, relates to the energizing function of drive, as discussed in Chapter 4. It results in emergency mobilization of the organisms so as to seek out or avoid the maximum number of stimuli evocative of the emotion. Tranquilizers reduce the intensity of this activating state.

Energizing is the basis for Bridges' (1932) classification of emotions, in which she starts with excitement, which is present from birth. Differentiating from general excitement at a couple of weeks of age is the well-known emotion of distress; delight follows somewhat later, at about 2½ months. The present author would like to suggest an earlier date, corresponding to the first social smile of 6 weeks. Anger, disgust, and fear are differentiated between 3 and 6 months, while elation and affection come into being between about 9 and 12 months. Jealousy is a product of about 15 months, a time corresponding fairly closely to Sewall's (1930) observations of the development of jealousy in young children.

Watson (1919) postulated three primary emotions: love in response to stroking; fear in response to loud noises and loss of support; and anger in response to physical restraint. Watson's original theory has been pretty well discredited by now: mild restraint actually seems to reduce activity, and some children take real pleasure in sudden loss of support. Loud noises evoke startle responses, as do any sudden and strong changes of stimuli.

Young infant's facial and behavioral reactions to emotion do not seem to be any better differentiated than their physiological responses, according to research conducted in the 1920s by Sherman, in which responses to hunger, dropping, restraint, and sticking with a needle could not be differentiated by observers who did not know the source of the stimulus evoking the emotion.

Children's Anger   This section of the treatment of emotion has been discussed under the socialization of aggression in Chapter 3, with further treatment forthcoming in Chapter 13, when the topics of frustration, failure, and aggression, are taken up. It should perhaps be repeated here that anger *per se,* while it may make the child feel better momentarily, is likely to provoke retaliation, thus setting up a vicious circle of anger, retaliation, more anger, and so on. While anger cannot be avoided in children, attempts to divert it once it has arisen and to organize the child's life so that frustration is mild enough to be handled by techniques other than anger seem desirable. When the child *does* become angry, retaliation for the sake of retaliation seems one of the least effective ways of dealing with him.

Children's Anxiety   This was discussed briefly in Chapter 7, where it was pointed out that strong anxiety, like any strong drive state, is crippling to intellectual functioning and adaptive behavior, probably because it evokes so many responses that conflict with the suitable response. The topic of anxiety is also dealt with in considerable detail in Chapter 13.

Children's Fears   Perhaps the most impressive bit of evidence we have regarding children's fears is that which suggest that the sources or stimuli for fear are learned. Hagman (1932) finds a correlation between children's fears and that of their mothers in the .60s. Children share fears of wild animals, probably due to fairy tales that have been told them. In general, as with all human learning, fears proceed from the concrete, although improbable, such as lions and tigers, to the abstract, such as religious fears and fears of failure in school. Middle-class children seem to fear school failure more than lower-class children. Within limits, this fear may be adaptive (see Chapter 4, the energizing function), but carried to extremes, it is disorganizing, as are all the unpleasant-disintegrative emotions.

Fear may be distinguished from anxiety in that the latter is floating— it seeks antecedent conditions, and is generally stressful and excitatory. The individual probably does not know what gave rise to it, nor what will allay it. As is pointed out in Chapter 13, many children and adults use the relative comfort of fear, where the stimulus and method of fear reduction are known, to alleviate anxiety. At least, the situation—the stimulus response complex—for fear is known and clear, while that for anxiety is ambiguous.

Holmes has a classical monograph (1936) that provides many guidelines to help in reducing children's fears. What she does is make practical application of the principles of extinction as these were discussed in Chapter 4. She points out that extinction occurs not only simply through lack of primary reinforcement, but through verbal mediation. Her youngsters were helped with their fears of a dark place by being an active participant in explorations, finding prized objects in the dark, being accompanied into the dark by an adult (having new conditioning set up where the pleasant stimuli are stronger than the unpleasant), and so on. This monograph should be read by all who are involved in helping to allay children's fears once they are established.

Fears seldom arise, at least fears of the intangible and unknown, in known circumstances, and when they arise, they do not generalize widely. It may be well to have a child fear a given fierce dog, but when he generalizes this fear to all furry objects, then the fear is maladaptive. Reduction of anxiety, accompaniment of new experiences by "throwing light on them," or accompanying a child with the physical presence of the adult giving reassurance; avoiding sudden changes of stimuli; explaining; anticipating; linking to past experiences—these are all methods of helping children to avoid developing fears, or in helping him recover from them once they have been developed. Blind fears, in other words (see Chapter 4) usually accompany classical conditioning without interpretation; whereas instrumental learning is helpful in preventing or curing them.

The Pleasant-Integrative Emotions   These accompany love and security, and are not dramatic, in that no particular physical changes go with them. They are adaptive and pleasant, and add to man's enjoyment of his life. Ironically, they have been little studied, although we have studies in the context of friendship and the dimensions of social development that have been discussed in the early sections of this chapter which give us at least some information.

A Theory of Emotions   There is little that can be said here that has not been said in the preceding pages. Without emotions, socialization is a dim shadow of itself, and without emotion life would be very gray indeed. There are tremendous differences in individual emotional reactivity: one of the more helpful concepts deals with a continuum from sensitizer (the person in contact with all aspects of his environment) to repressor (the person who denies threat and presumably new stimulation of all sorts). The former is alert and anticipative, the latter inert and denying. The former reaction is probably more adaptive than the latter, although it may give rise to more anxiety.

But to say that there is a well-developed, coherent theory of the puzzling field of emotion would be to falsify. Actually, adults cannot understand children's emotions very well, violent as the latter are and in general attenuated and socially cloaked as the former are. The author frequently says that for an adult to know or empathize with a child's fear or rage or love, he must go to his own primitive dream life, his nightmares, or his sexual dreams. Such a device is helpful in understanding the brutal power emotions hold over children.

Animal Research

As in the development of intelligence, research on emotional development of animals may throw some light on emotional development and behavior of humans. To be sure, the research is suggestive only, but is worth looking at. As has been mentioned earlier, research on animals can be more carefully controlled than research with humans, and the effects of stress can be better studied, as animals can be subjected to experimental treatments that would be impossible for humans. It is for such reasons that the following, concluding section on research with animals is included.

HANDLING AND GENTLING

Levine (1956) studied the effects of handling rats (1) very early in their lives (from the day after birth through 20 days of age); (2) later in their lives (from 50 through 70 days); and (3) not at all. When all the animals were 71 days of age, they were subjected to training designed to teach them to avoid an electric shock. The early-handled differed consistently from the nonhandled group in the speed with which they learned to do this (they were faster, and made fewer errors); and in the indications of emotional disturbance they showed—that is, they defecated less, and fewer of them "froze." (Freezing is a frequent maladaptive reaction of rats to stress.) On the whole, the later-handled group fell in efficiency between the early- and the nonhandled groups. On most measures it was not significantly different from either.

Weininger, whose work is based on Hebb's thinking, has published three papers, one of them with co-workers, on the effects of gentling white rats in infancy (Weininger, 1953, 1956; Weininger *et al.*, 1954). His technique of gentling, typically, is to take a rat from about the time of weaning (approximately 21 days) for ten minutes per day in his left hand, holding the rat gently against his chest and stroking it with the thumb of his right hand from the head to the base of the tail at the rate of about 50 times per minute. Weininger has found consistently that the gentled animals gain weight faster and to a higher eventual level than do nongentled rats. This is a symmetrical weight gain; that is, the gentled rats are not only heavier but longer and bigger. They do not, however, actually eat more than the controls, but presumably utilize their food better.

Weininger's gentled rats showed less fear of open spaces: they ventured further and more frequently into the middle of a 6-foot metal enclosure, where the light was brightest (rats fear open spaces and light). They hugged the walls of this open cylindrical space much less than the nongentled rats. When placed under severe stress (immobilized by bandages without food or water for 48 hours), more of the nongentled showed heart damage on autopsy, and suffered more extensive duodenal and stomach bleeding. The nongentled rats seemed to have enlarged adrenal glands *after* this experience of stress; another group failed to show this differential enlargement *before* stress. Still another group, exposed to even more severe (120-hour) stress composed of immobilization, food and water deprivation, and marked, though accidental, heat deprivation, showed the same symptoms on autopsy. More of the nongentled rats than of the gentled rats died under such circumstances. Levine and Otis (1958) also found that the earlier their albino-rat subjects were handled, the more resistant they were to stress.

At least three other studies (L. Bernstein, 1952; McClelland, 1956; Morgenson *et al.*, 1957) using rats as subjects support the findings reported above, including one which demonstrates that consistently handled animals learn faster than nonhandled ones, and that early handling is superior to later handling. The author of this last study (L. Bernstein, 1952) emphasizes that his results may be due, not just to an enriched objective environment, but also to the building of a positive "emotional" relationship between the investigator and the animal.

Gentling, then, as done in the studies reported above, seems to produce important differences in animal behavior. However, one apparently carefully done study (Scott, 1955), using the same gentling techniques as those used by Weininger, found no behavioral or weight differences between gentled and nongentled rats. There is no obvious explanation for this difference in results, and we must at present rest content with the conclusion that the bulk of the evidence favors positive results from gentling, but that some important research exists to discount its importance.

ISOLATION AND EMOTIONALITY

The influences of restriction (as described in the 1954 Thompson and Heron study) on the emotional responses of dogs have also been studied by Canadian investigators. Melzack (1954) studied seventeen Scottish terriers, eight of them reared from puppyhood to maturity in homes, nine reared for a similar period in the restriction cages described earlier. They were tested about one month after release from the cages, during which time they lived relatively normal lives; and again about one year after this. During the year, all had been normally handled.

Melzack exposed the dogs to a mannequin head, a bear and a chimpanzee skull, a toy car, a balloon, an umbrella, and a live rabbit. After an animal had been in the experimental room for one minute, one of these objects was moved toward him in zigzag fashion for one minute. The umbrella was opened to a 36-inch spread, and the balloon blown to a 10-inch diameter over a 30-second period before being moved toward the dog. Recording for behavior concerning the rabbit was not made until it had made its first move.

Table 10.1 shows the frequency of different kinds of behavior between the two groups. The third and last columns show the significance of differences between groups.

These differences are rather striking. The normally reared dogs showed relatively more adaptive behavior (attacking or getting out of the way), whereas the restricted dogs behaved in an "immature," excited, nonadaptive fashion. As can be seen from Table 10.1, these differences decreased with time, but were still in evidence nearly a year later. The

Table 10.1   *Differences in Emotional Behavior Shown by Melzack's Scottish Terriers, Raised Under Normal and Restricted Conditions, Tested Soon After Release from Restriction and About One Year Later.*

	TEST AT 3 TO 5 WEEKS			TEST 10 TO 12 MONTHS LATER		
BEHAVIOR	RESTRICTED	FREE	*P*	RESTRICTED	FREE	*P*
Excitement	3.9	0.5	.001	1.6	0.2	.045
Avoidance	1.9	5.5	.001	4.0	3.5	NS
Aggression	>0<	0.2	NS	>0<	2.2	.03
No emotional response	1.3	0.8	NS	1.3	1.2	NS

same dogs had also been tested for intelligence in about the same fashion as Thompson and Heron's dogs. Like them, they had been found less apt at problem-solving behavior.

It may be that "intellectual" differences account for some of Melzack's findings, although the emotional tests given to the animals seem to involve few elements of problem-solving. The study is not contaminated— that is, the experimenter did not know which dogs had been reared free, and which under restricted circumstances. Melzack states, in conclusion:

When the restricted dogs were first released, their level of excitement was higher than any yet observed in the normal controls and was maintained for longer periods of time. . . . (The study) adds further support to the view that diffuse emotional excitement is a primitive disturbed response out of which avoidance and other forms of emotional behavior develop. It demonstrates, however, that this behavior is primitive only in so far as it appears prior to integrated forms of emotional behavior. It may appear at any stage of the animal's life when the situation differs greatly from any that the animal has already encountered. (p. 197)[6]

In another study Melzack (1952) reports that the restricted dogs showed remarkably maladaptive reactions to pain; that is, they were much slower in learning to avoid an electric shock. Two of his seven restricted subjects never learned to do so during the experiment. In this situation (the experimenter was directing a mobile toy car that admin-

---

6 Reprinted with permission of the American Psychological Association and R. Melzack, from Melzack (1954).

istered a shock to the dog), the control dogs were smooth and coordinated in their avoidance responses, the experimental dogs wild and haphazard. A retest two years later showed that the experimental dogs were still much less adroit at this avoidance than the control dogs had been at about 9 months of age. The experimental dogs also used very little "sense" in avoiding lighted matches or pinpricks, or in moving from the "hot," or electrically charged, side of an apparatus to the safe side. They actually spent much more time around the experimenter after he had burned or pricked them than they had done before, whereas the control dogs shied away from him. Some of the experimental dogs came snuffling back up to the fire immediately after having been burned by it.

Melzack and Thompson (1956) tested dogs reared under the same circumstances as those described above for the adequacy of their social behavior. When the restricted animals were put into competition for a plate of food with normally reared animals of the same age, they consistently lost. The normal dogs scored 57 wins (drove the other dog away); the experimentals only 7 wins. This difference is significant at the .001 level. Even when the normals were substantially younger, the experimental animals lost. Their social curiosity, when exposed to a strange dog on the other side of a chicken-wire fence, was less adaptive: whereas the normal dogs soon tired of sniffing and exploring the other dog through the fence, the experimental dogs showed the opposite tendency. The experimental animals also showed less adaptive reactions to a human experimenter playing the part of a friendly, a timid, and a bold man.

EARLY EXPERIENCE AND AGGRESSION AND SEXUAL BEHAVIOR

Aggression is often thought to be an inborn trait for all species. We know that, in man, learning influences its expression strongly, but it might be considered relatively unmodifiable in lower species. However, one study (Kahn, 1951) demonstrates that mice, subjected while young to a severe beating by other mice, grow up to be relatively timid and unaggressive. Evidence also exists that mice reared in groups are more aggressive as adults than mice reared alone (King and Gurney, 1954). Rats reared in litters of six (Spitz, 1954) when contrasted with those reared in litters of twelve, seem emotionally more secure, are less fearful, eat more, but compete less effectively both for food and for sex objects. The future of any species depends upon its adequate sexual behavior. Such behavior should presumably be the least modifiable by environment, particularly in the lower species. Yet several representative studies illustrate how profoundly this presumably instinctual behavior may be modified by social learning.

In one study (Kagan and Beach, 1953) rats were separated from their kind just before puberty. At the time of their separation, their behavior with the opposite sex had been primarily playful. Males so separated and replaced at adulthood in cages with females in heat behaved inefficiently, consistently interrupting their adaptive sex behavior with the play behavior that had been appropriate during their "preadolescence."

In another study (Hayward, 1957) it was found that as adults, male rats that before pubescence had been consistently shocked in the presence of adult female rats in heat, but not shocked in the presence of adult males, avoided the in-heat female much more than a control group that had not been shocked in preadolescence. The experimental rats behaved inefficiently when they came into the presence of the female, and spent far more time with the available adult male rat than did the controls, although they did not show homosexual behavior. Actual ejaculation did not, however, occur for either the control or the experimental rats in this study. The author entertains the thought that the electric shock may have disorganized both groups.

Male guinea pigs with previous sexual experience (Riss and Goy, 1957) have been found to show much more sex behavior with an in-heat female following periods of living socially than they do after periods of living in isolation. When males were separated from other animals very early in life, the disturbance of sexual function was more profound than when separation occurred later (Valenstein, Riss, and Young, 1955).

Denenberg (1964) pinpoints these issues when he says that the amount of stimulus input in infancy acts to reduce emotional reactivity in a monotonic fashion. For tasks which are easy or difficult, the relationships between performance in adulthood and infantile stimulation should be linear, although opposite in slope. He treats of the following stimuli: handling and electric shock on the stimulus side, and different types of emotional reaction on the response side, such as the open field test, eating and drinking behavior; learning behavior, including avoidance learning, and behavior on emerging or being given the opportunity to emerge from the home cage.

Denenberg also suggests that the more rapid an organism's development, the greater the effect of infantile stimulation. He also believes that subjects subjected to a severe but nonlethal stress should be best able to survive a subsequent lethal stress if they have received a considerable amount of stimulation in infancy.

To summarize this section on animals, research that has been done to test the effects of early experiences on the later behavior of a wide variety of animals—dogs, rats, guinea pigs, mice—demonstrates that such experiences exert a profound influence on problem-solving behavior ("intelligence"); social behavior, including aggression; responses to pain; sex behavior; and even such presumably genetically determined phenomena as weight and size.

Summary

Socialization of children necessitates distinguishing between social response—the raw material of socialization, and impulse control, the refined behavior that goes into socialized responses.

One theory of socialization was presented: Erikson's eight stages of man. Through childhood to adolescence, these are learning trust versus mistrust, autonomy versus shame, initiative versus guilt, industry versus inferiority, and identity versus identity diffusion.

Children are trained through these eight psychosocial crises by thing-versus love-oriented techniques of control, exercised according to directions of reward or punishment, according to the degree of immediate, consistent, and generous reinforcement that is given. There are four sources of parental power: physical, sexual, wisdom or omniscience, and social and economic influence. The lower-class child, for example, may be confused when he finds that his physically powerful father is powerless in the wisdom or social and economic influence areas.

Two major philosophies of socialization were discussed: the shaping, or Fruedian-learning theory; and the self-actualization, or laissez faire theory.

Socialization depends on learning that other people are necessary, and first becoming dependent on them, then independent from them. Dependency must move from the crying clinging behaviors of infancy and early childhood to the sturdy "I am my own man phase," although the changes are less dramatic for girls than for boys.

Social and emotional development are mutually interdependent. Social interaction overlays emotional interaction, in which the language of expression and gesture are all important. Emotions may be characterized as pleasant approach, and unpleasant approach and unpleasant avoidance (anger and fear respectively). The unpleasant disintegrative emotions put the organism on an emergency physiological basis, although fear cannot be told from anger, while the pleasant integrative emotions, which have been little studied, affect the basic physiology to a slight degree. The latter are facilitative of adaptive behavior, the former disruptive. There is no coherent theory of emotions.

Animal studies of infantile effects on adult emotionality indicate that the more stimulation is given in infancy, the more able the adult organism is to withstand stress, and the shorter the period of infancy, the more important the effects of infantile experiences.

Sex-Typing, Identification, and Moral Development

The most basic category into which human beings, regardless of race, creed, or culture, are placed is the category of sex: male or female. Associated with the obvious biological differences between boys and girls and men and women, are psychological and behavioral differences that are perhaps even more important for individual adjustment than the biological differences.

To be genuinely happy, it is essential in almost all cultures that *biological* maleness or femaleness be accompanied by *psychological* and *social* maleness or femaleness. It is possible, of course, to be happy as, for example, a homosexual; but this happiness (at least in a culture like that of the United States) is gained at a heavy price, and there are few who would choose to have their children grow up with a homosexual adjustment.

Sex-typing, as it is discussed in this chapter, refers to the learning process by which children learn behaviors and adjustments appropriate to their biological sex. Along with sex-typing goes the process of identification (a psychological accompaniment of sex typing). Finally, identification—incorporation of the standards and adjustments of the parents, roughly speaking—seems to be essential before adequate moral or conscience development can occur.

Discussion of these closely linked and fundamental concepts forms the bulk of this chapter.

Sex-Typing

Sex-typing can probably be most plausibly distinguished from *identification* by saying that it is *imitative,* or *modeling,* behavior. The little boy with or without thinking much about it, practices ways of behaving that he has learned are characteristic of men; the little girl does things that she has learned typify women. Sex-typing is synonymous with sex-role differentiation, a term which covers all of the processes by which men become different from women (and women from men). We say that *sex-role identification* has occurred when masculine or feminine behavior is no longer deliberate or imitative, but automatic and generalized to all areas of the self, from the style of walking and thinking to the style of sexual behavior. The term *internalization*—a difficult one to define—is used by many to describe what happens when identification has been accomplished. To take an analogy from walking, for the 18-month-old the process is deliberate, self-conscious, painstaking, and poorly coordinated (imitative); but for the 12-year-old or the adult it is natural, smooth, and unself-conscious (identification has occurred).

Lynn (1959) considers three phases of the identification process: sex-role preference, sex-role adoption, and sex-role identification. A little boy, deep in his heart, may prefer to be a little girl; but social pressures cause him to adopt the behaviors of a little boy. Unless he changes his sex-role preference, of course, it is unlikely that he will ever make a genuinely natural and sincere masculine identification, although he may be able to live his life as a socially acceptable male. As will be seen later in this chapter, more little girls apparently prefer to be little boys than vice versa, although most of them seem to be able to live out their lives very satisfactorily as girls and women.

The fortunate child, of course, is the one who has so adequate a father (male model) and mother (female model) that he comes early to prefer the sex role dictated by his physiology, moves naturally into its rehearsal, and eventually identifies easily with it.

Another author (Colley, 1959) points out that there are three areas in which an individual may be said to assume masculinity or femininity. The first he calls the *biomode,* or physiological area. The boy with somewhat feminine characteristics will have a harder time here than the child who is ruggedly masculine in physique. The converse will be true for girls. The second is the *sociomode,* or the preferred way of behaving, which is, of course, similar to Lynn's (and D. G. Brown's, 1958) sex-role preference. The third is full identification, which Colley calls the *psychomode,* or internalized identity.

Miller and Swanson (1960) found the distinction between sociomode and psychomode relevant in their study of University of Michigan young men. They found young men who were consciously and unconsciously masculine, young men who were consciously masculine but unconsciously feminine, and young men who were consciously and unconsciously feminine.

Their measures are useful for adolescents and adults, and their measure of unconscious sex-typing could probably be adapted for children, although it has not been to date.

Measures of unconscious sex-typing are provided by the "It Test," which is discussed later in this chapter. The "It Test" is a stick figure test of a semiprojective nature. The Franck Drawing Completion Test, which could be adapted to children (Franck and Rosen, 1949); and by concealed tests of game and toy preference, such as De Lucia's (1963) toy preference test, where two equivalent sets of twenty-four tests each are designed for children's choices are other measures of unconscious sextyping. De Lucia's standardization population ranges from kindergarten through fourth grade. Sutton-Smith and Rosenberg (1963) also have a test of unconscious sex identification, a play preference schedule ranging from fifth grade through twelfth grade, consisting of 180 items.

Franck, in her figure drawing test, which is internationally standardized, but not for children to the present author's knowledge, finds that men expand the area of the original figure, close open objects, draw angular shapes, protrusions, and unsupported lines, unify figures, and also draw active containers, such as autos, as well as fountains, caricatures, faces, tools, eyeglasses, and engineered figures such as bridges and skyscrapers. Women, on the other hand, elaborate inner spaces, draw open objects, rounded and blunted shapes, and supported lines. They also draw interiors of homes, furniture, fruit or flowers, and passive containers such as bowls or rowboats.

Measures of conscious identification are provided by question and answer techniques of a disguised nature, but so arranged that faking is possible for a clever subject. These are the masculine-feminine tests of the Strong Vocational Interest Test, the Edwards Personal Preference Schedule, the Terman Miles, and the Minnesota Multiphasic Inventory. Alpern (1960) has brought the Terman-Miles scale up-to-date for college males as a part of his doctoral dissertation.

TIME OF APPEARANCE AND NATURE OF SEX-TYPING

By the time the child reaches the runabout age (from perhaps 18 months on), adults begin to expect sex differences in behavior. Many subtle as well as obvious pressures are placed on children to produce such differences. Sex-typing precedes and is a part of identification, and results from a pattern of rewards and punishments administered by parents, teachers, older brothers and sisters, and playmates. It is probably based on imitation. Other things being equal, it is likely that the adult figures who will be imitated are the ones whom the child sees as appropriate, rewarding, and capable models.

By the early preschool years, many signs of sex-typing have appeared, even for children who spend a part of their time in permissive preschool settings where there is no obvious pressure on little boys to "act like little boys" or on little girls to "be ladylike." The preference of boys for wheeled toys, gun play, rough block-building, running and tussling, rope play, and the like is striking in groups of children long before they reach the age of 3. Girls in the same age groups play more quietly, utilize dolls rather than guns in their play, and prefer dramatization and playing house over rugged construction and cowboy play. But during the pre-school period there is much crossing-over in type of activity. Girls frequently desert the sandbox or doll corner for the jungle-gym. Boys with equal frequency take part in quiet dramatic play with girls.

PARENTS' ROLE IN SEX-TYPING

Compared with that of girls, the fantasy play of little boys contains significantly more aggressive themes, particularly of the physical type. To what extent this is the result of imitation of their fathers and their perception of the father's masculine role is not clear, although imitation probably plays a part. There may also be a factor of frustration: fathers ordinarily assume the ultimate disciplinary role in the family, and probably discipline their sons more severely than they do their daughters. Fathers also very possibly monopolize some of the mother's time that the boy would like to have. If little boys, at these ages, are especially close to their mothers, this would prove frustrating to them—more so than to girls. Then if, as seems likely, frustration instigates aggression, boys growing up with their fathers around will be more aggressive (directly or in fantasy) than boys whose fathers are away; and girls less than boys will be affected by the father's presence or absence.

It has been demonstrated (for example, by Pauline Sears, 1951) that little boys whose fathers are not living at home show less aggressive fantasy play than those whose fathers are living with them—that is, they are more like girls. This result may be due either to lack of opportunity to imitate the father or to less frustration at his hands.

Another study by Pauline Sears (1953) suggests that warm, permissive, easygoing—in other words, *rewarding* fathers—have sons who are most likely to sex-type appropriately. Using 202 boy and 177 girl kindergartners as subjects, Sears obtained reactions to a standard set of family dolls and a doll house. Family conditions were judged from interviews carried out with the mothers. Hence, all information about what the father did was channeled through the mother and does not represent actual observation of interactions between him and his son.

It was found that boys who chose the father role (were appropriately sex-typed) were more often reported to have fathers who were warm, permissive, and fairly easygoing with their sons. Boys who took the mother role in play came from homes in which the mother, but not the father, was high in warmth. Mothers of such boys were quite permissive with respect to the child's sex behavior, restricted him in his mobility outside the home (in all probability constituting themselves the major source of authority and influence), and were critical in their evaluation of their husbands (perhaps mediated unfavorable impressions of the father to the children). As mentioned in Chapter 10, Moulton *et al.* (1966) provide recent data in support of this point.

Another study (Levin and Sears, 1956), although not directly relevant to sex-typing, suggests that when children have incorporated their parents' standards, they are likely to model their behavior on that of their appropriate-sexed parent. Aggression in a doll-play situation was studied with almost 250 boys and girls 5 years old as subjects. These youngsters were said to be "highly identified" with their parents if they gave indications of having achieved a measure of internalized control over their behavior. Signs of guilt, for example, were considered as evidence of identification. For the subgroup of highly identified boys who were usually punished by their fathers, doll-play aggression was most frequent and intense. Identification in girls was associated with a high degree of aggression only when the girls' mothers were severe punishers and usually did the punishing.

Parents begin selective reinforcement of sex-appropriate behavior very early. The father, in his playtime, is likely to be rougher and to play more boys' games with his son than with his daughter; the mother will do more playing and take part in more mutual activity with her daughter than with her son, and their play will be gentler. Toys bought for boys and girls differ almost from babyhood. Boys are given toy tractors, footballs, and bats; girls receive dolls, dishes, and doll furniture. Differential pressure is put on the two sexes for conformity, lack of aggression, quietness, neatness, and good manners, girls being subjected to more pressure than boys. Boys also appear to be more active and to have more energy than girls. Work by Garn and Clark (1953) indicates that boys actually may have higher basal metabolic rates than girls. This does not mean that boys have more energy available, but suggests that, as far as their bodies are concerned, they "live faster" and even in conditions of rest, they burn up more energy. All these factors result in the early appearance of sex differences in behavior.

We have seen in Chapter 10 that there are several sources of parental power on which a child may model, and have pointed out some of the confusions in socialization that may result when a child, for example, models on his parents' sex role purely, or when he comes to find out that his lower-class father's physical power is inferior to the types of power that come under the heading of wisdom (omniscience) or social and economic influence (see Wolowitz, 1965). Heilbrun, working with college students in 1965, has devised a test of identification based on modeling, and finds that male college students identified with their fathers are better adjusted, have a stronger sex identity, a higher development of conscience; that first and only children are better identified than those who come later in the family, that they imitate their parents and model on the social power of the parents; and that identification is stronger when the mother approves of the father. In a later paper, he emerges with about the same conclusions: identification for both sexes is best when a father is both strong and nurturant, and when the mother approves of the father. Identification was appropriate for 88 percent of the children of highly masculine fathers, 58 percent of highly feminine mothers, 47 percent of low feminine mothers, and only 43 percent of low masculine fathers.

Johnson (1963), in a survey of the literature on identification, reaches similar conclusions. She presents a convincing exegesis of the hypothesis that there is an initial, nonsex-typed identification with the expressive, loving mother, which must be followed for appropriate sex-typing *or* identification by identification with the instrumental father—that is, the father is the person who represents the harsh consequences of the real world, and orients the child to reality. She believes that, after the age of about 5, the father takes a less demanding and more appreciative attitude toward his daughter than toward his son. He is husband to the girl, mentor to the boy. The mother does not make a similar symmetrical distinction, but is loving and expressive toward both sexes, simply rearing them as children. Johnson's hypotheses are well supported, in that it is consistently found that girls identified with their fathers are better adjusted than girls identified with their mothers. Heilbrun's data are in the same direction.

Johnson also points out the importance of parental power, and the helpful mediating influence of the mother who loves and approves of her husband.

Epstein and Liverant (1963) find that subjects with a strong masculine ego ideal condition (form conditioned responses, see Chapter 4) more effectively for a male experimenter, who is more effective with high than with low scorers and that, in line with Johnson's ideas, both high and low subjects conditioned more to the father (the reality enforcer) than to the mother.

Sex-Typing and Social Class

Sex-typing may also be related to social class. In one study (Rabban, 1950), children were divided by sex into middle- and lower-class groups. Lower-class boys were the first clearly to identify themselves with masculine interests, whereas middle-class girls were the last to take on a pattern of feminine interests. Lower-class girls and middle-class boys were intermediate between these two extremes. The average lower-class little boy manifested sex-typed behavior quite clearly, according to reasonable criteria (choice of masculine rather than feminine toys), by the time he was about 4 to 5; not until some three or four years later did the average middle-class girl manifest similarly appropriate sex-typed behavior.

Speculations about the reasons for this discrepancy are various. It seems likely that masculine and feminine roles are more clear-cut among the lower- or working-class population than they are in the middle class, and that the masculine role is more attractive than the feminine. Working-class men do heavy work on their jobs and assume little care for their children or the house. Working-class women, when employed, usually take such traditionally feminine jobs as housekeeping, cooking, or laundering. But among the middle-class group, both father and mother may be teachers, or lawyers, or work in the family business. Wives frequently handle the family finances. Mother drives the automobile with equal or greater frequency, particularly when father commutes. Father helps with the dishes and may do the shopping as he comes home from the office. Hence, models for the child's behavior are less distinctive. It is also likely that lower-class parents have less tolerance for individual differences on the part of their children than do middle-class parents: not only are working-class boys encouraged to act like boys, for example, but they are punished or ridiculed for *not* acting like boys. This also seems to be true for middle-class boys (see Hartup, Moore, and Sager, 1963). Middle-class women may also be more restless, more in competition with their husbands, and less satisfied with their roles as housewives and mothers than lower-class women, although this is speculation. However, if such speculation should prove true, then middle-class mothers may be assumed to present a somewhat unenthusiastic and blurred feminine model for their daughters.

Indirect support for this hypothesis is provided by an ambitious study (D. G. Brown, 1957) done with 303 boys and 310 girls, aged $5\frac{1}{2}$ to $11\frac{1}{2}$ years, who were enrolled in public schools from the kindergarten through the fifth grade. The children were all from middle-class homes.

The technique Brown used in his study is called the "It Test." "It" is a modified stick figure, vaguely resembling some illustrators' conceptions of "The Gingerbread Boy," but executed as a line drawing without features. The assumption behind the test is that the child will consider or "identify" himself as "It," and that the sex role and activities he chooses for "It" are actually those that he would choose for himself. In other words, the test is a projective technique, although an unusually straightforward one, and thus a measure of unconscious identification.

The actual testing procedure consists of having "It" indicate a preference for being a boy or a girl; choose between a number of pairs of toys, one of which is clearly masculine, the other clearly feminine; indicate a preference for one of several differently drawn figures, which range from boyish boys through girlish girls, and so on. Masculine choices are given higher scores, feminine choices lower ones, so that the higher the score, the more masculine the sex-role preference is presumed to be. Following Brown (1958) and Lynn (1959), we might say that this is a test of sex-role preference rather than of sex-role adoption or identification.

At every grade level up to the fifth, a majority of girls indicated a preference for boys' toys, and a majority of them said that they would rather be the father in the family than the mother. Boys made appropriate sex-typed choices much earlier. Even among kindergartners, 75 percent of the boys preferred boys' toys, and 77 percent preferred the father role to that of the mother. Among boys the percentages for both these choices reached the 90s by the second grade and remained consistent from then on. But even at the fifth-grade level, 37 percent of the girls preferred masculine toys and 21 percent of them stated that they would rather be a father than a mother.

Hartup and Zook (1960) have done an interesting study using 3- and 4-year-old nursery-school children and find, as did Brown, that boys of these ages have more appropriate sex preferences than girls. Unlike Rabban, they did not find lower-class children to be more firmly sex-typed than middle-class youngsters. This finding may have reflected the youth of the subjects or perhaps the effect of nursery-school attendance. Since nursery schools are ordinarily quite permissive, lower-class children may have been under less pressure for sex-typing; or middle-class children, under such circumstances, may have more opportunities to learn appropriate sex-typing than they would have had in the absence of a group experience; or both of these factors may have been operative. Since 61 percent of the fathers of the lower-class children were absent from the home, the number of subjects from "normal" lower-class homes was small, hence subject to sampling error (see Chapter 2). Finally, the lower-class subjects in this study came mostly from the upper-lower class, which has much in common with the middle class. In other words, the conditions in the Hartup and Zook study were so different from those in the Rabban study that they cannot be directly compared.

The earliness of appropriate sex-typing for the lower-lower social classes may be forced by their identification with their peer group, a conclusion for which there is considerable clinical evidence. Lower-class parents are relatively devoid of power, except in the physical and sexual areas. They are short on wisdom or omniscience, and on social and economic power. They also tend to be casually or brutally rejecting, and restrictive and nonnurturant in their child-rearing practices. This is likely to force children to turn very early to the peer group, where sanctions are mercilessly exercised against inappropriate sex-typing. We have already, in Chapter 10, seen that boys are discouraged from feminine interests and presumably encouraged in masculine interests, while the directives are less clear for girls. This is presumably even more rigidly enforced in the lower classes, where exaggerated masculinity and femininity seem to be the rule rather than the exception.

Sex-Typing and Cultural Stereotypes

Another of Hartup and Zook's findings raises some questions about the "It" technique, *if* "It" is presented to girls with the sex unspecified. Girls more often than not may see "It" as a boy: hence their rather high masculinity scores may be earned simply because they assign to "It" the masculine interests and preferences that they consider appropriate for boys. The fact that there was a highly significant shift in the direction of femininity for girls when the experimenter identified "It" as a girl supports this contention. Regardless of this, however, 4-year-old girls scored as more feminine than 3-year-old girls, and 4-year-old boys as more masculine than 3-year-old boys. Lansky and McKay (1963) secured good results with girls by keeping "It" shielded in a box.

One interesting finding from the Hartup and Zook study was that the 4-year-old girls were more feminine than Brown's 10-year-old girls. A possible explanation advanced for this is that for 4-year-olds, the feminine model is almost entirely limited to mothers (and possibly preschool teachers), who are doing very feminine things such as cooking, washing, baking, tending children, and so on. But in school years, through television, reading, and observation, girls see women doing a much wider variety of things, including some high-prestige activities that may be thought of as masculine. In other words, with increasing age (up to fourth or fifth grade) the masculine role becomes more attractive, and girls change from their moderate preference for the female role at the preschool years to their relative rejection of it in elementary school. Boys with older brothers, girls with older sisters, sex-type more easily than those with different family relationships.

APPROACH-AVOIDANCE TENDENCIES AND SEX-TYPING

It is possible to relate the concept of sex-typing to the ideas of approach-avoidance gradients that have been discussed earlier. We might speculate, on the basis of evidence concerning child-rearing practices in different socioeconomic classes (Maas, 1951), that lower-class fathers provide less attractive and loving models for their sons than middle-class fathers, but that the latter offer less clear masculine models. Open aggression, a masculine trait, is, for example, frowned upon in middle-class society, but condoned by the lower class. Under such circumstances, the approach tendency toward masculine behavior will be stronger for middle-class boys than for lower-class boys, but it will be less clear to them precisely what it is they are to approach. On the other hand, girlish or sissy behavior on the part of the lower-class boy will be clearly and firmly disapproved of by both parents and peers; whereas in middle-class boys such behavior is more likely to be tolerated. The avoidance tendency for feminine behavior will therefore be very strong for lower-class boys, and substantially weaker for middle-class boys. It is probable that the masculine model provided by peers is not only clearer but also more compelling for the lower-class boy, since he is more likely to be dependent on his peers than his middle-class counterpart.

For lower-class boys, early, appropriate, and rigid sex-typing should occur, based as much on "avoidance of femininity" as on "approach to masculinity," or "attractiveness of the role." Middle-class boys would be expected to sex-type later, but more flexibly and with more genuine satisfaction.

The process of sex-typing for girls is less clear than it is for boys. Some of the reasons for this have already been touched on. Lynn (1959), for example, reasons that, although girls start out by identifying with their mothers (as do boys), the process of adequate sex-typing and identification is "corroded" for them by a number of social pressures. Males are accorded more prestige and privileges than females in our culture; boys are punished for adopting aspects of the feminine role, but the adoption of part-masculine roles is not strongly discouraged for girls. Lynn makes four predictions about differential identification: With increasing age, boys will become more firmly identified with the masculine; girls less firmly identified with the feminine role; more girls than boys will adopt aspects of the role of the opposite sex; and, whereas boys will tend to identify with a cultural stereotype of masculinity, girls will identify with aspects of their own mother's role rather than with a general cultural stereotype. It should be noted that Hartup and Zook's data, gathered independently of Lynn's predictions, support them quite directly, particularly when considered in conjunction with Brown's study. So do the data of Payne and Mussen (1956), although less directly. These are summarized later in this chapter.

The lower-class girl, like the lower-class boy, has a clearer (but again, on the whole, probably less warm, attractive, and successful) model for feminine identification than the middle-class girl. Probably she, like her brother, is punished more often than the middle-class girl for showing aspects of the role behavior of the opposite sex, although this has not been clearly substantiated. On the whole, the feminine role is relatively less desirable in the lower than in the middle class, so that her over-all push toward appropriate role behavior is weaker than her brother's; but the model, even though less attractive, is clearer than that for the middle-class girl. The lower-class girl, like the lower-class boy, may be more strongly pushed toward appropriate role identification by her peers, as well as by her early assumption of such feminine tasks as housework, baby care, and so on.

SEX-TYPING IN OTHER CULTURES

There is evidence for near-universality of sex differences in behavior. One study (Barry, Bacon, and Child, 1957) uses as data cultural anthropologists' records for a total of 110 cultures. For the five different traits studied, enough information was recorded to make possible judgments about sex differences in from 31 cultures (for achievement) to 84 cultures (for responsibility).

In the majority of cultures, girls were trained to be *nurturant* (to look after others) and *responsible* to a greater degree than boys. For boys, *achievement* and *self-reliance* were more heavily stressed. A majority of the 69 cultures for which information was available did not put differential emphasis on *obedience;* but 35 percent of the cultures stressed obedience more for girls, whereas only 3 percent stressed obedience more for boys. These data also suggest considerable variability among cultures.

In the cultures studied, stress on sex differences was greatest where the pattern of life included hunting or herding of large animals, following a nomadic rather than a settled residence pattern, and growing grain rather than root crops as the staple of diet. Sex differences also tended to be more clear-cut in cultures sanctioning multiple rather than single wives. The reasons are obvious: In hunting or herding of large animals, men, with their superior strength and speed, play a role sharply different from that of women. The nomadic way of life, because of its general hardships, sharpens sex distinctions. Grain crops require more land and muscle than root crops. When there are several wives, there is little likelihood that the man will have to take over the homemaking role at any time; with just one wife, he may be compelled to take on feminine tasks when, for example, his wife is ill, is having a new baby, and so on.

Sex-typing may be defined as imitative or modeling behavior. It should be thought of as sex-role *adoption,* rather than an indicator of sex-role *preference* or sex-role *identification.*

In our culture, starting at the runabout age—probably as early as 18 months—adults and older children begin to respond differentially to little boys and little girls. They reward masculine behavior in the former, feminine behavior in the latter and punish feminine behavior in boys. By the age of 2 or $2\frac{1}{2}$ years, clear differences in play preferences have appeared: boys prefer more rugged activities (play with wheel-toys, climbing, and so on); girls engage more in quiet activities (play with dolls, dramatic play). The play of boys contains more physically aggressive themes than that of girls.

Little boys whose fathers are living at home show more aggressive themes in their fantasy play than boys whose fathers are away from home, but fathers' absence seems to have little effect on girls' fantasy play. Boys manifesting appropriate sex-typing have been shown to have warm, permissive, and fairly easygoing fathers.

Lower-class children seem to achieve appropriate sex-typing earlier than middle-class children; and in both social classes boys sex-type earlier than girls. It is probable that the appropriate roles are clearer for lower-class children than for middle-class children: their fathers engage in rough work, and are more clearly the heads of their households; mothers do not engage in masculine activities, and are placed in an inferior role. Children in the lower class may also be punished for failure to sex-type appropriately. In our culture the feminine model, whether lower or middle class, is probably less attractive than the masculine model.

Children with older siblings of the same sex appear to sex-type earlier than children who do not have older brothers or sisters, and almost all cultures seem to put pressure on children for appropriate sex-typing. Training for girls emphasizes nurturance, obedience, and responsibility; for boys achievement and self-reliance are stressed.

Identification

DEFINITION

The problem of arriving at a definition of identification is a knotty one. Sanford (1955) agrees with others who have written on the subject before him that identification has probably been used in more ways— with more different meanings—than any other psychoanalytic term. From his own thinking and the writing of others, Sanford points out that the following meanings of the term have been employed: copying or modeling, adhering to a group of which an individual feels a part, acceptance of a cause, empathy and vicarious living, sympathy, love, closeness, and loyalty. In addition, workers with projective tests such as the Thematic Apperception Test say that the subject *identifies* with the central character or hero of the story he tells.

The definition used here stresses *sex-role identification,* and is essentially a learning definition. The boy who has made a male identification is the boy who has happily and thoroughly adopted maleness as his way of life; he thinks of himself as a male; he accepts and likes this state of affairs, its advantages and its disadvantages; and he assumes the responsibilities that being male demands. His fantasy behavior is male, just as his sexual behavior, pattern of interests, and style of walking, talking, and gesturing, are male. It is assumed that the boy has learned to be male for various social-personal reasons, and that ordinarily (and ideally) his best model for this role is his father. In other words, it is likely that a boy must be *identified with* (love, respect, and, in many ways, imitate) his father in order to arrive at a consistently and genuinely *male identification*.

With respect to the girl, identification can be defined exactly as it is in the paragraph above, substituting *girl* for *boy, mother* for *father,* and feminine for masculine pronouns, although strong cross-identification with the father seems desirable for the girl (see Johnson, 1963).

According to Freudian theory, full identification with the parent of the same sex takes place when the Oedipus conflict has been resolved. Incestuous wishes toward the parent of the opposite sex are repressed, and the child incorporates or introjects the image of the parent of the same sex. The boy then becomes genuinely male, the girl genuinely female. Psychoanalytic theory takes little note of what we have called sex-typing. Here again, we wish to distinguish between sex-role preference, sex-role adoption (based on imitation or modeling, and used synonymously with sex-typing), and identification, as defined above. Theoretically, it seems that appropriate sex-role preference certainly, and appropriate sex-role adoption almost equally certainly, must precede and accompany appropriate *identification.* Learning theory does not assume any literal *incorporation* of the image of the like-sexed parent in identification, but only a general modeling or patterning. Sex-role identification is possible, for reasons that will be discussed later, even when there is little warmth toward the parent of the same sex, but it is logical to assume that acquisition of an appropriate identification will be easier and probably less ambivalent when accompanied by good parent-child relations, just as imitation and sex-typing will be.

The term *identification* is usually employed to include sex-role identification and *other* important aspects of personality, although the present author has chosen to emphasize sex-role identification as being the clearest of the various meanings. Even those who have not made an appropriate sex-role identification, however, have assumed many of the attitudes, values, and beliefs of their parents and other significant figures in their lives. It is commonly held that such human attributes as conscience and self-determined morality, guilt, the motive to achieve, and so on, arise only through identification, which may be with either or both parents. As will be pointed out later, "cross-identification"—that is, assumption of some of the values and standards of the parent of the opposite sex—is advantageous in our culture.

IDENTIFICATION FOR BOYS

Freudian Theory In Freudian theory, the little boy first identifies with—incorporates in part—the mother. At around 5 or 6 years of age incestuous wishes toward the mother become very strong, but are counter-balanced by the child's fear of his father's strength and the possibility of punishment, particularly castration. Since this fear is great and the loss of his genitals unthinkable, and since the small boy cannot hope to vanquish his father and win his mother, he copes with his father's strength by "becoming one with him," by introjecting him and thus avoiding threat as well as, presumably, enjoining the mother vicariously. This process is sometimes called "identification with the aggressor," and might be summed up by the popular phrase, "If you can't lick them, join them."

Social-Learning Theory   The learning position on identification takes little account of the Oedipus conflict, although it would not deny that this conflict may be frequent in some cultures. It also grants that the young child, boy or girl, probably (although not necessarily) loves his mother more than he does his father. It may well be possible for boys to make an adequate male identification and at the same time continue loving their mother more than their father. Identification is probably easier and better consolidated if the boy has had a loving and a strong father than if he has not; and the mother who loves her husband *and* her son, and wishes her son to be like her husband, probably facilitates the identification process.

The boy in a normal family, during his early childhood, probably loves his mother best. But he also has affection for his father, and, under fortunate circumstances, this affection grows stronger with age. As a result of it, and of general cultural influences, the boy, early in his pre-school years, begins to imitate his father (to sex-type), and eventually makes his masculine identification.

In other words, learning theory holds that a father with whom a boy identifies, in the sense of loving and respecting him, facilitates appropriate sex-role identification in his son, and that this factor, rather than fear, is a major one in successful identification. A study done by Payne and Mussen (1956) bears on this topic. Junior- and senior-high boys were asked to complete a set of stories in which they were likely to reveal whether they regarded their fathers, their mothers, and the total family structure as rewarding or unrewarding. These boys, theirs fathers, and their mothers were given a series of tests, among which was a personality inventory and a test of masculinity-femininity. Boys whose scores on the personality inventory were much more like their fathers' than their mothers' were assumed to have modeled closely after their fathers: in the authors' words, to have identified with them. It was found that the most highly father-identified boys (those most similar to their fathers) also appeared to have the best male identification, since their scores for masculinity were substantially higher than those of boys showing little similarity to their fathers. They also saw their fathers as rewarders, not punishers; and as relatively more rewarding than their mothers; for them, the total family pattern was a happier, more rewarding one.

A distinction is often made between infantile and ego identification (for example, Bronson, 1959). In *infantile* identification, the child wishes to *be* the security-giving object in his environment—the mother or the father—in order to avoid frustrating reality. Under the stress of anxiety, he imitates (perhaps introjects) adult behaviors, believing that these, in a magical way, will make him identical with the model he is imitating. In *ego* identification, on the other hand, the realistic differences between model and child are perceived, the model is admired and loved, and hence the child wishes *to be like* the security-giving object *in the future*.

Bronson predicted that sons from families where there were stressful father-son relations would be more likely than sons who had nonstressful relations with their fathers to show signs of infantile identification, but not of ego identification. She obtained ratings of father-son relations for forty-two boys between 9 and 13 years of age, and measured the sons' covert and overt masculinity. The former was inferred from the boys' TAT stories, the latter from their tendency to choose masculine as contrasted with feminine toys.

Bronson also predicted that boys who had stressful relations with their fathers either would show extreme masculinity (that is, would attempt directly to copy their image of their fathers) or would reject the father-image and show feminine patterns of behavior, whereas boys with nonstressful relations would fall intermediate on the overt-masculinity test (could take from the father-image what was useful to them, but without need either to copy the father defensively or to reject him and what he stood for). Scores from the toy-preference test supported this prediction. Bronson also reasoned that boys with less rewarding fathers (with whom they had stressful relations) would not make a satisfactory covert male identification—that is, at the fantasy (or unconscious) level, they would reject masculinity—whereas boys with rewarding fathers would make satisfactory covert masculine identifications. The TAT data supported her prediction.

That the boys from stressful families actually rejected more often than they imitated their fathers' patterns is indicated by the fact that there was a —.74 correlation between their masculinity scores on the toy-preference test and ratings of the fathers' masculinity. This correlation for the boys from nonstressful homes was +.37.

The Payne and Mussen and the Bronson studies both support the notion that boys highly identified with their fathers do not necessarily pattern directly after them to any strong degree. Payne and Mussen found no relation between the masculinity scores of fathers and sons for highly identified boys, and the .37 correlation found by Bronson is not high. It might be said that the son who is securely identified as a male does not need to imitate his father slavishly, but can look to his environment for behavior models that may serve his purposes better than his father's. In other words, a ruggedly masculine but highly adequate father can rear a son with somewhat effeminate behavior, but with appropriate sex-role identification; or a rather effeminate but good father can rear a son who is ruggedly masculine in behavior as well as appropriately sex-identified.

The Power Theory A third theory of identification exists (Parsons, 1955), which is a logical extension of Freudian and learning theories. It argues that identification occurs, not solely because the father is a threat and not only because he is a benign model, but because he is *both* an effective rewarder and an effective punisher. In other words, a son identifies with him and models after him because he is *powerful.* This is the "instrumental father," referred to by Johnson (1963).

Mussen and Distler (1959) conducted an interesting test of these three hypotheses about identification (the "loving" parent; fear of the parent; and "power" of the parent), using a group of kindergarten boys as subjects. According to psychoanalytic theory, boys at this age should be intensely involved in the Oedipus conflict, hence should make ideal subjects. Mussen and Distler used scores on the It Test (described previously in this chapter) as their criterion for identification, which, like the present author, they consider to mean adoption of the appropriate sex role. It has been pointed out that the It Test may measure sex preference rather than identification, although it certainly seems a promising measure for the latter as well.

The authors secured experimental (highly masculine) and control (relatively feminine) groups of boys, ten in each group. The groups were matched on socioeconomic status. A structured doll-play situation, involving a mother, father, and boy doll and simple furniture, was used, and the boy was asked to play out a number of stories, of which the following is illustrative:

This boy lives on a very busy street. His mother and father have told him never to cross the street alone. He is playing in the front yard, and his mother and father are not there. His good friend on the other side of the street is playing with his new bike, and the boy wants to cross the street very much. What happens?

Mussen and Distler extracted a number of scores from the stories the boys told: *nurturance* (tenderness and care) from the mother and the father; *punishment* from the mother and the father; *nurturance* from *both* parents (when the child specified that it was not the mother or father singly, but the parents together who gave help and tenderness);

punishment from both parents; and a total *power* score for both mother and father. The power score was the sum of the nurturance plus the punishment scores for the mothers and for the fathers.

The clearest finding was that the highly masculine boys reported their fathers as significantly more nurturant than the less masculine youngsters did. There was also a tendency, although it did not quite reach statistical significance, for the highly masculine boys to report their fathers as more punishing. When the two scores of nurturance and punishment were added to constitute a "power" score, the fathers of the highly masculine boys were scored as much more powerful than the feminine boys' fathers (the probability was .007, a very high level of significance). The fathers' nurturance scores for the masculine boys were higher than the punishment scores (3.7 and 2.8 respectively), whereas they were almost identical for the feminine boys (2.2 and 2.1). None of the results for the mothers distinguished between the two groups.

Although the number of subjects is small, this study suggests rather clearly that boys identify with strength, that parental strength is a combination of reward and punishment (a sensible enough conclusion), and that, possibly, an excess of reward over punishment is conducive to appropriate identification (this last conclusion is the author's, not that of Mussen and Distler).

This study has been replicated with similar results for boys *and* girls by Mussen and Rutherford (1963). As has been stated, Moulton *et al.* (1966) report similar results, using different techniques and older subjects.

A Cross-Cultural Study of Identification   Following a theory of identification similar to that of Mussen and Distler, Whiting (1959) reports an interesting cross-cultural study. He reasons that "a person will identify with, hence accept the moral values of, any person who is a successful rival with respect to resources which he covets, but cannot control" (p. 188). In other words, when the father's relation with the mother is envied by the son—when she nurtures the father, and the son must at times do without—then the boy will identify with his father. Whiting reasoned that cultures high in guilt—in internalized control—will be cultures in which the son is most likely to be envious of the father.

He classified a large number of cultures according to the likelihood that within them the father is likely to be nurtured by the mother, with resulting denial of nurturance to the son, thus arousing the son's envy. This situation, Whiting believed, would be most likely to occur in nuclear households (where father, one wife, and children live together under one roof). It would be next most probable in extended households (where grandparents, grown children, and their families all live together and may provide nurturance for the child when he needs it). Third in order of predicted envy on the part of the son is the polygymous family living under the same roof; where two or more wives can nurture the father as well as the sons. Least envy was predicted for polygymous families where wives live with their children in separate houses, and the father only visits. Whiting's predictions were supported at a high level of statistical significance.

IDENTIFICATION AND OTHER PERSONALITY FACTORS

Sutton-Smith and Rosenberg (1959) argue that boys who are "indecisive, dependent, affectionate, and more prepared to admit to anxiety of weakness" (in other words, boys scoring high on the Castaneda, Palermo, and McCandless Children's Manifest Anxiety Scale, 1956) will show more signs of feminine identification than boys who score low on the test.

The authors selected the forty-two most anxious and the forty-two least anxious boys from a large original group of fourth-, fifth-, and sixth-graders, and gave them a game-preference test. This test includes a list of games, preference for which differentiates boys from girls. Girls, for example, clearly prefer Fox and Geese and Crack the Whip; more boys than girls prefer darts.

The results of the study indicate that boys scoring high in anxiety are clearly more feminine in their game preferences than boys scoring low in anxiety.

Miller and Swanson (1960) studied a group of University of Michigan male undergraduates. They used a projective drawing test to measure "unconscious" masculinity (what the man was in his "inner core"), and a conventional masculinity-femininity test to measure "conscious" masculinity. One might conjecture that these measures refer, respectively, to sex-role preference and sex-role adoption, as discussed by Lynn, and that, when a man scores "masculine" on both indices, he has made a genuinely masculine identification.

Miller and Swanson distinguished between men who were feminine at both the unconscious and the conscious levels (*FF*); feminine on the unconscious but not the conscious level (*FM*); and men who were masculine at both levels (*MM*). They reasoned that there would be no men who were unconsciously masculine but consciously feminine, and found only 3 men scoring thus out of their tested population of 522. This result provides some support for the validity of their techniques.

In the various tests taken by their subjects, no differences appeared between the *FF* and the *FM* groups. This finding suggests that the important variable in general adjustment is the unconscious or core identification. But the *MM* group differed from the other two in several important respects. Fewer of them came from families in which, it was assumed, severe demands had been placed on the child very early in life (more of the *MM*'s came from presumably relatively permissive homes). The

MM's also handled conflict and guilt in a more mature fashion than either the *FF* or the *FM* group.

What is the adjustment of the homosexual, the *FF* man of Miller and Swanson's categorization? Chang and Block (1960) have studied a group of well-adjusted, mature men, averaging about 32 years of age and relatively highly educated, and find that they are identified with their mothers.

On the other hand, Doidge and Holtzman (1960) took a group of much younger men found to be homosexual in preference and practice, and compared them with three other groups—one heterosexual, but with some homosexual experience, one heterosexual, but with discipline problems, and one heterosexual without discipline problems. The first group on a series of ten different tests of adjustment were "off the curve" as far as maladjustment was concerned. The authors conclude that homosexuals are likely to be suffering from an emotional disorder which is relatively pervasive and severe. They argue for the need to study similar populations of women.

With the sanctions against homosexuality in our culture, it is not surprising to find that a group of homosexually identified males from a young group where heterosexuality is the only admissible way of life would be maladjusted. The surprising factor is that Chang and Block find as relatively well adjusted a group of homosexuals as the ones they studied.

In other words, identification, in the sense of affiliation with the values of the opposite sex parent, can occur. It leads to difficulties, but persons so identified can incorporate the moral and conscience values of the culture, although at a considerable cost.

CROSS-IDENTIFICATION

Implicit in learning theory, and probably in psychoanalytic theory as well, is the idea that "cross-identification" is desirable—that is, that the boy should model *preponderantly* after his father as far as his attitudes, interests, and behavior are concerned (and entirely, as far as his "maleness" goes); but that some (sympathetic) modeling after the mother should also occur. In our complicated society, where masculine and feminine roles are often not clearly defined, a certain amount of cross-modeling seems to be desirable for boys. Some traits commonly labeled feminine make society run more smoothly: sweetness, tact, the willingness to compromise, intuitiveness, sympathy, interest in people as well as things, appreciation of the arts—all of these are as useful for the male in a Western European culture as they are for the female. It also seems likely that if a boy has genuinely liked his mother and respected—even incorporated—some of her traits, he will, as an adult, make a more sympathetic and understanding husband and father to daughters without necessarily losing any of his prowess as a male.

Siegman (1966) operates on the hypothesis that there will be a desperate attempt to identify with the father through delinquency for father-absent boys. He compared the acting out and delinquent behavior of fifty-one father-absent male medical students (a group who obviously eventually conformed) with that of eighty-nine comparable father-present students on an anonymous checklist, although Kulik, Stein, and Sarbin (1966) find that about the same amount of frankness comes from a group whose identity is known. Kulik, Stein, and Sarbin were also studying delinquency.

Siegman argues that, as he grows older, the young boy becomes aware of the cultural expectation that he behave in a masculine manner. Thus he frequently shows exaggerated masculine behavior as a reaction against a basic feminine identification. Goodness has been identified with femininity. A rejection of this feminine identification leads to antisocial acting out behavior. Siegman found that his father-absent group much more frequently had indulged in such behaviors as damaging and destroying public property, truancy, premarital and extramarital sex relations, theft of amounts ranging from $2 to $50, getting drunk, driving a car without a driver's license, and cheating on school examinations.

On the other hand, McCord, McCord, and Thurber (1962) do not find these characteristics for father-absent boys. However, few of the boys in their group had fathers absent from birth, many of them were delinquent, and most came from disordered, lower-class homes. Hence the two studies are not comparable, being based on very different populations with very different characteristics.

In summary, there are three theories that attempt to account for identification in boys. Classical Freudian theory holds that the boy identifies in self-protection and because of fear: the father is so powerful and so threatening that, to defend himself and to gain such power, the boy incorporates the father-image. Learning theory argues that boys identify with their fathers because they have been rewarded by them, love them, and wish to be like them. A sociological theory combines Freudian and learning theories, holding that children (boys and girls) identify with *powerful* parents—that is, parents who can both reward and punish. Whereas Freudian theory lays stress on the Oedipal conflict (the son's incestuous love for his mother, coupled with fear of his father's possible punishment directed against this love), neither the learning nor the sociological theory attends particularly to the Oedipal hypothesis.

Existing evidence supports the prediction that boys identify more completely with loving fathers and with powerful fathers, particularly when this power is preponderantly benevolent, than they do with rejecting and punishing fathers. It may be that envy is a motive toward identi-

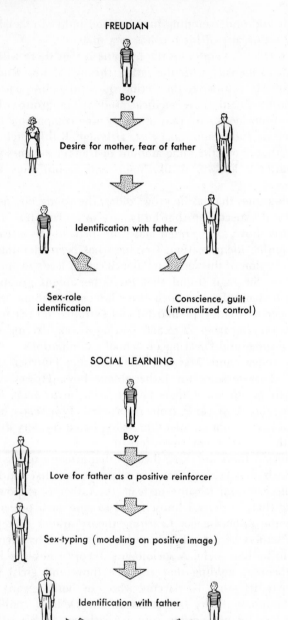

Figure 11.1 Contrasting motives for identification, according to Freudian (fear), social-learning (love), and power (love plus respect—possibly tinged with fear) theories, as applied to boys.

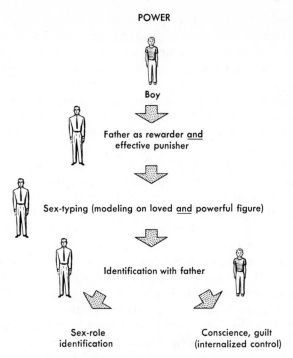

POWER

Boy

Father as rewarder <u>and</u>
effective punisher

Sex-typing (modeling on loved <u>and</u> powerful figure)

Identification with father

Sex-role   Conscience, guilt
identification   (internalized control)

Figure 11.1 *Continued*

fication: when mothers "look after" fathers, sometimes to the neglect of sons, boys may become envious of their fathers, see them as being powerful and as having desirable prerogatives, and hence be motivated to identify with them.

Some maternal identification appears to be desirable for boys. That is, society probably benefits when its males are interested in people, have positive regard for the arts and social welfare, and so on. It also seems likely that a man with some positive (or cross-) identification with his mother, even though thoroughly masculine in his own adjustment, would make a better husband and father of daughters than a man who rejected the mother-image and incorporated none of it in his own behavior.

IDENTIFICATION FOR GIRLS

Psychoanalytic theory holds that the identification process for girls is more complex than for boys. It involves, first, a close association with or love for the mother; then renunciation; then love, modeling, and identification again. According to Freudian theory, the little girl, at the age of about 2, discovers that she has no penis, and for this she blames her mother and turns away from her toward the father. Preference for him remains dominant until about 6, when she again turns toward the mother because, like the son in the family, she realizes that she cannot genuinely replace her mother and that, if she tried, she would lose the mother's love. So she too relinquishes her incestuous wishes and incorporates strength: her mother's image. Fear is less important for girls than for boys in this process.

Such a theory strains credulity and has no direct support. However, evidence exists that little girls of about this age *do* become extremely negative, and in many ways turn their affection from their mothers to their fathers. Some studies of parental preference find girls at around age 5 actually stating that they like their fathers better than their mothers, although the usual pattern for both boys and girls is to state a preference for the mother (Ammons and Ammons, 1949; and Simpson, 1935).

It may be that for girls, at about the age of 2, mothers begin to enforce the social expectations of good manners, obedience, and neatness to a greater degree than they do for boys. This change from a stage of permissiveness-without-substantial-demands that has existed between mother and daughter earlier is sufficiently frustrating to the girl to cause her to turn to her father. He is pleased: he loves the mother *and* her daughter, and responds warmly, thus increasing the strength of affiliation with him. But at the kindergarten to first-grade level, the little girl is faced with the inevitability of her femininity. If her mother is a successful person, she provides the best available model for the appropriate sex role. Then identification takes place. Mothers also exert more control over girls and discipline them more than they do their sons.

As for boys, it seems desirable that considerable modeling after, or cross-identification with, the parent of the opposite sex should continue to exist. The sex roles in our culture are *not* extremely clear-cut. Girls *do* compete. There is a place in their lives for striving, for doing well, for achieving, for being aggressive. Hence modified incorporation of these "masculine" traits is useful. Girls' marriages, and their mothering of their sons, should be helped if they have a sympathetic understanding of and liking for the male traits they will encounter in their husbands (and have grown to like first in their fathers); traits which, in a muted degree, they understand and respect as part of themselves.

One study (Lazowick, 1955) bears directly on this matter of identification of boys and girls, and is the only research study known to the author that deals with the matter of cross-identification. Although its subjects were college-age young men and women and their parents, and the number of subjects is not large (fifteen young men, fifteen young women, and their sixty parents), it is important because it bears on the end-result and reveals some of the dynamics of identification.

Essentially, the study deals with similarities between parents and their children; and with the children's associations of pleasantness and unpleasantness (like and dislike) with certain masculine or feminine terms (*father, man, mother, woman,* and the like). A measure of anxiety (used, in this study, as an index of poor personal adjustment) was obtained for the college men and women, and the low-anxiety (well-adjusted) were compared with the high-anxiety (poorly adjusted) subjects.

Among the more significant findings were the following: The lower the anxiety in boys, the more similar (the more adequate the identification) they were to their fathers. Boys resembled their fathers more than girls resembled them (but not at a highly significant level). The low-anxiety (well-adjusted) boys also resembled their mothers more than did the high-anxiety boys (support for the idea of cross-identification). Actually, low-anxiety boys (support for the idea of cross-identification) were more like their mothers than low-anxiety girls were. The fathers and mothers of low-anxiety subjects were more like each other (perhaps had a more harmonious marriage) than the parents of high-anxiety subjects.

When the male subjects were asked to talk about the similarity of the words *father* and *myself,* and women about *mother* and *myself,* the low-anxiety subjects gave more harmonious descriptions than the high-anxiety subjects. The terms *father, mother,* and *family* had more overlap, as far as their associations with the word *unpleasant* were concerned, for high- than for low-anxiety subjects. The low-anxiety subjects seemed, more than the high-anxiety subjects, to identify with both parents.

It should be noted that the association between good adjustment (as defined) and the degree of identification with *both* fathers and mothers is higher for boys than for girls.

A number of other studies fall rather well in line with Lazowick's, indicating that clear identification with the father is more important for the boy's adjustment than is clear identification with the mother for the girl. The reasons for this remain cloudy, unless, as has been mentioned, they have to do with masculine prestige in Western European cultures. Representative of these studies is that of Susan Gray (1959), who worked with fifth- through eighth-graders in an upper-middle-class school, and who found that boys with stronger identifications were judged as better adjusted on almost all of her tests than boys with weaker identifications (although they were not judged as more masculine). There were no real differences in adjustment for girls with low and high mother identifications. Johnson's (1963) and Heilbrun's (1965) data support the notion that girls need to be identified with the reality oriented, instrumental father.

Helper (1955), using a similar, very special population of adolescents, obtained very similar results. He worked with fifty freshmen and sub-freshmen in a small high school. His findings indicate that, for boys, patterning after the father in self-concept was at least in part a function of the praise or reinforcement the boy received for being like his father. The degree of "likeness" or "identification with" the father was also found to be related to popularity for boys. That the same findings did not hold for girls with respect to their mothers may be related to the fact that this high school was an intellectual and career-oriented one, in which standard feminine traits of homemaking and motherhood may have been less highly valued than traits of competitiveness and intellectual achievement. Helper's findings also fit with Johnson and Heilbrun's.

In summary, the process of identification appears to be more complex for girls than for boys. Girls who are strongly identified with their mothers do not seem to be superior in adjustment to girls who are less strongly identified, although this relationship does hold for boys. As for boys, however, some cross-identification with the parent of the opposite sex appears to be desirable: girls may have to support themselves; the girl who, while thoroughly feminine, has a certain amount of identification with her father should appreciate her husband more and be a better mother to her sons, and so on.

The lack of clear information about identification for girls may be due to the fact that, in our culture, the feminine role is less highly regarded than the masculine—hence, mothers may reject this role and provide unclear models for their daughters. Also, strong cross-identification with the reality anchored, instrumental father seems necessary for girls.

SOCIAL AND PERSONAL FORCES IN IDENTIFICATION

What happens to boys and girls with "defective" fathers or mothers, or both? With poor marriages and faulty child-rearing practices as common as they are in our culture, how do so many children nevertheless achieve adequate sex-typing and identification and become normally functioning, reasonably happy men and women?

There are at least four factors that may promote identification in the absence of adequate parental figures. The first is the transmission, through mediating processes, of favorable attitudes toward an absent or deceased spouse. There is some indirect evidence to indicate that mothers who pass on favorable opinions of their absent husbands rear children whose ideal father relationship, hence presumably their opportunity for adequate identification, is better than that of children whose mothers pass on unfavorable attitudes about the absent father (Bach, 1946; Helper, 1955).

Second, there are parent-surrogates in every culture and, in our culture, particularly for girls. A good kindergarten, elementary, or junior-high teacher can go a long way toward providing a favorable female model for the girl whose mother is weak, vicious, or absent. The average boy, on the other hand, does not encounter a male teacher until he is in junior high school, and often not then. But uncles, aunts, and neighborhood friends all can, and do, help provide models for the child of either sex who has no parental model on which to build. As has been mentioned, studies indicate that boys can make a satisfactory identification with fathers who themselves are not particularly masculine in their patterns of interest and activity. The reason for this may be that the boys can accept themselves easily as males if they see their fathers as warm, understanding, and rewarding. Then once this basic psychological identification has been made, the boys go ahead to copy from other males in their environment behaviors that are most suitable for them.

The popularity of Scouting with small boys may in part result from their need for a male model for identification. The hero worship that is given the good athletic coach may also originate in this need. Girls have some advantages over boys in our culture; their mothers are more available to them. Fathers go to work early; they come home late and, frequently, tired. Weekends are often so filled with activity that the father has little time for his son. The mother, in the ordinary course of the day, has more opportunity for informal interaction with her children. But, of course, if the mother is unsatisfactory, the girl is doubly threatened by this increased exposure.

A third factor pushing the child toward an appropriate sex-role identification is a general force in the culture. Boys are rewarded for acting like boys, punished for acting like girls. The same process holds true for girls. Teachers, the peer group, the community, all exert pressure for masculinity or femininity. These pressures, although not necessarily completely effective, are powerful.

Finally, there is suggestive although not definitive evidence that people have selective memories—that they remember the good, forget the bad. A child, even when his parent has preponderantly neglected, rejected, and punished him, forgets the bad times and remembers the good ones. He thus creates for himself a model for identification, however flawed the original may have been. Such a child may, of course, unconsciously follow the inadequate pattern set by his parent.

Identification is one of the most important of the socialization processes. Failure of identification seems to produce a variety of results ranging from schizophrenia through homosexuality, impotence, and frigidity to unhappy marriages and the repetition by parents of the inadequate parental performance they themselves knew as children.

Even in personality breakdowns, however, there remain evidences of the struggle toward identification, in the sense that the patterns of behavior of mentally ill young men resemble those of their fathers. Singer and Opler (1956) made intensive studies of the patterns of life of Irish-American and Italian-American families, and from these constructed family models for the two groups. They then predicted the consequences for sons. In Irish families, it was hypothesized, the mother is strong and chaste, the father weak, relatively inadequate sexually (it will be remembered that native Irish marry perhaps latest of any group in the world), withdrawn, and uninterested in wife and family. In Italian families, on the other hand, sex is an approved way of expressing affection; the father is dominant, the mother relatively passive and warm, and very feminine. Even in complete breakdown into schizophrenia, the authors predicted, sons would show patterns indicating both that they had attempted to identify, and the nature of their attempt. An investigation of the behavior of adult male Irish- and Italian-American schizophrenic males provided evidence supporting the predictions. The Irish-Americans showed more effort to control internally. They inhibited impulses more and manifested more fantasy. The Italian-Americans were assaultive, violent, and generally impulsive, and were rated as less cooperative on the wards. Each group, in other words, had struggled toward and modeled after the paternal model. Farina (1961) finds compatible results in a careful study of schizophrenic males with good and poor prognoses, and a control group of tuberculous men.

SOCIAL CLASS AND IDENTIFICATION

Socioeconomic effects on sex-typing have already been discussed. Evidence exists that, at least for men, identification is characterized by less warmth and affection in lower-class subjects than it is in middle-class subjects. In a study by Singer (1954) the Thematic Apperception Test was administered to normal and schizophrenic adult males who came from lower- and middle-socioeconomic classes. References to parental figures in their stories were scored for the presence and amount of warmth. In general, middle-class normal men made more warm and affectionate references to parental figures than lower-class normals. Normal men, regardless of social class, showed more warmth toward parental figures than schizophrenics; but even among the schizophrenics, the middle-class subjects showed more warmth than the lower-class subjects. These results are presumably due to the fact that children receive more over-all warmth in middle- than in lower-class homes; and that homes producing normal sons, when compared with those producing schizophrenic sons, are warmer and happier, whether middle or lower class. Sociological studies of adolescents, too numerous to cite, but proliferating in the 1960s, support a trend toward less warmth and more autocracy the further one descends the socioeconomic scale.

Two interesting studies, reviewed in more detail in the following chapter, indicate that middle-class mothers are more aware of the interests and activities of their adolescent sons and daughters than lower-class mothers; and that this awareness is significantly correlated with their children's identification with them (patterning after them). Cass (1952a, 1952b) found identification (similarity) less highly correlated with awareness for the lower-class mothers of nondelinquent children; the correlations were lowest when the children were delinquent. This suggests that the awareness of the lower-class mothers may well have taken the form of supervision or control rather than of a genuine, friendly interest. In line with this interpretation are Cass's findings that children of mothers who were highly aware of them, but exerted relatively loose control, were more strongly identified with the mothers than children of high-control, low-awareness mothers. The delinquent group of children, when compared with the matched normal group, reported more conflict with their mothers; their mothers showed less awareness of them, and were (as reported by the children) more strictly controlling. Of course, it may have been that such children required strict control, or that they resented even moderate control, or both.

This discussion of identification and social class has considerable relevance for those who work with children. Lower-class children, as a group, are likely to have less positive attitudes toward adult authority figures than middle-class children. But apparent coldness and indifference on their part may be based on previous experiences of rejection, and may well cloak a yearning for a warm relationship with an adult. On the average, lower-class children are less bright and less academically motivated than middle-class children. They may also be more aggressive and overtly sexual, as well as unkempt and ill-dressed. If, to these factors, is added an apparent indifference or even hostility to the teacher, the temptation to "give up on them" or even actively to reject them can become very strong. The teacher who is aware of some of the possible forces lying behind this façade will be less likely to yield to the temptation.

Moral Development

Hoffman (1963) has reviewed the research on moral development and relates it rather directly to parental child-rearing practices, love-oriented techniques of control, and identification. He believes there is such a thing as consistency of moral development, growing more pronounced at the older age levels, and showing itself at the younger age levels when tests of known reliability are used, such as in the area of honesty (Burton, 1963).

The only inconsistency occurs at the preschool levels. The studies at the college level demonstrate that psychological discipline by the parent contributes both to guilt and resistance to temptation. There is considerable generality at these older age levels, since cheating and expressing aggression were both considered. This leads to the idea that there is little behavioral generality in early childhood, but that there is an increase with age. The morality of the young child may well be a matter of rote learning of relatively specific acts and avoidances, which may not cut across different standards but which, in the absence of the ability to discriminate relevant cues and anticipate consequences, does not offer consistently strong competition to drives and pulls of moral conflict situations.

Hoffman cites a study of individuals from two different conscience, or moral development groups: one with humanistic consciences, one with conventional consciences. The humanistic group was made up of children who, in their moral judgments, considered extenuating circumstances and invoked principles in support of their judgment that were based on human need. The conventional group did not consider the circumstances, and they gave principles based more on convention and authority. Both groups were given projective story completion and sentence completion items. Each had an internalized moral orientation, but differed greatly in their orientations. The humanistic subjects indicated more guilt when the consequences of their transgression involved human life or were irreversible but, when the consequences were not major and could be rectified, they were likely to reduce their guilt through confession, reparation, and so on. The responses of the conventional subjects, however, lumped the minor with the serious. The humanistic subjects also showed evidence of being better able to bear the anxiety of thinking about a forbidden course of action and consider a forbidden act before rejecting it. There was considerable evidence for the relatively high degree of conscious integration between impulses and moral standards. The conventional group seems to be more likely to avoid facing such conflicts by repressing the impulse in question.

The main differences between the child-rearing practices for the two groups was that the mothers of the conventional subjects more often used techniques classified as "ego attack." Examples of this, taken from Hoffman are: "You ought to be ashamed of yourself," and "Can't you do anything right!" The mothers of the humanistic groups were more likely to indicate disappointment in the child for not living up to their expectations by such statements as, "I'm disappointed in you." While this conveys the idea that the parent has been hurt, it also tells the child that the parent thinks he is capable of living up to an ideal. Unlike ego attack, this is done without necessarily implying depreciation or disesteem for the child. The ego ideal—the flexible conscience—is thus strengthened for the humanistic child.

Love-oriented techniques of control are apparently designed to produce socialization and identification.

Kagan and Freeman (1963) report that adolescent conformity to adult demands and dependence upon mothers were associated with different early maternal practices for boys than for girls. Acceptance, affection, and protection during the early school years (the expressive role of the mother) predicted conformity and dependence for boys; while the instrumental, reality principle for mothers as evidenced by severe discipline and restrictiveness during ages four through seven were similarly predictive for girls.

Block and Turula (1963) report that degree of identification is strongly related to degree of ego control, which is one aspect of moral development.

McMichael and Grinder (1966) report an interesting cross-cultural study of moral development. They operate on the assumption that a Hawaiian-Samoan and a Japanese culture are based on shame rather than guilt, and that the further from the influence of the mainland American culture such children live, the more they will function according to shame rather than guilt. They studied such children from villages at different distances from Honolulu, and found their predictions supported. They used a five story projective technique measuring remorse, confession, and restitution as a function of guilt after transgression. The village children showed significantly less of this than the Honolulu children, although the Hawaiian-American and Japanese-Hawaiian-American children in Honolulu did not differ significantly from the old line white group there.

Median correlations between remorse, confession, and restitution of about .60 suggest that there is a generality of moral sense among the elementary school children with whom the authors worked.

According to Piaget, there are three stages of morality in children. He has developed these from a series of studies based on reactions to stories about children's transgressions. The first stage, the *Morality of Constraint*, exists until the child is 7 or 8 years old. It is characterized by automatic obedience to rules without reasoning or judgment, with adults viewed as omnipotent. The child sees punishment in terms of "immanent justice" and "moral realism," the former referring to the idea that all bad acts are punished either by human means or by nature or supernatural forces. The latter refers to the child's judgment of acts in terms of consequences rather than in terms of motives.

Between the seventh and eighth or tenth years, the child goes through an intermediary stage in which he either internalizes rules without evaluating them, or alternates in his responses to situations.

At the level designated as "Morality of Cooperation," the child begins to evaluate intentions rather than deeds or outcomes alone. Moral behavior is then engaged in for its own sake, not out of fear of punishment. Further, cooperation and mutual respect among peers takes the place of the former unilateral respect for adults.

Summary

Sex-typing makes its appearance very early, seems to be universal, is probably based on rewards and on imitative learning, and is the forerunner of identification. It should be thought of as sex-role adoption, rather than sex-role preference or identification. Early in children's lives (probably as early as 18 months) adults and older children begin to reinforce differential behavior in boys and girls. Boys whose fathers live at home show more masculine behavior, particularly in their fantasy play, than do boys whose fathers are away from home; and the sons of warm, permissive, fairly easy going fathers appear to be most likely to sex-type appropriately. Fathers' absence makes little difference in the fantasy play of little girls.

Lower-class children, probably because their parental models are clearer, sex-type earlier than middle-class children. Regardless of class, boys sex-type earlier than girls, perhaps because in our culture the feminine model is less attractive—has less prestige—than the masculine model. Boys with older brothers and girls with older sisters sex-type earlier than only children.

Almost all cultures apply pressure for appropriate sex-typing. Typically, girls are trained to be nurturant, to obey, and to live up to their responsibilities, whereas boys are trained for achievement and self-reliance.

The process of identification appears to be more complex for girls than for boys. Although boys who identify with their fathers are better adjusted than boys who have apparently failed to make this identification, the same cannot be said for girls in relation to their mothers. Both boys and girls would seem to profit from some "cross-identification" with the parent of the opposite sex.

Girls in particular seem to need to cross identify with the reality oriented, instrumental father.

There seems to be, at least at older ages, considerable generality of moral development, which is fostered by psychological techniques of child rearing in contrast to ego attacks. An example of the former is, "I'm disappointed in you," which conveys disappointment to the child, but the expectation as well that he can do better.

Other studies indicate that affection, acceptance, and protection during the early school years—the expressive functions of the mother—produce greatest conformity at adolescence, while the instrumental, reality oriented techniques of severe discipline and restrictiveness from 4 to 7 years produce the same results for girls.

A cross-cultural study indicates guilt in the sense of remorse, confession, and restitution following transgression for children growing up in a standard American situation than for those from a shame oriented culture. This study also suggests a consistency or generality of moral sense for elementary school children.

Authoritarianism and Prejudice

CHAPTER 12

Social attitudes affect our behavior profoundly. Such attitudes can be divided into many categories. Some people are generous and open toward others; some are cautious, reserved, and withdrawn. Some hold liberal, others conservative social attitudes that affect the way they vote, the policy of social action they advocate, and even the church to which they belong. Some believe in strictness as a way of dealing with delinquents and criminals; others believe that affection, understanding, and tolerance should characterize all approaches to such social problems.

Social attitudes in large part determine the way parents rear their children, and these child-rearing attitudes and practices, we believe, in turn shape the personalities of the children. As we have seen, one of the clearest dimensions of child-rearing practices is that of authoritarian-nonauthoritarian control. It pervades the family; it varies from culture to culture; and, in a rough way, it divides governments into two camps. Authoritarianism was one of the issues in World War II. Debate continues hotly about whether, for example, the United States should have friendly dealings with dictatorships, or should renounce them.

· This pervasive characteristic of social organization—the nonauthoritarian or equalitarian as opposed to the authoritarian—has been thought by many both to derive from and to influence the personalities of the individuals who make up a society. Many aspects of personality and social attitudes could be chosen for discussion in chapters such as this, but the one on which most research has been done concerns authoritarian as contrasted with equalitarian personalities: how each develops, and how equalitarianism and authoritarianism relate to other types of social and personal behavior. Concepts of authoritarianism and equalitarianism are so important that this chapter is devoted to an examination of relevant psychological research. Since it is impossible to review all of the research that has been done on personality variables and social attitudes, it seems appropriate to select a given *illustrative* and *socially important* area and develop it more fully and critically than would be possible if a policy of wider coverage were adopted. In other words, research on equalitarianism-authoritarianism is presented here as representative of research on personality and social attitudes in general.

Theories of Authoritarianism and Ethnocentrism

The concept of the "authoritarian personality" has been most influentially developed by Adorno *et al.* During World War II, a group of investigators centered at the University of California attacked the problem of race prejudice, believing that any answers that might be provided about its origins and social development would be helpful in understanding some of the roots of anti-Semitism and Nazism. Their investigations of race prejudice, most particularly prejudice against Jews and Negroes, led them to theories about personality—particularly the authoritarian personality—that were much broader than the ideas of prejudice with which they began.

Every general term must be defined by behavior. It is widely held that the authoritarian personality is rigid, or inflexible; that it is concrete in its thinking and does not handle abstractions easily; that it is conforming, being conventional, for example, in its morality and its politics; that it does not willingly or accurately examine its own thoughts and its own adjustment; that it manifests an exaggerated respect for authority, including "overprotestations" of love for parents. These protestations, however, are combined with underlying hostility toward parental or other authority figures. The authoritarian personality places extreme emphasis on masculinity or femininity, and is hostile (prejudiced) toward groups other than the one to which its owner belongs. It prefers absolutes: black is black and white is white; there are no grays—in other words it is intolerant of ambiguity. It suspects evil in others.

Measures of race prejudice correlate fairly highly (usually in the .50s and .60s) with measures of authoritarian personality. In this discussion it is necessary to assume that groups of people who are high in race prejudice are also high in authoritarianism. It will be made clear when measures of prejudice (a narrower, more specific concept) are substituted for measures of authoritarianism (a more general psychological construct).

Turning now to *prejudice*, there seem to be two types, equally troublesome in their effects but different in their origin. The first is "pathological" prejudice. Here the individual displaces his own frustrations, self-contempt, and self-destructive dispositions onto convenient scapegoats: he seizes upon a social situation, or a group in society, that enables him to project his own difficulties in hostile action or attitudes, thus (albeit in an unhealthy way) reducing his hostilities and anxieties about his own problems. All societies provide scapegoats, and in a great many societies minority groups are conspicuously available and safe candidates for scape-goat roles—prejudice is manifested against them.

The other type of prejudice is "normal." A reasonably well-adjusted and happy person may grow up in a culture that holds derogatory atti-tudes toward some peoples. Just as he assimilates or learns the positive attitudes of this culture, so such a person learns the negative ones and becomes "normally" prejudiced.

Many psychologists, psychiatrists, sociologists, and so on, believe that autocratic families (or nations) produce authoritarian personalities; and that one of a number of typical traits of the authoritarian is race preju-dice. There are at least two major theoretical explanations for the rela-tion between authoritarianism and prejudice. The first, and currently the most widespread, arises from Freudian psychology and concerns itself most with attempts to explain *pathological* prejudice; it has paid little attention to "normal" prejudice. The second has been advanced by sociologists and psychologists interested in learning theory. It attempts to account for both varieties of prejudice, and has drawn heavily from (yet been critical of) the neopsychoanalytic thinking of such people as Adorno, Frenkel-Brunswik, Levinson, and Sanford (1950).

THE PSYCHOANALYTIC POINT OF VIEW

The neopsychoanalytic theory of Adorno *et al.* holds though, as we shall see, the evidence is by no means clear, nor is the reasoning totally sound that the authoritarian personality is the result of child-rearing practices; and most specifically, those connected with toilet training. When toilet training is too severe or too early, it is believed that the child who has not yet acquired language learns, not only to be continent, but also to dread any situation that is unclear or ambiguous. Because he has been richly rewarded for being dry (when he did not know why he was being rewarded) and resoundingly punished for being wet or dirty (without recognizing why he was being punished), he expects unknown and very possibly unpleasant things to happen to him whenever he is in an unclear situation: he is intolerant of ambiguity. He attempts to reduce the anxiety engendered by ambiguity by forcing things into rigid molds and clear classifications.

The process described here also engenders in the child hostility against his parents. But because of their power, and the love (in addition to hostility) that he holds for them, he cannot express this hostility directly toward them. It is, therefore, displaced. The combination of these two tendencies—intolerance of ambiguity and the need to displace hostility —leads him to classify people as either in-group or out-group, fellow citizens or foreigners, whites or Negroes, Aryans or Jews. Toward the out-group, he expresses exaggerated rejection and dislike; toward the in-group, exaggerated fealty.

As we shall see in the course of this chapter, such a theory of prejudice is certainly oversimplified, and perhaps wrong, but the social importance of prejudice is such that any theory about it should be examined carefully. In many ways, prejudice resembles fixation (see Chapter 5).

Masling (1954), a sympathetic but critical viewer of the psychoanalytic theory of authoritarianism, has selected certain quotations from Adorno *et al*,[1] interspersing the quotations with comments of his own. In all, he provides a rather full presentation of the Freudian definition of authoritarianism. To quote Masling:

> . . . authoritarians . . . "worry about egocentric and material things. They think in terms of blame and they appear to express aggression against the weak". . . . authoritarians are conventional, submit uncritically in the face of authority, are anti-intraceptive, superstitious, and stereotypic in their thinking, are preoccupied with the "dominance-submission, strong-weak, leader-follower dimension," overemphasize the conventionalized attributes of the ego, have exaggerated assertions of strength and toughness, are cynical and destructive, tend to believe that "wild and dangerous things go on in the world," and have "exaggerated concern with sexual 'goings on'." In addition, authoritarian men are overly masculine and women overly feminine. . . . The authoritarian is characterized as achieving "social adjustment only by taking pleasure in obedience and subordination." This brings into play the sadomasochistic impulse structure both as a condition and as a result of social adjustment. . . . In the psychodynamics of the "authoritarian character," part of the preceding aggressiveness is absorbed and turned into masochoism, while another part is left over as sadism. . . . Ambivalence is all-pervasive, being evidenced mainly by the simultaneity of blind belief in authority and readiness to attack those who are deemed weak and who are socially acceptable as "victims". . . . He develops deep "compulsive" character traits, partly by retrogression to the anal-sadistic phase of development . . . (his religious belief is compulsive and punitive; he has overt rigidity of conscience with) strong traces of ambivalence. . . . The over-rigid superego is not really integrated, but remains external. (p. 316)

This is strong prose indeed, and Masling finds little evidence that the traits listed cluster together in the populations he studied. He states:

> . . . the characterization of the authoritarian has been overdrawn. All things evil have been positioned in one end of the distribution;

---

[1] In this volume, Adorno, the authority for psychoanalytically-oriented thinkers and researchers in the authoritarianism area, will be referred to repeatedly.

all things healthy and democratic have been attributed to the other. It has been natural to slip from a rigorous, scientific, "show-me" frame of reference, to one which has been heavily influenced by the researcher's concern about world conditions. The concept of the authoritarian personality may be a valuable, heuristic tool, but only if it can be divorced as much as possible from value judgments. There seems to have been a tendency to use the term "authoritarian" as a mild profanity which one could use to describe other people (never oneself). It is suggested that the concept be re-examined in the light of the data, purified of value judgments, and put to use again as a research instrument. (p. 318)[2]

Frenkel-Brunswik (1954), who is one of the co-authors of the important Adorno volume, has replied to Masling's critique, arguing that the authors of *The Authoritarian Personality* had no intention of linking this concept with "mental health" as it is conventionally thought of. She states:

We had even come to the conclusion that the use of projection mechanisms as manifested in prejudice helps rather than hampers the authoritarian in preserving his mental balance, especially in view of the fact that in this case defense mechanisms act through channels which are partially socialized. (p. 466)

Later, she adds:

In fact, as we have concluded on the basis of our interviews, the authoritarian may, and frequently does, function extremely well in most routine contexts of life; he probably even betters the equalitarian under certain narrowly circumscribed conditions, such as when the culture provides socialization for the mechanisms involved. (p. 468)

Frenkel-Brunswik also defends the empirical base of the value terms used:

Such terms as "aggression against the weak"—to which Masling objects as evaluative—acquire a different flavor as soon as we remember that "aggression" designates a certain way of functioning in a descriptive manner or as a dispositional term, and thus is a legitimate part of the behavioral vocabulary, and that "weak" is defined

2 Reprinted with permission of the American Psychological Association, and J. M. Masling, from Masling (1954).

by a certain objective locus in the social hierarchy. Similarly, "superstitious" designates nothing but the presence of a belief in supernatural explanations of natural phenomena. The sting that is bound to remain in any reference to such attitudes is given by the fact that they are in general ill-suited for coping adequately with the complexities of social and cognitive problems. They tend to lead to consequences that are detrimental to society, to others, and often to their holder himself; but this tendency is empirically verifiable like any other factual trend. (p. 468)[3]

Both Masling and Frenkel-Brunswik make sound points. Social scientists have overextended the theory of the authoritarian personality; they have often committed each of the research and interpretive errors discussed in Chapter 2. At the time Masling wrote, a "cold shower" was clearly indicated. On the other hand, the practical and theoretical problems presented by authoritarian personalities and by prejudice are so pressing and potentially fruitful that they merit major attention.

THE LEARNING-SOCIOLOGICAL POINT OF VIEW

Accounting for "normal" prejudice is not only important but probably simpler than trying to explain *pathological* prejudice, since the former seems to depend in a relatively straightforward fashion on the principles of *substantive* (nonemotional) learning; whereas for the latter, emotional learnings, drives such as anxiety and aggression, factors of personal security, fixation, displacement, and so on, must be taken into account. The argument about normal prejudice is that, if a person has been brought up in a culture which, for example, dislikes Negroes, he learns the attitudes, opinions, and stereotypes of the culture so that he, too, dislikes Negroes. But if he moves to a culture where such attitudes do not exist, his dislike of Negroes will be reduced or his frame of reference will be altered in such a way that he becomes less prejudiced.

Christie and Garcia (1951) have been interested in the implications of this point of view about the development of both authoritarianism and prejudice. They believe that lack of education produces authoritarianism: the less one has been taught about relativism (as opposed to absolutism), the less he knows about history, and the less information he has about cultural diversity, the more likely he is to be authoritarian—to subscribe to absolutes and immediacies. According to such a view, authoritarianism does not necessarily have its roots in psychodynamics. It is, rather, culturally determined. Authoritarian and/or prejudiced persons, given a dif-

---

[3] Reprinted with permission of the American Psychological Association, from Frenkel-Brunswik (1954).

ferent culture (anthropologically speaking), or *more* culture (educationally speaking), would become more equalitarian and less prejudiced. They are neither maladjusted nor evil, simply ignorant.

The social-learning theorist finds it difficult to embrace the version of psychoanalytic theory which holds that the authoritarian personality springs full-blown from the anal psychosexual stage, and is a direct function of fixation due to the trauma of early and severe toilet training. However, within social-learning theory, it is reasonable to entertain sympathetically the notion that the mother who is severe in her toilet training also engages in a number of other child-rearing practices that might well make a child an authoritarian.

According to Sears, Maccoby, and Levin (1957), the following childrearing factors were associated, at least to a modest degree, with severe toilet-training practices: tendencies to put relatively great pressure on children to use good table manners, to be neat and orderly, to be careful around the house and with furniture, to keep quiet, and to do well in school. Mothers who were severe in their toilet training were also likely to use physical punishment and deprivation of privileges (these are thing-oriented control techniques), and to reason little with their children. They strongly discouraged as well as punished aggression from their children toward themselves and their husbands, and expected strict obedience. They stressed modesty and were more concerned about masturbation and social sex play than the mothers who followed more lenient toilet-training practices. They suffered from marked anxiety about their child-rearing capabilities and (relatively) lacked warmth and esteem for themselves, their hubands, and their children.

They sound, in other words, as though they might be rearing children for a police state, where conscience or inner controls are not particularly necessary because external controlling forces are always present. Children so reared may well learn rather directly to fear insecurity and unclarity; to be hostile yet unable to express their hostility directly toward authority figures; to fear, distrust, and dislike minority groups; and to be rigid.

Prejudice and Personality

STUDIES OF NORMAL AND PATHOGENIC PREJUDICE

Authoritarianism as such has been little studied in children. But the assumption implicit in the preceding pages of this chapter, that authoritarianism and ethnocentrism (or race prejudice) are closely related to each other, has been widely accepted, and there have been a number of studies of ethnocentrism using children as subjects. Several of these studies have been selected for more intensive review here. It should be noted that most of them concentrate on pathogenic prejudice, and have been inspired by Adorno and his colleagues.

Mussen (1950) was interested in several aspects of prejudice: (1) Will prejudice decrease simply as a result of learning about members of a minority group, for example, by living with them for a time? Theories about normal prejudice would predict such a result. (2) What are the personality dynamics of those who increase, decrease, or do not change in prejudice as a result of greater familiarity with the minority group?

The subjects in Mussen's study were 106 white boys from 8 to 14 years of age, who had been placed for four weeks in an interracial camp. Early during their stay they had taken a test of anti-Negro prejudice, the Horowitz Faces Test. The test was re-administered when the boys left the camp. The Horowitz test is a picture test showing full-face views of eight Negro and four white boys. The higher a young subject ranks the Negro boys in a twelve-rank hierarchy of preferred friends, and the more frequently he chooses Negro boys as possible companions or associates in various activities or situations, the less prejudiced he is judged to be. Levitt (1956) has severely criticized this test. However, Mussen (1950) has shown that the prejudice scores derived from it for his sample of boys correlate moderately well (.52) with youngsters' actual choices of cabinmates during their stay in the camp.

Of particular interest to Mussen (1950) were various subgroups: those who, as a result of their camp experience, lowered their prejudice score; those who increased it; and those who stayed the same, whether originally high or originally low in prejudice. Although many individual children changed scores, *for the group as a whole* there was no significant change in the level of prejudice as a result of the interracial camping experience.

In addition to the test of anti-Negro prejudice, Mussen administered the Thematic Apperception Test to his group of subjects. Correlating the data obtained from the two instruments, he found that the boys who were initially high in prejudice, when compared with those who were low, appeared to be more hostile and to have a need to dominate others. In their TAT stories, they appeared to show more hostility toward their parents and to believe more frequently that "the world was against them."

Characteristic of the boys who *increased* in race prejudice as a result of their camp experiences were strong needs to defy authority and strong hostile feelings. These youngsters also seemed to feel that open expression of aggression was likely to lead to punishment, retaliation, restraint, and prohibition. They appeared to regard themselves as victims of aggression.

The boys who *decreased* in prejudice told TAT stories in which the heroes showed relatively few aggressive needs, and in which aggression was not necessarily followed by retaliation and punishment. Their TAT stories revealed rather favorable attitudes toward their parents and their general social environment. Interviews obtained as they were leaving camp indicated, tentatively, that they had enjoyed their camp experience more than the boys who had increased in prejudice.

Mussen's study offers evidence to support the thesis that prejudice serves personal needs; does not bear out the prediction that, for *groups,* "getting to know them" automatically reduces prejudice; but indicates that when prejudice is *not* related to personality needs, acquaintance with a minority group may reduce prejudice.

Pettigrew (1959), like Mussen, was interested both in normal and in pathological prejudice. If prejudice is considered to be normal—that is, a product of straightforward learning—then, in the United States, anti-Negro prejudice should be higher in the South than in the North; but in the South the correlation between prejudice and authoritarianism should be lower than in the North, where there is at least token disapproval of prejudice. It also follows logically that there should be a higher correlation between anti-Negro and anti-Jewish prejudice in the North than in the South. Both should be more closely related to personality needs in the North than in the South, where there are more opportunities to learn anti-Negro than anti-Semitic prejudice.

Pettigrew interviewed a random sample of 180 Northerners and 186 Southerners from four small northern and four small southern towns. On the whole, his southern sample was slightly younger, less well educated, and included a larger proportion of native-born than the northern sample. During his interviews (which were presented as attempting to determine the influence of mass information media), he asked a number of questions from the F-scale and from a Negro and Jewish prejudice scale. The set of questions about Negroes included two types: stereotyped beliefs (they are a happy-go-lucky people) and exclusion-discrimination (they should never mingle with whites).

As he predicted, Pettigrew found his southern sample to be much more prejudiced against Negroes than the northern sample, the difference being more marked for the exclusion-discrimination than for the stereotyped-belief items. This finding illustrates the influence of direct learning; but his results also indicate the presence of pathological prejudice equally in North and South. For example, in the North, the F-scale correlated, not highly but significantly (.27), with anti-Negro prejudice; the correlation for southern subjects was .34. Correlations between anti-Negro and anti-Semitic prejudice also supported the prediction that prejudice is related to personality. This correlation was very similar in the North (.55) and the South (.58). For both the northern and southern samples, the better-educated were less prejudiced and less authoritarian, but education affected these relations more strongly in the South than in the North (for example, in the North, the correlation between education and anti-Negro prejudice was −.30; in the South it was −.47).

Pettigrew's study illustrates clearly that both theories—prejudice as *directly learned,* and prejudice as related to *personality dynamics*—must be considered in any accounting for ethnocentric attitudes. The better-educated Southerner *and* Northerner have reduced their prejudice, but education has affected the former more than the latter because, usually, he has further to go. However, the authoritarian, whether Northerner or Southerner, has seized upon *general* prejudice (that is, against both Negroes and Jews) as a method of satisfying personal needs.

PERSONALITY CHARACTERISTICS ASSOCIATED WITH PREJUDICE

A study by Gough *et al.* (1950) sheds some light on personality characteristics associated with prejudice in children. Gough and his colleagues devised a test with each item of which the subjects—242 fourth-, fifth-, and sixth-grade pupils in two schools in a large midwestern city—were asked to indicate agreement or disagreement. Sample items, all of which concerned Negroes, are the following: They work hard. I would like to go on a picnic with them. They often hurt other people's feelings. I would like to see one of them get elected President of the United States. They are pretty dumb.

Other tests given to the children in this study concerned anti-Semitic prejudice and general intolerance. The characteristics of the most intolerant children were then compared with those of the most tolerant. There were approximately forty children, both boys and girls, in each of these groups.

On the basis of their findings, the authors conclude that children's race prejudice is related to general intolerance, thus supporting the frequently made assumption of a relationship between authoritarianism and ethnocentrism. There were indications that the more intolerant children were also more constricted (less free and more apprehensive about creative self-expression), more cynical, more suspicious, more fearful, and less confident and secure than the tolerant children.

It must, of course, be borne in mind that these conclusions were based, not on the children's real-life behavior, but on their answers to questionnaire items. There is not necessarily a one-to-one relationship between the two.

Although reactions to frustration and failure are discussed in more detail in Chapter 13, it is necessary to anticipate this discussion briefly. Rosenzweig (1944) has classified reactions to frustration into *intropunitive* (turned in upon oneself), *extrapunitive* (turned outward toward others), and *impunitive* (repressed). It has been suspected that persons who are prejudiced are more likely to be extrapunitive than those who are not. Rosenzweig has developed the Picture Frustration Test (1950) to measure the direction of expressions of hostility. This test is in the form of cartoons, in which, for example, someone has spilled soup on another person. The "balloon" above the soup-spiller is filled in with some statement, such as "Oops, I'm sorry"; and alternative possibilities are provided for filling in the balloon above the victim. These possibilities range from impunitive (for example, "Oh, that's all right. This suit had to be cleaned anyway.") to extrapunitive ("You clumsy ox. Just who do you think you are? I ought to poke you in the nose!") to intropunitive ("It's my fault—I have my chair too far out in the aisle."). The respondent's "punitiveness" direction is judged from the type of response with which he fills in the balloons.

Using this technique, Lesser (1958) investigated the relationship between anti-Semitism and extrapunitiveness. His subjects were fifth- and sixth-grade Jewish boys (twenty in number, from 10 to 13 years of age) and non-Jewish boys (twenty-four in number, aged from a little more than 10 to a little more than 13). Lesser's definition of anti-Semitism was sociometric: the number of Jewish boys chosen as being one of a boy's three best friends was subtracted from the number of Jewish boys among the three the boy most rejected. Scores ranged from $+3$ (very anti-Semitic) to -3 (very pro-Semitic). Scores for the non-Jewish boys average 0— they liked as many Jewish boys as they rejected. For the Jewish boys, the average was $-.44$. These average scores are not significantly different from each other.

Lesser then correlated anti-Semitism scores with extrapunitiveness scores for the two groups of boys separately. The correlation for the non-Jewish youngsters was .60, and for the Jewish boys .48. These correlations are high, and they are not significantly different from each other. Lesser thus provides support for the notion that youngsters holding anti-Semitic prejudices are also extrapunitive. They take out their wrath on the world; not on themselves. That this is not a healthy trait is suggested by Albee (1950), who found the prognosis (prediction of recovery) more favorable for adult schizophrenics and other psychotics who were intropunitive than for those who were extrapunitive. Albee, however, was dealing with actual behavior rather than test-inferred direction of punitiveness.

Berkowitz (1959) has used a research population of forty-eight women college students to demonstrate a similar point. His anti-Semitic college girls measured higher on a test of inclination toward hostility than girls low in anti-Semitism; and, when frustrated by a prestigeful outsider (the experimenter), vented (displaced) their aggression on their innocent working partners. Girls low in anti-Semitism actually said that they liked their partner *better* following than preceding frustration.

Research done by Cowen, Landes, and Schaet (1959) indicates that aggression displaced because of frustration is particularly likely to be directed toward Negroes. Using college students as subjects, Cowen and his colleagues administered an F-scale, an anti-Negro scale, a general anti-minority scale, and a patriotism scale. They then frustrated their subjects with two unsolvable puzzles, and retested them. Anti-Negro scores increased sharply and significantly, particularly for the men in the study, although there was no significant change in scores for the other tests.

Gough (1951a, b, c, and d) has published four studies in which he attempts to measure attitudes and traits that are associated with prejudice in high school boys and girls. He used a number of different samples of subjects and several research procedures, most of them involving pencil-and-paper techniques. It is not necessary for our present purposes to analyze these in great detail, although Gough's findings (as represented in his first two studies) are relevant here.

High race prejudice accompanied lower intellectual, social and educational levels, poorer grades, and less sociability and participation in school activities. Those highly prejudiced testified more to uneasiness and discomfort in social situations, and complained more than the low-prejudice subjects of personal dissatisfactions, problems, and annoyances. Their prejudice was not confined to one out-group but was spread to many. Politically, they were nationalistic and conservative, and stated feelings of being victimized and exploited (Gough, 1951a). These findings fit well with the Lesser study: the more prejudiced saw themselves as more frustrated, and indicated that they took out their frustration on others.

In his second study Gough (1951b) standardized a prejudice test. Five clusters of items characterized those who were high in prejudice: (1) anti-intellectualism; (2) a prevading sense of pessimism and lack of hope and confidence in the future (cynicism, distrust, doubt, and suspicion); (3) a hostile and bitter outlook, including admissions of temptations to injure the self or someone else; (4) grumbling and discontented evaluation of current status; and (5) a rigid, somewhat dogmatic style of thinking. The highly prejudiced high school students also showed signs of lack of poise and self-assurance; and underlying perplexity and an ominous fearfulness; and feelings of estrangement and isolation that mystify and frighten them (this is reminiscent of Erikson's adolescent "role diffusion").

From this study Gough concludes that "all of the tendencies mentioned are socially isolating in varying degrees and would be expected to interfere with and impair the efficiency of social interaction and response" (p. 253).

PREJUDICE AND AUTHORITARIANISM

Gough's studies, taken as a group, strengthen the assumption that prejudice is a special aspect of the authoritarian personality, since his highly prejudiced adolescents tend, as a group, to show characteristics that are usually combined in a definition of authoritarianism.

The assumption of a moderate-to-strong relation between authoritarianism and prejudice is further strengthened by Jensen's study (1957) of college students. Jensen used Gough's prejudice (Pr) scale to measure prejudice in 712 freshman students at San Diego State College. These young people were tested almost immediately upon entering college, as were the 312 of them who returned a year later. A number of college seniors and students at a nearby junior college were also tested. The California F-scale, or fascism scale, was also given to several of these subgroups. Some of Jensen's more striking results are summarized below.

Students who dropped out of college during their first year obtained higher Pr-scores than those who remained. Pr-scores were much lower for sophomores than for freshmen, 69 percent of the students who remained showed lowered scores. Of the 11 percent whose Pr-scores stayed the same, most had obtained exceedingly low scores in the first place.

The correlation of Pr with F (of prejudice with authoritarianism, as measured by these two scales) varied considerably from one subgroup to another. For education majors at San Diego State College, this correlation was only .27, but for the junior college students, it was .65.

Students with high Pr-scores also showed a number of scores on the Minnesota Multiphasic Inventory of the type considered to indicate maladjustment. Jensen says of their personalities, as judged by the MMPI:

> . . . the emphasis is on the obsessive-compulsive syndrome . . . , and there is comparatively little hysterical and repressive tendency. . . . The impression is that prejudiced, authoritarian persons have less well-developed ego defenses and are thus more exposed and vulnerable to psychological stress, in the face of which they develop tendencies toward pessimism, cynicism, low morale . . . and psychological isolation . . . , along with the more primitive defenses of a compulsive, ritualistic, and schizoid nature. (p. 310).

Jensen has also provided one of the few real-life tests of the relation of personality to prejudice. Members of the faculty of the college were asked to submit the names of students they knew personally and considered either well or poorly adjusted, in the sense of being likely or unlikely candidates for psychological counseling. None of the faculty had any idea of the reason for this request, nor was the faculty aware that a study of prejudice was being conducted. A list of thirty poorly adjusted and fifty-nine well-adjusted students was submitted. The mean Pr-score of the former was 9.9; of the latter only 5.6. This difference is significant at less than the .001 level.

No difference in Pr-scores were found between men and women.

PREJUDICE AND INTELLECTUAL FUNCTIONING

Kutner (1958) has made an elaborate study of the way prejudiced and nonprejudiced children attack intellectual problems. He accepts the assumptions that (1) rigidity and concrete-mindedness accompany and may even underlie prejudice; and (2) the person who is prejudiced is also authoritarian. His study is reviewed in some detail, since he has studied these phenomena with very young children.

Kutner used sixty 7-year-old public school children as his subjects, and measured their prejudice by interviewing them. During the interview they were asked such questions as the following: "Some people are Jewish and some people are Catholics. Some Jewish people say that the Catholic people are not very nice. They say that Jewish is a better religion than Catholic. They don't like to make friends with Catholic people. What about that? How do you feel about Catholic people?" (p. 48) The interviewer knew the children well, and obtained free and full answers to his questions.

On the basis of these interviews, children were classified as prejudiced or nonprejudiced. In the prejudiced group were eighteen children, ten boys and eight girls. The nonprejudiced group included forty-two children, twenty-seven girls and fifteen boys. The two groups were not significantly different from each other in IQ (although scores were not available for all), sex distribution, father's occupation, age, or religion.

Kutner defined "very unprejudiced" children as, for example, denying unwarranted assertions of virtues of their own group; or denying or enhancing denial of negative traits ascribed in the interview question to an ethnic group. "Prejudiced" children, on the other hand, spontaneously express hostility against ethnic groups quite aside from the interview statement; or they make enhanced spontaneous additions to attributed negative traits, with rationalizations, and so on.

Of the most defensibly usable of the children's responses to the interview items, Kutner found that an encouraging 58 percent were clearly nonprejudiced, and only 12 percent clearly prejudiced.

Besides the interview, Kutner administered three tests of mental functioning to his group of subjects. The first of these was a concept-formation test. Each child was presented with four large objects: a red square, a green circle, a white triangle, and a red triangle; and four small objects: a blue triangle, a red square, a white circle, and a blue square. These were cut out of desk blotters. The children were told that they must put the things together in groups so that each group included the same number of things and only things that belonged together. The possible solutions were either two groups, one of large and one of small objects; or four groups, consisting of two large and two small subgroups (although this is not clear from Kutner, two large triangles and a large circle and square in the large groups and two small squares and a circle and triangle in the small groups). The children were scored as obtaining a spontaneous correct solution, including verbalization of the correct principle; or a guided solution, in which the child did not verbalize the principle correctly or in which the experimenter had to guide him all the way to the solution through standard hints; or failure. Table 12.1 summarizes the results for the two groups of children.

Table 12.1   *Percentage of Nonprejudiced and Prejudiced Children Securing Various Degrees of Success on a Concept-Formation Test.*

	PERCENTAGE OF GROUP	
	NONPREJUDICED	PREJUDICED
Spontaneous solution	46.3	29.4
Guided solution	34.1	11.8
No solution	19.6	58.8

ADAPTED WITH PERMISSION OF THE AMERICAN PSYCHOLOGICAL ASSOCIATION AND B. KUTNER, FROM KUTNER (1958).

As can be seen from Table 12.1, the nonprejudiced children performed significantly better on this test than the prejudiced youngsters. This difference seems not to be a function of intelligence, since Kutner's analysis shows that passing or failing the test is unrelated to general aptitude.

Kutner concludes: "In situations requiring the formation of general concepts . . . more prejudiced children tend to be deficient in forming adequate concepts, less prejudiced children tend to develop adequate concepts" (p. 24). In other words, for these children, low prejudice is associated with better inductive reasoning.

Kutner next administered to his 7-year-olds a deductive reasoning test made up of nine problems. Of these, the first was an introductory item: "Electric lights never twinkle. This light is twinkling. Is it an electric light?" Four others were problems of "formal logic," in which the reasoning was straightforward and there was only one correct answer. Examples of this type of item are: "Jane is taller than Jill. Mary is shorter than Jill. Who is the tallest of all?" and "The green bug runs faster than the red bug; the red bug runs faster than the blue bug. Which bug is slowest of all?"

The second type of item was considered to be ambiguous, since it could be answered correctly in any of a number of ways. Illustrations of this type of problem are: "It runs but it has no feet; it roars but it has no voice. What is it? Why?" and "You're going to the store. On the right-hand side is a farm; straight ahead is a lake. Which way is it to the store? Why?"

The prejudiced group of children was not inferior to the nonprejudiced on the problems of formal logic, but did significantly less well on the ambiguous items. Kutner believes this difference results from rigidity, which, he thinks, underlies prejudice. He concludes: "It appears that the accuracy of deduction is dependent upon the nature of the problem to be solved: the more prejudiced children having much more difficulty in arriving at valid conclusions on problems involving some ambiguity than do less prejudiced children. Both groups, on the other hand, have equal success (or difficulty) on problems of formal logic" (p. 27). Furthermore, the nonprejudiced children, when baffled, seemed willing to give up by saying, "I don't know," and averaged 1.3 such responses for the whole test. The prejudiced children averaged only .56 such responses. Kutner says: "It would appear, then, that prejudiced children are not only less capable of producing valid conclusions but the invalid ones they *do* produce are *dogmatically held*. Another way of interpreting this result is that prejudiced children tend not to admit what, to E (experimenter), might be seen as an admission of weakness" (pp. 31–32).

The second-graders studied so intensively by Kutner, whose results are described in detail in the immediately preceding paragraphs, were followed up nine years later when they were 16 years old. He was able to locate twenty-three of the girls and ten of the boys who had taken part in his original study, and obtain their parents' permission to investigate them and their attitudes and cognitive functions as adolescents (Kutner and Gordon, 1964). Since the number of subjects who could be located and retested is small, not all of Kutner and Gordon's follow-up results are significant (it is interesting to note that ten who were located either themselves refused to submit to retesting, or their parents would not allow them to be retested). While at age 9 there were no IQ differences, at 16 the prejudiced averaged 111 and the nonprejudiced 119 IQ. The authors attribute this to a sampling error, but the difference is quite in line with their earlier findings about cognitive functioning and with other data cited in Chapter 8 about factors that produce change in IQ. There was a tendency for the nonprejudiced to score higher on tests of creative thinking, although this may be due to their higher average IQ. Those who had changed from being highly prejudiced at age 9 to low prejudice at age 16 seemed to perform cognitively better than those who had remained prejudiced, although the small number of subjects makes it impossible to evaluate this finding in any firm, statistical sense. The same thing is true of Kutner and Gordon's finding that those initially low but at 16 high in prejudice fared even less well in cognitive functioning than those who were consistent in being prejudiced. Finally, 16-year-old prejudice was not predictable from 9-year-old prejudice: eighteen of the children were consistent, fifteen inconsistent in their prejudice classification over the interval of nine years between the two studies.

O'Connor (1952) reports findings that support Kutner, even though she used Harvard college students as research subjects. O'Connor administered a test of abstract thinking and one of prejudice, and found that the two were significantly and negatively correlated (in the high .30s).

Using still another population (thirty senior medical students), Neel (1959) found that the higher the F-scale score of these young men (the more authoritarian they were), the less well they dealt with ambiguous psychiatrically related material (such as advising a young woman who complained about frigidity, and whose physical examination was negative, about "a good book on sex"). They also received lower test grades on course material related to "humanitarian philosophy," although they equaled the less authoritarian men in mastery of formal course content.

Neel's study had an interesting inspiration. For years, several senior medical students in each class had complained bitterly about a required course in psychiatry. All efforts to mitigate these complaints through improving instructional methods and materials had failed. The author finally conjectured that it was the human-relations material itself against which the students were rebelling. The study was based on the assumption that authoritarian personalities reject human-relations and adjustment content per se, and will do poorly with it (because of their own personality adjustment), regardless of how well it is presented. Neel's study offers moderate support for her assumptions.

STUDIES REPORTING NEGATIVE FINDINGS

The studies reviewed in the three preceding subsections, using different experimental populations and various measures of prejudice, authoritarianism, and personal adjustment, suggest strongly that prejudice is related to authoritarianism and general adjustment, and that it is associated with certain types of learning disability.

However, Masling (1954) has reported findings from studies of his own and others that (at least for adults) do not demonstrate a relation between authoritarianism (or prejudice) and adjustment. For thirty-four men and forty-eight women who were psychiatric patients, no relation was found between ethnocentrism and scores on the Minnesota Multiphasic Inventory; for 963 representative citizens of Philadelphia, scores on an authoritarianism-equalitarianism scale were not correlated with scores on a scale designed to measure personal security; for sixty-four summer-school students who took the F-scale and an incomplete-sentences test, there was no relation between authoritarianism and personal adjustment. Finally, forty-nine Navy recruits hospitalized for personal-adjustment problems did not differ in their authoritarianism score from 1,000 not so hospitalized.

Davids and Eriksen (1957) have reported similar results for a group of forty-eight naval men of college age (although few had attended college).

In this study, authoritarianism was significantly but slightly related (—.24) to intelligence, but no relation was found with three measures of personal adjustment. The authors argue that authoritarian college students, placed in the relatively democratic atmosphere that characterizes most colleges, become neurotic; whereas the same thing is not true for the Navy men.

McCandless and Holloway (1955) used the Horowitz Faces Test as a measure of anti-Negro prejudice for 154 fourth- and fifth-grade children in a midwestern public school. There were seventy-seven boys and seventy-seven girls in the group. The authors then tested the relations between race prejudice and various behaviors that, they reasoned, would characterize children who were intolerant of ambiguity. The general hypothesis was that prejudiced children would be more intolerant of ambiguity than unprejudiced children. An illustrative specific prediction was that there would be differences between the two groups in deciding which of two equal weights was the heavier. It was predicted that children intolerant of ambiguity would find a period of indecision unpleasant, and hence would "stampede" into a choice. For the thirty girls and twenty-five boys who took the test (this aspect of the study was dropped before all subjects had been tested, because there were obviously no differences), there were no decision-time differences between those high and low in prejudice. None of the other five hypotheses advanced by the authors (for example, prejudiced children will choose as friends other prejudiced children, whereas nonprejudiced children will not discriminate) was supported.

On the whole, it can be concluded that impressive relations exist between authoritarianism, prejudice, and personal adjustment, although in some populations no relation has been found between authoritarianism and maladjustment or intolerance of ambiguity, as measured.

PREJUDICE AS SEEN BY THE MINORITY GROUP

The research that has been summarized to this point in the chapter concerns the personality and social characteristics of those of a majority or core group who are prejudiced. What of those who receive the prejudice?

Goff (1949) interviewed 150 Negro children 10 to 13 years old, and a number of their parents, about the types of prejudiced treatment they had received, their reactions to it, and the type of advice parents had given their children about what to do when they encountered prejudice. These children were drawn from upper- and lower-income groups in New York City (where overt sanctions against the free movement of minority groups are relatively slight), and from St. Louis (where more restrictive practices are in effect with reference to Negroes).

Of the 150 children, 95 percent reported experiences that they interpreted as problems in Negro-white relations. The most frequent problem, mentioned by 77 percent of the children, was ridicule. More than half of them complained of radio and movie stereotypes, and almost half (41 percent) had actually experienced aggression from white children. A tenth (11 percent) reported physical ill-treatment from white adults.

Five percent of the children reported no difficulties. Goff believes that this figure of 5 percent is too high, since some children had been carefully protected by the community or their parents, or both; but that poor rapport in the interview, or difficulties in expression, may have been responsible for "no reported difficulties" on the part of some of the youngsters. In other words, she believes the percentage of children reporting problems should have been even higher.

The sex of the children was not related to the presence or absence of reported difficulty, but subtle manifestations of prejudice were more likely to be noticed (or reported) by girls. Lower-income children, who are more likely to be completely segregated from whites, seemed to be more sensitive to implied prejudice than upper-income children. There was some indication that heavily segregated communities bred cultural isolates.

The children reported that their most frequent feeling was resentment in situations where they encountered ridicule, physical ill-treatment, aggression, and indirect disparagement. Inferiority feelings most often were aroused by rude treatment and discrimination. Fear was not often admitted (probably because the children were ashamed to admit it), and occurred most frequently in response to aggression. Girls admitted fear more frequently than boys, as would be expected. Indirect disparagement was the derogatory treatment most likely to be accepted as "true" by the children (that is, such treatment caused them to question their own adequacy).

Interestingly enough, upper-income girls were more likely to fight in response to ill-treatment than lower-income girls, who were more likely to display inertia. Boys were more likely to fight than girls.

The counsel given by parents to the children stressed withdrawal and avoidance when confronted by discrimination. In only 42 percent of the cases where parental guidance had been given did the children report it as being helpful.

To sum up, from the victim's point of view, race prejudice is an ugly, hurtful thing, in the face of which he feels angry, inferior, and helpless. He is placed in a situation where there is "frustration and failure without solution."

Stevenson and Stewart (1958) have conducted an interesting study of the development of racial awareness in young children. They used as subjects 225 Negro and white children, boys and girls, aged 3 to 7 years, who lived in Austin, Texas. As one measure of racial preference, they gave each child his choice of playing with colored (Negro) or white boy-girl pairs of dolls. At the ages of 3, 4, 5, 6, and 7, respectively, the following percentages of white children chose the white dolls: 52, 60, 64, 82, and 82 percent. For the majority, in other words, a clear preference had been set up by the time they were 4, and by age 6 more than four fifths showed such a preference. Comparable percentages for the Negro children were 50, 39, 35, 33, and 65 percent. At the ages of 4, 5, and 6, Negro children appeared to be rejecting dolls that represented their ethnic group. Only at age 7 did a modest majority pick the Negro doll.

It should be noted that Stevenson and Steward did not equate the dolls "intrinsic" attractiveness, although the colored dolls were identical in dress and physiognomy with the white dolls, the only difference being "skin tone." Furthermore, it is almost certain that both Negro and white children have had more experience in playing with white than with colored dolls (indeed, the authors report that they had been unable locally to purchase Negro dolls to use in their study). An additional, although unavoidable, defect in this study is that the socioeconomic status of the Negro children was lower than that of the white youngsters. The Negro children therefore probably tested lower in intelligence, although this may have little or no effect on racial awareness or preference as such.

In another phase of the Stevenson and Stewart study, the authors showed the children a series of pictures, of which the following is typical: two Negro and two white boys are shown playing in the background, and a child whose ethnic group cannot be determined is lying in the foreground. The experimenters then said to each child: "This little boy was playing in the yard. Another little boy was very mean to him and pushed him down. Which one of these little boys do you think pushed him down? Which little boy is going to come over and see if he is all right?

A higher proportion of the white children than of the Negroes chose a child of their own ethnic group as the "hero" or "good guy"; the Negro children were more likely to choose a Negro child as the "bad guy" than were the white children to choose a white child.

At the ages of 3, 4, 5, 6, and 7, respectively, the following percentages of white children chose a white child as the villain in the picture described above: 32, 32, 40, 20, and 32 percent. But, in the same order, a Negro child was chosen as the villain by the following percentages of Negro children: 65, 56, 45, 71, and 85 percent.

For this picture, the differential trend in choosing a hero was not as clearly marked or statistically significant as the choice of a villain, but at five of the six ages, more white children chose whites as heroes than Negroes chose Negroes. The percentages for whites for the five age levels in order were 52, 76, 56, 56, and 60; and for Negroes, 48, 39, 41, 47, and 75. In other words, at each age level, a majority of the white youngsters believed that a white child would be the "good guy" in the story; but at each age level except age 7, the majority of the Negro children chose as the hero one of the two pictured white youngsters rather than one of the two pictured Negro children.

The implications of this study, although tentative, lead to the hypothesis that racial awareness, including differential preference, is developed very early in life; and that society is so organized as to lead the Negro child to devalue and perhaps even to reject his own ethnic group. The consequences of such a rejection for the self-concept of Negro children are serious, and should be investigated further.

Introduction to Authoritarian Personality

This section is concerned less with the personality characteristics of the authoritarian and the prejudiced than with the question of how authoritarian personalities and prejudiced attitudes develop among families with different child-rearing practices and in different social classes. Before proceeding to this question, however, it is necessary to mention again that in investigations of child-rearing practices and social class, our concepts and methods have frequently left something to be desired. For child-rearing studies, these difficulties have been discussed in some detail in Chapters 2 and 3. With respect to social class, although there are many disagreements about its measurement, almost everyone will agree that, at the very least, there is a blue-collar class and a white-collar class. Furthermore, regardless of how social class is defined and measured, quantitative expressions of it as it exists in our society exhibit solid relations with (that is, help to predict) human attributes ranging from IQ level to capacity for delaying impulse gratification.

We have, therefore, concepts—somewhat cloudy but useful—that we may call social class, patterns of child-rearing, and authoritarian personality. The concern of this chapter is with the relations among these three.

Child-Rearing Practices, Prejudice, and the Authoritarian Personality

None of the theories of authoritarianism and prejudice discussed in the preceding chapter holds that these attitudes come into being *spontaneously* or *automatically*. Both psychoanalytic and social-psychological theories accept the assumption that prejudice or an authoritarian personality is something that is *developed*. The theories posit different mechanisms for this development, but each assigns responsibility to *some* experiential, social factor; none, for example, endorses instinct or heredity as a causal dynamism.

Among the most prominent to suggest that child-rearing practices were dynamically related to later race prejudice and authoritarianism were Adorno and his colleagues (1950). As was mentioned earlier in this chapter, the research of this group began with efforts to investigate race prejudice. Studies of prejudice against various minority groups led them to the conclusion that prejudice was not usually confined to a specific minority group, but was general: for example, those prejudiced against Negroes tended to be prejudiced against Jews and Orientals as well. A broader term than prejudice—*ethnocentrism*—seems to describe this phenomenon accurately. Ethnocentrism is defined as an emotional attitude that one's own race or nation is superior to all others; and, in addition, it implies a rejection of other races, nations, or groups other than one's own.

Further studies in this general area led Adorno and his co-workers to the still broader conception of the authoritarian personality, as has been defined and discussed at length. The most general personality-attitude construct employed here, then, is the *authoritarian personality*. One of its most frequent manifestations—in fact, one of its *usual* manifestations —is *ethnocentrism*; ethnocentrism, in turn, is ordinarily accompanied by specific *prejudices* against minority and other out-groups. The most common measure of the authoritarian personality is the F-scale, but a very large number of specific prejudice scales exists. Some of the studies reviewed in this chapter relate to authoritarianism, but they employ only specific prejudice scales as their measure. Such studies, it should be kept in mind, relate directly to authoritarianism *only to the degree that the prejudice measure used correlates with a more general measure of authoritarianism*. In this chapter, authoritarianism is often inferred from the use in a study of a specific measure or measures of prejudice because of the often-demonstrated correlation between them; but such a study provides less convincing support for a relation between the independent variable (as child-rearing practices) and authoritarianism than if a direct measure of authoritarianism had been used.

STUDIES OF PARENTAL PRACTICES AND ATTITUDES

Type of Discipline Adorno and his colleagues (1950) made inferences about the childhood and the parent-child relations of their authoritarian and nonauthoritarian, prejudiced and nonprejudiced adult subjects from interview and TAT data. Frenkel-Brunswik (1948, 1951, 1953, 1954a) worked directly with children and their parents, and concluded that parents of very authoritarian and ethnocentric children used harsher and more rigid forms of discipline than parents of children scoring low in authoritarianism or ethnocentrism. She states (1954a) that ethnocentric adolescents describe "the perfect father" as disciplining, strict, punitive, and a good provider, whereas nonprejudiced children see him as companionable and relaxed. Frenkel-Brunswik found that ethnocentric children see the discipline that has been meted out to them as threatening, traumatic, overwhelming, and bewildering. She believes that these perceptions accurately reflect the type of home in which such children have been reared. Parents of ethnocentric children, she believes, do not use an individualized approach with their children, but concern themselves principally with transmitting a set of fixed rules and customs. This interferes with the children's development of a clear-cut personal identity and integration.

An interesting study by Block (1955), one of the few research workers who has used fathers as subjects, presents a picture of *actual* authoritarian parents that is very like the one Frenkel-Brunswik constructed from her interviews with authoritarian children. Block made a rather detailed personality study of the 20 high (restrictives) and 20 low (permissives) scorers on a test of child-rearing attitudes given to a group of 100 army officers. He describes the restrictives as follows:

> The picture which emerges of the fathers expressing restrictive attitudes toward child-rearing is almost a prototype of what has been variously labeled "the authoritarian personality" or "the over-controlled." These fathers are constricted, repressing, essentially dependent individuals with great feelings of personal inadequacy. Besides over-controlling their inner needs and tensions, they find it psychologically necessary to over-control the situations within their environment for which they hold responsibility. Their approach to child-rearing, while of particular importance for the forming of personality in the child, should be understood as but one of many manifestations of their basic personality structure. (pp. 45–46)

The restrictives, according to Block:

> . . . still lack in themselves a perception of self-integrity and a differentiation of the social environment which can enable them to treat their own children differently from the way they had been treated by their own threatening fathers. In effect, the restrictive father, acting upon the residues of his own childhood anxieties, is revenging himself upon the wrong generation. This cycle of personality transmission is thus self-perpetuating but *self-defeating*.[4]

Block's implication is clearly, "like father, like son." Frenkel-Brunswik and Havel (1953) present evidence to support this implication, at least

[4] Reprinted with permission of W. E. Martin, Editor, *Child Develpm.*, and J. Block, from Block (1955).

for ethnocentrism. They report correlations between ratings of parental prejudice and children's prejudice ranging from .20 to .60.

Harris, Gough, and Martin (1950) found that certain maternal attitudes toward child-rearing were related to prejudice in their child subjects. Although the results are not entirely clear-cut, they present evidence that mothers of prejudiced children were more authoritarian, fussier, tended to want quiet children, and were in general less effective with their children than mothers of nonprejudiced children.

Evidence that harsh parental treatment may result in personal attributes reflecting authoritarianism has also been provided by Mussen and Kagan (1958). They measured tendencies to yield, or to conform, by a technique similar to that discussed earlier in this chapter. They also gave the twenty male college students who took part in their study the TAT, evaluating the stories told according to how severely the heroes were punished by story characters judged to represent their parents or other authorities. The subjects whose TAT scores indicated that they had received high punishment from their parents (or, at least, believed they had) were significantly more often yielders than "independents"; those whose scores indicated mild punishment were more often independent in their judgments.

Harsh parents, Mussen and Kagan conclude, may have more conflicts with their children: their children, then, have more experiences with their parents in which yielding, or conforming, reduces anxiety. Consequently, through generalization, these children adopt yielding as a way of life. Mussen and Kagan also state that conformists have been shown to manifest marked distrust toward other people, which, they speculate, "may also be generalized responses stemming from original fear and distrust of the parents" (p. 60).

Further evidence supporting the fact that types of parental punishment affect the child's notion of appropriate punishment, as well as his need to direct hostility and punishment toward others, has been provided by Radke (1946) and Lyle and Levitt (1955). Radke's study indicates that children prescribe for others the same sorts of punishment they receive from their parents; and Lyle and Levitt have demonstrated, for a fifth-grade population, that there is a correlation between children's authoritarianism and their tendency to see their parents as punitive. Authoritarianism and punitiveness on the part of the children were also found to be related. These correlations, although not high, were statistically significant.

Such studies as those by Mussen and Kagan, and Lyle and Levitt, raise the extremely important question of whether children's *perception* of their parents' behavior accurately reflects the parents' *actual* behavior. Few studies have been done that bear on this important question, but what evidence is available indicates that children both perceive and report their parents' behavior more or less accurately, and that boys are as accurate as girls. Bronson, Katten, and Livson (1959), for example, found that children's ratings of parents' behavior in the areas of authority, affection, and involvement were in all instances highly and significantly related to psychologists' ratings of the parents. One hundred families who had been studied for eighteen years were involved in the study, making it quite convincing.

Still other studies suggest relations between authoritarian attitudes and methods of rearing children. For example, Hart (1957) administered the Traditional Family Ideology scale, which presumably measures authoritarian trends in child-rearing practices and family organization, to 126 mothers of children aged $2\frac{1}{2}$ to $5\frac{1}{2}$. She also conducted interviews with the mothers about their practices concerning feeding and oral activities, cleanliness training, sexual behavior, aggression, and dependent and independent behavior of their children. On the basis of the interview material, Hart classified the mothers' responses into two categories: love-oriented and nonlove-oriented techniques of control. She found that the higher a mother's authoritarianism score, the more she tended to use nonlove-oriented techniques. Correlations in the area of complex human behavior usually run rather low—in the .20s, .30s, sometimes in the .40s and .50s—but Hart found the correlation between mothers' authoritarianism and the number of situations in which nonlove-oriented techniques were used to be a highly significant .63. Such factors as the age of mother and child, sex and birth order of the child, and number of children in the family bore no relation to mothers' authoritarianism.

The scale used in Hart's study (the Traditional Family Ideology) correlates .73 with a version of the F-scale (as reported by Titus and Hollander, 1957, in a review of literature dealing with the F-scale).

An ingenious study of identification shows that young men reared harshly, according to their ratings of their parents on the Traditional Family Ideology scale, identify more strongly with an instructor who punishes them than they do one who rewards them (Baxter, Lerner, and Miller, 1965).

Child-Rearing Attitudes Zuckerman and his colleagues (1958) indicate that harsh child-rearing attitudes accompany high authoritarianism as measured by the F-scale. Their correlation between harshness, as measured by the child-rearing attitudes scale, and the F-scale was almost identical with that found by Hart: .61, despite the fact that they did not use mothers, but 88 student nurses, as subjects. Zuckerman and his coworkers took elaborate steps to eliminate the "yielding" or "response-set" influence on the F-scale. Even with this influence controlled, the correlation between their measures remained in the .40s.

Kates and Diab (1955) used both men and women college students as subjects in a study to determine the relation between authoritarianism and child-rearing attitudes. They found correlations for their women subjects to be in the .30s (for the most part) between presumably "pathogenic" (poor) child-rearing attitudes and authoritarianism; but uncovered *no* relation between child-rearing attitudes and authoritarianism for the men.

This last study, taken in conjunction with others reviewed in this section, suggests that, among college students, child-rearing practices may be of more concern to women than to men, perhaps because of the emphasis of our culture. It is appropriate, even necessary, for girls and young women to interest themselves in children, their care, and their development; but such an interest is not expected to be manifested by men, particularly unmarried men. In addition, college women, more than their male classmates, may have had experience in caring for younger sibs, baby-sitting, and so on.

Since psychology is a young science, its students, teachers, and practitioners must be tolerant of ambiguity, uncertain results, and the lack of flatly demonstrated generalizations. From the studies that exist for a given area, they must determine the most likely trend and hope for further definitive research—or, even better, do such research themselves. But they must not overlook negative evidence. Gallagher (1957), for example, has done a study with college students somewhat similar to those summarized above, but found no relation between authoritarianism and attitudes that were judged to represent harshness toward children. However, he did not perform separate analyses for the forty-four college women and the fifteen college men who took part in his study, and it may be that results for the college men reduced his correlations. In addition, the scale of attitudes toward children used by Gallagher was not a *direct* measure of child-rearing attitudes. It included, for example, items related to information about child development; and there is no particular reason to expect a relation between authoritarianism and factual knowledge about how children develop. In other words, Gallagher's results introduce a note of caution into our conclusions for this subsection; but, because his methods differed from those of investigators who obtained positive results, his study is not directly comparable and its results cannot be clearly considered contradictory.

Taken together, the studies reviewed in this section suggest that authoritarian and prejudiced children are more likely to have parents who are overcontrolling and who use predominantly nonlove-oriented child-rearing techniques. Fathers holding harsh child-rearing attitudes seem to have patterned themselves on their own fathers, to be rather unaware of the individual needs of their children, and to feel personally inadequate.

The evidence indicates that children adopt their parents' attitudes: prejudiced children tend to come from prejudiced homes, and children who have been reared punitively seem themselves to be punitive. At least one study indicates that parents who are perceived by their children as punitive may produce conforming or yielding children.

An important question about this area of research is: Do children's perceptions of their parents represent what the parents are *actually* like? At least one study, using a sizable sample of 100 families, indicates that the children's perceptions of their parents agree by and large with the judgments of professional psychologists who have studied the parents.

Other research indicates that relations between personality characteristics and attitudes toward child-rearing may be a function of direct personal involvement with children. At college age, such relations have been found for women (who, according to the dictates of our culture, should be interested in children, even though not yet mothers), but not for men. But correlations between child-rearing attitudes and personality characteristics have been found for older men who *are* fathers.

The emphasis in this section on the desirability of love-oriented techniques of child-rearing should not lead one to the belief that spontaneous expressions of feeling, even to the point of a spanking, are irreparably damaging to children. The important factor may be, not *absolute consistency* of love-oriented techniques, but their *predominance*.

SOME OTHER CORRELATES OF AUTHORITARIANISM AND PREJUDICE

The distinction was made earlier between normal and pathological prejudice. Christie and Garcia (1951) were interested at least as much in the determinants of normal prejudice as in the antecedents of pathological prejudice (which has been the focus of the preceding subsection). They selected fifty-seven pairs of college students, one of each pair from California, the other from "Southwest City." They characterize Southwest City as a town that might have come directly from Sinclair Lewis' *Babbitt.* Their pairs were well-matched: for example, on sex, age, fathers' median income, political preference, and so on. The distributions of F- and E-(ethnocentrism) scores for the two samples (as well as the larger samples from which the matched pairs were drawn) were very similar in type, but the *average* scores were much higher for the Southwest City subjects. F- and E-scores were highly correlated: .63 for Southwest City, .56 for California subjects. Christie and Garcia conclude:

> Less psychoanalytically oriented theorists than Adorno and his colleagues might speculate that lifelong immersion in an implicitly authoritarian subculture establishes the frame of reference under-

lying one's perception of the world and the value judgments made about human nature, and that this factor would account for the increased evidences of authoritarianism in Southwest City. (p. 469)

Young, Benson, and Holtzman (1960) have also published a study related to environmental influences on anti-Negro prejudice (although they did not concern themselves with the broader concepts of authoritarianism). They report that the prejudiced attitudes of University of Texas undergraduate students are remarkably resistant to change. The three years of ferment over desegregation between 1955 and 1958 had produced no *average* changes in prejudice score—that is, the average prejudice score of a sample of University of Texas undergraduates measured in 1955 was almost identical with the average score of a comparable group measured in 1958. However, there were *sex differences* in change: men students, as a group, had become *more* prejudiced; women less prejudiced. Since, according to theory, women (mothers and future mothers) transmit the culture, there is some encouragement about tolerance in their finding.

Young, Benson, and Holtzman divided their large sample of students (508 in number) into a number of subgroups in order to study various factors that might relate to prejudice. Eight personal and demographic factors were found to be associated with anti-Negro prejudice at a statistically significant level:

1. *Area of residence.* Students who came from east Texas were most prejudiced; those from west Texas were intermediate in prejudice; and those from the Rio Grande Valley were least prejudiced.

2. *Religious affiliation.* Of the major religious groupings studied, Baptists showed the highest prejudice; Catholic students were intermediate; and Jewish students were least prejudiced.

3. *Church attendance.* Those who attended church *very* regularly and those who did not attend church *at all* were less prejudiced than those who claimed that they attended church once or twice a month.

4. *Scholastic standing.* Students earning good grades (B average or above) had lower prejudice scores than those earning poor grades (C average or below).

5. *Type of curriculum.* Social science majors were the least prejudiced group; pharmacy and business majors showed the highest prejudice.

6. *Urban-rural residence.* Students who had come from urban areas

(cities of more than 50,000 population) were less prejudiced than students residing in small-town and rural settings.

7. *Fraternity-sorority membership.* Members of sororities and fraternities were more prejudiced than nonmembers.

8. *Fathers' reported income.* Students who claimed that their fathers earned more than $40,000 per year were significantly more prejudiced than those who reported paternal income as $5,000 per year or less.

Another interesting study investigated the relations between religious devoutness and anti-Semitic and anti-Negro attitudes (no direct measure of authoritarianism was used). O'Reilly and O'Reilly (1954) devised a scale of devoutness—the "extent to which the subjects (Ss) agreed with the Catholic Church on certain social, moral, and religious questions" (p. 378). This scale was administered, along with anti-Semitism and anti-Negro prejudice scales, to 92 men and 120 women attending Roman Catholic universities and seminaries. Almost all the subjects reported that religion had had a very marked influence on their upbringing.

For women, the devoutness scale correlated .29 with the anti-Semitism scale; for men the correlation was .31. The anti-Negro and anti-Semitism scales were rather highly correlated (.69 for women and .68 for men). Students scoring high on the devoutness scale also favored parish segregation for Negroes. Of those who favored segregation, 76.5 percent scored in the upper half of the devoutness scale, whereas 74.5 percent of those scoring low on the devoutness scale opposed parish segregation. As far as the present author knows, data do not exist concerning parental practices and children's devoutness, but it is reasonable to predict that there are significant relations of some type.

It has been argued, more often from clinical than from formal research evidence, that minority groups, or "inferiors," adopt (even *over*-adopt) the attitudes of the majority group, or their "superior"—perhaps as a matter of self-protection. The butler may be more snobbish than his employer, the headwaiter haughtier than the prosperous clientele he serves, the "poor white" more prejudiced toward Negroes than members of his ethnic group who are above him in social class. Two studies are interesting in this connection. Authoritarian ideology in Negro college students has been studied by Steckler (1957), who concluded that Negro students were very conservative and that, in general, there was evidence that they had "identified with the aggressor"—that is, adopted the values and attitudes of the majority group. C. U. Smith and Prothro (1957) actually found that southern white freshman students scored lower on the F-scale than Negro college freshmen from the same state.

In other words, the conditions of one's rearing and his own status are likely to be related to attitudes of authoritarianism or equalitarianism. Those growing up in authoritarian surroundings acquire authoritarian patterns of reaction; and those who experience prejudice may become even more authoritarian than those who exercise prejudice.

Authoritarianism and Social Class

Less is known about the relation between socioeconomic status and authoritarianism than about child-rearing practices and authoritarianism. Before the topic can be usefully approached, an attempt must be made to arrive at general but differential descriptions of lower- and middle-class child-rearing practices. This is a difficult task.

For present purposes, two papers have been selected that attempt to define the relation between lower- and middle-class parents and their children. The author grants his possible bias in selecting these particular studies, although his own general and professional clinical experience is congruent with their conclusions. This whole question is discussed more fully in Chapter 14.

Maas (1951), using interview techniques with a small sample of 10- to 15-year-olds, some from the lower-lower class, the others from the "core culture" (an amalgam of lower-middle and upper-lower classes), contrasted child-rearing practices of the two groups as he inferred them from the interview. There was greater social freedom and tolerance of physical aggression in the lives of the lower-class children; but, at the same time, they had experienced a psychologically closed, hierarchical, and quite rigid parental relationship. The core-culture children, on the other hand, reported a more open, relatively equalitarian and flexible relationship. Lower-class parents were seen as relatively closed and inaccessible to the child's communications, and the child was relatively mute with them because of the threat of explosive anger. Core-culture did not seem fearful of expressing either positive or negative attitudes toward their parents, nor did they either fear or identify with the potentially threatening power of adults; lower-class children often experienced intense fear of parents and expressed feelings of rejection or unworthiness because of disobedience. Such children, under duress, may explode in a manner similar to their parents, or redirect their hostile aggression (as well as tender feelings) toward siblings or other contemporaries.

Maccoby and her colleagues (1954) found that, in general, lower-class mothers espoused more rigid child-rearing practices, used more physical punishment, and allowed less aggression toward parents than did middle-class parents.

Viewed in this framework, the following results fit together moderately well:

Singer (1954), using TAT protocols obtained from a normal and a schizophrenic population of men, found some evidence for warmer family and father-son relationships among middle- than among lower-class subjects.

Cass (1950, 1952a, 1952b) investigated the relation between mothers' awareness of their daughters and the identification of the daughters with the mothers. To measure identification, she asked four different groups of mothers (two middle-class, two lower-class) to fill in a check list of favorite interests and activities. When the pattern of a daughter's check list was quite similar to her mother's, Cass considered her highly identified, and vice versa. The mothers were also asked to predict how their daughters would fill in the check list. The more accurate the mother was about her daughter, the more "aware" of her daughter she was considered to be.

A rather high relation was found between mothers' awareness and daughters' identification for the two groups of middle-class mothers of nondelinquent daughters ($r = .59$ and .48). For the two groups of lower-class mothers and daughters there was a low relationship between these variables. For lower-class mothers and nondelinquent daughters, the correlation was .32; for lower-class mothers and delinquent daughters, the correlation was only .11.

Cass also found that average scores for awareness and identification were higher for middle- than for lower-class mothers and daughters.[5] The average awareness scores for the middle-class mothers were between 13 and 14 (these figures represent the number of items checked by the daughter that were accurately predicted by the mother); the lower-class mothers of nondelinquents scored 12 items correct; the lower-class mothers of delinquents, 8. Identification scores for middle-class daughters averaged about 9; for lower-class daughters about 7.4.

Cohn and Carsch (1954) found significant F-scale differences between a group of 117 German factory workers who had attended only *Volkschule, or Volkschule* and *Mittelschule* (less well educated), and a better-educated group of 23 subjects who had attended *Hochschule*. The mean F-scale scores were 5.40 and 4.57 respectively, this difference being significant at less than the .01 level. (The higher the score, the more authoritarian the person is considered to be.)

Finally, Adorno and his colleagues report, among other relations, the following mean F-scale scores for combined University of Oregon and University of California groups: 3.39 for men and 3.82 for women; for middle-class men and women, 3.62 and 3.69, respectively; and for working-class women and men, 3.86 and 4.19, respectively. A proponderantly upper-lower-class group of Maritime Service men scored an average of

---

[5] These figures come from personal communication with Dr. Cass, and, although they are in the expected direction, the differences have not been tested for statistical significance.

4.06; and a group of San Quentin prisoners, mostly lower-class, scored 4.73. A group of professional women scored 3.43.

The evidence of a relation between lower-class socioeconomic status and authoritarianism is tenuous, but a connection is suggested. If verified, it seems logical to suggest that this relation is due to an interaction between child-rearing practices, general educational-cultural factors, and social threat, with lower-class parents as a group using stricter and less love-oriented ways of bringing up children, having a less adequate education, and being more vulnerable to threat from authoritarian figures in general (such as the police and the boss). In addition, they are more directly in contact and competition with minority groups; hence are more likely to be threatened by them.

The Development of Authoritarianism

A tentative theory of why authoritarian children differ from equalitarian children is advanced in this section of the chapter. It will be noted that in the present treatment, learning theory has been enriched by psychoanalytic theory, which, in turn, has been sharpened by learning theory. The latter, influenced by sociological theory, takes more account of normal prejudice than psychoanalytic theory does. It should be noted that a number of the predictions made from social-learning theory are similar to those that would be made within a Freudian framework, particularly as developed by Frenkel-Brunswik (1948, 1954a).

Theory can often be most economically developed by dealing with the extremes of the population distribution: hence, this section is concerned with children who are extremely authoritarian, considered as a group, and with children who are extremely equalitarian, considered as a group. The assumption is made that child-rearing practices for the two groups will differ sharply, with a minimum of overlap between the attitudes and methods of parents of authoritarians and parents of equalitarians. These extreme groups, of course, form a very small part of the total population, so that most parents fall somewhere between consistent and extreme authoritarianism and consistent and extreme equalitarianism. Similarly, few or no children or adults can be expected to be completely authoritarian or completely equalitarian in personality characteristics. The concept of the authoritarian personality is complex, so that a person may show high prejudice, for example, but at the same time be moderately flexible in behavior and attitudes. Nor, human nature being what it is, is it likely that the most extremely authoritarian parent is authoritarian in *all* his practices with his children *all* the time. But he will differ from the equalitarian parent in being *more* authoritarian *more* of the time.

CHILD-REARING PRACTICES AND INTOLERANCE OF AMBIGUITY

The first major hypothesis about authoritarian parents is that they are personally intolerant of ambiguity. They like things clear-cut; ambiguous and tentative situations or problem-solutions make them uncomfortable; and they prefer the absolute to the relative. Hence, in contrast to equalitarian parents, they tend to use an either-or approach to child-rearing: depending on the situation and the child's behavior, they are either all-punishing or all-rewarding. Discipline and punishment are not diluted with tenderness, acceptance, and reasoning. Conversely, love and approval, when given are unmixed with reservations or qualifications. This all-or-none attitude is perhaps due to the fact that authoritarian parents do not question the correctness of their behavior with their children, and at any given time they may actually perceive the child as "all bad" or "all good."

This either-or method of treatment will have very different effects upon the child, depending on his chronological age. Up to about 2 or $2\frac{1}{2}$ years of age, before he is able to use or understand complex verbal symbols, he will see this parental treatment as highly inconsistent and arbitrary. That is, from *his* point of view, the child is doing nothing more than behaving naturally. He does not discern his behavior as good or bad, right or wrong. His parents receive some of it with punishment and rejection, some with affection and reward; but he is unable to make the proper or appropriate reference of the parents; treatment *back to his behavior.* Such a state of affairs bears a reinforcement, and may produce at least two major effects. The first of these concerns the child's emerging self-concept and his relationship with his parents. Since the parents' treatment is perceived as arbitrary, the child's self-concept may become (at least temporarily) quite confused and his attitudes toward himself ambivalent. Similarly, his attitudes toward the parent-child relation will be confused and ambivalent—Erikson's mistrust and premature bipolarity.

However, the child will come eventually, but with difficulty and through trial and error, to associate a preponderance of reward with, for example, behavior A (keeping himself clean); and of punishment with behavior B (wetting his pants). Hence he will consolidate behavior A and extinguish B, even though the *earlier* history of both behaviors as *seen by him* has been one of partial or inconsistent reinforcement (it is perhaps not entirely justifiable to consider partial and inconsistent reinforcement as equivalent, although in principle they have much in common). However, even after the child has learned what his parents expect of him, the ambivalent attitudes engendered during this learning process are likely to be retained, although perhaps not at a conscious level.

After effective verbal mediation (true speech) sets in, the child will see his parents' reinforcements as they intend and practice them; that is, as highly consistent.

Equalitarian parents, on the other hand, may tend more than authoritarians simply to accept their children until they are old enough to make appropriate references of differential parental reinforcements to their behavior. Hence, during early childhood, the child of nonauthoritarian parents experiences relatively consistent and positive reinforcement: his behavior, undifferentiated by him, is met with equally undifferentiated acceptance and love on the part of his parents.

From this first hypothesis, that parents of authoritarian children are themselves authoritarian and intolerant of ambiguity, four predictions follow logically:

1. The things that the authoritarian child eventually learns through his parents' teaching are relatively difficult to extinguish, since, from the child's point of view, they have been not only excessively but partially or inconsistently reinforced. It may be that partial reinforcement for humans produces responses that are more difficult to extinguish than responses that have been established through consistent reinforcement. There is some evidence that this holds true for animals as well as children. It may also be that extreme reinforcements (either rewards or punishments) produce more rapid (and possibly better) learning than mild reinforcements, although evidence on this point is not clear.

2. The responses of the child of authoritarian parents will be more intense than those of the child of nonauthoritarian parents, since frustration has added to his ordinary drive level.

3. The child of authoritarian parents will develop clear, persistent, and widely generalized expectancies of punishment in new or unclear situations. With these expectancies will be associated subjective discomfort and anxiety, producing a condition resembling "intolerance of ambiguity."

This third prediction (as well as the first) is based on evidence that some of the responses associated with secondary drives, such as anxiety, are extremely difficult to extinguish. Hence, such intolerance of unclarity may be exceedingly persistent. Also, some evidence exists that punishment or reward administered in unstructured situations is generalized more widely than in situations that are clearly structured (Levy and McCandless, 1952). There is evidence that younger children (7 through 9 years of age) generalize more frequently and widely than children 10 through 12 years of age (Mednick and Lehtinen, 1957). Finally, it may be that anxiety and stress situations result in increased generalization. Hence, the child will be persistently anxious in a wide-ranging series of unclear or ambiguous situations, not *just* those similar to situations in which he has been punished; and his anxious responses will be extinguished with difficulty.

4. With age and increasing ability to mediate verbally, the child learns to refer the social rewards and punishments he receives to the appropriate behavior. Then, like his parents, the authoritarian child comes to react dichotomously (in an either-or fashion), and to make sharp distinctions between, for example, "right" and "wrong." Such distinctions are unusually intense and persistent because they help the child to ward off or allay anxiety; they are facilitated because he has become able, through acquiring language and increased time perspective, to realize the consistency of his parents' reinforcements, which are now seen as relevant to his behavior. It is possible that authoritarian parents are *objectively* more consistent than nonauthoritarian parents in their child-rearing behavior, although in his runabout years, their child may not have perceived this consistency.

CHILD-REARING PRACTICES AND CHILD CONFORMITY

The second major hypothesis about the families of authoritarian children is that the parents, themselves highly conforming to approved adult standards of behavior, will give strong positive reinforcement to their children for acting in socially sanctioned ("adult") ways, such as being quiet, orderly, and successful in competition. Deviant or "childish" behavior will be punished with equal strength. From the point of view of the parent and the *older child* (although not from that of the *very young child*), such reward and punishment are consistent as well as strong. This hypothesis leads to two predictions:

1. The child of authoritarian parents will develop clear, easily available, and consistent methods of responding to familiar situations, and will suffer from little apparent indecision, self-doubt, or conflict in such situations, although anxiety may underlie his seemingly assured behavior.

2. It will be more than usually difficult for the child of authoritarian parents to learn to make different or new responses to familiar situations and stimuli: he has a standard way of responding, and it is difficult for him to change.

QUALITY OF REWARD

The third major hypothesis argues that for the authoritarian as well as the equalitarian parent, rewards to the child will usually exceed punishments in frequency, since parents ordinarily prefer the positive to the negative approach, love their children, and want to do the best they know for them. But the rewards of authoritarian parents (see also the first hypothesis in this section) will be less diluted, or more intense. Two predictions follow from this consideration:

> *1.* The child of authoritarian parents will perceive his parents as need-gratifiers to a greater degree than the child of equalitarians, since authoritarian parents present themselves as "always right," whereas equalitarians are often frankly uncertain.

This situation may change sharply at adolescence, when the child seeks independence from his parents, begins to question the values by which he has been brought up, looks more searchingly at society and the value system of families other than his own, and often becomes rebellious. At this time, the child of the authoritarian parent, particularly if his upbringing has been short on love, may reject the parental image sharply; whereas, in the equalitarian home that has been rich in love, the child may see that his parents are really "not so bad after all," and make a final, adult, and lasting identification with them and their values.

> *2.* The authoritarian child will pattern his attitudes and behavior after his parents, perhaps to a greater degree than the child of the nonauthoritarian family, since by the nature of his training, he will strive more to please, and not to offend, his parents. They, having no conscious question of their own rightness, will reward him strongly and consistently for patterning after them. The equalitarian parent, more thoughtful, and at the superficial level at least, less sure of his own admirability, may view such imitative patterning with mixed feelings.

If equalitarian parents have given their child much love, and have used predominantly love-oriented techniques of control, we would expect the child to be sensitive to his parents' feelings and considerate of them— that is, to strive to please them, just like the child of authoritarian parents. He will not see a straight-line pattern of "modeling after them" as the *only* way to please them, nor will they themselves. But he *will* strive for behavior models that satisfy not only himself but his parents.

The behavior modeling of the authoritarian child may go in either of two ways: *copying,* which will involve close modeling on the parents' attitudes and values; or *rebellion,* in which the child seeks to make himself as different from his parents as possible in all of his values, beliefs, and behaviors. How many beatniks have come from authoritarian homes?

SOURCE OF REWARD

The fourth hypothesis about the development of authoritarianism is that authoritarian parents are more likely than equalitarian parents to teach their children that *all* rewards and punishments come from them. This hypothesis leads to two predictions:

1. For children of authoritarian parents, persons (including other "authority figures") who are easily differentiated (distinctly different) from their parents afford them little positive *or* negative reinforcement. They do not regard the rewards that such people can offer them as worth while (or they mistrust these rewards); and they are not afraid of the punishment such people can administer. Hence, their disregard and perhaps contempt for weak (including minority-group) persons, or permissive teachers, or kindly neighbors.

2. The child of authoritarian parents, who has been taught that his parents are all-powerful, will expect that all of his behavior, conforming or deviant, will come to light (will be judged). Hence, he will be more conforming than the nonauthoritarian youngster, will have a high expectation and fear of retaliation for misdeeds, and will be more accepting of and influenced by external techniques of control. He will not wish to be conspicuous, except possibly in such socially approved areas as academic competition. He may be uncomfortable even then, particularly if he is "too good." However, he will misbehave if he is quite certain that he will not be caught, or if he has no fear of (or respect for) the person who might possibly catch him.

CONCERN WITH STATUS AND POWER

The fifth hypothesis suggests that very authoritarian parents are more concerned with status and power than with love and affection. Their child may thus be viewed by them as an enhancer of their own status and power rather than as an individual in his own right. This hypothesis also leads to two predictions:

1. The children of authoritarians will learn to gratify their own love and affection needs by developing techniques for satisfying status and power needs, will frequently be unrealistic in their ideas of the socially valued goals they can reach, and will value external success (status and power) disproportionately. Ausubel and his colleagues (1954) have found that children who believe their parents to hold a primarily "extrinsic" valuation of them—like them for what they can do, rather than for what they are—*do* have unrealistically optimistic ideas of their ability to be successful, often have unrealistic levels of aspiration, and hold to these aspiration levels with a tenacity outside the limits of common sense or adaptive behavior.

2. The child of authoritarian parents will be relatively task-oriented and matter-of -fact, and will manifest relatively little overt affection-seeking behavior (not, at least, as an older child—as a preschooler, he may be more dependent than average, seeking to make up for what he does not get at home). He will seek to gain *approval* through independent, task-oriented behavior, but will do little direct seeking of *love*. This type of *task*-orientation rather than *person*-orientation may have been forced on him early in his life through control techniques mentioned in the discussion of hypothesis 1. That is, the methods of control applied to him as a very young child have resulted in his perception of human relations as anxiety-provoking rather than security-giving. He has also learned to devalue himself as a person, and has come to realize that he cannot be loved for himself but only *approved* or *disapproved* of on the basis of his *objective* performance.

This last consideration, coupled with the others that have been introduced, suggests why authoritarians have been said to be anti-intraceptive (to dislike thinking about and looking into themselves). They dislike intraception because, if they look too closely at themselves, they see the ambivalences, uncertainties, and insecurities for which they are compensating. It is more comfortable to keep thought and attention fixed securely on the objective world and on measurable achievement.

TRUST AND HOSTILITY IN AUTHORITARIANS

The five hypotheses that have been developed on the preceding pages, when considered together, lead us to two further general predictions. The first of these is that the child of authoritarian parents will lack trust, and probably be less optimistic than the child of nonauthoritarian parents.

Second, the child of authoritarian parents will have built up more of a reservoir of hostility than the child of equalitarian parents (Siegel, 1956). Because of the nature of his relations with his parents, he cannot reduce

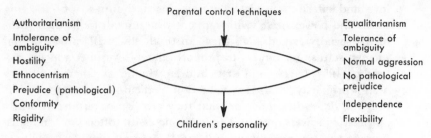

Parental control techniques

Authoritarianism | Equalitarianism
Intolerance of ambiguity | Tolerance of ambiguity
Hostility | Normal aggression
Ethnocentrism | No pathological prejudice
Prejudice (pathological) |
Conformity | Independence
Rigidity | Flexibility

Children's personality

Figure 12.1 One theoretical view of the relation between authoritarian-equalitarian and other personality dimensions. The necessary clustering of traits as diagramed has been questioned by some research workers, as has the concept of authoritarianism as a unitary trait.

this hostility by directing it at them or their surrogates. It seems permissible to conjecture that he relieves the pressure of this reservoir of hostility by displacement either to "safe" objects and persons, or to equally safe fantasy, or perhaps to both.

The term reservoir is not a satisfactory one. Nor do we have any plausible theory about how a "reservoir of hostility" might be built up and maintained, although we see that there are chronically hostile people around us. However, such a concept may not be necessary in this context. Because they are frustrating and threatening, an authoritarian has reason to be hostile to others who are not rule-bound, who present him with ambiguous situations, who (from his point of view) are immoral, who were or are disliked by his parents, or who are socially prescribed objects of hostility.

Three additional considerations may be advanced to account for authoritarianism in the lower class. First, lower-class children are not as well educated as middle-class children. Other things being equal, the lower the educational level, the higher the authoritarianism and prejudice. Second, lower-class children lead more difficult lives in all respects, from their experience of parental discipline on through personal insecurity, than middle-class children. Such frustrating circumstances produce aggression; this cannot, as has been mentioned, be safely expressed toward parents and peers. Hence it is displaced to, among others, those belonging to minority groups. Third, lower-class people have to live shoulder-to-shoulder with minority-group persons, who also compete with them for jobs, housing, and so on; hence, minorities are directly frustrating in a sense that they are not for the middle class.

TRANSLATION OF ATTITUDES INTO BEHAVIOR

It is to be hoped that the following generalizations have been made explicit:

Authoritarianism, ethnocentrism, and prejudice are related but not identical concepts and, like almost every other major social attitude, may be either normal or pathological, or both. This is another way of saying that they may be directly learned and, like any other direct, cognitive learning, fairly easily changed as a person acquires new information; or they may be expressions of deeply ingrained, even fixated, personality needs, in which case change will be much more difficult.

Regardless of whether an attitude is normal or pathological, parental attitudes and child-rearing practices have played a substantial role in its development; but the general culture has also affected it.

Authoritarianism is a very *general* concept, defined in many ways. Its various operational definitions are sometimes, in some groups and in some people, highly related to the general concept; but in other groups and in other people, the relations may be much lower. For *groups,* prejudice and authoritarianism usually show a high correlation; but for a given group (for example, in a stable, well-adjusted group of young people growing up in the Deep South), the correlation may be low. It should not be forgotten, either, that generalizations of only a moderate level of confidence (for example, based on a correlation of .50) cannot in any definitive way be applied to an individual. A correlation of .50 accounts for only 25 percent of the variance of the variable one is attempting to predict. In other words, an individual may be very rigid in some or many of his attitudes and behaviors, but at the same time be unprejudiced and equalitarian; hold little or no latent hostility toward his parents; and be thoroughly extroverted.

One cannot regard the conclusions reached from the literature on social attitudes as being as firm as conclusions reached from the literature on intelligence or physical growth. Attitudes are less tangible; research tools are more ambiguous and usually both less reliable and less valid; and theory is both looser and more complex. Nevertheless, important suggestions have come and are coming from research on personal-social attitudes; and the task of the researcher or writer in the area, while immensely difficult, is also immensely important both to the science of psychology and to society.

Summary

Attitudes of authoritarianism and prejudice have been selected as representative of the range of social beliefs and predispositions that children develop—beliefs that influence their behavior and have much to do with the conduct of society. A specific but representative attitude area was selected to permit more extensive review of appropriate theory and research than would have been possible with a wider range of attitudes and values.

The authoritarian personality is thought to be characterized by rigidity, concreteness of thought, conformity, intolerance of ambiguity, disinclination toward introspection, exaggerated loyalty and affection toward parents and members of the in-group (yet with underlying hostility toward them), and hostility toward the out-group.

Psychoanalytic theory views prejudice as pathological and believes it to be closely related to authoritarianism. A person is hostile toward alien ethnic or religious groups in order to satisfy certain unconscious or unadmitted personality needs of his own. His hate is *displaced*. Another theory regards prejudice as normal. If one lives in a prejudiced society, he learns prejudice directly and, given a different environment, will reduce his prejudice. Such a theory can be extended to include pathological prejudice on the assumption that certain types of restrictive child-rearing practices so circumscribe and frustrate the child, at the same time tying him to his parents, that he becomes basically resentful yet overconforming, and must find scapegoats on whom to vent his hostility.

The most widely used measure of authoritarianism is the California F-scale. This scale has been criticized because only affirmative answers contribute to the authoritarianism score. Critics maintain that the scale does not necessarily measure authoritarianism, but may instead measure a tendency to be agreeable—to acquiesce, or conform. Research indicates that there is merit in the criticism, but that as a group subjects *do* respond to the content of F-scale items, not just to their style; and that F-scale scores are related to many other behaviors that have been subsumed under the more general construct of authoritarianism.

A number of studies of authoritarianism and prejudice, using populations ranging from second-graders to senior medical students and noncollege adults from the South as well as the North, support the hypothesis that prejudice is both normal and pathological. For example, it has been found that whites living in the South are much more prejudiced against Negroes than those living in the North; yet at the same time a high level of education serves to reduce their prejudice more than it does that of Northerners. A study of boys in an interracial summer camp indicates that simply living with those of another race does not reduce prejudice, and may even increase it—particularly for boys who are initially rather prejudiced and who seem to believe that "the world is against them."

Although most studies indicate that authoritarianism and prejudice accompany maladjustive personality traits, such findings have not always been obtained. For example, "authoritarian" young men, not well educated, who were living in a military setting, showed no signs of maladjustment. Under such circumstances, the authors of the study conclude, authoritarianism is an "approved way of life"; hence does not bring the highly authoritarian person into conflict.

Studies including as their subjects second-grade children, college students, and senior medical students reveal that measures of authoritarianism and prejudice are associated with difficulty in solving abstract problems, difficulty in learning material related to a humanitarian philosophy, difficulty in handling ambiguous academic psychiatric material, and poor personal adjustment. They are also associated with a tendency to project hostility and blame, with general cynicism, and with underlying personal insecurity.

A study of the development of prejudice shows that for white children in Austin, Texas, racial awareness begins at least as early as 4 years of age; and that Negro children apparently learn to discriminate against those of their own ethnic group. Interviews with those against whom prejudice is directed (the minority group) suggest that serious personality difficulties may develop as a result of being "prejudiced against."

The last one half of this chapter has concerned itself with the question of how authoritarian personalities and prejudiced attitudes develop among families with different child-rearing practices and in different social classes. The three major concepts involved are *child-rearing practices, social class,* and *the authoritarian personality.* In some of the studies cited in this chapter, a measure of *prejudice* has been used to infer authoritarianism; although high correlations have usually been found between the two, such an inference supplies less convincing evidence for the conclusions reached than do studies using a more direct measure of authoritarianism.

With some exceptions, research on parental attitudes and authoritarianism indicates that overcontrolling parents who employ predominantly nonlove-oriented control and socialization techniques are most likely to bring up children who are authoritarian; and authoritarianism in parents is related to espousal of harsh child-rearing practices. Such a relationship between authoritarianism and severe child-rearing attitudes has usually been obtained in studies using women as subjects, whether the women were mothers or not; for men, the relationship has been found only when the subjects were *actually* fathers. This finding suggests that personality-attitude relationships may occur principally in areas that are of *personal* importance.

Studies of both fathers and mothers suggest that those holding harsh child-rearing attitudes are likely to be unaware of the needs of their children and to feel personally inadequate. Evidence also suggests that children emulate their parents' attitudes, including authoritarianism and prejudice, although correlations between the attitudes of children and their parents have not been uniformly high.

Many studies of parental attitudes and practices utilize a technique of asking the child to evaluate his parents, rather than observing the parents directly. In evaluating these studies, one must ask: How accurately does the child's perception or judgment of his parent reflect the behavior of the parent? At least one study indicates that the level of accuracy is rather high.

Several studies indicate that both authoritarianism and prejudice vary markedly depending (apparently regardless of child-rearing practices) on whether one has been exposed to a culture in which authoritarianism and prejudice are tolerated or approved. In communities where prejudice is accepted, children and young people manifest more prejudiced attitudes than where it is not accepted. Some evidence exists to indicate that members of minority groups may actually adopt the authoritarian and prejudiced attitudes they have experienced at the hands of the majority group.

There is moderately supportive evidence for a relation between authoritarianism and prejudice, on the one hand, and membership in the lower-socioeconomic class on the other, probably because of a combination of factors. Lower-class parents seem to employ harsher child-rearing methods than middle-class parents; lower-class children are more directly exposed to threat and receive less reward from authority figures in general; and lower-class children are more likely to live in a highly frustrating situation (characterized by overcrowding, poverty, and so on) where they are forced into competition with minority-group children first in play and school and, later, for employment.

In the concluding section of the chapter, five major hypotheses relating to the development of authoritarianism were formulated: (1) Authoritarian parents are intolerant of ambiguity; (2) authoritarian parents, much more than equalitarian parents, reward their children for social conformity and punish them for individualism or social deviation; (3) like equalitarian parents, authoritarian parents ordinarily give more rewards than punishments to their children, but their rewards are greater and less qualified; (4) more than equalitarian parents, authoritarian mothers and fathers set themselves up as exclusive need-gratifiers; and (5) authoritarian parents are relatively more concerned with status and power than with love and affection, whereas the reverse is true for equalitarian parents.

From these five hypotheses, a number of predictions were made. For example: It will be more difficult to change the behavior of an authoritarian than of an equalitarian child; authoritarian children, like their parents, will be intolerant of ambiguity, authoritarian children will have more latent hostility than equalitarian children, and will be less trusting; the authoritarian child, in familiar, well-charted situations, will behave at least as efficiently as, and perhaps more efficiently than, the equalitarian child.

Child Development and Childhood Education

CHAPTER 13

A society stands or falls according to its values. If these meet the needs of the majority of its citizens, and if it resists destruction from without, then a society stands. If its values do not provide for its citizens' welfare, or if they are intolerably threatening to other societies, or if the organization of the society cannot withstand outside pressure, then (at least this has been true in the past) the society falls. One of the most important—perhaps the most important of the factors in the continuity of a society is the transmission of knowledge and values to the society's young.

Earlier chapters (particularly Chapters 3 and 10) have discussed relations between parents and children and have explored the effect of the culture on the child's daily living. But little has been said about another profound influence on United States children—the public and private schools as they affect the academic, personal, social, intellectual, and physical development of their charges.

For understandable reasons, the areas of academic growth and change have been most carefully investigated. Measuring instruments have been devised for all sorts of academic skills. But only surface knowledge exists concerning the influence of schools on children's personal, social, motor, and intellectual development. The reasons for this dearth of knowledge are several. The community's first expectation is that the school should transmit the substantive (or factual) culture to its pupils. Dispute rages about its responsibility for other areas of development. Partly for this reason, research in such areas as personality has been neglected. Also, it is relatively easier to conduct research about academic growth: the questions to be asked are quite clear; no one quarrels about the legitimacy of the research; and techniques of measuring academic achievement are comparatively clear-cut and easy to develop.

But no phase of development proceeds independently, and all phases need to be studied. There is urgent need for more research dealing with such topics as teaching methods of all sorts, special educational procedures, and the effect of recreational programs on social skills and motor development. An example of a relatively simple (but as yet unanswered) question is: Do United States toys and recreational programs neglect the development of the child's torso, arms, and shoulders? We know that our children tricycle, bicycle, and run, thereby developing their breathing capacity and leg muscles. But do they pull and climb and lift sufficiently for the optimal development of their arms, shoulders, and backs? The incidence of creaking backs among the middle-aged (and not-so-middle-aged) suggests, but does not prove, that this type of development has been neglected.

There are more questions than answers about the impact of the public schools on the development of United States children. These questions can be answered only through research, and research in the public, private, and parochial schools demands conviction on the part of teachers and school administrators, flexibility and tolerance on the part of research workers, understanding by the public, and more research workers (either functioning as part of the public-school staff, or cooperating with the staff).

A detailed discussion of research concerning such things as teaching reading or arithmetic is best reserved for education textbooks. However, some of the points of view and theories that have been developed by child psychologists and developmentalists can profitably be brought to bear on selected phases of the child-training and educational process. That is the goal of this chapter.

General Assumptions About Curriculum

The elementary, secondary, and liberal-arts curriculum is primarily a learning experience. Its goal is to have students assimilate in increasing breadth and depth the most significant aspects of human knowledge. Every society selectively emphasizes that knowledge characteristic of and unique to it. For example, United States children learn more about United States than about British culture, and more about the traditions and ways of the Western world than of the Eastern. The "rightness" of this, of course, is open to question, although the factual correctness of it is not.

A second assumption (more often questioned than the first) is that to be effective, any curriculum, at any level of sophistication, must be geared realistically to the child's needs and level of development; and that each student should have available to him competent and realistic guidance.

The educational process has received considerable philosophical attention. Two major theories—the *classical* and the *progressive*—have been advanced, defended, and denounced, but all too little investigated. The classical theory regards the child as a learning machine, and accounts for his acquisition of reading or number skills in much the same way that sociologists and psychologists account for normal prejudice (as discussed in Chapter 12). If the child has a sufficient number of exposures to an idea (or a skill) and if he is rewarded for improvement and punished for failure, he will eventually master it. This educational philosophy is adequate enough as far as it goes, but, historically, it has tended to ignore differences among children, has been associated with authoritarian classroom practices, and has been naïve in failing to allow for the subtle effects of motivation, including frustration, level of aspiration, achievement motive, and achievement anxiety. These concepts are discussed in some detail in this chapter.

The classical philosophy of education places much stress on high academic standards, traditional subject-matter content, drill, and conventional discipline, but frequently fails to attend to some of the side-effects of these practices. An illustration of some of these side-effects is furnished by the following anecdote, concerning a young couple who acquired an irresponsible puppy. Among this puppy's other undesirable habits was that of chewing the drapes. The first time he did this, they decided to rub his nose against the rough wallpaper and throw him out of the ground-floor window. They repeated this process the second, third, fourth, and fifth times he chewed the drapes. On the sixth occasion, he chewed the drapes, rubbed his *own* nose against the wallpaper, and voluntarily jumped out of the window.

Many adult attitudes and behaviors reflect this type of teaching: learning occurred, but it was not what the parent or teacher intended. How many people in the United States regard art with near-distaste because their art-appreciation courses consisted of memorizing the titles and painters of 200 great works, or are utterly indifferent to poetry as a result of analyzing hundreds of lines for the type of meter and the number of beats to a line?

In contrast to the classical philosophy, progressive educational philosophy is strongly pupil-centered. Its extreme proponents hold that the child needs simply to be *exposed* to the opportunity to learn in order to become educated. This school of thought resembles the self-realization theory of social development as this was discussed in Chapter 10: accept the child, and he will "flower." In its extreme form, progressive educational philosophy neglects the contributions of learning research and theory, perhaps underemphasizes the value of classical knowledge, overemphasizes some of the superficial aspects of "adjusting to the society," and takes an oversimplified view of "discipline" and behavior control. However, the movement has been beneficial in forcing educators to consider individual differences among children. It has laid heavy stress on motivational factors in learning, and has made it possible to consider the effect of such crucial social and emotional factors as social-class differences, anxiety, and unresolvable frustrations. These factors have usually been neglected in the classical approach to education.

As this volume is written, education in the United States appears to be in a healthy ferment. The best of both of the extreme educational philosophies outlined above is being considered and incorporated into practice: Respect for traditional, substantive learning, application of the laws of learning (including practice), and so on, are being joined with regard for individual differences among pupils, concern for personal adjustment, increasingly sophisticated use of motivational principles, and other factors, in a fashion that should help improve the efficiency and happiness of students of all types.

LEARNING, LEVEL OF ASPIRATION, AND ACHIEVEMENT MOTIVATION

An effective curriculum must meet the children who take part in it at their ability level, must allow for their motive systems and their interests, and must move them forward as rapidly as possible toward its objectives. Foremost among these objectives are knowledge of the culture, development of a respect for knowledge, and acquisition and maintenance of self-respect.

Children's adjustment to a curriculum will be shaped to a substantial degree according to the principles of level of *aspiration* and *achievement motive*. This section reviews research and theory relating to both of these concepts.

DEFINITION OF LEVEL OF ASPIRATION

"Level of aspiration" refers to how well an individual wishes to perform in the future, compared with how well he has done in the past. As a concept, it is closely related to expectancy and the self-concept, as these were discussed in Chapters 5 and 6. Level of aspiration (a basic reference is Lewin *et al.*, 1944) is related to goal-seeking behavior: How difficult are the goals an individual seeks? If they are higher than those he has reached previously in performing the same task (that is, if he wishes to achieve more next time than he did last time), he is said to have a high level of aspiration. If his aim is low—as low as or lower than goals he attained before—he is said to have a low level of aspiration.

In other words, "level of aspiration" carries a personal connotation: it refers to a person's ambitions about his own performance. But level of aspiration can also be viewed in an absolute context. A great but aging scientist sets his goals so that he expects himself to do less in 1970 than in 1969. In terms of the *personal* frame of reference, his level of aspiration is low; but *absolutely* (compared with what the average man in the United States aspires to) his level of aspiration is high. A vigorous young day laborer may aspire to do better in 1970 than he did in 1969. Defined in personal terms, his level of aspiration is high; but the scientist's absolute aspiration is far higher than the young laborer's. In research, however, the term *level of aspiration* most often refers to the personal and relative, rather than the absolute, and is defined by what the individual aspires to in comparison with what he had done previously.

Like all abstract concepts, "level of aspiration" must be translated into observable behavior before it can be scientifically or practically useful. Many translations (behavioral measures) have been devised. Two studies, summarized below, have been selected to illustrate the methods by which level of aspiration may be measured. The conclusions of the first study illustrate the effect that parental aspirations may have on the aspiration level of their children. The second study illustrates the effect of social climate on level of aspiration.

REPRESENTATIVE LEVEL OF ASPIRATION STUDIES

Little and Cohen (1951), on the basis of their observations of asthmatic children referred for treatment to a university hospital, were led to suspect that mothers of asthmatics pushed their children harder than typical mothers do. They devised a simple but practical level of aspiration task: shooting darts at a bull's-eye target. Each child was given twenty-one trials at this task. Actually achieving the bull's-eye earned the highest possible score; attaining the concentric ring next to the bull's-eye gave him the next in highest score; and hitting each ring concentrically outward resulted in progressively lower scores.

After his first trial with a dart fired at the target the child was asked how well he believed he would do the next time, but was warned that he would be penalized if his "bet" or prediction was too wide of what he actually did on the next shot. The difference between his prediction and his previous performance was called his discrepancy (or D) score. If his bet was for the third ring away from the bull's-eye, for example, but his immediately preceding performance had been for the fourth ring from the bull's-eye, he would be assigned a D-score of $+1$ since his aspiration was one circle better than his previous performance. But, had he predicted the fifth ring from the bull's-eye, his D-score for that trial would have been -1. The study allowed for twenty such predictions, and D-scores were averaged for each child.

Thirty asthmatic children and their mothers were included in the experiment. They were compared with thirty nonasthmatic children, either their brothers or sisters who were not asthmatic, or children who were in the hospital for ailments other than asthma. The subjects ranged from 4 to 12 years of age. Before each child made a prediction, his mother (who was watching) predicted privately how well he would do next time.

The authors' technique worked well; even the 4-year-olds were able to get the idea and perform the task. Their results supported the predictions Little and Cohen had made before they started the study: mothers of asthmatic children appeared to expect more of their children than mothers of nonasthmatics did. The average D-score for the mothers of asthmatics was $+1.6$, whereas that of the mothers of nonasthmatics was only $+0.1$ (this difference was highly significant statistically). In other words, the mothers of asthmatics expected their children (on the average) to better their performance by almost two bull's-eye rings, whereas the mothers of nonasthmatic children predicted that their youngsters would do about the same next time as they had done last time.

The children's aspiration patterns followed their mothers', which perhaps indicates that their levels of aspiration were modeled after what they thought their mothers expected of them. The average D-scores (ambitions) of asthmatic children were twice as high as those of nonasthmatic children ($+1.85$ and $+.93$ respectively).

The second illustrative study (Pauline Sears and Levin, 1957) indicates that children in relaxed and permissive circumstances change their level of aspiration in the direction of assuring themselves maximal success. The authors used nineteen 4- and 5-year-old children as subjects, and devised interesting and ingenious techniques for measuring level of aspiration. Each child was given a pegboard, with different sections painted green (to indicate the easiest task), yellow (for next easy), brown (for intermediate), blue (for rather difficult), and red (for most difficult of all). The child inserted a peg into the colored section to indicate the level of difficulty of the performance he planned to undertake. The tasks, also identified by color (green easiest, red most difficult) were: jumping for balls at different heights over the children's head; copying designs with blocks, the designs ranging from very easy to quite complex; pulling weights on a pulley, the weights ranging from light to heavy; matching designs to a model; and broad-jumping. The children were given six trials for each task; for a first experimental session, the order of tasks was predetermined by the experimenters. All children had a second session a few days later in which *they* chose the order of their tasks.

After a success, the children tended to become more "ambitious" and they went on to a more difficult task. They showed no consistent pattern after failure. But during the second session with the very permissive experimenters, the children's choices were for lower levels of difficulty than during the first session. In other words, under circumstances of general relaxation and friendliness, the children "aimed" lower than when they were new to the situation.

A person's level of aspiration is undoubtedly affected by many things. His previous history has taught him to be generally optimistic or pessimistic about how well he can do at a given type of endeavor (he has formed expectancies about his performance, see Chapter 5). His level of aspiration will vary according to the importance of the goal he is seeking. He may be more cautious about important goals than about goals that hold no great value for him, although the literature is not conclusive about this. He tends to be either markedly more daring or the opposite, markedly more cautious, if he states his level of aspiration in public. His level of aspiration will vary more if his principal motive is to avoid failure than if it is to achieve success (this conclusion is treated more extensively a little later, in the discussion of achievement motivation). If he is competing against a group that he considers about equal to him in ability—that is, if he has been informed about how well such a group has done on a similar task—his level of aspiration may be higher than if he thinks he is "competing" against the standards of a group much superior to him.

Experimental evidence has not yet been gathered to illuminate all these influences on level of aspiration; but a brief, oversimplified, and general review of results in the area of level of aspiration studies can be attempted; and tentative inferences can be drawn for child development and training. Following success, level of aspiration is raised; it is lowered after failure. Following either success or failure, maladjusted children and adults react either more extremely, more variably, or both, than do normals. Following failure, the level of aspiration of maladjusted subjects may shoot far up, unrealistically; or some may go up very high, others down very low. Their reactions following success are more predictable than those following failure, but remain more erratic than those of normal subjects. For a normal middle-class population of children, the level of aspiration is moderately positive, but not unrealistically so. The principles implied by level of aspiration research appear already to be well established by the ages of 4 and 5. Under permissive, nondemanding circumstances, individuals appear to relax their level of aspiration to assure themselves the greatest chance of success, although they remain optimistic.

Most studies report only modest correlations between level of aspiration from one situation to another. Because of the differential learning histories of complex human organisms, such a finding might be predicted. On the other hand, there is probably a moderate relation between levels of aspiration for different tasks in similar areas, as for arithmetic and reading in the area of academics or for basketball and volleyball in the area of athletics.

In the present context, the findings summarized above are all interesting, but perhaps the most pertinent one concerns the hopeful or optimistic nature of aspiration level. Apparently most normal children seem both to expect and to hope that they will do somewhat better "next time" than they did the time before. Both the Little and Cohen and the Sears and Levin studies illustrate this trend. On the basis of their research (and the general body of research in this area), the general, practical prediction can be made that children actually like to "stand on their toes." Reaching for concepts and skills which are perhaps a little too difficult for them at the moment, but which can hopefully be attained, is both natural and challenging for children. In other words, the following practical recommendation might be made: Keep each child reaching, but see to it that he has some hope of grasping what he reaches for.

Experimental work on level of aspiration demonstrates that experiences of success result in a person's raising his level of aspiration, while, on the average, experiences of failure result in its lowering. It is reasonable to suggest that if patterns of success or failure persist over long periods of time, the level of aspiration may be affected relatively permanently. Long-time experiences of success may result in increasing confidence and optimism, and in redoubled effort, whereas persistently repeated failure may result in resignation, pessimism, and, possibly, reduction of effort. G. O. Johnson's findings (1950) concerning mentally retarded youngsters in regular classrooms fit well with these predictions. His retarded children fell academically further and further behind the standing of their class in each advancing year of elementary school during which they were studied. This has also been shown to be true for high school dropouts as a group.

Regardless of how social class is defined, there is little argument about the fact that the United States can be divided into at least two classes: the white-collar and the blue-collar class. Evidence was introduced in Chapter 12 suggesting that child-rearing practices differ according to social class, and that these practices influence the development of authoritarianism, and prejudice in middle- and lower-class children. It seems equally likely that social class affects the aspiration level of children.

One of the most ambitious studies of the relations between level of aspiration, social class, and various personal traits was conducted by Douvan and Adelson (1958, 1966). This study merits detailed discussion.

The most usual treatment of social class considers three strata: the upper class (relatively aristocratic); the middle class (professional and white-collar); and the working, or lower, or blue-collar class. It is generally held that upper-class boys aspire merely to hold their own—they have little hope of doing better than their fathers, and are content if they do as well; middle-class boys are thought to be quite ambitious, wishing to exceed their fathers' status; and lower-class boys are believed to possess little hope of bettering their fathers' position, although such a prospect does not cheer them.

Douvan and Adelson have done some interesting thinking about upward mobility (doing better than father), which they classify into three types. The first type, according to them, is that of the "desperately scrambling Philistine," who is exhausted in his pursuit of status. He defines his own identity and personal worth exclusively according to whether or not he is successful. His family teaches him to be competitive: don't be happy, make MONEY. He measures his success not by his actual achievement, but by how he compares with others. He is a "keeper-up-with-the-Joneses." But, as Douvan and Adelson point out, there are always some who have done better, and who have more money and social prestige than he has. He always runs the risk of being pushed off the social or occupational ladder by a competitor.

The second upwardly mobile pattern they describe is one that might be produced by the "authoritarian personality" family. Such an upwardly mobile person is ambivalent toward success (has mingled feelings of attraction and repulsion, approach and avoidance). Douvan and Adelson believe that the response of such upwardly mobile people is to the dominance and prestige of the more privileged stratum through a defensive identification with it (this stratum is strong, dangerous, and threatening, so one had best join it, not fight it). In the process, one denies and decries his own background and status. The origins of such feelings lie in the child's early encounters with authority and status in his own family. He is likely to have had harsh and forbidding parents who allowed him no expression of hostility. He has *accommodated* to parental strength through identifying with it. Arising from this process are manifestations of the authoritarian personality: a conscious overidealization of the parent and authority, together with unconscious rebellion and hostility, rigidity, conformity, and resistance to examination of one's own motives and thoughts. The motive to move upward socially and occupationally arises from the need to emulate the parents, yet this mobility arouses conflict because it implies a struggle with powerful authority figures.

Douvan and Adelson's third type of upwardly mobile child and adult is considerably happier. Young people falling into the third category have a "hope of success" pattern. They are high in Erikson's stage 1 of trust. Their interest in success is directed by a rational ego; consequently, they can mobilize their energies effectively. Their aspirations are realistic, not grandiose. When they aspire to very substantial improvement of status, this aspiration is based on a realistic judgment of their own capabilities, and in general their aspirations for improvement are relatively modest. They are likely to come from families that encourage autonomy (self-determination and independence). Such a family is not obsessed by status, yet accepts and transmits to its children in a straightforward fashion a culturally central value of solid achievement. The shifts in identity necessary for the child—from child to adolescent to young man or woman to successful independent adult—do not involve the child conflict, because he has been taught that such shifts are not only inevitable but desirable. Douvan and Adelson believe that this third, happy type of upward mobility is most frequent in our culture. They therefore predicted that upwardly mobile children, as a group, would show more desirable personal and social characteristics than downwardly mobile youngsters.

Douvan and Adelson studied 1000 boys 14 to 15 years of age, all of whom came from urban nonfarm families. The fathers of the group on which they reported in greatest detail were small business owners, self-employed artisans, or men who worked at white-collar jobs, including sales and clerical positions; or who were skilled and semiskilled manual workers. The boys were classified as upwardly mobile if they aspired to an occupation higher than their fathers'; downwardly mobile if their vocational aim was lower than their fathers'; and stable if they wished only to equal their fathers.

Table 13.1 shows the percentages of upwardly mobile, stable, and downwardly mobile boys of fathers in different occupational groups. In class one, the professional, it is impossible (because of Douvan and Adelson's methods) for a boy to be upwardly mobile or for the boys of unskilled workers to be classified as downwardly mobile.

Before continuing with a discussion of Douvan and Adelson's results, it should be pointed out that Table 13.1 gives scant support to the notion of occupational resignation on the part of lower-class boys; or of driving ambition, relatively speaking, on the part of middle-class boys. A substantially higher percentage of the former (84 percent) than of the latter (46 percent) wish to surpass their fathers.

Douvan and Adelson's results do not provide a direct test of their ideas about three types of upward mobility, but they *do* suggest that upwardly mobile boys are happier and more effective than downwardly mobile youngsters. When compared with downwardly mobile boys, the upwardly mobile excelled in the following characteristics: they took part in more group-membership and leisure-time activities; did somewhat more dating

Table 13.1   *Percentage of Boys from Different Paternal Occupational Levels Who Aspired to Do Better Occupationally (Upwardly Mobile), the Same (Stable), or Less Well (Downwardly Mobile) than Their Fathers.*

| | | PERCENTAGE OF BOYS WHO WERE | | |
FATHER'S OCCUPATION	NUMBER	UPWARDLY MOBILE	STABLE	DOWNWARDLY MOBILE
Professional	136	—	67	33
White collar	183	46	29	25
Manual skilled	335	58	34	8
Manual unskilled	70	84	16	—

ADAPTED WITH PERMISSION OF THE AMERICAN PSYCHOLOGICAL ASSOCIATION AND ELIZABETH M. DOUVAN, FROM DOUVAN AND ADELSON (1958).

(although no more of them held jobs); did more, and more intellectual, reading; and expressed more enjoyment in their activities. They also had more plans for future activities. More of them said that they had chosen an occupation because it was interesting and would give them status, but fewer of them had selected it because it was easy. They preferred success to security. They were more likely than downwardly mobile boys to save money and to plan for the future. They were more interested in getting satisfaction from assuming adult roles, less interested in simply being popular with their group. More of them said that they kept promises because they were trusted by their parents or other adults; fewer of them kept their word because they were afraid of punishment. More of them said they would be honest with their parents, but more of them also said they would not worry unduly about breaking a promise either because of an emergency, or because they felt personally mature ("I am sensible enough to judge what is right"). Fewer would break promises because of feelings of rebellion, or on impulse, or because their parents were not around to police them. Fewer of the upwardly mobile boys thought that there was such a thing as an unbreakable rule. More of them believed that friends can be just as close to one as family. More of them considered adult leaders as helpers rather than decision makers; fewer of them relied on authority; and fewer of them regarded one of their family members as their ideal. They were more humorous, less self-rejecting, yearned less for impossible changes. More of them believed that change of status was within their own power.

In general, they reported that they had received less physical punishment than downwardly mobile boys; their punishment had been more psychological, for example, "withdrawal of love." Fewer of them portrayed their parents as punishing and harsh, although they said that they had had more disagreements with their parents. The parents voiced more disapproval of how they spent their money. They were more likely to share leisure-time activities with their parents.

In general, there was no relation between mobility aspiration and degree of certainty about what would happen to them, nor were there relations between mobility aspiration and age, family economic status, or fathers' education. However, the upwardly mobile boys possessed significantly more verbal ability than those who were downwardly mobile. It may be conjectured that this is partly the result of the greater amount of time they have spent with their parents, and is also related to other child-rearing practices.

Douvan and Adelson (1966, p. 68) are the first to admit that differences in intelligence exist for their upward and downward mobile boys, but believe that the intelligence differences are more likely to be a result of the child-rearing practices and personal adjustment made by the boys than that intelligence is the "cause" of differential mobility. They ask: "Does low intelligence produce alienation, or does alienation produce 'low intelligence'?" Their conclusion, which seems plausible to the present author, is that "Our dispirited, despairing downward-aspiring may show very little alertness, very little curiosity, and very little zest because the game is not worth the candle, and not because their innate capacities are so limited" (p. 68). However, one wishes that Douvan and Adelson had better data on the effects of intelligence, or that they had pulled from their very large sample boys equated in verbal ability, but differing in social mobility aspirations, and checked to see whether the findings for the sample as a whole held for these selected boys as well. In other words, the failure to control for intelligence is a serious flaw in the generally interesting and stimulating Douvan and Adelson studies.

In general, the "stables" fell between the upwardly and downwardly mobile boys in the characteristics that have been summarized.

The Douvan and Adelson findings for girls (1966) are similar to but not so dramatic as for boys.

Rosen (1956) worked with male students in two New Haven high schools. His upper-class subjects, according to test, showed higher need for achievement on a TAT-like test, and seemed to be more future-oriented and individualistic. Their achievement-need score was positively related to their school grades; and their values included an ambition to attend college. Brim and Forer (1956) report similar results, adding that being Jewish and male is associated with the tendency to plan one's life ahead. They believe that the tendency to plan one's life is a function of having learned that planning is good, while at the same time possessing a social status that makes the future sufficiently predictable to permit planning with some degree of positive expectation.

Empey (1956) reports that lower-class high-school students aspire to lower occupational levels than upper- and middle-class youngsters, but that (as with Douvan and Adelson's sample) they *do* aspire to an occupational status higher than that of their fathers.

Hieronymus (1951), working with 910 ninth-grade boys and girls from a moderate-sized midwestern town, found that socioeconomic status was more highly related to socioeconomic expectation (how well the children expected to do) than was intelligence. For girls the correlation between socioeconomic level and socioeconomic expectation was .61, for boys .63. Similar correlations for intelligence were only .36 and .41. Socioeconomic status was also correlated (in the neighborhood of .30) with positive attitudes toward education, and seemed to be an important factor in determining a positive attitude toward education ($r =$ approximately .50). High socioeconomic status, favorable attitudes toward education, and high socioeconomic expectations all combine to assist the student in doing well at school. Hieronymus concludes that he has provided evidence to support the hypothesis that socialized anxiety (and by this he means simply the desire to do well, or ambition) is a factor in the selective process of American education.

Campbell (1955), working with New Zealand (presumably) secondary-school children 12 to 14 years of age, finds that those who are progressing at a greater rate than expected are not particularly different in intelligence from those making normal progress, but that they have significantly higher sociocultural scores. He suggests that of two types of secondary school (one more, one less academically oriented), placement for border-zone children (in terms of their academic achievement) should be made according to social class: the border-zone middle- or upper-class child should go to the academic, the border-zone lower-class child of the same achievement level to the nonacademic school.

Wyer (1965) adds to the generally consistent literature about males and achievement. The males in this study who were self-accepting and who were accepted by their parents were academically effective, although the same thing was not true for women. Where parents agreed that a college education was either intellectually or socially broadening, their sons were more effective than when they disagreed.

Oberlander and Jenkin (1966) add to the literature on first-born children, finding that the intense parent child interactions and verbal proclivity produce children who manifest relative superiority in academic pursuits.

In other words, a generally positive level of aspiration—the desire and intent to do better than one's father has done—seems to be associated with a complex of positive factors: greater optimism, greater orientation toward "doing the job well," greater self-determination, and more effective performance. There is no suggestion in existing research that more lower-class than upper- or middle-class boys are resigned to their status.

At the same time, the relative level of aspiration (how high one aspires to climb) appears to depend on the place in the social ladder from which one begins.

ACHIEVEMENT MOTIVATION AND ACHIEVEMENT ANXIETY

A discussion of the literature devoted to level of aspiration leads to the conclusion that (at least in United States culture) a *positive* level of aspiration is associated with many other desirable traits. A consideration of the concept of level of aspiration leads logically to the idea of an *achievement motive*—a widely generalized "wish to master" or "desire to do well." The achievement motive has much in common with such concepts as autonomy, independence, and generativity. These concepts have already been discussed, particularly in Chapter 10. Inevitably, in a culture like ours, any motivation as important as the wish to achieve is highly esteemed and is likely to be associated with *anxiety* about achievement, just as problems in any other important developmental area may result in anxiety.[1]

Anxiety and School Learning   These days, anxiety has become one of the most frequently, and probably loosely used motivational concepts. Books have been written about it. It has become the central motivational plank for both learning and psychoanalytic theories of personality (as it has always been for psychoanalysis). Scales to measure it have been developed both for adults and children.

One seemingly simple definition of anxiety considers it as a highly noxious drive state or stimulus condition. A child or adult will go to considerable lengths to avoid or reduce it.

This definition assumes that the existence of anxiety (considered as a drive or motivating condition) is accompanied by perceptible stimuli. These may be physical stimuli, as "My stomach is tied up in knots," or "I'm so tense I'm shaking like a leaf"; psychological, such as "I have this vague feeling that something awful is going to happen"; or a mixture of physical and psychological, for example, "I feel very nervous tonight."

The person experiencing anxiety may or may not identify it as such, but for the concept to be employed usefully, it must be definable:

> *1. indirectly* as is assumed, for example, in Rorschach Theories of "anxiety signs," through behaviors which can be reliably subsumed as "anxious" by observers; for example, repeated and probably

---

[1] The relation between delayed or inadequate physical development and anxiety was discussed in Chapter 9; the relations between the self-concept and anxiety were suggested in Chapter 6; and the association of anxiety and fixation was discussed in Chapter 5.

several headaches or stomach upsets for which no physical reason can be found; unusually high baselines for physical tension; frequent bad dreams or nightmares; unusual frequency and severity of such symptoms as nail biting, hair pulling, "nervous" sweating, tics, logically baseless fears; and so on.

2. *semi-directly* as is assumed by the Taylor Manifest Anxiety Scale for adults; the Sarason General and/or Test Anxiety Scales and the Castanada, McCandless, and Palermo Manifest Anxiety Scale. Sample items from anxiety scales for children are: "I get very nervous when I take tests. I worry a lot about my grades. I worry that something may happen to my parents. My hands sweat a lot." "Yes" answers to such items are presumed to indicate anxiety; "No" answers, a lack of anxiety.

3. *directly*, by speech or gesture.

It should be added that evidence is far from clear concerning the correlation between, let us say, *direct* and *indirect* indices.

This lack of established correlations among such different definitions of anxiety substantially reduces the practical (or theoretical) usefulness of the concept.

The most convincing current definition of anxiety, at least for children, is the score derived from the Sarason Test Anxiety Scale. This judgment is based on relational results obtained using the test (for example, Hill and Sarason, 1966).

To amplify the general definition given for anxiety, one might say that the antecedent condition for anxiety is most likely to have been physical or psychic pain. However, the original connection of the pain stimulus and its response has been forgotten. This "forgetting" or "repression" provides a practical distinction between anxiety and fear: in fear, the connection between stimulus and response is remembered or recognized. Another distinction has to do with the multiplicity of connections or associations of anxiety and fear, with anxiety stimuli being widely, but fear stimuli rather narrowly, associated or conditioned.

The time of greatest incubation or growth potential for anxiety is probably the preverbal year or years, although this is not definitely established. The opportunities in our culture for its acquisition and overlearning are so widespread as to be, for all practical purposes, universal. Hence, in considering its conceptual usefulness, it is unnecessary to argue about whether it is a primary (unlearned) or secondary (learned) drive. Logically, secondary drives are nothing more than deeply ingrained (extinction resistant) habits. Anxiety may be either situation specific (attached, for example, to test-taking situations, or high places); or chronic (as in the hypertense person) without logical inconsistency, just as under certain circumstances its social effects (in the sense of the responses made to the individual by those in his environment) may be positive or negative. Hill and Sarason believe it results from harsh evaluations by parents of children's products and performances in their preschool years.

One needs to consider anxiety as a response, as opposed to anxiety as a drive. Anxiety responses are ordinarily thought of as nonconstructive: we think of the anxious person as one who goes to pieces under stress, who is tense and jerky, who "gets tied up in knots." Such responses are not usually responded to positively by society, since they make other people tense themselves. But many anxious responses, even though they accompany discomfort in the person making them, can be socially constructive: compulsive neatness is a useful attribute in the scientist or the certified public accountant, for example; consistent promptness, even though motivated by the prompt person's discomfort about being "even one minute late" is behavior that is valued, although seldom practiced, in our society.

In any event, responses motivated by and associated with anxiety in a person are remarkably hard to change. Both anxiety and behavior designed to avoid or reduce it are likely to be most intense in areas of human endeavor that are most highly valued by society, or with which society most concerns itself, such as sexual behavior, school learning, vocational achievement, popularity, adequacy of sex-typing, and the like. In chronic anxiety, associated behaviors pervade all areas of living (as in eating, eliminating, and social relations).

The relation between chronic and situational anxiety is not clear. They should be positively correlated, in the sense that the stimuli belonging to a pervasive and general drive easily become associated with situations, particularly those that are relevant to the drive (are seen to pertain to or be connected with it). The chronically anxious person may be compared to an individual in a famine ridden country. For him, every act is designed to reduce hunger; and even far-fetched stimuli are seen as possible drive reducers (grubs, for example, in U.S. culture are seldom eaten except by the near starving). But for the comfortably situated resident of a district with a full larder, stimuli associated with hunger operate selectively, for example, three or four hours after a meal and in particular surroundings, such as restaurants and dining rooms. This is to say, under conditions of chronic *hunger* or anxiety, a disproportionate share of behavior is due to energizing and sensitizing functions of drive, and is directed toward its satisfaction (in this case, reduction). With *situational* hunger or anxiety, behavior is for the most part related to other motives. Only under selected and appropriate circumstances, biologically and/or socially determined does the individual behave so as to reduce hunger or anxiety. The two designations of anxiety, then, are not necessarily inconsistent with each other. Their apparent difference is one principally of threshold and facilities or opportunities for satisfaction (in almost all cases, for these drives, satisfaction is synonymous with reduction).

For a highly anxious or a very hungry person, a disproportionate amount of behavior is devoted to seeking comfort (relaxation, peace, pleasure) or food; and unusual stimulus objects (or behaviors) are also employed in this search. To reduce anxiety, thumbs are sucked, blanket edges become fetishes; tranquilizers or therapies are sought; compulsions are developed; specific but unreasonable fears are learned so that their reduction may reduce their formless and more general antecedent, anxiety. To reduce acute hunger, people ordinarily honest steal, substances usually considered inedible are eaten, and so on. Anxiety or food related dreams or fantasies perhaps serve, in a temporary and unrealistic way, as drive reducers.

It also seems likely that a person high in *chronic* anxiety will have more *situational* anxieties than a low anxious person; just as a chronically hungry person will be hungry across a broader range of situations than a "low-hungry" person. The correlations of about $+.60$ between test anxiety and general anxiety reported by Hill and Sarason support such a hypothesis. Indeed, it may be that a construct of general anxiety may best be quantified by subsuming number and intensity of situational anxieties.

Much of this reasoning is admittedly analogical. As drives, hunger and anxiety are very different: the former is admittedly physiological or primary, although heavily overlaid by habits (*what* one eats, *how* one eats, *where* one eats, and so on), and its intensity is partially but by no means entirely determined by "time of deprivation" (the amount of time since a person has last eaten). There is some dispute as to whether anxiety is a drive or a habit, and certainly time of deprivation does not relate to its strength (that is, a person does not become more anxious simply because a long time has gone by since he was last anxious).

Basic similarities also exist. The nonhungry person, given food, associated stimuli, or competition for food (see the competition literature for animal species), develops hunger. Stimuli associated with anxiety, equally inappropriate, also evoke it.

It is important to distinguish achievement motivation from achievement anxiety (a situational anxiety). For the person who is motivated toward achievement, achieving something (succeeding, solving a problem has reinforcing properties, is rewarding, constitutes a goal.

The definition of achievement *anxiety* is more difficult. Such an anxiety is probably situational (evoked only when stimuli associated with the achievement motive are present). A further assumption is that for either the child or adult, pain or punishment, as well as reward, have been associated with achievement or achievement-directed behavior; and that the reward-punishment ratio was close to 50–50, but probably tipped more in the direction of reward.

An achievement-directed child has developed *conscience*. His controls come from within, predominantly. For such a condition to develop, it is probably necessary that:

1. He sees one or both parents as powerful people in one or more of the following ways: (a) physically (strength), (b) socially (their friendship circle), (c) economically (their earning power), (d) possessed of knowledge (wise), and (e) dependable (he can predict their behavior, to a degree that does not cause him intolerable discomfort). This point is related to (2) below.

2. He sees one or both parents as loving: (a) They have conveyed to him that he is important to them as a person. (b) Their reward-punishment system has been psychologically rather than thing (tangible or bribe) oriented. (c) They have given more rewards, proportionately, than punishments.

3. They have let him know that his own success is important to *them* as well as valuable to *him*.

Anxiety about achievement can presumably develop in the absence of any obviously strong motive for it. Given the background sketched above and as a consequence of achievement behavior imposed on the child by, for example, the school system in the course of which the child is punished, he may begin to worry about success even though his parents have not stressed it. For such a child, however, a result more likely than anxiety will be simple avoidance learning. A fairly strong value **must** be present for anxiety with reference to it to develop.

For the child who does not value achievement, the schools' values are likely to result in avoidance behavior (under achievement). For the child who values achievement—and he has probably learned this at home—punishment at school triggers anxiety, and he begins to work harder. If he is capable, the schools eventually reward him for this. If he is not, the schools offer him only a situation of defeat, and he looks elsewhere for success (for example, he may become a school delinquent, or may drop out of school when he becomes old enough, to look elsewhere for success).

Achievement anxiety then, is likely to increase with the achievement motive. Hence, maximal achievement anxiety in, for our purposes, the context of school learning, should occur for the child maximally motivated to do well, but whose achievement history has been characterized by a ratio of punishment *of a given type to reward* (psychological) ranging from approximately 50–50 to 100–0, but probably with reward exceeding punishment.

The punishment of which we speak was probably originally externally imposed, but its aims have presumably been internalized, since the presence of a strong achievement motive or motives implies internalization of control, or development of super ego or conscience (see above). This, in turn, implies the adoption of self-punishing as well as self-rewarding behavior. For this reason, even the straight A student can experience a majority of punishments or failures, self-judging as he is, because despite his A's he is more often second than first in his class; while the straight C student, who considers himself lucky to avoid D's, may be on a 100 percent positive reinforcement schedule, in that he always manages to escape the D's which he fears.

Our society is so organized that in the middle class the individual like the second example is rarer than the first. However, the latter type may be more frequent, the former rarer, in the lower socioeconomic classes, and possibly in the upper classes.

To relate school achievement motivation and anxiety to social class requires that one examine the relation between school achievement need or motive and conscience. The connection between school achievement motive and parent control techniques must also be looked at, since it can be assumed that the need for school achievement is but one manifestation of conscience, in that it involves the incorporation of a set of standards that adult society holds valuable.

Conscience, as we have postulated, develops or fails to develop, as a function of control techniques used from about 1 to 5 or 6 years of age. To be precise, love-oriented techniques of control (psychological controls) perhaps operate on a continuum: if I behave in such and such a way, I significantly please others and my parents; if in another way, I displease them. This set of learnings applies to people in general. The child eventually includes himself as a person—an important and socialized person—and becomes his own rewarder or punisher. *He has developed a conscience, and its concomitants, guilt and anxiety.*

Nonlove (thing-) oriented techniques, particularly when punishment sharply exceeds reward, fail to achieve the same end. Parents punish, hence one must behave as they wish and modify behavior as they wish; significant others, through generalization, acquire the same punitive properties. But why label yourself as a socialized person if the only consequent is permission to punish yourself: There is no reward for such an internalization, so it is not made. Hence, there is developed the person who is low in anxiety, high in fear and shame, and high in direct self-gratification (including low need for school achievement, since good school achievement involves hard work and few tangible, immediate rewards).

How do control techniques correlate with social class? We know almost nothing about the control techniques of the upper class. We can speculate that they are diluted in their application to the child by upper lower-class maids, gardeners, and chauffeurs; and by middle-class nurses and tutors. Some evidence exists to indicate that competition with the father does not play the role that it does in the middle class, since papa's position is such that his children cannot realistically expect to exceed it. Children do well to live *up* to it. Competition with parents (particularly the father) may not be very strong in lower-class children, since their fathers are at the bottom of the social heap and hence, almost automatically, the child can only equal or excel their status. For boys, this may be particularly true in lower-class Negro families, where fathers are typically absent (in about 40 percent of the families), or powerless.

The lowest social class Negro father, when he is present, has only two sources of power: his physical strength and his sexual prowess. If his son identifies with him, seeking to gain his own identity, these are the only channels open. The consequences are obvious: exaggerated masculine, bully-boy, heterosexual behavior which, obviously, is opposed to the value systems of the schools, as they are currently organized. Such a lower-class Negro boy, to become achievement motivated, must identify with his mother, the dependable, economically sufficient, socially influential adult in the family. The resulting sex-identification conflicts are bound to be severe (see Pomeroy, verbal communication, for Kinsey's data, 1964; and Clark, 1965).

The control techniques of the middle class (Maas, 1951; and Maccoby *et al.,* 1954; and the author's own observations) are more love or psychologically oriented, less thing oriented, than those of the lower class. Additionally, sons as well as daughters can (and are encouraged to) compete with their mothers and fathers with more chance of success than is true for upper-class children.

In other words, the achievement motive should be highest in the middle class, lowest in the lower-lower class, and perhaps about the same for the upper-lower and the upper classes.

By the same token, and for reasons set forth, school learning anxiety should be highest for middle-class children, due to an interaction between their motives, parental love or psychologically oriented punishment or control techniques, and self-punishment for failure to do well; and lowest for lower-lower-class youngsters. Upper-lower- and upper-class children should be aligned somewhere in between.

Middle-class children probably have differentially more added to their achievement motivation (and anxiety) than children from other social classes because of the fact that their teachers are middle class, and hence provide them with models to be imitated; this may work both ways, with teachers being better able to understand, empathize with, and even identify with middle than lower- or upper-class children. Middle-class parents also provide academic achievement models that are not provided, certainly not by lower class, and probably not by upper-class parents.

There may not be sex differences in school learning achievement anxiety. Girls may *show* more of it, because they are less diluted in their needs for achievement between, say, school work versus athletics, than are boys; and a person can demonstrate *just so much* achievement anxiety. But boys can probably be as frequently characterized as anxious about achievement in school as girls. Hill and Sarason (1966) suggest that boys are more anxious about achievement than girls. Our culture emphasizes independence, initiative and success "on one's own" more for boys than girls. Girls are expected to be confirming, obedient, and responsible. Boys are expected to *stand out*.

Sex differences in school achievement anxiety probably vary with the age of the child. It is possible that, in elementary school, boys do not experience the same subjective pressure to achieve academically that girls do; but, by junior high and secondary school, the prospect of having, before too long, to be the breadwinner intensifies the pressure on boys. During college, it is predicted that boys will have more academic motivation and academic achievement anxiety than girls. Boys must be, not only self-sufficient, but able to take care of their future or actual wives and children. For girls, success depends more on the caliber of the men they marry. Situational factors also put extra pressure on older boys. Usually an ever-intensifying draft call awaits; and academically (achievement) successful boys get deferments but academically inadequate boys/ young men do not.

The literature suggests, as has been implied above, that the United States schools operate differentially by social class and caste. For example, we have the "gentlemen C" or the girls' academically superficial finishing school tradition for upper-class children and adolescents.

Most elementary school classes in the United States are taught by women. Conservative, obedient, and responsible as they are, they discourage independence and initiative (boys' prerogatives). Thus, the phenomenon exists of girls as a group receiving higher grades than boys, although there are few or no differences between the sexes in standardized achievement test scores.

This pattern is probably continued in junior and senior high school (see Payne and Farguhar, 1962), where overachieving boys follow feminine attitude patterns, while overachieving girls vary from the norms in being independent, curious, and intellectually nonconforming. Given the greater freedom of college, this pattern apparently changes again: the really good scholars are more likely to be boys than girls.

The material treated above brings us inevitably to the questions:

1. How does one treat (perform therapy) for anxiety, chronic and intense?

2. How does one handle achievement (situational) anxiety?

Therapy for anxiety is of many types. Some therapies, such as tranquilizers, do nothing for the drive state itself, but merely reduce the intensity of the symptoms. This reduction may also reduce the feedback from the symptoms to the organism: that is, if a person finds himself betraying anxiety, or behaving and feeling in ways that he labels anxious, this behavior or these feelings may further increase the intensity of the anxiety state. For example, odors from a bakery may intensify hunger. If he is not giving off anxiety cues, his anxious behavior may be reduced.

Insight therapy dwells lightly on the symptoms themselves, but seeks to help the individual discover (or recover) the origin of his anxiety. The assumption is that, once he understands how a given set of stimuli has come to arouse his anxiety, these stimuli eventually lose the power to evoke both the anxiety drive and the socially maladjusted responses designed to reduce it. It is actually doubtful whether such behavior changes are automatic. It seems more logical to think that, with the anxiety drive reduced, an individual can be more easily retrained along socially acceptable lines. Socially constructive, but anxiety motivated behaviors need not be retrained, but can simply be preserved, the difference being that they are no longer associated with personal discomfort.

One can predict that chronic anxiety will be higher for those who in their early childhoods have been "badly reared" than for those who have been "well reared." Admittedly, except in a clinical and subjective way, it is difficult to say what is meant by badly and well reared.

There are some teasing notions (Sears *et al.,* 1957) in the literature about the relations of anxiety and love (or psychologically) versus nonlove (or thing-) oriented child-rearing techniques and the relations of both of these (anxiety and control techniques) to the development of super ego (or conscience, or internalization of control). These have been discussed earlier.

Provisionally, for propaedeutic purposes, the position is adopted here that situational anxiety, guilt, and super ego or internalized control, are positively correlated with each other, and that their presence and correlation are useful, even necessary, in a democratic society. Shame, fear (in contrast to anxiety), and nonlove-oriented child control techniques may be similarly correlated; but the combination fits ill with a democratic society (see McCandless, 1961, Chapter 9).

Second, how does one handle situational, or achievement connected, anxiety?

To begin, in our culture, he is thankful that it exists. Its presence means that the child is socialized, conscientious, and amenable to the reward and punishment pattern accepted by our society. Such a child, basically, wants to succeed, to do well, to get into the "system." In other words he is, as the educators and psychologists say, motivated.

But what if this achievement anxiety is so intense as to interfere with the child's performance? If the interference is for all important life areas, we look for help for a "tense" child. If it is specific to tests or subjects (for example, some children do well in reading or social studies, but "go to pieces" in arithmetic and science; some children do well in free class discussions, but "freeze" on tests), then the teacher or parent attempts retraining.

First, he reassures the child that he is essentially capable.

Second, he emphasizes that he "likes or accepts" the child, regardless of his performance.

Third, he works to give the child all available cues about how to handle the subject matter that "panics" him, or gives him techniques about how to take tests, such as:

1. Read all the questions before answering any given question.

2. Answer the questions for which he is sure he knows the answers, leaving those about which he is unsure until last.

3. Encourage him to express his worry about examinations in general.

4. Tell him that if he does not understand a question, he should ask its meaning (a good reassurance technique is to say, "If you don't understand what the question means, then probably at least half the class doesn't understand").

5. If group testing situations bother him, let him take the examination individually, if this is possible.

6. Underplay the general importance of examinations by saying, "They are necessary. We have to check to see whether you know the material. This test is such a check, and *only* a check."

ACHIEVEMENT MOTIVATION VERSUS FEAR OF FAILURE

The preceding section suggests that the achievement motive may be a rather pervasive and stable trait and that, as far as academic achievement is concerned, it may be heavily concentrated in middle-class children.

This section also suggests that "fear of failure" is closely related to the concept of achievement anxiety.

An interesting body of literature has accumulated concerning achievement motivation (or need for achievement) and fear of failure (see, for example, McClelland, 1958; and Atkinson, 1958). This literature relates closely to the notions of expectancy and self-concept (see Chapters 5 and 6 of this text), and to level of aspiration, school achievement, and general "ambition," or desire "to get ahead." The theory and research chosen to develop this topic here have been provided by Atkinson and his co-workers (Atkinson, 1958; Atkinson *et al.*, 1960; and Atkinson and Litwin, 1960).

Atkinson reasons that any competitive situation—and for the average child, both his family and his school situation are likely to be competitive—arouses one of two major motives: either to achieve success (the achievement motive) or to avoid failure. Some children and adults work hard for success, without seriously considering the threat of failure. Others think less of succeeding than of avoiding failure (as, some work to get A's, others to avoid D's). Yet both motives operate in the same person: for the striver-for-A's, the drive toward success is stronger than the fear of failure, yet he undoubtedly also fears failure; for the avoider-of-D's, the threat of failure is paramount, but he would also like success, as represented by a B or an A.

Atkinson and his colleagues have made some interesting and generally accurate predictions about these two types of persons—the strivers-for-success (those who are achievement motivated) and the avoiders-of-failure. The first type, Atkinson reasons, is likely to be a middle-of-the-roader in his aspirations or ambitions; whereas the second type, the failure-avoider, will be either excessively cautious or extravagantly reckless in the things he tries.

Atkinson has developed a behavior theory about motivation, arguing that motivation is equal to the strength of the relevant motive, multiplied by the expectation of success for behavior related to the motive, which is multiplied again by the incentive (or value) of the goal. In other words, motivation $= f$ (motive $\times$ expectancy $\times$ incentive). In the context of this chapter (as for Atkinson), the important motives to which this equation is to be applied are the achievement motive and the failure-avoidance motive.

The three terms in Atkinson's equation may be thought of as follows: *Motive* may be innate, or it may be learned. It is analogous to *drive*. *Expectancy* is a function of the individual's learning. On the basis of his experience he expects, at some level of confidence, either to succeed or to fail at any given undertaking. If he is an excellent basketball player, he will expect to make 3 out of 4 of his free-throws; if a novice or unskilled, he expects to make 1 out of 10, or fewer. Atkinson reasons that *incentive* is an inverse function of the expectancy of success. Incentive (reward value) will be greatest for undertakings attended by little hope of success, least for undertakings accompanied by a high expectancy of success. In other words, Atkinson's definition of incentive is equal to 100 percent probability minus the expected probability of success: for the proficient basketball player, a successful free-throw will have an incentive value of 1.00 — .75, or .25; whereas for our novice, it will have an incentive value of 1.00 — .10, or .90.

This formula leads directly to the prediction that, for those with a high need for achievement, middle-of-the-road ventures, bets, and aspirations will be preferred to extreme gambits; whereas for those whose dominant motive is to avoid failure, middle-of-the-road courses of action will be avoided and extreme alternatives, as very conservative or very reckless, will be chosen. If such theoretical predictions can be supported, our understanding of children's attitudes toward competitive athletics, games in general, and academic aspirations will be much increased.

Let us consider first the implications of Atkinson's formulations for the child who is motivated more by the desire to achieve than he is by fear of failure. If motivation $= f$ (motive $\times$ expectancy $\times$ incentive) and incentive $= 1.00$ minus expectancy of success, and if an arbitrary weight of 10 is assigned to motive and three levels of expectancy of success are considered (90 percent success, 50 percent success, and 10 percent success), we can solve the Atkinson formula as follows:

$$\text{First instance: Motivation} = 10 \times .90 \times .10 = .9$$
$$\text{Second instance: Motivation} = 10 \times .50 \times .50 = 2.5$$
$$\text{Third instance: Motivation} = 10 \times .10 \times .90 = .9$$

This solution demonstrates that, with positive approach motives (the principle of approach and avoidance gradients or motives was introduced in Chapter 5), subjective expectancies hovering around the 50–50 level result in maximal motivation. An achievement-oriented child (and it has been demonstrated that teachers can select such children, see McClelland, 1958) will put forth greatest effort if he figures his chances of reaching the goal as about even.

The Atkinson formula applies to failure-avoidance as well as achievement. If the motive in the equations above is thought of as *avoidance-of-failure* rather than approach-to-success, it can be seen that the second instance results in the strongest avoidance tendency. Because failure is painful, the child will choose either extreme of caution or recklessness but will avoid the middle instance, the 50–50 probability.

This explanation may help account for the general finding cited earlier in connection with level of aspiration studies—that, following failure, people manifest more variable levels of aspiration than they do following success. If the experience of failure has raised their motivation to avoid failure and made it stronger than their motivation to achieve success, then they will have been driven to extremes of caution or recklessness; consequently, considered as a group, they will be much more variable (or erratic) in their level of aspiration bids. The Atkinson formula is also instructive when we consider neurotics (a group which probably lives more to avoid failure than to achieve success) and contrast them with normals, who as a group probably strive more to obtain success than to avoid failure. The summary statement about level of aspiration earlier in this chapter indicated that deviant groups were more variable (less predictable) in their level of aspiration bids following success than were normals, but that the difference in variability following success was less than the deviant-normal difference in variability following failure. If deviants are shaky in their self-confidence, whereas normals are fairly stable, an experience of failure will be more likely to move the deviants from an *achievement* orientation to a *failure-avoidance* orientation than it will be to alter the goals of normals. Hence, deviant groups should be more variable than normal groups after failure than after success.

Atkinson and his colleagues, and McClelland, have provided experimental evidence that gives modest support to the predictions they have made. They have used a variety of populations as subjects, ranging from kindergarten and second-grade children through college sophomores and juniors, and have employed experimental tasks ranging from playing shuffleboard to obtaining superior college grades.

Crandall (1963) has written an excellent review of the achievement motive. He defines it according to three criteria: (a) The inferred goal of the behavior; (b) The unique characteristic of the behavior which might be reinforced; and (c) The nature of the situations in which that behavior occurred. The goal of achievement was "the attainment of approval and the avoidance of disapproval. Such approval or disapproval could be internal or could come from other persons. But nevertheless, achievement behavior is directed toward a distinct kind of reinforcement . . . such as competence of performance and a standard of excellence which is attached to it." Crandall goes ahead to discuss the motives of creativity, curiosity, originality, and others that have been discussed in this volume.

In sum, it seems possible to separate children and adults into groups according to whether their dominant motive is to attain success or to avoid failure. The latter are likely to be higher in test anxiety. When they are success-oriented, they are likely to choose middle-of-the-road ways of behaving; but when their predominant motive is to avoid failure, they are likely to go to extremes, selecting either excessively cautious or excessively reckless behavior alternatives. The research that has been done (Atkinson *et al.,* 1960) indicates that they are more likely to be reckless than conservative. However, in the Atkinson study, the experimental subjects were always confronted with an audience, and this circumstance may have driven them in the direction of bravado. In private, they might have behaved differently.

Frustration and Failure

DEFINITION OF FRUSTRATION AND FAILURE

In the literature of child development, *frustration* typically has a "bad" connotation. It is not good to frustrate your child; failure is psychologically damaging.

A closer analysis of the two terms, *frustration* and *failure*, leads us to interesting and provocative conclusions that differ from the stereotypes. *Frustration* can be defined in either of two ways. First, it can be thought of as an *internal state* resulting from or accompanying partial or complete blocking as one tries to get to a goal or away from some stimulus he is avoiding. Second, it can be considered as the *act* of blocking.

The internal state idea (see J. S. Brown and Farber, 1951) includes the hypothesis that frustration adds to total drive or motivation level (frustration "stirs the person up," thereby adding a certain amount of drive to that which he already has). Frustration is an "irrelevant" drive, in that it is not related to the motivation initiating the sequence of behavior. A hungry child, blocked from getting food, is frustrated; but his "frustration drive" is irrelevant to the hunger drive that prompted his behavior in the first place. However, frustration adds to his total drive level, thus intensifying the responses he makes to obtain food. Frustration may lead him to attack whomever or whatever is blocking him.

Failure, very simply, means not getting what one is trying to get. It is a descriptive term that refers to "successful blocking," or the *mechanics* of frustration; hence, it is related to the second definition of frustration given above. Failure, of course, is likely to produce frustration (considered as an inner drive).

The most perfunctory examination of the day of the average adult or child forces one to the conclusion that blocking and its accompanying frustration are not necessarily either "good" or "bad." They simply exist. One is frustrated when the alarm clock goes off in the morning. One is frustrated if the meaning of a paragraph does not come clear during the first reading. One is frustrated if someone else gets a higher grade than he does on a test. One is frustrated if the pavements are icy. One is frustrated by having to set the table rather than read the comics.

If frustration is bad, and if each failure is psychologically damaging, then each of us is lucky to get through any given day without coming apart at the seams.

What earlier writers probably meant by "frustration is *bad*" is that *hopeless* frustration (particularly in areas of great personal or social importance), and failure with *no* alternatives, are bad. Prolonged partial or complete blocking, which has no possible happy solution and which occurs in important need areas, may be severely damaging to personal development and adjustment.

THEORIES OF FRUSTRATION

A widely accepted theoretical treatment of frustration has been presented by Dollard and his colleagues (1939). These authors postulate that aggression is always instigated by frustration, although, depending on the learning history of the individual, many reactions other than aggression may occur in response to frustration. Like Brown and Farber, Dollard and his co-authors regard frustration as a drive with highly unpleasant qualities, so that a person is strongly motivated to reduce his frustration. Hence, any behavior that provides escape from frustration or reduces the frustration drive is reinforced.

Research has revealed a number of ways in which individuals of different ages react to various types and degrees of frustration. They may, for example, become passive, or withdraw, or regress (revert to more immature ways of behaving). They may persevere, and work harder; or they may become dependent and ask for help. They may persist blindly in maladaptive behavior (demonstrate rigidity). They may displace their aggression, or reject the task, or "go all to pieces."

Dollard and his co-workers believe that, according to his learning history, an individual may respond in any of these ways, and any behavior which succeeds in reducing frustration will be more likely to appear when he is next frustrated. When a response does not succeed in reducing the frustration, it is weakened so that eventually the next strongest potential response appears.

For example, let us assume that a child has three potential responses to frustration, diagramed in Figure 13.1. Response A (the strongest) is to be polite and considerate; response B is to ask help of the adult (that is, to be dependent); and response C (the weakest) is to become angry and abusive. The prediction is that in the course of repeated frustration, the first few responses will be polite and considerate. If these responses do not successfully resolve frustration, this pattern of behaving will be weakened and the child will show dependent behavior. If, in turn, this fails to reduce the frustration, response C (aggression) will occur, and, if successful, will be strengthened.

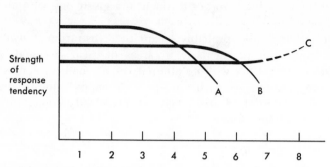

Figure 13.1   A schematic representation of the appearance, disappearance, and strengthening of three types of reaction to repeated frustration. A refers to politeness, B to dependency, C to aggression. The abscissa represents frustration episodes.

Otis and McCandless (1955) have demonstrated this phenomenon experimentally. Preschool children were placed in a mild frustration situation, in which two nursery-school building blocks were placed end to end as a "road." For each of eight trials, the child started with his car or doll from one end of the road and the experimenter (who adopted a very impersonal role) started from the other end. Upon meeting the child's car in the middle, the experimenter would say, "My car is blocking yours," and would leave it at that. She did not respond to the children's "good manners," nor to their requests for help. Three different groups of children dropped from their behavior repertoires the mannerly or dependent attempts to remove the road block and substituted for them, in the manner schematized in Figure 13.1, aggressive attempts at solving the problem. In other words, this study offers support for the idea that behavior (in this case, nonaggressive behavior) which does not reduce frustration will be weakened, or partly extinguished; and suggests that frustration is an instigator of aggression, which will appear overtly when the strength of the tendency toward other types of behavior is weakened.

As has been mentioned, Brown and Farber (1951) have worked with the conception of frustration as a drive. Their formulation of the theory fits well with (and extends) the formulation of Dollard and his colleagues; and the Otis and McCandless results are in accord with it.

Rosenzweig's theories of frustration (1938, 1941, 1944) were discussed briefly in Chapter 11, but will be reviewed more fully in the present context. Rosenzweig believes that there are at least three characteristic patterns of reactions to frustration: the *extrapunitive,* the *impunitive,* and the *intrapunitive.* The first type of reactor lashes out immediately at figures or people in the outside world; the second type attempts to remove emotion from the situation (perhaps denying the frustration, or simply persisting calmly in trying to solve the problem constructively); and the third type blames himself. Rosenzweig also classifies reactions to frustration as *need-persistive* (the need remains, and the individual keeps on trying to gratify it) or *ego-defensive* (the person is threatened and takes steps to save face, although he may do this constructively). Rosenzweig further distinguishes *primary* frustration as a situation of privation in which the goal-object of an active need is unavailable (for example, the absence of food when one is hungry); and *secondary* frustration, in which an obstacle prevents access to the goal-object. These obstacles are of several types: *passive* (such as locked door, or a state of dissatisfaction); *active* (such as the burglar who bars the way and threatens); *external* (to the person); and *internal* (such as a state of conflict).

Nothing in Rosenzweig's treatment is contradictory to the theories of Dollard or of Brown and Farber. However, Maier (1956), who has done most of his work with rats, introduces a different account of the effects of frustration. To him, the frustrated person's behavior is without a goal. When he is frustrated severely and for a prolonged time, task-orientation disappears and the person's behavior becomes goalless.

Maier's formulation is not unlike that of Child and Waterhouse (1952) who believe that because of previous learning, frustration stimuli arouse tendencies to respond in a manner that interferes with efficient, goal-directed behavior. The assumption that Child and Waterhouse make is that learning experiences during frustration are usually unfortunate. The things done when one is frustrated are maladaptive and become attached to the internal stimuli of being frustrated, perhaps because they have removed the unpleasant sensations of frustration. When frustration stimuli occur again, these interfering tendencies reappear. However, there is nothing in the formulation by Child and Waterhouse to say that constructive responses to frustration cannot be established.

Maier (1956) also speaks of fixation (blind adherence to a response that is usually or always wrong) which may occur as a result of frustration, particularly when blocking is prolonged and severe. Maier lists seven conclusions, based on research with rats and young adults, which are of interest at this point in our discussion; although it cannot be said with assurance that they are relevant to children's behavior, they may be useful in suggesting new hypotheses and developing new knowledge.

From a number of studies done by him, his students, and his colleagues, Maier concludes the following:

1. Animals placed for sixteen days in an unsolvable problem situation are more likely to fixate than when placed in a similar problem situation for eight days. The inference that may be drawn from this is that prolonged frustration is more damaging than shorter periods of frustration.

2. The rate of punishment accompanying an unsolvable problem seems to affect fixation. Mild electric shock given to human subjects on 75 percent of 50 trials produced more fixation than the same absolute number of shocks distributed over 150 trials. The implications for children seem clear: The higher the ratio of punishment to total behavior, the more likely it is that behavior will be disrupted.

3. Feeding animals after electric shock results in fewer fixations than does shock alone. To draw inferences from this result, one must speculate rather freely. After a child has been punished, or has failed severely, comfort and explanation will minimize the ill effects of the experience.

4. For rats, guidance during the early stages of learning prevents fixations later, when the rats are placed in an unsolvable problem situation. By implication, children who are familiar with or who understand a situation in which they experience punishment or severe failure will be less adversely affected than children for whom the situation is strange. In addition, if one has a "plan of attack" or a "cognitive map," punishment and frustration will damage him less than if he is proceeding aimlessly.

5. Difficult learning problems result in more fixation than easy ones. It is simple to draw implications for children from this conclusion, which seems to be closely related to the first conclusion: Severe frustrations or failures are more likely to disrupt behavior than mild ones.

6. For humans, the use of the word "wrong" instead of electric shock to indicate an error produces fixations about as frequently as the shock. Again, the implications for children's behavior are clear. The implications of verbally mediated generalization were developed quite fully in Chapters 4 and 5, and Maier's conclusion provides evidence for the effectiveness of this mediation. Human beings, after they have acquired language, can be punished just as effectively by the use of symbols—words, in this case—as by physical punishment. The jingle, "Sticks and stones can break my bones, but words can never hurt me," is not necessarily true.

7. Finally, Maier finds that failure to confirm expectancies seems to be an important influence in the formation of fixations in a discrimination learning problem for rats (when, for example, the rat must learn that the black card behind which he has learned to find food is no longer correct, but that the food is now concealed behind

the white card). This finding argues for consistency in handling children—or for giving advance notice if the rules of the game are to be changed.

Mallick and McCandless (1966) show that catharsis of aggression does not necessarily reduce it. In fact, the verbal suggestion that children may be aggressive to each other actually increases it. Girls, under conditions that assured they would not be known, were just as aggressive as boys, in terms of punishing a confederate who had previously frustrated them.

FRUSTRATION AND CHILD-TRAINING

Since frustration and failure are unavoidable, parents and teachers should seek ways to help children resolve their frustrations and arrive at accurate and constructive substitutes or explanations for their failures. Good child-training, including academic training, is aimed at such goals.

Avoiding Irrelevant Frustrations   Good parents, good teachers, and good schools seek to avoid *irrelevant* frustrations. Learning to read or to do long division are, by their very nature, frustrating. But we wish to confine the frustrations that necessarily accompany learning to those that are *task-relevant;* hence, learning should take place in esthetically and socially congenial surroundings. It is for this reason that teachers today more frequently than before use sociometric groupings, permitting children to work with and sit beside friends of their own choosing. It is partly for this reason that new schools are characterized by open, light, cheery, and attractively furnished rooms. It is for this reason that color and lighting schemes have been devised which will produce the least distraction or glare, and the old type of fixed desk has been abandoned wherever possible.

School psychology and counseling have come into being so that the academically irrelevant frustrations of social maladjustment or an unhappy home life can be reduced. Textbooks have been age-graded. Teachers increasingly study the development of normal children in order to understand the crises and frustrations (as well as the special satisfactions) of the different developmental stages and, whenever possible, reduce the academically irrelevant frustrations that may accompany them.

Most school systems now practice so-called social promotions, by which academically slow children are kept with their age-mates even though they may not be able to compete academically with them. The theory behind this practice is that the social frustration of being left back is greater than the increasing frustration of inability to compete. Grade-skipping for the superior student has been largely abandoned for similar reasons: fear that the social and personal frustrations encountered by the child in an advanced grade would more than offset the academic advantages. Both these points are debatable, and should receive more study than they have received so far. In the Brookline public schools (Hobson, 1956), for example, carefully screened children admitted early to kindergarten did better on all scores, including academic achievement, than children admitted at the normal age. By the time of enrolling in junior high school, the problems presented by socially promoted children who cannot cope with the advanced curriculum perhaps more than offset the intended advantages of social promotion. On the other hand, a gangling adolescent still in the fourth grade poses serious problems for other children in his class, for his teacher, and for himself. The accelerated child *may* be socially out of step for a time, particularly if he is male and especially at adolescence. However, he may be inordinately bored if kept in a homogeneously taught classroom where the average child is far below him in ability. Age-graded reading texts may be less frustrating *mechanically* to children, but many of them, with their endless repetitions and plot simplicities (even banalities), are thoroughly boring as well.

There are no simple answers to such problems. But, in principle, the steps taken to reduce irrelevant classroom frustrations are sound, and, as *experiments* (not dogma), they are worth trying.

Building Frustration Tolerance   A first principle, then, for dealing with frustration in child-training is to reduce irrelevant frustrations to a minimum. But, inevitably, frustrations remain. A practical recommendation for reducing their impact, and building up tolerance for frustration, is to start the child with mild frustrations and move him toward more severe ones. By such training, we try to help the child look for constructive ways of coping with frustration and failure. We do this by exposing him first to very clear-cut, black-and-white types of problems (or discriminations), providing guidance and emotional support as he works at them. As the child grows more and more capable of solving these problems, we narrow the discriminations and make the problems more complex and less clear-cut.

Excessive motivation is likely to impair performance in complex situations where a *correct* response or set of responses has not been established. The higher the drive state when such behavior choices must be made, the more likely it is that an already established "wrong" response will be made. Many inappropriate response tendencies that are ordinarily below threshold—that is, not likely to appear in behavior—will be strengthened under conditions of excessive motivation, and thus may interfere with performance. Since frustration is presumed to add to general drive level, and excessive frustration (or excessive anxiety) to add to it excessively, the recommendation follows that frustration should be kept within moderate limits. If it is not, it may cause an individual to perpetuate errors (behave in a rigid fashion) or be slow to select the single correct response or set of responses from competing but erroneous responses.

Providing for Individual Differences   Although the tremendous variation among children in a classroom subjects children to a wide variety of human-relations learnings, and adds interest to the teacher's task, this variation is also a major source of frustration for children. To confine this frustration to a minimum is a major and extremely difficult task for the teacher.

Almost everything that has been said earlier in this chapter relates to the topic of individual differences, and extensive literature on child development and education is devoted to this topic. By way of illustrating the problem, a hypothetical but not atypical fifth-grade class in a small town has been selected for description.

The teacher of such a group may have thirty-six or more children in her class, of whom about half are boys, half girls. Some of the girls in the class have already reached puberty, and most of them are in their prepubescent growth spurt. Two of the boys are pubescent. They are the oldest members of the class, and both of them have previously been "held back."

In terms of social status, this teacher's charges range from two children of itinerant farm workers, who come into her classroom shabby and ill-washed after an hour's ride on the school bus, carrying inadequate lunches in bags, to the daughter of the community's leading doctor, who walks the two blocks to school from her large and handsome home and goes home for a hot lunch.

The lowest IQ in the group is 77, the highest 145. One child in the room reads at the second-grade level, whereas another tests as high as the median for high-school seniors. The range in number proficiency is narrower, extending from second to ninth grade. The families of some of the children have never taken a daily newspaper, but one family subscribes to both a morning and an evening paper, and takes the Sunday New York *Times* as well. Some of the children have traveled no further than a few miles outside the town limits, but the doctor's daughter has toured Europe, and one of the itinerant farm worker's children has attended schools in thirteen states.

One child in the room is Negro and one Mexican American (his parents do not speak English). Religious affiliations of the children's families include orthodox Judaism, agnosticism, Roman Catholicism, and Protestant groups ranging from the so-called fundamentalist to the progressive or liberal. The age range is from 10 to 14 years. One child has spent a year in a school for delinquent and predelinquent boys.

This picture seems extreme. But for the elementary-school teacher in the small-town or consolidated school, and for junior-high teachers in all except the largest cities, it is not unrepresentative. In more populous urban centers, of course, the informal (and formal) residential segregation that exists restricts this variability in background. The school population becomes more homogeneous in high school because the less able students drop out, but even in high school variability remains very great.

With a population like that of our hypothetical fifth-grade classroom, individual differences in needs cannot be met in a fully satisfactory way. Most teachers are compelled to pitch their teaching at, or somewhat below, the median of the class, to spend a disproportionate amount of their time working with slow-learning or trouble-making children, and, to a regrettable degree, to allow the upper two fifths of the class to teach themselves. The result is severe frustration for the slowest-learning children in the room, and almost equally extreme frustration, due to boredom and too easily achieved success, for the two or three fastest-learning children.

One result of this procedure is that far too many intellectually gifted United States children do not learn to work by the time they reach college. Almost a third of Terman's "geniuses," for example, actually failed college for one or another reason (see Terman and Oden, 1947), although each possessed the potential to obtain advanced academic degrees. Accumulated hostility toward education may also have developed by the time a child becomes an adult and a taxpayer.

In the face of such difficulties, the American dream of universal education has nevertheless been achieved to a remarkable extent. The literacy rate is high, there is no hopeless schism between "aristocrat" and "peasant," and most children derive considerable satisfaction from their schooling. Individual needs are met, as best they can be, through the interested and dedicated teacher's knowledge of socioeconomic conditions, and through her efforts to understand the different problems of the children in her class. One of the most desirable characteristics in a teacher is the ability to put herself or himself to some degree in the child's place: to feel the lost-ness, the insecurity, even the hopelessness of the itinerant farm worker's child; to understand and sympathize with the doctor's daughter, who has always had everything (whereas teachers have often been forced, at least, in part, to work their way through school).

The most important tools for accommodating to individual differences are, then, compassionate knowledge of children's backgrounds and flexibility in dealing with them. Second, the schools must supply work materials of sufficient range so that no child needs to go unchallenged, yet no child needs to experience complete failure. Third, teaching should be done in subgroups formed according to modern principles of teaching and social grouping. As has been mentioned above, these groups should be as compatible as possible, and should be academically more homogeneous than the class as a whole. Modern testing techniques are sufficiently sophisticated to accomplish both of these goals. Sociometric tests (the determination, in strict professional confidence, of who are the good friends of each child in the class) are easy and quick to administer; and effective achievement tests exist for all areas of academics. Given social and educational data such as these, even our unwieldy class of thirty-six or more fifth-graders can be divided into "committees" for the benefit of all. It is probable that even such matters as classroom discipline can be improved by taking such steps.

Psychological literature now includes suggestions, based on experimental research, for dealing more effectively with special types of children in the classroom. For example, an experiment by Douvan (1956) suggests that concrete rewards are more effective in motivating lower-class children than are appeals to "intellectual excellence," which is the ordinary "coin of the realm" in the classroom. Douvan classified high-school seniors into three groups: middle class, working class, and "marginals" (children whose fathers held working-class jobs, yet who regarded themselves as middle class). All these young people were failed on an experimental task, but half the members of each social-class group were told that they were expected to do as well as other comparable children (the "internal intellectual standards" group), while the members of the other half of each of the groups were told that if they did well, each would receive a $10.00 reward.

After the failure experience, a measure of achievement motivation was made for each socioeconomic group. The average number of achievement motives recorded for middle-class children for the "intrinsic intellectual appeal" condition ("Do the best you can") was 7.6, whereas working-class children scored only 4.9 on achievement motive. The difference was significant statistically, and the marginals did not differ from the middle-class children. But, when the reward was tangible (hard cash) there were no differences between lower- and middle-class children: the average number of achievement-motive themes for the former was 8.1; for the latter, 8.3. The marginals obtained an average of 7.9, not significantly different from either of the other groups.

The implication of Douvan's study is that educational motivation—and perhaps motivation in general—should be made more concrete or tangible for lower- than for middle-class children. "Their academic consciences are not so well built-in."

The Schools, Human Relations, and Psychology

Among people concerned with education, controversy rages about the merits of "classical" versus "developmental" curricula. Although discussion of the merits of the controversy is outside the scope of this book, the following position is taken: Matters concerning human relations and social responsibility are not taught fully or adequately in United States elementary and secondary schools (and probably not in colleges). Covering them adequately does not preclude a "tough" substantive curriculum. Most people, upon serious thought, would admit that the world's and the nation's problems are less those of guided missiles and nuclear warfare than they are those of faulty human relations. The physical sciences are generations ahead of the social sciences.

What, basically, is homemaking: How to cook, or sew a set of drapes —or how to get along with a husband, children, and the neighbors? What is traffic safety: A matter of steering a car or a matter of using good manners and common sense? A local newspaper account tells of a driver passing on blind curves at a high rate of speed, with a load of strangers in his own car, who crashed head-on into a family-packed automobile, killing himself, most of his own passengers, and all of the family in the other car. This driver, only a few miles back on the road, had been stopped and warned by the highway patrol. Obviously, his driving skills were adequate, or he would not have got so far along the mountain road; but he had not learned that an automobile is a poor vehicle for expressing personal needs for power and aggression.

STUDIES OF CHANGE IN HUMAN NATURE

Objections to teaching human relations in schools are frequently expressed by some version of the cliché, "The idea is fine, but you can't change human nature." Research literature now includes enough studies (sociological and psychological, survey and experimental) to enable us to dismiss this generalization with confidence.

Two studies have been conducted to determine the effectiveness of the program of the Wayne County Training School, a residential center for high-grade mentally defective delinquent or predelinquent children. In a sense, it is a luxury institution: at the time these studies were run (during the depression years of the 1930s), there was a ratio of about two employees to every five children. The institution's grounds and buildings were attractive; the children were relatively well-dressed; counseling, therapy, and special education (both academic and vocational) were available for all children. Almost all the children, boys and girls, came from broken and disorganized families who lived in deteriorated urban slums. Children remained in the institution for an average of about three years.

In the first of these studies of children paroled from the institution into the community, Kephart and Ainsworth (1938) found that nearly three fourths of the boys had become law-abiding, self-supporting citizens, and had remained so for a period of from five to ten years after their return to the community. This was true despite the fact that the era of the study was also that of the social confusion and despair of the great Depression, and despite the fact that a population of this type is one of the least promising of the various problem subgroups of our society. Girls (Bijou, Ainsworth, and Stockey, 1943), who are more vulnerable than boys to accidental environment forces, were rehabilitated almost as successfully as boys and 70 percent of them did well in the community during the study period of five to ten years following parole.

A study of the Hawthorne-Cedar Knolls School (Curran, 1955) provides similar but even more encouraging results: almost 85 percent of its resident population of disturbed and delinquent boys were successful after being returned to the community. For children treated in the "standard" state reform or training school, the estimate of recidivism (continued delinquency) is between 70 and 80 percent; hence, only 20 to 30 percent are successfully rehabilitated.

Experimental studies of "change in human nature" include one demonstrating that it is possible to teach children constructive reactions to frustration and failure (Keister, 1937); two that demonstrate success in making shy children more self-assertive or ascendant in experimentally devised social situations (Jack, 1934; and Page, 1936); one showing that highly aggressive and competitive preschoolers can be trained to make more cooperative and socially approved responses (Chittenden, 1942); and one indicating that children's fears can be reduced through experience, reassurance, and explanation (Jersild and Holmes, 1935).

A summary of the first of these studies illustrates the methods (and the positive results) of the others. From a group of eighty-two preschoolers, Keister selected the twelve who showed the most maladaptive reaction to failure on a test she devised of fitting back into a flat box a number of gaily painted wooden figurines. The task is difficult for adults, almost impossible for children. The children's constructive and nonconstructive behavior while working on the problem was recorded. Examples of constructive behavior are: "Attempts to solve alone; shows interest." Nonconstructive reactions consisted of such behavior as, "No overt attempt to solve; asks another to solve; sulks, cries, whines."

After this test, the experimenter (a young woman trained in preschool teaching methods) worked with the children over a period of about six weeks, with sessions for the different children ranging from 8 to 33 minutes in duration. She taught them constructive approaches to a series of tasks ranging from quite easy to quite difficult, employing techniques of reassurance, praise, and sometimes direct suggestions, and putting the children through the training series in such a fashion that a child did not go on to a more difficult task until he had succeeded on an easier one. She provides a number of comments made by the children, of which the following is illustrative: "I'm sure havin' a hard time. But look! This is steadier now [his block construction]. I'm makin' him better. I think it will stay this time. Now it's gonna stay, I s'pose. See! It's gonna stay." (Keister, 1937, p. 70)

After these training situations the children were retested on a puzzle box similar to but different from the original. Table 13.2, modified from Keister, illustrates the dramatic nature of the differences in response to frustration before and after training.

Table 13.2   *Differences in Response to Frustration as a Result of Training to Produce Frustration Tolerance.*

BEHAVIOR	BEFORE TRAINING, MEAN MINUTES[a] $(N = 15)$	AFTER TRAINING, MEAN MINUTES[b] $(N = 12)$[c]	DIFFERENCE[d]
No overt attempt	6.0	2.1	3.9
Attempts to solve alone	8.5	11.2	2.7*
Asks another to solve	3.6	0.5	3.1
Asks help	2.5	2.4	0.1
Destructive behavior	0.6	—	0.6
Rationalizes	2.8	—	2.8
Shows interest	6.0	11.0	5.0*
No emotional manifestation	2.5	1.3	1.2
Indifference	1.0	—	1.0
Smiles	0.3	—	0.3
Laughs	—	0.1	0.1
Sulks	0.8	—	0.8*
Cries	1.7	—	1.7*
Whines	2.6	1.0	1.6
Yells	0.3	—	0.3
Motor manifestations of anger	0.2	—	0.2

a Mean length of the experimental period was 14.5 minutes.
b Mean length of the experimental period was 13.3 minutes.
c Keister lost three subjects, either because of withdrawal from school or because of irregular attendance.
d Differences marked * are significant below the .05 level.
ADAPTED FROM KEISTER (1937).

Keister used as a control group twelve children from the same nursery school who had showed moderately poor reactions to the initial frustration, and retested them when she retested her experimental group. Although the controls had experienced the general benefits of the preschool program, they did not show any significant improvements in reaction to the second frustration task.

Social climates may also affect behavior powerfully. Behavioral changes produced by variations in social climate have been demonstrated to be remarkably permanent by such "real-life" studies as the Wayne County Training School and the Hawthorne-Cedar Knolls studies discussed earlier. However, a more specific picture of these changes is provided by experimental studies.

The classical study in this area is that by Lewin, Lippitt, and White (1939). Four groups each made up of five 10-year-old boys, were placed under the guidance of leaders who were, by turns and with different groups, authoritarian, democratic, or *laissez-faire* (indifferent and passive).

The boys in one of the authoritarian groups were rebellious and, in the other, passive; they displayed little "we" feeling, "went to pieces" when the leader left the room, and showed much hostility toward each other. The *laissez-faire* boys disliked their groups, were bored, quarrelsome, inefficient in group projects, and disorganized. The boys in the democratic groups showed least hostility toward each other, were "we-minded," held together best when the adult leader was absent, and worked constructively and happily. Later interviews with the boys showed that all but one had liked their democratic leaders better than their autocratic leaders.

This study has had profound educational effects, and its results are pleasing to all of us who espouse the democratic way of life. But it must be pointed out that the study has certain defects. Perhaps the most serious one is that the design of the study included no "benevolent authoritarian" group climate. The author, because of this own experience, is convinced that such an atmosphere is probably the most effective and efficient one in which an adult can begin his relations with, for example, delinquent groups. Once accepted, respected, and liked by them, the leader can begin to help the children become self-disciplined instead of having to be controlled by others.

Fresh from his experience as one of the four group leaders in the Lewin, Lippitt, and White study (and ardent in his convictions concerning democracy, warmth, and child-centeredness), the author went into a situation where he was partially responsible for the conduct of two cottages (residential centers for thirty to forty boys each) of adolescent, mentally retarded, delinquent and predelinquent boys. Under the new regime of sweetness, light, trust in their better nature, and permissiveness, these youngsters went completely to pieces, making life miserable for their cottage personnel, themselves, and the writer. After some months of this nightmare, and after a particularly atrocious betrayal of trust, the author finally took one of the "gang" leaders over his lap and spanked him thoroughly—an embarrassing and temporarily painful experience for the gangling adolescent boy.

Following this incident, the atmosphere of the two cottages changed overnight; these slum youngsters had been talked to in their own language. Only then was it possible to put into action an effective democratic organization of the cottages. The effectiveness of this organization was attested by the fact that, after about two years, one of the cottages —during the acute manpower shortage early in World War II—operated well for some months with no adult living in it. During this time, an adult came in at meal- and bedtimes; but during the rest of the day, the residential group of 13- to 15-year-old low-IQ delinquent slum boys managed their own lives. There was no mayhem and there were no runaways, although on the average, under closely supervised conditions, one boy in thirty ran away weekly.

It is doubtful, however, whether democratic organization would have been equally effective had not the boys learned before the spanking episode that the adults responsible for them, though gullible, had real affection for them and were fair.

Another, but less obvious, flaw in the Lewin, Lippitt, and White study is related to the role-playing done by the four leaders in their three leadership roles. The four leaders were graduate students or postdoctoral fellows in child and clinical psychology. All were convinced and liberal equalitarians, living at a time when Hitler, the arch-authoritarian, was consolidating his power and preparing for world conquest. Each preferred and put his heart into his *democratic* leadership role, becoming perhaps the *warmest* and most dedicated democratic leader in recent history. But, when his turn came to play the authoritarian, he tended to become *cold* and *hard*—a veritable Captain Bligh. In the *laissez-faire* role, detachment of a profound sort became the order of the day. In other words, the crucial variable involved *may* have been warmth. Despite its flaws, this study was a pioneering one that should be replicated.

In another study illustrating the changes that can result from shifts in group climate, McCandless (1942) checked the social structure of one of the Wayne County Training School cottages mentioned above, but before democratic organization was introduced. This checking consisted in part of asking the 13- to 15-year-old boys to list their three best friends in order from first to third. The "stars" (the most popular boys) were those whom the cottage supervisors, who made their ratings without knowing popularity status, agreed were "muscle men" and physically domineering boys. Boys rated by the supervisors as "mature and interested in conforming to adult standards" were low in popularity.

Some months after the cottage had been reorganized along democratic lines, these measurements were repeated, and the social structure of the group was found to have shifted dramatically. The relatively mature boys had become the stars, whereas the muscle men had dropped sharply in popularity and no longer held positions of group leadership. One of these boys had become quite disturbed by what was happening to him and, during the period of the study, had run away from the cottage repeatedly.

Several experiments in public-school mental health are now under way in the United States and Canada. These programs and studies place their emphasis on *preventive* and *creative* mental health, in contrast to more traditional research emphases on remediation and cure.[2]

One of the most extensive of these programs is the Preventive Psychiatry Project directed by Ojemann at the Iowa Institute for Child Behavior and Development. Ojemann's approach to preventive psychiatry involves the concepts of a *surface* and a *causal* approach to human relations. He and his co-workers have made analyses (Stiles, 1950) of traditional curricular material (such as children's stories, and courses in civics), concluding from these that the United States approach to education is principally *surface,* fails partially to take account of human motivations, and neglects attempts at understanding the motivations of others.

Ojemann and his colleagues have prepared curricular materials which, although they do not ignore the traditional content of civics, for example, stress the motivations of members of society as these have been translated into social organization and law, and also consider how social organization and law in turn affect the individual. They have also prepared a number of causally oriented stories, which emphasize "psychological problem solving" and attempt to teach the child to look for the causes of behavior. The preventive-psychiatry program emphasizes the complexity of human nature and the multiplicity of causes that may underlie the "simplest" piece of behavior. The idea of "probabilistic thinking" is also stressed. For example, a child's fear may be caused by some specific unfortunate experience or set of experiences; but if this hypothesis does not work out, a secondary hypothesis may be that the child has a poor relation with his father; if this hypothesis is rejected, then we must look still further in our attempt to understand the child—operate, perhaps, on the assumption that his fear is symbolic of some apparently unrelated disturbance.

In the Ojemann project, it is assumed that the teacher's daily behavior (in addition to the more formal curriculum) is a vital causal (or surface) force operating on the child.

Ojemann and his co-workers are conducting research in a number of different school systems. Their undertakings include workshops in which teachers are trained in the causal approach; and the effects on school classes of being taught by such teachers are being examined. These studies provide for control classes composed of children similar to the

[2] The Group for the Advancement of Psychiatry (GAP, 1951) has summarized these programs.

experimental children, but taught by teachers without causal training. Although conclusions remain tentative, as such research is enormously complicated, preliminary results are encouraging. It cannot yet be said, however, whether the signs of improved mental health in the experimental children are due to the causal approach as such or to the lift in their teachers' morale. Whatever the cause, the teachers, after their training, appear to be more understanding of children, more interested in the general process of normal development, and more enthusiastic about their work.

The implication of the research reviewed in this section is that human nature can be changed. It is possible, by firm and intensive treatment, to turn delinquent children into self-supporting, law-abiding citizens. Children's methods of reacting to frustration and failure, their ways of handling fear, and their aggressive behavior can be modified radically and constructively. Children seem to "do better" in an atmosphere of democracy, although (particularly for delinquent and lower-class groups) an initial group climate of benevolent authoritarianism may be necessary. Several studies now under way, which emphasize preventive mental health rather than treatment, have yielded encouraging though tentative results.

EVALUATING A CHILD'S MASTERY OF THE CURRICULUM

A hotly debated issue in United States education concerns evaluation or "marking." Procedures for evaluating the progress of elementary-school children range all the way from interviews with parents, in which many phases of the child's development are discussed, to the traditional report card, on which everything from conduct to reading is graded by letter: A for excellent, F for "flunk," with no explanations given either parent or child. In junior and senior high school, such unqualified marks constitute the most typical form of evaluation.

Parent, child, teacher, and school counselor or psychologist (where there is one) must know at least three characteristics of the child's academic progress in order to guide him soundly: the child's personal potential, his ranking in his local group, and his standing on national norms. This is not to say that they do not need to know many things about his personal and social development as well.

The Child's Personal Potential   The first and probably most important piece of information about the child's progress is how well he is doing in relation to his ability. In our society, much is made of competition (successful or unsuccessful) with others, but very little is said about "competition with oneself."

There has been much talk about the evils of competition, by modern educators who have deplored its existence in the classroom. It has been pointed out that society requires cooperation more than it does competition, and that education should stress the former.

Research studies on competition and cooperation indicate that children do more work while competing than while working alone (just as hens eat more corn when another fowl is present and eating than when they are alone); that "natural" teams (as boys against girls) accomplish more when competing against each other than do "artificial" teams (randomly or arbitrarily assigned); and that children working toward a group goal, with no competing team, do the most work of all. For a fuller discussion of this subject, see Hurlock (1959), Jersild (1954), or Thompson (1952).

In the broad sense, ours is certainly as much a cooperative society as a competitive one, and perhaps more so: the flow of traffic (erratic as it often is) depends upon driver cooperation and conformity. In our daily living, we depend upon (cooperate with) the milkman, the postman, the grocer. To exist, labor and management cooperate more than they compete.

There is little question that a substantial share of our personal and social crises (our breakdowns in human relations) occur because of a lack of co-operation—because of our insensitivity to the needs of our fellow man, or his insensitivity to ours. While driving, we indignantly refuse to allow the pushing, honking, glaring motorist to pull in ahead of us from a side street; but should he smile hopefully and raise his eyebrows questioningly, we gladly accommodate him, and gain from this a pleasant sense of having done good.

For such reasons, one tends to agree with the liberal educator that cooperation is insufficiently stressed in our schools. The corollary that is often drawn, however—that competition is bad and should be eliminated from the classroom—must be argued. Competition is here to stay, just as frustration is. Like frustration, competition is neither good nor bad; it is simply inevitable.

Hopi and Zuni Indian societies have been presented to us (see Benedict, 1953) as free from competition. It is said that in these societies, each man lives as much for his neighbor and his group as for himself. However, Dennis (1955) obtained the *anonymous* wishes of Hopi adolescents about outcomes of competition, and found that in these circumstances the proportion who wanted to win was about the same as that of a population of non-Hopi Virginia adolescents. This competitive spirit may have been taught the Hopi youth in their "American style" schools, of course, although it seems unlikely that what has been said to be the spirit of the culture could be so easily contravened; more probably, the secret wish to win persists despite the well-documented public Hopi living pattern.

In our society, children and youth need to know how to compete effectively, realistically, and gracefully. Everyone wins and loses; each person must adjust to both circumstances, and it is perhaps as difficult to learn to handle a win gracefully as it is to lose in good style.

It might be very profitable for parents, teachers, and others who deal with children and youth to shift their emphasis from competing with others to "competition with the self"—that is, to living up to the potential one has. Certainly, the schools should provide information about a child's *actual* progress in relation to what he can do *potentially*. If children were assigned grades on such a basis, the pattern of many "report cards" would be greatly changed. For example, as a group, the intellectually superior perform much less well than would be expected even allowing for the statistical concept of "regression to the mean."[3] If grading were done according to potential performance, using conventional letter markings, many superior children might receive C's or F's even though their absolute performance is better than that of other children in a class. Using this "self-reference" system, the slowest child in the class, working up to his capacity, might receive an A.

The Child's Rank in His Local Group   The standing of a child within his classroom group typically determines the teacher's evaluation of his performance. This comparative evaluation is probably the most important single criterion by which a child forms his self-concept about his academic prowess.

Evaluation based solely on how children in a given class compare with one another can lead children to very inaccurate perceptions of their academic ability. A relatively bright child in a blighted neighborhood may develop grandiose notions of his ability; a bright child in a highly superior class may develop an unjustifiably poor notion of his ability. Isolated or rural communities frequently develop "delusions of grandeur" in at least the top students in a class.

Girls, who are more conforming, probably work somewhat harder, and are socially more mature than boys, typically get higher grades than boys, although their actual standing on standardized and objective tests of academic achievement is not higher (particularly after elementary school) than boys'. Teachers' grades correlate well with girls' achievement on objective and standardized achievement tests, but show much lower correlations with boys' ratings on the same instruments. The exception-

---

[3] Exceptional status (extremely high or extremely low) with respect to one trait does not imply equally exceptional status with respect to other traits (unless the traits selected have a very high correlation). Mentally retarded youngsters, for example, will be closer to the national average in height than they are in IQ; intellectually superior children will be closer to the national average in study efficiency and motivation than in intellectual status.

ally bright child who is young for his group may be graded no higher (or may be graded lower) than older children in the group who, intellectually, are less able. Grades often seem to be based on conformity and good manners almost as much as on performance.

Other deficiencies of the marking system, and a discussion of the difficulty teachers experience in selecting the bright children in their classes, have been discussed in Chapter 7.

Despite the weaknesses of a grading system based on relative standing in a classroom, knowledge of this standing is important in guiding children. Parents need to know, and their child *does* know, where he stands in relation to his classroom group. Teachers should, of course, mark with a scrupulous fairness. It is probable that boys are somewhat penalized by the average teacher's marking, and, since breadwinners in the United States are preponderantly male, this is a serious defect in the grading system. If relative academic failure discourages a substantial proportion of boys from going on to exploit their potentialities, educators should explore the problem thoroughly.

The Child's Standing on National Norms   The third major type of academic evaluation involves a comparison of the child's performance with national norms. In Iowa, for example, the top-ranking student in some high-school graduating classes stands lower on objective and standardized tests of academic achievement than the lowest-ranking student in other high schools. In some areas of the United States, as many as *two thirds* of high-school graduates fall below the *median* (mid-point) of high-school graduates from other sections of the country (Bloom, 1956).

Such discrepancies can (and do) lead to serious complications when, for example, the valedictorian of an inferior high school goes to college and begins competing with students who have been better trained than he. An equally serious problem, although perhaps not as traumatizing to the individual, is the lowering of self-concept that may occur for children in the middle or toward the bottom of the class distribution in highly efficient and rigorous school systems. Such youngsters may be quite capable of mastering advanced training, but be discouraged from trying to attend college by their relatively mediocre elementary and secondary-school performance.

For reasons such as these, the child and those responsible for his guidance should know how he stands on norms extending beyond his classroom and school. Such norms exist, and tests standardized on a large and representative population should be administered routinely to children in all schools. Only through the repeated use of such tests can all the important goals of evaluation be achieved: (1) comparing the child's year-by-year growth with his ability; (2) comparing his performance with the achievements of his classmates (thus giving the teacher a valuable check on her own objectivity); and (3) comparing the child (and the school) against broader norms. Certain disadvantages of such full reporting are inevitable—some children are moderately shocked, others made cocky, some parents push their children excessively, and so on—but the advantages of full and factual guidance seem to outweigh the disadvantages.

A fifth-grade friend of the author's attends a school where these three types of evaluation are routinely carried out. He is a bright but underachieving child, and such a picture of him appeared clearly on his progress report. At a conservative estimate, he could, at the end of his fifth-grade year, have been achieving about as well as the average United States child beginning the eighth grade; he was actually doing about as well as the average child at the beginning of the seventh grade. He stood at or near the top of his class in intellectual potential; but his actual achievement (whether measured by standardized tests or by teachers' marks) ranked at or slightly below the median of his class. According to the national norms for the test he was given, he scored better than 90 percent of United States children on all subtests but one.

From a study of his test profile (his scores on various subtests, such as reading comprehension, number performance, number comprehension, spelling, map reading, and so on), this boy provided his own educational guidance. The test profile showed that his two lowest scores were in reading comprehension and reading speed. This deficiency in reading, he was able to see, handicapped his performance in everything else, and the remedy was more free reading. As a result, he moved toward a goal that his parents and teachers had for some years been trying to achieve: he began to read extensively on his own, and subsequently improved in academic standing both within his class and according to broader norms.

Breadth of Evaluation   To this point, discussion of evaluation has been limited to description and measurement of academic progress. However, evaluation should be creative as well as descriptive. It should be designed to discover and record a range of talents broader than intellectual and academic proficiency. Parents, teachers, and schools in general should be on the lookout for such gifts as exceptional artistic and athletic ability. Floyd Patterson, as a case in point, attained championship status as a prize fighter; but he might have been an even greater champion, and some or many of his academic and personal troubles might have been prevented or alleviated, if his gifts of speed, power, and coordination had been discovered through creative evaluation when he was, for example, in the third grade. His talents must certainly have been present, at least in nascent form, as early as his elementary-school years.

Skill in such activities as music, art, tennis, and swimming are correlated only very modestly with measured intelligence and academic standing, and may easily be overlooked in a school system that is oriented exclusively toward academics (of course, this is not to deny that the basic function of schools is their academic function). Discovery and development of nonacademic talents may be a key to the adjustment problems of many children—the path by which they escape from the academic mediocrity that has given them a sense of failure. Thus, creative evaluation may not only make a positive contribution to society, but be of therapeutic value to many individuals as well. Currently, however, such evaluation is given a minor role—usually, lip service only—in most United States school systems.

Failure to stress creative evaluation may have later unfortunate effects on the schools' public relations. For example, it has been suggested that successful men in the business community often obtained poor or mediocre academic records as children. May not some of their later suspicion of—or, at best, lack of enthusiastic support for—the schools be an outgrowth of their school experiences? To become successful, they must have possessed attributes of drive, clear thinking, and initiative that could have been, but were not, recognized and rewarded during their school years. The next chapter portrays the adjustment of lower-class children to schools; usually this adjustment is frustrated and unhappy—certainly not of the type to cause the lower-class child, as an adult, to show much sympathy for the school system at whose hands he has suffered.

Acceptance of Evaluation If evaluations are to be accepted by children and their parents, they must be accurate, fair, and comprehensive. They must also be adequately interpreted. To achieve both of these objectives, teachers, school administrators, and counselors should acquire sound knowledge of evaluation procedures, including testing methods and sophisticated interpretation of test results. Weaknesses as well as strengths of tests should be recognized. Subjective influences on class grades should be recognized and allowed for. Aspects of evaluation other than the academic should be developed.

School people should have some training in counseling and should work to develop attitudes that accompany successful counseling—for example, tolerance of individual differences; acceptance, without condemnation and rejection, of parents and children *as they are;* recognition of the worth and integrity of the human personality; awareness that almost all parents no matter how misguided they may seem, genuinely wish to do the best they can for their children.

Some teachers seem almost to want the children in their classes for their own. Regarding themselves almost as substitute parents, they manifest a certain amount of resentment toward the children's real mothers and fathers. Although it is understandable and desirable that teachers should enter their profession because they like people, and *particularly* children, this liking should be realistically based and nonpossessive. Teachers should be on guard against rejecting parents because their own lives are empty, or because their own maternal or paternal needs are not fully satisfied.

Summary

This chapter has discussed emotional factors affecting all areas of the child's (and adult's) life. Topics have ranged from level of aspiration to evaluation of performance in and out of school.

Central to understanding both school and life performance is the concept of *level of aspiration*. This term ordinarily has a personal frame of reference: an individual has a positive level of aspiration if, for "next time," he predicts that he will do better on a task than he did the last time he tried it. However, the term can also be applied in an absolute sense: one man aspires to write great literature or to achieve fame through science, while another wants only to be personally secure.

Most children and adults believe and hope that their future achievement will be superior to their past performance. The implications of this finding are that children should be kept reaching, but that their reaching should be so structured as to afford reasonable hope for a successful outcome. The level of aspiration is usually raised after success and lowered after experiences of failure. Maladjusted groups of children and adults are more variable in their predictions about performance, following both success and failure, than are normal groups.

Suggestive evidence exists that persistent success or failure may have long-lasting effects on an individual's level of aspiration (his "ambition"). Success will buoy him up; failure will depress him. In the academic sphere, middle-class children seem to possess more positive levels of aspiration and stronger achievement motives than lower-class children.

The achievement motive may be thought of as a widely generalized *positive* level of aspiration. A person with high achievement motive regards problems, obstacles, and competition as a challenge to be met: he works for success. Others seem to be motivated more by fear of failure than by desire for success. An adjustment that is predominantly achievement-oriented appears to result in middle-of-the-road aspirations: the individual is neither overly cautious, nor is he reckless. But predominant motivation to avoid failure seems to result either in undue caution or, more frequently, in reckless attempts to achieve.

Achievement, of course, is heavily stressed in our culture. Both those who are generally motivated to achieve and those whose generalized motive is to avoid failure have acquired or learned such adjustments, usually in their family setting. Anxiety about achievement often accompanies both learning to value achievement and learning to fear failure. Achievement anxiety may be "situation-specific" (that is, it may arise only in situations where achievement is expected, and where competition exists), or it may simply be one of many manifestations of chronic anxiety. Achievement anxiety probably leads to inefficiency in performance more often than it does to efficiency, although if an individual possesses all the "right" or correct responses for dealing with a situation or solving a problem or taking a test, anxiety may increase his efficiency rather than interfere with it. Anxiety about achievement may have much in common with fixation, and may be very difficult to extinguish.

The author takes the rather widely accepted position that frustration can be defined in two ways: first, as failure to achieve a goal, or blockage (of a more temporary sort) of a person's efforts to reach a goal; and second, as a drive induced by such failure or blocking. Frustration in the first sense cannot be considered either "good" or "bad," but must be thought of as inevitable and ubiquitous. The important child-training consideration, then, is not how to avoid frustration, but how to handle it and resolve it constructively.

When frustration is considered in this light, the following recommendations emerge for parents and teachers: (1) attempt to avoid *irrelevant* frustrations in training and teaching children; (2) help children acquire a general "frustration tolerance" by starting them with easy learning tasks, discriminations, and problems; guiding their solutions; and moving them, after success, to more difficult problems; and (3) keep frustration (in the sense of a *drive*) moderate, insofar as this is possible, since severe frustration seems to interfere with performance more often than to facilitate it, particularly in complex learning situations for which there exist many competing responses, of which the majority are inappropriate (wrong).

A major source of frustration is the enormous variability among children in a family or classroom. In a typical classroom, the superior child is likely to be frustrated by lack of challenge to his abilities, while the inferior child is consistently frustrated by his inability to keep pace with the rest of the class. Meeting this problem of individual differences in ability, personality, physical characteristics, and so on, is one of the most difficult problems faced by the schools. Failure to challenge bright youngsters may result in their learning inefficient study methods, acquiring only low motivation, and failing to develop tolerance for future failures; while failure to meet the needs of slow-learning children may induce self-defeating attitudes of discouragement and pessimism. Similar, although perhaps less extreme, problems may arise in any family where there is more than one child.

Evaluation of children's performance is necessary, both in the family and in the school setting, although it assumes a more formal guise in school. Whether evaluation is done formally or informally, in the family or in the school, it should be guided by three principles. First, the child should be evaluated in terms of his own capacity: has he done as well as he is potentially able to do? Second, he should be evaluated in terms of his reference group, if for no other reason than that he compares himself with this group. Since his own comparison may be distorted (this problem was discussed in Chapter 6 in relation to the self-concept), it is essential that he be given an accurate evaluation. The immediate reference group may consist of either the child's brothers or sisters or his classmates at school. Third, the child's performance should be evaluated according to broad norms based, for example, on a state-wide or nationally selected population or even, conceivably, on a representative international population. Thus, the relatively able child who competes rather unsuccessfully with a superior set of classmates can be made to realize that he is quite competent according to broader standards; or, if he has been consistently compared with below-average children (as many bright lower-class or rural children are), he will know that the future may hold more competitive difficulties for him than he has met in the past.

United States public schools have tended to neglect teaching "human relations." A substantial body of research literature indicates that important aspects of "human nature" can be changed through education —for example, delinquents can be reformed; and children who are low in frustration tolerance be taught to meet failure constructively.

The Middle-Class Teacher and the Every-Class Child

Americans do not like to think of their society as being character-ized by social class. With the term is associated an idea of snob-bery that sits uneasily on the consciences of those who are proud to be citizens of a democracy and who, in their heart of hearts, believe that "every boy can become president."

On the other hand, everyone realizes that social class exists. It is prob-ably here to stay. There is no town so small that it does not have a "wrong side of the tracks" and a "right part of town." In small towns, these differences are less striking than in big ones, but they exist nonethe-less. In rural areas, some farmsteads are "nice," others are "slummy"; although residential distinctions are less clearly marked in rural than in urban areas.

Children from the lowest social classes in large cities may come later than rural and small-town children to recognize their low social status, living, as they are likely to, in segregated slum areas where everyone else is like them. The lower-class rural or small-town child is exposed very early to the fact that his house is shabbier, his clothing less good, than that of the child who lives two blocks away, or on the next farm.

People clique together, socially: professors are more comfortable with doctors than they are with businessmen. When businessmen gather socially, they are not likely to be found in company with members in good standing of the plasterer's union. The banker's daughter is more likely to marry the lawyer's son than the telephone lineman's boy.

There are social-class differences in tastes. An Associated Press article (February 22, 1959, Des Moines, Iowa, *Register*) tells of a beer that is popular with the working but not with the middle or upper social classes. According to this report, the company that makes the beer is trying dis-creetly to give it more snob appeal without at the same time losing the blue-collar clientele. Children of some social classes are more likely to go to college (even though they may not be any brighter) than children of other social classes. Although this difference is partly economic, it is not entirely so, as we have seen in earlier chapters.

Not only do social classes differ in preferences for beverages, food, clothing, and manner of speaking, they also differ in values, religion, intellectual interest, and social beliefs. These differences are exceedingly likely to lead to breakdowns in interclass communication: members of one class almost literally do not understand what members of another class are talking about, what they are striving for, or why their goals are important to them. When there is so gross a deficiency in communication, there is little understanding; and when there is little understanding, suspicion and even hostility are likely to develop. Adding to this likelihood of suspicion and hostility between social classes is the fact that there are frequently very important conflicts of interest between them. The middle- or upper-class landlord resents the cost of improving rental properties occupied by members of the lower class, and his tenants are justifiably bitter about the condition of their dwelling places. The aristocrat resents higher taxes on his inherited fortune; the lower-class widow desperately needs an increase in her "Aid to Dependent Children" funds. The successful medical practitioner resists any move toward "socialized medicine," while the poor neglect their health because they cannot afford doctor and drug bills.

This problem of breakdowns in communication and conflict of interest is particularly acute in public- and parochial-school education, where teachers, who are typically middle-class people, must try to communicate clearly and effectively with children of all social classes. Although the content of this chapter refers primarily to the child's life in school and to his relations with his teachers, it is equally relevant for other professional and lay people who work with children and families: nursing and public-health personnel; speech therapists; recreation, probation, and social workers; public-health oriented doctors and dentists; and members of youth-oriented service clubs. Members of all these groups are, in overwhelming majority, middle class; yet their clientele comes from all social classes, particularly the working or lower class.

The lack of communication between social classes can, and often does, have extremely unfortunate consequences in such areas as labor-management relations. A substantial portion of our difficulties with delinquents is the result of such failure of understanding and communication: the delinquent's difficulties often start as a result of the discrepancy between his lower-class standards and interests and the middle-class values of his teacher. When communication with the school has completely broken down, social work and legal agencies take over—but they too are staffed by the middle class, so that the situation may be little or not at all improved.

Problems of communication also exist between different ethnic and national groups. Education for vast numbers of Negro and Puerto Rican children, for example, is complicated both by their social-class position which is lower, on the average, than that of the so-called core culture, and by their membership in a minority group. To the Puerto Rican child's difficulties usually is added the handicap of speaking a foreign language.

Definitions of Social Class

One of the most widely used definitions of social class is that provided by Warner, Meeker, and Eells (1949). Their "Index of Status Characteristics" is made up by assigning points to four of five social characteristics. The most heavily weighted variable is occupation (of the father, for children; of the self for mature and established adults). A rating of 1 is given to doctors, dentists, judges, professors, and so on, or to persons with large capital investments or high status in business, management, or government. A rating of 7 is given to unskilled laborers, domestic servants, or migrant workers. Each social characteristic is given such a rating, from 1 (high) to 7 (low).

Next most heavily weighted is the source of family or personal income. A rating of 1 is given when at least half the income comes from inherited savings and investments; income from salary or commission, including pension, earns a rating of 4; and a value of 7 is assigned to income from public relief or "nonrespectable" income.

Housing is third in importance in calculating this index. An individual receives a rating of 1 if he lives in a large house of nine rooms or more, in good condition and set in adequate grounds; he is given a 7 if he resides in a house or apartment in bad condition, or in a dwelling not originally intended as a home (such as one that has a store front).

The fourth characteristic from which the index is computed is either the area lived in or the educational level of the father (or the self, for adults). Areas of residence rated as 1 are select residential areas in "the best part of town"; slum areas and neighborhoods in bad repute earn a rating of 7. Since it is difficult to rate "area" in small towns and rural sections, "education of father" may be substituted for the area rating. A 1 is assigned if he has completed as much as one or more years of graduate work at a college or university. For older people, a rating of 7 is assigned for education below third grade; for younger people, a rating of 7 is given for education stopping below eighth grade. This scale, although outdated in some respects (particularly in terms of income so that about 50 percent must be added to its classifications to bring it up to 1967 income levels) remains useful. It also neglects some of the newer occupations, such as astronauts and computer-programmer experts. Since 1949, the social status of elementary school teachers has also improved. Such updating is not difficult, and the present author and his colleagues employ it in their on-going research. Often it is desirable, for replication purposes (that is, it is scientifically profitable) to employ a widely used instrument about which much is known, even though it may have its faults, than to devise a new instrument which appears to be excellent, but about which we have little information. It is for this reason that the author continues to use Warner-Meeker-Eells. Anyone beginning research anew that involves an assessment of socioeconomic status would be well-advised to consult a professional sociologist as that discipline, in the author's judgment, has the greatest *expertise* on the subject.

Social class has been defined in a number of other ways, although most of the definitions involve either paternal (or maternal) occupation or education, or both. Centers (1950, 1951) has developed a "psychological" measure of social class: in effect, he has determined differential attitudes and beliefs that characterize different segments of the population. People are assigned by him to one social class or another depending on the pattern of their answers to his attitude and belief questions. However, Centers also often uses the more conventional variables (such as education or occupation), either independently or in conjunction with the psychological method of classification.

There are obvious deficiencies in these definitions of social class. In one city, the Presbyterian minister, a man trained to the doctoral level, lives in a "poor" part of town: his parsonage is in the same block with a filling station, a bar, and a beer storage warehouse. This man would receive an occupational rating of 1 according to Warner and his colleagues; on his source of income, he would be rated 4, since he is paid a salary; his house would merit a 3, since it is a medium-sized house in fair condition; if he were rated on the area in which he lived, he would receive a 5 at best, and probably a 6; but if the permissible alternative of rating his education were chosen, he would obtain a 1. If, of these last two ratings, area of residence were used, he would be classified as lower-middle class; however, if the basis of ranking were education, his social classification woud be upper middle. Actually, in the city in which he lives, he belongs to the highest social level. Usually, however, the numerical ratings are less variable from one "rating zone" to another than in the example chosen.

Although differential social-class ratings have been worked out for farm populations (Belcher, 1951; Kaufman, 1944, 1946; and Sewell, 1940, 1943) they are not widely used. In one classification system all farmers are listed together as being in class 4 of a hierarchy in which 1 is high and 7 low. But the social differences between the "gentleman farmer," who has inherited large blocks of land, the struggling tenant farmer, who pays rent either in cash or in kind, and the farm laborer are as great as those between a medical doctor or a lawyer and an unskilled laborer.

Despite varying definitions, however, almost all studies of social class have demonstrated differences between classes for variables ranging from intelligence through rate of delinquency to child-rearing practices.

SOCIAL-CLASS CHARACTERISTICS OF TEACHERS

For a number of years, the writer has been a "teacher of teachers." Repeatedly, after using the Warner Index of Status Characteristics as an illustration of how social class is measured, he has asked the students in his classes (who probably represent the more "ambitious" educators) to indicate (anonymously) their social class. Without exception (indeed, almost by definition), these teachers are middle class, and the overwhelming majority of them have improved their class status (they have advanced further educationally and, usually, economically than their parents). In other words, they are upwardly mobile, are proud of their status (although they deplore some of its disadvantages, such as poor salaries, community snooping into their personal affairs, and so on). They also want their own children to continue upwardly mobile—that is, to do still better than they themselves have done. The men, in general, come from humbler families than the women (are more "upwardly mobile").

THE VALUE SYSTEM OF THE MIDDLE CLASS

What are the values of the middle class? No one can say with certainty, nor can a complete list be constructed; nor, if one were constructed, would all members of the middle class agree with the inclusions in the list. However, the following set of values and beliefs appears to be subscribed to by a majority of the middle class, and perhaps particularly by those members of it who compose the professions and lay groups that work with children. Since, of all such groups, teachers ordinarily have the most extensive and immediate impact on children, this list and the discussion accompanying it are linked to teachers, although the broad reference is to middle class in general.

The list represents the author's experience and general reading. It has not been drawn directly from research, although many specific pieces of research are synthesized in it.

The majority of the United States middle-class population, and perhaps especially teachers, appear to support the following values:

1. Most members of the middle class believe in God and act on this belief to the extent of attending church. Usually they do more about church than merely attend. The majority of public-school teachers in the United States are Protestant.

2. Belief in personal cleanliness—clean clothing, clean bodies, clean teeth, clean hair, and clean fingernails—characterizes the middle class in general, and teachers in particular.

3. Teachers, like the middle class as a whole, believe in thrift. Teachers as a group do not have much money to save or invest, but by and large they believe firmly in the American adage that "a penny saved is a penny earned." Through their organizations, they have worked genteelly but with moderate effectiveness toward retirement plans, teacher annuity and group insurance associations, discount buying, and so on. Luxuries, including vacations, are planned for; it is disgraceful to be long overdue on debts. Payments on large debts or installment obligations may be small, but they are punctual. Falling behind in money matters causes real anxiety. For the middle class, possessions are both a sign of status and an indication of security. Ownership of a house, a lot, some real estate, some good stocks is important not only in and of itself, but because of what it represents.

4. Intellect should be used before emotion and should be the controlling factor in managing one's affairs, whether these are personal or concern the larger community. Teachers and the middle class in general are as emotional as anyone else, but they are somewhat ashamed of their emotions and believe that life should be handled according to the dictates of common sense and reason.

5. For such reasons as those expressed in (*4*), teachers and other members of the middle class try to avoid expressing strong emotion and are guilty and ashamed when they do. Of the various emotions, those that are openly aggressive or sexual in nature are particularly to be avoided. People should live peacefully and chastely together.

6. If aggression *must* be expressed, the avenues for expressing it should be socially acceptable. Teachers and other members of the middle class do not like to get into loud abusive arguments, physical combat, or barroom brawls. Their hostilities are likely to be expressed verbally, in the form of gossip (or, at the worst, sarcasm), rather than in more direct and violent ways. Physical aggression is seldom employed, except possibly behind the wheel of a car—honkings, inconsiderateness, glarings, and the like. Although poor driving manners are frowned upon, their use is a not uncommon way for the middle class to vent its spleen.

7. The middle class prides itself on sexual restraint. The stereotype of the teacher, probably as inaccurate as other stereotypes, is a prim and spinsterish woman or a repressed, dour, and somewhat effeminate (or at least not conspicuously virile) man. Coaches escape this stereotype, but they too are expected to lead lives that, sexually, do not go beyond the respectable joys of conventional wedded bliss.

8. Clean and correct language is a matter of middle-class pride. It is permissible for the middle-class male to swear, even sulphurously, if he bangs his thumb in a do-it-yourself project, but only if he is alone or, possibly, in the company of other men like himself. Most particularly, swearing should never be indulged in, no matter what the provocation, when children are within earshot. Shady stories are all right when men are together, but not when women are present. Verbal exchanges between the sexes should be well-laundered. This particular canon has been considerably relaxed in recent years, although the freedom and frankness of verbal exchange between the sexes almost never reaches the point that is typical of the lower class, particularly of the lower-lower class group. The standards of the upper-lower class are not far from those of the middle class, just as the standards of the upper-middle class are not far from those of the upper class. The greatest communication gap is between the lowest social class and all the others.

9. Since the middle class believes in restraint of impulses, particularly those of sex and aggression, and endorses moderation in all things, it follows logically that temperance in the consumption of alcoholic beverages is also advocated. The strictures in this regard are firmer for women than for men, but definitely apply to both sexes. Alcohol releases inhibitions, and alcohol is expensive. Hence it is to be used sparingly if at all. Although the absolute prohibition of teachers' drinking that formerly existed in many parts of the United States has been considerably relaxed, it still holds in many places in the South and the Midwest, where the teacher is expected to set a model of abstemiousness and virtue—all along the line and without exception—for the youth with whose education he is charged.

10. The middle class believes in, although it does not always practice, scrupulous honesty in speech and action (including financial dealings). Although in practice there is much "white-collar crime," in principle middle-class people do not condone lying and stealing (although the managers of hotels, as they tally their towels and ashtrays, have some reason to doubt the extent to which these values are binding). Teachers, being public servants whose salaries are a matter of community knowledge, are more constrained to financial honesty than many other occupational groups within the middle class. Not for them is the padding of the expense account or the partial evasion of the income tax. Their financial affairs are matters of public knowledge. The leading newspaper of one midwestern state, for example, periodically publishes the salaries of all employees of state-supported institutions of higher education. The teacher, if he has larcenous inclinations, must content himself with a few pencils or an occasional package of writing or typing paper. If he falls too far behind with his creditors, his job is likely to be forfeited—indeed, his creditors are not unlikely to be the members of his school board.

11. The middle class remains firmly convinced, although again does not necessarily act on its conviction, that hard work and self-discipline will bring success. That is to say, if one is not impulsive, if one does not gratify his immediate needs for pleasure but postpones them for the sake of later satisfactions, he will in the long run be happier, have more money

in the bank, and be more esteemed, both by the community and by himself. This middle-class ethic is as old as the fable of the grasshopper and the ant. In such a society as ours, the principle is sound enough although many regard it as dull—but it works better for middle- than for lower-class people who, usually, do not make it regardless of how hard they work.

Paradoxically, the middle class also holds such beliefs and values as these: "The breaks are a help. You have to get to know the right people. Influence will get you a long way."

12. Along with sentiments endorsing hard work and self-discipline goes a belief that one should acknowledge and live up to the expectations of others and should do his duty, unrewarding as this may often appear to be. Actually, the middle class believes that doing one's duty is virtuous in and of itself.

Examples of the esteem in which doing one's duty and working hard are held are such statements as these: "You can't let other people down. If you have an obligation, live up to it. I have always tried to do what my mother taught me at her knee was right. If a job is worth doing at all, it is worth doing well. All that I ask of any employee is an honest eight hours' work in a day. Genius is 90 percent perspiration and 10 percent inspiration. A man is just as good as his word. I must maintain my position, and live up to the obligations it entails. The devil finds work for idle hands to do."

13. Finally (and these thirteen points are meant rather as illustrations of middle-class beliefs and values than as a complete list), the middle class believes firmly in learning for learning's sake. Learning and schooling (which are by no means completely synonymous) are seen as vehicles for getting ahead, for bettering oneself. A college education is also viewed as a virtue in and of itself, regardless of the practical use to which it is put. A middle-class family feels disgraced if one of its children fails to finish high school. Girls should have a college education, whether they use it or not, because it "broadens" them. The reading of a biography has higher merit than the reading of a piece of fiction, and heavy or historical fiction is viewed with more favor than light or humorous fiction. However, appreciation of culture purely for its own sake is more an upper- than a middle-class virtue.

Paradoxically, *too much* learning is viewed with suspicion. The United States seems most to esteem the well-educated but practical man. It is uneasy about the scholar—unless he puts his great fund of information to work at some pursuit such as writing encyclopedias (which are held in high esteem because they are practical repositories of knowledge) or (in years not so far gone by) winning television quiz shows that emphasized breadth of information rather than depth of thinking or knowledge.

Such, then, is a crude, incomplete, and subjective map of the beliefs and values that characterize the middle class, one rather typical section of which is made up of teachers. Society not only entrusts these teachers with the imparting of skills, facts, and knowledge to its young, but (since school policy is set by middle-class people) explicitly expects them to pass these values on to their pupils by precept and example.

Middle-Class Values and Lower-Class Children

POPULATION BY SOCIAL CLASS

What is the distribution of United States school children by social class? This question is difficult to answer, but an approximation of the distribution of persons over 14 years of age by social class has been made from the 1950 federal census, and re-checked with the 1960 census, though in less detail. The census gives the occupational listings of people over 14. From these figures, the author has estimated that 39.4 percent of the population is middle or upper class; 55.3 percent belongs to the working class; and 5.2 percent are farmers. As has been pointed out, it is difficult, although not impossible, to classify farm population according to social class. Because of this difficulty, the farm-operating population will be omitted from the present discussion, although the 5.9 percent of the population engaged in farm labor and foremanship will be included. This group, for the most part, falls into the lower-lower socioeconomic bracket.

The 55.3 percent of the population belonging to the working class is made up in a ratio of about 3 to 2 of skilled craftsmen (who are usually classified in the group that Warner, Meeker, and Eells call upper-lower class) and unskilled workers (who, according to the same criterion, are considered lower-lower class). In other words, about one fourth of the adults in the United States are lower-lower class; almost one third, upper-lower class; and fewer than two fifths, middle and upper class. Since there is a tendency for lower-class families to have more children than middle- or upper-class families, one can estimate roughly that of pupils attending United States public elementary schools, nearly two thirds come from lower-class homes. At least one fourth, and probably more, of United States children come from lower-lower class homes. The 1960 census does not change this picture substantially.

The reader should keep in mind that these figures are approximations only (although Hollingshead in 1949 reported roughly these proportions in the midwestern "Elmtown" he studied), and that they are based on a strictly occupational classification. It may also be that distinctions between the middle and the lower classes have become increasingly blurred during the long period of prosperity dating from the early 1940s.

Regardless of the accuracy of the figures suggested above, the large number of lower-class children who must be educated remains beyond dispute. Their teachers, however, are overwhelmingly middle class, either having been born into the middle class or having worked themselves up to it. The implications of differences in social class between teachers and their pupils are set forth in the remaining sections of this chapter.

CONCENTRATION OF RESEARCH BY SOCIAL CLASS

Most psychological and sociological research concerning social class has been based on research populations ranging from the upper-lower to the lower-upper class. Little research has been conducted with lower-lower individuals or groups, except insofar as children from this class have served as research subjects, while attending public school or have been present in one or another type of residential treatment center. Their parents usually do not understand the purposes of research and hence do not cooperate with it. Neither have upper-upper subjects often served in psychological or sociological research. Their children are frequently "sequestered" in private schools, and they are themselves relatively unapproachable. It would, for example, take a psychologist or a sociologist with considerable temerity to request a research interview with, let us say, a senior Vanderbilt about her methods of child-rearing. It is not unlikely that, approached by an intensely devoted research worker, upper-upper class parents would take part in research; but their social position is sufficiently threatening to the conforming and usually somewhat deferential middle-class investigator that they are seldom asked.

This factor of subjective threat may also be partly responsible for the fact that lower-lower class parents have seldom been recruited as research subjects. A tough-minded, intensely motivated research worker could probably secure information about, for example, their child-rearing practices. But in the process he might be sworn at and even punched in the nose. He would have to go into residential areas that are objectionable to him, besides posing the threat of possible physical danger. He would have to translate his questions into simple and highly practical terms. Most research workers do not have these personal attributes of toughness, dedication, and flexibility. Hence, research subjects are rather generally drawn from the middle class, who talk the same language as the research worker, who hold standards similar to him, and who believe in "knowledge for knowledge's sake," just as he does. With such people, he is comfortable.

This focus on the middle class is more pronounced in studies of families (where the parents are involved) than it is in studies of the children themselves, although, as has been mentioned, upper-class children are not often available as research subjects in either public schools or institutions.

Some work has been done with them at the college level (MacArthur, 1955a; MacArthur and Stevens, 1955), since they attend such institutions of higher learning as Yale, Harvard, Princeton, Vassar, and Sarah Lawrence.

In other words, what is said here about the middle-class teacher and the social class of the children with whom she works is based on limited scientific information—information that does not include upper-class children and parents, and information that underrepresents, if indeed it represents at all, the values and beliefs of parents at the bottom of the social heap—the lower-lower class parents.

A substantial portion of the following sections is based on the author's experience with children from urban lower-lower classes, whose behavior had been sufficiently deviant to require their being sent to a residential treatment center for children of below-normal intelligence. In the course of working with them, it was both necessary and easy to get to know their brighter brothers and sisters (although these children and young people often had problems not much less severe than their institutionalized sibs), and their parents (who had their problems as well).

Some of the material is based on the author's close association with lower-lower class farm laborers and their families, both migrant and relatively stable.

The focus of this chapter is on the 25–30 percent of lower-lower class children in the public schools. It is they, more than upper-lower class children, who are referred to by the often-used designation, "lower class."

VALUES OF THE LOWER-LOWER CLASS

How do the beliefs and values of the lower-class child, particularly the child from the lowest socioeconomic stratum, jibe with the beliefs and values of his middle-class teacher?

1. First, how does the lower-class child regard God and religion? Lower-class parents are less likely than middle-class parents to belong to or attend church. When they do, their church is more likely to be one of the fundamentalist Protestant sects or the Roman Catholic Church than the Episcopalian, Methodist, Presbyterian, Baptist, or Jewish churches of their teachers. Hence, to begin with, there is often a religious gap between teachers and such children. This gap does not exist, of course, in parochial schools, where teacher and child are of the same faith. However, even in such schools, the teachers are principally middle-class people, while many of the children are from the lower class.

2. The second principle of middle-class belief, that of cleanliness, is again one that is not shared by lower-class children. These youngsters come typically from large families. If they live in town, their residence is not unlikely to be a cold-water flat; if they come from rural areas, their homes are not likely to include running water. The competition for the

bathtub, if there is one, is high; and water costs money on the meter, or effort if it has to be carried from an outdoor pump. The mother has many things to do besides scrubbing the children and their clothes. Baths, if taken, must often be taken semipublicly and, according to Kinsey (1948), there is a tendency toward taboo of nudity among the lower classes.[1]

Hence, for practical if for no other reasons, cleanliness is a luxury that lower-lower class parents and children find it hard to afford. Since they must live without it, it may well be that they relegate it to a low place in their hierarchy of values.

3. As far as thrift is concerned, the lower-class group has nothing to be thrifty with. One must *have* money to save money. A certain faith in the dependability of the future is essential if one is to plan for it. For the typical lower-class child, faith in the future has received little support. He has learned instead that he had better grab while the grabbing is good, because if he doesn't, one of his brothers and sisters, or his parents, or his peers, will grab instead; and the supply is limited. The lower-class child does not understand what the teacher means when she talks about or exemplifies thrift. As far as he is concerned, she probably "has extra holes in her head." He simply does not comprehend the principle of saving.

4. He is equally uncomprehending when he is asked to put reason before emotion. Reason has never won a street fight, nor enabled him to get the biggest share of the can of beans, nor served to keep his father from beating his mother when he got drunk. The virtues of reason and the desirability of suppressing emotion are values that the lower-lower class child has had no chance to learn. He sees only that reasoning breeds delay of action and serves to reduce the intensity of behavior. Without immediate action and intense drive, the child may not survive in the tooth-and-claw existence that for him is almost routine. Hence, he not only does not share his middle-class teacher's value but holds one opposite to it, and for reasons that in his experience have intense validity.

5. For such reasons, lower-class children fail to appreciate the fifth article of middle-class faith: that strong emotion, particularly sexual and aggressive emotion, should not be manifested. When one is battling for survival—for his fair share of the limited supply of food in the window cooler or ice box, for his turn with the local girl who will let the boys go as far as they want—intense emotion facilitates and spurs action. Standing back, thinking, and suppressing result in failure to reach the goal. Striking out, yelling, and pushing cause others to stand back so that you can go ahead.

It is true that the results of many studies of social class and personal

---

[1] Kinsey reports that although sexuality is freer among the lower classes, body exposure is permitted more often among middle- and upper-class populations.

adjustment have been influenced by the "admission phenomenon" (willingness to respond accurately to an interview or questionnaire). Middleclass children, for example, have been taught that aggression is "wrong." Queried, or given a questionnaire about aggression, they deny many of their aggressive acts and feelings. Lower-class children, on the other hand, have learned different values about aggression, and may be freer (more honest) in admitting overt and covert aggression. The admission phenomenon thus may increase the differences in expressed aggression between the social classes: the middle-class child denies some of his aggression; the lower-class youngster admits it all, or possibly even adds to it (since, for him, it may seem desirable to be aggressive).

McKee and Leader (1955), however, studied competitiveness and aggression as expressed in the *behavior* of middle- and lower-class 3- and 4-year-olds. The children were placed in pairs in a block-building situation. Table 14.1 shows the number of pairings of lower- and middle-class children in which neither child (0), one child (1), or both children (2) demonstrated aggression during the experimental situation.

Table 14.1   *Number of Children in Lower- and Middle-Class Groups Who Showed Aggression in an Experimental Block-Building Situation.*

	NUMBER OF CHLIDREN PER PAIR SHOWING AGGRESSION[a]		
SOCIAL CLASS	0	1	2
Lower	5	5	18
Middle	12	8	8

[a] Chi-square for this table is significant, with *P* between 0.5 and .02.
ADAPTED WITH PERMISSION OF W. E. MARTIN, EDITOR, *Child Development*, AND J. P. McKEE, from McKEE AND LEADER (1955).

This study, which supports the notion that lower-class children display aggression more openly than middle-class children, even as early as the preschool years, clearly was not affected by the admission phenomenon.

Griffiths (1952), in a study of 3,387 parents, 900 of their children aged 6 to 14, and 760 teachers of these children, found that middle-class children showed greater conformity to middle-class values than lower- (or upper-) class youngsters, were less aggressive in their behavior, and were more likely to be submissive and withdrawing. In general, the children, regardless of social class, became more conforming as they grew older.

It might be inferred that for lower-class children, open aggression would be related to status among their peers (that the more aggressive child would be the more popular one). Lesser (1959) became interested in checking this possibility, and asked upper-lower class children in two sixth-grade classes to name the boys (not the girls) who showed most of the following types of aggression: (1) provoked physical aggression (fought back vigorously when pushed around); (2) outburst aggression, of the temper tantrum sort; (3) unprovoked physical aggression; (4) unprovoked verbal aggression; and (5) indirect aggression, such as tattling or damaging other children's popularity.

Such estimates of aggression were obtained for seventy-four boys aged 10 to $13\frac{1}{2}$, and an estimate of their popularity as well as the degree to which they were rejected was also obtained. The index of popularity was the number of rejection votes the child received subtracted from the number of acceptance votes.

The results indicate that only the first type of aggression—fighting back when picked on—was positively related to popularity ($r = .31$). All other forms were negatively related to popularity, with indirect aggression (which in turn was negatively related to provoked physical aggression) correlating —.69 with popularity among one's schoolmates.

Apparently, at least for this population, only "legitimate" (provoked) aggression was positively associated with friendship status in the group, and even this not to a high degree.

One cannot assume, then, that aggression contributes to popularity among lower-class children, even though, as a group, they may be more aggressive than middle-class children. Most of the types of aggression studied by Lesser showed *negative* relations to popularity, and the one positive correlation he found was low and for "justifiable" aggression.

The lower-class child has more chance to acquire combative and aggressive sexual behavior through imitative learning than the middle-class child does. His world is full of fights, of sexual aggression, of the police. His mother may have "called the cops on" his father; his father may have made direct, open, and even brutal sexual advances toward his mother in his presence. The discipline that has been imposed on him is more likely to have been physical than verbal. One writer (LeShan, 1952) describes the discipline in a lower-lower class family as consisting, in the majority of instances, of threatening (and probably administering) immediate punishment (or reward). For example: "You go back to bed or I'll beat you with this leather strap." Of 101 observed instances of discipline in this study, 57 were of this type.

The lower-class child's inclination to use his reason, and to try to predict logically, is further discouraged by the inconsistent nature of parental discipline. LeShan reports that of the 101 observed instances of discipline, 28 were unpredictable both from the point of view of the child and from that of the observer. He gives the following illustration: "The father had brought a 3-year-old daughter some candy cigarettes.

The child pretended to smoke them, flicking off the ashes, and so forth. When she did this, the father took them away from her and spanked her for 'putting on the dog' " (p. 590). He also tells of a mother who described the weaning of one of her children thus: "Yeah, one day she threw the bottle out of her crib and I gave it back to her and she didn't want it so I never gave it to her again" (p. 591).

LeShan also states that "the lower-lower class child plays on the streets away from adult supervision. Here he is to a large degree at the mercy of his own impulses with reward or punishment following immediately on his actions. Rewards here may be in terms of motor activity, physical gratification, and so on. The parents are at work or are usually unaware of what he is doing" (p. 591).

For such reasons, the repression or suppression of strong emotion and the use of reason have, for the lower-class child, little familiarity or appeal. In his way of life, intellectualization and planning may actually be maladaptive.

6. The sixth middle-class value, socially acceptable expression of aggression, makes equally little sense to the lower-class child. He has not seen people, his parents or his peers, behave in such a fashion. For him, gossip is thin gruel; and sarcasm is likely to result in a beating.

7. Nor is it fashionable for the lower-class child to repress sex. As has been reported by Kinsey (1948, 1953), persons from the lower social classes are freer and more social in their expression of sex than are those from the middle class. This freedom undoubtedly includes talking about as well as indulging in sex. Lower-class children, partly because of their living arrangements, live openly with sex to a degree that is inconceivable in a middle-class family. Many children live together with their parents and other adult relatives in crowded quarters; several people sleep in the same bedroom; and uninhibited lovers are forced to do their courting on streets, in doorways, and in alleys. In one fatherless family the mother carried on her business of prostitution in the room in which her 7- and 9-year-old sons slept. MacKinlay Kantor, in *Andersonville,* gives a graphic account of the public nature of sex in a Civil War lower-lower class rural family. The present author has known many children of migrant farm laborers whose sexual sophistication was a source of amazement to him and a constant source of scandal to the author's middle-class parents.

What is sacred and taboo for the middle-class teacher in the area of sex may be a matter of indulgence and free expression for the lower-class child. Hence, the child may pose a distinct threat to the controlled and perhaps inhibited teacher.

8. The lower-class child shares little, if any, of the middle-class teacher's horror of filthy talk, "impure" accents, and messy grammar. He talks bluntly, in the argot he has learned in his particular portion of the wrong side of the tracks, and is interested only in communication, not in

form. The speech of the child from the New York City or Detroit slums may be almost incomprehensible to the midwestern professional worker or to the graduate of one of the good eastern colleges.

9. Nor is overindulgence in alcohol regarded with the same disdain by the lower-class child as by his middle-class peer or teacher. To people from the lower class, alcohol and sex often afford the only available, albeit transitory, escapes from an all too grim reality. The not uncommon case of the worker squandering his weekly pay in the saloon on the way home, leaving the family larder unstocked, provided powerful ammunition for those who worked to usher in the national era of prohibition. Almost the only way for a middle-class person to understand the role of drink in lower-class society is to spend a Saturday night in a bar in the wrong part of town, listening and observing. The function of alcohol and drunkenness as an escape becomes tragically obvious. Such a learning experience may be a little risky, is more open to middle-class males than to females, and is perhaps rather distasteful, but it provides an important insight concerning lower-class children. From babyhood and early childhood (when they cannot be left home alone), these children frequently accompany their parents on periodic excursions to the neighborhood drinking spot, which also serves as a neighborhood social club. Open sexuality and violent aggression typically accompany and follow evenings on the town, and the child is exposed to these manifestations as frequently and as early as to drinking itself.

10. It is probable that lower-class children and their parents endorse honesty as strongly as the middle class does. It takes a brave child, however, not to lie when the truth will be followed by a beating. It is easier to return a lost five-dollar bill when another one is available than it is to give it up when it is the only one you have ever had—and, perhaps, are likely to have in the foreseeable future. If you are well-fed and have an amply stocked toy chest, it is easy not to snitch from the bakery stall or the notions counter; but if your stomach is growling, or you have never in your life owned a doll, the drive to do a little shoplifting is substantial. Therefore, although the two classes may not be so far apart in endorsing honesty as they are in endorsing other values, there are genuine differences in drive, and probably in practice.

Dishonesty in the form of shoplifting, pilfering "souvenirs" from restaurants, lying, and other forms of deceit is, however, also characteristic of middle-class children, both during and prior to adolescence. It has been pointed out that, with reference to such things as hotel towels, their elders set them an example little better than that provided by lower-class parents. It is also probable that hypocrisy "Do as I say, not as I do" with its attendant disillusionment, is as frequent among the middle class as among the lower class.

11. The lower-class child has little reason to believe that hard work and self-discipline result in success. Middle-class fathers do not put in eight hours of brutal labor swinging a pick. Such labor is hard; it is done in the heat and the cold; it is dirty; and it obtains relatively few of the world's goods. Nor is the unskilled and uneducated father likely to win conspicuous advancement by his diligence. He remains a day laborer— secure, indeed, from being fired as long as times are good; but at the mercy of his boss, the times, and the weather. He does not get ahead. All he has to look forward to is more of the same. The relatively well-educated and well-trained middle-class father, on the other hand, can, given any breaks at all, demonstrate clearly to his child the advantages of diligence, night work, thinking about the job over the weekend, and so on. He gets a raise; he achieves a promotion; his self-esteem and his family's economic well-being are enhanced.

In other words, our society is not organized to demonstrate to the lower-lower class child the virtues of hard work and self-discipline; but his failure to appreciate these virtues leaves him, psychologically, far removed from his middle-class teacher.

12. The same type of argument holds for the twelfth middle-class value. The lower-class child's learning does not include convincing illustrations that doing one's duty and living up to the expectations of others pays off. If doing one's duty is rewarded only by being allowed to keep on working at the same dirty job, why do one's duty? If the expectation of others is that the old man will get drunk on Saturday night and beat up the old lady, and this state of affairs does, indeed, occur, wherein lies its virtue?

13. Finally, what is there in his life to teach the lower-class child that learning for the sake of learning is good? He grows up in a home where there are few, if any, books, magazines, or newspapers. His parents have probably done poorly in school and avoid rather than court culture because their memories of their own school days are bitter. Life is hard; intellectual satisfactions do not fill an empty stomach nor a pressing sexual urge; higher education, which might prepare the child for an "easy" job, is out of the question for practical reasons (no money; no family backing, either practical or psychological; and, all too often, not enough ability). The pleasures of the lower-class child are therefore likely to be those that are immediately available to the flesh, rather than those that delight the mind or result in advancement through education. The author strongly recommends Claude Brown's (1965) *Manchild in the Promised Land* as a "non-prettied up" autobiography vividly illustrating the above points and the gap in communication between middle and lower classes (and Negro and white).

One cannot escape the conclusion that the gap in values between middle-class teachers and lower-class children is enormous. Of the thirteen values and beliefs that have been examined, almost complete divergence exists for eleven. Although there is agreement in principle on the other two (religion and honesty), the style of implementing them —the actual practice—differs sharply from the middle to the lower class.

Shared values facilitate communication; disparate values estrange people from each other. The unreasoning bitterness between Israelis and citizens of the United Arab Republic has its roots in different values (including different economic interests), and precludes even the effort toward, let alone the effectiveness of, communication. We tend to condemn, reject, and exclude those whose values differ from ours; this tragic state of affairs quite generally characterizes relations between lower-class children and middle-class teachers. The failure of teachers to understand such youngsters probably retards the education of at least one fourth of a nation, and is certainly related to one of our most serious educational problems.

There are, of course, middle-class teachers who are very successful in reaching lower-class children. Such flexible, creative, and sensitive teachers succeed in bridging the values chasm and provide models for many youngsters in their classes. This sort of child-teacher relationship has probably played a role in the lives of most young people who have successfully escaped from the lower class. In such cases, however, the identification of the child with his teacher and her values often partially estranges him from his family.

SOCIAL CLASS AND SOCIAL ACCEPTANCE

It has been indicated earlier in this chapter that lower-class children are less well-accepted by their peers than middle-class children. Research supporting this point of view is provided by such papers as that of Grossman and Wrighter (1948), who found that social class was related to social acceptance among a group of 117 sixth-graders. The higher the level of the father's occupation, the more popular the child. The better-accepted children in this study were also better adjusted, according to a pencil-and-paper test of adjustment. A negative relation between popularity and poor adjustment has been found in a number of studies: McCandless and his colleagues (1956), for example, obtained a correlation of —.32 between anxiety and popularity for public-school fourth-, fifth-, and sixth-graders. Thorpe (1955) reports similar although lower correlations between neuroticism and popularity for British children, as does Trent (1957) for institutionalized delinquent boys. Holding the influence of rejections constant (delinquent boys tend to form gangs, so that members of one gang may, for loyalty's sake, reject the most popular boy in another gang or clique), anxiety and popularity in Trent's population correlated —.29, a figure remarkably similar to that obtained by McCandless *et al.*

Sewell and Haller (1956, 1959) have explored in some detail the relations between children's adjustment and their social class, and find indications that low social status is associated with poor personal adjustment (as measured by the California Test of Personality) of a type that seems likely to hinder social acceptance. In a study of 1,462 fourth- to eighth-grade children (1959), they found that lower-class children, when compared with those from higher social classes, showed more concern with their families' social status, worried more about how others rate their ability and achievement ("My classmates don't think I'm bright"), rejected their homes and parents ("I often wish I had some other parents"), and confessed to neurotic symptoms, such as stomach upsets, lack of appetite, dizzy spells, and so on. Sewell and Haller theorize that lower-class children adopt their parents' values during the years before they enter school, then find high-prestige people (teachers) endorsing standards and holding goals that are sharply different from those they have learned at home. The conflict engendered by this situation leads to anxiety, parental rejection, uncertainty, and confusion.

Brown and Bond (1955) provide some interesting suggestions that scoial class may be of greater importance in the social acceptance of girls than of boys, at least in the rather unusual (impoverished southern) community they studied. Their rural sixth-grade group was made up of thirty girls and twenty boys, all Negro, who came mostly from the lower-lower class. The correlation between social status and popularity for girls was an amazing $+.82$, whereas it was negligible for boys. The status factor that seemed most important for the boys was their proficiency at baseball and basketball, skills that cut across social-status lines. Davis (1957) reports similar results for ninety-seven public school eighth-grade boys in a "northeastern" city of about 23,000. McQuire, Lanmon, and White (1953), and McGuire, White, and Novak (1954) find, for high-school populations, that social-class discriminations are not made against lower-class children who accept the middle-class value of continuing into high school (into eleventh and twelfth grades) but that, for younger children, social-class bias exists. However, by the time he has reached the eleventh grade, the child has probably adopted middle-class values.

In general, we may say that the peer relations of lower-class youngsters do nothing to enhance their enjoyment of school; both teachers and classmates seem to reject them.

The Middle-Class Teacher
and Middle- and Upper-Class Children

No problem of unshared values plagues relations between teachers and middle-class children. Such children begin to absorb "appropriate" values and beliefs with their mothers' milk; and these are deeply, although not always consistently, ingrained by the time they are ready for kindergarten or first grade. If the child is assigned homework, his parents see that he gets it done. If his report card shows poor conduct marks and subject deficiencies, firm pressure is placed on him to better the conduct and remedy the deficiencies. Ordinarily, disciplinary emergencies in the school find the parent ranked solidly behind the teacher rather than the child. If the child does well as far as the teacher is concerned—that is, gets good marks and receives general approval—the parents reward him richly for it.

In earlier sections of this book, we have presented evidence indicating that the middle-class child (and probably the upper-class child) identifies more strongly with his parents, and consequently with the general standards of school and society, than the lower-class child does. He may have been toilet-trained and weaned more strictly and earlier than the experts judge advisable; but, at the same time, he has been more consistently loved and guided, and his major wants have been attended to. Hence his transfer of identification to the teacher is ordinarily quick and automatic, and meets with his parents' approval. This identification results in his respecting his teachers, conforming to their wishes, and adopting their goals. Consequently, the middle-class child is generally a docile, conforming, and respectable classroom citizen. Such behavior, and the achievement that ordinarily accompanies it, are in turn rewarding to teachers—a sign that they are doing well, are succeeding. Consequently, teachers give even more reward to middle-class children. Although often a disproportionate share of the teacher's total attention is of necessity directed toward the relatively recalcitrant and slow-learning lower-class children, this attention is, on the whole, more negative than that given to middle-class youngsters.

Although somewhat fewer teachers than in former years (Beilin, 1959) regard nonconforming and aggressive behavior as "the most serious behavior problem a child can have," they still view with jaundiced eye any child or episode that interferes with the orderly conduct of classes. Hence, lower-class children, because they are relatively nonconforming and aggressive, probably receive more than their share of teacher disapproval. On the other hand, and particularly in the lower grades, lower-class children are frequently apathetic and incurious (they have learned that this is the safe way to live). Thus, they bore and fail to challenge or even attract the attention of the teacher.

Hollingshead (1949), in his original data, and Opstad (1957), in a reworking of these data, show that lower-class youngsters are relatively slow-learning (a condition not to teachers' liking); and that, as a group, they receive a substantially greater number of low and failing grades than would be predicted even from their relatively low intellectual status.

In sharp contrast to his lower-class peer, the typical middle-class child conforms, is less aggressive, is brighter, and works harder. For these reasons, he reaps more academic rewards of all sorts. There are, of course, many middle-class children who are *not* conforming, who *are* aggressive, and who *do* underachieve. But, in general, their social class has taught them the attitudes and motives most conducive to success in the United States classroom.

It may be that there is an important distinction to be made within the middle class. The upper-middle class does not always solidly support teachers. Its members are often critical of teachers' methods and of the curriculum, although they agree on common goals. The very mobile parent of the upper-middle class often pushes the child beyond his capacities. Not to take note of this distinction is to ignore the common neurotic patterns shown by this group.

Nevertheless, the broad general principles that have been developed for the middle class probably hold for those upper-class children who attend public schools. According to some (MacArthur, 1955), the upper-class child (and adult), when compared with the middle-class child (and adult), is interested rather in making himself a "good" person than in achieving an objective success; is oriented more to the present and the past, and less to the future (toward which the middle class is primarily oriented); is more selflessly interested in his fellow-man; and is more strictly disciplined. If it is true that upper-class children have such attributes, they should fit even more easily than middle-class children into schools as they are now operated.

The School Situation of the Lower-Class Child

EARLY CHILDHOOD IN THE LOWER CLASS

It is difficult to reconstruct the infantile experiences of lower-class children. It has been assumed that such children are treated more casually and in a more relaxed fashion than middle-class children, although Bronfenbrenner (1959) suggests that this assumption may no longer be correct. Until fairly recently, however, the lower-class child is more likely to have been breast-fed on demand, weaned relatively late, toilet-trained later and less urgently, and given more freedom (not confined to a play-pen). He may also have had more total contact with adults.

But, by the time he is physically mobile, it is likely that a new brother or sister will have come along. At that point, observation suggests that he is likely to be abruptly "dropped" by his mother. Lower-class fathers seldom give their children the attention provided by middle-class fathers. Casual observations made in slum areas suggest that children from the ages of 2 or 3 years enjoy partial freedom from supervision, playing un-guarded on streets and sidewalks. What supervision they receive comes from an older sister or brother who resents being tied down, and whose supervision is something less than charitable.

As has been mentioned previously, the result of these practices may well be the production of a personality in the lower-class child which is moderately secure—secure enough so that he functions without social or emotional breakdown—but which includes an incomplete identification with adults (although, as we have seen, he is likely to sex-type (adopt mas-culine or feminine behavior) earlier than the middle-class child). He needs other people and will manifest a certain regard for their rights, but this social hunger, perhaps because of his obscure feelings of having been let down and deserted by adults, is likely to be satisfied through strong iden-tification with peer groups rather than adult figures and standards. In-deed, there may be strong hostility toward adults.

TEACHER-CHILD PERCEPTIONS OF EACH OTHER

As a result the teacher, with all of his or her proper middle-class values, is likely to face a class whose members share few of these values and, indeed, disagree sharply with the majority of them. In addition, lower-class children as a group, are rather distrustful of adults in general, par-ticularly those in authority positions.

The teacher sees sullen and indifferent, or actually defiant, children who are on the whole less bright, less clean, more aggressive, more overtly sexual, and less book-and-study oriented than the middle-class members of the group. The teacher needs his satisfactions, just as the child does. Because such children provide few rewards, they are rejected. Himmel-weit (1955) has shown that similar biases in favor of the middle class exist in Britain.

For their part, the children see a hostile foreigner, making new and (to them) unreasonable demands. Some psychological research indicates that one will conform to the values of groups in which he sees a possibility of being accepted, whereas he will reject (at least privately) the values of groups which he sees as rejecting him (Dittes and Kelley, 1956). Many, and perhaps most, lower-class children see little possibility of acceptance by middle-class groups. They are therefore unlikely to make any great effort to conform or accede to demands for such changes in their way of life as are typically made by teachers.

What, then, do lower-class children do in middle-class dominated classrooms? This depends greatly on the power of the teacher. If the teacher is weak (a poor disciplinarian) the child and his buddies will run wild, using all their energy destructively. With a strong teacher (and the typical middle-class teacher is by no means weak), the children will become passive. Their striking back will take the form of apathy and non-learning, feats they can manage very efficiently.

There are differences, of course, in classroom atmosphere between urban and small-town or rural classrooms. The almost automatic discrimination against lower-class children probably operates less strongly and automatically in urban areas. In cities, housing and school segregation by social class as well as ethnic group exists. Hence, teachers in a given school—particularly an elementary school—may be confronted by a class relatively homogeneous in social status. In such a situation children may be perceived more as individuals and less as representatives of an "inferior" or a "superior" social class. But in areas of less population density, classes will be more heterogeneous, and the conditions for discrimination by social class may be maximized.

LOWER-CLASS PARENTS AND THE SCHOOL

Teachers, in their struggle to control, motivate, and possibly inspire the lower-class children in their rooms, do not have recourse to the support of the children's parents, as they do with both normal and problem middle-class children. Lower-class parents have themselves had educational experiences similar to those their children are going through. They distrust the middle class in general, have had unhappy experiences with teachers in their youth, are likely to have dropped out of school well before the end of their senior high-school year and, in general, are not reinforcing to or supportive of public education. They do not see (and perhaps they have some justification) that education has done them much good, nor do they regard it as an important goal for their children.

One index of this attitude is provided by attendance at PTA meetings. Middle-class parents may complain that these are anesthetic experiences, and the stereotype of mother dragging father off to PTA has provided the basis for much cartoon and joke humor. But the fact remains that middle-class mothers and fathers attempt to work with the school, whether by policing junior's homework, attending PTA meetings, or backing the school bond issue. Only rarely do lower-class parents, particularly those of the lower-lower class, give even such token support of the school as is represented by PTA attendance.

Stendler (1951) interviewed 250 mothers of first-graders and analyzed her interviews in terms of attitudes toward school. In four of the five areas of analysis she found social-class differences, most of them indicating less school support by lower-class mothers. Lower-class children were less likely than middle-class children to have attended preschool (almost 100 percent of the upper- and upper-middle class parents had sent their children to preschool, but only 14 percent of the lower-lower class parents had done so). Head Start, to some degree, has probably changed this. There was, in the interview, little difference by class in the open criticism leveled against the school (this is not surprising; since the interviewers were middle-class, academic people, open criticism was not likely to be voiced). But the lower-class families had received their child's first report card with indifference; few of them had gone to school for a parent-teacher conference when this was substituted for a written card. Upper-class families were more likely to accept the report card with reservations, and to hold up higher standards for their children. More of the upper- and upper-middle class families had taught their children the alphabet, nursery rhymes, and writing or reading before they entered first grade, although all of the lower-class parents had at least taught their children to count to 10 before starting school. As one went down the social-class ladder, parents held progressively lower educational aspirations for their children, although half of the lower-class mothers reported that they hoped their children would finish high school.

Viewing the mother as the primary socializing agent for her child's educability, including his perception of the role of pupil, mothers' attitudes toward education and their position in the social structure of the public schools was examined. One-hundred-sixty-three Negro mothers of 4-year-old children from four social status groups were asked to respond to a photo of a mother and teacher and make suggestions for changes in the schools. The vagueness and passivity of the lower-class mothers' responses were assumed to serve as a model for their children's conception of the role of pupil and to interfere with successful adaptation to the school (Bear, Hess and Shipman, 1966).

Improving Relations Between Teachers and Lower-Class Children

The task of improving relations between teachers and lower-class children has received the scantiest possible research attention, although forward-looking educators have done considerable thinking, talking, and writing about this problem. The present section is based on clinical experience rather than research data. The 1960s are seeing more such work, although as this is written (1967), the state of our knowledge remains very incomplete.

APPRECIATION OF AND RESPECT FOR THE INDIVIDUAL

The first step toward improving relations between lower-class children and their teachers requires that teachers, either "naturally" or as a result of their training, have a sincere respect for human beings. Psychotherapists speak of the impossibility of doing constructive therapy if the therapist does not possess a deep respect and regard for the worth and essential integrity of the patient's personality. Such an attitude is also fundamental to many religions, and the teachings of Christ, for example, are quite explicit on this point. Such an attitude does not necessitate abandoning one's own values, but it demands willingness to listen to and understand the different value systems of others. This chapter has so far had a certain "snob" overtone—the middle class is better controlled, intellectually superior, more achievement-oriented, and so on. Snobbishness was not intended. However, for a stable society in which people cooperate and postpone their own immediate gratification for the good of others, standards similar to those of the middle class (although perhaps less harsh, less rejecting, and more flexible) seem to be necessary.

KNOWLEDGE OF CHILDREN'S PERSONAL AND FAMILY LIVES

If the psychological schism between teachers and lower-class children (and all children, for that matter) is to be closed, teachers must know in more detail, and regard with more sympathy, the circumstances of their charges' personal lives. For lower-class children, these circumstances are frequently tragic indeed. Biographies like those of the brother and sister discussed below are typical rather than exceptional.

Case Histories of a Lower-Lower Class Brother and Sister Elsie and Ronald Beal have been known to the author for many years. Their biographies as given here differ from their true life stories only to the extent of a change in name.

Elsie and Ronald were sequential in a family that eventually included fourteen children and depended, for its income, on the earnings of the father, a ranch laborer or hired man. Elsie was the sixth, Ronald the seventh child in the family, and their birthdays were separated by fifteen months. It was rumored in the community, and the physical appearance of the children gave the rumor an aspect of truth, that at least three of the children who preceded them in the family were the product of a temporary union between the mother and a man other than Elsie's and Ronald's father. The mother, a huge woman, had at least some ethnic characteristics of a group that, in the section of the United States in which these children lived, had attributed to it inferior status.

At no time during their childhood did the children live in a house of more than four rooms, and much of their life was spent in two-room shacks. Never, until late adolescence, did they encounter running water, a flush toilet, or electric light—except possibly, on an occasional Saturday visit to the conglomeration of frame stores and small houses that constituted the shopping and recreation center for the area.

Since part of their father's "hire" consisted of free eggs and milk, these rural lower-lower class children did not experience the malnutrition that might have been their lot in an urban slum. Consequently, they grew normally and, as elementary-school children, were sturdy and healthy. Elsie, beneath the dirt that caked her, was a beautiful, exotic-looking child. Ronald was a big, strapping boy whose appearance, while not handsome, was completely acceptable, particularly in the summer when he was able to go swimming occasionally to remove the dirt.

Elsie was bright and, in early elementary school, learned to read with ease, competing well with the "respectable" children of the men and women who owned the ranches on which her father and other fathers like him earned a meager living. Ronald was at best of dull-normal intelligence and repeated grades consistently, spending an average of about two years per grade until he dropped out of school at 13, when he refused to return to spend a second year in the fifth grade. At 13, being an early-maturing boy and having inherited his mother's impressive build, he was as big as the average man, and was able to work for nearly man's wages on the neighboring ranches.

These children were never accepted by other youngsters in the rural one-room school they attended. At noon they, with their numerous brothers and sisters, shared poorly balanced lunches from a common paper bag (metal lunch boxes were at that time *de regueur*). The "respectable" children laughed at them, and were prevented from more open aggression only by the fact that Ronald was a big, strong boy with a violent temper; and he and Elsie, along with their brothers and sisters, were well able to defend themselves and join in common defense against anyone who got too much out of line. Although Ronald (and his brothers) were well enough coordinated, they were never invited to play the boys' games of football and basketball. The rationale of their more prosperous schoolmates, had they been asked to express one, would perhaps have been: "They have none of the gear. Why should they play?" But a rationale was never solicited, either by the tribe of Beals or by any teacher. It was simply accepted by the Beals, by other children of their social class, by the middle-class children, and by the teachers that the Beals and "their like" were one group, and the children of the landholders another. The middle-class children as well as the teachers exercised constant vigilance over lunch baskets, desks, and cloakrooms, because everyone "knew" that, given half a chance, the Beals would raid lunch boxes for goodies and desks for pencils, erasers, compasses, and the like. Whenever anything disappeared, accusations were first leveled against the Beals and their group. This practice was never questioned, even though the possessions were usually found where their careless owners had left them.

Elsie was the brightest of the Beals, Ronald's academic performance being more typical of the family. But her brightness earned her little more praise and acceptance than Ronald received. She completed the eighth grade, as much alone socially as when she had begun the first. At this time she was 13, and (as the community realized shortly thereafter) pregnant. The father of the child was never identified, although there were many rumors about who he was. Her baby, when born, became simply one more Beal. Elsie, strikingly beautiful in her early maturity, found a "respectable" husband in spite of her illegitimate baby, and moved from the Beal hovel to a respectable farm home. However, no women's group, no church group, gave recognition to her new status. Following her marriage, she made a few somewhat flaunting but pathetic appearances at Sunday services, but since she was never greeted or talked to, she soon dropped the whole idea. Within two years of her marriage, her husband found her in bed with one of his hired hands and sued for, and was granted, a divorce and custody of the child that had been born to him and Elsie. She was not allowed visiting privileges, nor support.

Unable to face return to the Beal household, Elsie removed herself to the nearest good-sized city, entered prostitution (having had the way paved for her by one of her older sisters, who was already in the business), and was later arrested for defending with a gun a current boy friend who was being sought by the police for armed robbery. By the time she was 30, she had been through three marriages, was a professional prostitute, and had spent about six years in jails, reformatories, and prisons. She was also racked with venereal disease and had given birth to a total of four children, none of whom remained with her.

Ronald, after leaving school at 13 (a year after Elsie was graduated from eighth grade) worked on the ranches for a year or so; then joined the Beal migration to the "big city," where he too soon ran afoul of the law because of a clumsily executed burglary. Released from the reformatory because of good behavior, he married at 18 and settled down to steady work as a manual laborer. He managed to go straight for eight years, during which time he and his wife became the parents of five children. At that time he, along with some of his blood kin and some of his in-laws, was sent to the penitentiary for bootlegging.

Neither Elsie's nor Ronald's life has changed substantially in subsequent years. Both are now middle-aged minor criminals, and several of their children are following in their footsteps. Elsie's and Ronald's lives have been very similar to the lives of their older and their younger brothers and sisters. The community costs have, of course, been enormous in terms of social-work efforts, foster homes for the children, aid to dependent children, police workups, court trials, and incarceration.

But the Beals, as children, had possibilities. They were healthy, not unduly stupid, and, in Elsie's case, actually quite bright. Several, including Elsie, were strikingly handsome. Society, however, never did anything *for* them—and, eventually they did something *to* society (and, of course, themselves).

In terms of family circumstances, Elsie and Ronald certainly had at least two strikes against them. But, had teachers really thought about the lives these youngsters lived and stressed the positive characteristics they had instead of dwelling on the negative ones, something different might have happened to them. Had the members of the church congregation supported Elsie, as the tenets of their faith directed them to, in her tentative (although self-centered) moves toward respectability following her marriage, instead of concentrating on "putting her in her place," her life might have taken on a new look and a new purpose. But neither this nor much of anything else benign occurred, and Elsie and Ronald continue to live out their lives in a fashion destructive to themselves and society.

CONTROL TECHNIQUES OF WARMTH PLUS STRENGTH

The lower-class child, like the delinquent, approaches middle-class authority figures with suspicion. If authorities show weakness, the lower-class child will ride over them, in subtle or not so subtle ways. But if they show coldness, rejection, or unfairness, they only confirm him in his belief that he will "never get a square shake from a teacher." Hence, as has been said before, an initial (and experimental) attitude on the part of the teacher should combine warmth, fairness, and strength. Democracy in the lower-class schoolroom is a luxury that must wait until rapport has been built with the children and they have started along the road to self-control—a road along which, as a group, they have not traveled far.

REALISTIC EVALUATION AND APPRECIATION OF NEEDS

The statement, "To guide the child, we must know and appreciate his needs," has been made so often in the past twenty-odd years that it has become rather shopworn. It has often been made by intelligent people, but it is made equally often by those who truly believe that to understand is necessarily to condone and forgive.

The point taken here is not that to understand the need of a delinquent is to condone his behavior, but rather that to understand his needs, in a knowledgeable way, is to be able to guide him more effectively. Guidance may involve counseling, toughness, affection, remedial teaching. No technique should be arbitrarily ruled out, and all techniques should be regarded as tentative and exploratory. Certainly, love is not enough. Srtictness and punishment, by themselves, seldom seem to work much good, except to relieve the feelings of the punisher. Counseling alone does not help the adolescent who cannot read above the first-grade level; on the other hand, remedial reading doesn't seem to accomplish much if it is not accompanied by warmth and understanding (even a modified therapeutic atmosphere).

To be genuinely successful with lower-class children, middle-class teachers must face frankly the issues that have been discussed earlier in this chapter. Abstractions and social niceties have little meaning for children who may not have had enough to eat before they arrive at school in the morning. These children will learn things they see as related to their goals (and their goals are much more immediate than their teacher's), but if the subject matter presented to them has no discernible bearing on what they want out of life, they will not learn it.

Such children *can* learn to relate certain academic skills to their way of life. The author has seen child after child leave an institution for high-grade mentally defective and predelinquent children without a smattering of reading, even though they may have received regular and remedial reading instruction for ten or more years; and he has seen them return to the institution a year or two later for a visit, reading comfortably at the fifth- or sixth-grade level even though they have not had a minute's formal instruction in the meantime. The following experience is typical:

> All the teachers ever did was yell at me. I was the dumbest kid in the class. I just didn't care. I didn't know that reading could actually help me. But when I went out on parole, I got a job in the plant. I felt like a fool. All the other guys could read the paper. I couldn't hardly even write my name, let alone read. But I must of learned something all those years in school, because when I figured I had to read to get ahead in my job and keep from making a fool of myself in front of the other guys, why pretty soon I learned to read. It was dumb not to of a long time ago.

Why did these boys learn to read? Simply because they found that their needs were intimately and obviously connected with the skill of reading. Could this not have been accomplished earlier in their school career? The writer believes that it could have been. What is needed is, first, a teacher who is interested, warm, alert; who appreciates them as persons, and who can thus function as an identification model for whose approval and understanding they are "willing" to learn to read. Secondly, teachers must have sufficient insight into the problems of these children to be able to link reading (and numbers) convincingly with their later life: "Look, you're going to be working in the plant. How can you figure out the way to the men's room—the way to operate the spray gun—the menu at the company cafeteria—the deductions from your pay check—the union contract—if you don't know how to read? Ok, don't be a jerk! Let's get this show on the road!"

Unusual terminology for the elementary-school classroom, yes—but more effective than most of the methods typically used. Finally, a basic demand—perhaps *the* basic demand—children make of the school (though sometimes only implicitly) is that it help them become *competent*. This point, well-buttressed by research, cannot be too strongly made. The demand for competence training becomes more explicit and stronger the older the child, but is present from the earliest grades.

TEXTBOOK CHANGES

Another educational practice that would help lower-class youngsters is the use of reading texts that relate to their life experiences. In United States classrooms the standard introduction to reading is a bland diet indeed. The main characters are likely to be well-scrubbed, curled, and attractive children who almost invariably come three to a family: a handsome boy of 6 or 7, a winsome girl of 5 or 6, and an omnipresent, amusing, and cuddly "baby" of somewhere between 18 and 24 months. The parents of these children range in coloring from blond to very light brunet. They are youthful in appearance, lissome in figure, well-dressed, and endowed with a limitless amount of patience, pleasantness, and time for stories. Important activities include birthday parties and excursions from their pleasant suburban house to the country, where (often) grandma lives in an attractive frame house equipped with enough twin-bedded bedrooms to sleep the whole family. In the "farmhouse" there is running water, at least a bath and a half, electric light, and central heating. Grandma's conformance to "country" ways is likely to be limited to a pony that may be hitched to a freshly painted cart for the amusement of the grandchildren. She may also have a cow that the neighbor or hired man comes in to milk.

When the children in the family need a new blue coat, the matter is simple—their mother simply takes them to the store to buy it. The family almost always has pets, who share the large pleasant lawn with the children. These pets run to cocker spaniels and fluffy kittens with endearing ways.

It is possible for the lower-class child to share emotionally in the experiences of such a family to about the degree that he shares emotionally in the experiences of a family in central Afghanistan. His is a world of cold-water flats and not enough to eat at breakfast, of a rugged, adult-independent existence among the teeming life of sunbaked or ice-covered pavements. There should be some sort of story material—less harsh, admittedly, than his life actually is—that relates more directly to these experiences. Such stories would also, one suspects, add spice and zest to the reading experiences of the middle-class child, besides being more honest in their acknowledgment of what life is really like. Six-year-olds are reasonably sophisticated individuals. They have known people who are divorced. They have experienced anger from adults. They have seen or known of automobile accidents and death. They need not be fed a diet of lukewarm sugar water. Even the bland, positive relation between husband and wife and parents and children, as it is represented in typical readers, fails to catch the depth and intensity of true-life love and family relations.

The source books for arithmetic are less vulnerable to the criticism of complete separation from life; but they too leave something to be desired in their relation to the problems faced by lower-class children. For example, a study by Marshall and Magruder (1960) demonstrates that knowledge of money and skill in personal expenditure of money depend on how much money a child has had to spend. Regardless of the type of parental guidance he has received, a child will tend to be ignorant and foolish about money if he has had none to spend but relatively well-informed and sensible about financial matters if he has handled money of his own. It seems to make little difference in his practices whether his money has come via an allowance or has been handed out to him as he needed it. The lower-class child almost never has an allowance, and seldom does he have any money at all to spend. How, then, is the school to help him with monetary concepts and practices? No ready answers appear, but some effective approach to this vital problem might be found if capable educational minds would get to work on it.

EXAMINATION OF PERSONAL VALUES

Realistic evaluation and appreciation of the needs and goals of lower-class children does not mean accepting them as ideal for the children, nor does it mean that they should be accepted by the middle-class teacher or social worker. However, such knowledge makes possible communication with the children to a degree not now present; and where *communication,* both emotional and intellectual, is possible, *change* is possible. Some recent social research indicates, for example, that reformed criminals make more effective "social" workers than the conventional middle-class social and probation worker. Understanding and communication seem to be the relevant factors here.

Realistic evaluation and appreciation of the values of another group, and ability to face these without shock or rejection, involve honest examination of one's own value system. The middle-class teacher who comes honestly to grips with what he believes and holds valuable, who understands how he has come to be the way he is, and who has reasoned through the advantages and disadvantages of his value system, should be much better able to work with children of all social classes than the teacher who has made no such attempt at self-understanding. A certain prod toward understanding and tolerance of those of other social classes (or faiths) is to realize how strictly culture determines one's own value system, and by what a relatively circumscribed group similar values are held.

To conclude this section, it should be said—and urgently—that, in the interests of a genuine democracy, a lowered delinquency rate, a reduction in the intolerably large mental-hospital population, and the introduction of more reason and less adrenalin into the conduct of our social affairs, we need to employ our best brains and our greatest ingenuity in the education of our lower-lower-class youngsters. Again, the 1960s have seen real progress in this area.

Although the emphasis in these last sections has been on improving communication with lower-class children, the principles and practices advocated would improve the education of all children. Too often, for bright children of the middle or upper class, the teacher and the texts remain dull and generally unrewarding. It may be that the gifted are handicapped in their education for many of the same general reasons that hold back typical lower-class children.

COMPENSATORY EDUCATION

The term compensatory education is commonly used (and often criticized) as a summary term or topical heading for educational efforts to alleviate the damage to cognitive and personal function that has occurred for children who have grown up in barren but crowded, noisy, poverty stricken, and disorganized circumstances. Although the basic data documenting the perhaps irreversible damage that is done to children by such environments have long been available (for example see the dates of the research publications mentioned throughout Chapters 7 and 8, particularly the latter), only in about the last ten years have these data been brought forcibly to the attention of those responsible for United States education with some resultant action. The time lag between the publication of research and its educational applications has been pessimistically estimated by some as being as long as fifty years, and, although in principle we are relatively sophisticated in 1967 about what *can* be done to help children from socially disadvantaged backgrounds, almost no applications of procedures, even today, have been introduced into general school practice.

In 1967, there is, however, a large number of pilot or exploratory projects for some of which research data have been published. These fall loosely under the heading of compensatory education. There is substantial consensus that, to be maximally effective, compensatory education must be started much earlier than is possible under the current school organization, where school starts (with public support) at the kindergarten or first-grade level. Even where kindergarten programs exist on a permissive basis not all children attend (no more than about 50 percent), nor do kindergartens meet the needs of socially and culturally disadvantaged children much more effectively than do elementary, junior high, and secondary schools. Kindergartens, like first- or fifth-grades, are geared for middle- and upper-class children who have acquired, almost by osmosis, the knowledge and skills that go into "reading readiness" or "number readiness." Lower-class children (a disproportionate number of whom come from minority groups of Negro, Puerto-Rican, Mexican, and Indian ethnic or national origin) have not learned to listen, are deficient in memory span, are easily distractible, have had little experience with elaborative (descriptive, abstracting) language, have little time perspective, are inexperienced in linking the past with the present and future, have not learned to work for praise or adult approval (since they have had little of it in their lives), distrust adults, have not learned to control their impulses, are fearful, are handicapped in motor development, particularly in fine motor skills, have not learned to be curious. In short, they have not had the opportunity to acquire the multitude of basic skills or develop the attitudes that are essential either for reading readiness or for reading proper. Since reading is the foundation of all subsequent education, they are hopelessly handicapped and, as they move formally through the school system, fall consistently behind their middle-class classmates with all the despair, apathy, rebellion, and personal-social maladjustment that accompany school failure. Since *proficiency* in important areas is perhaps the most important single base for an adequate self-concept, and since school is the number one childhood arena in which proficiency can and should be gained, failure to develop such proficiency is disastrous indeed. No words are sufficient to portray the extremity of disaster of school failure.

Very briefly, the results from compensatory education projects, which have been heavily supported by such agencies as the Federal Government and the Ford Foundation, and which include among the better known projects, Head Start and Higher Horizons, are as follows:

Intervention, whether in the form of a well-structured (not a free play or custodial) nursery school working only with the children, or a nursery school interacting with the home, raises children's IQ's and provides them with skills needed for success in schools. They show material gains (average IQ gains of 10 to 20 points from a year of intensive, planned, and intellectually and socially stimulating nursery school experience are not uncommon) when compared to control groups of children not in nursery school. However, most frequently these differences completely or partially disappear by the end of first grade. Exceptions from unpublished data and personal communication with Dr. Susan Gray, George Peabody College for Teachers and from research on the socially disadvantaged being conducted by the present author with Drs. Walter Hodges and Howard Spicker occur when children receive first-grade instruction geared to the needs of each individual child. What happens (the author is speaking somewhat subjectively from general reports and personal observation rather than hard data) seems to be that the typical child who has attended a demonstration nursery school or been a part of a research project concerned with the socially disadvantaged continues his education in a school most of whose pupils come from backgrounds as wretched as his. The kindergarten and first-grade teachers, appalled by the lack of essential foundation skills possessed by the majority of pupils, concentrate on the majority, leaving the demonstration school project child more or less alone, since he already possesses such skills. Consequently, he coasts and loses ground progressively and rapidly. Where such demonstration project children have continued in demonstration kindergartens and first and second grades, their relatively rapid nursery school growth continues at the same rate, as it also apparently does when they enter heterogeneous schools (that is, schools that enroll all socioeconomic levels). In heterogeneous classes, the graduates of demonstration classes are placed with a "skills level" group consonant with their own status, and continue to achieve.

Similar results seem to occur with intervention or compensatory education at older age levels; the pilot project, successful in and of itself, washes out when it ends or when the child is graduated from it, because it has exerted no influence on the school to which it has been attached or to which its graduates return (see, for example, Silberman's summary of New York's Junior High School 43, "Demonstration Guidance Project," 1964, p. 256).

To summarize this all too brief section (brief because the literature has become very large, but much of it is of poor scientific quality; and because many of the research data have not yet been reported at the time of writing): Compensatory education at any level (from nursery school through secondary school) produces benefits for those receiving it. The benefits are more easily and economically achieved the younger the child is. When graduates continue in superior school settings—that is, where the ground rules of compensatory education have also become the ground rules of regular education—it is probable that the benefits to the children continue. Otherwise, they are eroded, or growth rate levels off. Israel's nation-wide compensatory education efforts from nursery through secondary school for the children of immigrant families, almost uniformly socially and culturally disadvantaged, who come from Morocco, Algeria, Egypt, Iraq, Yemen, or Kurdestan, suggest that education, begun early and on a broad rather than an isolated demonstration base, can permanently reclaim the disadvantaged. The Wayne County Training School studies reported in Chapter 13 indicate that, even taken in their early teens, training around the clock for an average of three years can dramatically and positively redirect children's lives.

In other words, we seem to have available to us the techniques to eliminate the borderline IQ, educational, and all too often social and emotional cripples who are a large share of the lowest social class population and who cost the nation so tragically much.

We move tragically slowly toward putting our knowledge into practice. The reasons for our lack of progress are complex and the problems are huge: ethnic prejudice, *de facto* (residential) segregation (and illegal partial segregation in the South), improperly prepared teachers, undersupported schools, overcrowded classrooms, ineffective school administration, inflexibility of school procedures, failure of middle-class educators to communicate with (or be adequately informed) about the socially disadvantaged members of their clientele, parental lack of sophistication about schools and the role that the home can play in supplementing the school, conflicting social class values—all of these and more impede the progress of schools in meeting the needs of "the submerged one fourth of the nation" (one fourth is a conservative estimate).

Summary

The United States population is often stratified according to social class by sociologists, educators, and psychologists. The most common division is into (1) upper class (relatively aristocratic, well-established people); (2) middle class (the great body of professional and white-collar workers); and (3) lower class, the upper-lower class being made up of skilled workers, the lower-lower class of unskilled workers. Research information, particularly about family practices, is for the most part based on studies of the middle and upper-lower classes. Research workers have been timid in approaching upper- and lower-lower class parents, although children of the latter have often been studied in public schools and residential treatment centers for delinquent, mentally retarded, and emotionally disturbed children. Upper-class children are relatively unavailable for research, since they often attend private schools.

Almost all teachers are members of the middle class, but perhaps two thirds of their students (particularly during elementary-school years) come from working-class homes, and about one fourth or more of them come from the lower-lower class. The values of the middle and the lower-lower class differ sharply, even dramatically. Middle-class people in general espouse hard work, ambition, cleanliness, and self-control (although their behavior is not always in line with their values); they tend to be inhibited in sexual and aggressive behavior. Lower-class individuals, on the other hand, tend to be more open and uninhibited and, as a group, are inclined toward immediate gratification of needs and impulses.

Major differences in values result in serious communication difficulties between middle-class and lower-class people; these are particularly troubling to the relations between teachers and lower-class children. Because of their failure to understand each other's behavior, standards, and goals, mutual distrust—even hostility—may result. The implications of this situation for the education of lower-class children are grave, and are made even more serious because lower-class parents typically do not support the schools' educational efforts. Middle-class parents, on the other hand, offer strong support to the schools; and teachers present about the same image to middle-class children as their parents do.

Lower-class children appear to be less well-accepted by their peers (as well as by their teachers) than middle-class children are. Boys may be more fortunate in this respect than girls, since they may be able to break the class barrier by means of athletic proficiency. For both boys and girls, social acceptance seems to be positively (although only moderately) related to good personal adjustment; middle-class youngsters appear to be better adjusted than those of lower social status.

Lower-class children seem to respond well to teacher techniques that combine fairness and warmth with strength. Their education might also be furthered by providing them with textbooks (particularly early in their school career) that have more in common with their way of life than the rather pallid reading fare ordinarily offered them. Compensatory education, if it can permeate regular education and extend downward to nursery school, offers great hope. Children strongly desire "training for competence."

Appreciation and respect for the individual can help bridge the gap between teachers and lower-class children. Specifically, teachers should strive to know these children and their families better, and to develop a more realistic understanding of their needs and standards. Developing attitudes of objectivity and acceptance toward others means that teachers must examine and justify—and, where necessary, modify—their own system of values. Such steps as these, thoughtfully and sincerely taken, can go far toward improving the education of lower-class children, and of all other youngsters as well.

References

Achenbach, T., and E. Zigler. Social competence and self-image disparity. *J. abnorm. soc. Psychol.*, 1963, *67*, 197–205.

Adams, Abby Bonime. Choice of infant feeding technique as a function of maternal personality. *J. consult. Psychol.*, 1959, *23*, 143–146.

Adorno, T. W., Else Frenkel-Brunswik, D. J. Levinson, and R. N. Sanford. *The authoritarian personality*. New York: Harper & Brothers, 1950.

Ainsworth, Mary D. The effects of maternal deprivation: a review of findings and controversy in the context of research strategy. From: World Health Organization: Geneva, "Deprivation of Maternal Care: A Reassessment of its Effects." *Public Health Papers*, 1962, *14*, 97–165.

Albee, G. W. Patterns of aggression in psychopathology. *J. consult. Psychol.*, 1950, *14*, 465–468.

Albers, Mary Elizabeth, and May V. Seagoe. Enrichment for superior students in algebra classes. *J. educ. Res.*, 1947, *40*, 481–495.

Aldrich, C. A., and Edith W. Hewitt. A self-regulating feeding program for infants. *J. Amer. med. Assn.*, 1947, *135*, 340–342.

Aldrich, C. A., C. Sung, and C. Knop. The crying of newly born babies: III. The early period at home. *J. Pediatrics*, 1945, *27*, 428–435.

Aldrich, C. A., M. A. Norval, C. Knop, and F. Venegas. The crying of newly born babies: IV. Follow-up study after additional nursing care had been provided. *J. Pediatrics*, 1946, *28*, 665–670.

Alexander, A. M. Teacher judgment of pupil intelligence and achievement is not enough. *Elem. Sch. J.*, 1953, *53*, 396–401.

Allport, G. W., and T. F. Pettigrew. Cultural influence on the perception of movement: the trapezoidal illusion among Zulus. *J. abnorm. soc. Psychol.*, 1957, *55*, 104–113.

Alpern, G. D. Children's performance in a socially reinforced learning task as a function of two characteristics of the adult reinforcer. Unpublished Ph.D. dissertation, *Child Welfare Research Station*, 1960.

Altus, Grace T. Some correlates of the Davis-Eells tests. *J. consult. Psychol.*, 1956, *20*, 227–232.

Altus, W. D. Birth order and its sequelae. *Science*, 1966, *151*, 44–49.

Ames, R. Physical maturing among boys as related to adult social behavior: a longitudinal study. *Calif. J. educ. Res.*, 1957, *8*, 69–75.

Ammons, R. B., and H. S. Ammons. Parent preferences in young children's doll-play interviews. *J. abnorm. soc. Psychol.*, 1949, *44*, 490–505.

Anastasi, Anne, and J. P. Foley, Jr. A proposed reorientation in the heredity environment controversy. *Psychol. Rev.*, 1948, *55*, 239–249.

Anderson, L. D. A longitudinal study of the effects of nursery-school training on successive intelligence-test ratings. *Natl. Soc. Study Educ.*, 39th Yearbook, 1940, Part II. Pp. 3–10.

Angelino, H., J. Dollins, and E. V. Mech. Trends in the "fears and worries" of school children as related to socioeconomic status and age. *J. genet. Psychol.*, 1956, *89*, 263–277.

Angelino, H., and E. V. Mech. "Fears and worries" concerning physical changes: a preliminary survey of 32 females. *J. Psychol.*, 1955, *39*, 195–198.

Angelino, H., and C. L. Shedd. An initial report of a validation study of the Davis-Eells tests of general intelligence or problem-solving ability. *J. Psychol.*, 1955, *40*, 35–38.

Appel, M. H. Aggressive behavior of nursery-school children and adult procedures in dealing with such behavior. *J. exp. Educ.*, 1942, *11*, 185–199.

Atkinson, J. W. Motivational determinants of risk-taking behavior. *Psychol. Rev.*, 1957, *64*, 359–372.

Atkinson, J. W., J. R. Bastian, R. W. Earl, and G. H. Litwin. The achievement motive, goal setting, and probability preferences. *J. abnorm. soc. Psychol.*, 1960, *60*, 27–36.

Atkinson, J. W., and G. H. Litwin. Achievement motive and test anxiety conceived as motive to approach success and motive to avoid failure. *J. abnorm. soc. Psychol.*, 1960, *60*, 52–63.

Ausubel, D. P. Prestige motivation of gifted children. *Genet. Psychol. Monogr.*, 1951, *43*, 53–117.

Ausubel, D. P., E. E. Balthazar, Irene Rosenthal, L. S. Blackman, S. H. Schpoont, and Joan Welkowitz. Perceived parent attitudes as determinants of children's ego structure. *Child Develpm.*, 1954, *25*, 173–183.

Avey, L. D. *Developmental anatomy.* Philadelphia: W. B. Saunders Co., 1954.

Bach, G. R. Father-fantasies and father-typing in father-separated children. *Child Develpm.*, 1946, *17*, 63–80.

Baldwin, A. L., Joan Kalhorn, and Fay H. Breese. Patterns of parent behavior. *Psychol. Monogr.*, 1945, *58*, No 3.

Bandura, A. Influence of models' reinforcement contingencies on the acquisition of imitative responses. *J. Pers. soc. Psychol.*, 1965, *1*, 589–595.

Barrett, Helen Elizabeth, and Helen Lois Koch. The effect of nursery-school training upon the mental-test performance of a group of orphanage children. *Ped. Sem. and J. genet. Psychol.*, 1930, *37*, 102–122.

Barry, H., III, Margaret K. Bacon, and I. L. Child. A cross-cultural survey of some sex differences in socialization. *J. abnorm. soc. Psychol.*, 1957, *55*, 327–332.

Bartlett, F. C. *Remembering: A study in experimental and social psychology.* Cambridge, England: Cambrige University Press, 1932.

Bartoshuk, A. Human neonatal cardiac response to sound: a power function. *Psychonomic Science*, 1964, *1*, 151–152.

Baxter, J. C., M. J. Lerner, and J. S. Miller. Identification as a function of the reinforcing quality of the model and the socialization background of the subject. *J. Pers. soc. Psychol.*, 1965, 2, 692–697.

Bayley, Nancy. Comparisons of mental and motor test scores for ages 1–15 months by sex, birth order, race, geographical location, and education of parents. *Child Develpm.*, 1965, 36, 379–411.

Bayley, Nancy. Consistency and variability in the growth of intelligence from birth to eighteen years. *J. genet. Psychol.*, 1949, 75, 165–196.

Bayley, Nancy. On the growth of intelligence. *Amer. Psychologist*, 1955, 10, 805–818.

Bayley, Nancy and Melita H. Oden. The maintenance of intellectual ability in gifted children. *J. Gerontology*, 1955, 10, 91–107.

Beach, F. A., and J. Jaynes. Effects of early experience upon the behavior of animals. *Psychol. Bull.*, 1954, 51, 239–263.

Bear, Roberta M., R. D. Hess, and V. C. Shipman. Social class differences in maternal attitudes toward the teacher and the school. Paper read at the APA, 1966.

Becker, W. C., D. R. Peterson, L. A. Hellmer, D. J. Shoemaker, and H. C. Quay. Factors in parental behavior and personality as related to problem behavior in children. *J. consult. Psychol.*, 1959, 23, 107–118.

Beilin, H. Teachers' and clinicians' attitudes toward the behavior problems of children: a reappraisal. *Child Develpm.*, 1959, 30, 9–26.

Belcher, J. C. Evaluation and restandardization of Sewell's socioeconomic scale. *Rural Sociol.*, 1951, 16, 246–255.

Benedict, Ruth. *Patterns of culture.* New York: New American Library of World Literature, 1953.

Beres, D., and S. J. Obers. The effects of extreme deprivation in infancy on psychic structure in adolescence: a study in ego development. In *The psychoanalytic study of the child*, Vol. V. New York: International Universities Press, 1950.

Berger, E. M. The relation between expressed acceptance of self and expressed acceptance of others. *J. abnorm. soc. Psychol.*, 1951, 47, 778–782.

Bergmann, G. The logic of psychological concepts. *Phil. Sci.*, 1951, 18, 93–110.

Berkowitz, L. Anti-Semitism and the displacement of aggression. *J. abnorm. soc. Psychol.*, 1959, 59, 182–187.

Berlyne, D. E., and Frances D. Frommer. Some determinants of the incidence and content of children's questions. *Child Develpm.*, 1966, 37, 177–189.

Bernard, J., and L. W. Sontag. Fetal reactivity to tonal stimulation: a preliminary report. *J. genet. Psychol.*, 1947, 70, 205–210.

Bernstein, L. A note on Christie's "Experimental naïvete and experiential naïvete." *Psychol. Bull.*, 1952, 49, 38–40.

Bexton, W. H., W. Heron, and T. H. Scott. Effects of decreased variation in the sensory environment. *Can. J. Psychol.*, 1954, 8, 70–76.

Bijou, S. W. Patterns of reinforcement and resistance to extinction in young children. *Child Develpm.*, 1957, 28, 47–54.

Bijou, S. W., Mildred H. Ainsworth, and M. R. Stockey. The social adjustment of mentally retarded girls paroled from the Wayne County Training School. *Amer. J. ment. Defic.*, 1943, 47, 422–428.

Bills, R. R. Self-concepts and Rorschach signs of depression. *J. consult. Psychol.,* 1954, *18,* 135–137.

Bingham, W. E., and W. J. Griffiths, Jr. The effects of different environments during infancy on adult behavior in the rat. *J. comp. physiol. Psychol.,* 1952, *45,* 307–312.

Bird, Grace E. The effect of nursery-school attendance upon mental growth of children. *Natl. Soc. Study Educ.,* 39th Yearbook, 1940, Part II. Pp. 81–84.

Blau, T. H., and Lili R. Balu. The sucking reflex: the effects of long feeding vs. short feeding on the behavior of a human infant. *J. abnorm. soc. Psychol.,* 1955, *51,* 123–125.

Block, J. Personality characteristics associated with fathers' attitudes toward child-rearing. *Child Develpm.,* 1955, *26,* 41–48.

Block, J., and H. Thomas. Is satisfaction with self a measure of adjustment? *J. abnorm. soc. Psychol.,* 1955, *51,* 254–259.

Block, J., and Emily Turula. Identification, ego control, and adjustment. *Child Develpm.,* 1963, *34,* 945–953.

Bloom, B. S. The 1955 normative study of the tests of general educational development. *Sch. Rev.,* 1956, *64,* 110–124.

Bonsall, Marcella R. Reactions of gifted high-school pupils to elementary education. *Calif. J. educ. Res.,* 1955, *6,* 107–109.

Bostock, J. Enuresis and toilet training. *Med. J. Aust.,* 1951, *2,* 110–113.

Bowlby, J. *Maternal care and mental health.* Geneva, Switzerland: World Health Organization, Monogr. Ser., 1952.

Bowlby, J., Mary Ainsworth, Mary Boston, and Dina Rosenbluth. The effects of mother-child separation: a follow-up study. *Brit. J. med. Psychol.,* 1956, *29,* 211–247.

Bradway, Katherine P. An experimental study of factors associated with Stanford-Binet IQ changes from the preschool to the junior high school level. *J. genet. Psychol.,* 1945, *66,* 107–128.

Brazelton, T. B. Sucking in infancy. *Pediatrics,* 1956, *17,* 400–404.

Brehm, J. W. Increasing cognitive dissonance by *a fait accompli. J. abnorm. soc. Psychol.,* 1959, *58,* 379–382.

Brehm, J. W., and A. R. Cohen. Re-evaluation of choice alternatives as a function of their number of qualitative similarity. *J. abnorm. soc. Psychol.,* 1959, *58,* 373–378.

Bridges, Katherine M. B. Emotional development in early infancy. *Child Develpm.,* 1932, *3,* 324–341.

Brill, A. A. (tr. and ed.). *The basic writings of Sigmund Freud,* New York: Modern Library, 1938.

Brim, O. G., Jr. Some basic research problems in parent education with implications for the field of child development. *Monogr. Soc. Res. Child Develpm.,* 1959, *24,* 51–68.

Brim, O. G., Jr., and R. Forer. A note on the relation of values and social structure to life planning. *Sociometry,* 1956, *19,* 54–60.

Brodbeck, A. J. The effects of three feeding variables on the nonnutritive sucking of newborn infants. *Amer. Psychologist,* 1950, *5,* 292–293.

Brodsky, C. M. *A study of norms for body form-behavior relationships.* Washington, D.C.: Catholic University of America Press, 1954.

Brody, Sylvia. *Patterns of mothering: maternal influence during infancy.* New York: International Universities Press, 1956.

Bronfenbrenner, Urie. Socialization and social class through time and space. In Eleanor E. Maccoby, T. H. Newcomb, and E. L. Hartley (eds.), *Readings in social psychology,* 3d ed. New York: Holt, Rinehart and Winston, 1958.

Bronfenbrenner, Urie. Soviet methods of character education: some implications for research. *Amer. Psychologist,* 1962, *17,* 550–564.

Bronson, Wanda C. Dimensions of ego and infantile identification. *J. Pers.,* 1959, *27,* 532–545.

Bronson, Wanda C., Edith S. Katten, and N. Livson. Patterns of authority and affection in two generations. *J. abnorm. soc. Psychol.,* 1959, *58,* 143–152.

Brown, C. *Manchild in the promised land.* New York: The Macmillan Company, 1965.

Brown, D. G. Sex-role development in a changing culture. *Psychol. Bull.,* 1958, *55,* 232–242.

Brown, D. G. Masculinity-femininity development in children. *J. consult. Psychol.,* 1957, *21,* 197–202.

Brown, J. S. Pleasure-seeking behavior and the drive-reduction hypothesis. *Psychol. Rev.,* 1955, *62,* 169–179.

Brown, J. S., and I. E. Farber. Emotions conceptualized as intervening variables —with suggestions toward a theory of frustration. *Psychol. Bull.,* 1951, *48,* 465–504.

Brown, W. H., and Lucille B. Bond. Social stratification in a sixth-grade class. *J. educ. Res.,* 1955, *48,* 530–543.

Brownfield, C. A. Deterioration and facilitation hypotheses in sensory-deprivation research. *Psychol. Bull.,* 1964, *61,* 304–313.

Bruce, P. Relationship of self-acceptance to other variables with sixth-grade children oriented in self-understanding. *J. educ. Psychol.,* 1958, *49,* 229–238.

Bruner, J. S. Education as social invention. *Saturday Review,* 1966, *49,* 70–72, 102–103.

Brunswik, E. The probability point of view. In M. H. Marx (ed.), *Psychological theory.* New York: The Macmillan Co., 1951.

Buros, O. K. (ed.) *The sixth mental measurements yearbook.* Highland Park, N.J.: The Gryphon Press, 1965.

Burton, R. V. The generality of honesty reconsidered. *Psychol. Rev.,* 1963, *70,* 481–499.

Byrne, D. Child-rearing antecedents of repression-sensitivation. *Child Develpm.,* 1964, *35,* 1033–1039.

Caldwell, Bettye M. The effects of infant care. Chapter in M. L. Hoffman, and Lois W. Hoffman (eds.). *Review of child development research.* New York: Russell Sage Foundation, 1964, pp. 9–87.

Calvin, A. D., and W. H. Holtzman. Adjustment and the discrepancy between self-concept and inferred self. *J. consult. Psychol.,* 1953, *17,* 39–44.

Campbell, W. J. The influence of sociocultural environment on the progress of children at the secondary-school level. *Aust. J. Psychol.*, 1955, 7, 140–146.

Carlsmith, Lyn. Effect of early father absence on scholastic aptitude. *Harvard Educ. Rev.*, 1964, *34*, 3–21.

Carlson, Edith Fox. Problems in educating the highly endowed. *J. except. Child*, 1947, *13*, 201–204.

Carmichael, L. (ed.). *Manual of child psychology*, 2d ed. New York: John Wiley and Sons, 1954.

Casler, L. The effects of extratactile stimulation on a group of institutionalized infants. *Genet. Psychol. Monogr.*, 1965a, *71*, 137–175.

Casler, L. The effects of supplementary verbal stimulation on a group of institutionalized infants. *J. Child Psychol.*, 1965b, *6*, 19–27.

Cass, Loretta K. An investigation of some important variables in the parent-child relationship. Data from unpublished Ph.D. dissertation, The Ohio State University, 1950.

Cass, Loretta K. An investigation of parent-child relationships in terms of awareness, identification, projection, and control. *Amer. J. Orthopsychiat.*, 1952a, *22*, 305–313.

Cass, Loretta K. Parent-child relationships and delinquency. *J. abnorm. soc. Psychol.*, 1952b, *47*, 101–104.

Castaneda, A., B. R. McCandless, and D. S. Palermo. The children's form of the manifest anxiety scale. *Child Develpm.*, 1956, *27*, 317–326.

Castaneda, A., D. S. Palermo, and B. R. McCandless. Complex learning and performance as a function of anxiety in children and task difficulty. *Child Develpm.*, 1956, *27*, 327–332.

Catalano, F. L., and Dorothea McCarthy. Infant speech as a possible predictor of later intelligence. *J. Psychol.*, 1954, *38*, 203–209.

Cattell, Psyche. *The measurement of intelligence of infants and young children.* New York: Psychological Corp., 1940.

Cavanaugh, Maxine C., I. Cohen, D. Dunphy, E. A. Ringwall, and I. D. Goldberg. Prediction from the Cattell Infant Intelligence Scale. *J. consult. Psychol.*, 1957, *21*, 33–37.

Chang, Judy, and Jack Block. A study of identification in male homosexuals. *J. consult. Psychol.*, 1960, *24*, 307–310.

Centers, R. Social-class identifications of American youth. *J. Pers.*, 1950, *18*, 290–302.

Centers, R. Toward an articulation of two approaches to social-class phenomena: II. The index of status characteristics and class identification. *Int. J. Opin. Attitude Res.*, 1951, *5*, 159–178.

Chapanis, Natalia P., and A. Chapanis. Cognitive dissonance: five years later. *Psychol. Bull.*, 1964, *61*, 1–22.

Charles, D. C. Ability and accomplishment of persons earlier judged mentally deficient. *Genet. Psychol. Monogr.*, 1953, *47*, 3–71.

Charlesworth, W. R. Instigation and maintenance of curiosity behavior as a function of surprise vs. novel and familiar stimuli. *Child Develpm.*, 1965, *35*, 1169–1186.

Chase, W. P. Color vision in infants. *J. exp. Psychol.*, 1937, *20*, 203–222.

Child, I. L. The relation of somatotype to self-ratings on Sheldon's temperamental traits. *J. Pers.*, 1950, *18*, 440–453.

Child, I. L., Kitty F. Frank, and T. Storm. Self-ratings and TAT: their relation to each other and to childhood background. *J. Pers.*, 1956, *25*, 96–114.

Child, I. L., and I. K. Waterhouse. Frustration and the quality of performance: I. A critique of the Barker, Dembo, and Lewin experiment. *Psychol. Rev.*, 1952, *59*, 351–362.

Chittenden, Gertrude E. An experimental study in measuring and modifying assertive behavior in young children. *Monogr. Soc. Res. Child Develpm.*, 1942, *7*, No. 1.

Chodorkoff, B. Adjustment and the discrepancy between the perceived and ideal self. *J. clin. Psychol.*, 1954a, *10*, 266–268.

Chodorkoff, B. Self-perception, perceptual defense, and adjustment. *J. abnorm. soc. Psychol.*, 1954b, *49*, 508–512.

Christie, R., and J. Garcia. Subcultural variation in authoritarian personality. *J. abnorm. soc. Psychol.*, 1951, *46*, 457–469.

Cicirellli, V. G. Form of the relationship between creativity, IQ, and academic achievement. *J. educ. Psychol.*, 1965, *56*, 303–308.

Clarke, A. D. B., and A. M. Clarke. Cognitive changes in the feebleminded. *Brit. J. Psychol.*, 1954, *45*, 173–179.

Clarke, A. D. B., and Ann M. Clarke. Some recent advances in the study of early deprivation. *Child Psychol. and Psychiat.*, 1960, *1*, 26–36.

Clarke, A. D. B., A. M. Clarke, and S. Reiman. Cognitive and social changes in the feebleminded, three further studies. *Brit. J. Psychol.*, 1958, *49*, 144–157.

Clarke, Ann M., and A. D. B. Clarke (eds.). *Mental Deficiency: The Changing Outlook*. London: Methuen and Co., Ltd., 1958, Pp. xvi, 513.

Cohen, A. R., H. I. Terry, and C. B. Jones. Attitudinal effects of choice in exposure to counterpropaganda. *J. abnorm. soc. Psychol.*, 1959, *58*, 388–391.

Cohn, T. S., and H. Carsch. Administration of the F-scale to a sample of Germans. *J. abnorm. soc. Psychol.*, 1954, *49*, 471.

Colley, T. The nature and origins of psychological sexual identity. *Psychol. Rev.*, 1959, *66*, 165–177.

Coopersmith, S. Self-esteem and need achievement as determinants of selective recall and repetition. *J. abnorm. soc. Psychol.*, 1960, *60*, 310–317.

Coopersmith, S. A method for determining types of self-esteem. *J. educ. Psychol.*, 1959, *59*, 87–94.

Cortés, J. B., and Florence M. Gatti. Physique and self-description of temperament. *J. consult. Psychol.*, 1965, *29*, 432–439.

Cowen, E. L., F. Heilizer, and H. S. Axelrod. Self-concept conflict indicators and learning. *J. abnorm. soc. Psychol.*, 1955, *51*, 242–245.

Cowen, E. L., J. Landes, and D. E. Schaet. The effects of mild frustration on the expression of prejudiced attitudes. *J. abnorm. soc. Psychol.*, 1959, *58*, 33–39.

Crandall, V. J. Achievement. *Yearbook of the National Society for the Study of Education*. 1963, *42*, Part I. Pp. 416–459.

Crandall, V. J., and Ursula Bellugi. Some relationships of interpersonal and intrapersonal conceptualizations to personal-social adjustment. *J. Pers.*, 1954, *23*, 224–232.

Crandall, V. J., and Anne Preston. Patterns and levels of maternal behavior. *Child Develpm.*, 1955, *26*, 267–278.

Crandall, V. J., Anne Preston, and Alice Rabson. Maternal reactions and the development of independence and achievement behavior in young children. *Child Develpm.*, 1960, *31*, 243–251.

Crowne, D. P., and M. W. Stephens. Self-acceptance and self-evaluative behavior: a critique of methodology. *Psychol. Bull.*, 1961, *58*, 104–121.

Crum, Janet, W. L. Brown, and M. E. Bitterman. The effect of partial and delayed reinforcement on resistance to extinction. *Amer. J. Psychol.*, 1951, *64*, 228–237.

Curran, F. J. Specialized techniques in the treatment of juvenile delinquency. *J. Amer. med. Assn.*, 1955, *175*, 108–113.

Davids, A., and C. W. Eriksen. Some social and cultural factors determining relations between authoritarianism and measures of neuroticism. *J. consult. Psychol.*, 1957, *21*, 155–159.

Davies, Carolyn M. Development of the probability concept in children. *Child Develpm.*, 1965, *36*, 779–788.

Davis, Allison, and J. Dollard. *Children of bondage*. Washington, D.C.: American Council on Education, 1940.

Davis, A., and R. J. Havighurst. Social class and color differences in child-rearing. *Amer. sociol. Rev.*, 1946, *11*, 698–710.

Davis, Clara M. Results of the self-selection of diets by young children. *Can. med. Assn. J.*, 1939, *41*, 256–261.

Davis, H. V., R. R. Sears, H. C. Miller, and J. A. Brodbeck. Effects of cup, bottle and breast feeding on oral activities of newborn infants. *Pediatrics*, 1948, *3*, 549–558.

Davis, J. A. Correlates of sociometric status among peers. *J. educ. Res.*, 1957, *50*, 561–569.

Davis, W. A., and R. J. Havighurst. *Father of the man: how your child gets his personality*. Boston: Houghton Mifflin Co., 1947.

Dawe, Helen C. A study of the effect of an educational program upon language development and related mental functions in young children. *J. exp. Educ.*, 1942, *11*, 200–209.

DeLucia, Lenore A. The toy preference test: a measure of sex-role identification. *Child Develpm.*, 1963, *34*, 107–117.

Denenberg, V. H. Critical periods, stimulus input, and emotional reactivity: a theory of infantile stimulation. *Psychol. Rev.*, 1964, *71*, 335–351.

Dennis, W. Are Hopi children noncompetitive? *J. abnorm. soc. Psychol.*, 1955, *50*, 90–100.

Dennis, W. Does culture appreciably affect patterns of infant behavior? *J. soc. Psychol.*, 1940, *12*, 305–317.

Dennis, W. A further analysis of reports of wild children. *Child Develpm.*, 1951, *22*, 153–158.

Dennis, W., and Yvonne Sayegh. The effect of supplementary experiences upon the behavioral development of infants in institutions. *Child Develpm.,* 1965, *36,* 81–90.

Deutsch, M. The disadvantaged child and the learning process: some social, psychological and developmental considerations. Columbia University, New York: paper prepared for The Ford Foundation "Work Conference on Curriculum and Teaching in Depressed Urban Areas," 1962.

Disher, D. R. The reactions of newborn infants to chemical stimuli administered nasally. Ohio State University Studies: *Contr. Psychol.,* 1934, *12,* 1–52.

Dittes, J. E. Attractiveness of group as function of self-esteem and acceptance by group. *J. abnorm. soc. Psychol.,* 1959, *59,* 77–82.

Dittes, J. E., and H. H. Kelley. Effects of different conditions of acceptance upon conformity to group norms. *J. abnorm. soc. Psychol.,* 1956, *53,* 100–107.

Doidge, W. T., and W. H. Holtzman. Implications of homosexuality among air force trainees. *J. consult. Psychol.,* 1960, *24,* 9–13.

Dollard, J., L. W. Doob, N. E. Miller, O. H. Mowrer, and R. R. Sears. *Frustration and aggression.* New Haven: Yale University Press, 1939.

Dollard, J., and N. E. Miller. *Personality and psychotherapy.* New York: McGraw-Hill Book Co., 1950.

Douvan, Elizabeth. Social status and success strivings. *J. abnorm. soc. Psychol.,* 1956, *52,* 219–223.

Douvan, Elizabeth, and J. Adelson. *The Adolescent Experience.* New York: John Wiley and Sons, Inc., 1966.

Douvan, Elizabeth, and J. Adelson. The psychodynamics of social mobility in adolescent boys. *J. abnorm. soc. Psychol.,* 1958, *56,* 31–44.

Duncan, O. D., and J. W. Artis. Social stratification in a Pennsylvania rural community. State College, Pa.: *Penn. agric. Sta. Bull.,* 1951.

Eagle, N. The relation of five cognitive variables to change in IQ between grades three, four, and eight. *Psychol. in the Schools,* 1965, *2,* 143–149.

Ebbs, J. H., F. F. Tisdall, and W. A. Scott. The influence of prenatal diet on the mother and child. *The Milbank Memorial Fund Quarterly,* 1942, *20,* 35–36.

Eells, K., A. Davis, R. J. Havighurst, V. E. Herrick, and R. Tyler. *Intelligence and cultural differences.* Chicago: The University of Chicago Press, 1951.

Eisenberg, R. B., E. G. Griffen, D. B. Coursin, and M. A. Hunter. Auditory behavior in the human neonate: a preliminary report. *J. Speech Hear. Res.,* 1964, *7,* 245–269.

Empey, L. T. Social class and occupational aspiration: a comparison of absolute and relative measurement. *Amer. sociol. Rev.,* 1956, *21,* 703–709.

Engel, Mary. The stability of the self-concept in adolescence. *J. abnorm. soc. Psychol.,* 1959, *58,* 211–215.

Engen, T., L. P. Lipsitt, and H. Kaye. Olfactory responses and adaptation in the human neonate. *J. comp. physiol. Psychol.,* 1963, *56,* 73–77.

Epstein, R., and S. Liverant. Verbal conditioning and sex-role identification in children. *Child Develpm.,* 1963, *34,* 99–106.

Erikson, E. H. Childhood and tradition in two American Indian tribes. *Psychoanalytic stud. Child.*, 1945, *1*, 319–350.

Erikson, E. H. The problem of ego identity. *J. Amer. psychoanal. Assn.*, 1956, *4*, 56–121.

Escalona, Sibylle K. An appraisal of some psychological factors in relation to rooming-in and self-demand schedules. In M. J. E. Senn, *Problems of early infancy*. New York: The Josiah Macy, Jr. Foundation, 1947, 58–62.

Escalona, Sibylle K. Feeding disturbances in very young children. *Amer. J. Orthopsychiat.*, 1945, *15*, 76–80.

Estes, W. K. An experimental study of punishment. *Psychol. Monogr.*, 1944, *57*, 1–40.

Farber, I. E. The role of motivation in verbal learning and performance. *Psychol. Bull.*, 1955, *52*, 311–327.

Farina, A. Patterns of role dominance and conflict in parents of schizophrenic patients. *J. abnorm. soc. Psychol.*, 1961, *61*, 31–38.

Farnsworth, P. R., Q. McNemar. *Annual review of psychology*. Palo Alto, Calif.: Annual Reviews, Inc., 1966.

Ferguson, G. A. On learning and human ability. *Can. J. Psychol.*, 1954, *8*, 95–112.

Ferguson, G. A. On transfer and the abilities of man. *Can. J. Psychol.*, 1956, *10*, 121–131.

Feshbach, S. The catharsis hypothesis and some consequences of interaction with aggressive and neutral play objects. *J. Pers.*, 1956, *24*, 449–462.

Festinger, L. *Conflict, decision, and dissonance*. Stanford: Stanford University Press, 1964.

Festinger, L. *Theory of cognitive dissonance*. Evanston, Ill.: Row, Peterson and Company, 1957.

Festinger, L., and J. M. Carlsmith. Cognitive consequences of forced compliance. *J. abnorm. soc. Psychol.*, 1959, *58*, 203–210.

Fey, W. F. Acceptance by others and its relation to acceptance of self and others. A re-evaluation. *J. abnorm. soc. Psychol.*, 1955, *50*, 274–276.

Findley, D. C., and C. McGuire. Social status and abstract behavior. *J. abnorm. soc. Psychol.*, 1957, *54*, 135–137.

Flavell, J. H. *The developmental psychology of Jean Piaget*. New York: D. Van Nostrand Company, Inc., 1963.

Fleming, Elyse S., and S. Weintraub. Attitudinal rigidity as a measure of creativity in gifted children. *J. educ. Psychol.*, 1962, *53*, 81–85.

Forgus, R. H. Advantage of early over late perceptual experience in improving form discrimination. *Can. J. Psychol.*, 1957, *10*, 147–155.

Forgus, R. H. The effect of early perceptual learning on the behavioral organization of adult rats. *J. comp. physiol. Psychol.*, 1954, *47*, 331–336.

Forgus, R. H. Early visual and motor experience as determiners of complex maze-learning ability under rich and reduced stimulation. *J. comp. physiol. Psychol.*, 1955a, *48*, 215–220.

Forgus, R. H. Influence of early experience on maze-learning with and without visual cues. *Can. J. Psychol.*, 1955b, *9*, 207–214.

Franck, Kate, and E. Rosen. A projective test of masculinity-femininity. *J. consult. Psychol.,* 1949, *13,* 247–256.

Frandsen, Arden, and Frances P. Barlow. Influence of the nursery school on mental growth. *Natl. Soc. Study Educ.,* 39th Yearbook, 1940, Part II. Pp. 143–148.

Frank, G. H. The role of the family in the development of psychopathology. *Psychol. Bull.,* 1965, *65,* 191–205.

Fredeen, R. C. Cup feeding of newborn infants. *Pediatrics,* 1948, *2,* 544–548.

Frenkel-Brunswik, Else. Further explorations by a contributor to "The authoritarian personality." In R. Christie and Marie Jahoda (eds.), *Studies in the scope and method of "The authoritarian personality."* Glencoe, Ill.: Free Press, 1954a. Pp. 226–275.

Frenkel-Brunswik, Else. Patterns of social and cognitive outlooks in children and parents. *Amer. J. Orthopsychiat.,* 1951, *21,* 543–558.

Frenkel-Brunswik, Else. Social research and the problem of values: a reply. *J. abnorm. soc. Psychol.,* 1954b, *49,* 466–470.

Frenkel-Brunswik, Else. A study of prejudice in children. *Hum. Relat.,* 1948, *1,* 295–306.

Frenkel-Brunswik, Else, and Joan Havel. Prejudice in the interviews of children: I. Attitudes toward minority groups. *J. genet. Psychol.,* 1953, *82,* 91–136.

Freud, S. *New introductory lectures on psychoanalysis.* New York: W. W. Norton and Co., 1933.

Friedman, I. Phenomenal, ideal, and projected conceptions of self. *J. abnorm. soc. Psychol.,* 1955, *51,* 611–615.

Gagne, R. *The conditions of learning.* New York: Holt, Rinehart and Winston, Inc., 1965.

Gallagher, J. J. Authoritarianism and attitudes toward children. *J. soc. Psychol.,* 1957, *45,* 107–111.

Gallagher, J. J. Clinical judgment and the Cattell Infant Intelligence Scale. *J. consult. Psychol.,* 1953, *17,* 303–305.

Garn, S. M., and L. C. Clark, Jr. The sex difference in the basal metabolic rate. *Child Develpm.,* 1953, *24,* 215–224.

Gesell, A. *The mental growth of the preschool child.* New York: The Macmillan Co., 1925.

Gesell, A. The ontogenesis of infant behavior. In L. Carmichael (ed.), *Manual of child psychology,* 2d ed. New York: John Wiley and Sons, 1954. Pp. 335–373.

Gesell, A., and C. S. Amatruda. *Developmental diagnosis: normal and abnormal child development.* New York: Paul B. Hoeber, 1941.

Gesell, A., H. M. Halverson, Helen Thompson, F. L. Ilg, B. M. Costner, L. B. Ames, and C. S. Amatruda. *The first five years of life: a guide to the study of the preschool child.* New York: Harper & Brothers, 1940.

Gesell, A., and Helen Thompson. *Infant behavior.* New York: McGraw-Hill Book Co., 1934.

Gesell, A., and Helen Thompson. Learning and growth in identical twins: an experimental study by the method of co-twin control. *Genet. Psychol. Monogr.,* 1929, *6,* 1–123.

Gesell, A., and Helen Thompson. Twins T and C from infancy to adolescence: a biogenetic study of individual differences by the method of co-twin control. *Genet. Psychol. Monogr.*, 1941, *24*, 3–121.

Getzels, J. W., and P. W. Jackson. *Creativity and intelligence.* New York: John Wiley and Sons, 1962.

Getzels, J. W., and P. W. Jackson. Occupational choice and cognitive functioning: career aspirations of highly intelligent and of highly creative adolescents. *J. abnorm. soc. Psychol.*, 1960, *61*, 119–123.

Gibson, Eleanor J. Development of perception: discrimination of depth compared with discrimination of graphic symbols. Chapter 2 in J. C. Wright, and J. Kagan (eds.), *Basic cognitive processes in children. Monogr. Soc. Res. Child Develpm.*, 1963, *28*.

Gibson, Eleanor J., and R. D. Walk. The effect of prolonged exposure to visually presented patterns on learning to discriminate them. *J. comp. physiol. Psychol.*, 1956, *49*, 239–242.

Gilliland, A. R. *Tests for infants 4–12 weeks' old.* Boston: Houghton Mifflin Co., 1949.

Glanzer, M. Curiosity, exploratory drive, and stimulus satiation. *Psychol. Bull.*, 1958, *55*, 302–315.

Goddard, H. H. *The Kallikak family.* New York: The Macmillan Co., 1912.

Goff, Regina M. *Problems and emotional difficulties of Negro children.* Contr. Educ., No. 960. New York: Bureau of Publications, Teachers College, Columbia University, 1949.

Golann, S. E. Psychological study of creativity. *Psychol. Bull.*, 1963, *60*, 548–565.

Goldberg, Susan. Probability judgments by preschool children: task conditions and performance. *Child Develpm.*, 1966, *37*, 157–167.

Goldfarb, W. Effects of psychological deprivation in infancy and subsequent stimulation. *Amer. J. Psychiat.*, 1945, *102*, 18–33.

Goldfarb, W. Infant-rearing as a factor in foster home placement. *Amer. J. Orthopsychiat.*, 1944, *14*, 162–167.

Goldman, Frieda. Breast feeding and character-formation. *J. Pers.*, 1948, *17*, 83–103.

Goldman-Eisler, Frieda. The problem of orality and of its origin in early childhood. *J. ment. Sci.*, 1951, *97*, 765–782.

Goldstein, K. M., and S. B. Chorost. Preschool and background factors in the school adjustment of culturally disadvantaged children. Paper read at the American Psychological Association, 1966.

Goodenough, Florence L., and Katharine M. Maurer. The mental development of nursery-school children compared with that of nonnursery-school children. *Natl. Soc. Study Educ.*, 39th Yearbook, 1940, Part II. Pp. 161–178.

Goodenough, Florence L., and Katharine M. Maurer. *The mental growth of children from age 2 to 14 years.* Minneapolis: University of Minnesota Press, 1942.

Goodlad, J. I. Some effects of promotion and nonpromotion upon the social and personal adjustment of children. *J. exp. Educ.*, 1954, *22*, 301–328.

Gordon, J. E., and E. Smith. Children's aggression, parental attitudes, and the effects of an affiliation-arousing story. *J. Pers. soc. Psychol.*, 1965, *1*, 654–659.

Gough, H. G. Studies of social intolerance: I. Some psychological and sociological correlates of anti-Semitism. *J. soc. Psychol.,* 1951a, *33,* 237–246.

Gough, H. G. Studies of social intolerance: II. A personality scale for anti-Semitism. *J. soc. Psychol.,* 1951b, *33,* 247–255.

Gough, H. G. Studies of social intolerance: III. Relationship of the Pr-scale to other variables. *J. soc. Psychol.,* 1951c, *33,* 257–262.

Gough, H. G. Studies of social intolerance: IV. Related social attitudes. *J. soc. Psychol.,* 1951d, *33,* 263–269.

Gough, H. G., D. B. Harris, W. E. Martin, and Marcia Edwards. Children's ethnic attitudes: I. Relationship to certain personality factors. *Child Develpm.,* 1950, *21,* 83–91.

Gray, P. H. Theory and evidence of imprinting in human infants. *Student Res. Univ. Chicago,* 1957, *1,* 19–40.

Gray, Susan W. Perceived similarity to parents and adjustment. *Child Develpm.,* 1959, *30,* 91–107.

Gray, Susan W., and R. A. Klaus. An experimental preschool program for culturally deprived children. *Child Develpm.,* 1965, *36,* 887–898.

Greene, Frances M. Effect of novelty on choices made by preschool children in a simple discrimination task. *Child Develpm.,* 1964, *35,* 1257–1264.

Greenfield, N. S. The relationship between recalled forms of childhood discipline and psychopathology. *J. consult. Psychol.,* 1959, *23,* 139–142.

Greulich, W. W. A comparison of the physical growth and development of American-born and native Japanese children. *Amer. J. phys. Anthrop.,* 1957, *15,* 489–515.

Griffiths, W. *Behavior difficulties of children as perceived and judged by parents, teachers, and children themselves.* Minneapolis: University of Minnesota Press, 1952.

Grossman, Beverly, and Joyce Wrighter. The relationship between selection-rejection and intelligence, social status, and personality among sixth-grade children. *Sociometry,* 1948, *11,* 346–355.

Gruenberg, E. M. Epidemiology. Chapter in H. A. Stevens and R. Heber. *Mental Retardation: A Review of Research.* Chicago: The University of Chicago Press, 1964.

Grusec, Joan. Some antecedents of self-criticism. *J. Pers. soc. Psychol.,* 1966, *4,* 244–252.

Guilford, J. P. Intelligence: 1965 model. *Amer. Psychologist,* 1966, *21,* 20–26.

Gurvitz, M. S. On the decline of performance on intelligence tests with age. *Amer. Psychologist,* 1951, *6,* 295 (abstract).

Haan, Norma. Proposed model of ego functioning: coping and defense mechanisms in relationship to IQ change. *Psychol. Monogr.,* 1963, 77.

Haggard, E. A. Social status and intelligence: an experimental study of certain cultural determinants of measured intelligence. *Genet. Psychol. Monogr.,* 1954, *49,* 141–186.

Hagman, E. R. A study of fears of children of preschool age. *J. exp. Educ.,* 1932, *1,* 110–130.

Hake, H. W., D. A. Grant, and J. P. Hornseth. Resistance to extinction and the pattern of reinforcement: III. The effect of trial patterning in verbal "conditioning." *J. exp. Psychol.*, 1951, *41*, 221–225.

Haller, M. W. The reactions of infants to changes in the intensity and pitch of pure tone. *J. genet. Psychol.*, 1932, *40*, 162–180.

Halperin, S. L. Human heredity and mental deficiency. *Amer. J. ment. Defic.*, 1946, *51*, 153–163.

Halpern, Esther. Effects of incompatibility between perceptions and logic in Piaget's stage of concrete operations. *Child Develpm.*, 1965, *36*, 491–497.

Hammond, W. H. The status of physical types. *Hum. Biol.*, 1957, *29*, 223–241.

Hanlon, T. E., P. R. Hofstaetter, and J. P. O'Connor. Congruence of self and ideal self in relation to personality adjustment. *J. consult. Psychol.*, 1954, *18*, 215–218.

Harlow, H. F. The formation of learning sets. *Psychol. Rev.*, 1959a, *56*, 51–65.

Harlow, H. F. Basic social capacities of primates. *Hum. Biol.*, 1959b, *31*, 40–53.

Harlow, R. G. Masculine inadequacy and compensatory development of physique. *J. Pers.*, 1951, *19*, 312–323.

Harms, Irene E. Development of intelligence in infancy. State University of Iowa, *Iowa Child Welfare Res. Sta.*, 1957. Unpublished ms.

Harms, Irene E., and C. C. Spiker. Factors associated with the performance of young children on intelligence scales and tests of speech development. *J. genet. Psychol.*, 1959, *94*, 3–22.

Harris, D. B., H. G. Gough, and W. E. Martin. Children's ethnic attitudes: II. Relationship to parental beliefs. *Child Develpm.*, 1950, *21*, 169–182.

Hart, I. Maternal child-rearing practices and authoritarian ideology. *J. abnorm. soc. Psychol.*, 1957, *55*, 232–237.

Harter, Susan. Discrimination learning set in children as a function of IQ and MA. *J. exp. Child Psychol.*, 1965, *2*, 31–43.

Hartup, W. W. Nurturance and nurturance-withdrawal in relation to dependency behavior of preschool children. *Child Develpm.*, 1958, *29*, 191–201.

Hartup, W. W., and Elsie A. Zook. Sex-role preference in 3- and 4-year-old children. *J. consult. Psychol.*, 1960, *24*, 420–426.

Hassen, Iftikhar, and B. R. McCandless. Self-concept and body build in elementary school-aged boys. Unpublished ms., 1966.

Havighurst, R. J., and Rhea R. Hilkevitch. The intelligence of Indian children as measured by a performance scale. *J. abnorm. soc. Psychol.*, 1944, *39*, 419–433.

Havighurst, R. J., E. Stivers, and R. F. De Haan. A survey of the education of gifted children. *Suppl. educ. Monogr.*, 1955, *83*, 114.

Hayward, S. C. Modification of sexual behavior of the male albino rat. *J. comp. physiol. Psychol.*, 1957, *50*, 70–73.

Heathers, G. Emotional dependence and independence in nursery school play. *J. genet. Psychol.*, 1955, *87*, 37–57.

Hebb, D. O. Drives and the C.N.S. (conceptual nervous system). *Psychol. Rev.*, 1955, *62*, 243–254.

Hebb, D. O. *The organization of behavior: a neuropsychological theory.* New York: John Wiley and Sons, 1949.

Heilbrun, A. B. An empirical test of the modeling theory of sex-role learning. *Child Develpm.*, 1965, *36*, 789–799.

Heilbrun, A. B. The measurement of identification. *Child Develpm.*, 1965, *36*, 111–127.

Heinstein, M. Child rearing in California. Berkeley, Calif.: Bureau of Maternal and Child Health, State of Calif. Department of Public Health, 1966.

Helper, M. M. Learning theory and the self-concept. *J. abnorm. soc. Psychol.*, 1955, *51*, 184–194.

Heron, W., B. K. Doane, and T. H. Scott. Visual disturbances after prolonged perceptual isolation. *Can. J. Psychol.*, 1956, *10*, 13–18.

Hetzer, H., and B. H. Tudor-Hart. Die frühesten reactionen auf die menschliche stimme. *Quellen und Stud.*, 1927, *5*, 103–124.

Hieronymus, A. N. A study of social-class motivation: relationships between anxiety for education and certain socioeconomic and intellectual variables. *J. educ. Psychol.*, 1951, *42*, 193–205.

Hilgard, Josephine R. Learning and maturation in preschool children. *J. genet. Psychol.*, 1932, *41*, 36–56.

Hill, K. T., and S. B. Sarason. A further longitudinal study of the relation of test anxiety and defensiveness to test and school performance over the elementary school years. *Monogr. Soc. Res. Child Develpm.*, 1966, *31*, 1–76.

Hilton, Irma. Differences in the behavior of mothers toward first- and later-born children. 1966. Paper read at Annual Meeting of the American Psychological Association, New York.

Himmelweit, Hilde T. Socioeconomic background and personality. *Int. soc. Sci. Bull.*, 1955, *7*, 29–35.

Hobson, J. R. Scholastic standing and activity participation of under-age high school pupils originally admitted to kindergarten on the basis of physical and psychological examinations. *News Letter*, Division of School Psychologists, APA, 1956.

Hoefer, Carolyn, and Mattie C. Hardy. Later development of breast-fed and artificially-fed infants. *J. Amer. med. Assn.*, 1929, *92*, 615–619.

Hodges, W. L., B. R. McCandless, and H. H. Spicker. The development and application of a diagnostically-based curriculum for culturally deprived preschool children. *U.S. Office of Education Research Proposals*, 1964–1966.

Hoffman, M. L. Child-rearing practices and moral development: generalizations from empirical research. *Child Develpm.*, 1963, *34*, 295–318.

Hoffman, M. L. Power assertion by the parent and its impact on the child. *Child Develpm.*, 1960, *31*, 129–143.

Hofstaetter, P. R. The changing composition of "intelligence": a study in T-technique. *J. genet. Psychol.*, 1954, *85*, 159–164.

Holland, J. G. The influence of previous experience and residual effects of deprivation on hoarding in the rat. *J. comp. physiol. Psychol.*, 1954, *47*, 244–247.

Hollingshead, A. de B. *Elmtown's youth: the impact of social classes on youth.* New York: John Wiley and Sons, 1949.

Holmes, F. B. An experimental investigation of a method of overcoming children's fears. *Child Develpm.*, 1936, *7*, 6–30.

Holway, Amy R. Early self-regulation of infants and later behavior in play interviews. *Amer. J. Orthopsychiat.*, 1949, *19*, 612–623.

Homans, G. C. Group factors in worker productivity. In Eleanor E. Maccoby, T. M. Newcomb, and E. L. Hartley (eds.), *Readings in social psychology.* New York: Holt, Rinehart and Winston, Inc., 1958.

Honzik, Marjorie P. Developmental studies in parent-child resemblance in intelligence. *Child Develpm.*, 1957, *28*, 215–228.

Honzik, Marjorie P. Biosocial aspects of thumb-sucking. *Amer. Psychologist,* 1948, *3*, 351–352.

Honzik, Marjorie P., Jean W. Macfarlane, and L. Allen. The stability of mental test performance between 2 and 18 years. *J. exp. Educ.*, 1948, *17*, 309–324.

Hopper, H. E., and S. R. Pinneau. Frequency of regurgitation in infancy as related to amount of stimulation received from the mother. *Child Develpm.*, 1957, *28*, 229–237.

House, Betty, and D. Zeaman. Reversal and nonreversal shifts in discrimination learning in retardates. *J. exp. Psychol.*, 1962, *63*, 444–451.

Houston, J. P., and S. A. Mednick. Creativity and the need for novelty. *J. abnorm. soc. Psychol.*, 1963, *66*, 137–141.

Howard, K. I. Concept of self vs. real self: discrepancy. *Student Res. Univ. Chicago*, 1957, *1*, 41–45.

Howe, Louisa, Fern French, Jessie Bierman, Angie Connor, and Dorothy Kemp. Longitudinal studies of pregnancy on the Island of Kauai, Territory of Hawaii. Paper presented before the American Public Health Association, November, 1956.

Hsu, E. H. On the application of Viennese Infant Scale to Peiping babies. *J. genet. Psychol.*, 1946, *69*, 217–220.

Hull, C. L. *A behavior system.* New Haven: Yale University Press, 1952.

Humphreys, L. G. Characteristics of type concepts with special reference to Sheldon's typology. *Psychol. Bull.*, 1957, *54*, 218–228.

Hunt, J. McV. *Intelligence and experience.* New York: The Ronald Press Company, 1961.

Hurlock, Elizabeth B. *Developmental psychology.* New York: McGraw-Hill Book Co., 1959.

Huttenlocher, Janellen. Development of formal reasoning on concept formation problems. *Child Develpm.*, 1964, *35*, 1233–1242.

Irwin, O. C. Infant speech: the effect of family occupational status and of age on use of sound types. *J. Speech Hear. Dis.*, 1948, *13*, 224–226.

Irwin, O. C. Infant speech: effect of systematic reading of stories. *J. Speech Hear. Res.*, 1960, *3*, 187–190.

Iscoe, I., and J. Pierce-Jones. Divergent thinking, age, and intelligence in white and Negro children. *Child Develpm.*, 1964, *35*, 785–797.

Jack, Lois M. An experimental study of ascendant behavior in preschool children. *Univ. Iowa Stud. Child Welfare*, 1934, *9*, 7–65.

Jackson, D. N., and S. J. Messick. Content and style in personality assessment. *Psychol. Bull.*, 1958, *55*, 243–252.

Jahoda, G. Children's concepts of nationality: a critical study of Piaget's stages. *Child Develpm.*, 1964, *35*, 1081–1092.

Jakubczak, F., and R. H. Walters. Suggestibility as dependency behavior. *J. abnorm. soc. Psychol.*, 1959, *59*, 102–107.

Janoff, Irma Z., L. H. Beck, and I. L. Child. The relation of somatotype to reaction time, resistance to pain, and expressive movement. *J. Pers.*, 1950, *18*, 454–460.

Jaynes, J. Imprinting: The interaction of learned and innate behavior: I. Development and generalization. *J. comp. physiol. Psychol.*, 1956, *49*, 201–206.

Jaynes, J. Imprinting: The interaction of learned and innate behavior: II. The critical period. *J. comp. physiol. Psychol.*, 1957, *50*, 6–10.

Jeffrey, W. E. The effects of verbal and nonverbal responses in mediating an instrumental act. *J. exp. Psychol.*, 1953, *45*, 327–333.

Jenkins, W. P., and J. C. Stanley, Jr. Partial reinforcement: a review and critique. *Psychol. Bull.*, 1950, *47*, 193–234.

Jensen, A. R. Authoritarian attitudes and personality maladjustment. *J. abnorm. soc. Psychol.*, 1957, *54*, 303–311.

Jensen, A. R., and W. D. Rohwer, Jr. Syntactical mediation of serial and paired-associate learning as a function of age. *Child Develpm.*, 1965, *36*, 601–608.

Jersild, A. T. *Child psychology*. Englewood Cliffs, N.J.: Prentice-Hall, 1954.

Jersild, A. T., and Florence B. Holmes. *Children's fears*. New York: Bureau of publications, Teachers College, Columbia University, 1935. Part III. Pp. 167–296.

Johnson, G. O. A study of the social position of mentally handicapped children in the regular grades. *Amer. J. ment. Defic.*, 1950, *55*, 60–89.

Johnson, Laverne C. Body cathexis as a factor in somatic complaints. *J. consult. Psychol.*, 1956, *20*, 145–149.

Johnson, L. R. The status of thumb-sucking and finger-sucking. *J. Amer. dent. Assn.*, 1939, *26*, 1245–1254.

Johnson, Miriam M. Sex-role learning in the nuclear family. *Child Develpm.*, 1963, *34*, 319–333.

Jones, H. E. Adolescence in our society. In *The family in a democratic society*, anniversary papers of the Community Service Society of New York. New York: Columbia University Press, 1949. Pp. 70–82.

Jones, H. E. The environment and mental development. In L. Carmichael (ed.), *Manual of child psychology*, 2d ed. New York: John Wiley and Sons, 1954. Ch. 10, pp. 631–696.

Jones, H. E., and H. S. Conrad. Mental development in adolescence. *Natl. Soc. Study Educ.*, 43d Yearbook, 1944, Part I. Pp. 146–163.

Jones, H. E., and Ada P. Jorgensen. Mental growth as related to nursery-school attendance. *Natl. Soc. Study Educ.*, 39th Yearbook, 1940, Part II. Pp. 207–222.

Jones, Mary C. The later careers of boys·who were early- or late-maturing. *Child Develpm.*, 1957, *28*, 113–128.

Jones, Mary C. Psychological correlates of somatic development. *Child Develpm.*, 1965, *36*, 899–911.

Jones, Mary C., and Nancy Bayley. Physical maturing among boys as related to behavior. *J. educ. Psychol.,* 1950, *41,* 129–148.

Jones, Mary C., and P. H. Mussen. Self-conceptions, motivations, and interpersonal attitudes of early- and late-maturing girls. *Child Develpm.,* 1958, *29,* 491–501.

Kagan, Jerome. Socialization of aggression and the perception of parents in fantasy. *Child Develpm.,* 1958, *29,* 311–320.

Kagan, J., and F. A. Beach. Effects of early experience on mating behavior of male rats. *J. comp. physiol. Psychol.,* 1953, *46,* 204–208.

Kagan, J., and Marion Freeman. Relation of childhood intelligence, maternal behaviors, and social class to behavior during adolescence. *Child Develpm.,* 1963, *34,* 899–911.

Kagan, J., and Barbara A. Henker. Developmental psychology. Chapter in P. R. Farnsworth, Olga McNemar, and Q. McNemar. *Annual Review of Psychology.* Palo Alto, Calif.: Annual Reviews, Inc., 1966.

Kagan, J., Bernice L. Rosman, Deborah Day, J. Albert, and W. Philips. Information processing in the child: significance of analytic and reflective attitudes. *Psychol. Monogr.,* 1964, *78,* 37.

Kagan, J., and H. A. Moss. Parental correlates of child's IQ and height: a cross-validation of the Berkeley Growth Study results. *Child Develpm.,* 1959, *30,* 325–332.

Kagan, J., and H. A. Moss. The stability of passive and dependent behavior from childhood through adulthood. *Child Develpm.,* 1960, *31,* 577–591.

Kahl, J. A. Educational and occupational aspirations of "common man" boys. *Harvard educ. Rev.,* 1953, *23,* 186–203.

Kahn, M. W. The effect of severe defeat at various age levels on the aggressive behavior of mice. *J. genet. Psychol.,* 1951, *79,* 117–130.

Kantor, M. *Andersonville.* Cleveland: World Publishing Co., 1955.

Karelitz, S., V. Fisichelli, Joan Costa, Ruth Karelitz, and Laura Rosenfeld. Relation of crying activity in early infancy to speech and intellectual development at age 3. *Child Develpm.,* 1964, *35,* 769–777.

Kates, S. L., and L. N. Diab. Authoritarian ideology and attitudes on parent-child relationships. *J. abnorm. soc. Psychol.,* 1955, *51,* 13–16.

Kaufman, H. F. *Defining prestige in a rural community.* Sociometry Monogr. No. 10. New York: Beacon House, 1946.

Kaufman, H. F. Prestige classes in a New York rural community. Ithaca, N.Y.: *Cornell agric. exp. Sta. Memoir,* 1944, No. 260.

Kaye, H., and G. R. Levin. Two attempts to demonstrate tonal suppression of nonnutritive sucking in neonates. *Perceptual and Motor Skills,* 1963, *17,* 521–522.

Kaye, H., and L. P. Lipsitt. Relation of electrotactual threshold to basal skin conductance. *Child Develpm.,* 1964, *35,* 1307–1312.

Keen, R. Effects of auditory stimuli on sucking behavior in the human neonate. *J. exp. Child Psychol.,* 1964, *1,* 348–354.

Keister, Mary E. The behavior of young children in failure: an experimental attempt to discover and to modify undesirable responses of preschool children to failure. *Univ. Iowa Stud. Child Welfare,* 1937, *14,* 27–82.

Kellmer Pringle, M. L., and V. Bossio. Early prolonged separation and emotional maladjustment. *Child Psychol. and Psychiat.*, 1960, *1*, 37–48.

Kendig, Isabelle, and Winifred V. Richmond. *Psychological studies in dementia praecox*. Ann Arbor, Mich.: Edwards Brothers, 1940.

Kent, Norma, and D. R. Davis. Discipline in the home and intellectual development. *Brit. J. med. Psychol.*, 1957, *30*, 27–33.

Kephart, N. C. Influencing the rate of mental growth in retarded children through environmental stimulation. *Natl. Soc. Study Educ.*, 39th Yearbook, 1940, Part II. Pp. 223–230.

Kephart, N. C., and Mildred H. Ainsworth. A preliminary study of the community adjustment of parolees of the Wayne County Training School. *Amer. Assn. ment. Defic.*, 1938, *43*, 161–166.

Kephart, N. C., and A. A. Strauss. A clinical factor influencing variations in IQ. *Amer. J. Orthopsychiat.*, 1940, *10*, 343–350.

Ketcham, W. A. Growth patterns of gifted children. *Merrill-Palmer Quart.*, 1957, *3*, 188–197.

Kimble, G. A. *Principles of general psychology*. New York: The Ronald Press Co., 1956.

King, J. A., and Nancy L. Gurney. Effect of early social experience on adult aggressive behavior in C57BL/10 mice. *J. comp. physiol. Psychol.*, 1954, *47*, 326–330.

Kinsey, A. C., W. B. Pomeroy, and C. E. Martin. *Sexual behavior in the human male*. Philadelphia: W. B. Saunders Co., 1948.

Kinsey, A. C., W. B. Pomeroy, C. E. Martin, and P. H. Gebhard. *Sexual behavior in the human female*. Philadelphia: W. B. Saunders Co., 1953.

Klackenberg, G. Thumb-sucking: frequency and etiology. *Pediatrics*, 1949, *4*, 418–424.

Klatskin, Ethelyn H., A. G. Lethin, and Edith B. Jackson. Choice of rooming-in or newborn nursery. *Pediatrics*, 1950, *6*, 878–889.

Klausmeier, H. J., C. W. Harris, and Z. Ethnathios. Relationships between divergent thinking abilities and teacher ratings of high school students. *J. educ. Psychol.*, 1962, *53*, 72–75.

Klineberg, O. *Negro intelligence and selective migration*. New York: Columbia University Press, 1935.

Knief, Lotus, M., and J. B. Stroud. Intercorrelations among various intelligence, achievement, and social class scores. *J. educ. Psychol.*, 1959, *50*, 117–120.

Knobloch, Hilda, and B. Pasamanick. Exogenous factors in infant intelligence. *Pediatrics*, 1960, *26*, 210–218.

Knobloch, Hilda, and B. Pasamanick. The relationship of race and socioeconomic status to the development of motor behavior patterns in infancy. *Psychiatric Research Reports*, 1958, No. 10.

Knobloch, Hilda, and B. Pasamanick. Exogenous factors in infant intelligence. *Pediatrics*, 1960 (in press).

Koffsky, Ellin. A scalogram study of classificatory development. *Child Develpm.*, 1966, *37*, 191–204.

Kretschmer, E. *Körperbau und character*, 2d rev. ed. Trans. by W. J. H. Sprott as *Physique and character*. London: Routledge and Kegan Paul, Ltd., 1925.

Krishef, C. H. The influence of rural-urban environment upon the adjustment of dischargees from the Owatonna State School. *Amer. J. ment. Defic.,* 1959, *63,* 860–865.

Kuenne, Margaret R. Experimental investigation of the relation of language to transposition behavior in young children. *J. exp. Psychol.,* 1946, *36,* 417–490.

Kuhlmann, F. *Tests of mental development: A complete scale for individual examination.* Minneapolis: Educational Test Bureau, 1939.

Kulik, J. A., K. B. Stein, and T. R. Sarbin. Disclosure of delinquent behavior under conditions of anonymity and nonanonymity. Paper read at American Psychological Association, 1966.

Kunst, Mary S. A study of thumb- and finger-sucking in infants. *Psychol. Monogr.,* 1948, *3.*

Kutner, B. Patterns of mental functioning associated with prejudice in children. *Psychol. Monogr.,* 1958, 72.

Kutner, B., and N. B. Gordon. Cognitive functioning and prejudice: A nine-year follow-up study. *Sociometry,* 1964, *27,* 66–74.

Kwall, Donna S., and F. M. Lackner. Ability, sociometric and parent-child relationship variables in the prediction of elementary school achievement. Paper read at American Psychological Association, 1966.

Lakin, M. Personality factors in mothers of excessively crying (colicky) infants. *Monogr. Soc. Res. Child Develpm.,* 1957, *22,* Ser. 64, No. 1.

Landis, J. T., and Mary G. Landis. *Youth and marriage.* Englewood Cliffs, N.J.: Prentice-Hall, 1957.

Lansky, L. M., and G. McKay. Sex role preferences of kindergarten boys and girls: some contradictory results. *Psychological Reports,* 1963, *13,* 415–421.

Lantz, Beatrice. Some dynamic aspects of success and failure. *Psychol. Monogr.,* 1945, *59.*

Lauer, D. W., and W. K. Estes. Successive acquisitions and extinctions of a jumping habit in relation to schedule of reinforcement. *J. comp. physiol. Psychol.,* 1955, *48,* 8–13.

Lazowick, L. M. On the nature of identification. *J. abnorm. soc. Psychol.,* 1955, *51,* 175–183.

Leahy, Alice M. Nature-nurture and intelligence. *Genet. Psychol. Monogr.,* 1935, *17,* 235–308.

Lee, E. S. Negro intelligence and selective migration: a Philadelphia test of the Klineberg hypothesis. *Amer. sociol. Rev.,* 1951, *16,* 227–233.

Leinert, G. A., and H. W. Crott. Studies on the factor structure of intelligence in children, adolescents and adults. *Vita Humana,* 1964, 7, 147–163.

LeShan, L. L. Time orientation and social class. *J. abnorm. soc. Psychol.,* 1952, *47,* 589–592.

Lesser, G. S. Extrapunitiveness and ethnic attitude. *J. abnorm. soc. Psychol.,* 1958, *56,* 281–282.

Lesser, G. S. The relationships between various forms of aggression and popularity among lower-class children. *J. educ. Psychol.,* 1959, *50,* 20–25.

Lesser, G. S., G. Fifer, and D. H. Clark. Mental abilities of children from different social-class and cultural groups. *Monogr. Soc. Res. Child Develpm.*, 1965, *30*, 115.

Levanway, R. W. The effect of stress on expressed attitudes toward self and others. *J. abnorm. soc. Psychol.*, 1955, *50*, 225–226.

Levin, H., and R. R. Sears. Identification with parents as a determinant of doll-play aggression. *Child Develpm.*, 1956, *27*, 135–155.

Leventhal, Alice S., and L. P. Lipsitt. Adaptation, pitch discrimination, and sound vocalization in the neonate. *Child Develpm.*, 1964, *35*, 759–767.

Levine, S. A further study of infantile handling and adult avoidance learning. *J. Pers.*, 1956, *25*, 96–114.

Levine, D., and D. W. Dysinger. Patterns of intellectual performance and the outcome of institutionalization in the mentally retarded. *Amer. J. men. Defic.*, 1964, *68*, 784–788.

Levine, S., and L. S. Otis. The effects of handling before and after weaning on the resistance of albino rats to later deprivation. *Can. J. Psychol.*, 1958, *12*, 103–106.

Levitt, E. E. The water-jar Einstellung test as a measure of rigidity. *Psychol. Bull.*, 1956, *53*, 347–370.

Levy, D. M. Experiments on the sucking reflex and social behavior in dogs. *Amer. J. Orthopsychiat.*, 1934, *4*, 203–224.

Levy, D. M. Release therapy. *Amer. J. Orthopsychiat.*, 1939, *9*, 713–736.

Levy, L. H. The meaning and generality of perceived actual-ideal discrepancies. *J. consult. Psychol.*, 1956, *20*, 396–398.

Levy, L., and B. R. McCandless. Expectancy of punishment as a function of type of differentiation in original learning. *J. abnorm. soc. Psychol.*, 1952, *47*, 520–525.

Levy, Ruth J. Effects of institutional vs. boarding-home care on a group of infants. *J. Pers.*, 1947, *15*, 233–241.

Lewin, K. *A dynamic theory of personality.* New York: McGraw-Hill Book Co., 1935.

Lewin, K., Tamara Dembo, L. Festinger, and Pauline S. Sears. Level of aspiration. In J. McV. Hunt (ed.), *Personality and the behavior disorders.* New York: The Ronald Press Co., 1944. Pp. 333–378.

Lewin, K., R. Lippitt, and R. K. White. Patterns of aggressive behavior in experimentally created "social climates." *J. soc. Psychol.*, 1939, *10*, 271–299.

Lewis, Hilda. *Deprived children: The Mersham experiment—a social and clinical study.* London: Oxford University Press, 1954.

Lewis, S. J. Thumb-sucking: a cause of malocclusion in the deciduous teeth. *J. Amer. dent. Assn.*, 1930, *17*, 1060–1072.

Lewis, S. J. Undesirable habits influencing the deciduous dentition. *J. Amer. dent. Assn.*, 1931, *18*, 1766–1778.

Lindzey, G. Thematic Apperception Test: interpretative assumptions and related empirical evidence. *Psychol. Bull.*, 1952, *49*, 1–25.

Lindzey, G., and P. S. Herman. Thematic Apperception Test: a note on reliability and situational validity. *J. proj. Tech.*, 1955, *19*, 36–42.

Lindzey, G., D. T. Lykken, and H. D. Winston. Infantile trauma, genetic factors, and adult temperament. *J. abnorm. soc. Psychol.*, 1960, *61*, 7–14.

Lindzey, G., and D. Kalnins. Thematic Apperception Test: some evidence bearing on the "hero assumption." *J. abnorm. soc. Psychol.*, 1958, *57*, 76–83.

Lindzey, G., and Charlotte Tejessy. Thematic Apperception Test: indices of aggression in relation to measures of overt and covert behavior. *Amer. J. Orthopsychiat.*, 1956, *26*, 567–576.

Lindzey, G., Charlotte Tejessy, and H. S. Zamansky. Thematic Apperception Test: an empirical examination of some indices of homosexuality. *J. abnorm. soc. Psychol.*, 1958, *57*, 67–75.

Lipsitt, L. P. A self-concept scale for children and its relationship to the Children's Form of the Manifest Anxiety Scale. *Child Develpm.*, 1958, *29*, 463–472.

Lipsitt, L. P., T. Engen, and H. Kaye. Developmental changes in the olfactory threshold of the neonate. *Child Develpm.*, 1963, *34*, 371–376.

Little, Sue W., and L. D. Cohen. Goal-setting behavior of asthmatic children and of their mothers for them. *J. Pers.*, 1951, *19*, 376–389.

Liverant, S. MMPI differences between parents of disturbed and nondisturbed children. *J. consult. Psychol.*, 1959, *23*, 256–260.

Loevinger, Jane. Intelligence as related to socioeconomic factors. *Natl. Soc. Study Educ.*, 39th Yearbook, 1940, Part II. Pp. 159–211.

Long, Barbara H., and E. H. Henderson. Self-social concepts of disadvantaged school beginners. American Psychological Association, 1966. Paper read at annual meeting.

Love, Mary I., and Sylvia Beach. Performance of children on the Davis-Eells Games and other measures of ability. *J. consult. Psychol.*, 1957, *21*, 29–32.

Lowe, C. M. The self-concept: fact or artifact? *Psychol. Bull.*, 1961, *58*, 325–336.

Lowrey, L. G. Personality distortion and early institutional care. *Amer. J. Orthopsychiat.*, 1940, *10*, 576–585.

Luchins, A. S., and R. H. Forgus. The effect of differential postweaning environments on the rigidity of an animal's behavior. *J. genet. Psychol.*, 1955, *86*, 51–58.

Lucite, L. F. Independence-conformity behavior as a function of intellect: bright and dull children. *Exceptional Children*, 1964, *31*, 5–13.

Luckey, Eleanore B. Marital satisfaction and parent concepts. *J. consult. Psychol.*, 1960, *24*, 195–204.

Lyle, W. H., Jr., and E. E. Levitt. Punitiveness, authoritarianism, and parental discipline of grade-school children. *J. abnorm. soc. Psychol.*, 1955, *51*, 42–46.

Lynch, Elizabeth I., and Alice E. Mertz. Adoptive placement of infants directly from the hospital. *Soc. Casework*, 1955, *36*, 451–457.

Lynn, D. B. Sex differences in masculine and feminine identification. *Psychol. Rev.*, 1959, *66*, 126–135.

Lynn, D. B., and W. L. Sawrey. The effects of father-absence on Norwegian boys and girls. *J. abnorm. soc. Psychol.*, 1959, *59*, 258–262.

Maas, H. S. Some social-class differences in the family systems and group relations of pre- and early adolescents. *Child Develpm.*, 1951, *22*, 145–152.

McArthur, C. Personality differences between middle and upper classes. *J. abnorm. soc. Psychol.*, 1955, *50*, 247–254.

McArthur, C., and Lucia Stevens. The validation of expressed interests as compared with inventoried interests: a fourteen-year follow-up. *J. appl. Psychol.*, 1955, *39*, 184–189.

McCord, Joan, W. McCord, and Emily Thurber. Some effects of paternal absence on male children. *J. abnorm. soc. Psychol.*, 1962, *64*, 361–369.

McCandless, B. R. Changing relationships between dominance and social acceptability during group democratization. *Amer. J. Orthopsychiat.*, 1942, *12*, 529–536.

McCandless, B. R. *Children and Adolescence: Behavior and development.* New York: Holt, Rinehart and Winston, 1961.

McCandless, B. R. Environment and intelligence. *Amer. J. ment. Defic.*, 1952, *56*, 674–691.

McCandless, B. R. Should a bright child start to school before he's five? *Educ.*, 1957, *77*, 1–6.

McCandless, B. R., Carolyn Balsbaugh, and Hannah L. Bennett. Preschool-age socialization and maternal control techniques. *Amer. Psychologist*, 1958, *13*, 320 (abstract).

McCandless, B. R., Carolyn B. Bilous, and Hannah L. Bennett. The relation between peer-popularity and dependence on adults in preschool-age socialization. *Child Develpm.*, 1961, *32*, 511–518.

McCandless, B. R., and A. Castaneda. Anxiety in children, school achievement, and intelligence. *Child Develpm.*, 1956, *27*, 379–382.

McCandless, B. R., A. Castaneda, and D. S. Palermo. Anxiety in children and social status. *Child Develpm.*, 1956, *27*, 385–392.

McCandless, B. R., and Helene Heye. The relationship of certain maternal attitudes, dependency, and nervous habits in preschool-aged children. *Amer. Psychologist*, 1949, *4*, 249 (abstract).

McCandless, B. R., and H. D. Holloway. Race prejudice and intolerance of ambiguity in children. *J. abnorm. soc. Psychol.*, 1955, *51*, 692–693.

McCandless, B. R., and Helen R. Marshall. A picture sociometric technique for preschool children and its relation to teacher judgments of friendship. *Child Develpm.*, 1957, *28*, 139–147.

McCandless, Elinore O. School achievement of newly institutionalized high-grade mentally retarded children. Wayne County Training School, Northville, Mich., 1943. Unpublished ms.

McCarthy, Dorothea. Child Development: Implications for mental retardation with special reference to language development. Unpublished paper presented at American Association on Mental Deficiency, Great Lakes Region Annual Conference, Columbus, O., 1964.

McClelland, D. C. Risk-taking in children with high and low need for achievement. In J. W. Atkinson (ed.), *Motives in fantasy, action, and society.* Princeton: Van Nostrand, 1958.

McClelland, W. J. Differential handling and weight gain in the albino rat. *Can. J. Psychol.*, 1956, *10*, 19–22.

McCord, W., Joan McCord, and A. Howard. Familial correlates of aggression in nondelinquent male children. *J. abnorm. soc. Psychol.*, 1961, *62*, 79–93.

McCloy, Emma McC. Discussion: Chapter 6, Techniques of behavior study for children, pp. 105–110. In: *National Institute of Mental Health. Child Research in Psychopharmacology.* Springfield, Ill.: Charles C Thomas, 1959.

Maccoby, Eleanor E., P. K. Gibbs, and staff. Methods of child-rearing in two social classes. In W. E. Martin and Celia B. Stendler (eds.), *Readings in child development.* New York: Harcourt, Brace & World, Inc., 1954. Pp. 380–396.

McGehee, W., and W. D. Lewis. The socioeconomic status of homes of mentally superior and retarded children and the occupational rank of their parents. *J. genet. Psychol.*, 1942, *60*, 375–380.

McGeoch, J. A. *The psychology of human learning*, 2d rev. ed. by Arthur L. Irion. New York: Longmans, Green, 1952.

McGinnis, J. M. Eye movements and optic nystagmus in early infancy. *Genet. Psychol. Monogr.*, 1930, *8*, 321–430.

McGraw, Myrtle B. Growth: *A study of Johnny and Jimmy*. New York: Appleton-Century, 1935.

McGuire, C., M. Lanmon, and G. D. White. Adolescent peer acceptance and valuations of role behavior. *Amer. Psychologist*, 1953, *8*, 397 (abstract).

McGuire, C., G. D. White, and E. Novak. Adolescent role behavior and age-mate acceptance. Paper read at Southwestern Social Science Association, Dallas, Texas, April 1954.

McIntyre, C. J. Acceptance by others and its relation to acceptance of self and others. *J. abnorm. soc. Psychol.*, 1952, *47*, 624–625.

McKee, J. P., and Florence B. Leader. The relationship of socioeconomic status and aggression to the competitive behavior of preschool children. *Child Develpm.*, 1955, *26*, 135–142.

McKelvey, R. K., and M. H. Marx. Effects of infantile food and water deprivation on adult hoarding in the rat. *J. comp. physiol. Psychol.*, 1951, *44*, 423–430.

McMichael, R. E., and R. E. Grinder. Children's guilt after transgression: combined effect of exposure to American culture and ethnic background. *Child Develpm.*, 1966, *37*, 425–431.

McNemar, Q. A critical examination of the University of Iowa studies of environmental influences upon the IQ. *Psychol. Bull.*, 1940, *37*, 63–92.

Mallick, S. K., and B. R. McCandless. A study of catharsis of aggression. *J. Pers. soc. Psychol.*, 1967 (in press).

Maier, N. R. F. Frustration theory: restatement and extension. *Psychol. Rev.*, 1956, *63*, 370–388.

Malzberg, B. Some statistical aspects of mongolism. *Amer. J. ment. Defic.*, 1950, *54*, 226–281.

Marshall, Helen R., and B. R. McCandless. Relationship between dependence on adults and social acceptance by peers. *Child Develpm.*, 1957, *28*, 421–425.

Marshall, Helen R., and Lucille Magruder. Relations between parent money-education practices and children's knowledge and use of money. *Child Develpm.*, 1960, *31*, 253–284.

Martire, J. G. Relationships between the self-concept and differences in the strength and generality of achievement motivation. *J. Pers.*, 1956, *24*, 364–375.

Masling, J. M. How neurotic is the authoritarian? *J. abnorm. soc. Psychol.*, 1954, *49*, 316–318.

Maslow, A. H. The instinctoid nature of basic needs. *J. Pers.*, 1954, *22*, 326–347.

Maslow, A. H., and J. Marie Sakoda. Volunteer-error in the Kinsey study. *J. abnorm. soc. Psychol.*, 1952, *47*, 259–262.

Maslow, A. H., and I. Szilagyi-Kessler. Security and breast feeding. *J. abnorm. soc. Psychol.*, 1946, *41*, 83–85.

Matsushima, J. An instrument for classifying impulse control among boys. *J. consult. Psychol.*, 1964, *28*, 87–90.

Mednick, S. *Learning.* Englewood Cliffs, N.J.: Prentice-Hall, 1964.

Mednick, S. A., and Laura E. Lehtinen. Stimulus generalization as a function of age in children. *J. exp. Psychol.*, 1957, *53*, 180–183.

Melton, A. W. Learning. In W. S. Monroe (ed.), *Encyclopedia of educational research*, 2d ed. New York: The Macmillan Co., 1950. Pp. 668–690.

Melzack, R. Irrational fears in the dog. *Can. J. Psychol.*, 1952, *6*, 141–147.

Melzack, R. The genesis of emotional behavior: an experimental study of the dog. *J. comp. physiol. Psychol.*, 1954, *47*, 166–168.

Melzack, R., and T. H. Scott. The effects of early experience on the response to pain. *J. comp. physiol. Psychol.*, 1957, *50*, 155–161.

Melzack, R., and W. R. Thompson. Effects of early experience on social behavior. *Can. J. Psychol.*, 1956, *10*, 82–90.

Mendel, Gisela. Children's preference for differing degrees of novelty. *Child Develpm.*, 1965, *36*, 453–465.

Menlove, Frances L. Aggressive symptoms in emotionally disturbed adopted children. *Child Develpm.*, 1965, *36*, 519–532.

Meredith, H. V. Comments on "The varieties of human physique." *Child Develpm.*, 1940, *11*, 301–309.

Meredith, H. V. A descriptive concept of physical development. In D. B. Harris (ed.), *The concept of development.* Minneapolis: University of Minnesota Press, 1957. Pp. 109–122.

Meredith, H. V. Physical growth. In *Encyclopedia Americana*, 1959, *13*, 499–502b.

Meredith, H. V. Status of Massachusetts children of North European and Italian ancestry. *Amer. J. phys. Anthrop.*, 1939, *24*, 301–346.

Miles, Catherine C., and W. R. Miles. The correlation of intelligence scores and chronological age from early to late maturity. *Amer. J. Psychol.*, 1932, *44*, 44–78.

Miller, E. L. Ability and social adjustment at midlife of persons earlier judged mentally deficient. *Genet. Psychol. Monogr.*, 1965, *72*, 139–198.

Miller, June. How infants three, four, and five months of age respond to sound. *Exceptional Children*, 1963, *30*, 149–154.

Miller, D. R., and Swanson, G. E. *Inner Conflict and Defense.* New York: Holt, Rinehart and Winston Co., 1960.

Miller, N. E. Comments on theoretical models illustrated by the development of a theory of conflict behavior. *J. Pers.*, 1951, *20*, 82–100.

Miller, N. E. Theory and experiment relating psychoanalytic displacement to stimulus-response generalization. *J. abnorm. soc. Psychol.*, 1948, *43*, 155–178.

Milner, Esther. A study of the relationship between reading readiness in grade-one school children and patterns of parent-child interaction. *Child Develpm.*, 1951, *22*, 95–112.

Milton, G. A. A factor analytic study of child-rearing behaviors. *Child Develpm.*, 1958, *29*, 381–392.

Mischel, W. Preference for delayed reinforcement: an experimental study of a cultural observation. *J. abnorm. soc. Psychol.*, 1958, *56*, 57–61.

Mischel, W., and R. Metzner. Preference for delayed reward as a function of age, intelligence, and length of delay interval. *J. abnorm. soc. Psychol.*, 1962, *64*, 425–431.

Mitchell, J. V., Jr. Goal-setting behavior as a function of self-acceptance, over- and underachievement, and related personality variables. *J. educ. Psychol.*, 1959, *50*, 93–104.

Montagu, M. F. A. *Adolescent sterility*. Springfield, Ill.: Charles C Thomas, 1946.

Montgomery, K. C. The relation between fear induced by novel stimulation and exploratory behavior. *J. comp. physiol. Psychol.*, 1955, *48*, 254–260.

Montgomery, K. C., and M. Segall. Discrimination learning based upon the exploratory drive. *J. comp. physiol. Psychol.*, 1955, *48*, 225–228.

Morgenson, G. J., G. A. McMurray, and L. B. Jaques. Effects of stress and administration of cortisone on weight gain in gentled rats. *Can. J. Psychol.*, 1957, *11*, 123–127.

Moulton, R. W., P. G. Liberty, Jr., E. Burnsetein, and N. Altucher. Patterning of parental affection and disciplinary dominance as a determinant of guilt and sex-typing. *J. Pers. soc. Psychol.*, 1966, *4*, 356–363.

Mueller, W. J. Need structure and the projection of traits onto parents. *J. Pers. soc. Psychol.*, 1966, *3*, 63–72.

Mundy, Lydia. Environmental influence on intellectual function as measured by intelligence tests. *Brit. J. med. Psychol.*, 1957, *30*, 194–201.

Munn, N. L. Learning in children. In Carmichael, L. (ed.), *Manual of Child Psychology*, 2d ed. New York: John Wiley and Sons, 1954. Pp. 374–458.

Munn, N. L. *Psychological development*. Boston: Houghton Mifflin Co., 1938.

Munsinger, H., and W. Kessen. Uncertainty, structure, and preference. *Psychol. Monogr.*, 1964, *78*, 24.

Murphy, D. P. *Congenital malformation*, 2d ed. Philadelphia: University of Pennsylvania Press, 1947.

Murphy, D. P. The outcome of 625 pregnancies in women subjected to pelvic radium roentgen irradiation. *Amer. J. Obst. Gynec.*, 1929, *18*, 179–187.

Murphy, C., Lois B. Murphy, and T. M. Newcomb. *Experimental social psychology*, rev. ed. New York: Harper & Brothers, 1937.

Murray, E. J., and M. M. Berkun. Displacement as a function of conflict. *J. abnorm. soc. Psychol.*, 1955, *51*, 47–56.

Mussen, P. H. Some personality and social factors related to changes in children's attitudes toward Negroes. *J. abnorm. soc. Psychol.*, 1950, *45*, 423–441.

Mussen, P. H., and J. Conger. *Child development and personality.* New York: Harper & Brothers, 1956.

Mussen, P. H., and L. Distler. Masculinity, identification, and father-son relationships. *J. abnorm. soc. Psychol.*, 1959, *59*, 350–356.

Mussen, P. H., and Mary C. Jones. Self-conceptions, motivations, and interpersonal attitudes of late- and early-maturing boys. *Child Develpm.*, 1957, *28*, 242–256.

Mussen, P. H., and J. Kagan. Group conformity and perception of parents. *Child Develpm.*, 1958, *29*, 57–60.

Mussen, P. H., and H. K. Naylor. The relationships between overt and fantasy aggression. *J. abnorm. soc. Psychol.*, 1954, *49*, 235–240.

Mussen, P. H., and L. W. Porter. Personal motivations and self-conceptions associated with effectiveness and ineffectiveness in emergent groups. *J. abnorm. soc. Psychol.*, 1959, *59*, 23–27.

Mussen, P., and E. Rutherford. Parent-child relations and parental personality in relation to young children's sex-role preferences. *Child Develpm.*, 1963, *34*, 589–608.

Nakamura, C. Y. The relationship between children's expressions of hostility and methods of discipline exercised by dominant overprotective parents. *Child Develpm.*, 1959, *30*, 109–118.

Nash, J. The father in contemporary culture and current psychological literature. *Child Develpm.*, 1965, *36*, 261–297.

National Institute of Neurological Diseases and Blindness. *Collaborative prenatal research project.* Bethesda, Md.: National Institutes of Health, 1963.

Neale, J. M. Egocentrism in institutionalized and noninstitutionalized children. *Child Develpm.*, 1966, *37*, 97–101.

Neel, Ann F. The relationship of authoritarian personality to learning: F-scale scores compared to classroom performance. *J. educ. Psychol.*, 1959, *50*, 195–199.

Newman, H. F., F. N. Freeman, and K. J. Holzinger. *Twins: a study of heredity and environment.* Chicago: The University of Chicago Press, 1937.

Newton, N. R., and M. Newton. Relationship of ability to breast feed and maternal attitudes toward breast feeding. *Pediatrics*, 1950, *5*, 869–875.

Nunally, J. C., A. J. Duchnowski, and R. K. Parker. Association of neutral objects with rewards: effect on verbal evaluation, reward expectancy, and selective attention. *J. Pers. soc. Psychol.*, 1965, *1*, 270–274.

Nye, F. I., and Lois W. Hoffman. *The employed mother in America.* Chicago: Rand McNally, 1963. Pp. v, 406.

Oberlander, M., and N. Jenkin. Birth order and academic achievement. *Amer. Psychologist.* Paper read at APA, 1966.

O'Connor, Patricia. Ethnocentrism, "intolerance of ambiguity," and abstract reasoning ability. *J. abnorm. soc. Psychol.*, 1952, *47*, 526–530.

Omwake, Katharine T. The relation between acceptance of self and acceptance of others shown by three personality inventories. *J. consult. Psychol.,* 1954, *18,* 443–446.

Opstad, P. Effects of social class in American secondary-school education. University of Iowa, *Iowa Child Welfare Res. Sta.,* 1957. Unpublished ms.

O'Reilly, C. T., and E. J. O'Reilly. Religious beliefs of Catholic college students and their attitudes toward minorities. *J. abnorm. soc. Psychol.,* 1954, *49,* 378–380.

Orgel, S. Z. Personality distortion and early institutional care. *Amer. J. Orthopsychiat.,* 1941, *11,* 371–373.

Orlansky, H. Infant care and personality. *Psychol. Bull.,* 1949, *46,* 1–48.

Otis, Nancy B., and B. R. McCandless. Responses to repeated frustrations of young children differentiated according to need area. *J. abnorm. soc. Psychol.,* 1955, *50,* 349–353.

Owens, W. A., Jr. Age and mental abilities: a longitudinal study. *Genet. Psychol. Monogr.,* 1953, *48,* 3–54.

Page, Marjorie, L. The modification of ascendant behavior in preschool children. *Univ. Iowa Stud. Child Welfare,* 1936, *12,* 1–69.

Palermo, D. S. Racial comparisons and additional normative data on the Children's Manifest Anxiety Scale. *Child Develpm.,* 1959, *30,* 53–58.

Palermo, D. S., A. Castaneda, and B. R. McCandless. The relationship of anxiety in children to performance in a complex learning task. *Child Develpm.,* 1956, *27,* 333–338.

Parsons, T. Family structure and the socialization of the child. In T. Parsons and R. F. Bales (eds.). *Family, Socialization, and Interaction Process.* Glencoe, Ill.: The Free Press, 1955.

Pasamanick, B. A comparative study of the behavioral development of Negro infants. *J. genet. Psychol.,* 1946, *69,* 3–44.

Payne, D. A., and W. W. Farquhar. The dimensions of an objective measure of academic self-concept. *J. educ. Psychol.,* 1962, *53,* 187–192.

Payne, D. E., and P. H. Mussen. Parent-child relations and father identification among adolescent boys. *J. abnorm. soc. Psychol.,* 1956, *52,* 358–362.

Penney, R. K. Reactive curiosity and manifest anxiety in children. *Child Develpm.,* 1965, *36,* 697–702.

Peterson, C. H., and F. L. Spano. Breast feeding, maternal rejection, and child personality. *Charact. and Pers.,* 1941, *10,* 62–66.

Peterson, D. R., W. C. Becker, L. A. Hellmer, D. J. Shoemaker, and H. C. Quay. Parental attitudes and child adjustment. *Child Develpm.,* 1959, *30,* 119–130.

Pettigrew, T. F. Regional differences in anti-Negro prejudice. *J. abnorm. soc. Psychol.,* 1959, *59,* 28–36.

Phillips, E. L. Attitudes toward self and others: a brief questionnaire report. *J. consult. Psychol.,* 1951, *15,* 79–81.

Pikas, Anatol. Children's attitudes toward rational versus inhibiting parental authority. *J. abnorm. soc. Psychol.,* 1961, *62,* 315–321.

Pinneau, S. R. The infantile disorders of hospitalism and anaclitic depression. *Psychol. Bull.,* 1955a, *52,* 429–452.

Pinneau, S. R. Reply to Dr. Spitz. *Psychol. Bull.*, 1955b, *52*, 459–462.

Pinneau, S. R., and H. E. Jones. Mental development in infancy and childhood and mental abilities in adult life. *Rev. educ. Res.*, 1955, *25*, 415–437.

Polak, P. R., R. N. Emde, and R. A. Spitz. The smiling response. II: Visual discrimination and the onset of depth perception. *J. Nervous and Mental Disease*, 1964, *139*, 407–415.

Pratt, K. C. The Neonate. In L. Carmichael (ed.), *Manual of Child Psychology*, 2d ed. New York: John Wiley and Sons, 1954. Pp. 215–291.

Pratt, K. C., Amalie K. Nelson, and K. H. Sun. *The behavior of the newborn infant*. Columbus: The Ohio State University Press, 1930.

Prothro, E. Terry. Patterns of permissiveness among preliterate peoples. *J. abnorm. soc. Psychol.*, 1960, *61*, 151–154.

Provence, Sally. Environmentally deprived infants. Paper read at Indiana State Pediatrics Association Meetings, Indianapolis, Ind., 1965.

Purcell, K. The TAT and antisocial behavior. *J. consult. Psychol.*, 1956, *20*, 449–456.

Rabban, M. Sex-role identification in young children in two diverse social groups. *Genet. Psychol. Monogr.*, 1950, *42*, 81–158

Rabin, A. I. Attitudes of Kibbutz children to family and parents. *Amer. J. Orthopsychiat.*, 1959, *29*, 172–179.

Radke, Marian J. Relation of parental authority to children's behavior and attitudes. *Univ. Minn. Inst. Child Welfare Monogr.*, 1946, No. 22.

Rank, O. *The trauma of birth*. New York: Harcourt, Brace, & World, Inc., 1929.

Reese, H. W. Relationships between self-acceptance and sociometric choices. *J. abnorm. soc. Psychol.*, 1961, *62*, 472–474.

Reymert, M. L., and R. T. Hinton, Jr. The effect of a change to a relatively superior environment upon the IQ's of one hundred children. *Natl. Soc. Study Educ.*, 39th Yearbook, 1940, Part II. Pp. 225–268.

Rheingold, Harriet L. The modification of social responsiveness in institutional babies. *Monogr. Soc. Res. Child Develpm.*, 1956, *21*, 3–48.

Rheingold, Harriet L., J. L. Gewirtz, and Helen W. Ross. Social conditioning of vocalizations in the infant. *J. comp. physiol. Psychol.*, 1959, *52*, 68–73.

Ribble, Margaret. *The rights of infants*. New York: Columbia University Press, 1943.

Ring, K., C. E. Lipinski, and Dorothea Braginsky. The relationship of birth order to self-evaluation, anxiety reduction, and susceptibility to emotional contagion. *Psychol. Monogr.*, 1965, *79*, No. 603.

Riss, W., and R. W. Goy. Modification of sex drive and O_2 consumption by isolating and grouping male guinea pigs. *J. comp. physiol. Psychol.*, 1957, *50*, 150–154.

Ritchie, B. F., B. Aeschliman, and P. Pierce. Studies in spatial learning: VIII. Place performance and the acquisition of place dispositions. *J. comp. physiol. Psychol.*, 1950, *43*, 73–85.

Robbins, Lillian C. The accuracy of parental recall of aspects of child development and of child-rearing practices. *J. abnorm. soc. Psychol.*, 1963, *68*, 261–270.

Rogers, C. R. *Client-centered therapy*. Boston: Houghton Mifflin Co., 1951.

Rogers, C. R. A coordinated research in psychotherapy: a nonobjective introduction. *J. consult. Psychol.*, 1949, *13*, 169–175.

Rogers, C. R., and Rosalind F. Dymond (eds.). *Psychotherapy and personality change.* Chicago: The University of Chicago Press, 1954.

Rogerson, B. C. F., and C. H. Rogerson. Feeding in infancy and subsequent psychological difficulties. *J. ment. Sci.*, 1939, *85*, 1163–1182.

Roff, M. Childhood social interactions and young adult bad conduct. *J. abnorm. soc. Psychol.*, 1961, *63*, 333–337.

Rosen, B. The achievement syndrome: a psychocultural dimension of social stratification. *Amer. sociol. Rev.*, 1956, *21*, 203–211.

Rosenbaum, M. E., and R. F. Stanners. Self-esteem, manifest hostility, and expression of hostility. *J. abnorm. soc. Psychol.*, 1961, *63*, 646–649.

Rosenblum, S. The effects of differential reinforcement and motivation on prediction responses of children. *Child Develpm.*, 1956, *27*, 99–108.

Rosenblum, S., J. E. Keller, and N. Papania. Davis-Eells ("Culture Fair") test performance of lower-class retarded children. *J. consult. Psychol.*, 1955, *19*, 51–54.

Rosenthal, Irene. Reliability of retrospective reports of adolescence. *J. consult. Psychol.*, 1963, *27*, 189–198.

Rosenthal, R. Experimenter outcome-orientation and the results of the psychological experiment. *Psychol. Bull.*, 1964, *61*, 405–412.

Rosenthal, R. Recent research on the effects of the experimenter's expectancy. Indiana Psychological Association, 1965. Unpublished paper.

Rosenzweig, S. Frustration as an experimental problem: The significance of frustration as a problem of research. *Charact. and Pers.*, 1938, *7*, 126–128.

Rosenzweig, S. Need-persistive and ego-defensive reactions to frustration as demonstrated by an experiment on repression. *Psychol. Rev.*, 1941, *48*, 347–349.

Rosenzweig, S. An outline of frustration theory. In J. McV. Hunt (ed.), *Personality and the behavior disorders,* Vol. I. New York: The Roland Press Co., 1944. Ch. II, pp. 379–388.

Rosenzweig, S. Revised norms for the adult form of the Rosenzweig Picture-Frustration Study. *J. Pers.*, 1950, *18*, 344–346.

Rossi, E. L., and Sheila I. Rossi. Concept utilization, serial order, and recall in nursery-school children. *Child Develpm.*, 1965, *36*, 771–778.

Rotter, J. B. *Social learning and clinical psychology.* Englewood Cliffs, N.J.: Prentice-Hall, 1954.

Ruja, H. J. The relation between neonate crying and length of labor. *J. genet. Psychol.*, 1948, *73*, 53–55.

Rynerson, Mary N. The relationship between scores on the Children's Manifest Anxiety Scale and clinical judgments of anxiety. Unpublished M.A. thesis, The University of Chicago, 1957.

Sandin, A. A. *Social and emotional adjustments of regularly promoted and nonpromoted pupils.* New York: Bureau of Publications, Teachers College, Columbia University, 1944.

Sarason, S. B. *Psychological problems in mental deficiency.* New York: Harper & Brothers, 1953.

Schaffer, H. R., and P. E. Emerson. Patterns of response to physical contact in early human development. *J. Child Psychol. Psychiat.*, 1964, *5*, 1–13.

Schonfeld, W. A. Inadequate masculine physique as a factor in personality development of adolescent boys. *Psychosom. Med.*, 1950, *12*, 49–54.

Scott, J. H. Some effects at maturity of gentling, ignoring, or shocking rats during infancy. *J. abnorm. soc. Psychol.*, 1955, *51*, 412–414.

Scott, R. First to ninth grade IQ changes of northern Negro students. *Psychology in the Schools*, 1966, *3*, 159–160.

Scott, T. H., W. H. Bexton, W. Heron, and B. K. Doane. Cognitive effects of perceptual isolation. *Can. J. Psychol.*, 1959, *13*, 200–209.

Sears, Pauline S. Child-rearing factors related to playing of sex-typed roles. *Amer. Psychologist*, 1953, *8*, 431 (abstract).

Sears, Pauline S. Doll-play aggression in normal young children: influence of sex, age, sibling status, father's absence. *Psychol. Monogr.*, 1951, *65*, Whole No. 323, No. 6.

Sears, R. R. A theoretical framework for personality and social behavior. *Amer. Psychologist*, 1951, *6*, 476–483.

Sears, R. R. Relation of early socialization experiences to aggression in middle childhood. *J. abnorm. soc. Psychol.*, 1961, *63*, 466–492.

Sears, R. R., Eleanor E. Maccoby, and H. Levin. *Patterns of child-rearing*. Evanston, Ill.: Row, Peterson, and Co., 1957.

Sears, R. R., and G. W. Wise. Relation of cup feeding in infancy to thumb-sucking and the oral drive. *Amer. J. Orthopsychiat.*, 1950, *20*, 123–138.

Secord, P. F., and S. M. Jourard. The appraisal of body-cathexis: body-cathexis and the self. *J. consult. Psychol.*, 1953, *17*, 343–347.

Seitz, P. F. D. The effects of infantile experiences upon adult behavior in animal subjects: I. Effects of little size during infancy upon adult behavior in the rat. *Amer. J. Psychiat.*, 1954, *110*, 916–927.

Sewall, Mary S. Two studies in sibling rivalry: I. Some causes of jealousy in young children. *Smith College Studies in Social Work*, 1930, *1*, 6–22.

Sewell, W. H. The construction and standardization of a scale for the measurement of the socioeconomic status of Oklahoma farm families. Stillwater, Okla.: *Okla. agric. exp. Sta. tech. Bull.*, 1940, No. 9.

Sewell, W. H. Infant training and the personality of the child. *Amer. J. Sociol.*, 1952, *58*, 150–159.

Sewell, W. H. Short form of the farm family socioeconomic scale. *Rural Sociol.*, 1943, *8*, 161–170.

Sewell, W. H., and A. O. Haller. Factors in the relationship between social status and the personality adjustment of the child. *Amer. sociol. Rev.*, 1959, *24*, 511–520.

Sewell, W. H., and A. O. Haller. Social status and the personality adjustment of the child. *Sociometry*, 1956, *19*, 114–125.

Sewell, W. H., and P. H. Mussen. The effects of feeding, weaning, and scheduling procedures on childhood adjustment and the formation of oral symptoms. *Child Develpm.*, 1952, *23*, 185–191.

Sewell, W. H., P. H. Mussen, and C. W. Harris. Relationships among child-training practices. *Amer. sociol. Rev.*, 1955, *20*, 137–148.

Sheldon, W. H. *The varieties of human physique*. New York: Harper & Brothers, 1940.

Sheldon, W. H. *The varieties of temperament*. New York: Harper & Brothers, 1942.

Sheldon, W. H., E. M. Hartl, and E. McDermott. *Varieties of delinquent youth*. New York: Harper & Brothers, 1949.

Sherman, M. The differentiation of emotional responses in infants: II. The ability of observers to judge the emotional characteristics of the crying of infants, and of the voice of an adult. *J. comp. Psychol.*, 1927, 7, 335–351.

Sherman, M., and I. C. Sherman. Sensorimotor responses in infants. *J. comp. Psychol.*, 1925, 5, 53–68.

Shirley, Mary M. The sequential method for the study of maturing behavior patterns. *Psychol. Rev.*, 1931, 38, 507–528.

Shuttleworth, F. K. The adolescent period: a pictorial atlas. *Monogr. Soc. Res. Child Develpm.*, 1949, 14.

Siegel, Alberta A., and Lynette G. Kihn. Permissiveness, permission, and aggression: the effect of adult presence or absence on aggression in children's play. *Child Develpm.*, 1959, 30, 131–141.

Siegel, S. M. The relationship of hostility to authoritarianism. *J. abnorm. soc. Psychol.*, 1956, 52, 368–372.

Siegman, A. W. Father absence during early childhood and antisocial behavior. *J. abnorm. Psychol.*, 1966, 71, 71–74.

Silberman, C. E. *Crisis in Black and White*. New York: Random House, Vintage Books, 1964.

Silverman, I. In defense of dissonance theory: reply to Chapanis and Chapanis. *Psychol. Bull.*, 1964, 62, 205–209.

Simpson, M. S. *Parent preferences of young children*. Contr. Educ. No. 652. New York: Bureau of Publications, Teachers College, Columbia University, 1935.

Simsarian, F. P., and P. A. McLendon. Further records of the self-demand schedule in infant feeding. *J. Pediatrics*, 1945, 27, 109–114.

Singer, J. L. Projected familial attitudes as a function of socioeconomic status and psychopathology. *J. consult. Psychol.*, 1954, 18, 99–104.

Singer, J. L., and M. K. Opler. Contrasting patterns of fantasy and motility in Irish and Italian schizophrenics. *J. abnorm. soc. Psychol.*, 1956, 53, 42–47.

Singer, J. L., H. Wilensky, and Vivian G. McCraven. Delaying capacity, fantasy, and planning ability: a factorial study of some basic ego functions. *J. consult. Psychol.*, 1956, 20, 375–383.

Skeels, H. M. Adult status of children with contrasting early life experiences. *Monogr. Soc. Res. Child Develpm.*, 1966, 31. Pp. iv, 65.

Skeels, H. M., and Irene E. Harms. Children with inferior social histories: their mental development in adoptive homes. *J. genet. Psychol.*, 1948, 72, 283–294.

Skeels, H. M., Ruth Updegraff, Beth L. Wellman, and H. M. Williams. A study of environmental stimulation: an orphanage preschool project. *Univ. Iowa Stud. Child Welfare*, 1938, 15, No. 4.

Skinner, B. F. *The behavior of organisms: an experimental analysis*. New York: Appleton-Century, 1938.

Skodak, Marie, and H. M. Skeels. A final follow-up study of one hundred adopted children. *J. genet. Psychol.,* 1949, *75,* 85–125.

Smith, Betty. *A tree grows in Brooklyn.* New York: Harper & Brothers, 1943.

Smith, C. U., and J. W. Prothro. Ethnic differences in authoritarian personality. *Soc. Forces,* 1957, *35,* 334–338.

Smith, H. P. A study in the selective character of American secondary education: Participation in school activities as conditioned by socioeconomic status and other factors. *J. educ. Psychol.,* 1945, *36,* 229–246.

Smith, J. M. The relative brightness values of three hues for newborn infants. *Univ. Iowa Stud. Child Welfare,* 1936, *12,* 91–140.

Smith, J. R., and J. C. Coleman. The relationship between manifestations of hostility in projective tests and overt behavior. *J. proj. Tech.,* 1956, *20,* 326–334.

Snygg, D. The relation between the intelligence of mothers and of their children living in foster homes. *J. genet. Psychol.,* 1938, *52,* 401–406.

Sontag, L. W. The significance of fetal environmental differences. *Amer. J. Obst. Gynec.,* 1941, *42,* 996–1003.

Sontag, L. W., and T. W. Richards. Studies in fetal behavior: I. Fetal heart rate as a behavioral indicator. *Child Develpm. Monogr.,* 1938, *3,* No. 4.

Sontag, L. W., and R. F. Wallace. The effect of cigarette-smoking during pregnancy upon the fetal heart rate. *Amer. J. Obst. Gynec.,* 1935, *29,* 3–8.

Spearman, C. *The abilities of man.* New York: The Macmillan Co., 1927.

Spears, W. C. Assessment of visual preference and discrimination in the 4-month-old infant. *J. comp. Psychol. Psychiat.,* 1964, *57,* 381–386.

Spector, A. J. Expectations, fulfillment, and morale. *J. abnorm. soc. Psychol.,* 1956, *52,* 51–56.

Speer, G. S. The mental development of children of feeble-minded and normal mothers. *Natl. Soc. Study Educ.,* 39th Yearbook, 1940, Part II. Pp. 309–314.

Spence, K. W. The differential response in animals to stimuli varying within a single stimulus dimension. *Psychol. Rev.,* 1937, *44,* 430–444.

Spence, K. W. The nature of discrimination learning in animals. *Psychol. Rev.,* 1936, *43,* 427–449.

Spence, K. W. The nature of the response in discrimination learning. *Psychol. Rev.,* 1952, *59,* 89–93.

Spiker, C. C. Stimulus pretraining and subsequent performance in the delayed reaction experiment. *J. exp. Psychol.,* 1956, *52,* 107–111.

Spiker, C. C., Irma R. Gerjuoy, and Winifred O. Shepard. Children's concept of middle-sizedness and performance on the intermediate size problem. *J. comp. physiol. Psychol.,* 1956, *49,* 416–419.

Spiker, C. C., and B. R. McCandless. The concept of intelligence and the philosophy of science. *Psychol. Rev.,* 1954, *61,* 255–266.

Spiker, C. C., and G. Terrell, Jr. Factors associated with transposition behavior of preschool children. *J. genet. Psychol.,* 1955, *86,* 143–158.

Spiro, M. E. *Children of the Kibbutz.* Cambridge, Massachusetts: Harvard University Press, 1958.

Spitz, R. A. Hospitalism: An inquiry into the genesis of psychiatric conditions in early childhood. In O. Fenichel *et al.* (eds.), *The psychoanalytic study of the child,* Vol. I. New York: International Universities Press, 1945. Pp. 53–74.

Spitz, R. A. Hospitalism: A follow-up report on investigation described in Vol. I, 1945. In O. Fenichel *et al.* (eds.), *The psychoanalytic study of the child,* Vol. II. New York: International Universities Press, 1946. Pp. 113–117.

Spitz, R. A. Reply to Dr. Pinneau. *Psychol. Bull.,* 1955, *52,* 453–458.

Spitz, R. A. The role of ecological factors in emotional development in infancy. *Child Develpm.,* 1949, *20,* 145–155.

Spock, B. *Baby and child care: revised and enlarged.* New York: Pocket Books, Inc., 1958.

Staffieri, J. R. A study of social stereotype of body image in children. *J. Pers. soc. Psychol.,* 1967 (in press).

Staffieri, J. R., and B. R. McCandless. A study of social stereotype of body image in children. Paper presented at the 50th Annual Meeting of the American Educational Research Association, 1966.

Starkweather, Elizabeth K., and Katherine E. Roberts. IQ changes occurring during nursery-school attendance at the Merrill-Palmer School. *Natl. Soc. Study Educ.,* 39th Yearbook, 1940, Part II. Pp. 315–335.

Steckler, G. A. Authoritarian ideology in Negro college students. *J. abnorm. soc. Psychol.,* 1957, *54,* 396–399.

Stendler, Celia B. Sixty years of child-training practices. *J. Pediatrics,* 1950, *36,* 122–134.

Stendler, Celia B. Social-class differences in parental attitudes toward school at grade-1 level. *Child Develpm.,* 1951, *22,* 36–46.

Stephens, W. N. Judgments by social workers on boys and mothers in fatherless families. *J. genet. Psychol.,* 1961, *99,* 59–64.

Stern, C. Hereditary factors affecting adoption. In M. Schapiro (ed.), *A study of adoption practice.* New York: Child Welfare League of America, 1956. Vol. II. Pp. 47–58.

Stevenson, H. W., and E. C. Stewart. A developmental study of racial awareness in young children. *Child Develpm.,* 1958, *29,* 399–409.

Stewart, Ann H., I. H. Weiland, A. R. Leider, C. A. Mangham, T. H. Holmes, and H. S. Ripley. Excessive infant crying (colic) in relation to parent behavior. *Amer. J. Psychiat.,* 1954, *110,* 687–694.

Stiles, Frances S. Developing an understanding of human behavior at the elementary school level. *J. educ. Res.,* 1950, *43,* 516–524.

Stippich, Mary E. The mental development of children of feeble-minded mothers: a preliminary report. *Natl. Soc. Study Educ.,* 39th Yearbook, 1940, Part II. Pp. 337–350.

Stolz, H. R., and Lois M. Stolz. *Somatic development of adolescent boys.* New York: The Macmillan Co., 1951.

Stolz, Lois M. *et al. Father relations of war-born children.* Stanford, Calif.: Stanford University Press, 1954.

Stott, L. H., and Rachell S. Ball. Infant and preschool mental tests: review and evaluation. *Monogr. Soc. Res. Child Develpm.,* 1965, *30.*

Stubbs, E. M. The effect of the factors of duration, intensity, and pitch of sound stimuli on the responses of newborn infants. *Univ. Iowa Stud. Child Welfare,* 1934, *9,* No. 4.

Sullivan, H. S. *Conceptions of modern psychiatry.* New York: W. W. Norton, 1947.

Sullivan, H. S. *The interpersonal theory of psychiatry.* New York: W. W. Norton, 1953.

Sutton-Smith, B., and B. G. Rosenberg. Manifest anxiety and game preference in children. *Child Develpm.*, 1960, *31*, 307–311.

Sutton-Smith, B., and B. G. Rosenberg. Development of sex differences in play choices during preadolescence. *Child Develpm.*, 1963, *34*, 119–126.

Sutton-Smith, B., and B. G. Rosenberg. Sibling consensus on power tactics. 1966. Paper read at Annual Meeting of the American Psychological Association, New York.

Taylor, C., and A. W. Combs. Self-acceptance and adjustment. *J. consult. Psychol.*, 1952, *16*, 89–91.

Terman, L. M. *et al. Genetic studies of genius:* I. *Mental and physical traits of a thousand gifted children.* Stanford, Calif.: Stanford University Press, 1925.

Terman, L. M., and Maude A. Merrill. *Measuring intelligence: a guide to the administration of the New Revised Stanford-Binet Tests.* Boston: Houghton Mifflin Co., 1937.

Terman, L. M., and Melita H. Oden. *Genetic studies of genius: IV. The gifted child grows up.* Stanford, Calif.: Stanford University Press, 1947.

Thomas, H. Visual-fixation responses of infants to stimuli of varying complexity. *Child Develpm.*, 1965, *36*, 629–638.

Thompson, G. G. *Child psychology.* Boston: Houghton Mifflin Co., 1952, 1962.

Thompson, W. R. The heredity-environment problem. *Bull. Marit. Psychol. Assn.*, Spring 1955, 30–40.

Thompson, W. R., and W. Heron. The effects of restricting early experience on the problem-solving capacity of dogs. *Can. J. Psychol.*, 1954, *8*, 17–31.

Thorndike, E. L. *et al. The measurement of intelligence.* New York: Bureau of Publications, Teachers College, Columbia University, 1926.

Thorpe, J. G. An investigation into some correlates of sociometric status within school classes. *Sociometry*, 1955, *18*, 49–61.

Thurston, J. R., and P. H. Mussen. Infant feeding gratification and adult personality. *J. Pers.*, 1951, *19*, 449–458.

Thurstone, L. L., and Thelma G. Thurstone. *Primary mental abilities scales: Primary, elementary, and intermediate.* Chicago: Science Research Associates, 1950.

Titus, H. E., and E. P. Hollander. The California F-Scale in psychological research: 1950–1955. *Psychol. Bull.*, 1957, *54*, 47–64.

Tolman, E. C. *Purposive behavior in animals and men.* New York: Appleton Century-Crofts, 1932.

Torrance, E. P. *Guiding creative talent.* Englewood Cliffs, N.J.: Prentice-Hall, 1962.

Torrance, E. P. *Rewarding Creative Behavior: Experiments in Classroom Activity.* Englewood Cliffs, N.J.: Prentice-Hall, 1965.

Trainham, G., G. J. Pilafian, and R. M. Kraft. Case history of twins fed on a self-demand regime. *J. Pediatrics*, 1945, *27*, 97–108.

Tredgold, A. F. *A textbook of mental deficiency.* Baltimore: The Williams and Wilkins Co., 1947.

Trent, R. D. The relationship of anxiety to popularity and rejection among institutionalized delinquent boys. *Child Develpm.,* 1957, *28,* 379–384.

Truax, C. B. Factors affecting intelligence change associated with preschool attendance. Manuscript in preparation, 1966.

Turner, Elizabeth A., and J. C. Wright. Effects of severity of threat and perceived availability on the attractiveness of objects. *J. Pers. soc. Psychol.,* 1965, *2,* 128–132.

Valenstein, E. S., W. Riss, and W. C. Young. Experiential and genetic factors in the organization of sexual behavior in male guinea pigs. *J. comp. physiol. Psychol.,* 1955, *48,* 397–403.

Van de Geer, J. P., and J. F. M. Jaspers. Cognitive functions. Chapter in P. R. Farnsworth (ed.), Olga McNemar, and Q. McNemar (assoc. eds.). *Annual Review of Psychology.* Palo Alto, Calif.: Annual Reviews, Inc., 1966.

Vincent, C. E. Trends in infant care ideas. *Child Develpm.,* 1951, *22,* 199–209.

Voas, W. H. Does attendance at the Winnetka Nursery School tend to raise the IQ? *Natl. Soc. Study Educ.,* 39th Yearbook, 1940, Part II. Pp. 363–376.

Waldrop, Mary F., and R. Q. Bell. Relation of preschool dependency behavior to family size and density. *Child Develpm.,* 1965, *35,* 1187–1195.

Walker, R. N. Body build and behavior in young children: I. Body and nursery school teachers' ratings. *Monogr. Soc. Res. Child Develpm.,* 1962, *27,* Ser. No. 84.

Wallach, Lise, and R. L. Sprott. Inducing number conservation in children. *Child Develpm.,* 1964, *35,* 1057–1071.

Walsh, Ann M. *Self-concepts of bright boys with learning difficulties.* New York: Bureau of Publications, Teachers College, Columbia University, 1956.

Warner, W. L. *Social life of a modern community.* New Haven, Conn.: Yale University Press, 1941.

Warner, W. L., M. Meeker, and K. Eells. *Social class in America.* Chicago: Science Research Associates, 1949.

Washburn, W. C. The effects of physique and intrafamily tension on self-concept in adolescent males. *J. consult. Psychol.,* 1962, *26,* 460–466.

Waters, Elinor, and V. J. Crandall. Social class and observed maternal behavior from 1940 to 1960. *Child Develpm.,* 1964, *35,* 1021–1032.

Watson, J. B. *Psychology: from the standpoint of a behaviorist.* Philadelphia: J. B. Lippincott, 1919.

Watson, J. B. *Psychological care of infant and child.* New York: W. W. Norton and Co., 1928.

Watson, J. B. *Psychology: from the standpoint of a behaviorist.* Philadelphia: J. B. Lippincott Co., 1924.

Wechsler, D. *The measurement of adult intelligence.* Baltimore: The Williams and Wilkins Co., 1944.

Weininger, O. The effects of early experience on behavior and growth characteristics. *J. comp. physiol. Psychol.,* 1956, *49,* 1–9.

Weininger, O. Mortality of albino rats under stress as a function of early handling. *Can. J. Psychol.*, 1953, *7,* 111–114.

Weininger, O., W. J. McClelland, and R. K. Arima. Gentling and weight gain in the albino rat. *Can. J. Psychol.*, 1954, *8,* 147–151.

Weir, M. S. Age and memory as factors in problem solving. *J. exp. Psychol.* 1967 (in press).

Weir, M. W., and J. C. DeFries. Prenatal maternal influence on behavior in mice: evidence of a genetic basis. *J. comp. physiol. Psychol.*, 1964, *58,* 412–417.

Wellman, Beth L. Iowa studies on the effects of schooling. *Natl. Soc. Study Educ.*, 39th Yearbook, 1940, Part II. Pp. 377–399.

Wellman, Beth L. IQ changes of preschool and nonpreschool groups during the preschool years: a summary of the literature. *J. Psychol.*, 1945, *20,* 347–368.

Wellman, Beth L., and Edna L. Pegram. Binet IQ changes of orphanage preschool children: a reanalysis. *J. genet. Psychol.*, 1944, *65,* 239–263.

Wheeler, L. R. A comparative study of the intelligence of East Tennessee mountain children. *J. educ. Psychol.*, 1942, *33,* 321–334.

White, B. L., and P. W. Castle. Visual exploratory behavior following postnatal handling of human infants. *Perceptual and Motor Skills*, 1964, *18,* 497–502.

White, R. W. Motivation reconsidered: the concept of competence. *Psychol. Rev.*, 1959, *66,* 297–333.

Whiting, J. W. M. Sorcery, sin, and the superego: a cross-cultural study of some mechanisms of social control. In R. Jones (ed.), Nebraska Symposium on Motivation. Lincoln: University of Nebraska Press, 1959, pp. 174–197.

Whiting, J. W. M., and I. L. Child. *Child training and personality*. New Haven, Conn.: Yale University Press, 1953.

Williams, Judith R., and R. B. Scott. Growth and development of Negro infants: IV. Motor development and its relationship to child-rearing practices in two groups of Negro infants. *Child Develpm.*, 1953, *24,* 103–121.

Winch, R. F. The relation between the loss of a parent and progress in courtship. *J. soc. Psychol.*, 1949, *29,* 51–56.

Winch, R. F. Some data bearing on the Oedipus hypothesis. *J. abnorm. soc. Psychol.*, 1950, *45,* 481–489.

Winder, C. L., and Lucy Rau. Parental attitudes associated with social deviance in preadolescent boys. *J. abnorm. soc. Psychol.*, 1962, *64,* 418–424.

Wolfenstein, Martha. Trends in infant care. *Amer. J. Orthopsychiat.*, 1953, *23,* 120–130.

Wolowitz, H. M. Attraction and aversion to power: a psychoanalytic conflict theory of homosexuality in male paranoids. *J. abnorm. Psychol.*, 1965, *70,* 360–370.

Wooley, Helen T. The validity of standards of mental measurement in young childhood. *Sch. and Soc.*, 1925, *21,* 476–482.

Worbois, G. M. Changes in Stanford-Binet IQ for rural consolidated and rural one-room school children. *J. exp. Educ.*, 1942, *11,* 210–214.

Worchester, D. A. Acceleration: good or bad? APA, Division of School Psychologists, Midwestern Psychological Association Meetings, 1959. Mimeographed, 31 pp.

Wurster, C. R., B. M. Bass, and W. Alcock. A test of the proposition: we want to be esteemed most by those we esteem most highly. *J. abnorm. soc. Psychol.,* 1961, *63,* 650–653.

Wyer, R. S., Jr. Self-acceptance, discrepancy between parents' perceptions of their children, and goal-seeking effectiveness. *J. Pers. soc. Psychol.,* 1965, *2,* 311–316.

Wylie, Ruth. *The self-concept.* Lincoln, Nebraska: The University of Nebraska Press, 1961.

Yamamoto, Kaoru, and O. L. Davis, Jr. Test instructions, test anxiety, and dependence proneness in relation to children's performance on a test of intelligence. *Psychology in the Schools,* 1966, *3,* 167–170.

Yarrow, Leon J. Maternal deprivation: toward an empirical and conceptual reevaluation. *Psychol. Bull.,* 1961, *58,* 459–490.

Yarrow, L. J. The relationship between nutritive sucking experiences in infancy and nonnutritive sucking in childhood. *J. genet. Psychol.,* 1954, *84,* 149–162.

Young, R. K., W. M. Benson, and W. H. Holtzman. Change in attitudes toward the Negro in a southern university. *J. abnorm. soc. Psychol.,* 1960, *60,* 131–133.

Zelen, S. L. The relationship of peer acceptance, acceptance of others and self-acceptance. Iowa Acad. Sci., *Proc.,* 1954, *61,* 446–449.

Zetterstrom, B. The clinical electroretinogram: IV. The electroretinogram in children during the first year of life. *Acta ophthal.,* 1951, *29,* 295–304.

Zook, Elsie. Sex role preferences in 3- and 4-year-old children. Unpublished M.A. thesis, University of Iowa, *Iowa Child Welfare Res. Sta.,* 1959.

Zubek, J. P., and Patricia A. Solberg. *Human development.* New York: McGraw-Hill Book Co., 1954.

Zuckerman, M., Beatrice B. Ribback, I. Monashkin, and J. A. Norton, Jr. Normative data and factor analysis on the parental attitude research instrument. *J. consult. Psychol.,* 1958, *22,* 165–171.

Index

Toilet training, 130–134, 140; bed-wetting, 132–133; bladder control, 131–133; practices in different cultures, 132; severity of, rating of, 130–131
Tolman, E. C., 213
Torrance, E. P., 332
Touch (pressure or contact), development of, 37–38
Tracking, 25, 26
Traditional Family Ideology Scale, 504
Trainham, G., 112
Training areas, universal, 93–94
Trait status, personal concern and, 407–408
Transfer, 209
Translation, attitudes into behavior, 518–519
Transposition, 197–198
Treatment, *see* Therapy
Tredgold, A. F., 339
Trent, R. D., 593
Trial and error, learning by, 45
Truax, C. B., 349
Trust versus mistrust, learning, 418–419
Tudor-Hart, B. H., 32
Turner, Elizabeth A., 226–227, 285
Turula, Emily, 477
Twins, studies of, 344–346, 372

Unconditioned response (UR), 181–188
Unconditioned stimulus (US), 181–188
Undesirability, 260
United States, child sexuality in, 135; culture in, 8–9; family in, 13; marriage customs in, 10–11
Universal training areas, 93–94
Unlearning, 184
Unsound generalization, problem in research, 73–75, 82, 99
Upper class, 12; children, middle-class teacher and, 594–596
Upper-lower class, 13
Upper-middle class, 13
Upper-upper class, 12

Valenstein, E. S., 445
Value system, lower-lower class, 586–594; middle class, 580–584;—lower-class children and, 584–594
Van de Geer, J. P., 47
Variance, definition of, 80
Verbal mediation, 176
Victorian theory of child-rearing, 104–105
Vincent, C. E., 58, 127
Vineland test of social maturity, 155
Vision, development of, 24–31, 54
Visual cliff, 29
Voas, W. H., 348

Waldrop, Mary F., 141
Walk, R. D., 369
Walker, R. N., 402, 403, 404
Wallace, R. F., 16
Wallach, Lise, 232
Walsh, Ann M., 270
Walters, R. H., 431, 434
Warner, W. L., 12, 578, 584
Warner Index of Status Characteristics, 580
Washburn, W. C., 404, 405
Waterhouse, I. K., 553
Waters, Elinor, 159
Watson, J. B., 39, 438
Weaning, 126–127
Wechsler, D., 295, 361
Wechsler Intelligence Scale for Children, 304
Weininger, O., 441
Weintraub, S., 333
Weir, M. W., 151, 221, 234
Wellman, Beth L., 347, 348
West Pakistan, child-rearing in, 105–107, 171
Wet dreams, 393
Wheeler, L. R., 353
White, B. L., 28, 40
White, G. D., 594
White, R. K., 60, 563, 564
Whiting, J. W. M., 93, 122–124, 132, 137, 139–140, 142, 146, 235, 431, 464, 465
Whole child, the, concept of, 3–5
Williams, Judith R., 112, 133
Winch, R. F., 166
Winder, C. L., 141
Winston, H. D., 151
Wisdom (omniscience), parental power of, 424, 446, 452
Wise, G. W., 115
Wolfenstein, Martha, 127
Wolowitz, H. M., 423, 452
Wooley, Helen T., 347
Worbois, G. M., 349
Worchester, D. A., 324
Wright, J. C., 226–227, 285
Wrighter, Joyce, 593
Wurster, C. R., 266
Wyer, R. S., Jr., 536
Wylie, Ruth, 259

X-ray treatment during early pregnancy, 16

Yale-Iowa theory of learning, 212
Yamamoto, Kaoru, 313
Yarrow, L. J., 116
Young, W. C., 445, 507